More praise for *Black Earth*

"The best non-academic book on Russia since the mid-Nineties. . . . *Black Earth* is like the best sort of love letter; mournful, obsessive and exquisitely readable." —*The Times* (London)

"[An] engrossing, beautifully written book." —*Publishers Weekly*

"Even after the fall of Communism, most American reporting on Russia often goes no further than who's in and who's out in the Kremlin and the business of oligarchy. Andrew Meier's Russia reaches far beyond." —Adam Hochschild, author of *King Leopold's Ghost* and *The Unquiet Ghost: Russians Remember Stalin*

"From the pointless war in Chechnya to the wild, exhilarating, and dispiriting East and the rise of Vladimir Putin, the former KGB officer—it's all here in great detail, written in the layers the story deserves, with insight, passion, and genuine affection." —Michael Specter, *The New Yorker*

"*Black Earth* . . . is a sprawling Baedeker of Putin's Russia, produced by a young man of vast energy and boundless curiosity. . . . Dozens of travel books about Russia have appeared during the last three decades. *Black Earth* is easily the best." —*Times Literary Supplement*

"A daring traveler, [Meier] . . . is particularly adept at weaving in just the right amount of chronology, history and literary allusion to illuminate the subject at hand. . . . Meier writes well too, especially when evoking landscape and atmosphere . . . a vivid yet necessarily inconclusive portrait of Russia in its current season of violence, corruption and sorrow." —Richard Lourie, *Washington Post Book World*

"[Andrew Meier's] knowledge of the country and his abiding love for its people stand out on every page, making his journey through Russia after the fall an informed and scrupulously researched one. But it is his linguistic fluency, in particular, which enables Mr. Meier to dig so deeply in Russia's black earth." —*The Economist*

"Since so much of the reality that Meier is getting at is ineffable, it helps that he is a fine, lyrical writer. . . . [*Black Earth* is] a wonderful travelogue that depicts the Russian people yet again trying to build a new life."

–William Taubman, *New York Times Book Review* (2004 Pulitzer Prize winner)

"This is the best piece of journalism written about Russia in English, and likely to remain so for a long time. It has almost all of the strengths which make American reporting, at its best, the envy and should make it the model of those aspiring to write journalism anywhere."

–John Lloyd, *The Glasgow Herald*

"This fascinating book . . . is part travelogue, part war reporting, part economic investigation. . . . Russia is a society simultaneously undergoing a series of revolutions–ideological, economic, demographic–its national self-definition changes from year to year, alternately proud, angry, defensive and embarrassed, and sometimes all at once. . . . Meier captures these contradictions eloquently."

–Anne Applebaum, *The Sunday Telegraph* (2004 Pulitzer Prize winner)

"If President Bush were to read only the chapters regarding Chechnya in Meier's *Black Earth*, he would gain a priceless education about Putin's Russia."

–Zbigniew Brzezinski

"[*Black Earth*] is more than a 'state of the nation' account. It is a lengthy journey, predominantly by public transport, into the soul of the people."

–Jason Burke, *The Observer* (author of the 2004 bestseller *On Al Qaeda*)

"A superb work of travel and reportage, and must reading for Russia hands."

–*Kirkus Reviews*

"What distinguishes Meier's book from many of its predecessors is the author's deep passion for Russia and its people. . . . *Black Earth* might not convince Westerners that living in Russia is a pleasant experience, but it might forestall an even worse fate for its citizens: being forgotten."

–Paul Mitchinson, *Newsday*

"[Meier] looks beyond Moscow, and below the level of the nouveaux riches, to what he sees as the common Russians. . . . *Black Earth* is a travelogue of epic proportions." —Georgi Derluguian, *The New Left Review*

"If you're going to Russia for the first time, take this book. You won't find better." —Lesley Chamberlain, *The Independent*

BLACK EARTH

A JOURNEY THROUGH RUSSIA
AFTER THE FALL

ANDREW MEIER

W. W. NORTON & COMPANY

NEW YORK LONDON

Grateful acknowledgment is made for permission to reprint lines from:
"Black Earth," from Osip Mandelstam, *Selected Poems*, Penguin Books, published 1991
and translated by James Greene (by kind permission of Angel Books, London);
Hadji Murad, in Leo Tolstoy, *Master and Man and Other Stories*, Penguin Classics,
1977, translated by Paul Foote; *Gubernatorskie romansy*, Moskovskii pisatel', 1994,
by Valentin Fyodorov. Every effort has been made to contact the copyright holders
of all translated material. Rights holders of any material not credited should contact
W. W. Norton & Company, Inc., 500 Fifth Avenue, New York, NY 10110.

For information about permission to reproduce selections from this book, write to
Permissions, W. W. Norton & Company, Inc., 500 Fifth Avenue, New York, NY 10110

Manufacturing by The Haddon Craftsmen, Inc.
Book design by Blue Shoe Studio
Production manager: Julia Druskin

Library of Congress Cataloging-in-Publication Data

Meier, Andrew.
Black earth : a journey through Russia after the fall / by Andrew Meier.
p. cm.
ISBN 0-393-05178-1 (hardcover)
1. Russia (Federation)–Description and travel. 2. Meier, Andrew–Journeys–Russia
(Federation) 3. Russia (Federation)–Social conditions–1991– 4. Post-communism–
Russia (Federation) I. Title.
DK510. 76.M44 2003
914. 704'86–dc21

2003006562

ISBN 0-393-32641-1 pbk.

W. W. Norton & Company, Inc., 500 Fifth Avenue, New York, N.Y. 10110
www.wwnorton.com

W. W. Norton & Company Ltd., Castle House, 75/76 Wells Street, London W1T 3QT

2 3 4 5 6 7 8 9 0

for Mia,
and for my parents

How pleasing fatty topsoil is to ploughshare,
How silent the steppe in its April upheaval!
Well, I wish you well, black earth: be firm, sharp-eyed . . .
A black-voiced silence is at work.

—Osip Mandelstam, "Black Earth," April 1935

❧ CONTENTS ❧

❧ AUTHOR'S NOTE ❧

One can transliterate the Russian language into Latin script variously. I have elected not to use the American scholarly standard, the Library of Congress system, in the hope of rendering the Russian as readable and recognizable as possible. (As such, the reader will find "Yeltsin" and not "El'tsin.") With regard to translations, I have sought to use existing English texts whenever possible. Only when such translations do not exist or fall short of the Russian have I resorted to my own. Lastly, in a few rare cases, to protect the safety of individuals I have substituted names.

BLACK EARTH

❧ PROLOGUE ❧

HE HAD BEEN THEIR FIRST CHILD, the elder of two sons. After his death they had turned the darkest corner of the spartan living room into a shrine. A hazy black-and-white portrait, blown up beyond scale from an army ID, loomed above the reedy church candles and a thin bouquet of plastic flowers. They had draped a black ribbon over the photograph.

"When I served," his father said, "I served the Motherland. 'To serve with honor and dignity.' That's what they told us to do and that's what I did. For twenty-eight years."

Andrei Sazykin died in the summer of 1996. He was killed on the northeastern edge of Grozny, before dawn broke on August 6, the parched day the rebels reclaimed their capital. The Chechens had swarmed back by the thousands. Seven other boys in his unit also fell that morning. Three weeks earlier Andrei had turned twenty.

For the Russian forces, the Sixth of August, as it became known, would live on. It would haunt them as a humiliation, the worst day of the war. For Andrei's parents, Viktor and Valentina, it made no sense. They would sit in the dim light of their two-room apartment in Moscow and wonder how the Chechens had so easily retaken Grozny that day. Until the letters started to arrive. One after another, Andrei's comrades began to write to his parents.

"And suddenly," his father said, "everything came into this terrible perfect clarity."

The letters were blunt.

" 'Your son served well,' " recited Viktor. He had read the words a thousand times, but he traced the lines with his forefinger. In his voice there were tears. " 'But he did not die in battle. He was sold down the river. We all were.' "

Valentina said the boys came to visit. They brought a video from their last days in Chechnya. It showed Russian officers, their shirts off in the severe heat of Grozny, playing backgammon with two Chechen fighters. They were smoking and drinking, all of them laughing.

"That was the afternoon on the day before Andrei died," Viktor said. "The boys later pieced it together. There was no battle that morning. There was a deal. The Chechens paid their way through the checkpoints. The boys were slaughtered. And when the others went looking for the commanders, they were gone."

Months after their son's death Viktor and Valentina brought a case, one of the first of its kind in Russia, against the Ministry of Defense. They sued to restore their boy's honor and not, as the papers claimed, to get rich on compensation. They called his death a murder and vowed to seek punishment for those who killed him.

Several Augusts later, nearly five years to the day after their son died, I went to see them again. We had spoken in the intervening years. But I had never brought them the kind of news they craved, for I had failed to convince my editors that their son's case was a story. I had, however, followed Viktor and Valentina as they waged their long campaign. They had started in their neighborhood court and fought all the way to Russia's Supreme Court. They even won a hearing in the Constitutional Court. But at every station they lost.

Along the way Valentina lost her job. For two decades she had taught biology in the local school. Viktor meanwhile had been forced to get a job. He now worked twenty-four-hour shifts, four times a week, at an Interior Ministry hotel, a hostelry for visiting officers in Moscow. Their savings depleted, they had also lost their hope. All they had, said Valentina, was *nashe gore* ("our sorrow").

"Tell me," Viktor said, fixing his eyes on mine. "Because I can't understand it. But you must know. Can a country survive without a conscience?"

In the days that followed our last conversation, I left Moscow after a stay of five winters and six summers. I had, truth be told, lived in the country for most of the last decade. I had seen out the last years of the Soviet experiment and witnessed the heady birth of the "new Russia." I had seen the romantic rise of Boris Yeltsin—and the wreckage his era wrought: the inglorious battle for the spoils of the ancient regime (an industrial fire sale of historic proportion), the military onslaught in Chechnya (the worst carnage in Russia since Stalingrad), and the rapid decline in nearly every index, social and economic, that the state took the trouble to record.

I had traveled far beyond the capital, to the distant corners of the old empire. I had lived for years in the remains of the Soviet state amid the millions of spectral dead souls who walked its ruins, as well as the rising new class of rent seekers, instant industrialists, and would-be entrepreneurs, who raced to accumulate and acquire, lest their new world vanish as quickly as the old. I had interviewed Politburo veterans and Gulag survivors, befriended oligarchs and philosophers. But I had no answer for Andrei's parents. I could only tell them that I hoped to write a book–not only to record my travels across Russia's length and breadth but, above all, to try to make sense of their plaintive question.

I. MOSCOW

ZERO GRAVITY

Vykhod est'! ("There Is a Way Out!")

–Moscow metro slogan, 2001

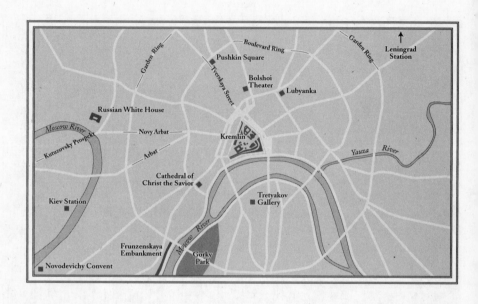

Garden Ring

Boulevard Ring

Leningrad
Station

Pushkin Square

Tverskaya Street

Garden Ring

Bolshoi
Theater

Lubyanka

Russian White House

Moscow River

Novy Arbat

Kremlin

Yauza River

Kutuzovsky Prospekt

Arbat

Cathedral of
Christ the Savior

Kiev Station

Tretyakov
Gallery

Moscow River

Frunzenskaya
Embankment

Gorky
Park

Novodevichy Convent

❧ ONE ❧

IN THE OLD DAYS, before the breakneck final decade of the last century, before the end of empire and the epochal shift that followed in its wake, in the days when dissenters were dissidents and poets were prophets, when "abroad" meant Bulgaria, Budapest, or Cuba at best, when leather shoes and silk ties were not bought but "gotten," when colleagues were "Comrades" and strangers "Citizens," when HIV and heroin were exotic plagues born of bourgeois excess, when artists and soldiers pointed to ceilings and dropped their voices, when churches held archives and orphans, when lovers met in parks because apartments housed generations, when everyone professed to believe in the Party, the Collective, and Vodka but in truth trusted only Fate, God, and Vodka, I first came to Moscow.

By the time I left, I had lived there longer than in any other city. But Moscow, like the country that surrounds it, eludes one. It defies measurement and loathes explanation, as if inherently ill disposed to definition. Longevity in Russia does not always yield understanding. Neither does intimacy guarantee knowledge. Nor does the first sensation of walking the city's poplar-lined boulevards and great avenues of granite, that first sense of awe and astonishment at the fairy-tale world turned nightmare, ever seem to diminish.

First impressions in Moscow fortunately do not lie. The city is built on an inhuman scale. Everything is by design inconvenient for *Homo sapiens*. The streets are so vast crossing them requires a leap of faith. The cars do not stop for pedestrians; more often they accelerate. The streets are so broad one can traverse only beneath them, through dimly lit passageways that shelter the refugees of the new order: makeshift vendors who hawk everything from Swedish porn to Chinese bras; scruffy preteens cadging cigarettes and sniffing glue; hordes of babushkas who have fallen through the torn social safety net and are left to sell cigarettes and vodka in the cold; the displaced stranded by the host of unlovely little wars that raged along the edges of the old empire. And everywhere underground the stench of urine lingers with the acrid aroma of stewed cabbage and cheap tobacco.

Aboveground the city seems to exist—as it did at its birth—to trade. Kiosks on nearly every corner, bazaars in every neighborhood. Even the outlying districts, more a part of the woods than the city, are overrun with feverish commerce. In the post-Soviet years, open-air wholesale markets, sprawling encampments of plastic tenting and cargo containers, lured tens of thousands each weekend. Here were the fruits of globalization, tinged inevitably with a Russian style: electronic and computer goods from the East and from the West, pirated software on CDs burned locally and on video, Hollywood blockbusters still unreleased in the States. The off-the-books trade united unlikely partners. A drug market sprouted one block from the Lubyanka, the once and present headquarters of the secret police, on a street where pensioners sold their prescriptions to hungry young addicts.

Slowly, too, the signs of the new opulence—the transfer of the state's vast wealth into the hands of a chosen few—came to dominate Moscow's implacable center. Vacant nineteenth-century mansions, the crumbling former residences of the prerevolutionary merchant class, became the ornate offices of new millionaires and billionaires, the men who soon took to calling themselves oligarchs. Even during the harshest years of the Communist era, Moscow had always been on the make. But in the mid-1990s, with the rise of powerful moguls like Boris Berezovsky, Vladimir Gusinsky, and Vladimir Potanin, among a half dozen others, the Great Grab began. In the bedlam of the Yeltsin years, the profit margin grew into a gaudy obsession. "The primitive accumulation of capital" was what the oligarchs, remembering their Marx, called their thirst for the riches of the *ancien régime*.

This of course was "the New Moscow." When I first stepped foot in the city in 1983, Moscow was grim and gray, a place of vast public spaces dominated by an eerie silence. It was the height of the age of Yuri Andropov, one of the last of the dour old men to rule the USSR. The Soviet war in Afghanistan was at its tragic height. I was then a nineteen-year-old undergraduate on a cheap one-week Sputnik tour. I had flown in from East Berlin with two dozen Bavarian high school students and, inexplicably, an older businessman from Buenos Aires who mesmerized the Kremlin guards with a new invention, a video camera.

My eyes glazed at the strange fairy-tale world. In the kaleidoscope of sounds and impressions, Moscow, it seemed, hosted another race on another planet. One encounter, above all the rest, remains indelible, fixed in the present. I sit on a low brick wall on a corner of Red Square. As I watch the crowds moving across the square, a young boy approaches. His name is Ivan. But I do not understand him when he tells me his age. He holds up ten fingers and folds down one pinkie. Nine, I understand. We cannot speak with each other. We only manage to establish two things. "*Lenin tut,*" Ivan says, pointing to the squat red granite mausoleum that sits across the cobbled square. "*I Mama tam.*" ("Lenin is here. And my mama's over there.") He waves a hand to swat the air, pointing to an office that lies far beyond this great busied corner of Moscow. That afternoon I made a vow to myself: I would return to Russia only once I had learned the language.

Five years later I did. In 1988 I came back as a graduate student from Oxford to study for a term. I never expected, of course, that I would stay on in Moscow to witness the USSR during its final gasps. After Oxford, there was only one place I wanted to be, where I had to be. I told family and friends that I was making my way as a free-lance journalist. In truth I was searching for any excuse to stay in Moscow. I was in love.

In those final, frenzied years of the Soviet Empire, Russian friends often wondered why I chose to live among them. My friend Andrei, then in the advanced stages of a doctoral dissertation on the liberalizing impulses of Josip Tito's economics, was no Soviet patriot. The son of a middling Soviet bureaucrat, Andrei had a fondness for tie-dyed jeans and peroxided hair. He had offered to let me stay with him and his young wife, Lera, and their five-year-old daughter, Dasha, in their *kommunalka*, a communal flat they shared with a young woman and an old lady in one of the city's most beautiful and crumbling prerevolutionary neighborhoods. Andrei and Lera were lucky; theirs was hardly the typical communal flat. The young woman worked in a sausage plant. She rose early, came home late, and at week's end without fail brought home frozen pork. The old lady was even more accommodating; she rarely appeared.

They lived a quarter mile from the Kremlin, but Andrei and Lera could not have been further removed from officialdom. Each night brought friends: rock musicians and military officers, actors and poets, tall, stunning women from Siberia, short, stunning men from Dagestan. Their cramped kitchen was always crowded with the voices of the emergent generation debating the issue of the hour, be it the chances for Gorbachev and glasnost, the Soviet pullout from Afghanistan, or the legalization of hashish in Copenhagen.

The gatherings grew so big that one Sunday morning Andrei axed his way through a wall, expanding the tiny kitchen into an unused closet. As the nightly assemblies ran their course, accompanied by the ceaseless flow of bottle after bottle, the attention turned to me.

"Just why are you here?" someone would ask.

"He's looking for a Russian bride," someone would joke.

"He's a spy," another would jibe.

Whenever doubt or suspicion arose, Andrei saved me. "He just enjoys watching dead empires in decay," he'd answer.

DAYS BEFORE THE COUP attempt against Gorbachev in August 1991, I left Soviet Russia. But in 1996, after a five-year remove, I returned again. This time I came with my wife, Mia, a native New Yorker and a photojournalist. We moved into a single room with a remarkable view. It was on the top floor of a fabled building that rose above the Frunzenskaya Embankment along the Moscow River. One side of the building overlooked the river and Gorky Park, the other–ours–had a view of the Novodevichy (New Maiden) Convent. On long walks along the river we would wonder at the glimmering cupolas of the Kremlin churches and savor the sweet air that wafted from the Red October chocolate factory across the way.

The building, erected in the lean postwar years, was a landmark. Stalin had built it not only as an elegant residence for his lieges but as evidence that their world would survive. This explained the decor. Our room stretched, at most, twenty-five by ten feet but boasted a corniced ceiling and an outsize crystal chandelier. Each month Nikita Khrushchev, the moon-faced grandson of the Soviet leader, came for the rent. The place belonged to his other grandfather, his mother's father. The quarters were tight, even by Russian standards, but more than we needed. I had a fellowship to report from the war zones of the former USSR, and our plan was to spend as much time as possible on the road, traveling across Central Asia and the Caucasus. We took the place for a few months, and we stayed there three and a half years.

That fall I joined *Time*, trading the freedom of free-lancing for my first monthly paycheck as a journalist. Nonetheless, we stayed on in our room. As a "local hire" I got a bare-bones contract. We still slept on the couch, did the laundry in the bathtub, and delighted in the discovery of Belgian flash-frozen chicken in the corner market. We installed a steel door and scoured the local street vendors for fresh vegetables. Mia made friends with an Azeri woman, a refugee from the war between the Armenians and Azeris in Nagorno-Karabagh, who set aside her fattest potatoes and tomatoes for us. When rare visitors from home arrived, we made sure to prepare them for the elevator. We lived on the fourteenth floor. The elevator was wooden, a rickety antique that screeched as it slowly ascended. Invariably, it was pitch black inside. Now and then a neighbor screwed in a light. But it did not stay for long. Ten bulbs, I soon learned, equaled a bottle of vodka. In all our years in Moscow we never lived in the ghettos reserved for foreign diplomats and journalists, and for this we would be grateful.

The house was filled with stories and sources. Lazar Kaganovich, one of Stalin's longest-serving henchmen, had lived on the next stairway over. (His daughter still did.) Next door to us lived Sasha, an aging underground painter who had been one of the first to stage avant-garde actions in the city streets. He still spoke proudly of the day under Brezhnev when he walked into a barren meat store and placed paintings of sausages and hams in its empty display counters. His wife, a restorer of fine art, worked for the Tretyakov Gallery, Moscow's grandest museum. Throughout the first winter that we shared a wall, she worked on canvases the soldiers had brought home from the Grozny Art Museum. Sasha was usually mild-mannered— except when he drank, which was often. One day he decided Mia would make a new drinking partner. He hovered outside our door, pounding it with a bottle of vodka, until as she refused, he sank to his knees, crying.

On the floor below lived Nina Aleksandrovna, a frail lady in her seventies who took a warm liking to us. Poor Nina was tortured by her son, Sergei, who seemed lost in a détente time warp. He wore faded denim shirts, unbuttoned low, and faded jeans. At least twice a week he would appear at our door to plead with me to translate some Beatles song. Sergei drank too much and worked too little.

Pyotr lived next door to Nina. A lanky hacker with a blond ponytail, he later showed me, as NATO jets bombed Belgrade, how he helped lead the attack on the North Atlantic Alliance's mainframe. When we first met, Pyotr was a nineteen-year-old who resisted wearing shirts, no matter the weather. He and I spent long nights on the landing between our floors. We would look out at Novodevichy, the most fabled convent in Moscow. He rolled cigarettes—no filters, Dutch tobacco—and talked of his course work. He was majoring in one of Moscow State's new fields, the Department of the Defense of Information. Pyotr was already one of Moscow's more established hackers; he anchored a TV show on pirated computer games and had bought a small dacha. One night he told me who was paying for his education, the FSB. He was on a full ride from the secret policemen who had taken over for the old KGB.

❧ TWO ❧

IT WAS EARLY ON A CRISP Saturday morning in the short Russian fall, and something was not right. The mayor had sensed it. He was sure of it, in fact. Tiles crack. They break. They splinter. Linoleum, he calculated, would last. The mayor sat in the center of the head table in a prefabricated construction office built of American aluminum siding and Finnish plywood in the heart of Moscow. He stirred slowly in his chair, staring straight ahead, as if seeing something far beyond the realm of all the eyes gathered here and fixed upon his tonsured square head.

All along the tables that spread out to the mayor's left and right big men sat stiffly. Early that morning they had stuffed themselves into dark suits. Now they wore faces of worry. The mayor folded his large, knuckly hands before him like a tent. The assembled understood: He was ready. Water was poured and cigarettes were stubbed out as the chatter subsided. The subject at hand—and the venue of this debate—was an important site, a new rehabilitation center for the city's veterans wounded on the battlefields of Chechnya. Russia's second campaign to defeat the Chechen fighters had entered its second year. The mayor was eager to show his compassion for the boys maimed in their service to the Motherland. The rehab center, an aide tugged me aside to whisper, was "especially close to the mayor's heart."

Yuri Luzhkov stood no more than five feet five inches, but he made his presence known. His outsize head was made even larger by the absence of hair and his large, piercing blue eyes. The mayor may have the build, and sartorial sense, of a head-banging enforcer in a James Cagney film, but he spoke softly and slowly. It was as if he had learned to rely on a lilting, unexpected cadence to disarm his interlocutors and draw them in. On this morning he sported a dark blue windbreaker and, even indoors, his trademark workman's leather cap. He was more than ready, once his minions came to order, to hold court.

It did not take much. The mayor called upon the engineers, and one by one they stood, with a slight bow, as Russian schoolchildren have recited their lessons for centuries, to report the status of their work. "The plan will be completed ahead of schedule," one boasted. "At least ten days ahead of schedule," he quickly added.

"We have all the permits in order," assured another.

"The windows have all arrived and been fitted," said a third.

Then came the debate. A structural engineer, a man too far into his fifties to be so nervous in this setting, confessed, "We aren't sure, just yet, quite how to proceed with the tiles or the linoleum for the flooring surface." A whisper rippled through the construction trailer. "We checked with the engineers from the building institutes, and they have tested the tiles," he hastened to add. "The tiles will last in terms of the pressure per square meter, and the longevity equivalency tests seem to have confirmed their preliminary findings. But the linoleum still has not been ruled out. We were"– and here, a long pause–"waiting to consult with you."

The mayor sat still, taking in the parade of reports. In a corner of the room, I noticed a luminary of his inner circle, Shamil Tarpishchev, once Boris Yeltsin's tennis coach, who fell from favor in a scandal involving the National Sports Foundation. Luzhkov, then Yeltsin's bitter rival, had sheltered Tarpishchev, taking him under his wing as his adviser on sport. All the same, allegations of underworld associations continued to dog Tarpishchev.[1]

Once the last of the speakers resumed his seat, the mayor gathered in his large hands and, massaging his knuckles, launched a barrage of questions. How much would the tiles cost to cover the requisite area? How much would the linoleum cost? Would there be wheelchairs? How many? Had both surfaces been tested for these wheelchairs? He demanded statistics.

Numbers were proffered. He asked for samples. Samples were produced. He wondered, Was the factory Russian? Or foreign? On it went. To his every question the mayor received a prompt answer.

And so it came to pass that Yuri Luzhkov, who on this chilly day could rightly claim a place among the most powerful men in all Russia, spent nearly an hour probing the virtues of linoleum versus tile. To the untrained eye, it was an inordinately detailed discussion of construction material. But to anyone who lived in the Russian capital in the final years of the twentieth century, it was a pageant of power intended to impress. For in a moment, once the mayor announced his decision—linoleum won out—the voice vote was unanimous. "*Da, da, da,*" rang out the chorus.

LUZHKOV HAS BEEN CALLED many things. A populist and an opportunist, Russia's most muscular godfather, its fattest oligarch, and a true *khozyain*, an autocratic boss in the patrimonial mold of the tsarist days of old.[2] Many of the sobriquets rang true. But one thing about Luzhkov always stood out: the need to make his mark. In the great Soviet tradition, Luzhkov was a builder. He had worked for decades in the Soviet chemical industry before taking over the Moscow city government in the early 1990s. Reelected in 1996 with more than 90 percent of the vote, Luzhkov would serve on into the new century. Muscovites adored him. As the decade after the Soviet fall closed, Yeltsin's political and physical prowess faded ignobly away, Putin rose, and Luzhkov was stymied in his desire to rule Russia. But the mayor had succeeded in remaking his city, "the city of Moscow, the capital of our Motherland," as he liked to call it, in his image.

"MOSCOW IS NOT RUSSIA." It is the refrain of Westerners and Russians alike who have ventured into the Russian outback and returned to tell of its miseries. But what, then, is Moscow? In the years after the Soviet collapse, when so many of its denizens mistook license for liberty, the city grew infamous for the Babylon of its nightclubs and the upheaval of its unbridled free market. Yet it remains Russia's heart, the grandest reflection, however warped, of its troubles and riches. With its wretched masses and gluttonous elite, Moscow is home to more than ten million, a population greater than that of many countries in Europe. Yet in its first post-Soviet decade no one so dominated the city as its boisterous mayor.

Lenin may have promised the Russian people a New Jerusalem, but Luzhkov set out to build it. In the mayor's mind, the messianic destiny loomed large. For centuries Russians have harbored a vision of themselves as a chosen people and of Moscow as the Third Rome. The Russian Orthodox Church, with its cult of martyrdom, is only partly to blame. There is also the bloodline: In 1472, when Ivan III, the grand prince of Moscow, wed the sole heiress to the throne of Byzantium, the niece of Constantine XI, Moscow claimed its right as the heir of Constantinople.

Zoë Paleologue took the name Sophia, and the Muscovites adopted the rituals and trappings of Byzantine power. Ivan III became the first Russian leader to call himself "tsar"–the Russified Caesar–and borrow the double-headed eagle as well.[3] In Constantinople, the emblem made only rare appearances. In the land of the northern Slavs, however, the two-headed eagle was featured prominently. The Muscovites were eager to parade their imperial inheritance.[4] It was only natural that Luzhkov set himself the task of restoring the symbols of the foundation myth. Yeltsin kept the red stars atop the Kremlin towers, but the mayor returned the gilded eagles to their perch. He also ordered that the Resurrection Gate, a fairy-tale entrance to Red Square of red and white brick, rise again. Stalin, eager to make room for the parade of missiles and tanks on Revolution Day, had leveled the seventeenth-century gateway. Once Yeltsin canceled the pageant, Luzhkov took the opportunity to rebuild it from scratch. Like so many other pre-Bolshevik edifices, the gate was duplicated, exactly. Luzhkov now had a style, joked the head of the city's Museum of Architecture: "Reconstructivism."

The mayor liked the myth of the Third Rome. The Orthodox elder Filofei, a monk in Pskov in the late Middle Ages, was among the first to raise the notion. At some time in the late fifteenth or early sixteenth century Filofei sent the grand prince in Moscow a stern warning: "Perceive, pious Tsar, how all the Christian realms have converged into yours alone. Two Romes have fallen, and the third stands, and a fourth there shall not be."[5] " . . . and a fourth there shall not be." Moscow would be the third and last Rome, completing a holy trinity. Even Byzantium had not made such a claim. How could the mayor not rejoice in the imperial inheritance? The myth entitled Moscow to the glory not only of Constantine's capital–with its shimmering churches of gold told of in medieval Russian chronicles—but also of Rome, and even Jerusalem as well. "We are the New Jerusalem," Luzhkov would purr on occasion. And he was not kidding.

IN LUZHKOV'S MOSCOW the appreciation of masonry work became something of a civic duty. As buildings went up around the city, construction sites became tourist attractions. When elegant shopping malls and business centers sprouted between the Stalinist facades, they came complete with viewing platforms for the citizenry to witness the new world rising.

One frigid night as the new millennium neared, I stood alone taking in one of the mayor's most beloved sites. On the naked northern bank of the Moscow River, in the bend where the water slowly begins to churn westward out of the city, Luzhkov had forced on his fellow citizens a twelve-billion-dollar construction project, the biggest in the former Soviet Union. He envisioned the Moscow Siti, so named after London's financial district, blooming into a bustling center of finance and trade, the heart of the new metropolis as it carried the country into the new age. A glossy brochure described the future "city within a city" in less than fluent English:

Having studied the experience of the world-famous centers: Wall Street and Manhattan in New York, the City in Greater London, Shinjuku in Tokyo, and La Défence in Paris, we have done our best to avoid certain mistakes ... Our "Moscow-City" will live a full-blooded life ... there will be dwelling blocks of corporate and profit houses, hotels, cinema and concert halls, exhibition grounds, clubs, restaurants and a unique aquapark with a series of basins, water chutes, amusement facilities, restaurants and cafés ... the central core will feature multi-level car parkings and a mini-metro line.

The project was a Luzhkov dream drafted on blueprints back in the rosy days when the image of Boris Yeltsin standing defiant on a tank still dominated Russia's political memory and the country's fledgling stock market impossibly topped the world's emerging markets.

I liked inspecting Luzhkov's Siti. I watched the masses of men, in the tradition of Peter the Great's minions, digging the enormous foundation pit, their thirty-foot-tall dump trucks crawling through the mud roads. Reduced by the size of the pit, they resembled armies of ants. By the time I began strolling by, the project had become the biggest of Luzhkov's white elephants. From the nearby glassed-in Wiener Hof, a cozy Austrian affair that boasts a dozen drafts and demure waitresses in petit lederhosen, the view of the site was spectacularly eerie. Or so I thought as I stood one night alone on the Hof's ice-glazed balcony, surveying the black expanse. It was well past midnight in Moscow, on a Sunday in midwinter, but in the construction site that sprawled before me in all dimensions, the welding brigades were clamoring away, their torches giving form to walls and girders of iron in the darkness below. Inside the Hof a cackling trio of Argentines were splashing through their expense account's final hours. Their female escorts, young locals with limited Spanish, were checking their watches. Below I could make out at least five Kamaz trucks, their broad backs loaded with brick, metal, and mud, groaning across the craters. Against the starless sky, a crooked line of cranes revealed the contours of one man's dream. I could see how, in the frozen mud of this mess, it would be easy to lose one's perspective.

Then, in the middle of August 1998, the Russian economy crashed. August, in Russian politics, has long been a fateful month, and the move to devalue the ruble had long been foreseen. But no one expected the market to fall so hard, so fast. Overnight the government defaulted on forty billion dollars in bonds. Within weeks the ruble lost more than two-thirds of its value. Expatriate bankers and brokers vaulted for the exits. But "the Crisis," as the politicians and the bankers called the crash, was kind to Mia and me. In the spring we were able to move from our one-room apartment into a beautiful flat on Kutuzovsky Prospekt. Moscow's criminally high rents tumbled as thousands of business ex-pats rushed to flee the sinking ship. We bought a bed from an oil and gas analyst and a sofa from a Big Eight accountant. We moved from a gray concrete edifice built for the elite of the Communist Party to another formidable postwar apartment block, this one built to house the dutiful officers of the NKVD—Stalin's secret police—and their families.

Russia's race to the free market slowed to a crawl. Luzhkov, however, saw no need to revise his grand plans. As I walked along Kutuzovsky Prospekt to work each day, I checked in on the progress of his Siti. Across the street from our new place, and down a block, a high-rise thirty-four stories tall began to take shape. Luzhkov had promised it would be a vital tower in the new financial hub, a luxury hotel for foreign bankers and brokers. After the crash, construction on the tower slowed. Luzhkov's aides quietly allowed that it would not, as planned, be a hotel, but an office building. They also got rid of the name. Once it had been dubbed The Reformer. Now they opted for something more neutral. Tower 2000, they rechristened it.

Luzhkov forged on in his drive to build the Siti. At the foot of the tower's concrete skeleton, and spanning the frozen river, was a "pedestrian shopping bridge." Inside, a mechanized walkway allowed Russians to glide along the glass corridor, as if between terminals at some anonymous airport. The walkway passed glitzy shops offering Murano vases, Finnish cell phones, and Milanese dresses for preteens. This was Luzhkov's bridge to the twenty-first century, intended as a conveyance to the free market. One day, the mayor imagined, the bridge would carry visiting capitalists across the river to Russia's Wall Street. German bankers, Japanese brokers, South African traders would float effortlessly to the gleaming financial colossus on the far bank of the river–globalization's Slavic headquarters. Throughout the years of construction the vast pit of mud received six football fields of concrete and the multilevel shopping bridge filled with popular boutiques and restaurants. But to many the Siti remained a pipe dream.

On the shopping bridge's lower floor–the sort of space where in an American mall Santa would sit in December or the balloon man in spring–a miniature Moscow sat on display. Centered beneath a domed ceiling of stained glass, the architectural model, some twelve feet wide, spun dizzyingly fast under a glass globe. In the sanitized mock-up of one of the most unforgiving cities in the world, Moscow's endless rows of Stalinist facades stood up orderly, tidily divided by non-existent trimmed evergreens. The rotting factories were stripped of their belching smokestacks. The city's byways, swept clean and paved smooth, were sprinkled with a few handsome trucks and new automobiles. The river, repeatedly diagnosed a cholera incubator, was a sparkling aquamarine. Upon it floated a barge and what appeared to be a cruise ship.

There were no people in the model city. Instead, the spotlights were fixed tight on a set of gleaming translucent skyscrapers that burst from the city's heart. Lit from above and beneath, they towered above the gray mass. The centerpiece, a tower far taller than all the others–part Empire State, part TransAmerica, but quintessentially Luzhkovian–lured the eye. On a mural on the wall nearby the radiant towers were transposed over an image of the Kremlin lit up at night. The towers dwarfed the Kremlin.

The lineage of the mayor's blueprint was Stalin's Dvorets Sovietov, the Palace of Soviets. This earlier design was immensely complex, but Stalin's aim had been simple: He wanted the world's tallest building. The blueprint called for the palace to be higher than the Empire State Building, capped by a statue of Lenin bigger than the Statue of Liberty. In 1931 Stalin detonated the world's largest Russian Orthodox Church, the Cathedral of Christ the Savior. The Dvorets Sovietov, however, was never built. Eventually a bog formed in the crater until Khrushchev filled it with a giant outdoor swimming hole for the proletariat. In 1991, Luzhkov, once an avowed atheist who found religion after his first election, set about to resurrect the cathedral. As a result of $330 million contributed by a legion of ignoble courtiers, Christ the Savior soon rose again.[6] And so, with God well housed, the mayor had turned to building a home for the free market.

One morning I saw a young couple, noses pressed to the glass, standing transfixed by the cardboard city. Like so many of the pilgrims who came to see this model of Moscow, they were eager and hopeful witnesses to the birth of the new Siti. They tried to locate their apartment in the model city, but it spun too fast. They spent another moment, then moved on.

"Think it'll ever be built?" the elfin girl, her long hair braided low below her waist, asked her companion.

"No," he replied. "Of course not."

❧ THREE ❧

IN MOSCOW I WAS AFRAID every day. Not that I would be attacked. I had been, but not harmed. No, my fear was derived from bad news, the flow of death, violent and early death, that courses through each day in Moscow. As luck would have it, we lived a floor beneath a celebrity, a would-be banker who helped run a notorious pyramid scheme that bankrupted thousands when it crashed in the first post-Soviet years. He was well protected.

In the morning, he posted flint-chinned bodyguards with short-stock Kalashnikovs buttoned inside their suit coats at his door and on every landing of our stairwell. At night, he didn't let us sleep. Big footsteps pounded overhead at all hours. One of his guards, it seemed, stood post all night. In the morning I would be sure to cough, sniffle, or shuffle loudly to let the guards know I was coming their way. I bade them good morning as they rebuttoned their jackets.

Paul Tatum, a onetime Republican fund raiser from Oklahoma and a well-known man about Moscow, was the most famous foreigner killed. *Pravda*, in 1990, had announced his arrival with creamy praise. Tatum, *Pravda* said, "has a dream, an American dream. . . . He dreams of the day when a tiny American oasis will grow in the center of the Soviet capital." The "oasis" was the Radisson Slavyanskaya, Russia's first deluxe Western-style hotel and business complex. Coowned with the Moscow city government, it grew into a bustling hotel that hosted visiting American presidents. "My baby" Tatum liked to call it. But as later was the case in so many of the so-called joint ventures, before long the natives made moves to muscle him out—at times literally. A long, nasty fight ensued.

Tatum was killed on Halloween night in 1996, the week I started at *Time*. I was working in the bureau on a Sunday evening when a few blocks away Tatum, as he entered an underground walkway, fell to the ground in a hail of bullets. Eleven of the twenty shots hit him. I had often seen him around town. The last time had been on the summer night earlier that year when Yeltsin won his improbable reelection. Tatum made the rounds at election headquarters. "I'm gonna win this war," he vowed to all who would listen. As the TV correspondents reported Yeltsin's "miraculous comeback" and "the end, perhaps forever, of the Communist threat to Russia's young Democracy," Tatum was his usual cocksure self. "United we stand," he declared, "and divided we fall."

Tatum was by no means alone. Each day I scanned the local wires: an English engineer found burned to death in his own apartment; an American television producer, a Californian in his thirties who came to Moscow to do good, stabbed to death; a young Canadian diplomat discovered dead in his living room (victim of a slipped mickey, the reports said); a German chef beaten to death on a central street, his face "torn." There were many more, but those who succumbed to Moscow's violence were rarely foreigners. We were invisible. Compared to the newly moneyed local elite, we were poor.

"Not likely these days," said my friend Lyona, the son of a Soviet general lavishly decorated for his service to military intelligence, when I told him how Mia and I had been robbed in Moscow once before, in 1991. That had been back in the old Soviet days, when foreigners were few in number and far richer than their neighbors. In one hour, as we shopped at a local market, our place had been stripped. The thieves took everything–and tidily hauled it off in our suitcases. They even took the telephone. "No one will touch you now," Lyona said. It was nothing against foreigners, he said. It was just that Russian thieves now wanted real money.

Now they went after the New Russians. The so-called *Noviye Russkie*–a deliberate play in Russian on "nouveau riche"–were those who had managed to grab a slice of the spoils and grown preposterously rich overnight. Most Russians, being Old Russians, naturally hated the New Russians. In the jokes that Russians addictively tell each other, they had replaced the Chukchi, a desperately poor native people of the Russian north who had long suffered as the favored butt of Soviet jokes. Lyona was right. The New Russians had become the new target.

I HEARD COUNTLESS TALES of horror from friends and neighbors. But none was more frightening than the one I heard T*** tell. I believed it right away because I believed everything he told me. He was the only Russian I ever met who had survived, flourished even, in the upper reaches of the Soviet Communist Party and the Russian Orthodox Church. His business, at least on the wintry day we met in the center of Moscow just off Pushkin Square, was oil. The church's oil. Early in the Yeltsin era, the Orthodox Church won the right to export, tax-free, millions of barrels of Russian crude each year. T*** now worked for the trading company the men of the cloth had set up. The work, he said, was pretty much the same as what he did in the old days. "Only now instead of the general secretary, I serve His Holiness."

T*** was fond of sushi, sweet Georgian wine, and sayings like "Creeds come and go, but I'm still here." Over lunch he digressed from a discussion of the church's role in building the market economy to a description of the forgotten world of Mikhail Andreyevich Suslov, Brezhnev's long-serving ideologist and gray cardinal. Though dead for decades, Suslov remained one of the few old Party bosses who still conjured fury among Russians. My neighbor Valery, a kindly retiree from the Soviet Foreign Trade Ministry, hated him as the symbol of Politburo excess. Valery's aunt, a nurse who spent her life ministering to the Party elite in the Kremlin hospital, had regaled him with tales of Suslov's enemas. Each morning he came to the Kremlin hospital for his daily fruit juice. Not to be outdone, his wife demanded fresh trout each week, flown in from Lake Sevan in Armenia. But none of this troubled T***. His tale concerned Suslov's grandnephew, a forty-year-old banker named Vladimir Sterlikov. Sterlikov, it was said, once lived in the dacha of Galina Brezhneva, Brezhnev's daughter, who had a weakness for diamonds, drink, and circus performers. For a time Sterlikov had worked for *Pravda*. Now he was the deputy head of the Russian Bank for Reconstruction and Development—"until recently," T*** added with relish.

"It was early one morning out on Rublyovka . . . ," T*** said, setting the scene. He was careful to call the Rublyovskoye Schosse by its nickname, the Rublyovka. He was letting me know that he too graced Moscow's most prestigious artery. Clogged morning and night with convoys of Bavarian sedans, the Rublyovka was the gateway to the off-hours realm of the elite. It was the road that bore the city's richest and mightiest into town from their fortified *cottedgi,* cozy five-story affairs nestled in the birches just beyond the city limit. Because it led directly to the residences of the mayor of Moscow, the prime minister, the cabinet, and, of course, the president himself, the Rublyovka was also the most heavily guarded road in Russia.

"It was early in the morning," T*** repeated, pausing between sips of green tea, "when Suslov's poor grandnephew met his bitter end."

A waitress in traditional Russian peasant dress, a nod to the prerevolutionary undertones of the menu before us, interrupted T*** to unveil his swordfish, a taste for which he had acquired, along with the affection for green tea, during an extended Asian stint, back in his days as a "journalist" reporting to the Central Committee's foreign relations office. T***, many whispered, was KGB in those Asian days. Some insisted that he still was. But T*** just laughed at all the talk and maintained that he was merely a journalist, a student of the Japanese language and culture, and, above all, a loyal, if less than devout, follower of the Party line.

As soon as the waitress took her leave, he continued.

"Sterlikov's driving his Saab, or rather his driver-bodyguard is, in from the dacha when all of a sudden a cop speeds past, cuts in front of them, and forces them to pull over. The cops ask the driver for his license. Then they say they want to check the engine number. So the driver opens the hood. Just as he leans over the engine—pop. They shoot him in the back of the head. Poor Sterlikov starts to get out of the car to see what's going on, and one of the cops shoots him. Six bullets in the chest. Died later in the hospital."

T*** took a sip from his bone china teacup and watched my eyes contract. But I had heard such tales before. The Moscow tabloids were full of them. "Never open a door for anyone in uniform" was one of the first rules a landlord taught a foreign tenant. The hit men, we were told, had access to the proper uniforms and even genuine IDs. Cop cars? No problem. T*** was undeterred. It was not the end of the tale, he said. "The cops were hit men," he said. "But they were also cops."

Another sip, right pinkie raised, to let it sink in.

"How do I know all this? Sterlikov worked for one of our banks. A recent hire and not the best. But he brought a certain pedigree, and we owed a favor to a friend. The poor guy was killed by real policemen. We don't know their names, but we know what happened." The bank, he explained, had conducted its own investigation. The cops had been hired to kill. They were moonlighting.

T*** returned to his fish. As for Sterlikov, he checked out clean. No extravagant debts. Nothing certainly to get killed over. And he hadn't been at the bank long enough to steal anything. He fell victim to a stupid blood feud. Banker for banker, that kind of thing.

"But the cops," T*** said, wiping the edges of his red lips with an ironed napkin, "now isn't that something?" He marveled at the accelerated evolution of the criminalization of the organs of law enforcement. He refolded the napkin and revealed a grin. Once we had left the restaurant, I watched T*** trundle off down the snowy boulevard and disappear into the noonday thicket of cars and passersby on Pushkin Square. He almost seemed pleased.

☙ FOUR ❧

BEYOND LUST AND FEAR, Moscow breeds power. You cannot help feeling that you are trespassing in its path. Every effort is made to impress upon the populace its privileged proximity to the unlimited power of the state. This is not just state power as in other countries. This is not merely the pomp of officialdom, but the deliberate demonstration of the state's power over the people, an ever-present slap in their face.

It is midmorning. You walk through the cold, dank underpass, lit by long fluorescent lamps. At one end stand two grandmothers, selling cigarettes, hand-knit caps, dried flowers. The underground walkway fills with the sounds of an accordion. A mournful Russian ballad. Every day the accordion player, a Moldovan refugee, is here busking. Every day he squeezes out the same song. It is a long underpass. When at last you emerge and climb the stairs up into the cold wind of the far side of the street, you suddenly hear it: the silence. Nothing announces the power like the silence.

Kutuzovsky Prospekt may well be the broadest street in Moscow. At its widest it has seven lanes in each direction. In its center the road is divided by a lane reserved for the political and financial elite, or at least any Russian sufficiently well moneyed or well connected to procure the coveted *migalka*, a little flashing blue light that, once affixed to a car roof, announces the right of the faceless passenger hidden behind the curtained, smoked windows to break any traffic rule or regulation. In the morning, as the city's bankers and bureaucrats rush toward their offices, the road is filled with cars and heavy trucks trying to tack their way into the center. The roar of the traffic, with all fifteen lanes fully loaded, is deafening. Walking the sidewalks of Kutuzovsky, as I did nearly every morning, can be unpleasant.

Until the silence comes. It happens at least twice a day, usually in midmorning and just before the sun sets. You are walking down the sidewalk, and then, in a single moment, you realize something has changed, something is amiss. All you hear is the crunch of your boots on the hard snow. On the street, the slow-moving river of cars has not simply stopped; it has disappeared. (In minutes a road as wide as a highway is completely cleared.) The trolley buses have pulled over and stand along the edge of the *prospekt*. The citizens too, waiting at the bus stops, stand still. Everyone waits. Hundreds of poor souls, trapped in the stilled traffic, sit mute in their parked cars. The street has frozen into a photograph, and you are the only one moving through it.

For several minutes nothing stirs. Then suddenly a black Volga, an illuminated *migalka* fixed to its roof, speeds down the middle of the *prospekt*. Then another, and a third, a fourth. And then the chorus of sirens accompanying the flashing lights. A convoy of automobiles, a dozen in all, each duly impressing the motionless citizenry with its size, speed, and cleanliness. As men, women, and schoolchildren (and the secret policemen in plain clothes sprinkled among them) stand and watch, a squadron of BMW *militsiya* sedans sweeps past, followed by an extended black Mercedes limousine and a quartet of oversize Mercedes jeeps. As the convoy passes, the cars leave a ripple of turned faces on the sidewalks.

A visitor might imagine the world had stopped because of a dire emergency. But the Muscovites frozen in place along this vast slate gray avenue recognize the scene for what it is: their president, the leader of all Russia, making his way to work. More than twenty miles of roadway in the Russian capital are closed in this fashion every day. In a city already paralyzed by too much snow and too many cars. And still no one complains, ever. It is the essence of power, Moscow style. It is *naglost*. In general, *naglost* is an unseemly blend of arrogance, shamelessness, and rudeness. In this instance it is the contemptuous disdain of the rights of ordinary Russians.

🕮 FIVE 🕮

IN THE COVETED neighborhood of Nikitskiye Vorota, nestled among small parks and large embassies and tucked behind the poplar-lined boulevard that circumscribes the city center stands a surprisingly modest apartment building where the new guard meets the old guard. No. 15 Leontievsky Pereulok, a squat seven-story building of beige brick and broad balconies, has an exterior that bears few distinguishing marks except for a row of Soviet-era plaques that honor a half dozen of its previous residents. Built in 1962 for Politburo members evicted from the Kremlin living quarters when Khrushchev tore them down to build his massive Palace of Congresses, the building housed Party overlords, titans of Soviet industry and arms, and even Dolores Ibárruri, the famed doyenne of the Spanish Communists. More recently, the chief of the International Monetary Fund mission in Moscow, a jovial bald economist with a hefty pinkie ring, lived here in the old flat of Andrei Gromyko, the long-serving Soviet foreign minister.

"That's the apartment of Mikoyan, designer of the MiG," Nikita Khrushchev told me one evening as we toured the building where he had lived since childhood. "And in that apartment," he exclaimed, "lives Lenin's niece!"

Just below the IMF chief, in a sprawling apartment filled, I imagined, with an overstuffed Warsaw Bloc living room set, lived Grigori Vasilievich Romanov, among the oldest of the old guard. One sub-zero afternoon in midwinter, as the air chilled to a glass-sharp edge, I set out to meet Romanov. He commanded me to stand, alone, on Ulitsa Tverskaya beneath the iron statue of Yuri the Long-Armed, founder of Moscow. Across the street looms Luzhkov's office, the lavishly remodeled Moscow Communist Party headquarters. A red electric sign at the Central Post Office flashed seventeen degrees below zero. I spent twenty minutes examining every passing face, but I had patience. I had been waiting to see Romanov for two years.

I spied him shuffling slowly, painfully, down the crowded sidewalk long before he spotted me. As he approached, a silver Mercedes, a For Sale sign taped to its rear window, nearly ran him down. He was short, no more than five feet five inches, and I remember hearing how Romanov, back when he was in the Politburo, had placed his desk atop a raised platform to make himself appear more imposing. He wore a gray topcoat, with a thin sweater beneath. A faint stubble shaded his sagging square cheeks; tuffs of gray jutted from beneath his brown fur hat. At seventy-five, and despite a recent heart attack, he was in far better shape than his phone voice had led me to believe. His pale blue eyes, however, were tearing from the cold wind.

"It's not that I don't trust journalists," he declared straight off, dabbing his eyes with an ironed blue handkerchief. "I don't trust anyone. But someone has to say what has happened here. Someone has to speak of Russia's misery."

Romanov came to the West's attention in the 1980s, when he and Mikhail Gorbachev served as lieutenants to Andropov and his ailing successor, Konstantin Chernenko. Romanov was the darling of the Politburo's hawks, the truest of the cold warriors, but upon Chernenko's death, he was ousted by Gorbachev. He had not spoken to a foreigner in years. "The only people he hates more than foreigners," joked Nikita, "are reporters." But I had long badgered him, calling him first thing in the morning once or twice a week. At last he relented. He agreed to meet—only in public, "in an hour."

His rant that winter day was almost pauseless. "Gorbachev will pay for his sins! I can't stand the sight of his pig's mug! He's a traitor! A traitor to the Motherland! He's sniveling about how no one here thanks him, about how ungrateful Russians are to him. To hell with Gorbachev. He started this disaster. He was a catastrophe, a peasant who had no right coming to the big city. . . . Yeltsin? Who is Yeltsin? A swine who drinks. He got drunk on power. I can't even speak of him. He's a criminal. A common thief who's robbed his Motherland and killed his people. All these Gaidars, Berezovskys, these so-called oligarchs, they're all Yeltsin's little children. Now they want to ban the Communist Party. Do you think all people are born the same? Of course not. Some are born to make things—to create, build, and work. Others are born to take, to steal. Gorbachev is one of the takers. He started the fashion. Now look where it's led us."

To some, Grigori Romanov was an oddity, a hapless relic shuffling toward his life's end. He was, to be sure, a diehard Communist who had chewed sour grapes ever since he fell hard from the Soviet Olympus. But oddly enough, in advanced retirement, far from his rarefied life among the Party elite, Romanov echoed the lament of many a common man in Russia. In the years after the Soviet collapse, he had found company. Romanov had no power now, but he took solace in the knowledge that millions of Russians shared his views. His principal conviction—*Ran'she bylo lushche* ("Things were better before")—had become the motto of his generation. And the dirty secret, only conceded in the capital sotte voce by the ascendant Young Reformers, was that they were right. For many of his generation, things were indeed better before—for them.

Romanov lived on some sixty dollars a month. As a veteran of the blockade of Leningrad, he said he deserved much more. "I'm entitled to several war pensions. I'm a veteran and an invalid. And I received the Hero of Soviet Labor. Politburo privileges? What a joke! We have nothing. No dacha, no car, no privileges at all. Only the apartment."

Once it was a very different story. After rising through the Party ranks, he ran Leningrad, Russia's second city, for twenty-five years, until he was summoned to Moscow by Andropov in 1983. He survived various Politburo wars, until he was finally outflanked by the ascendant Gorbachev.

"In February 1985, Chernenko called me out to the dacha," Romanov told me. "He was weak. He sat up in bed. I stood beside him. 'Just wait,' he said. 'Relax. It'll come to pass.' He relied on the defense sector. He knew the importance of our work. He never wanted Gorbachev. . . . We all knew Chernenko couldn't last long. He was in very bad shape. So were most of the others, for that matter. They were all old and sick. Gromyko and the rest. There were two candidates discussed at that time: Vladimir Shcherbitsky and Romanov. . . . No one talked about Gorbachev with any seriousness."

A few weeks later Chernenko died, and within hours Gorbachev wrested control of the Politburo in a late-night five to four vote. It was a bit of spectacular luck, or so his biographers have held, that the three committee members who were Gorbachev's chief opponents were absent from Moscow.

"The week before Chernenko died, my wife and I flew to Vilnius," Romanov said. "They had given us a trip to Lithuania, to a sanitarium. The day Chernenko died, we were there. They said the plane would only fly the next day. They met that day, hours after he died. But the three most senior members of the Politburo weren't present! Kunaev was in Almaty. Shcherbitsky was in the States. And I was in Lithuania. By the time we got back to Moscow he'd already done it. That fast. That was it. It was agreed to in public of course at the Politburo meeting and at the plenum. But he'd already cut the deal in secret with all of them. And you think the timing, Chernenko's death, I mean, was all accidental?"

In the aftermath Romanov was stripped of power. He had long been renowned as an epicurean lush, ridiculed as the "Last of the Romanovs." Gorbachev's cronies played upon that reputation, spreading the rumor that to celebrate his daughter's wedding, Romanov had ordered the caterers to use Catherine the Great's Sèvres from the Hermitage. Worse still, the story went, a few pieces had been smashed. By July Romanov had been summarily retired and sent, according to another rumor fed to reporters, to dry out.

Did he ever regret, I wondered, not making it to the top?

"No," he retorted. "I'm just sorry the wrong man did. The traitor. Because if it had been me, the invasion never would have happened."

❧ SIX ❧

Please, put it in a bank. . . . Please, let's put it in a foreign bank.

–Vladimir Putin advising the relatives of those who died on the nuclear submarine Kursk *on what to do with their compensation[7]*

EVER SINCE RICARDO, economists have built intricate mathematical models to explain and forecast how markets will move. Calculus, however, assumes reason. When Russia crashed in the summer of 1998, there was little rational about it. "Lenin is said to have declared that the best way to destroy the Capitalist System was to debauch the currency," John Maynard Keynes wrote in 1921. "Lenin was certainly right. There is no subtler, no surer means of overturning the existing basis of society than to debauch the currency. The process engages all the hidden forces of economic law on the side of destruction, and does it in a manner which not one man in a million is able to diagnose." Russia under Yeltsin was less a test market for the "Invisible Hand" or shock therapy than a new Babylon where the wheeling and dealing were nasty, brutish, and, for many in August 1998, lethal.

In the dawn of the new market those who would play its princes, if only for a while, needed gastronomic palaces where they could feast in the unreality of their reality. Across Moscow elite men's clubs sprouted, with reliable security and robust wine cellars. Fashioned from the pages of Tolstoy and Pushkin, the clubs were draped in pre-Bolshevik bliss. Whether or not such bliss had ever existed didn't matter. Artifice and excess were the object. In their urge to build a new world, the plutocrats imported Swiss chefs, Austrian furniture, English nannies. Having grown fat on the spoils of the Motherland, they could bask in the shimmer of their own money.

Tucked discreetly off Moscow's Ring Road, two blocks down from the

33

Institute of Biological Structures, which handles the annual repair work on Lenin's corpse, is Club T. For a time it was considered among the finest restaurants in Russia. It should be, since it was designed as a private reserve for the new plutocracy, its very own "21" Club. Guests are vetted by video-phone. The ten or so tables inside reflect absolute elegance, their pink table-cloths radiant under crystal and gold chandeliers. One corner of the dining room is heavy with the smell of Cuban cigars, another with the high notes of French perfume and Armenian cognac. Silk drapes keep the outside out-side. Gold seraphim dance on the walls, their pudgy arms hoisting aloft little gilded candles. Large mirrors announce your entrance, reassuring you that you belong, that you've arrived. The mirrors also assist the discreet diner to find the famous faces hidden across the room.

One evening, as the cold wake of the crash forced its survivors to renew their exit strategies, I invited four of the earliest American pioneers to join me at Club T. Paul Tatum of course was not the last American investor to see his dream sour in Russia. By the time Russia crashed in 1998, countless frontiersmen had been scalped, fled for home, or moved on to the next gold rush. But the quartet of Americans I invited to dinner—Bill Browder, Peter Derby, Charlie Ryan, and Boris Jordan—who, when their portfolios were at their fattest, controlled several billions of dollars of investments in Russia, remained.

Derby, a New Yorker of Russian descent, had arrived first, opening Russia's first foreign-owned commercial bank in 1991. Jordan, another prodigal son of Long Island's Russian diaspora, with roots among the Whites who fled the Revolution, had come in 1992 to help run Crédit Suisse/First Boston's Moscow outpost. By 1995, having reaped billions of dollars in the privatization scheme, he had left to found Russia's first Western-style invest-ment bank, Renaissance Capital. The 1998 crash forced a divorce that split the bank, and Jordan for a time found himself isolated and on his own.

Browder, the soft-spoken grandson of, ironically, the American Commu-nist leader Earl Browder, had also arrived in 1992, having run an equity fund for Robert Maxwell and later the Eastern European markets for Salomon Brothers. In April 1996 he founded the Hermitage Fund, a high-end hedge fund that at its peak boasted $1.2 billion in assets. By 1997 Hermitage had returns of 228 percent; Browder's return on his initial capital was 725 percent.

Ryan first came to Russia after working at the EBRD, the European Bank for Reconstruction and Development. Together with one of Russia's leading reformers, former Finance Minister Boris Fyodorov, Ryan founded the United Financial Group, which, by 1998, managed more than a billion dollars in assets. With his main line roots and mainstream résumé, he was an anomaly, a reflective banker. "Of course the money brings us here," Ryan told me in 1997. "But it's much more than that. We're building something entirely new. Okay, you can get stability and good returns in the U.S. But can you get the buzz?"

Over snails and caviar, king prawns, and medallions of New Zealand lamb, the evening's theme, at my request, was "What went wrong?" For the next three hours, the foursome pointed fingers at the IMF, former Prime Minister Sergei Kiriyenko, inborn Russian corruption, falling commodity prices, the global recession, prudish U.S. investors, prudent Asian investors, again the IMF. Jordan inevitably dropped the name of every player in Russia, from Kiriyenko to Soros, and declared early on: "This'll help them" ("this" being the crash, "them" being the Russians). Derby spoke in breathless arias on the chronology of the fall. Ryan waxed philosophical, and Browder concluded, "Sadly, this is a crash with too many morals." Sadly, too, the meal, by far the most expensive I had ever eaten, got lost in the burlesque of charge and countercharge.

"The basic problem is you can't control a company in this country," stated Jordan.

"You can have controlling stakes," said Browder.

"And get ripped off on every level," parried Jordan.

Derby announced that his number two, "a great Russian guy," would go to jail in days. (In fact, he didn't.) Derby paused, then said: "We will stay and try to be honest and fulfill our responsibilities."

"This country's so corrupt they fucked themselves," added Browder.

"Bill, you obviously don't believe that," replied Jordan, "or else you didn't do your fiduciary duty for your clients, investing a billion in the place."

At this moment the joust between Browder and Jordan was interrupted by the governor of St. Petersburg, Vladimir Yakovlev, a blithe opportunist, who stopped by for a round of handshakes. When the governor floated away, Derby seized his chance. "The worst thing about it was there was no reason to default," he said. "Absolutely none. There wasn't that much debt coming due, like twelve billion dollars over the six weeks. And it was ruble-denominated. There were reasons to take action, but not to default on the domestic debt."

"Any country will default if they can't roll over their debt," noted Browder. "If the U.S. couldn't sell T-bills for a month straight, they'd have a big fucking problem. But the thing that's most damaging is the collapse of the banking system. . . . "

"This place never had a banking system," scoffed Derby.

"It had a system where you made payments," Browder retorted. "You can't make payments now."

"The banking sector did not take savings, invest it, and get growth through investment," said Derby.

"There was no multiplier effect," Ryan summed up.

"And the reason you don't have people breaking the windows here is that they didn't deposit their money in the banks," said Jordan.

"This is one the great mysteries of Russia," Ryan noted. "No one's had a job in a lot of towns for years. But car ownership in those same towns has gone up by two hundred percent. Consumer durables are way up. And at the same time no one's rioting. That's a clear sign that no one's being very honest about their real net worth or about their real sources of income."

"Let's say you've got twenty-five percent of your money in the bank and seventy-five percent in your mattress," said Browder. "Eventually your mattress money is going to disappear."

Tuxedoed waiters unveiled course after course with remarkable flair, raising broad silver lids from big silver plates, making sweeping bows in unison. As the evening wound down, Browder, more puckish than the rest, observed, "There used to be Third World countries. Then they became Developing Countries. Then Less Developed Countries. Then the wall came down, and we got Emerging Markets. Well, folks, now they're gone, too."

With dessert the conversation drifted to talk of the price of bodyguards, the best tax havens for billionaires, and the travails of Bermudan citizenship. Over coffee, Jordan offered a parable: Back when it was flush, the Central Bank decided to buy an American satellite to monitor electronic trading across Russia's eleven time zones. No sooner had the satellite been launched than it spun out of orbit. Eventually it disappeared altogether.[8]

❧ SEVEN ❧

So many wonderfully fine women can hardly be seen in any country in one assemblage.

–Cassius Marcellus Clay, the Kentucky abolitionist Lincoln sent as America's emissary to Alexander II

ANOTHER STREAM OF PROSPECTORS had started in the last days of the old USSR. American men, weighted with middle age and regret, began to come to Moscow to troll. Back then they were searching for a woman they had heard of, the charming and servile Russian antifeminist, the alluring woman who could be wife, lover, cook, cleaner, and mother all in one. Moscow, the American lonely hearts believed, would be their mecca. For thousands, it was.

In the hotel bars and nightclubs you ran into all sorts: human rights lawyers and postdoctoral scholars, cardiologists, and even astronauts. Most of the men spoke no Russian, knew nothing of Tolstoy or Pushkin. To them, the girls were "Natashas," one and all, and Moscow was heaven. That was in the pioneer days. As time moved on, the marriage market slumped. "Russian bride" agencies still claimed a strong niche, but many of the men who came to Moscow now wanted only one thing. Sex ruled the night, and the dollar was the coin of the realm.

During Bill Clinton's last presidential visit to Moscow, Mia and I went for a beer at a new hotel on Tverskaya, Moscow's main drag. We found half a dozen Secret Service agents lining the bar. (After Tatum's murder the White House was relieved that a new American hotel had opened in Moscow.) Nearby sat several other Americans, from their banter, junior-level White House adjutants. The Secret Service on that night was more than happy to share a tip. "Go to Night Flight," one agent in a pinstriped suit said, "and you'll never regret it."

Night Flight was Swedish run and scarcely resembled a bordello, but it was famed for offering Moscow's most beautiful, and most expensive, prostitutes. ("DO IT TONIGHT," said its ads at the airport, tempting new arrivals.) The cover was steep, the Secret Service agent said, twenty dollars after 9:00 P.M. "But," he added, "it's the best twenty bucks you'll ever spend."

If Night Flight was the high end, the Hungry Duck anchored the low end. Run by a Canadian innkeeper who opened his first bar in Moscow in 1993 and housed in the old House of Culture for Soviet Workers in the Arts, a few minutes' walk off Red Square, the Duck, as the bar was known among ex-pats and natives alike, grew world famous. The *Washington Post* even dubbed it "the wildest bar in the world." While it lasted, it was certainly one of the most vulgar, with drunken sex in its dark corners and vomit on its floors.

The first time I braved the Duck, I ended up bartending. I had come to interview the club's impresario, Stanley Williams, a black deejay from Brooklyn who had recently emerged from a Moscow prison cell. Caught up in a sweep targeted against African students in a Moscow disco, Stanley had been arrested for possessing "less than an ashtray" of marijuana. In the end the charges were dropped, but by then he had spent nearly two years in Moscow's worst jails. I was writing a story on the miserable state of Russian prisons—the prison population had risen to more than a million, and the prisons had become one of the world's leading TB incubators—and I wanted to talk to Stanley.

I arrived too late. Stanley was already behind his turntables. So I was put to work, pouring beer behind the bar. All eyes were fixed on the male strippers who paraded on top of the long bar that ringed the center of the club. "We usually get upwards to eight hundred in here on Friday nights," Stanley screamed as Puff Daddy blasted out from huge speakers. (Nine hundred and twenty girls, he said, were the house record.) Stanley had stacked the speakers on top of one another, building a barricade to protect him from the sweating masses. "It can get a little–" I could not make out the end of his sentence. But I saw what he meant.

The Duck's managers, relying on the laws of physics and desire, had mastered the art of maximizing the sexual tension a single room can permit. The girls, many of whom had to survive long train journeys to get here, got in free. They drank—only hard liquor—for free. Men were allowed entrance only after 9:00 P.M. They gathered in a long queue outside the bar, like bulls locked in a chute awaiting a rodeo's opening bell. The effect naturally was dramatic. The sweating mass of Russian teenaged girls danced harder and harder as the music grew faster and faster, while the older, mostly Western men lusted all the more publicly. As the fever swelled, one, then two, then many more girls took to the bar to dance. Before long they had ripped off their blouses and bras. It was not rare, Stanley would say, for the action to go farther, much farther than that.

In the years that followed the crisis, Moscow's nightlife grew serious. As Yeltsin departed and Putin entered, a new stodginess threatened to reign. Many of the landmark stops along the ex-pat map of Moscow closed. The Duck was one of the last, but it, too, shut down. The woman who ran the former House of Culture that housed the club was eighty-two-year-old Olga Lepeshinskaya, a former Bolshoi prima ballerina. Still known as Stalin's favorite, Lepeshinskaya was not pleased her beloved building was hosting a bacchanalia. She launched a campaign to evict the foreigners. The Canadian owners had survived countless death threats and an attempted kidnapping, but eventually the police raids, even though the owners had paid out some two hundred thousand dollars in bribes, killed the business.

One of the final blows came when a clutch of Duma deputies, of the Communist and nationalist bent, checked in on ladies' night. They arrived just as Dylan, the Duck's six-foot male stripper from Nigeria, wearing little but gold spangles, was "dancing" on the bar, with several young Russian females, to the blasting strains of the Soviet national anthem. Weeks later one of the Duma deputies in a speech on the parliament's floor, grew red in the face. "If this were Washington," he screamed, "they would hang that Negro!"

EIGHT

IN ALL THE YEARS I lived in Moscow, I never had a car. Each day I would step out onto the curb and raise an arm—"voting" the Russians call it—and almost always in an instant at least one car, sometimes an entire lane, would screech to a stop. For a journalist, few modes of transport could be more rewarding. For Muscovites, and Russians in cities across the country, turning your car into a gypsy cab is what even the most educated and skilled did—and do—to get by. Over the years I enjoyed my share of ambulances, hearses, KGB Volgas, and Kremlin Audis. In the privacy of their cars, I sat beside the dispossessed and displaced: a nuclear engineer who had helped to design the SS-20s once pointed at the United States; a Yakut wrestler who pulled off the road, opened his palm, and tried to hawk a two-carat Siberian diamond; an ex-KGB colonel who had spent his career reading dissidents' mail and now complained that the state had abandoned him; an Armenian gas smuggler who drove an armored BMW he could no longer afford to fill with gas. Each day brought a new round of coincidental interlocutors. Rarely did they stay silent for long. Like the coachmen in the stories of Gogol or Tolstoy, they steered the talk effortlessly from the weather–the dreadful snow or the dreadful heat–to politics–the ineluctable triumph of the "den of thieves" in the Kremlin–before settling into a long disquisition on the country's dreadful past and dreadful predicament at present. Each, above all, was certain to recite, as if by rote, his–and occasionally her–own canto of loss.

One hot and humid summer morning in the final days of Yeltsin, I was sitting with such a stranger, an out-of-work air traffic controller whose dove gray face streamed with sweat. We were stuck in his 1986 Lada on a two-lane street that divides one of Moscow's largest cemeteries. For some unknown reason, he had turned onto this street even though it was bumper to bumper with cars. For nineteen minutes we had not moved. I watched the minutes tick off on the dashboard clock. The clear plastic cover of the clock was cracked, but the hands continued to move. I had long ago missed the interview I'd set out for when I met the man sitting next to me. He seemed a bright enough fellow, this man who once guided Aeroflot jets through the Soviet skies, but he did not realize that I was a foreigner and he had no understanding of why I could be exasperated.

He had a point. In Moscow, after all, time spent frozen in place was not without its lessons–even in a traffic jam. Soon the more enterprising drivers usurped the sidewalk. Still, they did not crawl far. Two black BMWs, their windows smoked, moved toward us, negotiating for space with the little blue *migalka* lights on their roofs: government cars. At the same time, a Mercedes 600, the largest model the Germans ever made, eased right to make good use of the sidewalk. In the Yeltsin years of excess the Mercedes 600 had become the chariot of choice among the Moscow elite. In one year in the 1990s, more *shestsoty*, as the luxury cars were known in Russian, were sold in the Russian capital than in all Germany. Others of course now tried to follow the Mercedes offroad, but almost immediately one follower, an old Zhiguli two-door, hit an asphalt crater and stalled. The sound of metal on stone hinted at axle damage.

The tension grew, but everyone stayed silent. A few men swore to themselves. No one honked. After nearly an hour we still had not seen the end of the block. I was staring at the same dozen drivers and their passengers and at the rows of tombstones that ran deep amid the lean trees. At the hour mark the honking started. It was naturally without purpose or direction. A Volga to our right gave out. The poor soul in it was forced to evacuate. There was nowhere to move the car and no one willing to help its driver. Instead, a burly fellow in a Land Cruiser read him the riot act. There is nothing as pleasing, it would seem, to a Russian driver as a stream of blue swearing. The yelling did no good. The Volga was rooted in place.

We inched forward. As the second hour approached, the driver said he did not mind the wait. When he worked the tower at the airport, he'd often have to stay awake for double shifts. Sometimes there were long stretches through the night when not one plane would land. I noticed that the gas gauge of the Lada was on empty, even to the left of empty. A young girl, perhaps fifteen or sixteen, rollerbladed through the maze of metal. She was blond and wore earphones. Three cars ahead of us, in the lane to our left, sat an army truck, with an open flatbed ringed by wooden slats. It held four or five large metal barrels. At first it was not clear what the barrels contained—until I saw the pool of liquid forming beneath the truck. Then I saw the trickle dripping from one of the barrels, the one lying on its side.

"Yes," the former air traffic controller said. It was gas. "And in a second, when some fool drops his cigarette out the window, that truck will go up like an open oil well on fire." We went on sitting in place. I began to smell the gas. We were in the middle of five lanes of cars. We could not move anywhere. I looked left and right. On all sides drivers and passengers and passersby were smoking. I counted nine lit cigarettes.

The scene became Felliniesque in its absurdity. Another car broke down. A young woman emerged from it. She had light brown hair and was wearing a white tank top and oversize sunglasses. Two volunteers abandoned their cars to come to her rescue. At the top of the second hour a crane, unattended and parked, appeared up ahead in the right lane. Nearby stood a truck with a green canvas roof. On the back of the truck a small yellow sign stenciled in black announced *LYUDI* ("PEOPLE"). The truck was filled with conscripts. Inside the heat of the canvas, the soldiers were sweating. They did not, as is the usual practice, extend a hand to cadge cigarettes.

We inched again. Up ahead a new obstacle, a parked trolleybus. Its power lines unstuck, it was forced from its lane by the cars that had occupied the sidewalk. At last we reached an intersection. In the sea of cars, the roads, two central arteries in the middle of the Russian capital, were unrecognizable. The traffic lights changed colors overhead, but no one paid them any heed. Only one lone Mercedes 600, big and black, tacked against traffic to the far side of the road and managed to move ahead. "A whale," the former air traffic controller said of the Mercedes as he and I sat in silence and watched it move slowly out of sight.

✻ NINE ✻

AN ADVENTUROUS documentary filmmaker, a friend informed me, spent a year touring the Russian outback as the last century closed. He visited dozens of small out-of-the-way towns and villages, everywhere asking the local children the same single question: "Who was Lenin?" Somewhere in his travels a little girl in an audience far from Moscow grew excited. "I know!" she exclaimed. "Lenin was the first amphibian who came ashore. He was the one who crawled from the water, learned how to walk, climbed atop an iron tank, and called for everybody to follow him."

DESPITE THE END OF the empire, the Seventh of November, Revolution Day, remained a holiday in Russia. In 1996, Yeltsin, having failed to bury the Party back in 1991, decided to try something different. He gave it a new name, the Day of Accord and Reconciliation. Like most of Yeltsin's grand gestures, the rechristening was a failure. Sergei Kovalyov, the Duma deputy who spent ten years in the Gulag and served as Andrei Sakharov's closest protégé after Gorbachev freed the physicist from his internal exile in Gorky, called it yet another foolhardy try at a top-down purification of the nation, the state's attempt to relegate the old way of life to history.

"What does this mean, 'Accord and Reconciliation'?" Kovalyov asked me one afternoon in his cramped Duma office. "These are empty words when people still carry Stalin portraits in parades. A day of national mourning would be a bit more appropriate. We don't need a new holiday. We need to teach our children that Lenin and Stalin were the progenitors of a criminal regime, that they were mass murderers."

Kovalyov, a shy, soft-spoken man who wore the same thick Soviet-style glasses as when I met him a decade earlier, was the first to say he had never wielded the clout of Sakharov. But amid the din of the Duma his voice resounded with moral sobriety. He shared a story that had stunned him. A student had come to see him. At one point in their conversation Kovalyov mentioned the passing of the writer Andrei Sinyavsky, once best known in the West by his pseudonym, Abram Tertz, who, along with another young Soviet writer, Yuli Daniel, was arrested in 1966 and imprisoned for publishing abroad.[9] As Kovalyov recounted for the student the saga of the Sinyavsky and Daniel trial that attracted worldwide outcry, the student had laughed. "How can you laugh at a writer who was arrested?" Kovalyov had asked him. The student said he'd imagined the story was a joke. "He just couldn't believe," Kovalyov said, "it was ever possible to be sent to jail for writing literature!"

Five years after Yeltsin renamed November 7, a poll in 2001 found 43 percent of those queried yearned for the return of Revolution Day. Another pollster asked: "Imagine that the October Revolution is happening before your eyes. What would you do?" Of the respondents, 22 percent said they would support the Bolsheviks; 19 percent said they would cooperate with them in part; 13 percent said they would leave the country. Just 6 percent said they would fight Lenin and company.[10]

IN 1990S MOSCOW the remnants of the Soviet intelligentsia liked to talk about expiating guilt. The villains of Soviet power, the forlorn and graying dissidents liked to say, needed their own Nuremberg. They knew there never would be one. Russians have not embraced any attempt at a *Vergangenheitsbewältigung*, what Germans, true professionals in matters of national repentance, call the process of coming to terms with the past. It is said to be cathartic, offering a kind of deliverance. Russian has no such word.[11] In Russia, no attempt on a social scale has been made to examine the totalitarian past, to learn not simply how the Soviet state functioned but how Russians themselves formed that state, to concede the crimes of the past.

One afternoon I stopped by a roundtable discussion held by several former KGB chiefs. Vladimir Kryuchkov, the true believer who had run the Lubyanka under Gorbachev until he turned against him in the coup of August 1991, went blank when a reporter, a Russian woman in her twenties, asked his opinion of the virtues of repentance. "What is there to repent?" Kryuchkov replied. He seemed more puzzled than angered. "We have nothing to regret; we only tried to save the Union. It's those who unleashed the present chaos who should think about repentance." History, I feared, had made a stunning return, only to be forgotten just as quickly.

IN SEARCH OF LEVITY in matters of remembrance, I learned to seek the gentle counsel of Semyon Samuelovich Vilensky. Semyon was in his early seventies when we first met, but his handshake, I was reminded each time I entered his two-room apartment on Moscow's northwestern edge, remained a nutcracker. A short, stocky man with a white curly mane, Semyon had bushy white brows and soft blue eyes that flashed when he smiled. His face, expressive and animated, invariably reminded visitors of Einstein.

Semyon established the ritual of our visits: first tea, strong tea; then a beloved cigarette; lastly crackers or cake, whatever the kitchen held. Only then did we get down to business. The apartment seemed sparse, but it was crowded. The wall of cabinets in the living room was filled with manuscripts. For more than four decades he had collected the works—memoirs, short stories, poems, plays, novels, diaries—of the zeks, the prisoners who suffered in Stalin's labor camps. "Zek" was camp slang, a word that grew out of the Gulag architects' bureaucratic shorthand; z/k stood for zaklyuchennyi, a prisoner.

By now Semyon had thousands of manuscripts. It was a miracle they had survived. With a wide grin, Semyon liked to share his secret. "The babushkas," he said. The grannies. "It's all thanks to the babushkas." For twenty-five years, from Khrushchev to Gorbachev, he traveled the country. He spent six months in Moscow, six months on the road. He was not wandering, though he said the warmth of rural Russia saved him. He was slowly, quietly saving the literary heritage of the camps.

"In those days where could you keep manuscripts written by zeks? Only in villages, far from Moscow, in the hands of old ladies. So I'd take to the roads of the countryside and walk. I'd go from village to village. And the babushkas took me in, and without fear or doubt, they took the manuscripts and hid them."

He did not think his archive a great achievement. "Camp survivors like to write," he said. "And by now their relatives know I will take anything and lose nothing." Moreover, he was not happy merely to have rescued the manuscripts. He had vowed to put them into print. In the late 1980s, once glasnost began to free Moscow's printing presses, Semyon started to reel in his scattered manuscripts. In 1989 he founded a group known as Vozvrashchenie (The Return), and although he was the sole full-time staffer, began steadily to publish the manuscripts. In 1990 he got a copying machine, a gift from George Soros. By 2001 he had published more than fifty volumes, but the copier remained his primary press. For a decade a repairman had fixed it gratis. "His father," he joked, "must have been in the camps."

Semyon of course was a survivor himself. He served on the Kremlin's Rehabilitation Commission, a body established by Yeltsin and chaired by Aleksandr Yakovlev, Gorbachev's former ideologist, that attempted to restore the good names of the victims of Stalinism. He was the commission's sole Gulag veteran. He did not, however, like to speak of his own experience. Only bit by bit did I piece it together. He had been arrested just after his twentieth birthday—"For poetry," he said. It was in 1948. He had been an eager student of literature at Moscow State, and he had done a stupid thing. He recited one of his poems to a circle of friends. One of his lines—"Agents surround us and the first among them is Stalin"—caught the ears of an informer. He was accused of "anti-Soviet agitation" and "terrorist intentions" and jailed first in the Lubyanka, then in a transit prison before being sent off to the dreaded mines of the Kolyma camps in the Far East. As Zek No. I-1620 he spent more than six years in Kolyma.

In 1955 Semyon got out. In 1962 he tried to get his first anthology of camp literature published–by the Kolyma regional government. "It would have been an important beginning," he said. He even secured a story from Varlam Shalamov, the camp survivor whose *Kolyma Tales* had earned Solzhenitsyn's envy. The book was typeset in 1963, but "at the last minute Moscow ordered all writers not officially residing in Kolyma excluded." They printed a collection of Kolyma works, but not any by camp writers, many of whom lay buried in the local cemeteries. Semyon vowed to right that wrong, a vow he had spent the next quarter of a century fighting to fulfill.

Tea at Semyon's lasted for hours. He took his time. His anarchic brows danced, his hands flew through the smoky air. As he braided old stories for a new audience, a smile coiled up and flashed. His conversation sounded Socratic, his tales almost rabbinical. He liked to end his discourses with a moral. He dispensed them like benedictions. But he always arrived at the same destination, the tragic conclusion that these first years after the Soviet fall were no exception. Russians had never come to terms with their past. "We barely had enough time to ask the right questions," he said, "let alone try to answer them."

🦚 TEN 🦚

"I JUST FLEW IN from Seoul," announced the voice on the phone, waking me at 4:17 A.M. "And from the height of thirty-five thousand feet, it suddenly made sense: This place was not intended for habitation." I hung up and soon fell back into a deep sleep. In the morning it seemed like a dream. But I knew who had called.

Viktor Pelevin, whom by then I had helped label "the voice of the new generation," had grown into a friend. Since the fall of the USSR, Russians have bemoaned the flood of pulp fiction as how-to manuals on everything from the Internet to the Kama Sutra filled their bookstores. But just as Moscow critics were ready to pronounce Russian literature dead, Pelevin came of age. His modern satires, laced with ontological meditations and wild flights of a psychedelic imagination, soared to the top of the best-seller lists. By his early thirties Pelevin had become the literary celebrity of the post-Soviet generation.

With a degree from the Moscow Institute of Power Engineering and a passion for Zen Buddhism, he did not seem the top candidate for the title. But in 1993 his first book of stories, *The Blue Lantern*, won an immediate audience and Russia's "Little Booker" prize. His first novel, *Omon Ra*, won high praise. Moscow's critics, never particularly cordial to newcomers, hailed it as the first landmark of post-Soviet literature. Ever since, Pelevin has proved spectacularly prolific, cranking out roughly a novel a year.

But it was his novella *The Yellow Arrow* that I kept close. In under fifty pages, Pelevin creates a metaphoric world that reveals Russia's predicament, a train bound for a broken bridge that neither stops nor arrives anywhere. The admixture of satire and mysticism is heady. The train's passengers, stranded in an iron coffin hurtling into infinite darkness, mimic the desperate last resorts of Russians, devolving into hunter-gatherers, swindlers, and madmen.

Pelevin soon gained a cult of envy. He was, rivals said, too clever by half. "But I'm not doing anything new," he pleaded. "I'm just writing what I see in my head." His works were sold in bookstores and kiosks across Russia. But his influence extended far beyond his readership. Pelevin changed the lexicon of Russia's hip urban youth, many of whom never read his books. By the time *Generation "P,"* a novel about the travails of a Russian copywriter, came out, it was hard to exaggerate his reach. The title was meant as a pun on Generation X and the Pepsi Generation. *P* stands for *pizdets*, a crude, but beloved, swearword that ends the sentences of young Russians everywhere. It means, alternately, "the absolute best" or "the absolute worst." Yet given the book's reach, the *P* might as well have stood for Pelevin.

On RuNet, the Russian Internet, Pelevin Web sites sprouted. Girls carried his novels in nightclubs and pored over them in the metro. In my travels I found Pelevin everywhere: a Pelevin band (heavy metal) in Pskov, a Pelevin disco (techno) in Samara, even a Pelevin movie (a bootleg film of a novel) in the works in Yaroslavl. In the West, meanwhile, his works became the focus of academic symposia. Pelevin had a constructive response to celebrity. He hid. He adopted the pose of a Slavic Pynchon or Salinger. He refused to be photographed or appear on television. Naturally, his fame only grew.

One night well into my last summer in Moscow, Pelevin and I met up at Justo, a sushi restaurant/nightclub high on the high end of the market. Justo was opened by the son of Iosif Kobzon, an aging crooner with a bad wig who was known as the Russian Frank Sinatra. For decades Kobzon has been the king of Estrada, the Soviet equivalent of a national lounge singer. For a time Kobzon was not able to visit the United States, thanks to the State Department's suspicions that he had mob connections, a charge he strongly denies.[12] His son's place attracted the city's most-traveled and, no matter the season, best-tanned crowd.

Viktor ordered sushi and tea. He had a fabled reputation as a chemical experimenter on a par with Jim Morrison. But he does not smoke or drink. He meditates. He is a devout Buddhist. He now shuttled among Moscow, Tibet, and South Korea, where he went for extended Zen retreats. In his work Pelevin spoke to Russia's bedlam, but he never preached. Too many generations of Russian writers, he said, had been priests of the state's propaganda. Stalin had demanded that writers be "architects of the soul." Too many Russian novelists had lived off "the literary collective farm." The reality of Russia, now more than ever, was too surreal, he said, to explain away in black and white.

Pelevin had just returned from a South Korean monastery. For a month he had eaten only rice and seaweed. For hours each day he had sat and stared at a blank wall. It didn't sound like fun, I ventured. It wasn't, he said. "But it's the best therapy I've found for living in this place."

Once he had asked advice on an English title for a novel. Now I returned the favor. He pushed for something that rang of Dostoyevsky or Tolstoy but echoed the new era as well: "Something Putinian."

"*Crime and Immunity*," I suggested.

"*Crime and Deportation*," he countered. "More in keeping with the times."

"*War and Crime*?" I offered.

"Too timely," he said. "What about *War and Piss*? Or even better, *Vor and Piss*." He was on to something. *Vor* is Russian for "thief" and to a Russian ear, "peace" and "piss" are hard to distinguish. And on it went for hours.

One of our best efforts was *Golaya Pravda* (*The Naked Truth*). We had met at the time of the Kremlin's attack on NTV, and as Putin drove Russia's first private network into friendly hands, freedom of speech, or the lack thereof, had dominated public discourse. Putin and his men tried to argue that Russia's airwaves were free and open. They had a point. The television channels were closed to political opponents, but they were certainly not straitlaced. *The Naked Truth* proved that.

Saturday nights at eleven a comely young brunette named Svetlana Pesotskaya appeared on a Moscow channel to read the news. She began the broadcast fully clothed, and then, as she ran through the news of the day, she slipped off her clothes. Soon she was topless. Svetlana did not let nudity get in the way of a good interview. Communist parliamentarians were her most frequent interlocutors. They sat next to her and, trying their best not to stare at her breasts, plowed on about the dire state of agriculture, the defense forces, or Russian-Japanese relations. *The Naked Truth*, at least among a press corps in search of a story, was a hit.

As a full moon rose and the club reached capacity, Viktor and I left. The street outside had become a parking lot of black German sedans and American Jeeps. The interior lights of the cars illuminated faces engrossed in crime thrillers, chauffeurs keeping warm. We walked for blocks, past the Tretyakov Gallery, past MinAtom, the Ministry of Atomic Energy, past the Central Bank, before we parted. I walked on alone toward St. Basil's and Red Square, across the broad stone bridge that spans the Moscow River. It was nearly two in the morning, and the streets were empty. Only the river churned darkly below.

Once, years before, Viktor and I had sat on a bench on the edge of Pushkin Square. The city seemed to stream before us. It was a chill spring day, and the sun had brought out the crowds. Zhirinovsky had commandeered a truck and turned it into a soapbox. He was hectoring a crowd to defend Saddam Hussein against the Satan in Washington. A man stopped to ask us the time. He also asked if we knew that Yeltsin was a war criminal. I told Viktor that day how lucky he was. As a writer in Russia, a hip young writer who wore black leather and dark sunglasses and protected his persona as religiously as Pynchon, he would find it hard to fail. The West was dying to discover a new voice in the Soviet rubble. "You'll be big," I predicted.

"You're the lucky one," he replied. "The old is over here, and the new has yet to begin."

We agreed; few people get to experience zero gravity on earth.

❦ ELEVEN ❦

HOW DO YOU EXPLAIN a state in decay? How do you explain a country where the death of an ideology has displaced millions? How do you explain a government that announces a 50 percent increase in defense spending when the poverty line cuts through a third of its households and its poor souls face new epidemics of HIV and TB, suicide and drug abuse and, most pervasive of all, the old scourge of alcoholism? Where people do not fear the future, they fear–with good reason–the past.

In Russia nothing political stays unchanged for long. Kremlin intrigues, however transfixing they may be, do not suffice to draw a faithful portrait of Russia a decade after the Soviet fall. Russia of course has changed. But for far too many of its inhabitants it remains an Old Testament land, a place of plagues and floods, of locusts and blizzards and power outages without end. I knew I would have to go far from Moscow, as far as the points of the compass could lead me, to chart a deep map of the country, to learn how Russians not only survive but struggle to find meaning in the ruins of empire.

"The death of the contemporary forms of social order ought to gladden rather than trouble the soul," writes Aleksandr Herzen, the Russian political philosopher, in *From the Other Shore*. "But what is frightening is that the departing world leaves behind it not an heir, but a pregnant widow." Herzen was writing of the European revolutions of 1848, but his words echo across Russia today. "Between the death of one and the birth of the other," he concludes, "much water will flow, a long night of chaos and desolation will pass."

I stared at the huge map on our wall at home and plotted my route. I would travel to the country's extremes, to the corners where no "Kremlin insiders" dwelt and few oligarchs set foot. I wanted to go to the Russian lands where no one had dined with Berezovsky or cut a deal with Luzhkov, where few cared about the Byzantine struggles that entranced Moscow and fewer still fretted about the price of Siberian crude on the world exchange. I wanted to go to the regions where Russians had seen little of the rewards of the new era but felt much of its pain. I wanted to listen to the land's survivors and survivalists, to those who lived in its far-flung corners without the slightest expectation that anything good should ever come to a people who deserved so much better.

II. SOUTH

TO THE ZONE

The way home was through a fallow field of black earth which had just been ploughed. I walked along the dusty, gently rising black-earth road. The ploughed field was squire's land and very large, so that on either side of the road and on up the slope you could see nothing but black evenly furrowed fallow land, as yet unharrowed. The ploughing was well done and there was not a plant or blade of grass to be seen across the whole field: it was all black. What a cruel, destructive creature man is. How many different living creatures and plants he has destroyed in order to support his own life, I thought, instinctively looking for some sign of life in the midst of this dead black field.

–Leo Tolstoy, *Hadji Murad*

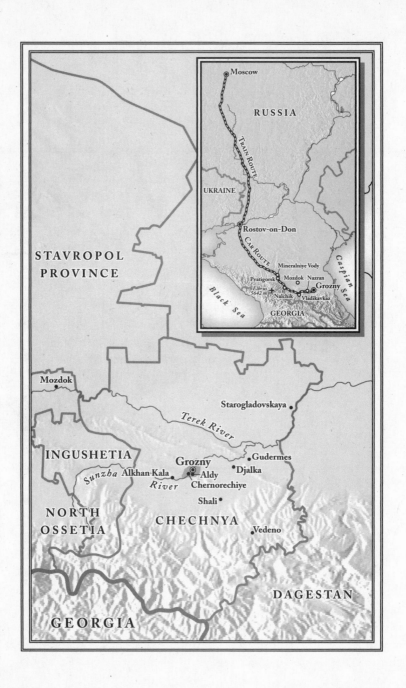

RUSSIA

Moscow

UKRAINE

TRAIN ROUTE

Rostov-on-Don

CAR ROUTE

Mineralniye Vody

Pyatigorsk   Mozdok   Nazran

Elbrus   Nalchik   Grozny
5642 m   Vladikavkaz

Black Sea

GEORGIA

Caspian Sea

STAVROPOL
PROVINCE

Mozdok

Starogladovskaya

Terek River

INGUSHETIA

Grozny

Sunzha   Alkhan-Kala   Aldy

River   Chernorechiye

Gudermes

Djalka

NORTH
OSSETIA

CHECHNYA

Shali

Vedeno

GEORGIA

DAGESTAN

✥ ONE ✥

WE WERE, AT LONG LAST, on the outskirts of Aldy, an ancient village of overgrown fruit trees and low-slung tin roofs on the southern edge of Grozny, the Chechen capital, and Issa was singing, "*Moi gorod Groooozny, ya po tebe skuchaaayu . . . no ya k tebe vernuuus, moi gorod Grozny moi.*"

He was an imposing figure, just over six feet, his chest and shoulders so broad he appeared taller. Issa liked to keep his silvering hair shaved on the sides of his head and at the back of his neck. The cut lent him the stern air of a military man or a Soviet bureaucrat of stature, an image, as was no doubt the intent, to intimidate at the checkpoints. More often silent, Issa broke into song when the air around him grew too quiet. Now, just as the roadblock, the last one before Aldy, rose into view, Issa was singing at the top of his lungs.

"*Moi gorod Groooozny,*" he wailed. "My city, the city of Grozny, oh, how I miss you, but I shall return to you. . . ."

There were four of us in the rattling Soviet Army jeep, known endearingly as a UAZik, pronounced *wahzik*, in the common parlance. Lord knows what image we projected to the well-muscled, sunburned, and deeply suspicious Russian soldiers at the checkpoints. Sometimes they were drunk. Nearly always they were scared. In Chechnya, I'd learned, checkpoints were the measure of one's day. People did not ask, "How far it is?" but "How many checkpoints are there?" Each day we crossed at least a dozen.

On this sweltering morning in July, we had already passed seventeen. The posts were the center of activity amid the ruins of the city. Conscripts maintained the constant vigil, checking the cars and their passengers, while their officers, hands on radios, sat in shaded huts off the road. But this post was nearly empty, and the OMON officer who stopped us, a pit bull from Irkutsk, was not in a good mood. His arms and neck glowed with the burned pink skin of a new arrival. He wore wraparound sunglasses and a bandanna over his shaved head. Tattoos, the proud emblems of Russian soldiers and prisoners, covered his biceps. "*Slava*" ("glory") adorned the right one. It could be a name or a desire. He wore no shirt, only a green vest fitted with grenades, a knife, and magazine clips to feed the Kalashnikov he held firmly in both hands. His fingers seemed soldered to it.

We may have looked legit, but we were a fraud. Issa ostensibly was a ranking member of the wartime administration in Chechnya, the Russians' desperate attempt at governance in the restive republic of Muslims, however lapsed, Sovietized, and secularized. He had the documents to prove it, but the man who signed them had since been fired. Issa knew the life span of his documents was limited. At any checkpoint his "client," as he had taken to calling me, could be pulled from the jeep, detained, interrogated, and packed off on the next flight to Moscow.

At fifty-one, Issa boasted a résumé that revealed the successful climb of a Chechen apparatchik. Born in Central Asian exile, in Kyrgyzstan, five years after Stalin had deported the Chechens in 1944, he had graduated from the Grozny Oil Institute in 1971. For twenty-one years he worked at Grozneft, the Chechen arm of the Soviet Oil and Gas Ministry. He spent the last Soviet years, until Yeltsin clambored onto the tank in 1991, in western Siberia, overseeing the drilling of oil wells in Tyumen. He spoke a smattering of French, a bit of Arabic, and a dozen words in English—all learned, he liked to tease, during stints in Iraq and Syria.

As the Soviet Union collapsed, life went sour fast. Djokhar Dudayev—the Soviet Air Force general who was to lead the stand against Moscow—returned to Grozny, and the fever for independence seized the capital. Issa, then a director of one of Chechnya's biggest chemical plants, took up arms against the insurgents. In the fall of 1993, more than a year before Yeltsin first sent troops into Chechnya, with Moscow's backing Issa and his fellow partisans rallied around a former Soviet petrochemicals minister and staged a pathetic attempt to overthrow Dudayev.[1]

He was careful not to dispense details, but the scars were hard to hide. His right forearm had a golf ball–size hole, remnants of a bullet taken on the opposition's line north of Grozny in September 1993. The bullet had pierced his arm and lodged in his left shoulder. A few months later Dudayev's freedom fighters got him again. Kalashnikov fire had ripped his stomach, intestine, and lungs, leaving a horrific gnarl of tissue in the center of his body. He'd moved his family—a wife, two boys, and a girl—to Moscow.

But he wanted to be clear: He never wanted to fight. "We never loved the Russians," he said. "We just hated that corrupt little *mafiya* shit." He was speaking of Dudayev, the fallen independence leader, the man many Chechens, much younger and more devout, now called the founding martyr of the separatist Islamic state, the Chechen Republic of Ichkeria, as Dudayev had ordered his native land rechristened.[2]

In front of me, behind the wheel, sat Yura. Projecting a genuine sweetness, he was a good-looking kid with blue-green eyes and blond hair that his mother cut short each week with a straight razor. He had thin cheeks, covered with freckles and shaded by the beginnings of a beard. Just twenty-two, he was lucky to have made it this far. He belonged to one of the world's most unfortunate species; he was an ethnic Russian born in Chechnya. "Our Mowgli," Issa had jibed, equating Yura with Kipling's jungle boy. Everyone laughed. There was no need to explain. Mowgli was raised by wolves. The Chechens, centuries ago, had made the wolf their mascot, the embodiment of their struggle.

The last of the crew, bouncing beside me in the back seat of the car, was Shvedov. It was a last name—few ever learned his first—that meant "the Swede." There was nothing, however, Swedish about him. He had a tanned bald head and a scruffy dirty brown beard and mustache. He carried an ID from the magazine the *Motherland*, but his paid vocation was what is known in the field as a fixer. For decades he earned a living, or something approximating it, by getting reporters in and out of places they had no business being in. Usually genial and often hilarious, he could be brilliant. But Shvedov's greatest attribute was that he did not drink. I had known him for years but never traveled with him. After only three days I discovered my own heretofore unknown homicidal urges coming on strong. Somehow I had missed Shvedov's worst sin: He talked without pause. (When he did not talk, he clacked his upper dentures incessantly on a set of lower teeth blackened by a lifetime of unfiltered Russian tobacco.) A colleague who traveled with him often had offered a tip: "Keep a cigarette in his mouth." But even smoking, Shvedov talked.

THE SIBERIAN PIT BULL barked at Yura. "Turn off the car," he instructed. Issa politely tried to ply his documents, but the soldier would have none of it. "Forget your papers, old man," he shouted. Shvedov, seeing the worst coming, proffered his press card from the *Motherland.* The OMON officer from Irkutsk had never heard of the honored Soviet monthly, which Shvedov insisted still existed, even though its readership could no longer afford to subscribe. "Stay in the car," the officer yelled at the insistent bald man in front of him, before turning his sights on me.

"Get out," he then commanded me.

One thing I'd learned about checkpoints long ago was it was best not to get out—ever. By now we had been stopped so often a routine had formed. A soldier would approach, profanities would rain, we would offer documents, another soldier would lean closer, we would wait, and then, the formalities exhausted, we would be waved through. Silence, I had learned, was the best policy. But this fellow wanted me out of the UAZik. He yelled again. He wanted to frisk the car, search its innards, rummage our bags. I tried to demur. I offered to help.

Undeterred, he opened the door and, with his Kalashnikov, nudged me aside. He lifted the seats, opened the metal canisters underneath, and, maintaining his silence, rifled our bags. When he was done, he grunted and jumped from the UAZik. Yura sat frozen until Issa ordered him, through his teeth, to turn the key, turn the goddamned key. As we moved on, I watched the soldier retreat to his roadside squalor, half a tent strung to a tree and a broken chair posted in the hot sun. With his back to us, he flicked his left hand sharply through the air, as if to swat an insect. We were beneath him.

We drove on, numb to everything but the sun, the dust, the bumps. Issa had stopped singing. Only the roar of the helicopters overhead accompanied us, and then, suddenly, as we turned off the road, the silence returned. We had entered a village without discernible life. No cars, no people. The first trees were tall, bare stumps, their branches shorn long ago. Then yards, all untended, their green veils grown too thick or too thin. Everywhere the branches, heavy with fruit, hung low. The season had come, but no one was picking. Everywhere there was only the weight of the still air. We had arrived.

I had marked Aldy, this Chechen village, on the map of Chechnya I had bought on a Moscow street corner months earlier. Aldy was the destination I'd set myself and shared with no one when I began the journey to the south. Something horrific, unspeakable, had happened here five months before. On a cold Saturday in midwinter, Russian forces had committed one of the bloodiest of the Chechnya massacres in this village. No one will ever know the true body count, but in Aldy on February 5, 2000, Russian soldiers had summarily executed at least sixty civilians.

A half circle of a dozen Chechen men, some lean and strong, others gray and bent over, huddled in a caucus as we drove in. Yura parked the UAZik across the road from them. They did not move from the lonely shade. One man, young, fit, and prominently armed, gripped the Kalashnikov on his shoulder. He wore full camouflage and tiny sunglasses. He could have been on either side, a fighter loyal to the rebels or a Chechen police officer in the Russians' employ. Issa didn't like the look of the sunglasses.

I got out, alone, and walked toward the men. One of the older men was separating leaves from a thin branch in his hands. As I approached, the young Chechen stepped forward. In his hands was the AK-47, shiny and new. Strapped across his chest was a leather bandolier, bulging with clips, grenades, and a pair of wooden-handled knives. A century and a half earlier Alexandre Dumas *père* had noted the Chechens' love of weaponry during a romantic romp across the Caucasus in 1858, a time when the Chechens struggled against the tsar. "All these mountain fighters are fanatically brave," wrote the creator of *The Three Musketeers*, "and whatever money they acquire is spent on weapons. A Chechen . . . may be literally in rags, but his sword, dagger and gun are of the finest quality."[3]

I told the armed man that I was a journalist, an American. I'd come to talk to people who were here the day "they" came. We did not shake hands, but he nodded and shifted the rifle from his hands to his shoulder. "Walk with me," he said. The sunglasses, their gold frame catching the sun, covered his eyes. Slowly we crossed the dirt road and headed away from the jeep, away from my guides, away from the Chechen men standing against the wall of metal gates and fences.

Oddly, a calm enveloped me. I kept walking, afraid to lose pace. Three options formed in my mind. This fellow is taking you around the corner, just out of sight of your companions, where you'll be summarily executed; or he's intent on kidnapping you, leading you to a house nearby to be sold on down the road from there; or he's bringing you to see someone–an elder?–who will listen to your best introduction and then either bless your presence in the village or send you away.

I had come to Aldy prepared. By March an amateur video, forty-six minutes long, made by the villagers had surfaced in Moscow. It featured corpses and widows. I had interviewed the lucky ones; the survivors who'd made it out. I had studied the reports, detailed and methodical, of the human rights activists. But I wanted to learn more than the extent of the massacre. I wanted to understand the motivation behind the horror. Aldy was not, as an American diplomat, a man of high rank and expertise in Russia, had tried to convince me, "just another case of Russian heavy-handedness." It was a conspicuous illustration, in miniature, of Russia's military onslaught in Chechnya.

The young Chechen led me on. But even before we reached the gate of the house, a wave of relief hit, and my shoulders settled. I knew where we were going. I had memorized a hand-drawn map of Aldy's long streets. We were calling on the man the fortunate ones had told me to see first, Shamkhan, the village mullah.

🐚 TWO 🐚

CHECHNYA LIES A THOUSAND miles south of Moscow, between the Black and Caspian Seas. Weeks before, I had opted for the slow route south. On an airless Moscow afternoon early in a summer of record temperatures, I boarded the *Quiet Don*, the North Caucasus express bound for Rostov-on-Don, nearly twenty hours to the south. From Rostov, the threshold to the Caucasus, I was to drive on across the steppes before coming to the foothills of the mountains and crossing into Chechnya. It was not the beaten path. Deadlines forced most correspondents to fly from Moscow to Nazran, the capital of neighboring Ingushetia, the tiny republic with the closest airport to Grozny. But I wanted to proceed slowly, to see the land that stretched between Moscow and Grozny, to mark the gradual descent into the lands of kidnapping, war, and a fast-evolving faith in Islam.

Like nearly every Russian, I knew something of the journey before it began. Tales of the Caucasus—martial epics featuring swarthy mountaineers with bejeweled daggers and mysterious black-eyed lasses—featured prominently in the nineteenth-century imagination. For Pushkin, and Mikhail Lermontov after him, the Caucasus was an exotic land to be envied, a realm free of the strictures of tsarist society. Both Pushkin and Lermontov, the poet and writer best known for *A Hero of Our Time*, were exiled to the south. Tolstoy went voluntarily. For young Tolstoy, the Caucasus proved a martial and moral training ground. In Chechnya he saw his first battle, wrote his first story, and heard a tale he remembered his entire life and returned to in his last work of fiction, *Hadji Murad*. Nearly a century after Tolstoy's death, relations between Moscow and the "small nations," the belittling term Soviet officialdom used for the peoples of the Caucasus, had grown only worse. Yet even among Russians, their name for the lands–Kavkaz–rarely failed to conjure, in its two clipped syllables that rose like a gallop, a romantic genie.

The Kazan station teemed so with sweating multitudes that I nearly missed the train. Inside, I found Kolya, lying on the opposite bunk in our narrow cabin. He was a bear of a man with a mop of ginger hair. Only hours later, once we'd emptied a bottle of Dagestani cognac, and Zhenka, the round-cheeked dining car girl, had thrice come and gone, delivering plates of glabrous chicken and half-fried potatoes, did I learn his last name.

"Nabokov," he said, without an inkling anyone had ever shared the name.

Freckles covered Kolya's red skin, and his left shoulder was tattooed with twin mountain peaks. "Mount Ararat," he said, rubbing a meaty palm over the skin. He had served in the Soviet border guards in Armenia, then a decade in the coal mines of the Don Basin–until the mines started closing. "Gorbachev," he said of the days when everything suddenly changed. "Glasnost, all that." When the work ran out, he'd gone to the far end of the empire, to mine gold in Magadan, once home to the Kolyma fields, the primary source of Russia's rosy gold, and the Gulag's largest labor camps. He lasted only a couple of years in the Far East, before coming home. Back in Rostov, he moved into the new world, "cooperatives," the Soviets' last-ditch experiment at small semiprivate enterprise.

Those were wild but good days, especially once he got to know the Chechens. "Best people in the whole union," Kolya declared. For years he'd partnered only with Chechens. They had joined forces in trade, jewelry, and electronics in the years before the war. He didn't know about now, but back then the Chechens were his best friends. "They'd do anything for me, and I'd do anything for them." He could not say the same of his fellow Russians.

"Walk into a Chechen's house," Kolya said, "and you are in his protection. I wouldn't suggest trying it in Moscow."

For a time we sat in silence, opposite each other on the hard bunks. We let the rhythmic clank of metal on metal fill the cabin. Beyond our curtained window, figures appeared in the blurred rush beside the rails: drunken wanderers roused to consciousness by passing thunder; Gypsy families bedding down in a dusky field; a babushka on a shortcut through the woods, the day's haul slung across her back. Even as the sun set, the temperature ran high. The window, however, remained locked shut. It did not matter. In such moments, I realized, as Kolya returned to the Chechens, there are few places in the world where strangers can find such closeness, with such ease, as on a Russian train.

We talked for hours. Kolya was not optimistic on the war. "They're not ones to give up," he said, looking into the woods. The pines and firs were aflame in the midsummer sunset. The musty compartment had caught the glow. "Chechens don't like to be screwed. This is no longer about independence. This is about revenge, honor, and this is forever." Before long the sun disappeared, and the cognac with it. Our little table grew crowded. Beer bottles swayed amid the plates of half-eaten chicken. Zhenka had warmed to Kolya. She now stopped by every time she delivered another meal to the far end of the train. Her cheeks red, and her brow aglow with sweat, she sat on the edge of Kolya's bunk, moving closer to him with each visit. As the hours passed, their giggling turned to laughter and then, as the last bottle emptied, to silence. Outside, as the woods gave way to black fields, the figures beside the tracks grew fewer and in the darkness lost distinction.

I managed a few hours' sleep before Kolya's snoring woke me. It was early morning, but we had reached someplace far from Moscow. Overnight, the world beyond our window had turned pastoral. In the first sun of the morning, we passed men baling hay, shirtless boys playing daredevil on Ural motorcycles, children swimming in rivulets in their underwear, brigades of large women weeding between the rails, old men fishing. The lands to the south may follow a farmer's schedule, but commerce seemed to center on the train. In the stations, men elbowed one another to board the cars and offer dried fish and vodka, while the babushkas lined the platforms, squatting behind buckets of apricots and walnuts, cherries and raspberries.

Kolya awoke with a groan just as we passed the town where he had mined coal, Shakhtnaya (Mining Town). At the station's edge a cluster of young men, their heads shaved, gathered by an olive gray army truck. Parents stood beside them, fussing. A farewell. One man pumped an accordion, while his wife clutched two bottles. They sang their son onto the train, through the corridor, and into a cabin down the way. In a moment the train jerked back to movement, and the forlorn parents barely escaped. At the end of the short platform a young couple kissed. They sat on a low wall of concrete under a weeping willow. The girl had tucked her knees up, beneath a long white skirt.

Kolya belched and stretched. He'd taken the train up to Moscow from Rostov only the day before. He'd been in the capital just a few hours, to visit "the big brother." His older brother had served in the KGB, first in Leningrad, then in East Germany. Now he'd been given a big job in the Kremlin. The résumé was strangely familiar. Putin had followed the same career path. Kolya had gone to Moscow, he said once we were well into the cognac, to get his brother's blessing. A deal was cooking. He needed a Kremlin seal to nail it down. He did not elaborate. He was just happy his brother had consented so fast. They'd had plenty of time to go to a big restaurant, just off Red Square. They'd gorged themselves. Kolya loved his brother and revered him. "Even up there," he said, pointing to the grimy ceiling above us, "he's still just like me, a normal guy from a shitty little town in the provinces."

THREE

ROSTOV STRADDLES THE broad waters of the Don. I climbed off the train and immediately felt the change in latitude. Everywhere the Caucasus announced itself. Dust-cloaked trains disgorged the pilgrims from across the steppes—Armenians and Georgians, Cossacks and Azeris, Ossetians and plenty of weary Russians. In the station the morning heat was spiced by the gristly shashlik and warm lavash piled high on wooden carts. The sweet smells betrayed the proximity of the mountainous lands to the south. So, too, did the OMON patrols, the stern officers who lined the exits, checking the documents of each new arrival before he or she could step into their city.

Rostov was not only the crossroads of the Caucasus in Russia but the last foothold of state power in the south. "The last Russian city," Kolya had called it, offering less of an acclamation than a warning of what lay farther south. "Beyond Rostov," he added, "it's only them." The OMON officers, sweating as they failed to keep pace with the elbowing hordes, betrayed their own fear, the anxiety that had stalked the city since the first urgings for independence stirred among the "small nations" of the south.

Rostov had long been a bulwark of Russian power. The narrow streets of its oldest neighborhoods were lined with nineteenth-century red brick merchants' houses from a past era. The filigreed roofs and wooden porches leaned with age but struggled to retain an elegant bearing. Once best known for its tractor plant, the USSR's largest, Rostov in recent years had gained fame as the unlikely breeding ground for one of Russia's most notorious serial killers. The 1994 prosecution of Andrei Chikatilo, murderer of at least fifty-two, became the first celebrity murder trial in the former Soviet Union. Theories abounded on why the city of sleepy hills and idled collective farmers had produced such homicidal intemperance. Explanations swirled but as always, never settled with any certainty.

Even before the advent of "the Rostov Ripper," the city had carried a reputation for crime–specifically, an illicit trade in just about anything. Odessa, went the old line, was the mama of Soviet crime, and Rostov the papa. Now the crime Lenin called speculation was known as *biznes*, and the city teemed with crowds buying and selling. The automobile market, one of the largest in Russia, stretched for miles. Moscow had its own sprawling open-air bazaars, where big-shouldered babushkas vied with Caucasian traders, but for any trader working Russia's southern reaches, Rostov was the dream.

The crossroads lured not only pilgrims from across the mountains, but a blond, blue-eyed Englishman raised and bred, as he put it, for the financial markets of London. John Warren had lived in the city on the Don for years. Brash and pink in the cheek, he seemed an eternal English public school boy, better suited to the world of Evelyn Waugh than Maksim Gorky. Yet in an unlikely post-Soviet evolution, Warren had risen fast in the turmoil of the new market–from a Moscow apprenticeship in the empire of Marc Rich, the elusive American financier living in Switzerland, to his current position as the honorary consul of Her Majesty's Government at the edge of the Russian steppes.

Warren had cause to be pleased with himself. He'd married a Russian beauty and fathered, a year or two back, a blond Sasha. He was fond of reiterating his conviction, gained by experience, that "Russia can work!" His service to the queen, albeit unsalaried, allowed him to affix a miniature Union Jack to the antenna of his Land Rover, an army green Defender, and to ensure, or so he hoped, his own small stake in the local economy. Warren was something of a local celebrity. He wore white shorts and dark sunglasses and careered around in the Defender, the only one in town. His fame, however, had another source: He had dared compete with the locals at their own game.

Rostov sold everything under the sun, but its first and primary product came from its soil, Russia's famed black earth, its chernozem. The city does not fall within the administrative borders of the *Chernozemie*, the Black Earth region that is centered on the Volga city of Voronezh and encompasses the five provinces north and east. Yet on the outskirts of Rostov, one found the same endless fields of rich silt loam that coat the steppes for three thousand miles from Ukraine to Siberia. Black earth is the dark, clumped-together soil that gleams like a black rainbow when its crevices catch the afternoon sun. Born of a thousand years' decomposition of ancient steppe grass, black earth holds no chalk and no dryness. Few soils are richer in nutrients, and fewer hold water better. Black earth is found elsewhere, but no nation has as much as Russia. Like a belt unbuckled across the country's girth, it spans its central regions, coating more than 150 million acres chestnut brown. "The tsar of soils," Vasily Dokuchaev, the nineteenth-century father of Russian earth science, called chernozem. "More valuable than oil," Dokuchaev called the soil, "more precious than gold."

Yet for all its promise, much of the great acreage lies fallow. Russia's black earth, perhaps like no other of its vast natural resources, betrays the burden of the country's abundance, the bequest that somehow seems too much to bear. Rostov, in the heart of the Russian breadbasket, seemed to carry the weight of its past, even the remote days mournfully evoked in the greatest literary work of medieval Russia. "The black earth beneath the hooves," writes the anonymous author of the twelfth-century epic *The Lay of Igor's Campaign,* "was sown with bones and watered with blood: a harvest of sorrow came up over the land of Russia."

THE CITY HAD LONG been the country's wheat, barley, and grain capital. John Warren, however, had seen something else, sunflowers. For hours on the train the yellow fields lit the cabin. In the endless stretches of gold, the tall plants stretched toward the sun, their faces black with seeds. Kolya spoke lovingly, almost romantically, of the seeds. It was a ballad sung across the country. Russians love their *semechki.* Every city, town, and village, no matter how small, was sure to have the seeds on sale–in the markets, at the bus stops, on the streets, and in the passageways below. Black bread and white water remained the first loves. But in the post-Soviet era sunflower seeds became the staple one could be sure to find no matter how bleak the outpost.

Seeds, Warren had to admit, were not gold. But they held oil. Rostov sunflower oil, he thought, could be shipped across the Black Sea and sold in Europe. Business had been good. Now forty-two employees helped him broker everything the black earth had to offer: grains, barley, hops, nuts. *Angliisky khleborob,* they called him in town, the "English peasant." He and his family enjoyed an enormous apartment, a floor above the local governor's. It'd been no fun, of course, to resettle the herd of eighteen who'd lived in it as a *kommunalka.* But the place really had a glow now. Tsarist antiques filled its elegant rooms, while gilt-framed canvases–"fabulous fakes," Warren boasted, of nineteenth-century oils–crowded its walls. Not long ago he'd bought a cigarette boat in Istanbul and motored home–"eight sublime days"–across the Black Sea and up the Don.

That evening I'd caught a report on the news that a worthy in local business had been killed. The deceased had resided, Warren explained, directly below. The apartment, now vacated, seemed a natural target for annexation. "Not a chance," he said. "Everyone would think I whacked him for it."

We went for a meal on Rostov's Left Bank, arriving at a line of tiered restaurants so gaudy with neon they resembled casinos. One was even called Vegas. En route, at the entrance of a dirt road running deep into a tall field of steppe grass, we passed a sign that read CHANCE. "Open-air bordello," Warren explained.

He pulled the Defender into Boris's Place and we were given the center table on the patio. Warren promptly requested a new waitress–Natasha was his favorite—and ordered deep bowls of sickly crawfish and shashlik sizzling in fat. He'd asked me to join him. English visitors were in town. They needed tending. "EBRD gents," he said, contract consultants from the European Bank for Reconstruction and Development. He feared boredom looming and intended to stave it off.

No sooner had Natasha lavished us with food and drink than the lights began to flash, the music blared, and a quartet of dancing girls sidled up. They wore pastel veils, red halter tops, loose trousers of gauzy white. To the electrified beat of "Hava Nagila," the Gypsies began to gyrate. The EBRD gents were overwhelmed. The younger of the two, newly married, tried to bury his head in his crawfish. His partner, however, a gray-haired economist recently retired and eager "to help out the poor Russians," forgot about food. Warren whooped and clapped and stuffed hundred-ruble notes into spandex straps.

"From all of us," he shouted.

"No, allow me!" cried the elder economist, tucking his own rubles into the elastic wiggling beside him.

Our host, Boris, stopped by. It was not his real name. Like most of the men who ran the clubs of the Left Bank, Boris was Armenian. Would we desire company? he wondered, nodding toward a table of gaunt girls in a corner. They wore black and looked bored. No, we were fine, Warren said. Before long the table of girls merged with a table of men next to us. They were a grim crew, anchored by two large pockmarked gentlemen. One wore a white suit, the other black. They both bore gold chains and bracelets. Kingpins from the local Azeri and Georgian mobs, Warren explained. "Colleagues and competitors." Didn't he ever worry about safety? "No," said the honorary consul. "We've got a simple arrangement. I control twelve percent of the market. That's my limit. Anything more, I'm dead."

🦢 FOUR 🦢

THE TALE READ AS IF it had been lifted from Gogol. It was just one of hundreds, testimonials collected in a book hanging in the half-light of the dank entranceway on Lermontov Street.

My boy went missing back in January '95, when his tank burned in Grozny. Write down his name: Aleshkin, Kostya. Went in when he was nineteen. From the Orenburg region, station Donguzskaya. They only told me in the spring that he'd gone missing. I went to Chechnya, found his commanders. They were kind, didn't kick me out. They fed me and told me to go home, that my Kostya was not among their dead and not among their wounded. So I went to the Chechen fighters. They didn't insult me either; they swore to their Allah that my Kostya wasn't among their prisoners. Then someone said: "Go to Rostov; that's where the unknown are kept in refrigerator train cars." I only came now. I wasn't up to it before and I had no hope. Here I met a young doctor, Borya. He took me to the train car. It was all corpses, some without heads, some without arms, others without legs. I looked through them—but my Kostya wasn't there. I went to bed, and just as I fell asleep I saw Kostya. He said, "Mama, how could you walk past me? Come back tomorrow. I'm lying in the first row, third from the end. Only I've got no face. It burned off. But there's still that birthmark under my arm. You remember." The next day I went to the train car and found Kostya straightaway—just where he said he was.

Chekhov in his diary wrote, "Alas, what is terrible is not the skeletons, but the fact that I am no longer terrified of them." The words raised a bitter smile on the lips of Vladimir Vladimirovich Shcherbakov. He was a military doctor, the head of Military-Medical Laboratory No. 124, known more precisely among the women who traveled to it from all corners of the country as a morgue. Rostov was not just a city of trade. It had a second life as an army town, the military headquarters for the North Caucasus. Its cafés were filled with camouflage, and its streets with UAZik jeeps. Lying, as a matter of considerable convenience, nearly halfway between Moscow and Grozny, the city also served as the main repository of the dead from Chechnya. Since 1995 Shcherbakov and his team of forensic sleuths had tried to return Russia's dead sons to their mothers. When I walked into his morgue, more than three hundred unidentified corpses remained locked in its refrigerated recesses. Two hundred and seventy had been there since the first Chechen war.

Tall and thin, Shcherbakov coiled his long legs behind a big desk piled with red files. He wore thick glasses and a yellow sleeveless shirt with three gold stars on its epaulets. A double-headed eagle adorned a tie clip that held a short blue tie tight against his frame. The office was small, spare. Over his shoulder hung a faded poster of the Virgin Mary in repose. For years now the women of the Soldiers Mothers' Committee had tirelessly dispatched mothers to his door. He had never tried to dissuade them. "What can I do," he said, "but let them search?" The mothers, in turn, called him the Good Doctor.

The morgue took them all, but the dead who remained, the doctor explained, were "the most severe contingent"–those impossible to identify visually. In contrast with the U.S. Army, the Russian military sent its soldiers into war without keeping fingerprints, let alone dental histories and DNA samples. The sleuths were lucky to get ID mug shots. In a room down the hall a balding man in a white lab coat peered into a computer, his eyes only inches from the screen. The monitor was filled with smudge lines, the inked tips of a man's fingers. The technician, Valery Rakitin, had just inked the prints from the corpse. "Wasn't much left," he said. The dogs had made a mess. "Only four fingers and a couple of toes."

The soldier had died at twenty-two. His mother, a forty-four-year-old teacher from Kemerevo, a coal-mining city in Siberia, had called that morning. She had come to collect him. In another age, a decade earlier, I'd been in Kemerevo. Lera, my friend who'd hosted me with her husband, Andrei, in their *kommunalka* in Moscow, came from there. In those days Kemerovo was synonymous with worker unrest; the miners had been among the first to strike as Soviet power ebbed. The boy who had died in Chechnya, been abandoned to the strays, and lain for months unidentified had left a hometown cold and bleak, a blighted city shorn of Siberia's beauty long before his birth.

On the screen, Valery compared the squiggles of a right palm with the whorls of a right forefinger. "Not perfect," he said. But the odds were "extremely good" it was the young man from Kemerevo. He pointed to the prints. "Almost identical," he said. "A match at a degree of one in a thousand." I got the idea–comparing prints and weighing the frequency of like patterns–but the calculus was beyond me. A local programmer had designed the software that tallied the probabilities pertaining to every known fingerprint pattern. Probables were matched, and the composite comparison yielded a percent range for positive identification. The system was far from perfect, Valery conceded, but it gave a fair estimate. Short of genetic analysis, it was the best the state could afford.

Across the narrow room sat Valery's wife. Svetlana had no computer on her desk, only a small white candle that stood before an icon framed in aluminum. "Valery takes care of the boys," she said, "and I take care of the mothers." She lit the candle. The mother from Siberia would be here soon.

NEARLY FIFTY, Shcherbakov could have retired. He was a local, born in the Don village of Aksai. He'd studied in Petersburg, then Leningrad, at the prestigious military medical academy there. Then it was the navy–Pacific Fleet destroyers, tours from Mozambique to Vietnam. His wife, Zina, worked at his side. She was his head nurse. They'd met over an operating table. Their daughter, Yelena, was in medical school, and their son, Andrei, fourteen, was heading for the military academy. Shcherbakov could have been enjoying the quiet at home. Theirs was a small house; an apple orchard lined the creek out back. But he couldn't quit. Returning an identity to the dead was more than a duty. It had become a calling.

There was nothing dramatic, Shcherbakov said, nothing unusual or heroic in the work, nothing that deserved any sympathy. Orthodoxy, he said, did not allow it. Everyone, he was certain, was given his own cross according to his abilities and had to carry it with dignity. At times, when he could deliver a mother and a father from uncertainty, a sense of relief did come. For the parents, he said, not knowing was worse than knowing. "If they can leave here with certainty, they can go home, defeat their grief, and find peace."

Down the hall the mother from Siberia had arrived. The fingerprints remained enlarged on the computer. She sat with her back to the burning candle and stared at the screen. "There you see it," the technician said. He leaned back in his chair.

The mother called him Doctor–in deference to the white lab coat–but was not convinced. "I see absolutely nothing," she said. She rubbed her eyes with a yellow handkerchief in tight, furious circles. "I see nothing," she said again. "But if you say they're his, I believe you. I do. I must. What else can I do?"

❧ FIVE ❧

ROSTOV HAD ITS pleasures, but the hotel was not among them. The phone rang incessantly each night–always females, always the same question: *"You need girl now?"*–before I pulled the plug from the wall. Then they took to knocking on the door. Worse, one morning I got out of bed to discover the sheet blackened with blotches–dozens of dead cockroaches. So when after a week Shvedov flew down from Moscow, I was happy to see him.

He arrived kitted out for battle. He wore Red Army surplus: old khaki jacket and trousers, layered with pockets and liberally frayed. It was Shvedov's idea of camouflage for journalists. He'd also brought the satellite phone I'd rented in Moscow and an old army backpack stuffed with six cartons of *papirosi*. Native to Russia, foul-smelling and absurdly strong, *papirosi* do not even pretend to be cigarettes. Stuffed with rough tobacco, they end not with a filter but with a long, hollow tube of rolled cardboard. Their drag, made famous by Jack London, is so coarse even hardened smokers–Russian, French, Vietnamese–beg off. *Papirosi*, however, have a singular virtue, never lost on Shvedov. They are cheap. A pack runs under five cents.

By then the world had heard of Andrei Babitsky, the Radio Liberty reporter who had dared report from the Chechen side of the war and been arrested by the Russians. Babitsky had suffered a dubious POW "swap," when the FSB staged a videotaped handover, turning the reporter over from its officers to masked men, who were almost certainly FSB operatives. Held captive for months, Babitsky had become a *cause célèbre*.[4] Nobody, however, outside a small circle of Moscow journalists, had ever heard of Shvedov. He did not write much, and he did no radio. But he was one of the best in the business. Born to a father who toiled in the upper reaches of GOSPLAN, the Soviet planning ministry, Shvedov did have a degree in journalism–Moscow State, late 1970s–and a string of credentials–BBC, NTV, *Moscow News*–not all of them false. Given the Kremlin's strict ban on journalists' traveling independently in Chechnya, the robust kidnapping market, and the only other option a government tour in a press herd, I sought out Shvedov.[5] I came to regret it, but he was well recommended. Just as it was hard to imagine Chechnya without war, it was hard to imagine Shvedov without the war in Chechnya. Since Moscow had moved to quash Dudayev's rebellion in 1994, he may have traveled to the region more than any journalist. Oddly, he never called the republic by its name. To him, it was always the Zone.

I had hoped things would get better farther south. I tried to talk Zhenya, the shy Cossack, all elbows and bony arms, who had driven me around Rostov, into delivering us to our next stop, Nalchik, capital of Kabardino-Balkaria. The small republic was sleepy and well within the borders of Russia, but Zhenya hedged. He had long been out of work. His income now derived from his Lada, but his face contorted at the prospect of crossing the city limits. "Down there," he said quietly, "you never know quite where you are."

Zhenya would go only as far as Mineralniye Vody (Mineral Waters), the first of the weary tsarist spa towns that lay a long day's drive to the south. We left Rostov as the car market opened, well before dawn, moving southeast along the Rostov–Baku Highway. The Route 66 of the North Caucasus, the road had once carried Soviet travelers directly through Grozny to the shores of the Caspian. Now, thanks to the years of bombings, assassinations, and war, it was clogged with checkpoints.

As we drove south, the road itself seemed to take a leisurely, southerly dip. All the while, Shvedov smoked without pause and rarely let a moment pass unbroken by commentary. He drove poor Zhenya crazy. He tried the radio but caught only static. Zhenya had mastered the Russian technique, passed down through the generations, of economizing on gas. He would accelerate only to take the car out of gear and coast, repeating the procedure every time the road regained its slope. I sat in the back of the Lada, alone, watching the landscape evolve. Thin stands of willows now ran through the sunflower fields, lining the creeks that rent the earth. Every so often pastures appeared, stretches of green where mottled cows grazed, the fattest I had seen in Russia.

By afternoon we had driven eight hours and crossed into the *krai*, or administrative region, of Stavropol. We had also, even before we saw them, felt the mountains. As we approached Mineralniye Vody, the dark massifs of the Caucasus appeared, giant shadows like clouds against the summer sky. At first the peaks stood stiffly in a tight row. Yet as we drove on, they rose ever higher, each revealing its own grandiose contours. One peak towered above the others: Elbrus. Too large for Zhenya's cracked windshield to compass, it seemed a castle in the sky, insurmountable and unreal. At 18,510 feet, Elbrus, the two-headed cone of a sleeping volcano, was not only one of the pillars of the Caucasus but also the highest mountain in Europe.

We had reached a fault line. After the green fields and streams, now before us spread the dusty foothills of the mountainous bridge that linked the Black Sea to the west with the Caspian to the east. For centuries the mapmakers have marked the Caucasus as the dividing line between Europe and Asia, Christendom and Islam. Stretching more than six hundred miles, since the Soviet fall the range has separated Russia from the former Soviet states of Georgia, Armenia, and Azerbaijan to the south. The lands north of the massifs, known collectively as the North Caucasus, comprise seven ethnic homelands, some gerrymandered, some legitimate, that fall within the borders of the Russian Federation. In all, the region is a linguistic and ethnic labyrinth, where as many as fifty different peoples speak their own tongues. In the first post-Soviet decade the pot boiled, gaining fame as the Caucasian Cauldron, an impossible corner of the world fated to suffer "ethnic hatreds," "religious divides," and unwanted attention for its oil. Yet as our little Lada chugged on south, taking in the expanse of rock, snow, and ice, I could not help wondering if geology, not geopolitics, still governed these lands.

We drove on, trading Zhenya for Khassan, Cossack for Caucasian, to Pyatigorsk, the Town of Five Mountains, a resort, founded in 1780, where the Good and the Great took the waters. For the aristocracy of nineteenth-century Russia, it was their Baden Baden. In 1841, Lermontov, at twenty-six, died here in a famous duel. The spot in the woods nearby where he fell remained a destination for Russians. The town still offered grand vistas and poplar-lined promenades, but it no longer looked noble, much less restorative. Even on a fine summer day Pyatigorsk looked depopulated and defoliated. The warfare to the east and west had taken a toll. The tourists now stayed away.

By dusk we had reached Nalchik, the inert capital of the tiny republic of Kabardino-Balkaria. We settled into a white-columned sanatorium, an old Soviet retreat among the firs, refashioned by a Turk into a hotel, the Grand Kavkaz. Kabardino-Balkaria was best known as a source of mineral water, mountain horses, and soccer stars. But it was also a prime example of the Bolshevik manipulation of the peoples of the North Caucasus. Kabardino-Balkaria, like its neighbor Karachaevo-Cherkessia, was a Leninist creation.

The genius of Lenin, Ali Kazikhanov, editor of *Severny Kavkaz*, explained, was to throw the Kabardins and Balkars together in one hyphenated republic in 1921, separating them from their natural allies the Cherkess and Karachai. As Kazikhanov told it, the history sounded like a Bolshevik game of checkers, with national destinies at stake. The Kabardins, by far the majority, were related to the Cherkess, while the Balkars shared a Turkic tongue with the Karachai. Each had a separate history, but Moscow entangled them, forcing rivals to share homelands. "It wasn't just 'divide and conquer,'" said Kazikhanov. "It was 'divide, conquer, and tie up in trouble.'"

I remembered Lenin's pushpins. Years earlier I'd driven into the woods outside Moscow to Gorki Leninskie, the estate where Lenin died in 1924, to see a replica of his old Kremlin office, complete with his desk, books, and paperweight–a bronze chimpanzee knitting its brow. (Yeltsin had ordered the original office removed–along with Stalin's–as part of his extravagant renovation of the Kremlin.) One wall of Lenin's study was covered with a map, its southern edges dotted with pins, each a different color. Lenin had kept a close eye on the ethnic and religious labyrinth of the Caucasus.

The Soviet map was drawn to maintain a false balance, the editor Kazikhanov said. Contradictions intended to preoccupy the natives. It was easy for him to explain the history of hatred between the Kabardins and Balkars. He belonged to neither group. He was a Kumyk from Dagestan. And he edited, naturally, a newspaper printed in Russian, the only language common among the peoples.

SIX

FOR THREE LANGUID days in Nalchik, I had to avoid the local president. A Kabardin–his prime minister was a Balkar–he had "requested" that I interview him. With no interest in being drawn into a squabble between Kabardins and Balkars, I decided to abandon both. Outside the Grand Kavkaz, I found Ismail, asleep in an ancient Audi. We struck a deal to head farther south, to travel in the shadows of the mountains to Vladikavkaz, capital of the next small republic on the road to Chechnya, North Ossetia.

With the fat end of his fist Ismail banged the tape I'd pulled from my bag into the Audi's cassette player. And so as we drove on through the operatic scenery, two Russian helicopters now limning the foothills to our right, Eric Clapton accompanied us, singing of tears in heaven. When we reached Vladikavkaz, the sun was a giant ball of burnt orange sinking behind the peak that towered behind the town, Mount Kazbek, another giant of the Caucasus range, on the Georgian side.[6] The streets, to my surprise, were crowded. Only the day before, a bomb had produced havoc in the central market, killing six and wounding forty-three. The remote-controlled device, a police investigator later told me, had been well made, designed to rip as much flesh as possible. We had descended a rung lower into the cauldron. Vladikavkaz, however, had grown inured to bombings. They had become seasonal. The previous spring a bomb had killed sixty-two. "Market squabbles" the locals called the explosions. With Chechnya so close, the North Ossetians affected an easygoing air, a rare commodity in the region and one they were eager to promote.

"Welcome to the oasis," said the president of the republic, Aleksandr Sergeyevich Dzasokhov, gesturing grandly like a cruise ship director as we sat down in his office. It was a long suite of oak-paneled rooms, so long it seemed without end. "Surrounded by war, we live in peace with our neighbors and, most important, with Moscow." Dzasokhov had been a member of Gorbachev's Politburo. Tall and elegantly dressed, he was more than a silver-haired survivor. He was a patrician master of Caucasian deal making. Dzasokhov knew he was only telling half of the truth. He was well aware of the difference between an oasis and a mirage.

Vladikavkaz, christened as a garrison town in 1818, means "To rule the Caucasus." The North Ossetians have yet to live up to the bravado, but they have long served as the proxies of tsars and general secretaries in helping tame the unruly tribes of the south. In August 1942 Hitler's troops planted a Nazi flag atop Elbrus. Hitler wanted the Grozny oil fields and dreamed of taking Baku, with its vast reserves of Caspian oil.[7] Not surprisingly, in some Caucasian circles, the Germans found support.[8] How many sided with the Nazis is a matter of historical debate. No one will ever know. To some, the Germans doubtless offered a chance to oppose Soviet power. The Ossetians, however, stood loyal. The Nazi forces got no farther than Vladikavkaz, then called Ordzhonikidze after a Georgian aide-de-camp to Stalin.

In recent years North Ossetia had distinguished itself as a singular outpost of fidelity. Things, however, could have gone very differently. In the last years of the old empire, as minor satraps across the south raised the sword of religion and the shield of sovereignty to revive "ancient hatreds" remembered by few, North Ossetia was the first Soviet tinderbox to explode. In the late 1980s, tensions boiled between the North Ossetians and the Ingush, the ethnic minority to the east—and the Chechens' next of kin. Both sides claimed the pastoral land east of Vladikavkaz known as Prigorodny, just on the North Ossetian side of the border with Ingushetia.

The roots of the trouble, like much of the present turmoil, began with Stalin, who in 1944 ordered the Ingush and the Chechens deported en masse to Central Asia. On February 23, 1944, Red Army Day, and the twenty-sixth anniversary of the founding of the workers' and peasants' army, Stalin tricked the Ingush and the Chechens into coming out to their town squares. They were rounded up and packed off—in lend-lease Studebaker trucks.[9] For the next thirteen years, until the liberalizing thaw that followed Khrushchev's secret speech of 1956, when they started to return to the lands, the Chechens and the Ingush disappeared from the pages of officialdom. The Soviet Union had established a tradition, as Robert Conquest notes in his seminal book on the deportations, *The Nation Killers*, of erasing the existence of intellectuals who had earned the wrath of the state. "Unpersons," George Orwell had famously called the writers and poets who were erased from Soviet society, if not killed. But as Conquest points out in regard to Stalin's rounding up of the Chechens and Ingush, among other minorities, "the 'unnation' was a new phenomenon."[10]

Before the deportation Prigorodny was Ingush. In the last years of the USSR the Ingush began to exhibit their intention of reclaiming it. In 1992, their Soviet bonds loosened, the Ingush and the North Ossetians went to war over the scrap of land. The fighting cost hundreds of lives on both sides, but the North Ossetians, backed by Moscow, kept their hold on the dry pastures of Prigorodny.

There had been another small war, across the mountains in Georgia, beyond the famed Darial Pass, among the Ossetians trapped in another contrivance of Soviet mapmaking called South Ossetia. In 1989 the South Ossetians, with a population of some ninety thousand, had risen up, seeking to break free of Georgia and reunite with their brethren to the north. No

nation on earth, however, recognized their sovereignty.[11] The North Ossetians meanwhile remained loyal to Moscow. Fealty had its rewards. The tiny
republic of fewer than a half million now led the Russian Federation in
vodka production. "Ours is a special relationship," President Dzasokhov said
of the coziness with the Russians. "We have a history of understanding."

In Moscow the North Ossetians had long been seen as kindred Orthodox amid the sea of Muslims, yet they led a double life. The first clue came
outside the president's office: an oil painting depicting a white-bearded warrior charging through the air on a white stallion. "A local hero" the president
had called him. "Our own St. George." The second clue came on a winding
road through the mountains. Rusik, a proud native of Vladikavkaz and an
old friend of Shvedov's, was doing his best to keep us on the road, its edges
fast giving way to the craggy scarps. He was once a KGB major but in the
spirit of the times had reincarnated himself. Rusik had made an enterprise
out of the town's aspiring entrepreneurs. He headed the new Small Business
Association. The group was "still growing," he conceded. There was plenty
of downtime. When I asked about Dargavs, known as the Village of the
Dead, he'd reached for the keys to his jeep.

The village lay high in the mountains a hundred turns above
Vladikavkaz. On a terraced hillside in a steep green valley dotted purple and
red with wildflowers, the tombs at first looked like giant beehives. But when
we neared, they came into focus as tapered mounds of slate stacked tight.
The oldest tombs dated from the thirteenth century. Each was a family sep-
ulcher, a resting place open to the mountain breeze and, bizarrely, the eyes
of strangers. Peering into the half-light of the shrines, one could not miss the
skeletons of generations of sheep farmers. Stretched out atop one another,
they lay as straight as they had been put to rest. In the shadows, skin, yellow
and thick like burlap, gave glow to the bones.

The balance of the sun, mountain air, and crossing winds, Rusik heard,
was perfect here. It had preserved the dead. The Russian guidebooks and
the villagers below claimed the tradition had long ago yielded to Soviet
secularism. Rusik, however, led me in silence farther up the hill, to a female
corpse. "Look closely," he said, "and judge for yourself." I could see fabric
wrapped around the bones. It was machine-woven, a skirt of faded cotton. The Ossetians, it seemed, had maintained the practice well into the
modern era.

Arguably the most Russified of the peoples of the North Caucasus, the Ossetians claimed ancient roots. They were the modern heirs of the Sarmatians, Indo-Iranian sun-worshipers who had pushed the Scythians from the southern steppes by the second century B.C. While their neighbors spoke tongues native to the Caucasus or Turkic languages, Ossetian derived from Persian. North Ossetia had even rechristened itself Alania, after the Alans, a Sarmatian tribe.

Officialdom may have wished to deny it, but the locals remained devout in the old ways. Outside Vladikavkaz I visited Hetag's Grove, a sacred stand of giant trees amid brown fields where Ossetians bowed before an ancient god named Wasterzhi.[12] I spent a morning in the wood toasting the god with homemade fire brew in the company of three Ossetian soldiers on home leave from Chechnya–and desirous of deliverance. Shvedov dismissed the idea of any local paganism from the start. "Ossetians are Christian," he insisted, "as Orthodox as Russians." Rusik, however, kept silent. It was not right, he said, catching my eyes in the jeep's mirror, to talk of such things.

❦ SEVEN ❦

WE MADE IT TO NAZRAN, the would-be capital of the would-be statelet of Ingushetia, in time for lunch. Rusik arranged for Soslan, the Small Business Association's driver, to take us. We drove slowly through the eerie silence of the old Prigorodny battleground–its houses burned out, its fields still fallow– before coming to the border with Ingushetia. Soslan, of course, being Ossetian, could go no farther. Shvedov and I walked across the dirt road to the border post, a hut, and, after haggling for an hour with the Ingush guards, entered the last little republic in the foothills of the Caucasus before Chechnya.

Nazran in the Soviet era was a market town, a dusty assemblage of collective farms that raised cattle and sheep and little else. When in the late 1950s the Ingush and the Chechens returned from their Central Asian exile, they resettled in a single administrative province, first established by Moscow in 1934 and generously named the Chechen-Ingush Autonomous

Republic. In 1991, when the Chechens unilaterally opted to end the curse of their hyphenated past, Ingushetia was born by default. Like any fledgling state, it soon gained a president: Ruslan Aushev, a homegrown general and a mustachioed hero of the Soviet war in Afghanistan. Naturally, a president required a seat of power.

Shvedov had dreaded Nazran. There was only one place, he'd said, that scared him more than the Zone, Ingushetia. He'd said it again and again. In Nazran, he'd warned, the price on my head doubled, and his confidence in the authorities vanished. The fighting remained across the border, but the war had seeped everywhere into Ingush life. Nazran was a breeding ground for kidnappers, assassins, bombers. It was also, as a result of a 1994 quid pro quo with the Kremlin, an *ofshornaya zona*, a new term in post-Soviet jurisprudence that denoted a realm known in the West as an offshore tax haven.[13] Everywhere the red-brick palazzi, as big as any in the woods outside Moscow, testified to the local growth industries in bootleg vodka, petroleum products, and arms. The Ingush hated to say it, and few did, but the war in Chechnya had been good to them.

The Ingush and Chechens speak closely related tongues. Brothers in the Vainakh nation–the word means "our people"–they share many cultural and religious traditions. But the years of war had strained the fraternity. Never ones to fight in the Chechens' defense, by now the Ingush had turned hostile. In the first campaign they had taken in Chechen refugees. But in the second round, Chechens had flooded across the border. As the storming of Grozny loomed, nearly two hundred thousand Chechen refugees had fled to Ingushetia, nearly doubling the tiny republic's population.

Outside Nazran we found two dozen Chechen families living in an abandoned pigsty. Shvedov found the irony–Muslims sleeping beside pig troughs–amusing. The camps farther on, however, left even him speechless. Here, for miles on the parched earth, thousands of Chechen refugees were trying to live. They were eating, sleeping, and, on a rare occasion, washing in a city of tents, the likes of which the world saw with regularity now, thanks to CNN and the end of the post–cold war bliss. At the height of the second Chechen war, the Sputnik and Karabulak camps had housed tens of thousands. Six thousand remained.

It was a stifling summer day. In the tents, skin streamed with sweat. The train cars were even worse, much worse. The old Soviet cars, four dozen in all, had been dragged to the edge of the barren field and left to stand in place. There was no breeze and no water, nothing but flies and a rising rate of infection. For 3,657 Chechens, the train was home. The men squatted in the shade of the carriages and watched the day go by. Their wives said they had ceased to be men. There was no work and no money. How could they be men? The women offered dry crackers and black tea. Had it been "back then," they said, had we been "over there," they could have hosted me properly. Not all them knew, but nearly all suspected, that the homes they had left behind were no longer.

The talk came to a end when the water truck arrived. The water came from the canal, two miles away. In an hour another truck came. Bread. There was no water here, the women explained. And no flour. There were only children. Everywhere, in the dirt, by the outhouses, under the train cars stopped in their tracks, the children played. So there would be a future, the women said, but what kind?

IF VLADIKAVKAZ BREATHED with the mystique of the nineteenth-century Caucasus, Nazran still lived by Soviet deal making. Whatever it was you wanted—a bottle of beer or a rack of lamb, an interview with the president or a ride to the camps—it was always negotiated through a side door, in the back of the shop, under the table. The epicenter of the negotiations was the Hotel Assa. A place of legend, the Assa was built in the euphoric first years after the Soviet fall as a Western-style hotel and business center, the first to grace this side of the Caucasus. Given the bloodshed and misery a few miles away, the Ingush investment climate had failed to lure many prospectors. The Assa instead since its first days had played host, and faithfully hustled, the journalists and relief workers drawn to the war. On a good day the foreigners nearly outnumbered the agents of the Ingush arm of the Federal Security Service, the FSB. The hotel claimed three stars and possessed, at first glance, the reassuring appearance of a tidy refuge from the dust, an outpost of modernity, if not air-conditioning.

Shvedov had looked forward to the Assa. For days it had been all he could talk of: the balcony one could eat on, the little artificial lake it overlooked, the presidential town houses across the way, the sweet waitresses he knew by name. His dreams all came true. Within a day he was dictating, in a painful recitation of no less than ten minutes' duration, his four-course meals without a menu. At the Assa we stopped dining together.

It was not hard to see why the hotel had earned a reputation as a hell-hole. The Assa had taken a beating. Hotels in the West often offer lists of local restaurants and recommended boutiques. At the Assa, rooms came with price lists—each item and what it would cost if destroyed: "Broken door: $200. Broken window: $200. Broken bed: $300. Broken shower stall: $400. Broken mirror: $200." The inventory closed with the administration's sincere wish that its guests enjoy a pleasant stay.

The place at least had color. The restaurant each night filled with Belgian doctors, Danish food distributors, even a crew of Irish clowns in from Bosnia to entertain the children in the camps. There was also a German engineer, a veteran relief worker who'd struck out on his own. Over coffee in the morning and drinks at night, he sat on the balcony, mumbling urgently about the *verdammte Chlor*, the damned chlorine. He was gripped by an obsession with the cisterns of chlorine gas in Grozny. I had heard of the cisterns, leftovers from an old Soviet plant. The Russians had claimed the Chechens had blown them up, in an improvised attempt at chemical warfare. The Chechens in turn blamed the Russians for shelling the gas tanks. Now here was the German insisting all the cisterns had not been blown up.

"*Sie sind tam!*" he cried, blending German with Russian. They are there! "*Sie sind* in very bad shape, *diese* tanks! They could explode any day, today, yesterday, *Morgen*. When they do, they kill any brave Chechens who make it *nach Hause*."

The German failed, it seemed, to recognize that I spoke English. But he was passionate about preventing the chlorine cisterns from exploding. He had a simple plan. He would cool the gas, liquefy it, and store it in trucks while the cisterns were repaired. He figured he needed only a few thousand dollars, but no relief organization would help him. They all ran, he said, at the word "Chechnya." And so the poor German had been left stranded at the Assa. Each night he retreated to the balcony on his own, to drink his furies away.

IN THE REFUGEE CAMPS I had sat in a stifling tent drinking strong tea from glass cups with Kuri Idrisov. He was a rarity, a Chechen psychiatrist. In the first war, he'd worked with a syringe, administering morphine day and night. The hospital in Grozny had been destroyed–twice. In the interregnum, now in his forties, he had joined the French crew of *Médécins du Monde*. For more than a year he had tended to the refugees. His family had moved back to Grozny, to his native village of Aldy, the destination I'd marked on the map I carried every day. The psychiatrist had heard of what happened in Aldy. His relatives had been in the village that day. He had wanted to return with his family, but he said he could not leave. He was hoping to salve the psychic wounds of the children in the tent city.

In another tent the children were listening to Musa Akhmadov. Akhmadov had written a series of books on the Chechens' customary law, the traditions that governed relations among children and elders, lovers and enemies, known as *adat*. The psychiatrist had recruited the writer to spend time with the children. *Adat*, Akhmadov explained, had suffered in the war. It was not a religious but a social code. "The backbone of Chechen culture" he called it. Since the Chechens' earliest days, *adat* had drawn the lines between right and wrong. But in the turmoil of the years of war, a new code–*Shari'a*–the Islamic religious law imported by young men with beards who called themselves Wahhabis had threatened the continuum of *adat*. Wahhabism, a strict form of fundamentalist Islam that originated in Saudi Arabia, had been carried to Chechnya from the Arab diaspora.[14] The two were incompatible, Akhmadov said. He feared that the youngest refugees, with no knowledge of the laws of old, would fall prey to the Wahhabis. The children, the writer worried, would lose their Chechen heritage in the tents.

As we walked outside, threading among the children, Idrisov did not smile. After the first war he had believed it was the Chechens' fault. "We'd won our freedom," he said, "but hadn't learned how to use it." Now he thought differently. This new round had convinced him. "Look around you," he said. "The Russians don't want our land or our oil or our mountains. They want us to die out."

DESPITE SHVEDOV'S HOURLY assurances, Issa had yet to appear in Nazran. For days we called Moscow, trying to relay a message to him in Chechnya. Shvedov, for some reason, insisted on code. "The package," he screamed into the satellite phone, "has arrived and is waiting." Issa turned up at last, claiming car trouble and the backup at the checkpoints from

Grozny. We'd come back late to the Assa when I noticed a large man sitting at a pink plastic table beside the hotel. He was trying to crack pistachios with his fist on the plastic. Shvedov had walked right past him. The man, without looking up from his pursuit, had whistled. Shvedov, fearful the kitchen would close, kept walking. The man called out: "Is that any way to say hello?"

Issa had come to me with the résumé of an opportunist loyal to Moscow. Colleagues he had previously ferried had passed on the collective intelligence: Issa was once a high-ranking official in the anti-Dudayev camp, a staunchly pro-Russian Chechen of the Soviet era. He could be trusted to get you into Chechnya and around the republic—to almost any place no journalist could otherwise get to. But he could not be trusted in any other respect. Rumor cast him as an intermediary in the kidnapping trade.

He looked at me directly, the barest of smiles curling the edges of a thin gray mustache. "My dear Andrei," he said, "I wish you a pleasant stay in the land the world has forgotten."

I don't know what it was. Maybe it was the singing. (He was fond of Joe Dassin, the bards of the Soviet underground, and old Chechen ballads sung, naturally, in Russian.) Maybe it was the way he affected a wordly air. (He mixed, in a single sentence, the few words he knew in French with the few he knew in English.) Maybe it was his gentlemanly manner. (He wore a pressed shirt, a sleeveless undershirt, and polished shoes.) But against my better judgment, Shvedov's insistent counsel, and all that I had heard, I took an immediate liking to Issa.

It was too dark to set out. Issa, however, did not want to stay in the hotel. He knew it was infested with Ingush security agents, men who had no desire to see him working with an American journalist. We would leave before dawn the next day. This time Shvedov was right: It was best not to let Issa out of our sight. The Assa was short on comfort, but it was long on protection. Each night we ate in the restaurant beside men wearing camouflage bodysuits, their Kalashnikovs slung over their chairs. They were the bodyguards of aid workers. Each night there was gunfire outside, but inside, it was quiet. Until our last night.

It was around ten in the evening. I was alone in my room when I was startled by pounding on the door. I opened it and saw only an ID card shoved in my face and a trio of well-armed men in plain clothes. Two had automatic rifles in their hands. The third, a pale fellow dressed all in black who now refused to show me his ID again, wore two holstered guns, one under an armpit, another in his waist. They said they were police, but I knew they were Ingush FSB.

"You have failed to register with the police," the lead man said when I showed him my documents. The hotel should have done that, I said. Like all hotels in Russia, it was required to do so. I had given the clerk my passport and visa. "You've committed a crime," he said. It was a bluff, and one poorly orchestrated. All the same the next hour consisted of a spectacle of pounding on doors, rousting aid workers, and seizing passports. It dragged on to midnight.

In the lobby I found an Austrian relief worker screaming at the Ingush FSB agents. He was pleading for his passport. He knew no Russian, had just arrived, and was justifiably confused. He had come from Vienna to build latrines in the refugee camps. I intervened to tell him that the gentlemen said he could retrieve his passport tomorrow. Did he know where the Interior Ministry was? Of course he did, he cried. His bodyguards worked there.

All the while, the agents of the Ingush secret police spoke of arrests, jail, court orders. In time, however, the threats eased. They spoke of "fines" and then of "exemptions." Before long they simply handed my documents back–with apologies. The lead man in black even offered to buy me a drink. I took a whiskey, a double. Later, once the men had vanished into the starless night just as suddenly as they'd arrived, the relief workers huddled in outrage in the lobby.

What relief organization did I represent? they wanted to know. They were relieved, oddly, to learn I was a journalist. "That explains it," said a Belgian nurse, a longtime Assa resident. The Ingush agents, she said, hadn't given them so much attention for months. Moreover, this time they hadn't really seemed to be after bribes. My presence, the nurse said, explained the goon squad's interest. She had a thought: "You're not going into Chechnya tomorrow, are you?"

✖ EIGHT ✖

THE POISONED EMOTIONS that pervade relations between Russians and Chechens have ample literary precedent. Lermontov's "Cossack Lullaby" is still sung to Russian children at bedtime:

> Over the rocks the Terek streams
> Raising a muddy wave,
> Onto the bank the wicked Chechen crawls,
> sharpening his dagger as he goes;
> But your father is an old warrior,
> Forged in many a battle,
> So sleep little one, be calm . . .

For Russia's "people of color" there is no political correctness, no cultural police to purge Russian literature of its jingoism. Russian writers have long coveted, and feared, the Caucasus. Although slurs emerged–Lermontov's "wicked Chechen" is only the most famous–the Chechens were not always cast as bloodthirsty bandits. Pushkin, in his 1822 classic "The Prisoner of the Caucasus," used the south as a lusty backdrop to probe the nature of freedom. To the poet, the Chechens were noble savages who enjoyed a "Circassian liberty" he could only envy. Lermontov, ironically, was no defender of Russian hegemony. In an early poem, "Izmail-Bey," he even undermined the imperial campaign to subdue the mountaineers.[15] Still, by the middle of the nineteenth century, as the Caucasian wars raged, a singular image of the Chechens had formed in the Russian imagination. They were merciless thieves, head choppers who would slit their own mothers' throats should a blood feud demand it. Worse, they lived by taking Russians hostage and holding them in a *zindan*–a dark pit carved into the earth.

If the Russians had poets and writers to blame for their bias, the Chechens owed their opinion of the Russians in large part to one man, General Aleksei Petrovich Yermolov. Under Alexander I and Nicholas I, from 1816 to 1827, Yermolov served as viceroy of the Caucasus, the prime mover of the effort to pacify the mountaineers. In the post-Soviet decade, as the Chechens again acted on their yearning for sovereignty, the old bigotry rose anew in Moscow and across Russia. So, too, as Yeltsin's failed campaign gave way to Putin's new and improved offensive, did the tsarist military strategy. Yermolov was the progenitor of the Russian notion that there was only one way to defeat the Chechens: burn all their villages to the ground. Early in the second Chechen war one of Putin's field marshals struck an uncanny echo of Yermolov's conviction. "Our strategy is simple," General Gennadi Troshev said. "If they shoot at us from a house, we destroy the house. If they shoot from all over a village, we destroy the village."[16]

Yermolov boasted an illustrious résumé even before he reached the Caucasus. A giant of a man–"the head of a tiger on the torso of a Hercules" is how Pushkin portrayed him after an audience in 1829–Yermolov had won the Cross of St. George for heroism in battle when he was sixteen.[17] At the fall of Paris in 1814 he had led both the Russian and Prussian Guards. With the deaths of Kutuzov and Bagration, Yermolov became the most revered officer in the imperial corps.[18] His cruelty was famed. "I desire that the terror of my name should guard our frontiers," he is said to have declared, "that my word should be for the natives a law more inevitable than death. Condescension in the eyes of Asiatics is a sign of weakness, and out of pure humanity I am inexorably severe. One execution saves hundreds of Russians from destruction, and thousands of Mussulmans from treason."[19] By his career's end he had become a legend. "Nothing has any influence on Yermolov," wrote the head of Nicholas's secret police, "except his own vanity."[20]

In short order, Yermolov set out to subdue the south. He built a line of fortresses along the Sunzha River. Forward bases in enemy territory, they bore names declaring his intentions: Groznaya (Menacing) was founded in 1818, the same year as Vladikavkaz, followed by Burnaya (Stormy) and Vnezapnaya (Sudden). He wrote Alexander I, Napoleon's most unyielding foe:

When the fortresses are ready, I shall offer the scoundrels dwelling between the Terek and the Soundja [Sunzha] and calling themselves "peaceable," rules of life, and certain obligations, that will make clear to them that they are subjects of your Majesty, and not allies, as they have hitherto dreamed. If they submit, as they ought, I will apportion them according to their numbers the necessary amount of land . . . if not, I shall propose to them to retire and join the other robbers from whom they differ only in name, and in this case the whole of the land will be at our disposal.[21]

It was psyops, tsarist style. Fortress Groznaya presaged not only the terror to come but the Russians' misguided strategy as well. Yermolov succeeded only in uniting the Chechens and their neighbors to the east, the Dagestanis, in a rebellion led by Imam Shamil, the fabled nineteenth-century Muslim warrior. Shamil's holy war, the *Ghazavat*, lasted more than twenty-five years. As early as 1820 one wise contemporary of Yermolov's foretold his failure. "It is just as hard to subjugate the Chechens and other peoples of this region as to level the Caucasian range," wrote General Mikhail Orlov, who did not fight in the campaign. "This is not something to achieve with bayonets but rather with time and enlightenment, in such short supply in our country. The fighting may bring great personal benefits to Yermolov, but none whatsoever to Russia."[22] In 1859, surrounded by imperial troops, Shamil gave up. But as the Russians knew well, the surrender was tactical. His *Ghazavat* would live on.

WE ARRIVED IN GUDERMES, Chechnya's second–largest city, as the sun set, moments before the shoot-on-sight curfew fell. Chechnya is only slightly larger than the state of Connecticut, covering some six thousand square miles. Once it took a couple of hours to drive from Nazran to Gudermes, the town that rose only a few concrete floors off the dry ground to the north and east of Grozny. Now thanks to the vagaries of the checkpoints and the Russian convoys on the road–the endless caravans of tanks, trucks, and kerchiefed soldiers clinging atop armored personnel carriers (APCs)–it took us the whole day. Gudermes had little to offer. But the Russians, in an attempt to lend a semblance of governance to their military adventure had made it the republic's temporary capital. Grozny was in no shape to host the officers and bureaucrats visiting from Moscow.

Issa, exhausted, went to his bedroom to undress. He rolled a small rug across the uneven floor and, stripped down to his sleeveless T-shirt and undershorts, bent to his knees to pray. Shvedov meanwhile was overjoyed. "Not a bad day's work," he said, declaring it over, as one shoe removed the other. He pulled off a sweat-soaked shirt, lay across an old sofa, and reached for another *papirosa* cigarette. As he smoked, the sweat continued to drip from his bald head.

It had been a long day. We'd started out early in the morning, crossed into Chechnya, driven across its dry northern plains and into the remains of Grozny. I had seen Kabul in the summer of 1996, just before the Taliban took the Afghan capital. Leveled so many times, Kabul had no cityscape. Little, save the remnants of the old Soviet apartment blocks, distinguished it from the Stone Age. Grozny, however, looked worse, much worse. When the USSR collapsed, the Chechen capital had been a modern city of Soviet architecture and European aspirations. It had been a city with promenades and parks, where the sweet smell of jasmine mingled with the smell of grilling lamb at sidewalk stands, where mammoth industrial works—one of the USSR's largest petroleum refineries, a chemical factory, a cement plant—belched black plumes day and night, ever reminding the residents of their service to the empire. The square blocks downtown had once boasted the landmarks of Soviet power—Party buildings of stone that lengthened the reach of the ministries in Moscow. Grozny had once been a destination for the ambitious from across the North Caucasus, a center of education (with a university, technical institutes, sixty schools) and culture (with a national library, fine arts museum, museum of national culture, puppet theater, drama theater, and concert hall).

There had also been people. Grozny before the first war was home to nearly half a million residents. Between Lenin Square and Lenin Park, university students had gathered in the long summer evenings at the square named in honor of the *druzhba narodov* ("friendship of peoples"). Nearby stood a famous statue that pretended to testify to the ethnic solidarity. Three Bolsheviks—a Chechen, an Ingush, and a Russian—were sculpted in stone, shoulder to shoulder. The years of war, however, had laid the myth bare. The heads of the happy trio had been blown off by a rocket-propelled grenade.[23] Now everything was different. Nothing functioned, and little remained. Grozny was a city of ruins.

We entered the long Staropromyslovsky district. Block after block had been bombed and burned out. Of the few buildings that still stood, many were sliced open. Walls and roofs had fallen, revealing the abandoned remains of homes inside: sinks, burned cabinets, old stoves. Furniture, belongings, anything of value had disappeared long ago. We drove on, accelerating between the checkpoints, now approaching the city center. Each turn revealed only more concrete carcasses, more black metal twisted and torched, more gaping holes that held only darkness. "This," announced Issa, though the images required no captions, "is the wreckage of Putin's War."

FOR THE CHECHENS the winter of 1999–2000 may have been the harshest ever. While the West greeted the new millennium with apprehension, fearful that computers and fiber optics might usher in the Apocalypse, Armageddon had already arrived for the Chechens. The fortunate ones had survived one horrible war, the campaign that began on New Year's Eve 1994 and ended for all practical purposes on August 6, 1996, the day the Chechen fighters swarmed back and retook Grozny. The first war left as many as one hundred thousand dead. Launched to quell a nationalist movement for independence, it dragged on thanks largely to Yeltsin's vanity, the shambolic state of his armed forces, and the resolve of the Chechen rebels. In the summer of 1996 Yeltsin won reelection, and "the Chechen question" was put on hold. On August 31, 1996, Yeltsin's envoy, General Aleksandr Lebed, cut a deal with Aslan Maskhadov, the shy military leader of the insurgency.[24] The pact, signed in the Dagestani town of Khasavyurt, brought a cease-fire but put off the critical issue of the region's status for five years. The deal haunted both sides. "Khasavyurt," in the coded lexicon of Moscow politics, lingered as a metaphor for Russia's weakness.

David had beaten Goliath but not killed him. The rewards were few. For Chechens the interregnum brought an ugly period of isolation, dominated by banditry, kidnapping, and arbitrary attempts at *Shari'a*. In January 1997 Maskhadov was elected the first Chechen president, but even he had no illusions the republic had attained sovereignty or peace.[25] In Moscow, Chechnya was pushed to the back burner, its troubles relegated to the expanding realm of the country's political taboos, another embarrassment best left unspoken and forgotten.

Then, one warm morning in August 1999, the back burner caught fire. The two most famous fighters of the first war, Shamil Basayev and the Saudi-born mercenary known as Khattab (his single *nom de guerre*), opened a new front. The Kremlin had made Basayev Russia's most wanted man after he had led a daring, and homicidal, raid on a hospital in the southern Russian town of Budyonnovsk in the summer of 1995. Basayev had led the rebels' return to Grozny on August 6, 1996, but struggled after the war. For a time he tried governing, serving briefly as prime minister under Maskhadov. By his own admission, Basayev as a politician was a disaster. His talent lay in warfare. Khattab, meanwhile, had become the most odious rebel to the Russians. An Islamic militant with a sinister giggle and long, curly hair, on Russian television he was branded the Black Arab. Khattab had joined the Chechen fight in 1995, having fought the Soviets in Afghanistan. In Afghanistan, by his own admission, Khattab had consorted with Osama bin Laden. But the rebel commander's ties to bin Laden were obscure at best.[26]

Basayev and Khattab led a convoy of fighters across the mountains of southeastern Chechnya, east into neighboring Dagestan, the mostly Muslim republic, firmly within the Russian Federation, on the Caspian Sea.[27] A caviar-rich republic the size of the Austria, Dagestan is a complex mélange of obscure ethnic groups—more than thirty in all—long ruled by Soviet-bred officials loyal to Moscow. The rebels, several hundred by the best estimates, marched in broad daylight, two by two, well armed with grenade launchers, wearing new camouflage uniforms. When they seized a handful of Dagestani villages across the border, in Moscow the move was seen as an attempt to fulfill an old vow to unite Chechnya with Dagestan in an Islamic state that would reach the Caspian.

The remote stretch of Dagestan had long been a center for the Wahhabi movement. Sergei Stepashin, the Russian prime minister at the time of the incursion, had even once visited the villages under Wahhabi "occupation." In August 1998 Stepashin, then Yeltsin's interior minister, had gone to Dagestan to hear grievances from the village elders. He left convinced that "the Wahhabis are peaceful people, we can work with them." The day after Basayev and Khattab entered Dagestan, Stepashin again flew to Dagestan. This time as prime minister he spoke in stern tones. He said he'd come to take charge, but his face was ash gray. The next day, August 9, 1999, Yeltsin sacked him.

Stepashin had personified loyalty, long considered the president's favorite attribute. However, this was not just another of Yeltsin's seasonal cabinet cleanings. Stepashin's shortcoming, said Oleg Sysuev, a Kremlin aide at the time, was that "he had a heart." Yeltsin needed more than fidelity; he needed strength. He turned to Putin, who had been his FSB director for only a year, and named him prime minister. In eighteen months Yeltsin had sacked five prime ministers. This time, however, he added a shocker. He spoke on television of Putin as his successor. At the time the former KGB officer was unknown. Polls put his popularity ratings at less than 2 percent. The dynamics, however, of the political vacuum had been proved. "Yeltsin could put anyone in the prime minister's job," said Aleksandr Oslon, Russia's best pollster, "and his numbers would rise."

Putin's numbers were aided by more than his new seat of power. The August march into Dagestan, fixed on Russian television screens as a slap in the Kremlin's face, gave him a perfect opportunity to avenge the mistakes of the past. But Putin wanted more: to permit Russia, insulted and injured after the crash of 1998 and burdened by Yeltsin's calcified rule, to imagine itself again a *velikaya derzhava*, a great power. Moscow dispatched helicopter gunships to pound the mud villages the rebels had seized. Basayev and Khattab, however, and nearly all their men, it seemed, had already fled. The new prime minister promised a short operation—he would mercilessly cleanse Dagestan, but under no condition reignite the embers in Chechnya.

During his brief tenure as FSB chief Putin had hung a portrait of Peter the Great in his Lubyanka office. In his first months as prime minister, his aides liked to assure foreign reporters that Peter, the tsar who opened Russia to the West, was Putin's model. Yet Peter had also begun his career with an onslaught against the heathens in the south, conquering the port of Azov in 1696 from the Ottoman Turks, gaining access, after a failed attempt the previous year, to the Black Sea.

For years, in Russian politics the month of August seemed to carry a curse. Both the coup of 1991 and the crash of 1998 came in August. But August 1999 hit Yeltsin particularly hard. His physical and mental health had moved from a topic of concern to ridicule among the Moscow elite. Worse still, scandals brewed on several fronts, conspiring to ruin his fishing vacation. There was the Mabetex mess, a tangled affair that reeked of money laundering on a massive scale and of egregious—even by Russian standards—bribery. The Mabetex story, gaining ground since the spring, had already ensnared Pavel Borodin, the president's drinking partner and chief of one of the state's largest internal empires, the Kremlin Property Department. In August the scandal threatened to drag in Yeltsin's two daughters, their spouses, and a host of family consiglieri. Borodin was alleged to have accepted bribes from a

Kosovar Albanian, Behgjet Pacolli, for multibillion-dollar contracts to refurbish the Kremlin.[28]

August also brought a second scandal, the Bank of New York affair. The story, which first appeared in the *New York Times* on August 19, 1999, alleged that Russian crime bosses, in cahoots with Moscow officials, had washed "as much as ten billion dollars" through the U.S. banking system.[29] The BoNY scandal unfolded as Russian forces bombed and shelled the Wahhabi villages in Dagestan. Then, on August 25, the *Corriere della Sera* ran a detailed exposé of the Mabetex case that linked, for the first time, the Yeltsin family to the misdeeds.

Six days later the bombing season began. Days after the rebels had retreated from Dagestan, a series of bombings rocked Russia. On August 31, as Mia and I sat in an Indian café two blocks away, a bomb exploded in one of Luzhkov's proudest creations, the Manezh, a subterranean shopping mall next to the Kremlin. Placed beside a video arcade, the device wounded forty-one. Two later died from their burns. On September 4, 1999, an apartment building housing Russian officers and their families in the Dagestani town of Buinaksk exploded in the middle of the night. Sixty-two died. Back in Moscow, one after another on September 9 and 13, massive chemical bombs leveled two whole apartment blocks. Three days later a fourth building blew, this time in the south, in the town of Volgodonsk. By then nearly 300 people had been killed in their sleep. Yeltsin denounced the "barbaric acts of terror."

No one came forward to claim responsibility. But the prime suspects naturally were the Chechens. Few facts surfaced, but, as always, theories in Moscow swirled. *Rossiiskaya gazeta*, the daily newspaper of the Russian state, saw a host of possible culprits: Chechen rebels, who "want[ed] to create a great state in the Caucasus," global oil barons, "who want[ed] to redraw the map of a rich region in their favor," and Russophobes, who wanted Moscow to "sink into local conflicts and retire from the world stage." Viktor Ilyukhin, the chairman of the Duma Security Committee and an unreconstructed Communist prone to fulminating without facts, saw the bombings as a Kremlin campaign to bring down Mayor Luzhkov. *Moskovskii komsomolets*, Russia's best-read tabloid and the newspaper closest to Luzhkov, accused his archfoe Berezovsky of masterminding the invasion into Dagestan. The paper even aired an accusation that many–members of the military included–

feared true: that the FSB had set the bombs. No evidence, however, surfaced that the blasts were the work of Chechen extremists.[30]

Questions lingered. There was the choice of targets—working-class districts—and the timing—just when things seemed quiet—and the fact that the Chechens had never set off a bomb in Moscow during the first war. Most disconcerting of all was a strange episode in Ryazan, a city 130 miles southeast of Moscow. On the night of September 22, 1999, just six days after the Volgodonsk bombing, residents of a twelve-story apartment house at 14/16 Novosyelov Street called the police. A bus driver had seen two men carrying something into the basement and feared it was a bomb. The police discovered three sacks bound by wires and a detonator set to go off before dawn. They evacuated the building and called the bomb squad. The next day Putin declared that "vigilance" had thwarted a "terrorist threat." On September 24, 1999, however, in the glare of the television lights, the new head of the FSB, Nikolai Patrushev, a man Putin had brought from Petersburg, apologized. The security service, he said, had put the sacks there itself. It was only "a training exercise," Patrushev said awkwardly. The sacks, he insisted, were filled with sugar.[31]

The bombings, coupled with the invasion of Dagestan, united the nation—against the Chechens. By September's close Putin's War had begun. Russian troops, this time a force of nearly a hundred thousand, were back in Chechnya. This war, the new prime minister vowed, would be different. Moscow would restore order in the lawless region that had enjoyed de facto, if not de jure, independence since driving the Russian forces out after the 1994–96 war. The first campaign had been a humiliation riddled with political indecision and military incompetence. The second round, as one of its architects, General Troshev, promised early, would be "a merciless battle, with Moscow refusing to abstain from any of our weapons, for every square foot of the Chechen republic."

Led by the new strongman in the Kremlin, Russian troops moved with purpose across the northern plains of Chechnya. On television Russians watched with pride, and muted amazement, as Chechen village after Chechen town fell without a shot. When Gudermes fell without a fight, Moscow imagined the war was won. "Only mop-up work remains to be done," announced Putin's unctuous spokesman for the war, Sergei Yastrzhembsky. A spin doctor who had served both Yeltsin and his rival

Luzhkov, Yastrzhembsky held daily briefings to assure reporters the new campaign was an "antiterrorist operation" not a war. "It will be over within days," he promised as New Year's 1999 neared. In the first war Russia's fledgling private media had tested their independence. This time, however, the state drew a new line: To report from the Chechen side was to support the enemy. The local media largely complied, glossing over reports of civilian massacres and Chechen resistance.

In Moscow the politicians and generals now tried to downplay the fate of Grozny. In the first war the city had become known among the troops as a meat grinder. The rebels had mastered the art of urban guerrilla warfare, using underground passages and fortified buildings to entrap Russian tank columns and destroy them. "Grozny is not critical," insisted General Valery Manilov, the logorrheic spokesman for the high command. "We will not storm Grozny" became his mantra at weekly briefings, as reporters wondered how the Russians could win the war without entering the capital.

The answer was simple—and brutal. Early in Putin's War, Aleksandr Zhilin, a former MiG pilot and one of the keenest military journalists in Moscow, mapped the new strategy for me. "You take up positions as far away from your target as possible," Zhilin said, "and shell the hell out of them. You use jets, attack helicopters, artillery—whatever has lead and metal and flies. You hit them day and night without pause. You send in men only once you've leveled everything." The onslaught was calculated to lose as few Russian soldiers as possible, while killing as many Chechens, armed or not, as possible. "Costly in terms of hardware," Zhilin called the plan, "but effective."

Almost immediately the Chechens felt the difference from the first war. This time they fled. At one point more than three hundred thousand abandoned the republic. While most went to Ingushetia, some went south—on foot across the mountains to Georgia. In October 1999 in Duisi, a village at the mouth of the Pankisi Gorge across the border in Georgia, I found hundreds of Chechen refugees crowded in an abandoned hospital.[32] For days they had walked in deep snow, beneath Russian bombers. At times the road was no more than a narrow path, much of it mined. They were the lucky ones, they said. Dozens more had died along the way. During World War II Leningrad residents trapped by the Nazi siege escaped on an ice road across Lake Ladoga to the north of the city. The Soviets later named it the Road of

Life. The road from Grozny into the Pankisi Gorge, the Chechen refugees said, had been a Road of Death.

The refugees had no trouble recognizing the Kremlin's new tactics. "In the first war," said Roza, a nine-year-old girl from Urus-Martan, "we'd sit in the cellar and count the bombs." But in the new war, she said, "there are so many you can't even count them." The hospital, long abandoned, had no heat. Plastic sheets hung over the empty window-frames. Khassan, a village elder from Samashki, spoke of a new level of brutality. "I never imagined I'd feel nostalgia for Yeltsin," he said. "I never imagined war could be worse than what we saw before. But this is not war. It is murder on a state level; it is mass murder."

Despite the generals' assurances, few in Moscow doubted that the Russians would have to storm Grozny. This time, however, Kremlin officials were sure the city would fall easily. After all, little of its infrastructure remained, and given the mass flight of refugees, this time around there would be few civilians to shelter the rebels. By November 1999 Russian forces had invested the city, hoping to sever the supply lines to the last Chechen fighters within it. The siege had begun.

By December 1999 the so-called *chastniye sektora* (private districts), the stretches of little single-story houses that had spread around Grozny in the years since Gorbachev, had been scorched. The tall apartment buildings along the long avenues were now shells, dark eye sockets in the city's skull. The center, leveled once in the first war, had fallen silent. Civilians, both Chechen and Russian, still lived in Grozny. No one knew how many remained—some said as many as twenty thousand—but they were invisible. Day and night they crowded together in dank cellars beneath the ruins.

The siege lasted 102 days. On January 31, after two weeks of the second war's bloodiest fighting, Minutka Square, the intersection long considered the key to the city, fell. There was in the end no great battle for Grozny. Both sides exaggerated the numbers they had killed and wounded. However, the Chechen fighters, even the generals in Moscow had to admit, made a strong stand. Some had retreated earlier to their traditional refuge, the mountains south of Grozny. In the final days of January 2000, the last rebel contingent in the city, some three thousand men in all, started to decamp. They moved at night, in two columns through a corridor on the city's southwestern side.

By February 1 the fighters, now several hundred fewer in number, had reached the village of Alkhan-Kala, eleven miles southwest of Aldy. Fighters who survived the trek later told me how they crossed frozen pastures covered with mines. Knowing the fields were mined, they moved forward one after another, in a suicide walk. "We shall see each other in paradise," they screamed as they stepped out into the field. *"Allah akbar!"* others cried. As they walked, explosions, feet triggering mines, lit the darkness. "The only way to cross the field," said a young Chechen who was there that night, "was to walk across the bodies." The exodus cost the fighters several top commanders. Basayev lost his right foot to a mine. Among the dead was Lecha Dudayev, the mayor of Grozny and nephew of the late former leader Dudayev.

Every village the retreating fighters passed through became the object of fierce Russian bombing: Shaami-Yurt, Katyr-Yurt, Gekhi-Chu. Aldy had suffered surprisingly little damage–before February. Bombs and shells had fallen on the village, hitting scattered houses and the train station. But it had not figured in any clashes between the Russian forces and the rebels. Only later did I piece it together. On their bloody retreat from the besieged capital to Alkhan-Kala, one column of fighters had come straight through Aldy.

GRIM AS IT WAS, Gudermes became home. In Moscow the town was considered under Russian control. In reality, the Russians' hold here was as illusive as in any other corner of Chechnya. The officers kept to their barracks, a Soviet-style housing project laced with several cordons of fortifications. Even still, their sleep was routinely interrupted by grenades, remote-controlled bombs, and Kalashnikov fire. In the local bazaar stocked by Dagestani merchants, Russian soldiers shopped warily, moving only in packs. Moscow's Chechen proxies, however, the natives recruited in the latest pacification effort, may have had the most to fear. Akhmed Kadirov, once the grand mufti of the republic, now Putin's choice to rule it, lived in Gudermes, but no one ever saw him. They only heard him–each morning and evening, coming and going in a Russian helicopter. "The invisible mufti," the Chechens called him mockingly.

Issa's apartment had all the warmth of an IRA safe house. He liked to keep the windows papered over, visitors at a minimum, and his Makarov pistol handy. The apartment was a gift from Nikolai Koshman, a feckless

Russian apparatchik who had risen in the Railways Ministry and had served as a deputy in the brief puppet regime Moscow had tried to foist on Chechnya during the first war.[33] In the new campaign, before settling on the former mufti Kadirov, Putin had recalled Koshman to duty, naming him his viceroy in the republic.

By his own estimation, Issa was equal parts Chechen and Soviet. Every morning he slapped on French cologne and prayed to Allah. Each night he prayed again. Yet when time and resources permitted, he drank. His usual drink, as beer and wine ran scarce in Chechnya, was *spirt*, denatured ethyl alcohol. As a reward for his taking on Dudayev, Moscow in 1995 had given him a sinecure, a position atop the Foreign Relations Department in Russia's puppet regime of Doku Zavgayev, a Soviet bureaucrat and Chechen loyalist. At one point Issa headed the negotiations for seven hundred million dollars' worth of contracts for the reconstruction of Grozny. Mabetex, the Swiss-based construction firm that had brought the Yeltsin family a flood of bad press, had a five-million-dollar slice of them. Issa was proud of his snapshots, pictures of himself in Grozny with Pacolli, the Kosovar Albanian who ran Mabetex. The Turkish firm Enka had been the lead partner. But it had all been run through Borodin. Nothing of course had come of it. "Only more war," Issa said. "And more reason to hate the Russians and distrust your fellow Chechens."

Early in Putin's War, Moscow had again turned to Issa. The Russians made him an aide to Koshman, with the promise of his old job back at Grozneft. By then he had made the rebels' blacklist, an honor bestowed on him by Movladi Udugov, Dudayev's onetime minister of ideology who had long since gone underground and now ran Basayev's and Khattab's multilingual Web site, Kavkaz.org. The rebels, Issa explained, had sentenced their enemies to death under *Shari'a*. With pride he proffered the list of names. Yeltsin topped it, but there, just a few lines below Putin, was Issa. He had few socially acceptable things to say about Udugov, Basayev, and Khattab. However, after six months of Putin's War, and hopeless attempts to work with his generals—Vladimir Shamanov, Ivan Babichev, Viktor Kazantsev, and Gennadi Troshev—he had even fewer nice things to say about the Russians.

Early one morning before the heat of the sun started to fill the apartment, we rose and, without tea, climbed into the UAZik. We drove slowly through Gudermes on its rutted roads. Scattering stray dogs, we creaked past the half-guarded officers' headquarters, beside the string of forlorn stalls that now pretended to be the local bazaar, and through the first checkpoints of the morning. We left town and headed west, following the old asphalt through brown fields, until at the eastern edge of Grozny, we came to Khankala, the Russian military headquarters in Chechnya. Journalists who had covered the war in Vietnam said Khankala reminded them of Da Nang. The base seemed like a small town. Everywhere tents and helicopters stretched as far as you could see.

We continued on, coming again to the ruins of Minutka Square, then on into the center of Grozny. The streets were as empty as before. In the concrete remains nothing stirred. Not cats, not dogs. Every so often, among the burned shells of the apartment houses, flecks of color flashed. Clothes dried on a line strung between two walls that a shell had opened to the street. The city's water supply was tainted with disease. There was no plumbing and no electricity, no shops and no transport, but someone did, after all, live here. Chechens, men, women, and their children, were coming home.

At a barren corner, near where the old Presidential Palace once stood, young girls sold candy, gum, and glass jars filled with home-distilled kerosene. They stood by their wares but didn't smile or wave. They had no customers. The only people moving among them were soldiers. They did not walk. They traveled on top of their tanks, trucks, and APCs. Only at the checkpoints did the soldiers, bare-chested in the hot sun, stand.

Issa hated taking lip from young Russians with Kalashnikovs. But they were becoming harder to avoid. "You take the same route twice in one day," he said. "If there's no checkpoint the first time, it's there the next time you go by." Amid the ruins the checkpoints often marked what had once been city blocks. The Russians stopped each car, scoured the occupants' papers and searched the trunk. They feared the suicide bombers who had taken to blowing up their checkpoints and barracks with regularity. The tactic of turning your body into a bomb may have come from the Middle East, but the Chechens made a significant advancement in the technique. Long before Palestinian women and girls joined the bombers' ranks, Chechen women had done so. Issa was never happy at the checkpoints. But the worst, he would later say, had been the last one we'd negotiated that morning, the final checkpoint before Aldy.

✿ NINE ✿

OFFICIALLY IT IS A district of Grozny, but to its residents Aldy is a village. Once it had its own bakery, clinic, library, and bazaar, where the locals sold vegetables. In those days, at School No. 39, nearly a thousand children studied each day. That was all before the first war in Chechnya, back when nearly ten thousand people lived in Aldy. The village lies in the Zavodskoi (factory) district of Grozny. Whoever worked back then, hardly the majority, worked at the plants across the way, producing petroleum and chemicals, cement and bricks. Now, under banners of black clouds, the factories nearly blended into the surrounding ruins. Some stood out. They were still burning.

Aldy sits above a dam, across from Grozny's largest reservoir. The village comprises a broad rectangle of a dozen streets lined with squat single-story houses, each with its own sheltered courtyard. In the middle of thick greenery, the branches of old trees—apricot, pear, cherry, peach, apple, walnut—twist above the low roofs. Bound together by fences of metal and wood taller than a man, the yards appear linked in a line against the world outside.

Inside, on the other side of the fences, the survivors of the massacre were still numb. Bislan Ismailov, a soft-spoken Chechen in his forty-second year, spoke in a detached monotone. His eyes were fixed on me, but his mind was not here. He was there. For him, February 5, 2000, was not fixed in time. When he spoke of it, he switched tenses without cause. Bislan had not left Aldy. He had been here throughout. Once he'd worked at the fuel plant across the way. Back in the days of Brezhnevian slumber he'd become an engineer. But throughout Russia's second war in Chechnya, he had collected, washed, and helped bury the dead.

"For months that's all I did," he said. "Whoever they bring in, we bury them. Eight, ten, twelve people a day. They brought in fighters and left them. Have to bury them? Have to. They bring them in beat-up, shot-up cars from the center of town . . . and we buried them, right here by our house, in the yard of the clinic. Right here, sixty-three people—all before February."

Bislan was thin but not frail. He had dark almond-shaped eyes and long black lashes. His thin black mustache was neatly trimmed. His appearance was impeccable. In fact he struck me, given the words that poured from his mouth, as inordinately clean.

In the last days of January 2000, a few weeks after the New Year's Day when the Western world breathed with relief at having survived the millennial turn without catastrophe and Putin, in his first hours as acting president, flew to Chechnya to award hunting knives to the troops and tell them their task was to keep the Russian Federation intact, the Chechen fighters had abandoned Grozny. In Aldy, life by then had taken on a strange, brutal routine as it had in nearly every other corner of the city. The nights were filled with shelling, and the mornings brought only more of the encroaching thunder.

"They fired everything they could," Bislan said. "Bombs, missiles, grenades. They shot from all sides. There were times when we could not collect the dead. We would bury them days later."

On the morning of February 3 nearly a hundred of the men in Aldy decided to take action. They left their homes and cellars and walked to the neighboring district of Grozny, District 20. They carried torn bits of white sheets as flags and went in search of the commander of the Russian troops, the ones closest to Aldy. They wanted to plead with him to stop the shelling, to assure him they were sheltering no fighters. As the group crossed the field of frozen mud where the Russians had dug their positions, shots were fired. One of the villagers fell to the ground. His name was Nikolai. He happened to be an ethnic Russian.

Until then the villagers had not seen a single Russian soldier during the second war, but in the middle of the afternoon on February 4 the first troops arrived. They were not friendly, but they were "businesslike." The first group of soldiers came to warn them. They were *srochniki*, conscripts, drafted into the war. They were young, the villagers recalled, almost polite. "So young the beards were barely on their cheeks," said Bislan. They wore dirty uniforms, and their faces were covered with mud. They were exhausted. They went house to house, telling the men and women of Aldy to get prepared. "Get out of your cellars," they said. "Don't hide and don't go out in the street. Get your passports ready," they said. For the next soldiers to check. "Because we're not the bad guys," they said. "The bad guys come after us."

On the next morning, the morning of February 5, the villagers, some seven hundred who remained, sleeping in old coats and blankets in cramped basements, heard something strange. As first light came, and the slopes of the snowy peaks far to the south brightened, as they rolled their prayer rugs out toward Mecca, bent to their knees, and praised Allah, they heard silence. No thunderclaps. Only the sounds of chickens, sheep, and cows. The numbing monotony had broken. The shelling had stopped.

For months the families of Aldy had waited. For months they had been transfixed by one question. They knew the Russians had surrounded Grozny; they only wondered when the attack would come. For days they had stored water from a nearby spring and kept the few fish the men could catch, the *belyi nalym* that once grew three feet long in the reservoir, frozen under the snow. When the Russians come, they thought, it would be good not to go out. The silence disturbed them, but they welcomed an hour for urgent repairs.

Bislan climbed up onto the low roof of his single-story house with a hammer and three scraps of plastic sheeting. From the roof he saw that his neighbor Salaudi, a mechanic in his forties, had done the same. Salaudi, deaf since birth, had done better. He'd found a sheet of aluminum siding. He was trying to nail it over a hole the shelling had left.

At just after nine, smoky layers of chill mist still blanketed the corners of Grozny. Aldy sits up high. It commands a vantage point over the lowlands that edge the city. But Bislan could not yet see the sun. He only heard the shouts. From the northern end of the village, APCs churned the asphalt of Matasha-Mazayeva. Three bus stops long, Matasha-Mazayeva is Aldy's central street, the only one that runs the length of the village. At the same time, the Russians came along the frozen mud of the parallel streets, Almaznaya and Tsimlyanskaya. Still more men and armored vehicles filled the roads that run perpendicular, Khoperskaya, Uralskaya, and Kamskaya. Within minutes the village was clogged with APCs and, running on each side of them, more than one hundred soldiers.

They did not all wear the same uniforms. Some wore camouflage. Some wore white snow ponchos. Some wore only undershirts or were naked to their waists. Nearly all wore dark camouflage trousers covered in dirt. Some had scarves wrapped around their necks, and some bandannas. Some wore knit hats pulled down close to their eyes. Some had tattoos on their arms, necks, and hands. Some carried five-liter canisters, marked only with numbers stenciled onto the plastic. But they all carried Kalashnikovs.

These were not *srochniki*, the conscripts of the day before. These were *kontraktniki*, contract soldiers. The distance between the two is vast. Conscripts stand on the far edge of puberty, often just a few months over eighteen. Contract soldiers, however, are older, more experienced, and fighting for the money. They earn much more than the newly drafted soldiers, and they are in the main far more battle hardened.

Kontraktniki were easy to spot, Shvedov said. "They look like criminals." With their shaved heads, bandannas, tattoos, and muscles, they tended to look like convicts who had spent too much time on the prison yard weights.

At the edges of Aldy, the soldiers had parked APCs and olive drab trucks whose open flatbeds sat high off the ground. They had blocked all the exits, sealed off the village.

Bislan was nailing the plastic sheet onto his roof when he heard the first screams. He looked down Matasha-Mazayeva, to the houses at the northernmost corner of the village. Two plumes of blue-gray smoke swirled there. The screams grew louder. He clung to his roof and looked down the other end of Aldy. Smoke had begun to billow as well at the southern end of the village. House by house, from either end, the men were moving down Matasha-Mazayeva. House by house they tried to get into the locked courtyards. First they kicked the gates with their boots. When that failed, they shot the locks.

The killing began at the northern edge of the village, on Irtyshskaya Street. The Idigovs were among the first to face the Russians. They were brothers, Lom-Ali and Musa. They stood at the door of their uncle's small house and tried to reason with the soldiers. There were a lot of soldiers. Too many. There would be no pleading. They were not listening. They screamed at Lom-Ali and Musa.

"Get in the basement!" one barked.

"Come on!" another yelled. "Don't you want to be in the action film?"

There was no cellar in the house, so the soldiers took them to the house next door. They forced the brothers into the cellar and threw a grenade in. It hit the cold floor and bounced. Lom-Ali, the younger of the brothers, threw himself on the grenade. He was in his late thirties. The shrapnel tore him to bits. Those who collected his body later were certain there must have been more than one grenade. His body had been cut into too many parts. The force of the explosion threw his elder brother, Musa, against the concrete wall. He was knocked unconscious, but came to as the smoke seeped into the basement. He looked for his brother and started to climb out of the cellar.

It was still not yet ten when the men reached the heart of Aldy and started to shoot–in every direction. Smoke and screams filled the air. Bislan climbed down from his roof. He saw people gathering at the corner of Kamskaya and the Fourth Almazny Lane. They had come into the middle of the street to show the soldiers their documents. The soldiers encircled them. They were shooting into the sky, and they were yelling.

"Get out of your houses!" one screamed.

"Go collect your bodies!" another yelled.

Not everyone that morning in Aldy was making repairs. In his small square house on the corner of Matasha-Mazayeva, No. 152, Avalu Sugaipov was making tea. Avalu, like his brothers, was a bus driver. He was forty, and driving a bus was all he had ever done. There was no food for breakfast. He could only put the kettle on. He would make the morning tea for his guests, two strangers who had come from the center of Grozny. One man was in his sixties, the other his late fifties. In Aldy, they had heard, there were still people. Safety, they imagined, was in numbers. Avalu had taken them in. They sat at his small kitchen table, waiting for the water to boil.

A woman, Kaipa, sat with them. No one knew her last name. She and her nine-year-old-daughter, Leila, had come from the town of Djalka. Her husband had died long ago. She had seven other children. The war had scattered them all save her youngest. The shelling in Djalka had become unbearable. They'd moved to another village, and then another, before coming to her mother's house in District 20 next door to Aldy. At the end of December 1999 she came to Aldy. Shamkhan, the mullah, was her distant cousin.

Avalu lived in his mother's house. His mother and younger brother had gone to Nazran in November. There were two small houses here–six rooms and a cellar in all. Avalu took in Kaipa and her girl, Leila. They had been living in the second house for a week now.

As Avalu poured the tea, they heard the screams. The men did not want her to, but Kaipa went out. They rushed after her. Just as she stepped out into the courtyard, the soldiers lowered their guns. Kaipa was hit twice, in the head and chest.

"Mama jumped in the air and then fell to the ground," nine-year-old Leila would later say.

The next bullets hit the two men. They were shot in the face.

Avalu stood at the threshold of his house and held the little girl tight. He told her to go back into the house, and he took a step forward. She turned around and saw his body leap into the air, too. Avalu fell backward, into the house.

Leila ran through the house to the room in its farthest corner. She crawled under the bed and hid behind a sack of onions. She lay there in silence as two soldiers entered the house.

"Pour it," one said.

She heard something splash against the floor.

"But where's the girl?" the other asked.

"Don't kill me," Leila said, coming out from under the bed.

One of them lifted her out. He covered her eyes with a scarf and, stepping around the bodies, carried her from the house. In the yard, from under the cloth, she saw her mother, lying facedown in a circle of blood. In the street he put a can of meat in her hands. He tried to calm her down. He looked up and found two women staring at him.

"Take her," he told them, and returned to the courtyard of the house.

The house was already on fire. The women grabbed the girl and ran to the far side of Matasha-Mazayeva. Every night for weeks the girl would need a shot of sedatives to sleep.

BISLAN WAITED FOR the soldiers to turn the corner before he opened the metal gate of his house. He crossed the street and walked into Avalu's yard. That was when he saw the bodies: two men, badly burned, one shot in the eye, and a woman. Bislan had known Kaipa. He stepped into the house. There, he saw the body of his friend Avalu, lying faceup in the middle of his kitchen. Bislan looked around the kitchen. The teapot sat on the stove, the cups on the table.

ASET CHADAYEVA RAN from her family's house on the Fourth Almazny Lane. She threw open the gate and ran into the street. She had heard the APCs, but when the screams grew close, she could wait no longer. There in the street, some thirty feet to the right, four houses down, she saw two

Russian officers. They were staring up at Salaudi, the deaf mechanic who persisted in trying to fix his roof.

"Look at that idiot," one said.

"Bring him down," yelled the other.

As one of the soldiers raised his rifle, Aset screamed, "He can't hear you! He's deaf!"

The soldier turned toward her and fired.

"Get on the ground!" they yelled.

Aset fell to her knees. The days had warmed since January. In the first days of February the snow had even begun to melt. The ground was icy and black, half-frozen mud. Her younger brother Akhyad, who'd turned twenty-five weeks earlier, ran from the house. "Come here and show us your documents!" the soldiers screamed. Aset and Akhyad walked slowly, arms in the air, toward the men. As they went through Akhyad's papers, Aset measured the men's faces. One, she sensed, was the commander. Aset's father and brother Timur came out into the street. They pleaded with the commander to let Aset and Akhyad go. Several more soldiers joined the two in the middle of the street. One of them screamed curses at Aset, her brothers, and her father. Tall and reeking of vodka, he stuck the barrel of his Kalashnikov into her ribs, pushed her to the fence.

The commander had had enough. *"Svolochi!"* he yelled at his own men. "You bastards! Get the fuck out of here! Move it!"

Aset saw an opportunity. There were still many people in the houses, she said. "I can collect them," she told the commander. "I can bring them to you. That way," she said, "your men can check their documents faster." Timur, Akhyad, and their father said they'd stay with the soldiers if the commander let Aset gather their neighbors.

He agreed but turned to Timur. "Walk behind me," he ordered.

"Don't worry," Timur said. "Our people won't shoot you."

The commander looked at Timur. "But mine might," he said.

Aset went down all the houses on Fourth Almazny Lane and on the side streets left and right. She came back with a crowd, two dozen women, men, and children. The soldiers pushed them forward, out into the intersection of Kamskaya and Fourth Almazny.

"You'll stand here," they said, "until we're through."

The commander came close to Aset. She was carrying as always a green plastic bag. In its folds, a gray wolf, the symbol of the Chechen people, howled. It was the flag of Ichkeria, the free state Dudayev had founded.

"What's in the bag?" he asked.

Aset had spent the war in Aldy. She too had helped bury the dead. She had collected the bodies, and body parts, and washed them for burial by the mullah Shamkhan. She was a nurse. She had finished her nursing studies at Grozny's medical college in 1987, in the heyday of Gorbachev and glasnost. She had worked in a children's clinic in Grozny until December 1994, until the Russians first stormed Grozny. In Putin's War, at thirty-two, she had become a one-woman paramedic unit. Day and night for months she had nursed the wounded and foraged to feed Aldy's elderly and sick. She had prepared food for her neighbors, both Chechen and the few stranded Russians, old men and women who had nowhere to go. She had also tended the fighters. They brought medicine from their fortified basements in the city and fish from the nearby reservoir. When the fighters passed through, she had sewn them up. She had cleaned their wounds—with *spirit*—pulled the metal from their flesh, and sent them on their way. Aset had feared the day they would abandon the city, and when at last they did, it was the first time in Putin's War that she cried.

"Bandages, medicine, syringes," Aset answered the commander. "I am a nurse."

"Then you can help me," he said.

He grabbed her by the sleeve and pulled her close, away from the crowd gathered at the corner.

"There's been a mistake," he said. "Some of my men have killed some of your men. They've got to be covered up quickly."

She looked at him but did not understand.

The commander had blue eyes and light hair. He was neither tall nor short. He was average, Aset said. "A typical, average Russian man." As she stood next to the commander, his radio crackled. Across the static, she heard a soldier's call name—*Kaban*—clearly: "Come in Boar, come in." In the street his men had shouted the names Dima and Sergei.

The commander seemed stunned. "What the hell are you assholes doing?" he screamed into his radio. "Have you lost your minds?" He looked at Aset and said, almost softly, "Stay with me. Don't leave my side. Or they'll kill you too."

At the corner the men and women and children stood still. They stood close to one another. They did not move from the corner. They stood there, as the smoke grew thick, for nearly two hours.

IN MOSCOW THAT SAME Saturday afternoon I had heard on Ekho Moskvy, the liberal news radio station of the Gusinsky media empire, that in the settlement of Aldy on the southern edge of Grozny a *zachistka* was under way. To many Russians, the word, meaning "a little cleanup," resonated with positive overtones. It meant "they're cleaning out the bandits." By the time Aldy burned and bled, *zachistka* operations had become routine, a staple in the "counterterrorist operation." A *zachistka*, it was understood, was a house-to-house search for members of the armed opposition. Broadcast on television back home, the endeavor was meant to impress. On the evening news the footage resembled scenes from American real crime shows. Russian soldiers moved house to house in search of bandits, not unlike the cops, guns drawn, who sidle down crack house corridors to ferret out dealers. On the ground the news carried a different meaning.

BISLAN KEPT RUNNING. He went to the next house on Matasha-Mazayeva, No. 160. The Magomadov brothers, Salman and Abdullah, lived here. Flames licked at the porch and the roof above it. He looked left and right. Three houses in a row were on fire. Salman was sixty, Abdullah fifty-three. Bislan had seen them the day before.

The stench of burning filled the winter air. Bislan could not find the Magomadovs in the yard. The Russians set the basements on fire first. He knew that, but he could not get through the front door. It was already aflame. He knew the brothers were in there. The stench was so strong. Then he heard the screams. Bislan broke a side window and climbed in, but in the dense smoke he became disoriented. He could see nothing. A staircase led to the basement, but he couldn't find it. He couldn't even find the window again. He ran to a wall, felt the glass pane and smashed it. He pulled himself through and fell into the yard.

The remains of the Magomadov brothers were found days later. They had been in the cellar. Both had been shot and then set afire. In the yard, to the right of the front door, bullet casings were on the ground. Among the ashes in the basement were bullets from 5.45-mm and 7.62-mm automatic rifles, the new and old standard-issue Kalashnikovs. There was also a wristwatch. It had stopped at eleven twenty-five.

Next door, in front of No. 162, Gula Khaidaev was already dead. He had left his house and been shot before he could step onto the street. Maybe he had heard the screams; maybe he had come out to show his passport. He was seventy-six. Shot three times, in his knee, chest, and forehead, Gula still held his passport in his outstretched hand. A few feet away lay his cousin Rakat Akhmadova. She had been shot in the neck and chest. She was eighty-two.

Malika Khumidovna, a widowed schoolteacher in her forties, who had guided a generation of Aldy children through School No. 39, stood with her back to a wall in the yard of a house on Khopyorskaya Street. Her three girls and mother stood near her. So did thirteen other women. They had slept and eaten together in the basement of the house. It was large, and they had kept glass jars filled with water and *kompot*, homemade fruit juice, there. Up until the day before, there had been many more women and children here. In January as many as thirty had slept in the cellar.

The soldiers had told them to stand at the cement wall, in the cold. Hours passed. The women dared not move. They stood there, their backs to the wall. The soldiers brought chairs out of the house and sat across from the women. Two soldiers ventured in the cellar and found the jars of *kompot* the women had kept there. They emerged with smiles and passed the sweet drink among themselves. Every so often the soldiers shot into the wall. The bullet holes traced an arc a few feet above the heads of the women and their daughters.

When their squad leader came upon the scene, he yelled. He told the men to get rid of the women. The soldiers went to work. Two took the children aside, while one led the women into an abandoned house next door.

Malika had already said her prayers. She had asked Allah not for mercy but to light her path. She did not look at the soldier. She averted her eyes. As the women walked into the house, the soldier stuffed a note into her hand. On the paper, he said, was his home address. He told Malika not to worry. He wasn't going to shoot her or any of the women. She reminded him, he said, of his mother. "So write my mama," he said. "Tell her I didn't kill you."

BISLAN PASSED TWO houses before he entered the yard of No. 170, nearly tripping on the first body. Just by the gate, half on the road, half in the yard, lay Rizvan Umkhaev, a seventy-two-year-old pensioner who in recent years had guarded the parking lot of the TB hospital in Grozny. The bullets had ripped right through him. Issa Akhmadov, a short, muscular man who at thirty-five had never held a job and spent too many years in jail, lay near him. It had been a close-range execution. They, too, still clutched their passports.

Bislan turned toward the house and took two steps forward. He could go no farther. Behind him lay the ghastly remains of Sultan Temirov, whose head had been blown off. He was forty-nine. His body was mangled, destroyed by a mass of metal. His head would never be found.

A few steps on, behind the high metal fence of No. 140, seventy-two-year-old Magomed Gaitaev lay dead. He had driven a tractor in the fields beyond the reservoir his whole life. He had lived for years alone. A bullet had pierced the base of his neck and torn his left cheek open as it exited. His chest pocket was open. It held his passport. His glasses hung on the top of the gate to his house.

Across the road, a scene had unfolded that revealed that the villagers were not the only ones afraid. Malika Labazanova, a plump round-faced woman in her forties who wore her dark brown hair in a bun, stood between two soldiers and her front door. They told her they wanted only to search her house. She opened the door. Once they checked the house, one of the soldiers turned to Malika and raised his gun at her. She fell to her knees and pleaded.

He stood over her in the front room of her house and said, "Lie down and don't move."

He shot into the air. If anyone knew, he said, that he had not killed her, he'd be killed as well.

At No. 1 Podolskaya Street, a ten-minute walk from the center of Aldy, the terror struck mercilessly. Sixty-seven-year-old Khasmagomed Estamirov, a disabled former chauffeur, had sent his wife, two daughters, and toddler grandson away to the refugee camps of Ingushetia. But the rest of his clan was home: his cousin Said-Akhmed Masarov; his son, Khozh-Akhmad, who had returned to care for his ailing father; and his daughter-in-law, Toita. At twenty-nine, Toita was eight and one-half months into her third pregnancy. Her one-year-old, Khassan, was also with them. He had taken his first steps that week.

By noon his older brother, Khusein, the toddler who had been sent off to the camps of Ingushetia, had been orphaned. The soldiers had killed everyone in the Estamirov house. The old man. The little boy. His pregnant mother. They even killed the family cow. It was trapped when the soldiers set everything they saw aflame. They torched the yard and the house. They burned the family car as well. Then, as the flames engulfed the cow alive, they left.

Khasmagomed's cousin found the bodies. As he approached the burning house, a mud-splattered APC was driving away. Father and son lay in the yard, side by side. Khasmagomed had been shot in the chest, several times. His wallet was on the ground, empty. The corpses were burned. Toita and her little boy Khassan lay under the awning in the courtyard on the concrete floor. The concrete was pockmarked with bullet holes. Toita, due to give birth in two weeks, was shot in the chest and stomach. Her ring and earrings were gone. Across the threshold to the small house lay the body of the cousin, smoldering. Blood covered the floors and walls.

In the house Khasmagomed had built a small iron stove to keep the family warm. Thirty-two bullet holes had pierced it. Khasmagomed had asked his cousin Said-Akhmed to come live with him. "It's frightening on your own," he had said. "Here we'll be together."

Here, too, the young conscripts had come the day before, February 4. They had warned the Estamirovs. "The *kontraktniki* are coming next," they said. "You'd better leave."

Khasmagomed, a proud grandfather who could count at least seven generations that tied him to the Chechen land, had stayed in the house he had built. He was retired, and his health was bad. But he had earned Hero of Labor medals for his decades of driving Party officials around Grozny. He did not believe the soldiers. He did not think the Russians would do anything. "They'll just come," he told his family, "and check our passports."

He and his wife had remained throughout the first war on Podolskaya Street. They had lost their first house but rebuilt it from the ground. He did not worry about the Russians coming. He believed they would bring order. So as soon as the conscripts left, Khasmogamed and his son went into their yard. They hung white sheets in front of the house, and on the fence, in white paint, they wrote, "*Zachistka* done."

IT WAS NEARING THREE in the afternoon and the sun had still not appeared when the soldiers came back to the center of Aldy, to the Abulkhanov house at No. 145 Matasha-Mazayeva. Five members of the family were living there: the elderly owner, his wife, their daughter-in-law, Luisa, their niece, and her twelve-year-old son, Islam—an old man, three women, and a boy. The soldiers first came early in the morning. They shot the family dog. All day long other soldiers had come—some wore white snowsuits; some had faces so dirty you could see only their eyes.

This time the owner of the house, seventy-one-year-old Akhmed Abulkhanov, tried to give them his passport, but they threw it on the ground. They lined them all up—Abulkhanov, his wife, their niece, her son, Islam, and their daughter-in-law, Luisa—against a wall at the side of the house.

The soldiers swore at them all and grabbed Islam.

"You'll make a good little fighter," one said as he laughed.

"Look, you guys," the old man said, "what are you doing?"

A soldier butted him with his Kalashnikov. They asked for whatever the family had: jewelry, money, wine. The women undid their earrings and surrendered them. The old man said he had no wine in the house and no money. He said if they let him, he'd go borrow money from a neighbor.

Several soldiers went with Abulkhanov as he went to his friend's house, around the corner on Third Tsimlyansky Lane. Khusein Abdulmezhidov, forty-seven, and his elder sister, Zina, both were home. Zina, a short black-haired woman, had turned sixty not long before. For years she had manned the counter at the bakery in Chernorechiye, the adjoining district just across the dam from Aldy.[34] They gave the soldiers all they had, three hundred rubles. It was not enough. There in the yard of his friend's house the soldiers shot Abulkhanov. They did not spare Zina or Khusein. Alongside their neighbor they both were killed in their own yard.

Aldy lay in flames. Black smoke filled the sky, and the stench was heavy. Whatever the liquid was that the soldiers poured on the houses, it burned well. And long. All along Matasha-Mazayeva Street, Aldy's central road, the houses were aflame. Even those villagers whose houses went untouched could only stand and stare as the fires gained force. All the while the screams, wave after wave, continued to rise behind the fences. But they were screams of discovery now—of horror, not pain.

By late afternoon, when the soldiers finally left, the list of the dead was long: at least fifty-two men and eight women. In English we call such an event a massacre. The Russian military command, and the investigators who later exhumed the bodies, persisted in calling it a *zachistka*. Given its privileged place in Putin's War, the term had moved from the front line into the political vernacular. Although the Russian military command likes to translate *zachistka* as a "mop-up operation," the word derives from the verb *chistit'*, meaning "to clean" or "to cleanse." Linguistically, at least, Putin's *zachistki* were related to Stalin's purges, the *chistki*. For Chechens, however, a *zachistka* had little to do with mopping up and everything to do with cleaning out. To them it meant state-sponsored terror, pillage, rape, and murder.

IN MOSCOW THE following day, a quiet snowbound Sunday, sheets of thick flakes, buoyant and motelike, fell steadily and kept the avenues empty and white. No one had yet heard of the horrors wreaked on Aldy, when Putin, now acting president of Russia, went on television to announce the end of the military operation in Grozny.

"As far as the Chechen situation is concerned," he said, "I can tell you that the General Staff has just reported that the last stronghold where terrorists were offering resistance—Grozny's Zavodskoi district—was seized awhile ago and that the Russian flag was raised on one of its administrative buildings."

Grozny's Zavodskoi district is where Aldy lies.

"And so," Putin concluded, "we can say that the operation to liberate Grozny is over."

The troubles, however, were far from over. All that spring and into the summer, when I arrived in Chechnya, the pace of the war may have slowed, but to those on the ground, both Chechen and Russian, it remained as devastating as ever. After the fall of Grozny the Chechen fighters turned increasingly to a new tactic, low-intensity, but persistent, guerrilla warfare. As in the first war, they bought grenades, land mines, and munitions from Russian soldiers–some corrupt, but some just hungry or awake to the grim reality that Putin's War would drag on with or without their patriotic duty. Almost daily Chechen fighters ambushed Russian convoys, checkpoints, and administrative headquarters. They killed at night and in the day, choosing their targets at random–a clutch of Russian soldiers buying bread in a local market–or with precision: high-ranking Chechen officials whom Moscow had appointed their administrative proxies in the region.

At the same time, the civilian population grew rapidly. By the summer of 2000 more than one hundred thousand Chechens had returned from Ingushetia. They came home to more than destroyed homes and fresh graves. Chechnya was now under Moscow's arbitrary rule. The sweeps continued, and with them, the cases of extrajudicial reprisal. Human rights advocates collected new reports of extortions and beatings, rapes and summary executions. For young male Chechens, however, the primary fear was detention. Each month more and more young men disappeared from the streets. At best the detentions were a rough form of intelligence gathering. At worst they served the enforcers' sadistic urges. But perhaps most commonly, the men were taken hostage merely for ransom. It was also not uncommon that days or weeks later their bodies would be found, dumped at a conveniently empty corner of town.

WE SAT UNDER A TRELLIS heavy with grapevines, in the still, hot air of the narrow courtyard of Aset Chadayeva's home. Aset, the nurse who survived the massacre, was not here, but I handed a note from her to her mother, Hamsat. Aset told me that without it, her parents would not talk. No one would. Such was the fear, she had warned, in Aldy.

"This man is a journalist," Aset had written. "You can trust him. Tell him about the Fifth."

Hamsat had dropped the note and was crying. She wore a dark blouse, a long black skirt faded gray, and a cloth apron around her waist. She wiped her eyes with the end of the apron. Aset's seventy-two-year-old

father, Tuma—I recognized him by his great bald head—came into the yard
to embrace me. Around us, sisters emerged (Aset was the eldest of seven
children), then cousins and grandchildren. In all, there must have been a
dozen members of the Chadayev family here, but only Aset's father and
brother, Timur, sat at the table with me. Timur was in his early thirties. He
wore no shirt, only a well-worn jeans jacket. His ribs were protruding.
Beneath his long lashes, his eyeballs bulged slightly. Timur, I knew from
Aset, remained in shock. "When you gather the burned pieces of flesh of
your friends and neighbors," she had said of her brother, "it affects how
you think."

Aset's mother, shifting her weight nervously from her left to her right
foot, stood behind her son and husband. Her grandchildren brought bowls
of candies wrapped in brightly colored wax paper. Her daughters produced
flat, hard pillows for me to sit on.

Tuma wandered the square concrete yard, under the green of the arbor,
mumbling to no one in particular. Occasionally he turned in my direction,
and I could make out what he was saying. The afternoon, like every afternoon for weeks, was stifling. It must have been over ninety degrees.

"We've never had such heat," Tuma said softly. "Never. Such heat. Look
at the grapes."

It was all he could say. He, too, I could see, was crying. Tuma, long
retired, had spent his life helping build the concrete edifices of power in
Grozny. A construction engineer, he had worked on most of the government buildings that lined the center. In 1992, after the Soviet fall, when
everything suddenly changed, he had dreams of his own construction firm,
Tuma & Sons. War of course intervened. In the first campaign his house
was leveled. Tuma had rebuilt it by hand. Then there had been plumbing,
hot water even. Now there was only the outhouse and the well down the
road.

"Never had such heat," Tuma repeated. He wandered beneath the tall
walnut tree that dominated the yard. "There're so many grapes. And all
dried up. We've never had such heat."

Timur brought Bislan. They had not always been good friends, but now
they were bound for life. Together they had collected the bodies after the
massacre. Together they had watched that night as the Russians returned,
this time with trucks, big open flatbed trucks. They had watched as the sol-

diers returned to the houses that had not burned and emptied them of their belongings, of televisions and sofas, carpets and refrigerators. In the morning Bislan and Timor began to collect the bodies. Several they just put in the empty houses. They nailed the windows shut, so the dogs wouldn't get them. It took six days to find all the bodies.

Timur and Bislan spoke softly. They had had to tell what they had seen more than once already. They had had to tell it to the men who came here before me, the Russian "investigators." Men who carried video cameras and tape recorders. Men who showed no identification and did not give names. Men who were interested only in what the villagers knew.

As Bislan talked, Timur sat in a far corner of the yard. Hunched over, he stared at the rough ends of his short fingers. He was haunted by more than his memory of the massacre. Since the Fifth the Russians had come for him several times. Each time they took him away he came home with bruises. Only rarely did he interrupt Bislan.

"Forever," Timur said, when I asked if he would remember the commander's face. "A typical face, one of those simple Russian faces," he said. His men, too, he was sure were Russians, not Ossetians or Dagestanis or even Chechens, as some in Moscow had wanted me to believe.

EVEN BEFORE GOING to Chechnya, in Moscow and Nazran I had met survivors of the massacre. I sat and listened, often for hours, at times for days, as they told of the events of the Fifth. I took notes and wrote up the sessions, but these were not interviews. It was testimony.

In an empty hovel on Moscow's outskirts, where refugees from the Caucasus often lived, lying low from the Moscow police, I spent hours talking with Aset. She had risked arrest, or worse, and come to the capital to tell the human rights advocates what she had seen. I was to meet many others who had been in Aldy that day, but even years later I was convinced that Aset knew more about the massacre than anyone who had survived that day.

The first time we met she spoke in a breathless stream for nearly six hours. She had details on command, chronology in perfect place. She could quote her neighbors verbatim. She was, I feared, too good a witness. I worried that in her shock she had reconstructed the day in greater detail than she could possibly have known. I even entertained the idea that she might have been sent to Western human rights groups and Western correspondents to enhance the story of the massacre. But as I sat and listened to her talk not only of the massacre but of the war that preceded it and the war that had preceded that war, I came to believe her without pause, and I admired her courage. Given the prominent threat of retribution, only a handful of survivors had spoken publicly of the massacre. None spoke more eloquently than Aset. In the years that followed, we spoke often. I played and replayed the day as she saw it. Never once did she stray from her first telling. Never once did she retract or recast those first words.

To her the commander had been human. He had looked at her, she said, and nearly pleaded.

"What do you want me to do?" he asked as they stood together in the midst of the carnage. "My men shoot old men? Well, sometimes old men and young children carry things hidden on their bodies that blow up when you get too close. You know it yourself."

Aset did. She had seen others do it, and once the men had left that day, she, too, would tape a grenade to her waist. For two days she wore it hidden beneath her blouse.

"I told Timur I was worried about being raped," she said.

"Don't worry," her brother told her, "tape a grenade to your body, and if anyone comes at you, pull the plug."

Aset bought the grenade from a Russian soldier for four packs of Prima, the cheap Russian cigarettes that Shvedov, when he couldn't find his beloved *papirosi*, smoked.

Months later, after we had met countless times, Aset told me what her name meant. It was derived from Isis, she said, the Egyptian goddess. But Aset did not know what Isis had done. Isis had collected and reassembled the body of the murdered Osiris. Isis had impregnated herself from the corpse, becoming the goddess of the dead and funeral rites.

Aset's black hair hung sharply above her shoulders. Her eyes were deep-set and almond-shaped. Her cheekbones, high and round, were pronounced. Hers is hardly a typical Chechen face. Rarer still, for a woman in her fourth decade of life, Aset was single.

"The war," she said, when I asked why.

SHAMKHAN, THE MULLAH of Aldy, closed his eyes. He lifted his large hands and opened his pale palms to the sky. Every other man, including Issa, at the table did the same. The mullah led the prayer. He began: "*La ilaha illa allahu. . . .*" ("There is no God but Allah. . . .") In a moment, he drew his hands together and, with his eyes still closed, swept them down his broad face.

"I cannot speak of the events of February fifth," he said straight off. "I was not here. I left with the fighters on the night of January thirty-first."

Shamkhan was not a typical village mullah. Well over six feet and barrel-chested, he was slightly larger than a good-sized refrigerator. Moreover, he was impeccably dressed. Despite the high temperature, he was draped in a brocaded frockcoat. It was made of white cloth and lined with gold stitching. It lent Shamkhan a religious aura that impressed. So, too, did the staff of carved wood he carried in his hand. On his head he wore a heavy *papakha*, a tall gray hat of Astrakhan lamb's wool. I was hardly surprised, given his physique, to learn that Shamkhan had been, during his tour of duty in the Soviet Navy, the wrestling champion of the Black Sea Fleet.

He was the son of a mullah, but he came to the clergy "late," he said, in his mid-thirties. Shamkhan was born in Kazakhstan in 1953, the year Stalin died. He had been the mullah of Aldy since 1996—since the end of the first war. A graduate of Grozny's technical institute, before the war he worked as a welder in the Chechen gasworks.

"Gas or electric, I could do either, and I earned a lot. But after the death of my father my brothers wanted me to continue my education. So I entered the Islamic University here in 1992. I was about to complete my sixth year in the *Shari'a* department when the war started. And now two wars and still no degree."

Shvedov liked to remind Issa and me that before declaring their independence in 1991, Chechens were not the most observant Muslims. "Of all the peoples of the Caucasus," he said, "the Chechens were the last to find Islam." As with much of his ramblings, Shevdov's claim was at best half right. It was true that for decades a folk Islam, not a strict adherence to the laws of the Koran, had predominated among Chechens. It was also true that Dudayev, when he seized power in Grozny, had led a movement for independence first and for religious freedom second. The first chief justice of

Dudayev's *Shari'a* court smoked Marlboros during interviews. But as the first war raged, more and more young Chechen fighters donned green head-bands that declared "Allah akbar" in Arabic. The Russian onslaught did what Dudayev had never envisioned: It turned the rebels ever more funda-mentalist. By the time the second war began, the talk was less of independ-ence and more of jihad.

THERE WAS A THEORY on why hell visited Aldy on February 5. It had to do with the brutality of Basayev and his comrade Khattab. I had heard it in Moscow from Russian journalists and in Nazran from Ingush bureaucrats. I heard it from Issa as well. It had to do with the abuses suffered after the end of the first war by the Russians who lived in Chernorechiye, the district border-ing Aldy. It was once a workers' district, home to those who traded shifts at the nearby cement, chemical, and oil works. In Chernorechiye, the story went, the Russians enjoyed the best apartments. After the first war, once the Chechens had retaken Grozny, they exacted revenge. "That they kicked out Russians for apartments, this is absolutely true," said the reporter Andrei Babitsky. "It happened everywhere in Grozny, but Chernorechiye had a large Russian population. And in the months before the second war, the practice there is said to have grown more and more violent, with Russians leaving their apartments through their windows."

Chernorechiye suffered a *zachistka* the same day as Aldy. The theory held that the Russians who had come on the Fifth had come to avenge the Russians killed in Chernorechiye. "WE HAVE RETURNED," read graffito painted in large letters during the *zachistka* in Chernorechiye, "YOUR VIL-LAGE NEIGHBORS."

There was another theory, one that concerned the question of fighters. In the wake of the Aldy massacre, news stories and human rights reports downplayed the possibility that Chechen fighters had been in Aldy. But the fighters had been there. Babitsky had been there with them. On January 14, in his last radio broadcast from Grozny before disappearing, Babitsky told Radio Liberty's Russian listeners, "In the village of Aldy, where I was also today with armed Chechens, bombs and missiles hit literally two hundred to two hundred and fifty meters from us." The fighters had come through the village, Aset said. Some had stayed a few days, only to rest and have her treat their wounds. The nearest rebel base, everyone insisted, had been in the adjoining district, District 20, three bus stops east from Aset's house.

Babitsky, when I asked him later what he had seen in Aldy during his hellish last weeks in Grozny, was forthcoming. "I was in Aldy nearly every day. In the middle of January I did spend two days there at my close friend's house." His friend, Babitsky said, was Kazbek, the commander of Aldy. "I'd thought Kazbek had surely died, but he survived the *zachistka*. He'd dug a hole in his cellar so deep that even though the Russians threw a grenade in, he lived."

Aldy, however, was never a rebel stronghold. The fighters were too smart to stay for long. Chernorechiye, Babitsky and other reporters who had been going to Chechnya since the first war told me, was by far the better defensive position. Chernorechiye sat high above the road and, unlike Aldy, boasted multistory buildings. For the wounded, Aldy offered a sanctuary, a rare corner of Grozny where there were still people, good water, and, most of all, medicine. But given the number of villagers who remained in Aldy, the fighters were reluctant to use it as a position. The fighters, Babitsky said, deemed the village too important to risk the inevitable reprisal. "They thought," he said, "Aldy was a good refuge."

THE CARNAGE THAT DESTROYED so much of Aldy is not peculiar to our time. Indeed Aldy, unbeknownst to the Russians who arrived on February 5, had a history. A river of violence and sadness found its source there in the eighteenth century, during the reign of Catherine the Great. In 1785 one of the first battles between Chechens and Russians took place when Catherine ordered her troops to storm Aldy, the village that at the time spanned the area of modern-day Aldy and Chernorechiye.

Catherine chose the target with purpose. Long before Yermolov built the line of forts that began with Grozny, Peter the Great had built the Line, a Great Wall of Russian forts and Cossack stánitsas. By 1784 the Russians had finished their critical garrison in the North Caucasus, the fort at Vladikavkaz. But in the following year Catherine's men suffered an unprecedented defeat on the Sunzha River—at the hands of the followers of a mysterious Chechen holy warrior.

In 1785, Prince Grigori Potemkin—Catherine's viceroy in the Caucasus and the favorite among her lovers—learned of a potent force emerging from

Aldy, a resistance movement led by a shepherd. Potemkin heard the news from his cousin Major-General Pavel Potemkin, who sent an alarming communiqué from the field: "On the opposite bank of the river Sunzha in the village of Aldy, a prophet has appeared and started to preach. He has submitted superstitious and ignorant people to his will by claiming to have had a revelation."[35]

Many believe that Imam Shamil, the holy warrior who led the longest resistance to the tsar, was the first great Chechen fighter. He was not. The title belongs to Sheikh Mansour. (Shamil, an Avar from Dagestan, was not even Chechen. Sheikh Mansour was.) History tells Mansour's story variously. His genealogy, theology, even name, have never been definitively revealed. But in the Caucasus what motivates men and triggers their weapons is not reality, but a perception of reality. In the realm of perceived reality, Mansour is revered as the first in the long line of Chechen holy warriors. He was born a peasant named Ushurma in Aldy. He had the good fortune to come of age just in time for Russia's southern onslaught.

"Muhammad paid this simple peasant a visit," Shamkhan told me. "He revealed himself to this young man because he was the purest of believers. The time had come, the prophet told him, to lead a *Ghazavat* on the Russians."

In 1783, Ushurma took the name Mansour—"conqueror" in Arabic—and later added the honorific "sheikh." A devout believer in Sufism, a mystical strain of Islam, Mansour already had a following. Sheikh Mansour led the Naqshbandi Tariqa, or path of belief.

Eager to please the empress, his lover and lord, Prince Potemkin dispatched three thousand troops to capture Mansour. They stormed Aldy but did not find him. Frustrated, they torched the village. Mansour's men got their revenge. They ambushed the Russians in the nearby woods and killed, the chronicles attest, more than six hundred men. Potemkin had to tell Catherine that nearly half his force had been lost. Many had drowned, trying to flee, in the Sunzha's muddy waters. An "unfortunate occurrence," Prince Potemkin called it in his report to Catherine.[36] The blood feud had begun.

As Catherine's men routed his followers, Mansour took refuge in the Ottoman fortress of Anapa. In 1791 he was captured and shipped off to St. Petersburg, where he spent his last years in the Schlüsselberg Fortress, an island prison in the Neva River near Lake Ladoga.[37] But Mansour's spirit never left Chechnya. In Aldy it was especially strong.

"We all know the history of this village. Sheikh Mansour lives on in each of us," the mullah Shamkhan said, leaning forward on his staff. "We feel his strength every day. We know the struggle began here." Shamkhan had just come from leading a service for one of the *shaheed*, the martyrs of the Fifth of February. At the service, dancing the *zikr*, a religious dance, was Magomed Dolkaev, an elegant elder with a flowing white beard who claimed Sheikh Mansour as an ancestor. No one knew the true genealogy. But as Shamkhan told me, it was not important.

A year and a half later Dolkaev was dead. He, too, had fallen victim to the new times–shot four times in the head by an unknown gunman in his home in Aldy.

ISSA, WHO SAT IN silence as I listened to Shamkhan, could no longer hold his peace. He had observed it all, taking in the mullah and his story with the weary eyes of a crocodile. When he begged permission to interrupt, I consented with a shrug to the inevitable.

Issa leaned forward, squaring his elbows on the table across from the mullah, with a question. "How come Maskhadov," he said, referring to the military commander elected Chechnya's president after the first war, "couldn't build a state that could defend any citizen, no matter his faith?"

His voice had lost its usual calm and was rising. "Where were all these brave fighters when there was not one Russian soldier here? When all you had to do was bury one, or two, or three bandits so that none of this would have happened?"

Shamkhan invoked the name of Allah. He swore that he was "against any embodiment of evil," that he could not "tolerate Wahhabism," and was a foe of "any extremism."

Issa did not let up.

"You say you left with the fighters. Abandoned the village during the siege. You and I speak the same language. Tell me, as the spiritual father of these people, how did we come to this? How can we live like this?"

Shamkhan struggled for a rejoinder. He stiffened his broad back and condemned the plagues that had visited Chechnya since the Soviet fall: the militarism of Dudayev, the romanticism of Maskhadov, the banditry of Basayev, the foreign Wahhabi virus of Khattab, and the venal hunger of the rest of Chechnya's warlords. "All this we have earned," he said, "because of our ignorance. Thanks to our lack of enlightenment, we were unable to establish any order."

The mullah was talking to Issa but looking at me. He said he had never led anyone to any jihad. He said the fighters had wanted to take him earlier from Aldy, that they were afraid the Russians would kill him on sight. He swore to Allah that everything he had done was done not in the name of Dudayev or Maskhadov or Basayev or Khattab, but in the name of Allah and Allah alone.

As the torrent of words poured forth, I realized Shamkhan was talking too much. Then, suddenly, he dropped his guard. He declared his conscience clean. He said he had done all that had been asked of him, that he had journeyed "the path from beginning to end," the path that was "written in blood."

Shamkhan, I realized then, had been with Basayev and the fighters the night they broke through the siege of Grozny. "The path" was the fighters' macabre retreat through the minefields to Alkhan-Kala.

I pressed for details.

"They needed someone to bless and bury the dead," he said. "So I made this journey with them and with my own eyes saw how they died. If someone were to sit and tell me what they had seen along this path, I swear to Allah, I would never believe him. I would not believe people could die like that."

The fighters had taken him from Aldy on the last day of January. Before he left, the mullah told his followers to stay in the village. "Do not abandon your homes to the Russians," he had said. The words, as Shamkhan recalled them, weighed heavily.

The minefields killed hundreds during the fighters' retreat. Others froze to death. He had stayed with the fighters for the entire trek, from Grozny to the snowbound mountains in the south. He had left the fighters in their mountain hideaways.

Would they fight until the end? I asked.

"What lies in their hearts," Shamkhan said, "is to me a dark wood."

❧ TEN ❧

THE CREEK WAS DARK green and cloudy. As Issa and I bathed in it, resting our hands on the sludgy rocks below, our feet and arms stirred the water the color of burned sugar. Issa was telling me tales of the glory of his youth in Grozny, but I was preoccupied. I was wondering what else lay in the mucky creek of Shali.

We walked here together, through the nettles of the overgrown orchard that was the backyard of the small house where Issa's mother and two sisters lived. His mother was eighty; his sisters were in their fifties. Throughout the years of war, Shali, lying in the plains just south of Grozny, had been spared the wholesale destruction of the capital and nearly every other town and village in Chechnya. Issa's mother and sisters lived here throughout the shelling, the bombings, and the military sweeps.

Inside the house it was dark and cool. There were two rooms and a kitchen. Issa did not say it, but the house was all he had in Chechnya now. Once he had a comfortable apartment in Grozny, but it was lost to the first war. He managed to save some of the furniture–a gold-rimmed mirror, a lacquered table, a velvety divan–vestiges of the Chechen elite of the Soviet era that now sat like islands in the biggest room of the house. Except for the salvaged treasures, the house was empty. The second room was filled with rolled-up carpets and chairs stacked against a wall, more remnants of a lost life.

The creek, no matter what toxins of war lay in its waters, was cooling. Like the children who jumped into it, we were naked to our underwear. Our shirts and trousers, stiffened with dirt and road dust, hung from a low cherry tree that twisted above the muddy bank. One side of the creek was lined by the overgrown yards. The other was a steep bank the children used as a diving platform. Behind them were only empty fields. The children leaped in, hands over knees, shouting as they fell through the air.

In the evening, after we dried ourselves with worn hand towels and dressed again in the same clothes, Issa's mother, Sabiat, took me on a tour. She was so thin and her back so bent that it was remarkable she could walk, let alone cook and clean. "We have everything here," she said, pointing to the trees that stood amid the weeds: "Apricot, pear, apple, cherry." The heat of the afternoon brought the smell of the fruit close. Sabiat squinted at the cloudless sky. "Why?" she asked. She needed no more words; she meant the war. "Somebody must want it," she said.

Everywhere there was greenery. Vines climbed high along the back wall. On a tall wooden fence, roses, pink and red, bloomed. The garden, Issa's mother said, was all she needed now. Nothing more. "But the fruit of the trees," said Issa's younger sister, "is not as good since the war." She was called Zulei, and her elder sister Zura.

The courtyard, the summer living room of houses across Chechnya, was clean and quiet. Here the routine of the day unfolded. In the morning the sisters washed clothes in metal basins. In the afternoon their mother fried potatoes and boiled lamb. And in the evening Shvedov lounged on a faded threadbare couch that sat in the middle of the narrow porch. Above the porch, in the corners of its slanting roof, swallows nested.

"Our mama's life has been a hard one," Zura said.

"Mama," Issa commanded, "tell him about the deportation."

There was no need, and he knew that. The deportation was not history. It informed the daily conversation in Chechnya. Issa's mother had been twenty-two in 1944. She remembered clearly how the NKVD soldiers had herded them into the freight cars—in all, more than fourteen thousand cars were needed—and sent them off to the remote Soviet republics of Central Asia. Along with hundreds of thousands of Chechens and Ingush, Sabiat survived thirteen years in Central Asia. Exile was hard, of course, she said. But it was better, much better, than this war. "They gave us a small plot of land and a little house. We could grow a garden."

Tired of talk, Sabiat went back to her chores. In her slippers and a flowered cotton dress, she reached for a short brush, a dozen switches tied to a stick. She was intent on sweeping the dirt from the concrete of her courtyard. She stooped low and, despite the heat, worked the brush with purpose and without pause.

"Every night and every morning our mama cleans," Zulei said. "Only the water from the well will she let us get ourselves."

She had survived Central Asia, the road back to Grozny in 1957, and the loss of her husband, to a car accident years ago that came on the Prophet's birthday. "She must work or else . . ." said her daughter Zura.

As Issa's mother swept, Shvedov stubbed out another *papirosa* in the tin coffee can on the sofa. After he got up slowly from the old couch and disappeared into the coolness of the house, Sabrat continued to sweep. A month later Issa would call and tell me that his mother's heart had at last given out.

ELEVEN

ILYAS CAME TO SEE me after dark. Darkness unnerved the Russian soldiers in Chechnya but liberated the locals.

"Why do they say," he asked, "that every journalist who comes here now is a spy?" Ilyas was a fighter and not afraid to probe. Chechens are, without effort, obsessed with spies. Cultural legends and historical mythologizing were one thing, but in Chechnya there was a veritable industry in conspiracy theories. The war was not Moscow's fault alone. Washington, Wall Street, world Zionism had also colluded against the Chechens. Intelligence agencies—the CIA, Mossad, MI6—loomed large everywhere. The plots and subplots were infinite but followed one story line. "They have hijacked our fight for freedom," Ilyas said, "in a global geostrategic fight for our oil."

The worst culprits of course were the journalists. In the Zone every reporter was a fifth columnist in poor disguise. Sitting with Ilyas, I was not in a particularly comfortable position. (At the time Issa had announced with unsettling confidence that he thought I was the only foreign correspondent in Chechnya.) I had never worked with Fred Cuny, the Texan genius of emergency relief, who had been killed in Chechnya in 1996. But I knew well several people who had. They remained convinced Cuny had been killed by Chechens acting at the behest of the Russian security service. Moreover, every day I was made amply aware of the price tag on any foreigner's head in these parts.

Ilyas lived in Urus-Martan, the third-largest town in Chechnya and a place known as a center of the new Wahhabism. He agreed to meet in Gudermes, in an apartment with little furniture and less light, one short block from the Russian military headquarters. Although he moved about the city freely and was unafraid to meet a foreign correspondent, Ilyas said it was better to meet at night.

At first we sat in silence. I tried a few entreaties without luck. Ilyas was short and stocky, with wavy hair that curled long behind his ears. A reddish brown beard was coming onto his square cheeks. Failing to engage him in small talk—where he was from ("here and there"), what he did ("this and that")—I decided to up the ante.

"Why do they call you an *amir*?" I asked.

"Because I lead a group, a group of fighters."

I had heard the term *amir* before. In Afghanistan, in the summer of 1996, weeks before the Taliban took Kabul, their leaders in Kandahar spoke reverently of their *amir*, their leader, the one-eyed mullah Muhammad Omar who had taken to calling himself the *Amir ul Momineen*, Commander of the Faithful. When I met Ahmed Shah Massoud, the military genius who stood behind the Afghan government then clinging to Kabul, Massoud spit the term out.

"No one can call himself the *amir*," Massoud said. "It is sacrilege to all Muslims."

In Chechnya being an *amir* meant Ilyas had gone Wahhabi. "Wahhabism," at least in Chechnya, is an imprecise term. Religiously, it could mean nearly anything. Yet militarily, its meaning was clear: It meant Ilyas had joined Jama'at, the fighting arm of the would-be Islamic fundamentalists who were now claiming recruits across Chechnya—even in Gudermes, the Russians' administrative center. Being an *amir* meant that Ilyas, though scarcely twenty years old, controlled six fighters, who, as he put it, "would do anything I ask."

"The Wahhabis," Ilyas explained, "are anyone who believes in the need to cleanse our nation and who will sacrifice himself in the jihad against Russia," and, he politely added, "against the United States and its allies as well."

In Kandahar that summer of 1996 the Taliban had convened a gathering of mullahs, one of the largest ever. In the dark of night, their high-pitched prayers woke me. I had never heard a more terrifying sound. To me, their cries did not ring of piety, but of a dark passion laced with bloodlust. Later I told a UN worker, a gentle Somalian who had survived the worst of Mogadishu, what I had heard. The Somalian pulled me aside and whispered: "You have heard the sound of evil. You may think me paranoid, but these Talibs are dangerous. They will only grow and foster more evil. You must warn your government, tell them not to support them. They will take this country and turn it into the world's terrorist camp."

In Putin's War, Kremlin aides and Russian generals had grown fond of spinning tales of "thousands of Taliban fighters" flooding into Chechnya to aid their brothers. Although the Chechens had boasted of the aid their Islamic brothers had provided, chiefly mercenaries and money, the ties among the Chechen rebels and the Taliban and Al Qaeda were shadowy. So as we sat across a small table, cupping our hands around thin glasses of tea, I asked Ilyas if he could refute Russia's claims.

"It's nonsense," he said. "We have no Taliban here. Did we have Arabs fighting on our side? Yes. But a hundred or two at most. Do we support the Taliban? Of course. They are our spiritual brothers. They, too, are fighting to purify Islam and liberate it from its oppressors."

As we sat together in that corner of Chechnya, the horror of September 11, 2001, lay a year in the future. But the Kremlin had long emphasized reports of Khattab's ties to bin Laden.

"Khattab is our *amir*," Ilyas said. "He is a man of great purity who knows how to bring *Shari'a* to our land." But as pro-Chechen Web sites had long made obvious in numerous languages, the Black Arab's expertise was not restricted to religion. An adept commander, Khattab had become renowned as the mastermind of one of the first war's deadliest ambushes. Russian and Western intelligence agencies also considered Khattab an able fund raiser, reaping financial support, if not large numbers of mercenaries, from Islamic radicals around the world.[38]

"New money comes every week," Ilyas boasted, refusing to name the country or organization of its origin. "For this we can thank Khattab as well." Ilyas did not disguise the fact that some of his fellow Wahhabi fighters had come from Saudi Arabia and elsewhere across the Arab world, but the majority, he insisted, were Chechens. And their arms, he added, were Russian. Russian officers and soldiers were more than willing, for a price, to keep the enemy well armed.

Ilyas had clear ideas about the future, his own and his people's. As we sat in the dank apartment in Gudermes, and scattered gunfire pierced the night air outside, he laid out for me—in far more detail than I felt safe knowing—the fighters' plans. I pulled out my well-worn map of Chechnya and spread it on the thin carpet. Ilyas's eyes danced. In Soviet times such maps were restricted to government eyes. I'd bought it from a street vendor in Moscow, a block from the Lubyanka. But like many fighters, Ilyas had never seen a map of his land.

Excited, he charted, town by town, gorge by gorge, where the resistance forces now bided their time. He traced the roads in and around Grozny. He knew where each curve and hill lay. His voice quickened as he talked of the rebel leaders Basayev and Khattab, and the lesser field commanders now spread across Chechnya. His fingers danced over the map as he shared his best estimates of how many men each commander controlled. Tasks differed, he said, from assassination to suicide bombing to intelligence, but one mission united the fighters: to carry the war on, to keep the occupiers in a vise, to ensure they suffer a slow, but constant, loss of life.

"We have no other choice," he said when I asked why he had chosen the Wahhabi path. "Once we believed our elders. We believed it when they told us moral virtue would bring victory. But we are a new force, and we know we must purify the soul of our nation. Today. Before it is too late."

Ilyas was educated, intelligent, and impatient. He wore a Swiss mountaineering watch, a state-of-the-art piece that boasted a digital compass, a barometer, and an altitude gauge. He had a clear sense that the struggle would be long, perhaps even without end. Yet he was convinced it was just. Fighting the Russians, he said, was the only way for a morally pure Chechen man to live and the most righteous way to die. Ilyas was not a big fighter, just one of thousands in the new scaled-down resistance. Small teams, young, well armed, and dedicated to the *ghazavat*, were now forming to run sabotage and reconnaissance missions. They would take out Russian soldiers in the markets. They would take out Chechen traitors in their sleep. They would blow up checkpoints. They would ambush convoys at will.

I had seen Ilyas's handiwork up close. That afternoon, as Issa, Shvedov, Yura, and I were making our way from Grozny to Gudermes, four agitated young Russian soldiers bade us stop at their checkpoint near the town of Djalka, just ten miles from Grozny. At first we thought another convoy was coming and we would have to let it pass. But when I got out of the UAZik, I saw that was not the case. Half a mile or so beyond the checkpoint, in the dense woods that divided two brown fields, a firefight raged. I could hear the exchange of automatic rifle fire and, through the shafts of billowing smoke, see a trio of helicopters swoop down and fire into the woods. The Russian soldiers, suntanned OMON officers from Irkutsk, checked our documents. Shvedov asked what had happened. They shrugged their shoulders.

"Something," one said.

"Nothing," said the other.

They would not let us through, so we stood at the checkpoint and watched the spectacle.

After half an hour a bus that had crossed through the firefight approached. Issa went to talk to its driver.

"It's the train," he said when he returned. His wan smile revealed delight.

The Russians had recently started running trains again between Gudermes to Grozny to supply their headquarters with food, fuel, and weapons.

"They hit the train," Issa explained.

As more cars joined the line behind us, Issa talked to the drivers. No matter where we went in Chechnya, Issa seemed to know everyone and everyone knew him. It was not always a comforting equation. He returned with details: guerrillas in the woods, remote-controlled bombs on the tracks, an armored car with a cache of Russian weapons blown up. "It will soon be over," Issa announced, with the confidence of a man who had grown used to the timetable of guerrilla warfare. He was right. In an hour we were back in Gudermes, and several hours later I was sitting with Ilyas.

"You saw the remains of the train, didn't you?" Ilyas asked. We had been going over the map when he paused an index finger on Djalka. "You must have been there when the train was hit this afternoon, no?" he asked, revealing a knowledge of both the attack and my whereabouts. It was a polite way of letting me know that his group had helped bomb the train. The ambush was effective. The train was hauling two carloads of soldiers and several wagons of matériel to Khankala, the Russian military headquarters at Grozny's eastern edge, when four remote-controlled bombs exploded in succession. Six soldiers were wounded, and one woman, a cook, was killed. The train ground to a stop. The soldiers walked the ten miles to Khankala on foot and in fear.

"We will not give up," Ilyas said. "We will hit them in small ways, but every day. Some colonel gets up to go to work, ties his shoes, puts on his coat, starts his car, and he is gone."

Given the frequency of assassinations in Chechnya, I knew this was not a rhetorical flourish. In fact, as we spoke, another squad was moving through the darkness toward its target. In the early morning, a quiet Sunday in the town of Alkhan-Yurt, the town's Chechen administrator, accused of serving the occupiers, was to be assassinated outside his home, shot by more than a dozen bullets.[39]

"When will it end?" I asked.

"When they leave."

Like many Chechens, Ilyas did not refer to the Russian soldiers in their midst as anything but "they."

As our talk stretched into its third hour, I sensed that if there were enough young men in Chechnya like Ilyas, the Russians might succeed in bringing a semblance of governance to the region but would never again rest comfortably as its guardians.

The hatred, Ilyas assured me, would always burn. A group of young men in Urus-Martan were now back in school, learning how to blow themselves up. The suicide bombers, he said, were not mentally disturbed, drug-addicted, or eager to earn money for their families, all motives the Kremlin had provided reporters in Moscow. They were Chechens, he said, who had been through the so-called filtration camps, the jails the Russians had established in the republic since the days of the first war, ostensibly to weed out terrorists from civilian men. The filtration camps were notorious locales for torture.[40]

"They ram steel rods into your anus until they nearly kill you," Ilyas said. "It would be better to be killed, because you come back to us humiliated. For a Chechen man there is only one thing to do: avenge."

As the kettle boiled a second time, Ilyas fell silent. Then he raised his eyes and bore them into mine. "Are you a Christian?" he asked.

"No," I said. "I am a Jew."

"So you're an American, a journalist, and a Jew. Are you not scared?"

It seemed as much a warning as a question. I said, banally, that for years, ever since I had first heard of the Chechens, back in 1989, when my friend and host in Moscow Andrei had laughed at the Chechens' first stirrings for sovereignty, I had dreamed of coming to Chechnya.

Ilyas did not allow his eyes to drift. He only tightened his dark brows. "But you have no fear?"

I mumbled something about the nature of journalism in the modern world, how you had to measure risks and walk appropriately, how you never knew, of course, but you set your itineraries with care and trusted your judgment. Ilyas did not nod or smile. He kept on staring. I said no more. But as the panic began to pull at my neck and the breath in my lungs tightened, I wanted to tell him, "Yes, yes, you raise a good point. A great point. I am in fact scared out of my mind."

🏵 TWELVE 🏵

IN THE YEARS SINCE the first Russian onslaught in 1994, the kidnapping industry replaced petroleum crude as the primary contributor to Chechnya's gross domestic product. No full tally exists, but by the best estimates, several thousand people fell prey to the trade in hostages. Reporters, technical advisers, and aid workers were among those kidnapped. Anyone of course was a target, but by far the majority of those "stolen," as the Chechens put it, were natives of the Caucasus: Chechens, Dagestanis, Ingush, Georgians, Armenians. Things had gotten particularly bad of late.

"Kidnapping's the only business that works in Chechnya," Shvedov announced one night as we dined on boiled potatoes and fatty squares of boiled lamb. We sat beneath a dying moon in the yard of Issa's mother's house in Shali. We listened to bullfrogs croaking in the creek and nightingales shrilling in the trees.

"Strange," Issa said, "the nightingales are still here."

Shvedov lit a *papirosa* and spun the dial on his transistor to Radio Free Chechnya, the station Moscow had launched days earlier to enlighten the Chechens. The voice of General Troshev filled the courtyard. He was promising his interlocutor, an army press aide, that from now on "every human right" would be respected during *zachistka* operations. Every so often a thunderclap of artillery guns buckled through the air. The Russians were outside Shali, aiming at targets a few miles from the house. The shelling punctuated the talk of kidnapping.

"Don't you worry about someone stealing us from here?" Shvedov asked Issa.

The thought had crossed my mind. I was not the first journalist to stay in his mother's house. The word was certainly out.

"If they want you," Issa answered, "they can get anywhere."

Issa knew a lot about the kidnapping industry. For months he had tried to secure the release of an Armenian teenager kidnapped in Moscow and now held near Vedeno, the town that anchors Chechnya's southeastern corner. ("A favor of the heart," he explained.) The boy, he said, was the son of an old comrade from his oil-drilling days in Siberia. Wherever we traveled, Issa was in deep negotiations to get the boy back. "That Armenian kid is keeping me going," he said. He meant his fight to save the boy's life. But I had heard another motive, the fifty-thousand-dollar share of the ransom Issa would get for bringing the boy to his father alive.

The trade in humans, and their remains, brought all the players in the Zone to the table. There were the Islamic wise men: the mufti of Vedeno, a slight fellow with a stiff manner and a beard that seemed too well trimmed, and his taller, quieter cohort, the mufti of Elistanzhi. One's eyes never stopped smiling, the other's were cold. (They both made my skin crawl.) Then there were the Jama'at fighters, young men like Ilyas with grand ambitions and the first signs of facial hair. And the local FSB, the men from Russia's security service. "Necessary intermediaries" Issa called them.

A few nights later Issa and I lay on opposite sofas in the big empty room in the house in Shali, trying to get to sleep. It was too hot to cover oneself with anything. I had rolled my dirty jeans into a pillow. In the darkness Issa continued to talk. He had been sullen all day. The deal for the Armenian had gone south. The boy was dead, killed some time ago. The body, he said, might even be impossible to retrieve. "How do I tell his father?" Issa asked. He was struggling, it seemed, less for an answer than for a way to accept the revenue loss.

KIDNAPPING WAS ONLY the most notorious plague bred in the years that followed the first war. The interregnum, above all, had yielded a dismally poor effort at self-rule. Perhaps the urge for revenge was too great, or the desire for personal power too strong, but the Chechens, the would-be victors of the first war, proved unable to win the peace.

A few months after I received the video from Aldy, the villagers' desperate attempt to send word of the massacre to the outside, I got a second video from Chechnya. This one did not feature Chechens butchered by Russians. It featured a Chechen killed by Chechens. In Kandahar in 1996 I had heard tales of public executions, of adulterers stoned to death. In the interregnum the Chechens did not establish the Taliban's vice squad, the Committee for the Prevention of Vice and the Promotion of Virtue. But they did mete out *Shari'a* in its bloodiest form.

During Putin's War the Russian Interior Ministry got smart. They culled all the snippets of video they could find that testified to the abuse—kidnapping, starvation, head and finger chopping—suffered by Russians and foreigners at the alleged hands of Chechens. The ministry then invited reporters to come view their snuff films. Not eager to savor the barbarism, I declined.

This second tape would have better served the ministry's purpose. It offered a scene from a *Shari'a* court, in early August 1996, on the day before the Chechens retook Grozny. Five Chechen fighters sit in a bright wood, their legs crossed on a blanket spread on the grass. The bearded man seated in the middle is Basayev, the most famous of the fighters. Across from them stands an older man, gray-haired. He is tall and frail. His hands are tied behind his back, and a bandage is wrapped around his forehead, but the old man does not cower. The dialogue is ruthless and revealing. Basayev, for the sake of the camera, interrogates the old man.

BASAYEV: *Acting what?*

OLD MAN: *Acting head of administration.*

BASAYEV: *Whose head?*

OLD MAN: *The region's.*

BASAYEV: *Who put you in that job?*

OLD MAN: *Bugayev. Koshman recommended it, gave him the paper. He signed it and gave it to him.*

BASAYEV: *And who are they? Who's this Koshman?*

OLD MAN: *The head of the government.*

BASAYEV: *Of what?*

OLD MAN: *The Chechen republic.*

BASAYEV: *Oh, I see. That makes you a national traitor. Know that?*

OLD MAN: *I never was. And am not now.*

BASAYEV: *Yes, you are, you're a traitor. You've been afraid since '93 that the Russians wouldn't come. Ever since you stood on the Theater Square [in Grozny]. Now you say you're the prefect of the Vedeno region.*

OLD MAN: *I am the acting head.*

BASAYEV: *Makes no difference to me. It was you pigs who brought this misery to our people.*

OLD MAN: *When you are done, I will explain.*

BASAYEV: *I am done.*

OLD MAN: *The people, when they stood on the Theater Square, said that the Russian troops were coming. We had to come together so they couldn't enter. We had to prevent this tragedy. And we all stood there with economic demands.*

BASAYEV: *Don't give me propaganda. Better you tell me why you sold out to the Russians.*

OLD MAN: *I swear, I brought no one any misery, and I never sold out to any Russians.*

BASAYEV: *You're just working for them?*

OLD MAN: *I am not working for them. I am a teacher. I taught our Chechen children.*

BASAYEV: *How is it you never worked for them? Who is this Koshman?*

OLD MAN: *Chairman of the government of the Chechen republic.*

BASAYEV: *Which republic? Where is the Chechen republic? You let in these Russians, pushed them forward, leading the people to this misery.*

OLD MAN: *Not because of me.*

BASAYEV: *That's what you say—"not because of me"? So who destroyed this land?*

OLD MAN: *Those who have sinned, they are the sinners.*

BASAYEV: *God will judge, is that it?*

OLD MAN: *He will judge. Soon we shall know.*[41]

Basayev flattens a piece of paper on the blanket spread across the grass. He takes out a rubber stamp and, after warming it with his breath, stamps the paper sharply. Then, switching into Russian to lend his voice an air of state authority, he reads the death sentence: "The military field court of the Central Front of the Armed Forces of the Chechen Republic of Ichkeria, for crimes against the state and the Chechen people, committed under aggravating circumstances, resulting in numerous victims among the population and the barbaric violation of the Chechen Republic of Ichkeria, in accordance with Article 50: 'Violation of the Constitutional Order'; Article 51, Part A and B: 'Inciting War against the State'; Article 52: 'Collaboration with Enemy States'; Article 53: 'Espionage against the Country' of Chapter Five of the Criminal Code of the Chechen Republic of Ichkeria, all of these qualifying as a crime against the state sentences Zakayev, Amir Abdullakhavich, born in the year 1940, living on Veterinarian Street, House 4, village of Dyshnee Vedeno, Vedeno Region, to the highest form of punishment, execution. The sentence is final and not subject to appeal."

Zakayev stands against a broad tree. His hands remain tied. He does not flinch.

"Bear witness that you are a Muslim," a voice offscreen says.

As shots ring out, the camera lurches close. A ribbon of automatic fire cuts through the air. The old man's knees buckle as he falls to the ground.

"Maybe after burning in hell, you'll end up in heaven," the voice says, "*inshallah*."

The execution appeared in a video made by pro-Russian Chechens. Issa had provided the narration. The scene seemed staged and, given the source, a potential fake. I showed it to a number of Chechens in Moscow who doubted its authenticity. Then I showed it to Adam, a former Chechen fighter, once an associate of Basayev's. Adam had long ago put down his gun and taken to working as a fixer, getting foreign reporters in and out of Chechnya. He recognized the scene. It was not an interrogation, Adam said, but "a trial." "Some teacher," he said of the man executed. "A son of a bitch. He worked for the Russians."

Chechens everywhere told me the same thing: that the worst were the enemies within, the Chechens who crossed to the Russian side. They were the ones, they said, who had brought the nation to its knees and now threatened to cut out its heart.

"Men like this old man were not innocents," Adam said when I stopped the videotape. "They were traitors. Not enough of them were killed."

✦ THIRTEEN ✦

THE RUSSIANS, I HAD come to believe, had convinced themselves they needed only one ally to win hearts and minds in Chechnya. The decimation of the Chechen people and the destruction of their homes could do only so much. To establish a lasting rule, as General Troshev proclaimed more than once, Moscow would have to rely on the Good Chechen. In Raibek Tovzayev, they imagined they found one.

"Salaam aleikum," I said, extending my hand. "Peace to you."

"Va aleikum salaam," Raibek said in the customary return. "Come in peace."

Raibek was a muscled man with unshorn silvering hair and clear blue eyes. He was eager to show me his ID, a Russian military pass encased in red leather. It declared him deputy chief of the administration of his native Vedeno region, not only Chechnya's most fabled corner but its most strategic as well. General Troshev had put Raibek on retainer, made him a free lance in the employ of the Russian military. His men, some one hundred irregulars who in times of peace tended fat cows and thin goats, were now fed, uniformed, and armed on Troshev's budget. Raibek's task was daunting: to secure Vedeno for the Russians and make a good show, at the very least, of keeping its peace.

In Putin's War, Troshev had long spoken passionately of the new, "humane" plan. Raised in Grozny, the general considered himself a native, someone who appreciated Chechen traditions. Moscow, Troshev assured viewers in nightly appearances on Russian television, would not make the same mistakes twice. This time the generals would meet with the *Shura*, the local council of elders, in each town and convince them of the need to cleanse their land of "illegal bandit formations." Chechens would rush to Moscow's side, Troshev reasoned, for they, too, hated the terrorists and bandits, kidnappers, and cutthroats. Troshev struck a historic echo: "the good Chechen" had been the elusive ideal of his nineteenth-century forebear General Yermolov.

Raibek's attraction had little to do with loyalty to the federal cause–he professed an undisguised disdain for it–and everything to do with geography and history. His fiefdom spanning a ridge above the Vedeno Gorge was the best line of defense against Basayev and Khattab, who had retreated to the forbidding hills to the east, the Nozhai Yurt region. The Russians also liked Raibek's history. A native of the village of Pervomaiskoye, which overlooks Vedeno, Raibek had known Basayev since both were small children, and it was no secret, in Grozny and in Moscow, that Raibek and the most wanted man in Russia were mortal enemies.

It was not easy to visit Raibek. We left Shali just after dawn and followed a well-worn road south through the pink haze of the midsummer sunrise. Layers of mist clung to the brown fields at the foot of the mountains. After a series of checkpoints we came to the mouth of the Vedeno Gorge, a deep ravine of rock cut by centuries of snow melting from the Caucasian massifs. As we headed south, the black mountains rose ever higher around us.

Vedeno, centered in the depths of the ravine, had long loomed as the vortex of the war. Once the home of Imam Shamil, it was now renowned as the birthplace and base of his namesake Basayev. Here, in the 1990s, Basayev rekindled the legend of the nineteenth-century Shamil to rally his compatriots against their Slavic masters. Now Vedeno was the dark crossroads where seemingly incompatible forces met, the kidnapping industry flourished, and firefights flared easily. More than any other town in Chechnya, it was saturated with young men who carried plenty of ammunition and few loyalties. "Vedeno is the key," Ilyas, the would-be Wahhabi, told me. "Vedeno is the heart of the new Islam. From there the cleansing of our nation will come." It was also considered, by many Chechens and Russians alike, the heart of the conflict. From here the road south leads through the mountains to Georgia. For the fighters, it had become a vital supply line. "Whoever wins Vedeno," Ilyas said, "wins the war." It was a prophecy I heard again and again.

"YOU'LL LOVE RAIBEK," Issa told me as the UAZik slipped up the steep gravel road to his mountain redoubt, "because he's a modern-day Hadji Murad." Tolstoy had first heard the tale of Hadji Murad as a young man in the 1850s, when he lived among the tsarist troops in a Cossack stanitsa in Chechnya's northern plains. It is the story of a famed Chechen warrior who, facing death at the hands of his former ally Shamil, goes over to the Russians. But Murad, as I reminded Issa, does not end up well. He escapes from the Russians, hoping to free his family from Shamil, but is killed by bounty hunters–Russian, Cossack, and Chechen–eager to claim the price on his head. The tale turns tragic as a Cossack delivers Murad's severed head to the Russians who once praised his strong will and gentlemanly manner.

"To hell with the literary allusions," Shvedov barked from the back of the jeep. "You'll love Raibek for one reason. The Zone is covered in fog. No matter how many times you come here, you hear myths and legends, tales of global conspiracies and ancient blood feuds, devout lectures on jihad from Chechen bandits." Raibek, he promised, was different. "He doesn't give a damn about Mr. Putin or Mr. General Troshev or the *Izvestia* newspaper. He cares only about his villages, where he is the tsar, God, and boss of the land. Whatever it is–gas, food, protection–he'll find it for his people. No one pays taxes. They pay honor to their lord. Raibek is a classic Chechen feudal baron."

Raibek sat out the first war. He sided with neither Basayev nor the Russians. For a time he even lived in Germany. "Trade," he said, when I asked what had brought him to a town along the Rhine. Yet given the elaborate allegiances of the *teips*, Chechnya's ancestral clans, it was inevitable that he would be drawn into the war.[42] In August 1995 a Chechen warlord from Argun, Allauddin Khamzatov, staked a claim to the ridge along Upper Vedeno. Raibek was in Europe, but his father, the ninety-year-old patriarch of the *teip*, was home. He refused to give in to the interloper.

The result was painful to remember. Khamzatov shot Raibek's father dead, right in front of his family. The feud open, Raibek came home and, as is required by *adat*, evened the bloodletting. He and his men hunted down the warlord and killed him and his accomplices. His troubles with Basayev and Khattab, however, had yet to begin. The next spring, in March 1996, as Raibek drove into Grozny, dozens of Basayev's men encircled him. A shootout ensued, and he barely escaped. Then, in June 1996, he was arrested on Basayev's orders and thrown into a jail run by the commander in the town of Dargo near the Dagestan border. He spent nearly eight months in jail before escaping one night in February 1997. He fled on foot through the frozen mountains to Dagestan and a month later was back in Vedeno.

As the UAZik pulled into his compound, a fortified lair of stone, brick, and wood, it was clear Raibek was not expecting guests. He extended his

arm around my shoulder, in the half hug that Chechen men perform in salu-
tation, but he did not smile. Raibek was not in a buoyant mood.

He had reason to be angry. In the first, critical months of Putin's War, he
and his lieges stood their ground. While Troshev's troops moved south by
shelling from afar and bombing without pause, even before the Russian
paratroopers landed on their ridge, Raibek and his men took on Basayev
and Khattab and several hundred of their fighters. In February 2000, he
boasted with a grin, he and his men "liberated" Vedeno.

The Russians had rewarded him with the job of deputy military and
administrative head of the region. It was not a sinecure to envy. Basayev and
Khattab were eager to retake Vedeno, the town that now housed thousands
of Chechen paramilitaries and several thousand more Russian soldiers, who
manned Moscow's military headquarters in the district. The paramilitaries,
moreover, would pledge allegiance to whoever paid a premium.

The job was sure to bring criticism, and in Vedeno, disfavor often took
the form of assassination. Raibek, I'd heard, had already survived five
attempts on his life. "Six," said one of his bodyguards. Raibek had lost count.
On the sole road that switchbacked from his compound down into Vedeno,
the gravelly road we had come on, Raibek's convoy now came across mines
with increasing regularity. The woods were thick with enemies, he said.
Basayev and Khattab, Raibek said, stood behind most of the attempts on his
life, but not all.

The most recent attack had been the work of his new patrons, the Russians. One night a few months earlier a helicopter had roused Raibek and
his family from their sleep. He got up in time to see a pair of APCs roll into
his yard, as Russian soldiers, doing the bidding of their commander in
Vedeno, shot their way into his house. They stole his furniture, rifles, bullets,
and, most distressing of all, his Mercedes. Raibek did not feel betrayed. He
knew better. "I never gave them my trust," he said. "I just wanted my property back." He succeeded in retrieving the Mercedes. He traced it to
Khankala, the Russian base on the outskirts of Grozny, and, with help from
up the Russian chain of command, repossessed the prized sedan.

Raibek's brother was a boxer who'd fought all over the world, even winning championships, it was said, in Europe. Looking at Raibek, I did not
doubt it. At forty-two, he was not particularly tall or broad-shouldered, but
when he moved, muscles rippled across his arms, shoulders, and neck. He

wore a maroon shirt opened to the waist, sweatpants, and Adidas flip-flops. Gray stubble covered his sharp cheekbones, and a half grin revealed two chipped teeth. Issa made sure to tell me Raibek's blue eyes were a sign of his *teip*, the Gunoi, who, legend had it, owed their ancestry to mixed marriages of Chechens and Russians. The Gunoi were deemed less than pure Chechens.

Raibek took me on a tour. We walked through an open yard that had neat rows cut in its concrete floor where small flowers bloomed. Grassy hills, sloping down the steep mountainside, surrounded the main building. It was a two-story house made of hand-cut beams and square stones. The house, without a fourth wall on the courtyard side, was open to the mountain air. Raibek apologized that it lacked windows.

"A work in progress," I said.

"War," he said.

Scores of children ran underfoot. Women, teenagers and grandmothers, worked in every corner. As in every other home I had seen in Chechnya, they were the ones kneading, washing, stoking the stove. Playroom, kitchen, dining area, and garage were all one vast room without walls. A trio of children stood at a pool table, wielding cue sticks twice their height. Beyond the pool table, a Nissan Patrol and an old Lada were parked.

We lunched at a long table covered with hot flat bread, tomatoes and cucumbers, green onions and cloves of garlic. Three girls emerged from the smoke of the woodstove with bowls of mutton soup and plates of rice stacked with mutton. Over lunch Raibek told of a recent spectacle. It was night, he said, when the gorge grew "noisy." The sky lit up. A firefight ensued—from one side of the valley to the other. The Russians were firing from their base nearby on their own command post in Vedeno. Only later did he learn the reason: The soldiers hadn't been paid for weeks. They were hungry.

THROUGHOUT LUNCH a secret smile played on Raibek's lips. Over the three rounds of black tea that followed, I sensed him taking me in. By the time he offered to drive me out to his new checkpoint at the edge of his territory, I wondered if he'd finished doing the math, calculating the price an American journalist would bring. All the same, I agreed to see his check-

point, "the only post in Chechnya," he boasted, "not manned by Russians."
An elderly woman–"one of the wives," Issa informed me–delivered two AK-
47s to the table. Raibek took them in his hands, strapped on a pistol, holstered a knife, buttoned his shirt, and led me to the Nissan Patrol.

Shvedov was not overjoyed that I had accepted the invitation. The checkpoint, he said, was on the far edge of Raibek's ridge. It bordered the preserve
of Basayev and Khattab. "You go with Raibek," he said, "at your own risk."

I was slightly reassured when Mogamed, Raibek's mammoth bodyguard,
jumped into the Patrol. "Raibek's best fighter" Issa called him. "And one he
trusts," Shvedov added. Cradling a shiny automatic rifle between his knees,
Mogamed sat to my left. Shvedov sat on my right, and Issa reluctantly up
front. As Raibek set off on the road, his foot barely touching the accelerator,
the bodyguard sat in silence, scanning the bushes beside the road. My calm
deserted me, however, when I realized we were stopping to pick up another
guard, a young fighter. He carried five grenades across his chest, two knives,
one pistol on his belt, and a Kalashnikov in his hands. He crawled, without
saying a word, into the rear of the Patrol.

We drove on, past scatterings of sheep and goats and a string of stone
villages along the green ridge. "These are my people," Raibek said, but he
meant "This is my land." Soon we stopped again, in the village of Marzoi
Mokh (Sweet Earth), to add yet another body to our mission. We walked
into the grassy yard of a low-slung wooden house where Raibek's best fighters, a family of four brothers, lived. The brothers, each the size of an ox,
emerged and after an elaborate exchange of half hugs and salutations, one of
them joined us, squeezing in next to me. I was now surrounded by three of
Raibek's men, each heavily armed.

As we left Sweet Earth, Raibek did not drive more than ten miles an
hour. He let each tire turn slowly over the rock. The road was torturous, at
times so rutted it seemed impossible to traverse. Raibek tacked across it
carefully, as if the massive Patrol were a dinghy on rough seas. For long
stretches we saw no people. The woods ran thick and silence filled the car.
The farther we drove from Raibek's last village, as the wheels spit out the
rocks from underneath them, the more anxious I became. The farther on we
drove, the more I found myself staring at the back of Raibek's head. His
neck was tanned and creased, ringed by a gold chain. As the woods grew
close, I thought of the bounty hunters who, like their forefathers who had

done in Hadji Murad, were now angling for Raibek. For several miles, as he eased the Patrol along the gravel, the only sound in the car was Shvedov chewing his dentures.

As we drove on, Raibek pointed to a series of craters beside the road.

"From the last war," Shvedov said.

"From last week," Raibek said.

At last we reached the checkpoint. Five young Chechens in torn T-shirts and plastic slippers manned it. "My partisans." Raibek laughed. "If they do not stand here, this road is Khattab's highway into Vedeno, and from there he moves into Grozny." We joined a half dozen fighters more on the crest of the ridge. "Congratulations," Issa said. "You now stand where no journalist has been."

I tried to enjoy the view. The steep hills, cloaked in bush and woods, stretched before us. To the north, beyond the haze of the hot afternoon and the banners of smoke from the burning oil wells, we could see the plains of northeastern Chechnya.

One of the thin boys guarding the ridge tugged at my sleeve. "Don't stand here long," he said. "We do get fire." Three days before there'd been an attack. Snipers had shot two of his colleagues. To the east, said Raibek, waving to the mountains on our right, lay Dagestan. His ridge, he boasted, was now the first line of defense against the last of the insurgents. The lands that rose and fell from here to the border constituted the last refuge of his sworn enemies Basayev and Khattab.

We drove back along the narrow road, just as deliberately as on the way out. We were still far from the village of Sweet Earth when Raibek stopped the car, suddenly and without explanation. He pulled over beside a bright grove at the edge of a cluster of stone and corrugated metal houses. The small houses made up the village of Haji Otar. Issa got out of the Patrol, and soon everyone else, without a word, did as well. Raibek sat beside the road on a jagged boulder. He tugged at the tall grass in front of the rock. I sat nearby, on another stone. Together we watched as Issa crossed the road and walked up the hillside across from us. He had gone to pray. He knelt before a tiered shrine, each level a different hue, that filled the hillside.

It was the tomb, Raibek explained, of Heda, the mother of the holy man Kunta Hajji. Known to scholars of Sufism as al-Shaykh al-Hajj Kunta al-Michiki al-Iliskhani, Kunta Hajji brought an alternative to Chechnya to the

Naqshbandi path, the Qadiri order. Issa had long lectured me about the benevolent nature of Kunta's teachings. "Kunta was like a Tolstoy, a Gandhi, a Martin Luther King of the Caucasus," he had told me one night in Shali. "He offered Chechens a different road. He believed in nonviolent resistance. Where Shamil was militant, Kunta was contemplative."

As usual, Issa had folded legend into fact. Little, to be sure, is known of the holy man who introduced the Qadiri order to the Chechens. But in the middle of the first war, in 1994, one of the last surviving Chechen historians, Vakhid Akayev, scoured the archives in Grozny and wrote a life of Kunta Hajji.[43] Born in the Chechen village of Isti-Su, Kunta was eighteen when he embarked on his first pilgrimage to Mecca, or hajj, in 1848. (When he returned, he earned the surname Hajji as an honorific.) Initiated into the Qadiri order on his first hajj, Kunta brought the new movement with him when he returned to Chechnya.[44]

For the Chechens, Kunta opened a realm of purification. He urged withdrawal from the world, self-cleansing through prayer. A Muslim, he preached, must "clean his soul and interior from the dirt and everything that is forbidden and . . . from evil intentions and falsehoods."[45] In earthly matters, Kunta urged his believers to cease their resistance to the infidels of the north. He considered the struggle not only futile but a sin. He did not embrace Russian rule but sought to develop a pacifist resistance. Kunta Hajji, above all, offered a way out to a people whose only hope of deliverance had been found in war.

Kunta's teachings gained so many followers that in the late 1850s a religious divide rent Chechnya. Islam had always separated Russians from Chechens, but the advent of the Qadiri order alienated Chechen from Chechen. The emergence of two Sufi orders threatened to split a brotherhood bound by *adat*. Kunta Hajji had grown to rival Imam Shamil. And so in 1859, months before giving up to the Russians, Shamil sent Kunta off on a second hajj.

"The divide lasts to this day," Raibek said, as we sat at arm's length on opposite rocks across from the shrine to Kunta's mother. Issa was still across the road, praying. For Qadiris, Raibek explained, Heda's shrine was the most sacred in Chechnya. Kunta's own grave lies somewhere in Russia's northwestern corner. In the winter of 1864 the Russians arrested Kunta near Shali, and Alexander II ordered him brought to Russia to serve a life sentence "under police supervision."[46] Because Kunta died in 1867, poor, starving, and surrounded by Russians, in a village in the far-off province of Novgorod, Chechens came here, to Heda's tomb, to pray to him.

Many among the Qadiris had long since strayed and become just as militant as their Naqshbandi brothers. (Dudayev, for example, the man who led Chechnya's rebellion in the first war, was a Qadiri.) Yet among Imam Shamil's spiritual descendants, Kunta Hajji's teachings still stirred enmity. Basayev and Khattab's fighters had tried to destroy Heda's tomb. "To this day," Raibek said, "they're not happy that Kunta offered us a way out."

🕮 FOURTEEN 🕮

TOWARD THE END OF *Hadji Murad*, Tolstoy describes a raid that lays waste to a Chechen village, in much the same manner as the *zachistka* in Aldy. The Russian soldiers destroy houses, wreck roofs, bayonet (in the back) a young boy, and burn the villagers' fruit trees and gardens. The raid's grim aftermath, as written by Tolstoy, oddly echoed the testimony from Aldy that I had gathered in my notebooks: "The wailing of women sounded in every house and in the square where two more bodies were brought. The young children wailed with their mothers. The hungry animals howled, too, and there was nothing to give them. The older children played no games and watched their elders with frightened eyes."

In the tale, once the Russians leave, the elders gather to debate what to do. They face the same dilemma as those who survived the massacre in Aldy: How to respond? "Nobody spoke a word of hatred for the Russians. The emotion felt by every Chechen, old and young alike, was stronger than hatred. It was not hatred, it was a refusal to recognize these Russian dogs as men at all, and a feeling of such disgust, revulsion and bewilderment at the senseless cruelty of these creatures that the urge to destroy them—like the urge to destroy rats, venomous spiders or wolves—was an instinct as natural as that of self-preservation."[47] And so the blood feud widened. Tolstoy's villagers chose to follow Imam Shamil and his *Ghazavat*.

ON A PARCHED AFTERNOON in the steppe of Chechnya's northeastern corner, in the Cossack *stanitsa* of Starogladovskaya, I met Khusein Zagibov. Unlike Raibek, Khusein, a lean forty-eight-year-old former journalist, was overjoyed to have unannounced guests. Khusein ran the Tolstoy Museum in Starogladovskaya, sleeping in it at night with a shotgun by his side. He could not remember the last time he had been paid, but he had spent three winters fending off looters. Born during the exile in Central Asia, he had no illusions about the Russians' goodwill. Nor did he defend his compatriots. His brother had been kidnapped after the first war. The toll, Issa warned, was heavy. Khusein's eyes were rheumy with apprehension, and his long face bore a look of perpetual defeat. Yet he seemed to believe in the providence of the gods of literature. He took it as a sign of Tolstoy's saintliness that the museum honoring the writer's appreciation of the Chechen people still stood.

"I am writing in the stanitsa of Starogladovskaya, at ten in the evening on the thirtieth of June," Tolstoy wrote in his diary of 1851. "How did I end up here? Don't know. Why? Also, no idea."[48] Tolstoy came to Chechnya in the company of tsarist troops. He was twenty-four and, having run up unseemly gambling debts, felt an urgent need to leave Moscow. Here, in Starogladovskaya, in extended stretches from 1851 to 1853, Tolstoy first saw war. He also wrote his first book, *Childhood*. The young count, loosed from the strictures of Moscow, fell in love with the freedom and courage of Cossacks and Chechens alike.

Despite Khusein's stand, the museum languished in a desperate state. Gaping holes threatened to cave in its ceiling. The floor had rotted through. There was no electricity, let alone an alarm. Every night Khusein bedded down in the back office, lying beside a makeshift stove. The shotgun was handy, he said. It kept the thieves at bay. Yet there were no real artifacts of Tolstoy's to guard, only yellowing photocopies of pages he wrote here, a reproduction of a Cossack saddle, a white Cossack tunic. The prized object was a red carpet featuring Tolstoy's image as a young officer, beardless and dashing, as seen by a collective of Soviet seamstresses a century after his death. The carpet had been stolen in the first war, Khusein said. But a few weeks ago, after a *zachistka*, it had reappeared on a street nearby.

We made our way through the dark rooms with care. As Khusein spoke of the Great Writer, emotion filled his voice. "We are proud Tolstoy chose to live among us," he said, "and that he remembered his entire life the lessons our people taught him."

Tolstoy in his works on the Caucasus blamed neither Cossack nor Chechen. In his 1863 tale *The Cossacks*, he marveled at the Cossacks' fortitude on the empire's edge. Yet he depicted both Cossack and Chechen as just and their cultures as equally exotic and endangered. Tolstoy left little doubt: Moscow's heavy hand would bring only ruin to the peoples of the south. In a draft of *Hadji Murad*, he wrote:

. . . what always happens when a state, having large-scale military strength, enters into relations with primitive, small peoples, living their own independent life. Under the pretext of self-defense (even though attacks are always provoked by the powerful neighbor), or the pretext of civilizing the ways of a savage people (even though the savage people is living a life incomparably better and more peaceable than the "civilisers") . . . the servants of the military states commit all sorts of villainy against small peoples, while maintaining that one cannot deal with them otherwise. That was the situation in the Caucasus . . . when Russian military commanders, seeking to win distinction for themselves and appropriate the spoils of war, invaded peaceful lands, ravaged villages, killed hundreds of people, raped women, rustled thousands of cattle, and then blamed the tribesmen for their attacks on Russian possessions.[49]

Khusein was eager to draw out the visit, to keep life in these rooms as long as he could. But I had hoped to leave Chechnya that day, before the sun set and the curfew fell. As we came around to the threshold again, Khusein recited Tolstoy's memory of his days in Chechnya: "Never, neither before nor afterward, did I attain such heights of thought. . . . And everything I discovered then has remained my conviction."

As we stepped outside, the hot sun of the late afternoon enveloped us. Shvedov was happily smoking a *papirosa* beside the silver-painted statue of the Great Writer that dominated the museum yard. Tolstoy had offered a prophecy that still entranced Khusein. He had seen the futility of any military resolution to the discord in the south and foreseen the cost of imperial ambition. He had understood the Chechens' traditions and honored them. Chechnya loomed large in Tolstoy's imagination until his last days. When the writer, in his last escape from Yasnaya Polyana, his estate south of Moscow, died in 1910 in the snows at the train station at Astapovo, he was heading for the Caucasus. "At least there was one Russian," said Khusein, "who understood what it means to be Chechen." Emotion again filled his voice. This time it was not love but regret.

The Russians, he said, had reason to be unhappy with the pseudostate Maskhadov and Basayev and Khattab had won. "No order, no law, no *adat*, no *Shari'a*" had existed in his land after the first war. Russia had been right, Khusein said, to cut Chechnya off. No one but the Taliban had recognized the free state of Ichkeria. In the yard, someone had lined up a row of uprooted headstones, leaning against an old wooden fence. The stones were broken and engraved with Arabic script. Our commanders grew rich, he said, but who built a school or a hospital, let alone a museum? And now there was only *proizvol*, the arbitrary rule, of the generals and the warlords.

Shvedov had joined Issa and Yura in the UAZik. As I climbed back in the jeep, Khusein stood still, a hand at his forehead to shield against the sun. His museum may have lacked artifacts, but it was something singular and irreplaceable, a haven of humanity. As we pulled away, he remained in the yard, motionless beside the silvery statue of Tolstoy.

WE DROVE ACROSS the brown northern steppe. Hot air streamed through the open windows as the dry fields blurred left and right. The hay, uncut, had grown tall. The air seemed thin, filling the car with the smell of the fields. The road followed the Terek, and in the sky above it a hawk traced the turns of the narrow river. We had driven a half hour from the museum when a checkpoint appeared through the windshield. Suddenly a helicopter, only faintly heard moments earlier, swooped down across the road in front of us.

"Bastard," Issa mumbled. He was tired and ready, I was sure, to say good-bye.

The chopper flew wide to the right, before circling back and descending directly toward us. Yura drove steady on. The helicopter lifted its nose and rose suddenly, passing us by. As we neared the checkpoint, we pulled even with a battered Ural motorcycle. Its sidecar attached, the bike was overloaded with a Chechen family. A man drove it. Behind and beside him four children and an old woman clung tight. I looked at the woman–she had pulled her gray hair under a scarf and folded the hem of her long skirt under her legs—and wondered whose mother she was, the children's or the man at the wheel.

At the checkpoint the soldiers, three OMON officers from Lipetsk, wore black plastic sunglasses. They were in no mood for Issa's humor. They peered into the back of the UAZik. The officer on my side of the car, a blond fellow who revealed two gold lower teeth, asked for my documents. I complied.

"What the hell are you doing here?" he asked. His colleague had raised his Kalashnikov. It was now centered on Shvedov's chest.

"We've been to see Tolstoy," Issa said.

"Think you're funny, Grandpa?" the blond officer retorted.

Shvedov came to the rescue. "Look, fellas, look at this," he said as he undid a tiny pin from the pocket of his tattered army jacket. It had been a gift from Khusein, a button of soft gray metal that bore a relief of Lev Niko-layevich's profile. "From the museum," Shvedov said. "Keep it."

The OMON officers crowded close to examine the pin. They turned it over twice in their fleshy hands. They were intrigued.

"Tolstoy actually lived here?" the blond officer asked.

"What the hell for?" one of his colleagues said.

"I don't believe it," a third said.

I imagined Khusein taking in the scene. It was a shame, he'd said as we parted, no one seemed to read the Great Writer anymore.

🕮 FIFTEEN 🕮

We cannot term the Russian soldier, by any perversion of language, a brave and gallant warrior [wrote Edmund Spencer in 1836.] But then, on the other hand, he possesses many qualities highly valuable in the military subordinate: he is robust by nature; and, being accustomed to the hardest fare from infancy, bears patiently the severest privations; he is also bigot, slave, and fatalist; knows no will of his own. The first lesson that falls on his ear, is obedience to his lord, and love for his emperor; and, when led to the field, he becomes a complete machine, capable of being driven to the mouth of the cannon, or transformed into a target! [50]

I SPENT MY FIRST NIGHT out of Chechnya in Mozdok, the Russian army town just across the border in North Ossetia that had long been the staging ground for the war. For twenty dollars I got a room in the center of town. Ever since the first war Rima and Viktor had turned their house into an informal bed-and-breakfast for journalists and relief workers. They seemed like good, gentle people, but there was no mistaking that I had left behind a different world.

Rima ordered me to take a shower, while she filled a large metal bowl with chopped cucumbers, tomatoes, and onions. Viktor was busy preparing for the evening's festivities. In the small courtyard, he dragged tall glass jars of home brew.

What was the party? I wondered after I'd showered for the first time in weeks. Her younger boy's eighteenth birthday, Rima said. His brother had already served in Chechnya. "He was sent there, and we didn't even know," she said. "He wouldn't tell us."

Viktor busied himself with an elaborate rubber contraption to fill a row of bottles with the moonshine.

"Now they'll come for my youngest," Rima said. "Who needed this?" she asked, staring at the broken linoleum of her kitchen floor.

Before I could say anything, Viktor, who had been born in Grozny and served his years in the Red Army in East Germany, answered for me. "No one," he said as he left the kitchen, "no one needed it."

CHECHNYA WOULD HAVE been sufficiently surreal, even without Sergei Tsygankov. Few Russian officers in Putin's War could claim a good job. But Tsygankov, a lieutenant colonel only months from retirement, may have had the worst one of all. Throughout the first winter of Putin's War, he ran the body collection point closest to the battleground. No matter whether the temperature fell below zero or rose over a hundred degrees, Tsygankov, with a supporting crew of twelve unfortunates, ran the tents that were the Mozdok base's approximation of an army morgue. It was his job to collect, sort, and send on north the dead to the Good Doctor's morgue in Rostov.

From the outside of the apartment block, nothing foretold the night-mares that resided inside. It was a long, drab block, home to officers, their wives and children. I knocked a second time before the door opened. A blond woman, in her early forties and wearing a yellow sundress, appeared. Both she and the unshaded lightbulb above her head were swaying.

"Sergei cannot be disturbed," she said.

I understood. He was drunk. And so, it seemed, was she. I told her I'd be back in the morning, early. The birthday party was still in embers the next morning when I peeled a thin sheet from my body, got dressed, and headed back across town. By seven Tsygankov stood in front of me. A tall, thin man, he opened the door in a sleeveless undershirt and khaki trousers.

"Five minutes," he said, shutting the door. A few minutes later he reappeared, in uniform. The morning was hot, near ninety degrees. We drove toward the Mozdok base, stopping a half mile from its gate. We sat down by the side of a swiftly moving creek. It was the Terek, the thin river that runs strongly through Vladikavkaz and across the breadth of Chechnya. We sat on the grassy bank for two hours, as the words poured from Tsygankov. Rarely did he stop for breath. Not once did he utter the words "corpse," "bodies," even "the dead."

Tsygankov was all limbs, like a stick figure. His eyes were a poor, dulled brown; his face was so attenuated there was no flesh to it. When he talked, you could see his bones at work. He had run the makeshift morgue for five months. His nerves were shot. In all, more than two thousand bodies had passed through his tent.

He told me what I knew: "They're lowering the figures." And what I did not know: "For every ten soldiers we get, only three have been killed in battle. All the rest have frozen to death, or died because someone wasn't careful with a weapon, or died from disease, especially in winter. Even from the flu." The dead, Tsygankov explained, fell into two categories: killed and deceased. "Killed" meant they had died in battle, but "deceased" meant they had died in the hospital. And if a wounded man died in the hospital, he was not included in the casualty figures.

Sometimes, Tsygankov said, the dead arrived in horrific form. Sometimes, for instance, when a poor soul had suffered a direct hit by a rocket-propelled grenade, they came in pieces. No flak jacket, he said dryly, could save you. The arms and legs would be blown right off. Sometimes the bodies revealed evidence of executions. One guy, he remembered, had come in with a notebook still stuffed in his breast pocket. A 5.45-caliber bullet had pierced its pages and then his heart.

"A Kalashnikov," he said, "at short range."

Drinking became Tsygankov's salvation. Everyone who worked the morgue drank, day and night. No one ever gave them a hard time about it. Morale was not low, he said. It did not exist.

"I'm gone, I know that," he said. "But what kind of life is it for the young guys? You never leave this work behind. You go home, take a shower, and then at night you're back in that tent again. You can shower, use vinegar, but it's no use. You can't get rid of the smell. And forget about saving money. Guys work two weeks straight. When they get two days off, of course they're going to go out, get drunk, and throw their whole paycheck away with a whore."

Tsygankov offered a grim measure of how far the Russian Army had fallen since Afghanistan. A career officer, he was a long way from his specialization. At eighteen he had graduated from the elite academy of the Soviet missile forces in 1971. After the academy he had served first in the north, near Arkhangelsk, then in Tajikistan, during the Soviet war in Afghanistan. He had been there when Gorbachev ordered the pullout, ending the Soviets' greatest military debacle. He had, as he put it, "absolutely nothing to do with this business."

His tour in the first Chechen war had erased any vestigial notions of patriotism or duty. Yet nothing had prepared him for the macabre service to come. The worst, he said, were the shortages. He told how he had to fuel his refrigerator truck by trading body bags for gasoline with other officers. The bags were in demand; the officers used them to insulate makeshift banyas at their encampments inside Chechnya. The bosses were forever promising gas money, he said. They even sent an officer in from Moscow to bring him cash. "Never saw the guy," he said. He took the money and never made it to Mozdok.

For most of the nearly one hundred thousand Russian troops in the region, Mozdok was merely the last transit point before Chechnya. For Tsygankov, it was home. His parents were from here, he had grown up here, and his grandfather had been the chief of police here. He had also married a local girl. Now they had a son and a daughter, two teenagers he could no longer afford to house, let alone educate.

Dark bags hung under his eyes. The left side of his face had developed a twitch. He laughed without cause, and more often than not, his answers did not follow my questions. He had seen more than enough in his waking hours, but now the nightmares terrorized him. At first the bodies, waxen and bloodied, had visited him only in his sleep. Then the daytime hallucinations began. He would be at work, in the hot tent, when suddenly the bodies began to come alive.

"They'd start to move," he said, "writhing in pain on the stretchers, reaching up toward my face if I got too close."

He had suffered two heart attacks in the tent. The last one landed him in the hospital. But after two weeks, he had been sent right back to work. At last one night he exploded, "like a bottle," as he put it, "hitting concrete." A Chechen had driven up to the front gates of the Mozdok base. In the back of his Lada was a corpse he had found by the road. It was the body of a Russian officer, a senior lieutenant.

"A normal Chechen," Tsygankov said. "It happens."

The general in charge of the base called in Tsygankov to deal with the body. Because it was a hot night and he had been working almost nonstop for a month, Tsygankov was not wearing his cap. The commander unleashed a verbal assault. "Where's your goddamned cap?" he screamed.

"Comrade General," Tsygankov replied, "why give me a hard time? What am I, some kind of fucking kid standing here? Some punk? You and I are the same goddamned age." The general said he would fire him. Tsygankov, overjoyed, urged him to go ahead. The paperwork went out, but the order came back, overturned.

"Who else they'd get to do that job?" Tsygankov said.

Before long he tried to take early retirement. His superiors would not let him. Unable to get fired or to quit, he was promoted–to the deputy commander, in charge of the rapid reaction force, of the base.

Tsygankov had been to a psychiatrist. "Sergei Vladimirovich," the psychiatrist had told him, "you must take a vacation, spend time in nature, go on picnics, go fishing."

Tsygankov laughed. His pension, he said, would be eighty-nine dollars a month. It was not enough to take care of his family, let alone to take a holiday. Now he wanted just enough money for "the only cure," to drink.

For all the ravages the war had brought him, Tsygankov still yearned for the old days, the days when he had entered the academy. "For a young kid," he said with a short laugh, "to be an officer was the height. It was real work for real men." The girls back then didn't love carpenters or welders. They loved soldiers. It wasn't just the uniform or the honor that attracted young brides. Military men earned more and retired younger. They also earned enviable pensions and long vacations on the Black Sea.

Yet what Tsygankov missed most was the professionalism. Mozdok, he said, was a *bardak*, a complete and utter mess, where SNAFUs, in their original U.S. Army sense, were the norm. A week earlier Anatoly Kvashnin, head of the Russian chiefs of staff, had come visiting. He had flown in from Moscow to tour the troops. The helicopter carrying him tried to land in Mozdok. It could not. A group of drunken *kontraktniki*, who had finished their tour of duty but been denied a flight home, refused to let Russia's top general land. "They got stuck here for days," Tsygankov said. "There were no planes. So what did they do? Got shit-faced. Then they heard the big boss was choppering in. So they got clever. They covered the landing pad with their bodies. He couldn't land." In the end, the *kontraktniki* got what they wanted, a plane out. "There was no other way," Tsygankov said. "It's a *bardak*, an absolute *bardak*."

FROM ROSTOV TO Vladikavkaz to Gudermes I had heard Russian officers offer their prognosis for "how the war would end." Tsygankov, too, had his theories. But sitting beside him in the thick grass along the Terek, I heard a rare sermon, a blend of propaganda, legend, and experience collected at ground zero. He may have ranted, but his prophecy was not easy to dismiss.

"Just look at history. Go back to the first Great Caucasian War, when Shamil was captured. Yermolov moved wisely back then. But this war is far from over. Even under the tsar, the conclusion was: You have to pack up all these tribes and disperse them across Russia. That's what Stalin eventually did.

"As long as the Chechens lived in Central Asia, there was no problem. As soon as they came back here, they went back to thievery, not least because they had been spoiled by the fat compensation the state gave them. They had grown lazy. Before then this land produced something. Cossacks, and even Chechens, worked it. Slowly the level of civilization rose. But now? The land is absolute shit. There's nothing left. The only idea still alive in Chechnya is the worst one for Russia, Wahhabism."

Tsygankov was facing a hard year. His son was moving to Petersburg, to enroll at the Suvorov military academy. Given Russia's culture of bribes, Tsygankov had gone deep into debt to pay nearly fifteen hundred dollars for a place there. His daughter had another year in high school. Then he'd have to bribe her way into the local institute as well. I asked if he would rather have his son close by. For a moment he thought it over.

"In Vladikavkaz there's another military academy," he said. "But I don't want him there. It's the Caucasus. And the Caucasus is still the Caucasus. It's eternal war."

SIXTEEN

AFTER A MONTH ON the road I did not leave the south with much hope. When I returned home to Moscow and Russian friends asked, "What will become of Chechnya?" I could find few encouraging words. But as Chechnya settled in my mind into a stream of dust, fighters, helicopter gunships, and tattooed OMON officers, I found myself thinking most often of Andrei Zhivoi.

His name alone astonished. *Zhivoi* means "alive." He was a former sapper who had lost his legs to a mine in Grozny in the first war. It took me the better part of a day trip from Rostov to find him in Taganrog, the town of Chekhov's birth off the Sea of Azov. He had come home from the war with a grievance but had not sunk into regret. He walked now with new legs, German prostheses procured by the Soldiers' Mothers Committee in Rostov.

I found him in Taganrog's one-room Center for Social Rehabilitation. The office was hidden behind a police station and above a row of garbage bins. It was filled with young people working silently. There were none of the computers and fax machines that decorated the offices of "grass-roots" initiatives favored by Western foundations across Russia. The center gave free legal advice to the disabled, the retired, and the indigent, anyone who walked through its door. Zhivoi had little time for me. He was preparing for court.

Before Chechnya, he had been certain to become a metal worker at the local factory. But he had come home from the war with a grievance. He had served not one but two tours, and the second extended, as was all too common, beyond the legal limit. His commander had simply refused to let him go home. Some may have called Zhivoi unlucky. As a deminer he'd been among the first into Grozny on successive waves. He did not see his fate as misfortune, nor did he blame the Chechens. He blamed the desperation of Russia's armed forces, their stubborn refusal to obey their own laws. If Russia had had a rule of law, Zhivoi was sure, he would still have had his legs.

He had recovered, learned to walk again, and gone to law school. He did not seek retribution or compensation but a weapon to rectify the ills he and so many others had suffered. The journey had not been easy. Taganrog, when Chekhov was born there in 1860, had been a sleepy hamlet of traders and fishermen. Then the city had been a disheveled corner of the south—"not a single sign without a spelling mistake," the playwright later recalled.[51] The Soviet century had little changed its provincial air. When Zhivoi returned home, no one knew his rights, and he had no one to turn to but the Mothers Committee in Rostov.

Born in a village outside Taganrog, he had moved to the city as a young boy for schooling. He'd grown up in his grandmother's home, a ramshackle collection of red brick that now housed an assortment of relatives. The yard reeked of rotting cabbage, the outhouse, and too many cats to count. It seemed an unlikely place to begin anew. The hardest he said was the first winter, when going to the toilet meant dragging himself across the frozen courtyard. For a time he'd returned to his parents' village. There he met his wife. A nursery school teacher, she had learned accounting to help pay the bills. He'd won a stipend for law school, but his military pension came in just under twenty dollars each month.

If the Chechen question is ever to be resolved, I imagined, it would take the strength of men like Zhivoi. He had lost nearly everything but returned to the living with dignity and hope. Zhivoi, at least, saw only one future—not just for Chechnya but for Russia as well. The country, he said, had to follow the rule of law. His insistent words on that stifling day in the south lingered as I traveled again across his country.

"Without that foundation," Zhivoi said, "without a legal order, it's impossible to achieve anything. Anything at all."

III. NORTH

TO THE SIXTY-NINTH
PARALLEL

Russia is an enormous plain across which wander
mischievous men.

> –Chekhov in his notebooks

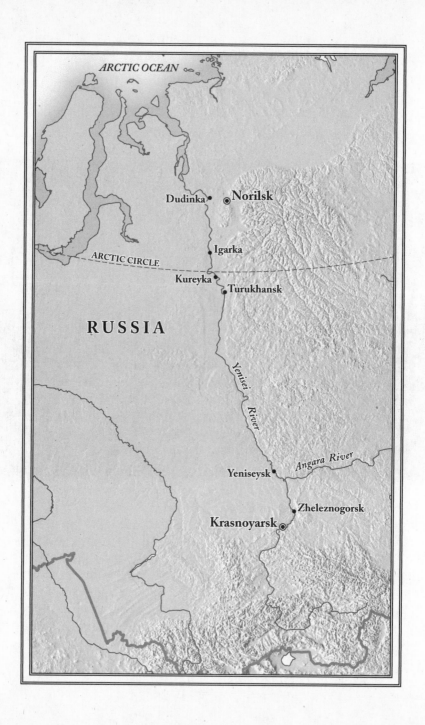

ARCTIC OCEAN

Dudinka • ○ **Norilsk**

Igarka •

ARCTIC CIRCLE

Kureyka •
• Turukhansk

RUSSIA

Yenisei River

Angara River

Yeniseysk •

• Zheleznogorsk

Krasnoyarsk ○

❦ ONE ❦

WITHIN WEEKS OF MY return from Chechnya, I headed in the opposite direction, traveling far above the Arctic Circle to Norilsk. As Russia opened again to the West, Norilsk gained fame as one of the world's most prodigious suppliers of precious metals. I had visited the city once before, in the middle of its ungodly winter. Then I'd braved a blizzard and flown. This time I wanted to feel the far north coming before I saw it. I wanted to let time expand as I ventured into the depths of Siberia. Above all, I wanted to go in the path of the men and women who had founded the city.

I was to fly twenty-five hundred miles from Moscow to the city of Krasnoyarsk in southern Siberia, the seat of Governor Aleksandr Lebed's power and the battlefield for Russia's bloodiest aluminum wars. From Krasnoyarsk, I would board a steamer–the *Aleksei Matrosov*, built in the German Democratic Republic in 1953, the year Stalin died–to sail thirteen hundred miles up the Yenisei, Russia's second-longest waterway and one of the world's most impressive rivers, which forms near Mongolia and runs to the Arctic, nearly dividing Siberia in half. The boat trip was to last a week, as we were to wind our way north, at a sixteen-mile-per-hour clip, gliding past the decaying remains of the tsarist-era exile villages that punctuated its shores. We were to decamp at Dudinka, the port near the northernmost end of the Yenisei, which existed solely to serve as the gateway, across the moonscape of the tundra, to Norilsk.

Born of the Gulag, Norilsk was the quintessential Soviet company town built over the bones of prisoners. Lured by the riches hidden deep beneath its permafrost, Stalin ordered the city constructed in one of the world's most forbidding climates. By now, a founding member of the Moscow moguls' club that called themselves oligarchs, a balding young banker named Vladimir Potanin, ruled it. Potanin did not own the town. But as the primary force behind the holding company that ran the metals complex, he in essence controlled the fate of everyone who lived and worked in the city.

On our wall map at home Norilsk loomed at the edge of civilization. It seemed a place at once ominous and illuminating, a corner of Russia where one could measure not only the gap between the newly rich and the long poor but the haunting legacy of the unfinished past as well. Everywhere across Russia, in the years since the Soviet collapse, the past had been exhumed, laid bare, only to be abandoned, unexamined and unburied. Nothing had resettled right. In more cosmopolitan corners, life had of course moved on. In Moscow and Petersburg, sushi bars, casinos, and soup kitchens had quickly appeared. But Norilsk, for all its riches, remained a severed world, a Pompeii of Stalinism that the trapped heirs of the Gulag still called home.

LEAVING MOSCOW AS the clouds darkened on a sweat-drenched evening in late July, I flew through the night in the company of Syrian and German natural gas executives. The air conditioning was out on the plane. The Syrians sweated in their suits. The giant boat of a plane was one of the old Aeroflot fleet now in the commission of Krasnoyarsk's fledgling local operator, KrasAir. The German seated behind me could not help himself. "Thank God," he said, "there's no *h* in KRASair." To those who flew frequently across Siberia, the joke was worn out. Western aviation officials liked to reassure reporters that Russian planes had suffered a worse press than their safety record deserved. All the same, the native aircraft had fallen so often from the sky Aeroflot officials had adopted a disconcerting habit of calling crashes "unanticipated descents."

The clouds above Moscow looked like giant pillows soaked in tar. The river, the lights, the avenues glowed below before we finally broke through the blackness and into the night sky. After an hour, in the middle of the night, the prim flight attendants served a meal. It was either chicken or fish. Chicken, I guessed, from the hair. The Germans, the Syrians, and their two chaperons from Gazprom spent the flight smoking, drinking, toasting, and reminiscing about old days in Damascus. I did not even feign sleep.

Krasnoyarsk, as the still-drunk Gazprom honchos informed their guests once we'd landed in the morning, means "Red Cliffs." Everyone in town insisted that I drive out to see these magnificent landmarks. I never did. There was too much to see in town.

Krasnoyarsk surprised. I had expected belching smokestacks and sprawling factories. They were here, to be sure, but upriver, beyond town. In its heart the city was quiet, and instead of post-Soviet industrial decay, an unexpected sense of the past prevailed. Downtown offered a tidy array of narrow thoroughfares–Lenin, Peace, and Marx streets–that paralleled the river. There were more nineteenth-century private houses than twentieth-century apartment blocks. I passed the house with ornate columns where Vasily Surikov, a nineteenth-century painter, spent his most productive years.

Governor Lebed, the general once favored to succeed Yeltsin, who two years earlier had retreated from the intrigue of Moscow politics, now ruled the Krasnoyarsk region. I had followed the general's career since 1991. He had then commanded the Tula Division that advanced on the parliament building in Moscow during the coup against Gorbachev. He had led his men to the White House, as the building holding the parliament (now the seat of the federal government) was known, but never fired a shot. I had interviewed Lebed a number of times and watched his reputation as a peacemaker grow–from curbing the Trans-Dniester conflict between Russians and Moldovans in 1992 as head of the Fourteenth Army to signing the cease-fire accord in 1996 with Maskhadov that ended the first Chechen war. Now in the heart of Siberia, I wanted to watch Lebed as governor in action, to see how he ruled one of Russia's largest regions, a fiefdom rich in minerals and *mafiya* that extended from the Arctic Ocean nearly to the Mongolian border.[1]

I was lucky. I had arrived on Paratroopers Day. Lebed, a battalion commander in Afghanistan, was a paratrooper's paratrooper. He would be hosting, I could be sure, the festivities in the city's enormous Ballet and Opera Theater. I walked along the western bank of the Yenisei, following the river's grassy embankment, past the little old steamer that had once delivered Lenin into tsarist exile. Its paddles, long out of use, were corroded, but the boat had been repainted and retrofitted. Now it was a floating bar. At the docks, a throng was pushing to get their worldly possessions onto a riverboat. The river here flows over a mile wide, bisecting, the locals say, without paying attention to geography, the heart of Siberia.

On the far bank were the concrete high-rises of the newly dispossessed, the working poor who kept Krasnoyarsk's aluminum plants stoked. If the left bank seemed quaint, across the river the dark past announced itself.

North of the apartment towers, a small lonely-looking red-brick church marked the site where, from the era of Nicholas I to the late 1950s, the old *transitka*, the main transit camp for prisoners and exiles, had stood.

I arrived at the theater just as the paratroopers' fest neared its crescendo. Thousands of soldiers, young and old, each resplendent in a pressed parade uniform, filled the seats. A choir of preteen cadets lined the stage, their trumpets and flutes at the ready, while a military ensemble strummed electric guitars and sang martial ballads. Paratroopers came out onstage, squad by squad, to break bricks on one another's backs. In the center of the stage sat Governor Lebed. He wore a smart blue and gray uniform. Gold braids hung from his shoulders, and medals adorned his chest. Lebed not only glittered, he radiated.

The governorship had proved a less than desirable sinecure. Berezovsky had generously financed Lebed's campaign–in large part to nurture a potential presidential candidate who could stand in opposition, should the need arise, to the Kremlin. Lebed had run a respectable third in the 1996 vote, tipping the scales in the runoff against the Communists when he lent Yeltsin his support in exchange for becoming his national security chief. But in Krasnoyarsk, Lebed had not had an easy time of it.

"Don't be mistaken, Krasnoyarsk's a mob town," the governor's adviser had whispered as we sat on a bench overlooking the river. I had treated him to an ice-cream cone, and he was rushing to finish it. In the heat it was melting fast.

"It's personal now," the aide said. "It's a fight: Bykov versus Lebed."

Bykov was Anatoly Bykov, like Lebed a former boxer, and for a good stretch of the 1990s, the boss of KRAZ, the city's aluminum plant, the biggest in Russia. Bykov was known locally as the Bull, *byk* being the Russian word for the animal. A fight for power was now joined, Lebed's adviser said. He had grown worried of late about the general. Things had gotten out of hand, indeed had grown personal. Reports had long held that Bykov had backed Lebed with funds, hoping for a cozy relationship. But the enmity, the aide said, had run deep from the start. When Lebed arrived in town to assume the governorship, Bykov had come calling. The two had locked themselves in the governor's office, told everyone to go home, taken off their suit coats, and brawled. "They beat the hell out of each other," the aide said. "And the fight continues to this day."

As the celebrants filed out of the theater, I found Lebed surrounded by a double scrum of paratroopers. On home leave from Chechnya, they had no questions for the governor. They wanted only to take their pictures with him. Lebed obliged. I stood a few feet away, trying to stay out of the way. I was on the edge of the huddle when an elbow hit my ribs. It was not a bodyguard. It was Yevdokiya Georgievna, a stout pensioner in her seventies who wore a chestful of medals across a forest green uniform. She had a question for the governor.

"Why aren't you answering my letters?" she thundered at close range.

Lebed froze.

"It's my car," she shouted. "You must do something about it."

The governor did not shift his weight. The paratroopers moved close, but he had nowhere to hide.

"I don't need the car," Yevdokiya said, "but my grandson does." She told her story briefly: She'd been a nurse on the Ukrainian front in the war, her pension at nearly fifty dollars more than sufficed, and the car, a tiny Russian-made two-seater, had been an unexpected bonus. As she had no use for it, she gave it to her grandson. But now, she told Lebed, the army informed her she couldn't leave the boy the car when she died. "It goes back to them," she said, "the *chinovniki*."

Yevdokiya had hit one of Lebed's favorite enemies–"the bureaucrats." The governor guided her into a mutual attack on "the great morass of brainless bureaucrats who slither beneath our legs, threatening to strangle the heroes of our Motherland." The invective seemed a touch too sexual, but Lebed won over everyone in earshot. The paratroopers peeled off, exulting in the radiance of power and eager to reach the beer kiosks across the square. Yevdokiya only smiled and nodded faster. Even the governor's bodyguards grinned. As Lebed and his entourage vanished in a convoy of Land Cruisers and Mercedes 600s, I asked Yevdokiya if Lebed's response had sufficed. She shook her head. "*Da nyet*," she said, two words that on their own mean "yes" and "no" but when conjoined form a wondrous idiom in which *nyet* strips *da* of its force. *Da nyet* means "come off it," "not a chance," "forget it"–pronouncements that betrayed the national fatalism few could shake. "Nothing of course will happen," she said, "but I got it off my chest."

I walked her home. She lived alone now, not far away. As we moved through the afternoon crowd shopping on an elm-lined street, Yevdokiya offered a warning. Privileges, she said, stopping in her tracks and clasping my arm, were for the folks in Moscow. Promises were for the poor souls in the provinces. "But out here in Siberia," she said, "you learn there's only one person who'll help you survive, yourself."

CHEKHOV, ON HIS EPIC journey east to Sakhalin in 1890, had stopped off in Krasnoyarsk. At thirty, and already coughing up blood from the consumption that was to kill him at forty-four, he crossed the Urals to become the first Russian writer to travel to Siberia of his own will. After enduring a tortuous ride by tarantass, an open horse-drawn carriage, across the Urals and western Siberia, Chekhov's spirits soared at the sight of the Yenisei. In Krasnoyarsk, he could take the measure of the distance he had traveled from Moscow. His journey to the empire's edge would continue to be arduous, but here it acquired the depth of discovery. In Krasnoyarsk's cultural circles Chekhov found unexpected proof that "intelligent life existed in Siberia after all."

One hundred and ten years later the city afforded the same relief. It offered a chance to measure how far into Siberia Moscow cast its shadows. Here, too, to be sure, were the corruption, the venality, the health crisis, and the undisguised law of post-Soviet economics that raw muscle plus political patronage equals absolute financial power. At the same time, Krasnoyarsk told another story. It testified to the adage I had heard so often in Russia's remote corners: "The farther from Moscow we live, the better."

On a building on Karl Marx Street downtown I read a plaque: "The leaders of the Bolshevik Party met here in 1905." Around the corner of the same house a poster announced: "Test for AIDS here." On nearby Lenin Street, I passed a pair of Jehovah Witnesses from Michigan looking lost. I tried to steer them in the right direction. But they were searching for an old Soviet House of Culture, and I could not help. A girl standing at the bus stop, however, knew the way.

I came to the city's main square. At one edge loomed the Ballet and Opera Theater, where the paratroopers had gathered. A vast rectangular fountain dominated the square's center. The fountain, a labyrinth of lanky pipes that spun slowly and delicately sprayed water in a choreographed spectacle, lured crowds from the heat of distant apartments. A statue of

Chekhov marked the square's southern edge, above the graduated river-bank. Chekhov stood looking out over the Yenisei. His lips seemed pursed in some secret knowledge.

I sat on a bench in the square between two young couples sipping canned gin and tonics. It was dark, but the square, the heart of the city in summer, was filled with people. They walked slowly, mesmerized by the fountain's long arms, which danced and sprayed wet streams of cool air. A girl stood nearby. Two drunks, beer bottles in hand, were failing, loudly, to entice her to their hotel room. They were Russian tourists who had spent the day raising shot glasses to the paratroopers' health. The girl stood her ground, arms folded at her thin waist. She stared straight ahead, at the fountain. In a moment with a razor laugh and a shake of her head she fended them off.

The fountain was new, she said. She loved it—and all other new ones the mayor had built across town. It was only water, of course, but the fountain gave the people something. "It softens the city at night," she said, staring at the turning pipes, "and lightens our souls."

She was, I realized, the girl from the bus stop who had shown the missionaries from Michigan the way to the House of Culture. Aleysa was twenty, a student, the daughter of two mathematicians, and she had never met an American.

"You must think we're crazy to live out here," she said. "But this is a different world. You look at the television; Moscow, Petersburg, Vladivostok—they're losing their own culture. We're so cut off things come here late, and some things never come." It did not sound like a lament. At one end of the square, on a wooden stage raised off the concrete, a circle of boys, fourteen or sixteen years old, entertained the crowd with updated improvisations of old Cossack dances. In a blur of tightly wound bodies, they spun circles on the square stage, marking its edges loudly with one-foot stomps. The crowd kept pace, clapping out their appreciation.

Where would she go, I asked, if she could live anywhere?

Aleysa thought for a time, staring at the boys dancing. "Nowhere," she said. "This is Siberia, not Moscow. The air's lighter here, and the people are more open." Of course everyone now was trying to get ahead, and many would do whatever it took. But Krasnoyarsk was nothing like the tales she heard of Moscow. Here you could still be honest and survive. She had started waitressing at a new café, Domino, off Karl Marx Street. She worked from noon until 2:00 A.M. and earned less than five dollars a day. She had no complaints. Her father was a professor, and he of course earned far less.

We stood on the far edge of the crowd before the stage, watching the blur of dancers in their Cossack routines. Their shirts, soaked with sweat, caught the dim light of the beer kiosks that ringed the square. The boys fell, arms crossed, to one knee, then rose again. They were still spinning and stomping when I bade Aleysa farewell. As I crossed the square and headed back to the hotel, her last words rang in my ears: "I love our Krasnoyarsk."

🦢 TWO 🦢

I HAD NOT INTENDED to travel with General Nikolai Vladimirovich Numerov. I wanted to take a Gulag tour. For years a Moscow travel agency had offered trips to the ruins of Stalin's camps. The tours, I imagined, would attract ideal company, the curious descendants of those who had perished in the Gulag. But by the time I set out for Norilsk, I discovered the tours were passé. "The fashion's gone," a Moscow travel agent said. "The Gulag didn't sell."

General Numerov was only too pleased to have me join his expedition. "Our general," as everyone on the *Matrosov* grew to call him, was on his way back, for the first time in fifty years, to Norilsk, where he had been imprisoned in one of Stalin's most notorious labor camps after World War II. Not only had he survived, but in the years of Gorbachev he became something a celebrity among Gulag veterans. In 1989 he attended the founding congress of the Memorial Society. Known simply as Memorial, the group, led by dissidents and liberal historians, bloomed into one of Russia's rare grass-roots associations with promise. Backed by Western foundations, Memorial became one of the few national organizations dedicated to ending Russia's moral and historical eclipse. It was not the general's crowd. He soon broke with the "longhairs" and "squabbling dissidents" to found his own Association of the Victims of Political Repression. He now claimed three hundred thousand members across the country.

At eighty-one, with his great shock of white hair, ramrod frame, and booming tenor, the general still commanded attention. Months earlier I had gone to see him in the barren headquarters of his association in Moscow. The office revealed a lack of funding. It was spacious enough to impress but too large to heat. The decorations on the wall behind his desk warned of what I heard in the months ahead. On the left hung an old black and white portrait of Marshal Georgi Zhukov, the Soviet general who had staved off Hitler's march on Moscow in 1941. On the right hung a small metal icon in a wooden frame, an image of Nikolai the Miracle Worker, the general's patron saint. A glossy portrait of Putin at his Kremlin desk dominated the space in between. Putin sat awkwardly, as if he had stolen a chance to pose for the photo while the boss was at lunch. (The portrait, a Kremlin aide had said, was taken just hours after Yeltsin had resigned.)

"Let me tell you something, Anders . . . " For some reason, apparently discerning Scandinavian features I do not possess, the general decided to call me Anders. I tried to correct him, but he persisted. "Having you with me helps. You will record my journey for posterity." He had left, however, little to record. The general had just published the second volume of his memoirs, *The Golden Star of the Gulag*. The back cover offered a modest summary: "Perhaps everything that could befall the destiny of a Russian man in the past eighty years—this is what Nikolai Vladimirovich Numerov survived. Fate, merciless to millions of his peers, for some reason saved him. Was it not to try to embody in one man the history of an entire country, the history of Russia?"

It was, he promised, a great epic. Not only was he an honored son of the Motherland, a distinguished son of the Don Cossacks, but he was one of the few Russians alive who had survived imprisonment under both Stalin and Hitler. He had fought valiantly on the southern front against the Nazis only to get shelled, lose consciousness, and awaken a prisoner of war. He was, moreover, the last survivor of the Communist underground that had worked behind enemy lines in Berlin. The others had been tortured to death. He alone escaped. And for that, upon returning to his Soviet homeland, he had suffered—and still suffered.

"I have seen the inside of the Lubyanka, the KGB interrogation cells in Lithuania, the black hole of a barge's hold traveling up the Yenisei. Packed like sardines! Then the miserable, indescribable horrors of Norilsk! Then the mine I ran in Norilsk for seven years. The Medvezhka, one of the world's biggest mines! The labor, endless labor! This is not something any man can tell you. And my life after the camps. A wife destroyed by KGB lies and sadism. A little boy whose childhood I missed. A life where my every step is watched. But all this you will see."

The timing of the general's return voyage was auspicious, but I had my doubts about him and his story. Norilsk would be celebrating a jubilee, the sixty-fifth anniversary of the giant metals complex, the Kombinat (Combine), as the locals called it. The general's trip was to coincide with the festivities. However, the folks at the Krasnoyarsk branch of Memorial, the sponsors of his return, were clever. They planned to use his trip as an occasion to mark not the Kombinat's birthday but the anniversary of Noril'lag, the first Gulag camp that grew into the city of Norilsk.

The general required an entourage. He didn't really want one, he assured me, but Governor Lebed had insisted. Lebed had hired the general as an unpaid adviser. Lebed despised Communists, Stalinists all the more. He had, the general said, taken a liking to him and an interest in his trip back to Norilsk. Lebed, he added, had suggested memorializing the trip in an exhibit in the Krasnoyarsk museum. Out of his respect for the general's wisdom, Lebed even dipped into his coffers to fund the production, soon to be known among its members, as "Return to Norilsk."

No one made the distinction, but I did not belong to the general's promotional team. However, everyone else in his entourage–a motley quintet– did. There was Oleg, the designer; Vladimir, the videographer; and Volodya, the archivist. Leading the way, by virtue of her status as the directress of the Krasnoyarsk History Museum, formerly the Krasnoyarsk Lenin Museum (a terrifying red brick edifice that towered above the left bank of the Yenisei), was Galina. A stocky platinum blonde with a Soviet sense of propriety and a weakness for Crimean champagne, Galina adored the general. She made his tea and squeezed his lemons. Galina had slipped into the traveling crew thanks to a dark conspiracy that reached all the way to Lebed.

That at least was the tale rich in betrayal and greed that Olga told me. Petite, well coiffed, and in her forties, Olga worked as Galina's deputy in the museum. The two, it seemed, were engaged in a twenty years' war. The latest skirmish had come that day. Galina had managed to push Olga off the manifest on the eve of our departure from Krasnoyarsk. Olga appeared at my hotel room in tears. As her mascara ran, she pleaded that she had been the real producer of "Return to Norilsk." The trip was all her idea. She'd arranged everything from the general's suite on the boat to the museum's illuminated glass displays. Norilsk, Olga said, as convulsions neared, was her first home, her lost home. The daughter of a Pole who had died in the camps, she had lived in Norilsk for more than a decade. She just had to go back.

It was too much to take. I caved in. I volunteered to buy her a ticket on the boat. Neither compassion nor pity moved me. I only wanted to see Galina, the Soviet ogre, blanch when Olga climbed aboard. But Olga now bubbled. "She'll think I'm an American spy," she shrieked with joy.

EARLY THE NEXT morning I boarded the *Matrosov*, falling in with the families and teenagers. Standing against the rail of the uppermost deck, I noticed an old man in the crowd of well-wishers on the concrete shore. He wore a gray suit and a gray cap. In his hands was a white plastic bag filled with cedar cones from the woods nearby. When I climbed down to buy one, he leaned close and confided: "They sell the oil from these seeds to the Japanese and Germans for millions. They help you where it counts. They nourish your organ." He was charging not quite two cents a cone for this all-natural virility boost. I handed him a hundred rubles and took one to taste.

Aleksandr was eighty. For thirteen years he had worked the mines of Norilsk. He was first arrested in Kiev, during the war, for the crime of being a Ukrainian peasant. He was arrested the second time in Krasnoyarsk. That time he had not even been given a reason. Sentenced to a dozen years, he spent thirteen in the camps. Now he had no teeth left and no family either. His wife had died last year, killed on her way home by a tram. His pension had fallen to twenty-seven dollars, he told me, translating the rubles into dollars to flaunt a knowledge of the exchange rate. These days, he got by only thanks to the cones. His industry was impressive, but he refused any praise. "I'm nothing unusual," he said. "We all get by like this—surviving, not living. Everyone around here, we're all orphans of the Gulag."

As we pushed off, the loudspeakers along the *Matrosov*'s three decks blared a prerevolutionary battle march, and the boat creaked out onto the vast riverway. "Capacity load," a deckhand said. "Two hundred and sixty eager tourists on the river." We eased slowly out of the city, passing the gray hulk of the aluminum plant. Beneath us the river's dark waters churned. First the well-wishers waving good-bye from the shore, then the dark contours of the city itself faded from view. A sinking dread arose in me. Instead of the Gulag tour I had envisioned, I feared a booze cruise. The boat was packed with teenagers, students on a summer holiday. For them the fortnight up and down the Yenisei offered opportunity: drinking and dancing and long nights without parents or obligation.

Lunch brought relief. There was no sign of the Siberian mall rats. The dining room was elegant. It overlooked the ship's bow and was lined with windows draped with gold lace. "A mini-*Titanic*," noted Oleg, the artistic designer of the museum exhibit our trip was destined to become. Tall and sinewy, Oleg was soft-spoken and eager that I join him before meals in emptying his "aquarium," a jug of home brew, a vodka base tinged with berries and wild grasses. It was delicious. Oleg never talked of his time in the army, but Olga did. He was, she whispered, a former *spetsnaz* officer, a veteran of the Soviet special forces, who'd served in Vietnam and Africa.

Next to Oleg sat Olga. Buying her a ticket, I realized, raised a problem. We would have to share a cabin. Thankfully, Volodya Birger, the trip's designated archivist, seconded from the Krasnoyarsk branch of Memorial, was also on board. A shy, pony-tailed computer programmer who seemed innately incapable of guile, Volodya had volunteered to work in Memorial from its founding. In the years since the Soviet collapse, he had struck an unlikely partnership with the Interior Ministry officers in Krasnoyarsk who held the archives of the Norilsk camps. Volodya was permitted into the archives in exchange for saving the policemen from the pleas of the children and grandchildren eager to rehabilitate relatives. And so, for nearly a decade now, Volodya had set himself an unenviable mission: to scour the archives for the scant details of the lives lost to the camps.

By the second day I had had enough of the general's production. I started to walk the decks with greater frequency and expectation. While the boat did not brim with the yearning for historical recovery, it held promise. Russian couples on holiday lined the decks. Some in their early thirties wore shorts and sunglasses; others in their seventies had cotton stuffed in their ears. By the second afternoon I had met most of them. They had come from all over: Vladivostok in the Far East, Yekaterinburg in the Urals, Samara on the Volga, Chelyabinsk in central Siberia. We had yet to stop, but the passengers had already divided into camps. The cardplayers and the smokers held firm to the top decks, while the choralers and piano players retreated behind the lace curtains of the music parlor. The crew, all the while, remained in a private realm, the windowless bottom tier of the boat, well below the waterline.

To my amazement, I was not the only American on board. I was standing out on deck with Volodya when I first heard the thick Boston accent: "No more bang-bang! We're friends, friends, now! Peace, not war!" Jim Conboy, a seventy-three-year-old retired pulp mill worker from Massachusetts, was a tall man with a long, ruddy face. His gray hair stood on end in a razor-sharp buzz cut. By the third meal he had attracted the boat's attention. Jim had become Dzhim. In the years since the Soviet collapse he had taken to coming to Russia, leaving Peg, his wife, and three grown children at home. Each year he spent months traveling the outback of the old USSR.

Jim wore two hearing aids and spoke one word of Russian, *normal'no*. "Normal," he said with a laugh. "Everything's always normal. No matter what I ask these kids, the answer's always *normal'no*." Jim could not fathom it. "Just what in this country would you call normal?"

Jim was a hit. Wherever he went, a circle of kids followed. "No more bang-bang!" he'd tell them. "No more boom-boom! The cold war is dead. We're friends now, friends." The declaration was accompanied by hand signals. To illustrate the cold war's aggression, he extended his forefingers and shook them like a cowboy with six-shooters. For peace and friendship, he clasped his hands together and smiled. If he failed to elicit a smile, Jim covered his heart with both hands.

He soon found a partner to play cards, a shy blond woman on the cusp of middle age. Galina introduced herself as a member of "the new professional class." Warm and without pretense, with a penchant for ironed white slacks and thin cashmere sweaters, Galina spoke conversational German—"residue of an ex-boyfriend"—and a smattering of English she had picked up during an extended Swiss sojourn. She was a marketing director for a security company—"from apartment steel doors to car alarms to bodyguards." For years ads for the Spanish bouillon Gallina Blanca had flooded Russia's airwaves. Within hours the school kids in our midst had nicknamed her Galina Blanca.

Then there was the German, as he was known. For the first day he kept to himself. Well equipped with rain gear, thermos, and compass, the German wandered the boat in silence. On the second day he started to talk. His fluency in Russian betrayed an extended stay in the country. Once Jim got to him, the German warmed up. We learned he was an agricultural engineer who had come to lend Bavarian experience to a farming project on the banks of the Volga. His name was Kristoph. But for the duration of the trip he remained the German.

I HAD BEEN STANDING astern on the top deck when I heard the shouting. "Come, Andrew, quick."

It was Oleg, one deck below. Only a hour or so north of Krasnoyarsk, and already he was showing me the sites. I knew we were going to pass one of the Soviet Union's most secret atomic sites, the subterranean labyrinth code-named Krasnoyarsk-26, once one of the world's most prodigious producers of plutonium. Built to make the fissile material for nuclear warheads, the entire complex had been constructed inside the mountain. It never appeared on Soviet maps. The map I carried, printed during Yeltsin's reign, marked the site's location with a single word, *izba*, a hut.

I did not want to miss it, but I had not expected help. Oleg knew just where the secret complex started. He had worked as a welder there for years. He pointed to the fences, three that ran evenly spaced from the riverbank to the top of the mountain. Trees covered the hills, but Oleg made sure I saw the holes, lined by cement, in the side of the mountain. "Tunnels," he said. He pointed to banners of black clouds that rose softly above the horizon. "Waste," he said, from the invisible smokestacks. He still remembered the size of the flowers on top of the mountain. They were huge, he said, "unbelievable."

The general, coming on deck for the first time, was not pleased. "Now wait a minute, Oleg," he commanded. "You know such sites mustn't be shown to eyes of NATO." He was only half joking.

"What's the worry?" said a blond woman standing at the rail. She wore dark sunglasses and a pantsuit of yellow linen. Her hair was short, cut at a fashionable angle. "We know every secret about the place," she announced. "We live there."

Irina introduced herself. To her the secret complex was Zheleznogorsk

(Iron City), a city of ninety-eight thousand people that boasted apartment high rises, trams, restaurants, nightclubs, and one struggling casino. Zheleznogorsk had come out since the Soviet fall, shedding its code name in 1994. Life there, Irina attested, was *normal'no*. She and her husband, Sasha, and their teenage son, Andrei, loved it.

Irina and Sasha had long dreamed of cruising the Yenisei, but this was their first river trip. Invariably, no matter what the time was, they stood out on deck and smiled as the lifeless banks passed. Irina was a lawyer. She had spent her "Soviet career," as she put it, in the prosecutor's office. She had specialized in rape and domestic violence. But recently she'd gone out on her own, opened an office and delved into corporate law. She wore elegant clothes, no matter the hour, and changed nightly for dinner. "It's a good place to raise kids," she said of their atomic city. "They grow bigger there than anywhere else."

As Oleg and Irina debated in jest the merits of child rearing in heightened radioactivity, the loudspeaker blared: "Respected passengers, we are now passing the city of Zheleznogorsk, once a top secret location established in 1950 by the Council of Ministers of the USSR." The invisible tour guide sat in the upper reaches of the boat, never making an appearance. She burst forth periodically to give the weather forecast, a short history of a passing exile village, or the starting time for a Schwarzenegger film in the video hall. Whatever the subject, she maintained a monotone that belied any interest in her own pronouncements.

"In the days of the cold war," the loudspeaker proclaimed, "this location was a critical point in our Motherland's defense. In those days this area was closed to citizens. Now, however, the cold war has ended, and we can again take pleasure in the flora and fauna of this region along our beautiful Yenisei."

Fortunately, I had Volodya for a bunkmate. He filled in the blanks. In 1950 the Soviets had ordered the construction of Sibkhimstroi, the Siberian Chemical and Mining Combine. It took years and sixty-five thousand prison laborers to build the secret complex, a thousand feet beneath the Jurassic ore. The fences I'd seen circumscribed an area of fifty square miles. Of its twenty-two divisions, three were most important: the plutonium production reactors. The underground complex also housed a reprocessing facility for separating plutonium from spent nuclear fuel. After Stalin died, troops replaced the zeks on the construction, and in

1958 the first reactor went into operation. Two more came on line in the 1960s. (The Krasnoyarsk-26 reactors served as the template for the infamous Chernobyl RBMK reactors.) The design was ingenious, if mad. The complex was built not only to avoid detection but to survive a nuclear attack. After Armageddon, Krasnoyarsk-26 would keep making bombs. "It's a catacombs," Oleg said, "worthy of its fame." Seven million cubic meters in all, nearly as big as the Moscow metro system. Pollution, however, was a worry. The water used to cool the reactors came from the river.[2]

I asked Irina and Sasha, loyal residents of the radioactive town, what they made of the MinAtom plan. The Ministry of Atomic Energy was pushing for a law allowing the importation of nuclear waste. The proposal stirred sentiment. Greenpeace activists had dumped radioactive soil on the steps of the Duma. One lawmaker had worried Russia would become "the world's nuclear toilet." MinAtom promised a windfall, twenty billion dollars over a decade if Russia imported twenty thousand kilograms of waste.

Nikolai Kharitonov, leader of the Agrarian party, was outraged at the attempts to block the law. "When the Russian people find out how valuable this so-called waste is," he declared on the Duma floor, "they'll be running by the thousands to pick up a barrelful and put it under the mattresses. They will realize they'll be sleeping on gold."

Irina and Sasha were not worried about the gamma rays that poured from the mountain. Irina said the problem was how to employ all the people who had lost their jobs as a result of the cold war's end. "If only we'd stayed enemies," she sighed. "All those poor people could now buy European clothes!"

Sasha looked on the bright side. Two reactors had been shut down. The third still produced plutonium, but it also delivered heat and electricity to the locals. "The way I see it," he said, "we're lucky. Now we get heat in the winter."[3]

IT WAS A BLESSING to bunk with a loner. Volodya Birger, as I had sensed the moment I picked him out of the throng that stormed the ramparts of the *Matrosov*, proved the antidote to Shvedov, an ideal companion for the week on the Yenisei. Volodya had just turned forty-nine. But on the night of his birthday he never made it to the cake. He had suffered, he told me one morning as we puffed away on his cheap cigarettes, a heart attack.

Volodya was slight, with a body more befitting a teenager. No one would guess his age. He wore, every day, black jeans and a T-shirt emblazoned with a blurry image of a young boy and girl. The boy appeared to be Leonardo DiCaprio. Volodya had a morning ritual of brushing out his long black hair and tying it back with an old red rubber band. He wore thick glasses that did little to discourage the impression of a forlorn, vulnerable outcast. Yet when he removed the glasses, you caught a glimpse of Volodya. Freed of their shield, his eyes brightened.

He, too, was a victim of the camps. His father had traveled the Yenisei by barge to serve five years in Norilsk. Released in 1944, he had returned—with his young family—within a decade. Volodya had spent his first years in Norilsk. The family had left when he was five. He had not been back since. Though Volodya did not like to speak of it, he, too, had suffered Soviet officialdom. As a student he'd been kicked out of the institute in Kharkov, deemed an undesirable, not Komsomol material. His, he grinned, had been "an embarrassingly mild form of dissidence," but enough to earn "a dissident's ID," a rare document that termed his offense "the holding of views not in accordance with the status of a Soviet student."

Our cabin, like the dining room, possessed a well-worn elegance. A rounded half table separated our bunks, a porcelain washbasin stood behind the door, and a curtain of white lace covered a fogged window. On the wall above Volodya's bunk a romantic landscape hung in a frame. It was a snow-capped mountain, more Caucasian than Siberian, we agreed, more Vladikavkaz than Krasnoyarsk.

In public, Volodya had perfected the art of disappearing. But in the narrow fraternity of our cabin, he shone. He would grab his guitar and without a word begin to play. He played every day, first after a morning smoke and last just before bed. As his fingers plucked at the worn metal strings, the resonance seemed to calm him, to carry him to a gentler realm than the one he had to inhabit. He played folk songs, the treasured inheritance of the bard poets of the Soviet century.

"Kipling Soldier," a Leningrad ballad from the 1960s, was a favorite:

Again, the road, I'm with you, my desire all burned out
I've got neither God nor the devil nor a wife
The West is still a foreign land, and the East is not my East
While at my back is the smell of burning bridges.
Today I see tomorrow differently from yesterday.
Victory, like revenge, depends on the cost.
As the thirteenth soldier I shall die, and to hell with it–
I don't even know how to live, let alone to kill.

It seemed an odd anthem for a bookish man-child who would suffer swatting a wasp. Yet as the days passed, and he strummed it out again and again, the more sense the song made. Like Kipling's soldier, Volodya could not find his place. He reminded me of the *yurodivi*, the holy fools of Russian lore. Tolerated by the church, they lived in society's margins. They did not claim spiritual superiority; they gained it by their mystery. Other than his wife and son, Volodya had few cares and fewer desires. He was, however, passionate about his cards.

Each night he took out a tall stack of index cards and a pen and methodically recorded the details of a life lost to the state. "Name, Hometown, Date of Birth, Statute, Transit Prison, Year of Arrival, Year in Camp, Year of Departure . . ." He'd been compiling the cards for thirteen years. His goal was to document everyone who had passed through the camps of the Krasnoyarsk region. He knew it was a Sisyphean task, but his archive of cards was formidable. It comprised nearly thirty-six thousand cases. Recently he had begun to compile them in a digital database.

This mission to memorialize the dead was painstaking. Volodya interviewed the survivors and their relatives who walked into the Memorial office in Krasnoyarsk, tracked down living relatives who did not, dug up prison records, corroborated oral histories, and all the while cultivated the policemen who guarded the camp archives. But when he described his work, it was as if he were speaking of mushroom picking. "All depends on the week," he said. "In a good one, sometimes you'll get twenty." Twenty new cards, he meant, twenty fates to add to the catalog.

It was not simply the admirable pursuit of an amateur historian. Thanks to the Law on Rehabilitation passed in the last days of the USSR, the heirs of Stalin's victims were entitled to compensation. The maximum allowed by law was "one hundred times the minimum wage." "Not much, of course," Volodya conceded, "but for many it's a hundred times what they make."

IN THE AFTERNOONS, when I tried to escape the general and his entourage, I spent time at the edges of Jim's circle on deck. He entertained the kids and Galina Blanca and the German with talk of life back in the States. The Russians could not fathom Jim. He held court in the long afternoons, talking of his twenty-eight years in the machine factory in South Walpole. He told how he'd saved all his life, and now he and Peg had more than enough. He told of his grandson, a medical student, who worked hard in off hours to pay his way through school. He told of the boy's father, a Vietnam vet who had come home, got married, and got a good job, only to leave one spring night sixteen years ago and never reappear. In story after story, Jim may have had more to say about Jeffersonian democracy and the limits of the free market than any of the well-funded Western consultants who had trespassed deep into Russia with the best intentions of helping the natives replicate, preferably as soon as possible, the American way of life. Each day Jim's story hour followed the same theme: how to build a life on hard work and doing what's right. "Peg and I've been together forty-nine years," he said one day. "When I get home she'll ask, 'How'd it go?' And I'll say, 'Okay.' She'll say, 'Fine,' and then go to the market. We've both got our passions. She has line dancing at the town hall with the girls. And I have Russia."

ONE EVENING, AS the teen horde flooded the disco that roosted each night on the top deck, I found Sasha and Irina, the couple from Krasnoyarsk-26, sitting on plastic chairs and sipping Crimean champagne from plastic cups. They were sitting near the railing with two other tourists, a man and a woman, both doctors, but traveling separately. The foursome was giddy.

"It's the most wonderful coincidence!" Irina cried. "We're all from radioactive cities!"

The doctors had come from Chelyabinsk, a city in the Urals also famed as a production center of the Soviet nuclear arsenal. "So here's to growing supersize vegetables!" the female doctor shouted.

I joined them in the toast. But as the loudspeakers again blared Ricky Martin, I headed down to the hold, to the only room on the *Matrosov* where all its contingents commingled. I went down to the bar for a beer. Inside its smoked glass doors, I ran into Sergei. We had played cards on the aft deck. He sold spare parts back in Krasnoyarsk, for air conditioners from Italy. Siberia was a new niche for the company, but so far a profitable one. Sergei was short, in his forties, and, he lamented, fast going bald. He had a round face, a bushy mustache, and gentle dark eyes. He was vacationing alone and determined to have a good time.

Sergei clutched me. "I need you," he said. "Lyosha's dead." He explained: He'd just bumped into an old acquaintance and asked after a mutual friend, only to learn that Lyosha was dead. "So please sit with me," he begged, "and drink." It was not right, he said, to drink to the dead alone.

We sat at a small wooden table, one of four in the bar. It was nailed to the floor and covered with a burgundy plastic tablecloth. He ordered tall shots of vodka, followed by beer. Behind us were a group of young toughs, seven or eight in all. Half-empty vodka bottles crowded their tables. The boys were smoking and boasting loudly.

"He was a good friend, Lyosha," Sergei said. "But let us not think of what's gone. Let's drink to new beginnings! To friendships among nations!" In another shot, I knew, there would be no more mention of the dearly departed. After years in Russia, little frightened me more after midnight than an opened bottle of vodka. Once opened, bottles in Russia are never corked.

As we poured down the vodka, we crossed, as expected, the Handshake on the Elba and moved on to the Apollo-Soyuz union in space. Our meeting, Sergei was certain, was "a great moment in the history of two nations. Your great land," he added, "and our shitty one." So began Sergei's confessional, an epic of regret that, after an hour or two, left its mark. It haunted me for days, till we reached Dudinka, the old timber port that was our final stop on the Yenisei. And it haunted Sergei.

We were halfway down the bottle of vodka when his cheery air deserted Sergei. His face darkened, and his voice fell to a whisper. He said he wanted to tell me a story he'd never told anyone. These days, he said, who was going to care? "Now," he added as if to reassure himself, "we've got no more secrets, right?" Behind us heads thumped against wood with greater frequency. Sergei stepped out on the limb. His mother, he said, his eyes no more than a hand from mine, had served in the KGB. Her whole life. Worse than that, he said, she had worked with the Stasi, the East German secret police.

I was not sure how to take the news. When he had spun jokes on the sunny deck, I'd known how to play. I knew the rules. But here, in the bar that had suddenly grown dark and stuffy, I had no idea how to proceed.

"I've lived my entire life lying. I was born in Leipzig. But I've always had to lie whenever anyone asked why. I say, 'My parents were working in East Germany.' I could never tell the truth. We were there because of my mother's job. My father left when I was a kid. She's a good person, but this is what I have to live with. She knew what she was doing, but she did what she was told."

Sergei lapsed into silence. When he surfaced, he had found clarity. "They were criminals, weren't they?" he said, looking hard into my eyes. "The KGB, the Stasi, their armies of informants. They were the ones who kept the people enslaved, no? They could not now be excused, could they?"

I looked at Sergei. His eyes were no longer round and smiling. He was crying.

"Someone had to suffer for their sins, right?"

"Someone did," I said. I filled the shot glasses and proposed a toast: "To living as honest a life as possible."

Sergei lifted his glass and offered his own. "To finding a friend to tell one's lies to."

❧ THREE ❧

THE CREW OF THE *Matrosov*–the cooks and engine room men, wait-resses and waiters–kept to the lower depths. Only by accident or necessity did they reveal glimpses of their world. There was the furtive trade, of course. At twilight, for no apparent reason we'd quietly drop anchor in the middle of the river. A metal dinghy with an old motor would chug off to rendezvous with the local fishermen. It was a simple barter: beer and vodka for gleaming fat sturgeon. And there was the sex. The showers were narrow cabinets, three in a row down in the hold. One morning I nearly ran into a cook, a lithe boy in his twenties, as he stepped out of one. Behind him, holding his hand, was a sloe-eyed girl of no more than sixteen.

In the afternoons everyone seemed to come out on deck. The villages came onto the horizon less frequently, one before lunch, another before dinner. We watched the water ripple beside us and the steep shores that lined our course. For days the setting had not shifted. The soft roar of a sudden motorboat, two fishermen hawking their wares, was enough to spark a rush to the rails. As the sun set port, the moon rose starboard, and we pushed on past a logger's train. A rusting trawler pulled a tail of timber nearly half a mile long. Bound by a perimeter of chained logs, the rectangle of floating wood filled the river's middle. The logs, hundreds in a jumbled row, spun in the river's darkening waters but did not stray.

The Yenisei is one of the great rivers; from its start in Mongolia it runs thirty-five hundred miles to the Arctic. As we glided on north, but downriver, the banks flattened. It was as if the earth were stretching its arms, over the pole, to touch its feet. The *materik*, the mainland, as the people of the far north call the rest of Russia, slipped away, behind us.

ON THE FOURTH DAY we stopped in Turukhansk, the first Russian settlement on the Yenisei. Here, as in all the desolate hamlets this far north, there was no dock, no jetty to greet us, only wind-bent huts and stray cows. We walked across a narrow gangplank and climbed the long, steep stairs up to the village.

Turukhansk, connected to the world by three radio séances a day, is one of the better-known villages of these reaches. On the eve of the Revolution, Stalin lived here. Exiled in 1913, he gained his freedom after the February Revolution, but he made good use of the secrecy the isolation afforded. In Turukhansk he plotted with his fellow Bolsheviks. For most of his exile Stalin lived in the village of Kureika to the north. He left his mark there, fathering a son with a fourteen-year-old orphan. The story of Stalin's lost son had long been rumored, but its details surfaced only when a sleuthing historian in Moscow came across a KGB report in the archives. More than twenty years the girl's elder, Stalin vowed to marry her—and avoid jail time—

when she turned sixteen. Instead he abandoned her and their boy, Aleksandr. (After reports of the historian's find made the press, a grandson even emerged, in Novokuznetsk.)[4]

The general joined me for a stroll through the village. We walked to a wooden cabin, the local museum. Once it had been the home of the Bolshevik Yakov Sverdlov during his tsarist exile. One of Lenin's closest comrades, Sverdlov would now be the answer to a good trivia question. He was the first Soviet president. He also happened to be Jewish. As we toured the museum, the general unburdened himself.

"You see, Anders, again the Jews." He was not whispering. "This mess we're in—all their fault. From the beginning they ran the Revolution. Their goal? Kill off as many Russians as they could. It's in their genes. Bloodthirsty bastards."

The disquisition on the ruinous Semitic conspiracies, I had learned by now, was a favorite of the general's. The Jews, he declared, had stolen Lenin's revolution. Trotsky? Nothing more than a saboteur seconded by the world Jewish movement. Feliks Dzerzhinsky, founder of the Cheka, the first Soviet secret police? Only the first of the generations of Jews who subverted the Okhrana, the tsar's noble secret police, into a brotherhood of vampires.

I was not alarmed by the rant. In Russia, after all, *The Protocols of the Elders of Zion* and *Mein Kampf* sold briskly at sidewalk kiosks.[5] I had grown used to, but not inured to, impromptu anti-Semitic tirades. The Jews, I had come to learn, were behind all the trouble that followed the Revolution: the murder of the tsar, civil war, famine, and seventy-plus years of suffering at the hands of Soviet central planners, who were themselves, of course, Jewish. The charges resounded in the strangest places. Once, in Yekaterinburg, I sought out the man who had unearthed the remains of the Romanovs. After years of fighting incredulous apparatchiks, Aleksandr Avdonin, an avuncular geologist turned amateur historian, was proved right about the bones of the last tsar and his family. But when he talked of their executioners, my skin crawled. He had amassed an impressive library devoted to the secret world of the great Judeo-Masonic conspiracy. The collection was so extensive that it seemed to betray more than a passing interest.

THE TURUKHANSK MUSEUM boasted three display cases. One, dedicated to Sverdlov, held copies of the letters and manuscripts he wrote during his exile here. Next to it stood a tall glass case that contained a few yellowed photographs of a woman with a broad face lit by giant luminous eyes. The third case displayed stuffed birds.

I recognized the woman in the photographs. Ariadna Efron was the daughter of Marina Tsvetaeva, one of the greatest Russian poets of the twentieth century, and Sergei Efron, a literary scholar turned Soviet spy. Ariadna, known as Alya, had spent six years in exile here. The museum case offered a paragraph on her parents' tragic lives. Soviet power destroyed millions of families. Few were as famous as Alya's. Born in Moscow, Alya as a young girl traveled with her mother in 1921 to Europe. With Efron, they settled in Paris, where Alya studied book illustration at the Louvre. In the spring of 1937 she returned to Moscow. Her father joined her later that year. By the summer of 1939 Tsvetaeva had also come home, bringing with her Alya's brother, Georgi. Within weeks of her mother's return, Alya was arrested. Her father was jailed a month later. Charged with espionage, Alya was sentenced to eight years. In August 1941 her father was shot. That same month Tsvetaeva hanged herself. And so by 1943, when Georgi fell at the front, Alya, at age thirty-two, had lost her entire family. (A sister, Irina, had died earlier, in a Moscow orphanage at age two.)

Alya had been exiled to Turukhansk for *vechnoe poselenie* (eternal settlement). Yet she later reminisced almost fondly of her years here. She worked in the village first as a janitor, then as an artist in the House of Culture. Here she began a relationship with Ada Federolf, a cultured teacher of English who had once lived in London, that spanned twenty-five years. In 1955 Alya was rehabilitated—"for the absence of evidence of a crime"—and resettled in Moscow. Ten years later, in 1965, she and Ada revisited Turukhansk. They, too, sailed on the *Matrosov*. As soon as Alya had climbed to the village plateau and again beheld the Yenisei—"the view imprinted in my heart forever"—she felt her soul lighten. "I felt this physical lightness, this vast relief," she wrote in a memoir of the pilgrimage. "Why? I do not know and never will know. I did not understand where this sense of peace and clarity came from. . . ."[6]

As we walked the sparse hamlet, it was clear that the last of the exiles had left long ago. Little remained of that "rail stop between life and death," as Alya called the Turukhansk she and Ada had known. The village in fact seemed worse off. Now it encompassed only four dirt roads, two small stores, one (closed) post office, and clouds of gnats everywhere. In front of one store a shingle read COLD BEER in Russian. The door was padlocked. "Boat's a week late," an old man explained. Throughout the village raised walkways, curling planks nailed into the earth, lined the dirt roads. When the snows melted and mud came, only the walkways, the old man said, made it possible to cross the village.

In the museum I found Baba Mariya, a round-faced grandmother from Kemerovo, the bleak city of coal miners far to the east. Baba Mariya smiled whenever I passed. She was traveling with her granddaughter, Katya. Every day, nine-year-old Katya wore pale pink ribbons, tied around the tips of her braided pigtails. They stood in front of the glass case that enshrined Alya's years of exile. Baba Mariya read every line in the display to Katya. Alya's enormous aquamarine eyes gazed out at the girl. "Have you understood what's written here about this lady?" her grandma asked. "How they sent her here even though she hadn't committed a crime?" The pigtails nodded. "Now be sure you never forget it."

IN THE EVENING I was sitting alone at the bow of the boat when the general put on his gold-rimmed sunglasses and came out to join me. After the museum he had retreated to his cabin. Turukhansk, it seemed, had taken its toll. The closer we got to Norilsk, the more he talked of Russia's future and not its history, of Putin's chances of survival and the need to rein in the oligarchs, the secret policemen, and NATO. The general, I realized, was having second thoughts about this voyage to his past.

"Anders," he said, "you seem like a fine young man."

He clasped my elbow.

"American, yes, but fine all the same. Did you know that I was arrested as an American spy? I'd never even met an American! I went to the Bolshoi with a girl. Took her to see *The Fountain at Bakhisarai*. Two couples, foreigners, sat in front of us. My girl spoke French with them. A phrase or two. I had no idea they were from the American Embassy! But from the loge across the way the fellows from Lubyanka filmed it all. Me, a spy for Uncle Sam! That's what they thought. And so that was it: I went to the ballet and ended up in Norilsk."

Even for a man who had survived, and survived nicely, surfacing from the camps only to rise again as a Soviet boss, there could be no nostalgia for the Gulag.

That night the crew treated us to fireworks. Where an old wooden sign on the shore read ARCTIC CIRCLE, they dropped anchor and organized a show. "Neptune's Holiday," they called it. Volunteers performed an hour of comic sketches in which girls danced as water fairies and the men from the Krasnoyarsk smelters donned white sheets and played vengeful Greek gods. Even the German got in the act. He painted on a goatee, robed himself in purple silk, and sat among a harem of young girls. It was not clear what it all had to do with the Arctic, but the spectacle entertained the crowd.

By midnight the disco had returned. The nightly standards, a mélange of post-Soviet pop, punctuated, almost on the half hour, by more Ricky Martin, blared as the sulfur lingered in the warm air. Volodya and Olga and the vacationers from the nuclear cities danced on the open deck. The horizon no longer hung low in front of the boat, pulling us north. As we sailed farther on, the earth's round edges seemed to close in. Thin streaks of pink spread across the bluish gray sky. An hour later both banks of the river were still visible. Darkness no longer separated day from night.

WE WERE HALFWAY along our journey up the Yenisei when the general at last was given the floor. He feared a low turnout, but the cruise director had taken to the loudspeaker that afternoon to announce the presentation of *The Golden Star of the Gulag*.

Half the boat had filled the disco. Near the front sat Baba Mariya, little Katya on her knees. At the back were Rinat and Alyosha, blue-eyed sixteen-year-olds from southern Siberia. I had stood with them at the rail as we crossed the Arctic Circle and the fireworks filled the bright night. We had talked until late. The boys had tried to lip-synch their way through a Petersburg rap, while I tried to translate the deeper meaning of Britney's "Oops! I Did It Again!"–and failed.

A few rows ahead sat Alyosha's parents. The trip was to celebrate their twenty-fifth anniversary. His father worked at the petroleum plant back home. He had a gray crew cut and a smile broken by gold- and silver-capped teeth. Maman, as he tenderly called Alyosha's mother, was stout, in her late forties, and proud of her men. Alyosha's folks, bemused to find an American in their midst, had shared their home brew with me. They took me into their circle, taught me their card games, and told me their greatest hope for their son. "He can have all the girls he wants," Maman said. "We just pray that God will keep his hands off the needle." Heroin, Alyosha had told me, had not only hit their small town but taken nearly all his friends under its wing.

The general did not disappoint. By the time his book reading came, the crew of "Return to Norilsk" had heard his stories several times. But as we sat in the front row of the crowded room, listening to him tell how the Lord led him, time and again, down the path between life and death, none of us could honestly say that our general was not indeed in his prime.

After the performance Volodya retreated to our cabin. He had picked up his old guitar, and his fingers were popping hard against its strings when I entered the room. He was fuming. "The old man's a victim of his own distorted memory, of course," he blurted out as he kept playing.

The general had declared, with his usual certitude, that "forty-five million had died" in Stalin's terror. Volodya knew well that no accurate tally of Stalinism's victims existed. He did not take errors of fact lightly. "And the bit about Lebed, you got that, of course." I had. The general had made sure to plug his beloved Lebed, saying that the governor sought only to bring justice and order to the Krasnoyarsk region, not to use it as a platform for presidential ambitions. The truth was closer to the opposite.

"And the pathological hatred of Gorbachev, glasnost, Yeltsin, and privatization?" I nodded. The general had digressed on a rant that described the decade and a half since Gorbachev's ascent as the worst years Russia had suffered since the Tatar yoke.

"Then you know he's right?"

I was confused.

"Oh, sure," said Volodya, "the thousand years of Russia's torture at the hands of enemies, the loss of our great Soviet forces, and of our once-great Olympic machine, not to mention the terrible and sudden melting of the permafrost in Norilsk and across the Arctic: This is all the fault of privatization. These are self-evident facts." It wasn't just the inaccuracies. Volodya could not brook the general's proselytizing, or that he'd donned the mantle of Memorial to make such an antireform stump speech. But even in anger,

Volodya only crossed his thin legs, picked up his guitar again, and strummed out "Kipling Soldier."

IGARKA, 150 MILES north of Turukhansk, looks like any other forlorn village atop the Yenisei's westerly bank. However, among historians and Gulag survivors, Igarka is famous. It once housed the headquarters of Construction Site No. 503, Stalin's railway to nowhere. Had it been completed, the project—so secret it had no name, only a number—would have been the world's most northerly railroad. The rails would have run across thousands of miles of frozen tundra, connecting Igarka with Salekhard, a forbidding settlement in northwestern Siberia. The project was not just an inefficient means of exterminating undesirables. Stalin dreamed of linking the far north with European Russia. He ordered construction to commence in 1949 even before the surveyors had charted the route.

As in Turukhansk, little trace of the prison labor remained. The dilapidated huts verged on collapse. They blended in with the barren landscape. We walked the dusty narrow streets for an hour, swatting the swarms of gnats and mosquitoes and trying not to swallow them. Other than the insects, Igarka had little to offer. A small new museum valiantly attempted to memorialize the lethal railway project. Its guests, it seemed, were a tough lot. At its entrance a scrawled sign announced: IT IS FORBIDDEN TO VISIT THE MUSEUM IN AN UNSOBER STATE. Across the way the general and his constant escort Galina were overjoyed to find the world's only Permafrost Museum. For them, venturing down iced-over stairs nearly fifty feet to touch genuine permafrost was the highlight of the afternoon. After an hour or so we all trudged back to the *Matrosov*, in silence, fighting the gnats and mosquitoes all the way.

I walked up to the top deck. It was almost deserted in the hot sun. At the rail stood the cop from the bar. In my mind, he had earned the moniker the first night, when I'd seen him in the bar downing shot after shot of vodka. He was tall, well over six feet. He had stood there, staring at the mirror behind the bar and saying nothing. He'd only nodded to the bartender when he required another shot. Now he was standing alone again, looking out at the gray shacks of Igarka.

"What a godless place," he said. His name was Shurik, short for Aleksandr. He did not move. He only stared at the empty shore. He said he had never seen such a desperate corner in all his life. He was from Novokuznetsk. He wasn't a cop. He ran security at the metals plant there. As we talked, Shurik looked at me out of one eye. "Every year," he said, "we take a vacation at the sea, Sochi, the Crimea, that kind of thing. But this year I told the wife, 'It's time. We're going to see where Grandpa died. We're going to take that Gulag tour.'"

His grandfather had been an ethnic German, sent here to work on Stalin's railway. For years Shurik had put it off. But now he knew he had done the right thing, to see this place. "To see where he walked, where he worked himself to death." Shurik stared straight ahead. We stood there together, taking in the silence. "Hey, why do you think," he asked after a moment, "all these people are still here?"

THE ISLAND LAY in the middle of the river. Improbably, it boasted a beach of golden sand. Dunes with bulrushes rolled on beyond. This was billed as a "leisure stop." The location, to believe the handwritten schedule on the dining room door, was a spit of land called Green Island. The sky was a cloudless blue. The sun was hot. The *Matrosov* was anchored in midriver. The crew had lowered the lifeboats and ferried us by the dozen to shore.

Everyone went swimming. The general emerged from a lifeboat sporting his sunglasses and a new crimson swimsuit. It was a Y-front affair that Galina had purchased for him in the Turukhansk store. He was tanned and, true to his words, "in fighting shape."

"Come on, Anders!" He beckoned across the teenagers sunbathing amid the black clouds of gnats. "Don't desert now! Where's our Soviet-American friendship?"

He didn't want me to swim with him. He wanted to race. We would swim, he commanded, using only one arm and going against the current. I followed him into the cold water. We swam parallel to the shore. From the river the beach seemed a mirage. Three times the general and I fought the current. Each time he won.

"Perfect blood pressure," he announced as we stepped again onto the hot sand. "I may be ancient, Anders, but nothing on this earth is stronger than the heart of a Don Cossack."

SIBERIA. AS LONG as I can remember, Siberia was never a metaphor but a destination. *Siber'* had been the tsars' quarantine, the prison of dissenters and criminals. The Soviet century brought even greater havoc, destroying lives and contaminating forests, lakes, and rivers. Flooded with toxins, the Yenisei no longer froze in Krasnoyarsk. Yet as I sat alone on the prow in the light of the moon on my last night aboard the *Matrosov*, I wondered if Siberia was not reverting to its original state, if the realm of isolation and hard labor had not become Russia's last resort, the sanctuary for its free men and women.

As four in the morning neared, voices filled the foredeck. Behind me, from the dark side decks, giggles drifted over the water. The teenagers by now had coupled. In the morning we were to reach Dudinka and from there drive across the tundra to Norilsk. An incandescent sky covered the boat. The river here was at its widest, nearly four miles across. There were no more little villages. Only now and then smoke puffed above the banks. "What a strange incomprehensible attraction there is in a light like this in the forest," wrote the Norwegian explorer Fridtjof Nansen, who came this way, in the opposite direction, in 1913. Nansen, too, had sat on deck, watching "the endless flat forest country" pass, and found himself yearning to see "what the faces are like that are staring into the fire over there. . . ."[7]

The tundra unfolded. The shores left and right were nearly level, each littered with stunted gray trees, like stumps left by a forest fire. The landscape was unlike any other—"deserts, immense plains filled with frozen marshes and wretched shrubs. . . ." wrote a French mapmaker in 1818.[8] A young couple came out on deck to take photographs. I wondered how their camera could capture the beauty. We sat there, a few feet apart at the bow, mesmerized by the ripples the boat cut in the silvery water.

Maybe it was the overwhelming beauty of the north or the luminous light that poured into our cabin, but sleep did not come easily. Rather than wake Volodya, I headed in search of company. The bar, I figured, was closed. Its doors were shut, but life resounded inside. Singing and laughing. I ducked in for half a second and pulled back.

A voice shouted out: "No, come on in, Endru!"

I took in the scene. Half the crew was at a private feast. I recognized the faces: waiters, cooks, engine room toilers. They all seemed to know me. "Endru, what'll you have?" asked the blond boy who had waited on the general's table at every meal. They were Krasnoyarsk kids on summer jobs. They didn't get paid much, but the months on the river were ample compensation.

I scarcely recognized the bar. The stench was the same, the stale smell of tobacco and flat beer. But they had turned it into a living room, a corner of a home. One by one they introduced themselves, like actors backstage after a show. Pyotr worked the bar. On the stool next to him sat Sveta, the waitress who hadn't smiled all week. Now she laughed.

Vadim, a lanky twenty-year-old, anchored the party. An old guitar rested across his knee, and his long blond hair, dyed bright orange in streaks, covered his eyes. He was not nearly as drunk as his companions. Around the table sat the guys, no longer boys and not yet men, who conducted the secret trade of the boat. Next to Vadim sat Vova, the shy deckhand with scars the color of burgundy running across the back of his hands. I had seen Vova at the dock in Igarka, shouldering crates of potatoes and beer off the boat. At his elbow sat Styopa, the cook with two chipped front teeth who steered the motorboat to the middle of the river each afternoon to barter with local poachers for the day's catch. By my side sat Roma, a twenty-eight-year-old whose good looks, Vadim informed, had earned him the nickname Johnny.

Why Johnny? I wondered.

"Just look at him. He's so pretty," Vadim said with a belly laugh, "he doesn't even look Russian."

Johnny was embarrassed. He had three years of the university behind him but said he'd never finish. What was the use, he told me, if working the *Matrosov* was the best work he could get? He was older and quieter. After Vadim had finished teasing him, largely for my benefit, I was sure, Johnny sat in silence.

I had come in on the end of their night. In a moment, when their revelry regained its pace, I became invisible. They had come to the bar for not only the buoyancy of the drink but the warmth of the company. They had come here to fight the coming dawn. Vadim picked up his guitar, cleared his blond and orange hair from his eyes, and let his fingers drift across the strings.

"*Eto vsyo,*" he sang. "This is all . . ."

It was the title of a popular song.

"This is all that will remain after me."

Wherever you went in Russia you heard it. It blared from sidewalk kiosks and stalls at outdoor bazaars. It blared from chrome CD players in refurbished cafés and old radios in beat-up Ladas. It blared from tentlike beer stands in the city parks where grandmothers aired newborns in ancient perambulators. It filled the air everywhere, from the smoky basement clubs of the capital to the barren cafeterias of the most remote workers' settlements, where no workers lived anymore. For years, in places public and private across Russia, "*Eto Vsyo*" had set the mood.

> *This is all that I will take with me*
> *Two dreams and a glass of sorrow*
> *That we, arisen from the dead, drank to the end.*

At that moment Olga, the assistant curator from the general's crew, stepped into the bar. At her side stood the gentleman doctor from Chelyabinsk. She listened for a moment before blurting out her displeasure. "What a depressing song!" she announced. Olga was tipsy. The doctor escorted her out.

Sveta's eyes soon fell to half-mast. Johnny grabbed her thin hand, and they disappeared through the doors. No one noticed that they had gone. The party plowed on. Vadim used his teeth to tear the metal top from the last bottle of vodka. It was warm, but that did not stop them. The table, half its Formica top long ago lost, was covered with empty bottles and empty cigarette packs. Only the song, as the drunken chorus joined Vadim, hung in the air.

> *I don't know why I am given to you.*
> *The moon rules me.*
> *Don't cry now, but if you can, forgive.*
> *Life is not sugar, and death is not tea.*
> *I will bear my way. So good-bye my friend and farewell.*

I climbed the stairs and walked out on deck. The sky was no darker, no lighter than when I had left it hours earlier. It must have been six in the morning, but I would not sleep. I had never felt closer, more at one, with Russians in my life. By eight we were to reach Dudinka.

✣ FOUR ✣

"THIS IS IT," THE general announced as we piled into the rickety minibus. "At last, the road to the inferno." From Dudinka, the grim port city near the northern tip of the Yenisei, we embarked on the two-hour drive through the tundra to Norilsk. An old minivan met us. The general sat in front, beaming. Galina and Olga sat in the middle seat with our guide, a bouffant-haired woman with horn-rimmed glasses. I sat with Volodya and Oleg, the former *Spetsnaz* exhibit designer, way in the back. We drove in silence past the rows of rusting cranes that lined the port and Soviet housing projects that still bore Communist slogans on their roofs. Dudinka had once been noisy, when freighters, waiting for days to dock, crowded the Yenisei. Now a solitary ship from Murmansk, stacked high with used German cars, sat near the dock in the hot sun of the early morning. In the streets there were more giant crows than people. The entire city seemed tinged a pale gray. Dudinka was bleak, but nothing portended what lay ahead.

"In the North," wrote Varlam Shalamov, "trees like people die lying down." On the road from Dudinka to Norilsk, it was clear what he meant. There was no soil for trees to take root in. The tundra was dotted with dwarf pines and larches. There was, however, an odd mantle of beauty. During the brief summer "the carpet" came out. Everywhere a floor of spongy vegetation spread. If you pulled at it, even gently, whole swatches lifted off the ground. And in the desolation there was color: berries of brilliant red and purple; wildflowers that flashed yellow and blue as we drove past.

For József Lengyel, the Hungarian writer and friend of his compatriot the Communist leader Béla Kun, the severity and beauty of the far north were forever haunting. Lengyel spent eighteen years in the camps and exile, including four in Norilsk. He could never forget the yellow poppies. "No matter where I go," he said in a memoir, "they force me to remember." Under different circumstances, Lengyel wrote, he could even imagine falling in love with this place. If he had come "as a free man, a hunter or explorer or geologist, in this mooncrust land of the pale and yellow ores."[9]

Just as the tundra rose to a peak, the strip of asphalt split. To the south, it bent toward Kayerkan, a desultory coal-mining satellite of Norilsk's that bears a name appropriated from an indigenous Arctic tribe. *Kayerkan* means "valley of death." To the north the road led to Norilsk, which rose suddenly out of the tundra, a blackened oasis of the unimaginable. Norilsk is the world's northernmost city of those with at least one hundred thousand residents. Just north of the sixty-ninth parallel, this is isolation in extremis. The railroad stops six hundred miles to the south. To the west unfolds the great Putorana Plateau, a mass of ice and volcanic rock unchanged since prehistory.

I had first come to Norilsk in the winter of 1997, not long after it opened to Westerners. On the drive from the airport, my eyes were blinded. I searched the white horizon for a sign of life—human, animal, or vegetable—and found none. The city sits in one of the world's cruelest environments. In winter the polar nights draw a curtain across the sky, the sun disappears altogether, the temperature sinks to minus sixty, and the snows and the winds force the tiny airport to close for more than fifty days. "Summer" is the five- or six-week respite when the polar days come: when the sun does not set, the wildflowers emerge, and the mosquitoes and gnats again swarm. Norilsk, perhaps more than any other city in Russia, is a place apart. To its residents, the mainland is a realm of childhood memories, television news, and summer vacations. "Time somehow passes," the locals like to say, "but we remain."

FROM ITS BEGINNINGS Norilsk has beguiled. The first Russians to arrive, the geologists, were lured by the promise of its hidden riches; the last Soviet migrants, by its romanticism—and higher pay. Everyone in between, whether guard or prisoner, did not come, as people say, by goodwill.

Gulag is an acronym. As if driven by a latent desire to destroy the language of Pushkin, Soviet officials bred acronyms, abbreviations, neologisms to disguise the business of the state. Gulag is short for the *Glavnoe Upravlenie Lagerei* ("Main Administration of Camps"). By Memorial's best count, there were 476 camps in all. Norilsk, however, enjoyed special status.

From the mid-1930s through the early 1950s, armies of prisoners were shipped this far north to raise the riches deep within its frozen ground. Had it not been for Stalin, no one would have dared try live north of the Arctic Circle save the native peoples who have roamed these lands for centuries, surviving, albeit with markedly less success in the last century, on little but reindeer meat and wild berries.[10] Had it not been for Stalin, permafrost would still be the most vital force in this territory. Unlike Hitler, Stalin intended to put his imprisoned enemies to work. The Soviet camps did not set extermination as their primary goal. Zeks were not to be killed off like flies but, even while kept in the worst of conditions and on the poorest of diets, bled of their muscle and brains. The secret policemen devised a cynical formula: Prisoners would be sorted by their health and fed according to their work. The camps would foster high rates of attrition. Torture and sadism would thrive, but Stalin understood the virtues of slave labor. And Norilsk, he knew, held great promise.

As early as the seventeenth century, Russian explorers had surmised that the uppermost reaches of the Arctic peninsula boasted immense mineral wealth. Peter the Great had commissioned geologists to survey the empire, fixing his sights on unearthing its riches. More than 150 years later, in 1860, the Petersburg doctor and zoologist Aleksandr Middendorf noted the "great coal shoals" of the frozen lands near Dudinka. Before long, Fyodor Schmidt, geologist, botanist, and paleontologist, discovered the veins of copper ore. The word soon spread. In Dudinka, in 1913, the Norwegian explorer Nansen wrote: "Some sixty miles across the tundra here from the Yenisei there are rich coal measures; the coal is as good as the best that comes from Cardiff, it is said." He had "no doubt that these coal measures might become of great importance in the future."[11]

The Bolsheviks were determined to mine the coal. On July 2, 1918, Lenin signed a decree ordering a navigational route to be cut through the north. In the summer of 1920 the first Soviet expedition arrived: fifteen people, a dozen sleds, 140 reindeer. Seven young horses bore kasha, cooking oil, dried fish and biscuits, shovels and picks. Nikolai Urvantsev, a bespectacled tall geologist from the Siberian city of Tomsk, led the way with his wife, Yelizaveta, the crew doctor. A grainy photograph of the Urvantsevs, double-barrel shotguns in hand, hangs in the Norilsk museum.[12] Dzerzhinsky, the Cheka founder, soon set his sights on the ore beneath the permafrost. On May Day 1925 *Izvestia* printed his speech at the Sixteenth Party Conference. "The issue of ferrous metals," Dzerzhinsky declared, "is the most fundamental one in our industrial economy."

Urvantsev had come home with ore that revealed high levels of platinum and its related metals. Moscow, however, was preoccupied with collectivization (the Bolshevik project to destroy the old ways of farming and herd the peasantry into new collective farms), famine, and the struggle to bring Soviet power to the ends of the old empire. Only a decade later, on June 23, 1935, the Council of People's Commissars passed the resolution that gave birth to the mining venture. In Moscow I pried a copy of the top secret directive, No. 1275-198ss, from the archives. It was just four pages. Here was the whole plan, in materials and money. From cargo ships to pipes to drill bits, the commissars laid out Norilsk's future with confidence and simplicity: " . . . for 10,000 tons of nickel a year . . ."; "with production beginning in 1938"; a "special camp" to be founded, run by "administrative-technical personnel." The grand scheme was sketched in strokes so spare and bold that one could not help feeling the hubris of the planners, and the absence of any consideration for their endeavor's human cost.

The commissars set forth thirteen commandments. They ordered the blueprints finished in just over a year, the plan lavished with ten million rubles, machinery shipped in from Arkhangelsk and Murmansk, and the air route extended from Krasnoyarsk into the tundra. In sum, they ordained that Norilsk would become the site of the biggest metals complex in the USSR.

AT THE HOTEL NORILSK—$13.65 a night—they had been waiting for the general. Four men in dark suits, officials from the Kombinat, emerged from a polished black Volga. They offered handshakes, not hugs, and whisked him off to a welcoming lunch. The rest of us were not invited. Volodya and I set off down the main street, Leninsky Prospekt. He wanted to walk the streets of his childhood.

Today the camps are long gone, but some 240,000 souls, many of them heirs of the zeks, remain. Thanks to them, Norilsk still produces nearly all of Russia's nickel and platinum, copper, and cobalt and has seized the attention of Japanese carmakers as the world's primary source of palladium, a rare metal used in catalytic converters that in recent years has traded at multiples above the price of gold.[13] Norilsk remains, as it was under Stalin, the most prodigious center of precious metals in Russia.

Few Russian cities better illustrate the strictures of the Soviet city plan. Norilsk is High Stalinist. As one walks downtown, the eight-story blocks of cement apartment houses file neatly into lines. A dozen avenues, equally spaced, cut the lines into a grid. The stores are the Soviet shops of the 1950s. The central planners' blueprint is unmistakable. The House of Culture, Drama Theater, Sports Hall, Party Headquarters—all stand on Leninsky Prospekt in one prim row. Leading the way, in the place of honor, is the tall white-stone headquarters of the Kombinat.

In the Yeltsin years, when the Kombinat suddenly passed from state to private hands—in a sleight of hand that fooled few of the locals—the complex was rechristened. It was to be called RAO Norilsk Nikkel, the Russian Joint-Stock Company Norilsk Nickel. By the time our crew arrived, it had just acquired another name, the Norilsk Mountain Mining Company. Try as they might, the new owners failed. In the mines that run a mile deep and the smelters that ring the city, the workers still called the complex by its old name. To them, it would always be the same old Kombinat.

THE COLD, THE WINDS, the snows, the blizzards shaped the city. Norilsk was divided between the world of "here"—aboveground—and "there"—everything that lay belowground, far belowground. Everything aboveground was designed to fend off the cold. Shop entrances had not two- but three-door thresholds. The courtyards formed by the empty center of each apartment block were treeless squares of broken cement, nearly enclosed to keep out the freezing winds. The apartment houses were built on foundations planted deep in the permafrost, the first floor set high off the ground to allow the cold to circulate in the space below. The result was an aboveground catacombs, a crawl space where kids took refuge. Condoms and broken bottles, syringes and Snickers wrappers littered the ground. A jumble of heating pipes twisted among the stilts, connecting each house to the network of warmth that ran through the city aboveground. In winter the streets and buildings belched clouds of steam.

The permafrost, however, was melting. Global warming was not to blame; the aboveground pipes were. Over the decades the heat had caused the buildings to list and fissure. Some had already collapsed. The wreckers had brought down others and quietly marked eighty-six more for detonation.

The ecological damage was not limited to the permafrost. Norilsk is one of Russia's most contaminated cities, a remarkable achievement in a country covered with environmental disaster zones. For months only the smoke-stacks pierce the jaundiced sky. On rare afternoons of blue sky, the city, built directly downwind from the first smelters, is enshrouded in a yellow fog, as the gases—sulfur dioxide, nitrogen dioxide, and hydrogen sulfide—descend. When mixed and exposed to moisture, the gases form sulfuric acid, acid rain. Outside the city, the rutted roads of the plateau are laced with blood-red pools of iron oxide.

In recent years, the Kombinat had gained fame as the leading single source of atmospheric sulfur emissions in the world. Its smelters have spewed, on average, more than two million tons of sulfur dioxide yearly since the 1950s—six times the pollution generated by the entire U.S. nonfer-rous metals industry.[14] Given the geography and the way the winds blow, Norilsk's bad air reaches all the way to Canada. "It's quite something," declared my breakfast partner one morning, a Finnish environmental scientist in town to survey the damage. "Norilsk is one of the largest landmasses on the globe ruined by air pollution."

The locals recognized the ecological troubles, but they were proud of their hospital. Built by the Yugoslavs in the last Soviet years, it towered over the tundra outside the city. Its ICU, however, was filled with young men, cancer and lung disease topping the list of illnesses. Male life expectancy in Norilsk was never high. Now few of its workingmen could expect to live much beyond fifty. Once upon a time the Kombinat carried its workers and their families from cradle to grave. Nurseries and schools, sanatoriums and Black Sea vacations: Everything was provided. The days of all-inclusive care were long gone. Salaries were now paid on time, but dozens of the kinder-gartens, two-floor affairs that sprouted across the city in the 1970s and dom-inated its courtyards, stood empty.[15] The Kombinat had launched a campaign to shed its social programs. It paid mothers who worked in the factories and smelters half their salaries to stay home with their children. The stockholders in Moscow, and far beyond, were pleased.

❧ FIVE ❧

AT THE HOUSE OF CULTURE the stage had been set since morning. The general's reading was to kick off a weeklong celebration of his triumphant return. He had spoken of this day when we first met in Moscow and he looked forward to it each day on the river. The presentation of *The Golden Star of the Gulag*, he had confided, was to be the denouement of his life—"justice at last served." The Norilsk House of Culture, true to Stalinist design, was grand. The walls were freshly coated with pastels, a reminder of the recent sixty-fifth anniversary. The general commandeered the head of a long table in an elegant room in the upper reaches of the hall. Galina and Olga had scoured the city to put out a spread. They had sliced apples, red and green, and peeled oranges. They laid out chocolates and cut cubes of cheese. They carefully placed bottles of champagne and vodka at equidistant positions along the table. Everything was right. Except only a dozen people showed up.

The general met the low turnout with aplomb and hit his stride early. But soon it all went awry. Only minutes had passed when, before his eyes, "Return to Norilsk," the pilgrimage he had waited half a century to make, went terribly, irreparably wrong. No sooner had he launched into his tale of "how the Lord led me down the narrow path between life and death" than a tidily dressed little old lady wearing fire engine red lipstick let out a high-pitched sigh. More sighs followed. Then the whispering began.

"Who is he to tell us?" hissed the woman, who could no longer control herself.

"The nerve of him!" her neighbor said.

"What kind of general is he anyway?" asked a third.

Then, as whispers gave way to shouts, the heckling began. "We know all about working in the mines! Who do you think you're talking to?"

General Numerov began to sweat. "Now, *girls*," he pleaded, "keep calm!" Later he said he'd been "ambushed by the grannies." But the truth was plain: In Norilsk, General Numerov hit a wall. On the boat our cruise-mates feted him at his reading in the disco; they gave him a standing ovation. But in Norilsk when he unfurled the same speech, the locals refused to sit in silence. "Girls, please!" he cried. "For the love of God, let me speak!" It was no use.

I couldn't help smiling. Neither could everyone else in our crew. Except Galina. Galina sat beside the general and reddened. She seemed to have difficulty breathing. The general tried to forge on. His deafness perhaps shielded him. He could hear little ever since the blasts of the guns at the southern front, when he fell into the hands of the Germans and the Lord led him down that narrow path between life and death.

Olga Yaskina heckled the loudest. At seventy, Olga was a sturdy, compact woman with bouncy dark crimson curls and eyes that flashed. The women who ambushed the general, the eight who were his Greek chorus, had also survived the Norilsk camps. One by one, in the weeks that followed, I visited them to learn how the city, both its horrors and unexpected joys, had misshaped their lives. After a month in Norilsk I ran out of notebooks. I left town carrying with me a dozen voices, each recounting a different tale of survival and loss. Olga was the women's leader, the chair of the Norilsk association of surviving zeks. Their group was not big—fifty-six members in all—and it was shrinking fast.

The address Olga gave me did not make sense. It was a new apartment house that stood apart from the surrounding decay. For Norilsk, its red-brick exterior seemed luxurious. It was the residence of the Kombinat bosses. I found her seated in the entryway, behind a small desk beside the elevator. She was still working for the Kombinat, now as a *dezhurnaya*, a Soviet-style concierge. "It's not so bad," she said. "I only have to stay through the night three times a week." Like many of the survivors I met, Olga was a lost Pole. Born Olga Petryga in the city of Yaroslav in eastern Poland, she'd grown up, as these Poles turned Russians proudly put it, "under capitalism."

"In 1939, when Hitler came, they divided the town along the San River. All of our relatives ended up on the German side, and we on the Russian side. They arrested me on the twenty-first of March 1952. But by then we'd already been living in exile, and under guard, for six years. In 1946, we lost our freedom when my father came home. That was when we all ended up in this paradise."

She was sixteen when they came. The Soviets rounded up her family and sent them to the Urals. In a barracks deep in the taiga, Olga, her siblings, and her parents made do. Perm, a city whose name can cause Russians to tighten their shoulders and rub their folded arms, became civilization, the nearest city.

"For miles there was nothing but trees," she said. "It was as if they'd cut a window in the forest and stuck in the barracks. Farther on there was a men's camp, and in time they moved us there."

By 1951 she had been sent to work at Ural-Almaz, a vast diamond-processing plant, as an accountant's apprentice. When she passed her exams with honors, they let her stay on. For the first time in her life Olga had good work. But she could not rejoice long. Within three months she was arrested. The charge was Article 58. "What else?" she asked. In the years of Stalin's terror, Article 58 of the 1934 Criminal Code—"counterrevolutionary activities"—swept millions into the camps and exile.

A military tribunal sentenced her to ten years in the camps and five without rights. She was sent to a "special prison" for "politicals," a jail reserved for political prisoners. The cots were iron and the floor was iron—and they were welded together. The prisoners could neither lie down nor sit. The guards forced them to walk all day unless they were taken off at night to interrogations, which lasted for hours.

Many went to the camps without any notion of their offenses. Nearly all the survivors I met had believed they'd been caught up in a "mistake," a "mixup," something that would be "worked out." It would take only "a day or two." Olga, however, had known exactly why she had been taken away. She had written a letter to her best girlfriend. She had told her, "Marusya, don't cry, the sun will rise for us as well."

"It was enough," she said, "to make a case."

She was shipped from one prison to the next, from Perm to Sverdlovsk, from Sverdlovsk to Krasnoyarsk, then up the Yenisei. She was packed in with other girls into the hold of the *Mariya Ulyanova*, a freighter named after Lenin's sister. The trip north lasted three weeks. The women were each given four herrings and a handful of dry biscuits. From Dudinka they were herded into cargo wagons on a narrow-gauge train that creaked its way for hours to Norilsk. She arrived at the camps on October 30, 1952, prepared for the worst.

"Everyone had said, 'As soon as you get to Norilsk, you'll die.' So when they took us to the banya, I was thinking, How come I'm not dying? That night they finally gave us food, horsemeat. The next day, dried fish and a scrap of bread. Then they led us straightaway to work."

The women of the Sixth Female Gulag had dug the foundation pits of the city. But Olga considered herself among the fortunate. In 1955, on March 8,

Women's Day, she was released. While she was recalling the day, a family entered the stairwell. Two little boys clambered up the stairs in Rollerblades. Their parents, young and robust in Nike sweatsuits, trailed. A Kombinat family. Olga was not hushed. "It was all thanks to Stalin," she said, with a smile. "Joseph Vissarionovich died just in time."

❧ SIX ❧

TROUBLE WAS BREWING, and I knew it. Norilsk, on the books at least, remained what is called in the old Soviet parlance, a closed city. It required all visitors, Russian or otherwise, to register with the authorities. Just who these "authorities" are is never explained. It has to be intuited. In the Soviet days the rationale for the city's closed status was arguably legitimate: Given its mineral riches, it had more than its share of military and industrial secrets. Now, however, the Kombinat exploited the status as an excuse to exclude undesirables.

Ever since my first trip to Norilsk, I'd wanted to get inside the oldest nickel smelter, a colossal red-brick monster known affectionately among its workers as the Crematorium. The zeks had built it on the eve of World War II in merciless speed. I knew, however, the Kombinat officials would not look favorably on a foreign journalist wandering in their midst, unchaparoned and in no rush to make a plane back to Moscow. I had already come up against the folks from Economic Security.

I never hid my intentions. I had informed the company's press office in Moscow of my trip. I just did not say that I'd be coming by boat. The Kombinat did not take kindly to the omission. It had posted a minder at the airport for a week, expecting to intercept me upon arrival. Unamused, it dispatched a team from the Economic Security Department to find me. It was not hard.

At the general's book party I felt a sharp tap on my shoulder. "Time for you to go," announced a whippet-thin blonde in a pink pantsuit. Where? I wondered. "Moscow—your interview with the head of the Kombinat is set for tomorrow. In Moscow."

I laughed. I had, it was true, tried to see the director in Moscow, but was told it would be impossible. "I'm afraid there's been a mistake," I said. The interview, I explained, would have to wait until my return.

"This is impossible." She persisted. "No one turns down a chance to meet our director." She introduced herself as a high-ranking representative from the External Relations Department of the Kombinat.

I said I was sorry, but I'd be staying on a few weeks. She was not pleased. She demanded to know when *did* I plan on leaving town. "Depends how things go," I said with a shrug.

As the women finished chastising the general, the blonde from External Relations lurked in the hallway, whispering to a well-scrubbed adjutant in a gray suit. She pointed in my direction. Disobedience was one thing, but a refusal to set a departure date was another. Such audacity, I could be sure, would come back to haunt me.

🜲 SEVEN 🜲

FROM *THE GULAG HANDBOOK*, an encyclopedia of camp life compiled by Jacques Rossi, a Frenchman who had served as a young courier in the Comintern, the Communist International, until he was arrested in the purges and sent off to Norilsk:

KOROVA, cow.
Person intended for use as food. Completely unsuspecting, any novice criminal may play this role if senior comrades propose that he participate in an escape. The trust invested in this novice flatters him and he usually agrees. If, during the escape, the escapees do not succeed in augmenting their diminishing stores, they slit the "cow's" carotid artery, drink his blood, and eat the still-warm kidney (it is dangerous during an escape to light a fire). If the escape turns out successfully, the novice will realize only much later what he has risked.[16]

The camps appeared in Norilsk shortly after the engineers. The first zeks, twelve hundred in all, arrived by barge, in August 1935. Noril'lag–the

Norilsk *lager*, or corrective labor camp—was at first no more than a line of wooden barracks. Construction, however, advanced at a ruthless pace. By March 1939 the settlement's first factory, the so-called Small Metals Plant, had produced its first copper and nickel. By the start of World War II, the Kombinat had grown to include factories for oxygen, coke, and machine repair, a power station, three coal and three ore mines, limestone quarries, and its own airport.

At the same time, the army of prison laborers had grown to nearly twenty thousand. During the war, as the demand for metal for armor and armaments grew, the population swelled. In Moscow a camp official, Vasily Ksintaris, who had run the Dudinka port, had shared a disquieting anecdote. He had told me how during Lend-Lease, a foreign ship, British or American, he never knew, arrived in Dudinka with canned American meat and corn. The officials fretted that the foreigners would discover that the gaunt men who unloaded the supplies were in fact prisoners. So the guards hid their guns under civilian clothes, while the prisoners wore smocks that did not have their camp numbers stitched onto them. Still, the ruse did not work. The sailors on the foreign ship pitied the sallow-faced laborers. They threw loaves of bread onto the dock, bread that the guards, Ksintaris said, later made the zeks throw into the river.

The prisoners had no illusions about the wartime alliance with America. Yevfrosiniya Kersnovskaya, one of the most extraordinary survivors of the Norilsk camps, was keenly aware of the consequences. A polyglot daughter of Bessarabian aristocrats, Kersnovskaya was sent to the camps twice. The first time she escaped and traveled on foot nearly a thousand miles through Siberia only to be rearrested. She served twelve years in Norilsk as a prisoner, then stayed on for another six. Kersnovskaya was one of the first female miners at the Kombinat. In her memoir, a testament that runs nearly fifteen hundred pages, she lays bare the irony of Lend-Lease:

It is 1944. The war. The mines and pits in the European part of the mainland were blown up, filled with water, or occupied by the enemy. Norilsk is nickel. Nearly all the nickel, so vital for the war, came from there. That's why Norilsk must live and function. And the prisoners, nearly one hundred percent of the city's population in those years, couldn't simply die. They must work, and they must work productively.

That's why they had to be fed. The Americans understood it. We understood it, too,
because the food we unloaded from the barges and into the wagons came from
America. . . ."[17]

After the war Stalin, seeing the Soviet POWs returning from the Nazi-
occupied lands as spies and collaborators, embarked on a new round of
purges. More barracks went up. On January 1, 1948, the Noril'lag, according
to the camp directors' own tally, held 56,779 prisoners.[18] Russians and
Ukrainians numbered the greatest, but the camp also mirrored the Soviet
"brotherhood of nations." It held Belarusians and Azeris, Georgians and
Armenians, ethnic Germans and Poles, Tatars and Tajiks, as well as vast contingents from the Baltic, nearly all of them military men accused of aiding
the Nazis. There were foreign nationals, too: Germans and Japanese, Chinese and Finns, Koreans and Greeks.

In 1948 the order came from Moscow to build *osobye lagerya*, "special
camps," for "especially dangerous state prisoners"–the politicals.[19] The new
camps were for a new generation of victims: ". . . spies, saboteurs, terrorists,
Trotskyists, right-wing forces, Mensheviks, Social Revolutionaries, anar-
chists, nationalists, White émigrés, and participants in other anti-Soviet
organizations and groups and all those posing a danger by their anti-Soviet
relations and activities."[20] Only four regions were deemed worthy to host
these camps. Norilsk of course earned the honor. "Special Camp No. 2" in
Norilsk was christened Gorlag–short for "Mountain Camp."

In Moscow, in the Gulag archives, I unearthed a curious document,
instructions, printed by the Interior Ministry in early 1948, on how to
build a "Tula fence," the most effective perimeter to prevent the new class
of prisoners from escaping. The blueprint detailed the best combination of
barbed wire, wooden posts, and guard dogs that the Gulag architects had
devised.

Beginning that spring, the Yenisei was crowded with barges, as fifteen
thousand political prisoners were sent north in short order. In 1949 the
Norilsk bosses duly informed Stalin of their success: The Gorlag camp had
exceeded its plan for 1948. Norilsk was producing nine million tons of ore a
year. In 1951 the prison population reached its peak: at nearly 100,000 men
and women. Noril'lag, the first camp, held 72,490 alone.

MANY YEARS AGO, when I was still living in the Moscow *kommunalka* a few blocks from the Kremlin with my friends Andrei and Lera, they took me to visit a dacha far outside town. It belonged to a friend of Lera's, an old Jewish woman, the soft-spoken matriarch of five generations of women. She had lived several lives, had survived the ravages of World War II and Stalinism. If anyone, I thought, she would know.

What was the difference, I asked, between Stalin and Hitler?

"Hitler," she replied without pause, "killed only his enemies."

AS WE DROVE through the outskirts of Norilsk, past the edge of Mount Schmidt, Sasha's screed came pouring forth. He drew a forefinger across his thin neck. "We're up to here in bones," he said. Sasha needed little prodding. In Norilsk the mountain, named after the geologist, is known by an affectionate diminutive, Schmidtikha. It looks more like an overgrown hill than a mountain. Its westward tilt is not a geographical formation but a leaning tower of slag, the leftovers of six decades of mining.

I had met Sasha and his wife, Irina, on my first trip to Norilsk. I had hoped to talk with miners at an old mine, but the Kombinat would offer only a press tour of the most modern ones. Sasha and Irina had made it happen. We had become friends. In their early forties, they were enjoying a kind of second adolescence. Theirs was a second marriage for her, a first for him. Not only were they happy to be in Norilsk, but they were among the happiest people I ever met in Russia. Both worked of course for the Kombinat.

Irina had steep cheekbones and dark lashes that batted with each word she spoke. She was tall and gentle, slow in her movements and speech. Her voice was that of a lilting soprano. There was something stereotypically Slavic, something outwardly feline, about Irina, how she spoke, how she walked, how she folded her long hands into her lap. She seemed somehow more Russian than the Russians I worked with and had known for years in Moscow. She had been born, of all places, in Grozny. Her family had moved to Norilsk when she was twelve. Papa had worked as an engineer, Mama in the chlorine-cobalt plant. Irina remembered her first Norilsk winter well. She had gone one day to see her father at work. They had had to carry her out of the copper factory; she passed out. Irina now worked in the seamstress department, making uniforms for the miners and blasters. It brought a decent wage but demanded, she lamented, "no thought at all."

Sasha, too, was bored. He was thin and wore metal-framed glasses that he was forever pushing back to the bridge of his nose. He had grown up in Norilsk. In 1965 his mother had followed her husband north, bringing Sasha in tow. His father had driven a Belaz, a giant truck and one of Belarus's greatest gifts to the USSR, at the oldest and biggest open-pit mine in Norilsk, Medvezhy ruzhei (Bear Creek), or the Medvezhka, as everyone called the mine on top of Mount Schmidt. It was a giant quarry edged by a thin road that descended, rung after rung, to its depths—less a pit than the hollowed-out inside of the mountain itself. Sasha had served in the armed forces here, helping man the secret missile sites that lined the low hills outside the city. The missiles, he explained, had been aimed directly over the North Pole—"at you." Now the sites were scars in the earth; abandoned, they had been stripped of their metal in the first post-Soviet years. After tending the missiles, Sasha had followed his father up the mountain.

Sasha and Irina were eager to show me how the memorials had multiplied. Since the Soviet fall, the crosses had begun to rise in an uneven row at a clearing in the slag at the base of Mount Schmidt. Clustered together, the ceremonial graves were marked by unadorned plaques. Poles and Lithuanians and Latvians who returned to the site of their internments had erected Orthodox and Catholic crosses above the "graves." Close by stood a small chapel, large enough for a solitary worshiper.

We walked across the clearing. The city stretched out beneath us. Irina tried to point out their apartment house. She could not. Gassy clouds hung over the city like an orange-yellow curtain. The ground beside the memorials was cut by rivulets of red clay, fissures filled with toxic sediment from the smelters. Just beyond the memorials, a bit up the incline, two bulldozers carved long, deep trenches in the steep earth. A few yards ahead, a squad of women, robust in bright orange vests, busily fitted pipe. As we walked among the crosses, I noticed how the bulldozers had opened seams in the dark slope of the mountain.

I stepped into the tiny chapel. Three shriveled apples, once red, were piled in front of an icon. A cross, broken and rusted, leaned against a wall. When I came out, one of the women who had been fitting pipe approached. She was broad-shouldered, with large red hands that could snap, you could be sure, the neck of a chicken. She pointed to a white plastic shopping bag leaning against the wooden cross of a memorial.

"One day's work," she said.

Bones protruded from the bag. She pointed over her shoulder, to the bulldozers at work. One of the guys, she said, collects the bones as he plows. Someone, she said, ought to give them a proper burial. At the bottom of the bag, she told me, lay a skull.

"This whole side of the mountain, right down to the edge of the city, was a cemetery," Sasha said. "I remember playing up here as a kid. You could still see the graves then. Rows and rows."

As we walked, we watched the bulldozers at work. "They're building a spillway," Sasha said. He pointed to a pond at the base of the mountain below. A bright yellow dragging boat sat in the middle of the pond. It looked new, distinctly foreign. The Kombinat, Sasha had heard, had signed a deal to use American equipment to extract the most minute particles of gold from the slush of rock. The bulldozers had not intended to draw back the curtain on the past. They were here to carve ditches for pipes. Irina said it seemed like a lot of work for gold dust.

🌼 EIGHT 🌼

I KNEW POTANIN. All Russia did. Vladimir Potanin, Moscow banker of world renown and good standing on the *Forbes* list of the world's richest men, was the man who, despite all claims to the contrary, controlled the fate of the city of Norilsk and the paychecks and pensions of nearly all its inhabitants. Potanin was one of the original oligarchs, the man who had bought the Kombinat and all its subsidiary holdings at an astounding discount.

"So do you know who this Potanin is?"

It was the second time Aleksei had asked the question. Again, he looked at me sideways. This time he did not wait for an answer. Aleksei was on a riff, as we careered across Norilsk at night. We were looking, without luck, for a club named Hell. It was supposed to be the best nightspot in town. We had already driven past three places. Two candidates remained.

"I'll tell you who Potanin is. A little Soviet bureaucrat who never climbed beyond the middle ranks of the Foreign Trade Ministry. What was he making back then? Three hundred rubles a month, maximum. Berezovsky at least was a scientist with degrees, a member of the Academy of Sciences." He dragged out the resonant syllables of *aaakaaadeeeemiiiyaaa*, to let me know the establishment carried clout with him. "Berezovsky had a Ph.D. before he had billions. He's a Jew, so he's got brains. Like Marx–maybe too much brains. But Potanin? The kid, I have to tell you, fails to impress me."

Aleksei was squeezed behind the wheel of a dustless Volga that dated from the late 1960s. He had a barrel chest, graying hair shorn close to his square head, and pale blue eyes that bulged when he grew animated. He wore strong cologne and a faded jeans jacket two sizes too small. Many in the West, as Aleksei knew, did not share his opinion. From George Soros to British Petroleum to the Harvard University endowment fund, Western investors had believed in Potanin's touch. After all, in late 1995, he had bought the controlling stake, 38 percent, in the Norilsk complex. In the infamous loans-for-shares auction, Potanin had paid $100,000 over the starting price of $170 million.[21]

The auction was not an auction. It was the crux of the scheme that Potanin himself had devised in the spring of 1995. The oligarchs were to lend the cash-strapped government millions for the right "to manage" the state's stakes in the country's fattest enterprises. No one believed the state could ever repay the loans. Everyone knew the oligarchs would simply resell the shares–to themselves at massive discounts. In 1997 Potanin did sell the 38 percent stake to himself, for $250 million. At the time he was thirty-five years old.[22]

Unlike many of the men who rose to call themselves oligarchs, Potanin was a child of the Soviet elite. Growing up, he lived with his parents in Yemen, Turkey, and New Zealand. In the spring of 1990 he founded a trading company. True to the Soviet penchant to abbreviate, he christened it Interros. By 1993 he had founded a bank as well, Uneximbank. He had not of course risen all on his own. But Potanin had skill. Fluent in the vernacular of modern finance, he caught on fast. He coaxed capital from the West, admiring profiles from foreign reporters, and untold funds–"to manage"– from the state coffers. By the end of 1995 Uneximbank's assets had hit three billion dollars.[23] By 1996, when Yeltsin won reelection, Potanin had built one of the largest financial and industrial empires to emerge from the Soviet ruins.

In his oak-paneled cocoon in Moscow, Potanin spent hours detailing for me his latest plan for restructuring the Kombinat and modernizing its mines. He wanted to rebuild Norilsk and return its poor pensioners to a warmer clime. He said all the right things. He promised to do good. Aleksei would hear none of it. To Potanin, he said, Norilsk's bloated work force, not to mention its elderly and ill, was only an inconvenience on a balance sheet.

Aleksei of course was right. I remembered the corporate strategy I had heard on my first visit to Norilsk, articulated by a young public relations aide flown in from company headquarters in Moscow. "Cities like Norilsk should never have been built," he said. "Now they're just not necessary." In the Soviet era the complex had employed 150,000 workers. Nearly 30,000 had lost their jobs by 2000. More layoffs no doubt would follow.

THE HUNT FOR THE club named Hell had taken longer than expected, but Aleksei did not mind. He had time. He had just quit, after twenty-five years, the Kombinat. I asked about the shares. The miners and Gulag veterans all said that in the early 1990s, during the first round of mass privatization, everyone had received shares in Kombinat. I had made it a routine to ask people what they'd done with their shares. No matter whom I asked, the answer was always the same: They had sold them.

Aleksei had sold his early. The big Moscow brokerages had flown in the young scalpers. "Hordes of them, slick kids who bought shares by the thousands and then sold them on the Moscow exchange." Not a bad business, he mused. The workers and their families, Aleksei explained, were trapped in an information vacuum. But one day they had opened up *Polar Pravda* and read that in Moscow the same shares sold for much more. "We're not fools," he said. "We saw the two prices and the distance between them." All the same, he said, the practice continued to that day. In fact it had only grown. Kiosks where the locals could sell their shares had sprouted across town.

"If you're good at it," Aleksei said, "you can make good cash—five, ten thousand bucks a month. Buying and selling stocks in the West may be hard work, but here, they're just exploiting our ignorance and inability to get to Moscow. It's *rafinat*." He explained the term. It was thieves' slang. In the days of the Romanovs, *rafinat* was fine sugar, the best the nobility could serve. The underworld had appropriated the term. Now it meant "easy money," sweet profit. Yet to Aleksei *rafinat* was something to disdain. It was "soft work" for men who had never had calluses. "There's no lifting," he said. "No loading, no digging, no blasting."

Aleksei maintained, even unconsciously, a Soviet admiration for hard labor. His was an affection unwarranted by experience. After twenty-five years at the Kombinat, he could not even live on his pension of a thousand rubles–little more than thirty dollars–a month. Five hundred went to his one-room apartment and telephone. The balance he spent on bread, half a loaf a day. To buy food, he had to drive his old Volga around town. Yet he said he was lucky. He had no wife and no kids and lived alone.

For Aleksei, at least, the future was clear. He could have stayed on at the Kombinat. Lots of workers were doing that, collecting their salaries and pensions simultaneously. It was the only way, they had told me, they could put something away. But he had done the math, and every way he tried it, he lost.

"Look," he said, pulling the Volga off the road to make his case. "Potanin came out of one of the world's biggest bureaucracies ever, the Soviet system, where planning was everything. He's got it all worked out. He's got computers and accountants working on it. Every cent's calculated: plus a million here, minus a million there, move some here, push some there. In this man's profit margin, there's no such thing as an accident."

We both knew Aleksei had a point. For weeks I had heard miners talk of how things were getting better, how the Kombinat had upped their pay, imported new equipment, paid heed at last to their concerns. The cheery talk had sounded like rationalization. The Norilsk complex paid high salaries–among the highest in Russia. The average was seven hundred dollars a month, a fortune by Siberian standards. In Soviet days there had been a waiting list of several years to get on the payroll. Now there was no list. The Kombinat was not taking newcomers. It was trying to shed thousands. The workers knew that. They knew that management would now streamline production. They also knew, whether they admitted it or not, that Norilsk's riches, as in its beginnings, were unlikely to return to the men and women who raised them from the ground. They knew, in short, that Aleksei was right. The arithmetic left little doubt. In 2000, Norilsk Nickel cleared well over one billion dollars in profits. In the same year it paid out a little more than ten million dollars in dividends.[24]

YOU HAD TO LOOK at the context, Potanin had told me in Moscow. He might have bought Russia's biggest nickel producer, but he had also inherited its bills, trillions of rubles in back taxes. All the same, Potanin, as every sentient investor in Russia knew, had done well by Norilsk. The 1998 crash had hit his empire hard. He had lost his beloved bank and his oil company as well. But he held on to Norilsk and survived.

In 2000 Potanin again stood among the richest men in Russia. I had long heard stories of his European vacations–skiing in Switzerland, sailing in the Mediterranean. Then there was the tale of the Champagne Wars, a favorite among Moscow bankers. In St. Tropez there is a famed restaurant, La Voile Rouge. With tables on the beach and naked girls dancing on top of them, for years it's been the hottest spot on the Riviera. The crowd was always the same: middle-aged multimillionaires with twenty-something girlfriends enjoying breaks from their yachts. By the mid-1990s, the Yeltsin years of excess, the Russians had hit La Voile Rouge. Potanin, it was said, was a regular.

More than one Moscow banker told me of the day when the Russians entered the Champagne Wars. The music was blaring, and the girls had begun to undress when one Russian diner ordered champagne, Dom Pérignon, at three hundred dollars a bottle. He didn't drink it. He shook the bottle and sprayed it all over himself. The gauntlet was thrown. At a nearby table another Russian followed suit. The Champagne Wars were not new– the French had been wasting money for show for years–but the Russians took the battle to heart. Soon they were dueling, each trying to spray more bubbly than the other. By the end of the lunch, in a restaurant that accepted only cash, the bill for the champagne hit thirty thousand dollars.

🌺 NINE 🌺

AFTER A WEEK IN Norilsk, the general and his entourage parted ways. The crew from Krasnoyarsk returned to Dudinka and the *Matrosov* to make their way home by water. The general had already left. He'd seen enough. He got up one morning, summoned a black Volga from the Kombinat, and boarded a direct flight back to Moscow. He never recovered. The Kombinat had treated him well enough, but his return had not been the gala he had expected. On his last night in town he sent word for me to join him in his room. He wanted to share a farewell shot.

"Anders, it's strange," he said. "It's the same place, that's for sure. It's the people who're different. These guys running it now—they don't know the blood and the bones that went into it." He seemed, for the first time on the trip, to carry the weight of concern. The whole town, he said, had depressed him. He poured the vodka into two cloudy water glasses and let them stand on the table. For a time he sank into silence, his eyes fixed on an unknown spot on the dark floor. "How can they do it?" he asked, finally raising his head. "How can they keep on living here?"

THE HOTEL NORILSK was now nearly empty. In the long corridors I ran into only an occasional environmentalist—Finnish or Swedish—flown in to survey the source of the damage. For two weeks Sasha and Irina had been patient as I spent the days with the camp survivors. They wanted to take me on a picnic. "We love picnics," Irina said, her blue eyes covered in a glaze. She said they loved to hunt for berries among the hummocks of the tundra. Sasha went to the store and bought black bread and cheese. Irina harvested the cucumbers and tomatoes in their bedroom. The vegetables, the result of a winter's care under twenty-four-hour grow lights, were enormous. "The cucumbers keep us going," Sasha said. In the kitchen Irina displayed the shelves of glass jars that held pickles.

We drove the only road east out of town. When we came to what looked like the beginnings of the city dump, Sasha pulled over. "Urvantsev's hut," he announced. I had heard of the "First House," as it was called, where the geologist who opened this land had spent his first winter swaddled in reindeer hides. We got out of the car to look closer. The ground was covered with piles of burned nail-studded planks and cement chips. A blood-stained syringe lay among the ruins. "Poor Urvantsev," Irina said. "He did so much good."

A simulation of the geologist's home, a log cabin akin to Lincoln's, stood downtown off Leninsky Prospekt, squeezed between the concrete apartment blocks. It was a museum, but now shuttered, whether marked for destruction or repair no one knew. In Norilsk, Urvantsev was worshiped as the city's founding father. But even he had not been spared the terror. Residual bourgeois, merchant class, White Guard leanings, his accusers claimed, had led him to stall the development of the northern sea route. Urvantsev was jailed first in Kresty (Crosses), the infamous nineteenth-century prison in Leningrad, before being packed off to the Norilsk camps.[25]

We drove on, back up Mount Schmidt, and beyond its hollowed-out peak. A single-lane road took us to gentle hills where thousands of larch trees stood ghostly pale in the brown grass. "The Dead Forest," Irina announced. For miles the stunted trees barely rose above the ground, their branches twisted in tightly around their trunks. They were spectral, bleached of life. Over the past two decades, more than fifteen hundred square miles of forest around Norilsk had succumbed to the gas.

As we walked among the dwarf trees, Irina twirled a long blade of dried grass in her hands. She told me a story. She and Sasha had tried an experiment. Last year they'd planted a radish plant here. It had not lasted long. "I bet no other country would tolerate it," Sasha said. "First you kill off your own people. Then you kill off the world they lived in. What does that leave you with?"

IT IS DANGEROUS, Russian historians liked to tell me, to compare the German experience with the Russian. It is unfair, they said, to hold Russians to German standards. The historians were not talking about industrial efficiency, academic stipends, or lagers. They were talking about guilt.

In Germany the past has been opened wide—in part by the victorious Allies but far more significantly, in the years since World War II, by social demand and the law. In German society, after the war and again after the fall of the Berlin Wall, excavating the past and telling its secrets became national obsessions. The West need not worry that German schoolchildren grow up not knowing who Hitler was. The evils of national socialism are taught from a young age. For all the failings of denazification, Buchenwald and Dachau were not allowed to disappear in decay and overgrowth. They became museums. Among West Germans, with the rise of the generation of 1968, the urge for self-examination only gained strength. The fall of the Wall brought the craving to the East. The Stasi headquarters were not only stormed but opened. The state established the right, and means, for every citizen to access his or her secret police file.[26] Most important of all, the line between perpetrator and victim, so clearly drawn by self-deception and betrayal, was not allowed to fade away. To be exposed as a Stasi officer, agent, or informer is today to wear the stigma of the offender. Germans, whether confronted by the Allies or their sons and daughters, faced the issue of moral complicity and bore its weight.[27]

Nothing could be further from the case in Russia. The state awarded scant reparations to the victims of Stalinism. Parliament passed only the most cursory attempt at curative legislation. The history textbooks have yet to be rewritten. Thousands, if not millions, of Russian children do not know the truth about Stalin and the terror. Moreover, a decade after the Soviet fall a former secret policeman rose to rule the Kremlin. Had Norilsk been a German city and Potanin born a German, things would no doubt be different. One of Potanin's first orders of business, upon taking over, would have been to build a new museum, a hall of remembrance to honor the victims of Stalinism, a place to expunge collective guilt for mass murder and enslavement. Yet the German comparison may be unfair. Germany, after all, started to examine its past only after an economic miracle, one of history's greatest. Russia has enjoyed no such recovery. In a nation economically, socially, and ideologically adrift, reopening old wounds is not a priority. For Potanin, the past is not an issue. I had in fact never heard him utter a word about the origins of the city he now controlled. He had a hard enough time justifying its economics.

❧ TEN ❧

IN THE HOTEL NORILSK the restaurant had been closed for as far as anyone could remember and the shower water ran black. Then there was the battleaxe in the lobby. She had taken to asking me each day when I would be leaving. Trouble, I knew, was brewing. I had been stalling them for weeks when one morning Economic Security struck back.

I was in the lobby watching the news from Moscow—"The search for signs of life from the members of the crew of the submarine *Kursk* goes on . . ."—when I was caught. The hotel clerks were also glued to the television.

Word that the *Kursk* had sunk had come only days before. I heard the enforcer before I saw him. A young man with a serious demeanor, he asked at the desk for "the American." He wore a black blazer and black jeans. There was no room to maneuver. At least he was polite.

"There's a warrant out for you," he said. "Your name is on my wanted list." I asked how that could be. He said I had failed to register with the authorities and that he was only doing his job. But I had registered, I explained, first with the hotel, then with the Kombinat. I had handed over my press accreditation and my passport and visa to a woman who professed to be from Economic Security a week before. She had said she would register me. "No," he explained, "you did not register with the appropriate authorities."

I felt as if I were back in the Assa, the listening box that masqueraded as a hotel in Nazran. Déjà vu told me it was no use arguing. It could all be settled with a fine, my visitor from Economic Security said. It had added up every day that I had not registered. It totaled just shy of twelve dollars. I acquiesced. He took my rubles and documents and disappeared as suddenly as he had appeared.

The woman anchored behind the counter stared coldly. I was a delinquent in her eyes. "This is Norilsk," she said. "You know the rules."

In the winter of 2001 the Kombinat cut the pretense of openness. The city again declared itself officially closed. No one, neither foreigner nor native, could even buy a plane ticket to Norilsk without first obtaining permission from the authorities—and the blessing, of course, of Economic Security.

IN MOSCOW I HAD grown used to hearing Americans visiting Russia for the first time say that they felt as if they'd fallen into a time machine. "It feels like years ago," people said, substituting the number of years depending on the topic. The boxy Russian cars, they said, brought back the 1950s. Sexual relations, the 1960s. Capitalism, the nineteenth century. Russians, however, suffered the time travel all the more. In Norilsk, the past intruded daily on the present. Sometimes the intrusion was physical. The lines that circled Mount Schmidt, like stitches yet to be removed, were remnants of the earliest railway, a small-gauge line that carried the coal from the mines. More often, the past returned in people's minds. As I sat with the survivors of the camps, they seemed to drift rudderless between temporal realms. Making a home in the city of their imprisonment, they struggled to preserve the chronological threads of their lives. I could not see the barbed wire that once spread like vines, the guard towers, the dogs. But they could. They glided unknowingly between tenses. Talk of the tragedy of the *Kursk* gave way to a discourse on the joys of pouring cement on a minus-forty morning with a line of guards, guns in their hands, watching over you.

Two words, more than any other, could trigger the collapse of the present: Stalin and *zabastovka*, the strike. Everyone remembered March 5, 1953, the day Stalin died, and everyone remembered the strike that followed. To millions of Soviet citizens, Stalin's death brought despair and panic, but in the Gulag it brought hope for a loosening of the strictures on prison life and labor. By March 25, 1953, Lavrenty Beria, the new head of the secret police, had stopped an entire slate of Gulag projects, from the tunnel under the Tatar Strait in the Far East that was to tie Sakhalin to the mainland to the "Railway of Death" in the far north. (The rails Stalin had ordered laid from Igarka and Salekhard ended up hundreds of miles apart.)[28] In Norilsk, Stalin's death unleashed something rare in the Soviet world: rebellion. Here and later in two other islands of the Gulag—in the camps in Vorkuta, also in the Russian north, and in Kengir in Kazakhstan—the prisoners stood up.[29]

By 1953 Norilsk had grown into a sprawling complex of camps. Noril'lag now had thirty-five zones, or *lagotdeleniie*, and fourteen sections, or *lag-punkty*. Noril'lag held nearly four times more prisoners than Gorlag. The camp for politicals worried the bosses most. With six zones for men and one for women, it was desperately overcrowded. Each zone held between three and six thousand men. The trouble began in the men's zones. The guards had never required a reason to abuse, but in the days after Stalin's death the provocations grew frequent and severe. Then the killing started.[30]

On May 25 the crackle of automatic-weapons fire was heard across the fifth zone of the camp. Versions diverged on what happened. Rygor Klimovich, a Belarusian zek and one of the strike leaders, remembered a group of prisoners who were sitting on a barracks roof, watching a convoy of female prisoners march off to work, and accompanying them with a Ukrainian folk song on an accordion, when a guard sprayed the roof with gunfire. Other survivors said the first murder came randomly, during a routine escort of prisoners between zones. A former prosecutor wrote that it all started when a prisoner had screamed at a passing guard, "Hey, you Stalinist son of a bitch!"[31] Whatever the cause, the murder was enough to spark the strike. The men across the camp let their hands fall and stopped work. The strike lasted, in various zones of the camp in varying degrees, until August.

The women did not sit idle. "It was Leysia," recalled Olga Yaskina, the woman who had led the charge against General Numerov. As Zek No. X-401, Olga endured the strike in the Sixth Female Camp of the Gorlag, the camp for politicals. Leysia Zelinskaya was barely into her twenties. Born in the Ukrainian countryside, she had been arrested after the war, charged in 1946 with treason. She was pale, pudgy, and not particularly tall. But Leysia, Olga said, started it all. She rallied the women to strike.

"Leysia and I slept side by side on wooden bunks. One morning we got up as usual and went to breakfast. Katya Kutz was with us. Katya was much older, but she always walked with me. We'd walk arm in arm as we were led out to work at the cement factory. That morning, when we got to the camp gates, we had to wait. The guards letting in the last shift were counting the prisoners. When I tried to walk through the gates and down to the factory, another prisoner, this giant of a woman, knocked me off my feet. No one would be going to work that day. But I had no idea, that's how well organized they were. Some girls knew, and some didn't."

It began with a hunger strike. For a week none of the women ate. Leysia and the strike leaders made sure of that, even though the bosses boiled up kasha and kept the canteen open day and night. For three days Olga ate nothing. Then she got dystrophy. "I had no strength," she said as her eyes grew moist. "I would have died if I hadn't eaten. So yes, I went and ate." The sense of shame, at her having given in to hunger, remained. "The girls beat me, but I ate."

The women's strike lasted until July 9, 1953. Olga remembered well how it ended. The women stood in a ring around the camp, all together, at least a thousand of them, arms locked. The guards stood on the other side of the fence, trying to coax them to go to work. One young officer, quite a nice-looking young man, stood across from Olga on other side of the fence.

"What are you doing here?" he yelled at her. "You're nothing but a scrawny little thing."

"Me!" she screamed back. "You tell me what am I doing to you!"

The guard only yelled louder, "Come out!"

But Olga simply looked at him and said, "I have as much strength as you have."

Both sides knew the standoff could not last. Within minutes the guards began to beat the women. The nice-looking young officer picked up a plank and hit Olga over the head with it. She fell to the ground, but the women behind her stood strong. Until the fire trucks came.

"The guards opened their hoses and flooded the camp. We were thrown backward. Anyone who resisted got clubbed on the head . . . and that would be it. They'd be done in there and then." That day, out of fear or out of shock, Olga still did not know, the strike ended.

An emergency MVD commission convened, as the bosses attempted to sort the leaders from the led. "It was a farce," Olga said. "Our side was made up of *zhuchki*," camp slang for female recidivists. Even before the strike, the *zhuchki* had their own barracks. The guards had favored them, and the *zhuchki* returned the favor. They did the guards' bidding, Olga said. "They were the ones who beat us even before the strike." Now they were put on the commission because they weren't politicals. The women strikers were divided: Some were sent back to the camp, while the organizers were moved to a men's camp. That night Olga and her bunkmates returned to their barracks and began to organize new brigades. The next day they were back at work.

For the women who had led the strike, things did not end as well. Twelve prisoners sat on the commission with the camp bosses. "Don't worry," they told the women, "you won't be punished. Speak out." Leysia, still pudgy but paler than before, took a seat to testify. The guards took their places across from the women. The bosses let the prisoners make their statements, and the next day they took them all off to solitary. Before long they sent them back down in barges to camps on the mainland. Olga never heard from Leysia again. "The girls," she guessed, "didn't make any more statements."[32]

The camp authorities did not wait long to quell the men's revolt. The worst killing came on August 4, 1953. "They drove in trucks covered with steel plates," one of the survivors, Bronius Zlatkus, said. "They'd mounted machine guns on each truck, and they simply opened fire on the camp." By the most modest tally, more than one hundred men were killed and more than two hundred wounded. Zlatkus, who in the summer after Stalin's death was a twenty-five-year-old Lithuanian imprisoned in Norilsk since 1948, remembered his near execution vividly: "They herded about four hundred of us in one camp and about six hundred in another. We were out in the tundra, in barracks surrounded by four guard towers and a line of machine guns. They were going to shoot us. They told us the tundra would be our grave."[33]

Only Beria's sudden fall saved them. The secret police chief was arrested on June 26, 1953, and on July 10, *Pravda* spread the word that the former head of Lubyanka was an enemy of the people.[34] The executions were halted. By early August two planes had arrived in Norilsk with MVD officers. They moved the strike leaders—more than three hundred men—south, first to the infamous Vladimir Prison and then east on to Kolyma. Zlatkus was among the few who survived. He had long since found his way back to Vilnius, where he served as the reunion chair of the two hundred or so Lithuanian veterans of the Norilsk camps.

SEMYON VILENSKY, my friend in Moscow who had set himself the task of collecting and publishing the works of the survivors, liked to argue about the origins of the Norilsk revolt. Arching his brows, he pronounced it a provocation, a cynical but expedient plan to cull the worst offenders and reduce tension in the camps. Others pointed to the softening that followed Stalin's death and argued that the camp directors did in fact provoke the strike, but only to justify, and prolong, their reign. Yet to those who participated in it, the uprising was genuine, a natural result of hellish conditions.[35]

The ground, according to all the available evidence, was more than ready. Vladimir Zverev, the fourth boss of the Kombinat, had tried to warn Moscow. Camp conditions, he wrote in a secret report in January 1953, had become "unacceptable." Zverev did not varnish. His litany of complaints was long. There were never enough supplies or food. In 1952, he wrote, there had been numerous escapes, and six zeks remained at large. His prisoners had yet to be segregated by the severity of their crimes. Common criminals bunked alongside politicals. There was also insufficient supervision in the factories, he cautioned, that enabled prisoners to make "knives, spikes, and even grenades."

Zverev's greatest headache, however, was not the prisoners but the guards. I had seen such complaints before, in the archives of the Soviet prosecutor's office. By the 1950s Norilsk, the documents made clear, had also become a place of exile for wayward NKVD officers. Zverev reported that in 1952, among his four thousand officers and guards, there were 1,240 disciplinary violations. Twenty-two of his men were tried for crimes. There had been drinking, debauchery, and desertion. Guards had succumbed to "contact with prisoners"—and suicide.[36]

Zverev's report was a storm warning and a last plea for help:

If you will allow me, comrades, to address a few words to the Gulag administrators. The Gulag is well aware that the prisoner contingent of Norilsk is a very severe, difficult one. Those collected here are the worst from all the camps of the Soviet Union. It is known that in the work of the camps there are a great number of major shortcomings. Nonetheless, even despite the orders of a minister, the Gulag deals with the Norilsk camps without care or caution. This is particularly evident in the selection of cadres, including the administrative officers.

Zverev was no reformer. His complaints were devoid of a moral voice. He wrote cursorily of the lack of the prisoners' living space—he would love to increase it, one day, to the Gulag standard of two square meters—and fumed over the improper storage of spoons in the canteens. Insubordination, however, had driven him to despair. Drunks surrounded the camp director. There was his deputy, a man so fond of the vodka that the prisoners brought him he had to be pensioned off early. He was duly replaced by another "scoundrel," sent north "for reforming."

When an officer elsewhere in Russia was fired for drinking, Zverev wrote, he was packed off to Norilsk. He disagreed with the practice: "Although the Arctic gets cold, even extremely cold, the idea of turning Norilsk into a drying-out tank is not the best." The camp director did not lack for evidence. Not long before, Moscow had sent up a new deputy director of the political department of the guard corps, a certain Lieutenant Colonel Barybin. "We did not even have time to size up the lieutenant colonel," Zverev quipped. "He drinks so much that he succeeded in losing both his hands to frostbite, a loss he explained by saying that he did not realize it got so cold in Norilsk."

In the years following Stalin's death, the Norilsk camps were gradually liquidated. The Tula fences came down, but the barracks stayed. In 1956 the first contingent of "volunteers" arrived, thanks to the *orgnabor*, the organized selection orchestrated by Moscow. The so-called enthusiasts, Komsomol students and former military men, were ferried in by the thousands to replace the prisoners. The state now dangled incentives–chiefly, better pay–to lure workers to Norilsk. The campaign worked. In the 1960s Norilsk even acquired an odd allure, as the romanticism of the remote and exotic sparked the imaginations of the ascendant generation. By the end of the 1970s, the Kombinat had opened new mines and smelters and the city's population had doubled since the end of the camps. Throughout the Brezhnev years Norilsk grew faster than almost any other Soviet city. It also grew younger. In 1973, some fourteen thousand children attended its kindergartens. By 1987 the figure had doubled.[37] When Gorbachev came to town the next year, Norilsk's population was at its height, and its miners were among the best-paid workers in the USSR.

❈ ELEVEN ❈

"MEN ARE CLEVER at forgetting what it is not pleasant to remember," wrote József Lengyel, the Hungarian writer who survived the Norilsk camps. "They scrape earth over their memories, as dogs do over their excrement." [38] Aleksei Borisovich Loginov had much to forget. He had served, in all, seventeen years in Norilsk, from 1941 to 1957, retiring as an engineer-colonel. He became an engineer in 1936, when he had graduated from the USSR's top mining institute in Leningrad. He became a colonel as he rose through the ranks of the men who ran the Gulag, having joined the NKVD in 1939. Loginov had headed the Kombinat during its time of greatest change, in the years after the strike. Two weeks after Stalin's death, on March 18, 1953, the Norilsk camps were transferred from the Interior Ministry to the Ministry of Ferrous Metallurgy. It was more than a bureaucratic distinction. Starting in the fall after the strike, and extending for several years, tens of thousands of prisoners were released or sent south into exile in the wilds of the Krasnoyarsk region. That year Norilsk lost its title as a settlement. It became a city.

I found Loginov in Moscow, on the eve of his ninety-fifth birthday. He was a tall, elegant man with a glistening bald head. His eyes were large and brown, softened by milky rings of pale blue. He wore a gray cardigan, zippered to the neck, brown slacks, and well-worn checkered slippers. He got right to the point. "We couldn't do it any other way," he said. "Everyone knew that." He would not brook any softhearted talk of human rights or inhumane work conditions. Industrialization in the West was one thing, and Norilsk quite another. The city and the Kombinat, he said, could not have been built without the prison labor. Few men alive knew more of the early days of Norilsk. He had arrived in the fall of 1941. For a time after the war he left the city but always returned. He had won the Lenin Prize and the Red Labor Banner, had met Stalin and Beria—"many times."

The Soviet leaders, in the glow of the triumphant war effort, dispatched him to America in 1947. He crisscrossed the country on a buying spree for Norilsk and the entire Soviet mining sector. (He'd also purchased American machinery for the gold mines of Kolyma.) He held his memories of America close, a joy he never relinquished. He kept a gold-leafed diary of the trip on his desk, but even now he would not open it. Made that mistake once, he said, when he first came home. He'd shared the diary with a friend who read of the fraternizing in San Francisco and New York and told him to burn it or he'd regret it one day. In Norilsk people had gone wild over Loginov's lectures on his American adventures. "The hall overflowed," he recalled, flashing a smile. "The ladies all wanted to hear what the Americans wore." Detroit and the Colorado mines had awed him, to be sure. But the Americans had done it all so "differently" it was hard to compare. They had money, he said, and equipment. "They didn't need to do things the way we did."

Tea was served, but he did not drink it. He sat on the edge of a high-backed chair, staring through the flowery lace that covered his living room window. I tried to ask again about the legacy of the camps. Was his conscience not troubled? He turned and looked at me blankly. A cat ran underfoot. He had known that the prisoners' lot was not the best. "Conditions of course were difficult." His own first impressions of Norilsk had been "the worst." But he tried to explain the gulag away. "It was necessary," he said.

The Soviets had needed the metals, first for building the Soviet state, then for the war. "There was," he repeated, "no other way." For Loginov it was too much. He lasted only until 1957 as head of the Kombinat, before asking to be relieved. His nerves shot, he was demoted south, back to Moscow.

Loginov's birthday was February 23, Red Army Day and the anniversary of the day in 1944 Stalin deported the Chechens. In 2001 he turned ninety-five. But that spring, on a cold wet morning in Moscow, his heart gave out. No need to be sad, an old Kombinat colleague, the editor of his memoirs, informed me. "The old man had been praying for death for weeks," he said. "He just got weaker and weaker and the last few days he lost all sense of the world. In the end he went peacefully, in his sleep. It was a blessing, really."

DISOBEDIENCE, THE NATIVES of Norilsk liked to say, was bred in their bones. They liked to talk of the strike of 1953. They also liked to remind you that in 1989, when miners began to rise up across the Soviet Union, Norilsk again stood in the vanguard. Gorbachev was stunned by Norilsk's anger during his visit in 1988. At an orchestrated "meeting with workers" on the need for reform, the workers did not disguise their defiance. Gorbachev announced that he had received a letter suggesting he give the order to "Fire on headquarters!," intending the suggestion as an example of what not to do. But the workers cried out, "Absolutely right!"[39]

Defiance, to be sure, ran strong in Norilsk. Yet at the same time, a tangible, disquieting irony pervaded the city. Once freed, thousands of the zeks had remained. Like so many of the freed slaves in the American South who settled beside the plantation gates, the former prisoners stayed on to work for the Kombinat. Despite the deprivations of the far north and the abundant medical and environmental reasons to evacuate, no one, it seemed, wanted to leave. No matter how often or rapturously they pined for the places far away where they had been born, schooled, or once worked, they stayed.

"It would be hard for you to understand," said Olga Yaskina, the heckler of the general. "But where were we to go?" The whole country, as she put it, was "in camps." Here at least there was work and a one-room apartment. And a husband. Like so many of the female survivors I met, Olga had married a guard.[40] Later he left, trading her, she said, for "a young tramp in heels." But in the first years of freedom he was good to her. They had had a son, a son who had just lost his job at the Kombinat.

Marriage was not the only reason to stay. Vasily Romashkin stayed so his past wouldn't follow him everywhere he went. An engineer who had helped pour the foundations of each of the city's factories, Romashkin, a spry eighty-six when we met, had been among the first prisoners to arrive. He came in 1939 and never left. A new life, he said, would have been impossible. Even freed, former prisoners were often given long terms of exile or suspended rights.[41] Few zeks could gain a *propiska*, or residency permit, to go back home. Even for those who succeeded in winning back passports, they were "dirty," branded with the details of their camp time. They knew they would be considered *vragi naroda*, enemies of the people, and it would be hard to get a job or an apartment anywhere else.

Romashkin lived in a bright apartment on Leninsky. The windowsills, as in so many homes in Norilsk, were lined with unruly plants, their overgrown vines climbing the glass. He was a compact man with large brown eyes. He wore a black beret that he pushed back when he had a pronouncement or a joke to make. Nothing about him seemed old, least of all his eyes, which lit up when he laughed. A man who would rather talk concrete than terror, when he spoke of the past, it was with pride.

In his life one could read much of the history of the Soviet century. Born in a village not far from Moscow, he had suffered the famine of the 1920s and collectivization. There had been a train journey of desperation to the Urals. Romashkin remembered how his parents had run from the train during stops to steal wooden crosses from the cemeteries to stoke the makeshift stoves. He remembered, too, the hope of the early 1930s. In flight, his family had struck upon an idyll. They resettled in a farming commune on Siberia's edge, one that in retrospect at least had adhered to common ideals. He soon enrolled at the local institute. Then, just months before graduation, came his classmates' false accusations and, afterward, the camps. Romashkin was released in 1947. The years that followed he now called "the best of my life." He continued then to serve the Kombinat, however, as a chief engineer, a man of stature.

The years since the Soviet collapse had been unkind. His daughter had divorced, his son, he said, drank so much he had disowned him, and his pension barely covered the groceries. Romashkin had taken in his daughter and her son. Still, he refused to complain. The Kombinat had asked him, as a veteran of fifty years' work, to join the parade that marked the sixty-fifth anniversary. He had marched down Leninsky Prospekt behind Potanin, Governor Lebed, and the new bosses. A withered bouquet stood on a table nearby, a present, he said, from the after-parade party.

It was late, and Romashkin had yet to take his walk. He walked every day. He changed only his route, depending on the direction of the gas. "I watch it on the horizon," he said, "and adjust my path accordingly." His daughter and grandson would be home soon. The boy represented Norilsk's third generation. His grandfather had no intention of letting him go astray like so many young people of late. He wouldn't stand for the boy's leaving Norilsk for the mainland, let alone falling for some dream like Moscow. Romashkin wanted him to stay here. "After all," he said, "why did I build all this?"

THE PROPENSITY OF the zeks to put down roots in the place of their incarceration raised inconvenient questions. It got to the contrarian point that Semyon Vilensky liked to raise in Moscow but few dared admit: The vast majority of those sent to the camps for "political" crimes had not been politicized at all. Only the minority had been opposed to the regime. A great many of the zeks not only had believed in the system but had yearned to be recognized as supporters. In Paris, Jacques Rossi told me a story, recounted in his *Gulag Handbook*, of his witnessing the power of the word *tovarish* ("comrade"), when employed by an officer talking with prisoners. He had seen a head engineer, a major in the secret police, ask a brigade that had just finished their day's work, nearly twelve hours, to stay and do a double shift with no sleep. "They all agreed," Rossi said, "and only because the officer addressed them as comrades!"

Even the strike leaders of 1953 believed in the system. They believed Moscow would heed their concerns, recognize their plight. Moscow still held curative power. As Yevhen Hrycyak, one of the strike leaders, wrote in his memoir of the uprising, ". . . we did not take a hostile stand in relation to the central government itself, because we expected that after Stalin's death, the newly formed government would at least attempt to lead the country onto the straight and narrow path. Therefore we declared to the government: 'Our goal is freedom . . .' and 'We want to be talked to not through sub-machine guns, but in a language of father and son.' "[42] It was as if the zeks had held true to the illusions of their first nights in jail: "It can't be intentional," "it will all work out," "if only the people at the top knew."

As the twenty-first century opened, however, few believed in Moscow anymore. They did not imagine, as many of the eldest Chechens in Aldy had, that the representatives of the state would come and take care of them. Still, they stayed. Some, no doubt like prisoners too long in jail, had become institutionalized, unable to live on the outside.

The Kombinat had tried a resettlement program, baited with cash incentives to entice the laid off and retired to move south. It backfired. The workers took the money and stayed. Then the officials devised a new plan. This time they would use free apartments, not cash, to lure the "excess population" to the mainland. The former workers, however, were quick to recognize fungibility. They accepted the apartments, only to convert them into cash and stay in Norilsk. In June 2001 the World Bank approved a long-overdue eighty-million-dollar loan to the Russian government to assist with resettlement from three northern regions: Norilsk, Vorkuta, and Magadan. By 2002 the bank program had still not moved a single person.

The fatal allure confounded. I had begun to wonder if the city had not inspired a Soviet version of the Stockholm syndrome, the strange psychological transformation in which prisoners assume an affinity for their captors. But Norilsk, I realized as I walked the length of Leninsky Prospekt one last time, was shaped, perhaps more than any corner of Russia I had seen, by juxtapositions of the incompatible: a city built in a clime where there were no cities; a city where factory furnaces burned at a thousand degrees while the air outside was so cold that spit, as Shalamov wrote, froze in midair; a city where an industrial complex built on terror had become a showcase for the ravages of unbridled capitalism; and a city where the heirs of the Gulag, whether camp survivors or recent arrivals, shared a sense of belonging. Norilsk engendered a secret warmth. Money no doubt had something to do with it. (A Kombinat salary, by Russia's dismal standards, remained high.) Yet the greater pull seemed the strange consolation, pride even, of inhabiting one of the world's most uninhabitable places.

ON MY LAST NIGHT in Norilsk I headed over to a Caucasian restaurant with no name on Leninsky. A month had passed since I had boarded the *Matrosov* in Krasnoyarsk. It was dark inside, but Romanovich, the house singer with attenuated black sideburns and flaring white trousers, was just warming up. Before long the disco ball turned, the tiny dance floor filled, and Romanovich was back in form. Everyone danced, women with men, men with men, women with women, and boys with girls. A broad-busted grandmother twirled on the arm of a teenage boy whose baby fat still hung from his cheeks.

The restaurant used to be across the street until the melting permafrost leveled the building next door. Then it had been called the Sixty-ninth Parallel. No one had come up with a new name yet, but it remained Norilsk's hot spot, the place families came to christen marriages, children, jobs. The dance floor, five square feet beside the bar, was bathed in blue light. Romanovich, a velvety crooner from Dagestan, was clearly the town's favorite. As the crowd swelled and spun, now and then someone would shout a request from the floor.

"This one," Romanovich relayed, "goes out for our friend Pasha." Pasha, he said, had just graduated and was heading out tomorrow, flying south to the mainland. "This one's from his loved one, Yekaterina. She's gonna miss you, Pasha, but we know how much you've looked forward to this. . . . We wish you the best of times in the big city, we wish you a safe journey, and most of all, we wish to see you back here among us, where you know, Pasha, my friend, we're going to be right here waiting for you. . . ."

Romanovich clutched a glass-beaded microphone close and sang.

> *He's flying away, my friend, flying beyond the cordon*
> *He flies somewhere where winter never comes*
> *He's flying away, my friend, far away . . . beyond the cordon*
> *He flies far away . . . with a broken wing.*

The next morning, by the time I at last boarded an aged Tupelov, bound once again for Moscow, a cold certainty had settled in. As long as there are riches to pull from the frozen ground—and the ore reserves are expected to last another half century—the heirs of the Gulag will not be going anywhere.

IV. EAST

TO THE BREAKING POINT

I arrived on Sakhalin thinking Russia would be like
Germany or Japan after the war. But it turned out to be
more like Germany or Japan during the war.

> —An American pilgrim who spent years on the
> island trying, and failing, to run its largest timber
> concern

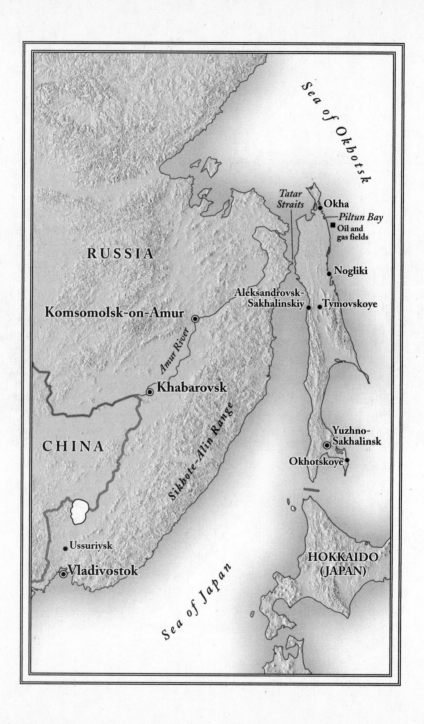

🕸 ONE 🕸

SAKHALIN, EVER SINCE I first read Chekhov's account of his 1890 journey to the island, had loomed as an alluring challenge at Russia's farthest edge. The writer had faced a wretched road, "the Siberian *trakt*, the biggest, and it would seem, the most absurd, road in all the world."[1] The trip, however, proved a tonic for a young man with consumption. The farther east Chekhov ventured, the more he seemed invigorated. As the distance from the capital grew and the taiga thickened, worry and regret gave way to renewed hunger and sexual appetite. In Irkutsk, with two thousand miles at his back, Chekhov took the measure of the provincial lasses and disdained them: too square-shouldered. He passed Baikal, the oldest and deepest of the world's lakes, and caught a steamer to begin the last, and steadiest, stage of the journey. As the boat chugged along the vast Amur River to Nikolayevsk, the port for Sakhalin, the frontier enveloped him.

Once back in Moscow, Chekhov summed up the trip aptly: Everything before Baikal was prose, he said, everything after, poetry. In the isolation and expansiveness of Siberia, girls smoked cigarettes, men professed liberal streaks, and everyone everywhere shared the same complaints. They railed against the miseries of their roads and the ineptitude of their officials. Deep in the lands where the spring mud never dried, Chekhov felt closer to the American West, even the Australian outback, than to Russia. He had entered a stateless realm where the forests never ended and the locals asked, "Are you from *Russia*?" as if it were a foreign land, because to them it was. Chekhov's journey to Sakhalin covered nearly sixty-five hundred miles, more than a quarter of the globe's circumference. The trip across the continent alone stretched eighty-one days.

For months I tried out itineraries, hoping to retrace Chekhov's route. I wanted to approach the island as he had, by boat, but found no reliable conveyance that would bear me along the Amur and across the narrow

Tatar Straits to Sakhalin: no ferry, barge, or even cargo ship. In tsarist days, it seemed, traversing the wilds of the Far East was easier. After months of telegrams and calls in the middle of the night—Sakhalin lies seven time zones ahead of Moscow—I gave up assaying the virtues of the train and bought a one-way ticket on VladAvia, Vladivostok's proud new air carrier, one of the so-called babyflots that had sprouted across Russia since the Soviet collapse. Most of the planes in the new regional fleets were old Aeroflot jets, the ones parked on local tarmacs when the empire died. The planes were seized, repainted, and, one hoped, occasionally tuned up.

Flying to Russia's Pacific coast can take, if the winds run strong against an old Tupelov, nine hours. I had flown to Vladivostok before, but this flight, the ticket lady in Moscow informed me, featured a new shortcut. "The Chinese finally gave in," she said with a smile. Russian planes could now fly over the land once known as Manchuria.

THE CHILL RAINS of autumn had descended on Moscow by the time I boarded the plane. The interior lights dimmed, and the cabin filled with a deep rosy light, as the sun dipped behind the horizon to the left and we headed due east. The sun streaked through the windows, as if it were taking us in, not yet ready to disappear on the far side of the earth. We crossed the Urals, and then for hours, the length of Siberia stretched below. A river emerged, writhed through the steppes, only to disappear as mysteriously as it had appeared.

The Ilyushin 62M is a fat, superfat, passenger jet. When it takes off, it enters the sky in slow motion, in an ascent more horizontal than vertical, on a trajectory that seems carefully calibrated to challenge the laws of gravity. The plane is so large it seems best suited to carry tanks, not people, and its thin seats an afterthought, a concession to the necessities of the new economy. I had flown countless times in Russian skies. All the same, as the VladAvia jet began to shudder over southeastern Siberia, forebodings flooded my mind. The plane did not fall, as it would have had we hit an air pocket. Nor did it shake sideways. Instead, it jerked up and then down just as suddenly. As it became a piggy bank shaken by an impatient child, and the passengers the coins inside, I wondered if the pilot, if indeed he was a pilot, was having a seizure. At last a copilot emerged from the rear kitchen. As he rushed past, the smell of cigarettes lingered in his wake.[2]

The turbulence, even by Russian standards, was bad. The Ilyushin had just cleared the deep blue of Baikal when the flight attendants abandoned their tea service. The plane continued to dip and duck. The gasps grew louder. The attendants struggled to their seats. I wondered what the American couple behind me was thinking. Wearing matching sweat suits and carrying Stephen King novels in their laps, they were en route to adopt a Russian orphan. They had been friendly and chatty. Now they were not conversing. They were crunching through a stash of PowerBars.

The plane steadied. The harried attendants delivered food, the usual still life on a tray. Again fibrous chicken. I stared at it, and somehow the food, dove gray and tasteless, was calming. The sky slowly changed color, from the rainbow of a fireball sucker to the palest blue, absent of any red. From here on, the lines separating the colors of time became sharp, distinct.

VLADIVOSTOK, POPULATION six hundred thousand, is the capital of Primorsky Krai, the Maritime Territory, known locally by its short name, Primorye. Vladivostok means "to rule the east." The echo sounding back to Vladikavkaz, the fortress in North Ossetia, was deliberate. Tsarist hubris yet again. Vladivostok has long been more of an end than a beginning: the terminus, since its completion in 1903, of the Trans-Siberian Railroad and the limit of first tsarist, then Soviet power. In the final Soviet years, however, it had increasingly become the USSR's exposed edge to the outside world.

Vladivostok owes its founding, in 1860, to Nicholas I's governor-general of eastern Siberia, Nikolai Muravyov. A hero of the battlefields in the Caucasus, Muravyov wrested the coastline from the Chinese and the British, whose naval surveyors had only a few years earlier christened its bays and inlets with English names. Petersburg had not rushed to the idea, but the geography possessed a commanding logic. The city, centered on hills above two majestic bays, seemed destined to become the empire's outpost in Asia. Some sixty miles from the Chinese border, and a few hours' sail from the Japanese main island of Honshu, Vladivostok held not only strategic import but great promise. With the humiliating loss of Port Arthur in the Russo-

Japanese War of 1905, the city became Russia's largest naval base in the Far East.

Vladivostok never grew into a stronghold of power. Instead, in the years after the Revolution, it became a stronghold of opposition, a refuge for Whites, and a harbor for the Allied intervention. In 1918 the Allied head-quarters occupied the largest building on its main street, and the United States maintained a consulate here until the dawn of the cold war. The city had long been a cosmopolitan crossroads, home to a mélange of French hoteliers and Austrian shopkeepers, Swiss jewelers and American sailors. The actor Yul Brynner was born here in 1920; his Swiss grandfather was an important trader in the city. After the Revolution, the Japanese and Americans, the French and British, occupied Vladivostok.[3]

Kolchak, the White commander, ultimately disappointed his Western backers. In 1920 the Bolsheviks captured Kolchak and executed him in Irkutsk. That spring, in Blagoveshchensk, a Bolshevik commander founded the Far Eastern Republic, which united nearly two million Russians in lands across the Far East and the north of Sakhalin. It did not last long. By 1922 the interventionists had retreated. Moscow subsumed the would-be republic and ruled this corner of the east unchallenged.[4]

Within a decade the isolation at the eastern end of the Trans-Siberian attracted the attention of the architects of the Gulag. They turned Vladivostok into a seething entrepôt in the archipelago of camps. As the cargo cars delivered the zeks en masse, sprawling transit camps grew on the rough northern outskirts known as Vtoraya Rechka (Second River). From here the prisoners were sent north to the gold fields of Kolyma.[5] The poet Osip Mandelstam was not as lucky. For him, the Second River camp was his last. Just how and when we may never know, but Mandelstam died here not many months after he arrived in 1938. He was forty-seven.

Geography paid off handsomely. Vladivostok became the USSR's most muscular arm in the east, the base of the Pacific Fleet. During World War II it served as a major port for Lend-Lease. Franklin Roosevelt's vice president Henry Wallace even visited in May 1944, and stopped by Magadan, the headquarters of Dalstroi, the far eastern arm of the Gulag founded as a con-glomerate of gold-mining camps. Wallace, who later fell from power famously under Truman, told his Soviet hosts how impressive it all looked. Owen Lattimore, a prominent China hand who accompanied Wallace on the trip, came home to publish a glowing report in *National Geographic*. Lattimore, who later suffered the glare of Joseph McCarthy, described Dalstroi as a "a remarkable concern" that could be "roughly compared to a combination Hudson's Bay Company and TVA."[6]

In the state archives in Moscow I found out just how carefully the secret policemen had stage-managed the Americans' visit. The spirit of Potemkin had been very much alive. A three-page, single-spaced telegram, dated June 6, 1944, from the head of the Dalstroi, Ivan Nikishov, to Beria, Molotov, and Stalin detailed Wallace's misadventure. The local NKVD boss faithfully recorded every question the U.S. vice president had posed: How many workers did Dalstroi have? How much gold did they mine? What was the better transport for the region, rail or airplane? Nikishov was most struck by Wallace's pronouncement made upon leaving: "We heard a lot about Dalstroi in America and knew it was a big trust. But having been here, we've become convinced and must confess that in America we haven't such a big trust, one that encompasses so many tasks. . . ."

By 1948 the warmth had dissipated. With the advent of the cold war, the United States closed its consulate in Vladivostok, and the Soviets, in time closed Vladivostok altogether to the outside world. It remained out of bounds until the Soviet fall.

❧ TWO ❧

"YOU'LL LOVE VLADIVOSTOK," a native son, one of the nightly horde of visitors to Andrei and Lera's communal apartment in Moscow, had assured me long before. "It'll remind you of San Francisco," he said. It had the same hills, streetcars, views of the water. My first impression was indeed of San Francisco—but of Chinatown. The architecture, at least what was not Soviet cinder block, bore a distinctly Asian influence. Much of the city was built by Korean and Chinese labor, and many of the once-grand houses that lined its avenues were the work of Japanese POWs. But there the resemblance to the city of the Golden Gate ended.

In 1992 the locals surveyed their bountiful inheritance—a huge merchant fleet and a cornucopia of timber, fish and furs–and dreamed of becoming a Russian Hong Kong. They envisioned a free economic zone blooming as freighters filled the ports, forming a bridge to the Asian markets close by. Some still believed the dream. Primorye, no longer a pliant colony of Moscow, said the new optimists, will join arms with the Pacific Rim, and, in a case study of globalization's fruits, arise from its post-Soviet slumber.

The dream informed conversations from the governor's office to the Chinese cafés along the city's main streets, but sadly, a decade after opening up again, Vladivostok still awaited its revival. Instead of a boomtown, the traveler found the corrupt heart of the far eastern frontier, the modern update of the unbridled market that nineteenth-century visitors discovered.

"Whatever it is you're looking for, you can find it in Vlad," a dark-eyed prospector from Belfast assured me one night in the casino bar of the lavishly rebuilt Hotel Versailles. The locals pronounced the hotel's name as it was spelled in Russian: *Versal.* "And you can be sure," the Irishman added, "that it's for sale."

The city bordered not just one frontier but many. China, Japan, the Koreas all lay within broadcast, trading, and smuggling range. Japanese and Korean cars, old compacts discarded to the Russian market, clogged the hills. The Hyundai, a graceless concrete tower that was Vladivostok's finest hotel, loomed above the sparse city center, while cargo ships from Japan and Seoul stewed in the harbor, awaiting their turn in port. At night, neon from the new Chinese cafés mottled the downtown streets pink and green, while in the hotel corridors and lobbies Chinese shuttle traders tempted Russian tourists with thin necklaces of gold and pearls. The city, to be sure, had its share of indigenous mafiosi and thugs, as a U.S. marine found out one spring night in 2000 in the Blue Bird Café, when he was shot in the back by one. But somehow everywhere I looked I saw well-fed Korean businessmen, Russian girls at their sides, luxuriating in the largess created by post-Soviet windfalls.

The fear of the Yellow Peril had made a strong comeback. Locals fondly quoted Governor-General Pavel Unterberger, who, in the age of Alexander II, declared his jingoist preference for "a Russian desert over a Korean-made paradise."[7] Now the xenophobia was fueled by the corps of out-of-work military and naval officers. The end of the empire had displaced hundreds of thousands of military men. It had hit its sailors particularly hard. They suffered not only the decline in prestige but the absence of a paycheck. They bridled at the word *konversiya*, the ambitious plan, amply funded by American taxpayers and George Soros, to try to beat the Soviet military-industrial complex into plowshares. While most could do little but grumble, their once-mighty Pacific Fleet rusted and its arms depots were looted. The admirals meanwhile made annual additions to their triple-tiered dachas.

With scant hope on the horizon, the displaced officers feared Russia's last frontier would be ravaged by Asia, the Chinese traders, Korean loggers, Japanese fishermen, and Vietnamese laborers. "We're trapped in a press between the masses of China and the wealth of Japan," a former border guard groaned as we drove through Vladivostok in his old Toyota pickup. "We know our days are numbered. The only question is who we'll surrender to."

Although the influx of Asian immigrants was far below the "millions" Russian officials spoke of, locals looked about and saw their worst fears coming true. In the town of Ussuriysk, just a few miles from the border, a Chinese bazaar of cargo ship containers had swollen into a village alongside the tracks of the Trans-Siberian. The stalls brimmed with knockoff clothes emblazoned with imaginary Western labels ("DKZY"), touting fictitious origins ("Santa Acapulco"). "Junk," Russians said with sneers. But they were less likely to admit that the inexpensive Chinese goods found a vast market, appealing to Russian tastes. Similarly, reports of illegal border crossings by Chinese laborers filled the local papers almost daily. Yet the stories failed to mention the demand that lured the workers, from one of China's poorest regions, into Russia. The locals knew the truth: Be they Chinese, Korean, or Japanese, the return of Primorye's neighbors was but a convenient excuse to revive the fear of the Asian Other.

For the politically astute, however, the favored target lay far to the west, in Moscow. The Kremlin, they sighed, knew how to take but not to give. Moscow, they said, created their misery by failing to domesticate the regional governor, Yevgeny Nazdratenko. For nearly a decade Nazdratenko made Primorye his duchy. He had long gained renown–"Nasty Naztradenko" local U.S diplomats dubbed him. He relished the limelight and even the role of the rogue. He flouted public mores, ignored the mounting discontent, and throughout the Yeltsin era disobeyed the Kremlin itself. At one point he even made a point of presenting the skin of a Siberian tiger, a fine example of the endangered Amur species, to his good friend–the Belarusian leader Aleksandr Lukashenko, Europe's last dictator. At his peak, Nazdratenko performed on a split screen: He played to the Russian love of the outcast while currying the requisite favors among the elite in Moscow. In the end, however, the cold did him in.

In Primorye, thanks to the freezing winds off the Sea of Japan, winters chill to bone. For years Nazdratenko so mangled the region's delicate energy policy that millions spent the winters without heat. The combination of mismanagement, embezzlement, and political brinksmanship was stunningly callous. Each winter the governor reprised the spectacle. Each year he blamed the crisis on rivals in Moscow. Vladimir Putin was not one to tolerate such insolence. Putin's ascent spelled Nazdratenko's downfall, although he did not fall hard or far. The new president named him head of the State Fisheries Committee. The position, as the Moscow press commented loudly, offered more than sturgeon and caviar.

IN MOSCOW, WHERE the climate seemed comparatively temperate, my elderly neighbor Nina Aleksandrovna used to watch the evening news and wonder how they did it. How did they survive the winters of blackouts with no heat? She knew the answer: Like her, like so many millions of Russians, the hardy souls of Primorye relied on a long tradition of self-preservation. The Far East was isolated. Even Siberia, the mapmakers insisted, ended to the west. Little beyond the weekly lists in the newspapers of the local boys killed in Putin's War and the daily vigil on the fate of the ruble betrayed the region's ties to Moscow. Yet as is almost always the case in Russia, in isolation there was relief.

"We'll never starve," Zhenya Voropaev assured me on my first night back in Vladivostok. It was late, but he was in a mood to chat. Zhenya worked the tiger patrol. A former submariner who had traveled the ports of the Soviet bloc, he was a loner, a trapper since childhood and a lifer on Russia's far eastern edge. He was a cheery sort, a barrel-chested man with a ginger mustache, reddish brown hair, and a perpetual half grin.

We had met a year earlier, on a field trip to visit the Siberian tigers. The famed beasts of the Far East were facing extinction. Their skin, bones, and body parts had become local currencies, and a smuggler's trade flourished, feeding Asia's medicinal recipes. I had come then to see the unlikely environmental warriors, the wilderness officers, nearly all hunters themselves, who sought to fend off the poachers. In an old Soviet Army truck we had crisscrossed the low-slung Sikhote-Alin range, fording the frozen creeks that laced its valleys. The entire Far East was suffering one of its worst winters. At night in the taiga, the temperature dropped to minus forty. Bones grew so cold that the numbness was welcome. We found dozens of drunken hunters, but no tigers. Still, the trip was a revelation.

Zhenya taught me the survival strategy of the Far East. The woods, he was fond of saying, held the *zapas*, the reserve. No matter how blighted life in the city turned, he could always return to the taiga, where he'd forage and hunt. "Berries and shotguns"—Zhenya was certain—"will be our salvation." There was great truth to his humor. Separatist talk might still find followers in Chechnya and other corners of the federation, but in Primorye the stalwart inhabitants favored self-reliance over secession. Once a sanctuary for tsarist explorers and scofflaws, then a refuge of White partisans and Old Believer sectarians, the taiga here had become a preserve for twenty-first-century hunter-gatherers.

One morning on the tiger trip, in the village of Vesyoli (Happy)—the ravages of the new order revealed themselves. The "village" was no more than a dozen huts tilting left and right on either side of a single road—Soviet Street, of course. We arrived on a momentous day. It had snowed all night, but the sun was bright, and the temperature had risen to minus thirty-eight. In every little yard along the frozen street, amid the cacophony of chickens and dogs, the families were out. Listless souls in slippers and in shock, they stared numbly down the street, to where an old black truck from Dal'energo, the Vladivostok electricity company, stood. In the cab of the truck two officials checked their watches. They wore fur hats and overcoats. At the same time, all along the road, Dal'energo workers climbed the telephone poles to sever the thick wires that ran to the sad huts. The sky was cloudless, and it was too cold to snow. "You're a lucky traveler," Zhenya said in disbelief. He had never seen such a thing. "Something to tell the folks back in Moscow," he said as the men from the power company proceeded to cut the village of Vesyoli off from the world of electricity.

On the road from Rostov to the southern reaches of the North Caucasus, I had driven past countless miles of fields where bare telephone posts stood, their wires having been stolen long ago. Once, outside Samara, along the Volga, I had seen young boys climb to the top of such poles. Stealing wire, in much of rural Russia, had become a common, and often lethal, pursuit. But I had never seen the electric company cut away its own wires.

DENIS DYOMKIN MAY have been the only resident of Primorye to take on Governor Nazdratenko and win. Denis was a reporter. Like many of the best journalists in Russia, he was scarcely in his twenties and already a veteran.

I tracked down Denis in Vladivostok. I'd heard of his triumph. Among Russian reporters, it had been something of a celebrated case. We met one evening to sort out the options for traveling the rest of the road to Sakhalin. In the midst of a crowd of Chinese jewelry traders from Harbin, we sat at a plastic table and sipped viscous Nescafé from plastic cups. The cups were so thin the coffee melted them. Above us, a Latin American soap opera blared on a color television. The front of the set was emblazoned with a brand name: Great Wall.

Denis had never heard of anyone sailing by cargo ship to Sakhalin. Or on a ferry up the Amur. He counseled flying, directly from Vladivostok. But I wanted to see the lands along the Chinese border and those to the north, along the long road to Khabarovsk, the city on the Amur that is the second largest in the Russian Far East. We struck an easy deal. I needed a ride, and Denis needed money. I would hand him two hundred dollars for the day's work, and he would provide wonderful company—and the tale of how he had beaten the tall odds.

We had passed the last kiosk on the outskirts of Vladivostok when Denis began to retrace his saga. He saw no reason to boast. To him it was a simple matter, a clear case. The governor had tried to bar him from doing his job; he had sought relief in the courts and won. The story seemed too equitable to be true. Denis explained. As the local reporter for *Kommersant*, the leading business daily in Moscow, he had long before earned the governor's scorn. Things had gotten personal. The governor's aides had made his life misery. Then one day he arrived at the governor's office, where Nazdratenko held press conferences, and the guard would not let him in. He said Denis's pass had expired. In fact it had been invalidated. So he had sued. Still, Denis refused to gloat. He did not see the case "as some David versus Goliath thing." It did not even seem a fight for free speech. He only wanted to work.

We had been in the car for two hours and passed accident after accident before we both seemed to conclude, however silently, that this road trip was a crazy idea. We had left town early, in the chill darkness before dawn. Chinese tourists, men and women, had filled the hotel parking lot to do tai chi. The rains had started early, when the skies were still dark. Sheets of rain swirled in a squall. Worse still, the road, the main highway, comprised two uneven lanes, backed up with trucks bearing goods inland from the port. On a good day, Denis figured, the drive took seven hours. Today it would take ten.

The road, as we approached Ussuriysk, brought us close to the Chinese border. When the car climbed a low hill, the rolling forests of Heilongjiang Province came into view to the left. "The trains with foreigners still run through here at night," Denis said, "so they won't see the border." The city was steeped in military slogans; the majority of its residents were border guards. We passed Russian graffiti: RESPECT US OR LEAVE! A warning, no doubt, from the cocky young nationalists to the Chinese in their midst. Later, as we approached Bikin, the garrison town where the radar half globes spun atop the rain-soaked hillsides, more graffiti greeted us: RUSSIANS FOR RUSSIAN POWER!

The rain fell ever harder against the windshield, as the bald tires of Denis's old Mitsubishi thudded rhythmically over the ruts in the Soviet asphalt. "There's nothing really to celebrate about my victory," he said, apropos of nothing. "It's not like life here for me or anyone else has gotten better because of it." The windshield wipers scraped across the glass, keeping time to Denis's laments like a metronome. He was divorced. "Married too young." He now lived with his mother. He yearned to get to Moscow, maybe to a job in the main offices of the paper. Everything in this country, he said, happened only in Moscow. Vladivostok, the biggest city in the Far East, was a village. Reform there had no prospect. A free economic zone to these crooks meant only one thing, a free criminal zone. And politics? What did they matter? Politics were not even real. Life was shaped by the brute force of business, big business. Even his legal victory had paled. "You can beat the governor only once," Denis said. "In the end he wins."

We entered the *krai* of Khabarovsk. The forest had thickened. And the rain had slowed. For long stretches of the road, however, low, heavy fog clung to the sudden mountains that rose above the swampy valleys. The villages, on the first day of fall, were flooded. The region was immense, nearly twice the size of California. But as we drove on, I felt the burden of the land—the boon and bane of its vastness. For hours we passed no sign of industry or of agriculture.

When we at last reached Khabarovsk it was nearly as dark as the dawn had been when we set out. A Japanese-run hotel offered rooms for $250 a night. We fought our way into a Soviet dormitory, $4 a cot. At the telegraph office I placed a call to the port of Vanino, which sits across the inlet from the better-known Sovetskaya Gavan (Soviet Harbor). Once it had been the starting point for the boats to Kolyma. Semyon Vilensky, and countless others, had been herded through it. Now, on occasion, it hosted boats to Sakhalin. Or so I had been told.

I made one last try to retrace Chekhov's route from Khabarovsk. Today, however, the only way to preserve that leg of Chekhov's trip appeared to be to travel the Amur by hydrofoil for five hours to Komsomolsk, then to take a small-gauge train for thirteen hours to Vanino, and finally an overnight ferry to Sakhalin. The journey, with luck, would last three days. Without luck, there would be no boats to Sakhalin, and I would have to return by the same route. For months I had tried unsuccessfully to call the port to learn the ferry schedule. I vowed to give it one final shot.

A woman, the harbor dispatcher, answered. "This *is* Vanino port," she shrieked. No, she announced, she had no schedules for the ferries and no knowledge of any boats to Sakhalin. Then she hung up. So it was decided. Instead of three days by hydrofoil, train, and boat, I would fly, one hour from Khabarovsk to Yuzhno-Sakhalinsk, the capital of Sakhalin.

❧ THREE ❧

"Despite all our sins," said the minister of natural resources, "despite seventy years of communism, and a privatization program that many state enterprises were not ready for, we are still the richest country—in natural resources—in the world." The numbers do indeed impress: Russia boasts a third of the world's natural gas, 17 percent of its oil, and more than a fifth of precious metals. Yet in the first post-Soviet decade the riches were plundered. In Moscow many surveyed the damage and wondered, Would history judge it the crime of the century? Some in the capital, however, as Putin and a new sobriety took hold, posed a weightier concern: Would Russia succeed in squandering its resources? The answer, I imagined, lay in Sakhalin.

I did not come by sea, but I arrived, like Chekhov, in darkness. Outside the airport the Japanese tour group I'd flown in with from Khabarovsk, a dozen men and three women, jumped into a waiting bus and vanished. I was left to haggle with the cabbies. One, a Russian Korean, demanded fifty dollars for the short ride into town. It sounded like a felony. "This is Sakhalin," he said. "What laws can there be here?"

The streets, with every fifth lamppost aglow, were pitch black as we drove into Yuzhno, as the locals call the capital. The only hotel with room, the Eurasia, lit a dark corner on the dismal square by the train station. Built under Brezhnev, and freshly refurbished by Japanese entrepreneurs in the early throes of the post-Soviet exuberance, the Eurasia had foundered. Like many of the hopeful ventures of the new era, it had reverted back to local ownership and languished. Outside, dark figures crowded the threshold, enveloped by clouds of cigarette smoke. Inside, there was no lobby, no front desk, only a heavyset woman who seemed reluctant to smile. She scoured my passport, unable to read the English. Her blond hair was piled in a bun, and her lips were painted fluorescent pink.

In the dining room, at large, round tables beneath small black paper lanterns, I discovered the Japanese tourists from the plane. They were energetically tucking into deep bowls of jellied fish and gray rice, as if they had arrived with the secret knowledge that Yuzhno offered few dining options. The Japanese were not foreigners. They were native sons and daughters of the island, returning to their birthplace. In 1905 the Treaty of Portsmouth that sealed Tokyo's victory in the Russo-Japanese War split Sakhalin along the fiftieth parallel. The southern half became a Japanese colony, Karafuto. Yuzhno to the Japanese was, until the end of World War II, Toyohara. Since the Soviet fall, as Sakhalin opened again, the Japanese had come trickling back. The Karafuto Renmei, the Japanese association of former residents of Karafuto, claimed more than six thousand members.

Not all the Japanese, however, came to step back into time. A Tokyo securities firm built a gleaming bank downtown. A graying Japanese hippie, despondent at the dearth of edible cuisine in Yuzhno, opened a vegetarian place across town. Toyohara, he called it. A group of Tokyo investors constructed a deluxe hotel complex, the Santa Resort. The Japanese, however, like their Western counterparts in the European realm of the country, soon learned the perils of investing in Russia. Before long their enthusiasm—and start-up capital—disappeared.

The Santa Resort, the would-be Ritz of Yuzhno, became the most infamous of the failed joint ventures. The Moscow press had followed the legal saga closely: A Japanese firm had sunk twenty million dollars into the Santa, outfitting it with sushi and espresso bars and health and beauty spas. Once it was completed, their Russian partners proceeded to muscle out the Japanese investors. The Japanese went to court and won at every instance, but no one in town imagined they would ever recover their investment or feel safe on the island again.

Inhospitality was not the only reason the Japanese had soured on investing. The other was the Kurile Islands, the disputed archipelago that fans out to the east. Seized by the USSR in 1945, along with the southern half of Sakhalin, as part of the deal Stalin cut at Yalta, the Kuriles remained part of the Sakhalin federal region, the oblast. The Japanese still call the islands the Northern Territories. Throughout the Yeltsin years the Russian Foreign Ministry, while privately bargaining for the best selling price, publicly maintained Stalin's claim to the islands: that the Soviets had rightly taken the Kuriles as their due, the minimal compensation for taking on the Japanese after Yalta.

To pay for dinner—a total of three dollars, green tea included—I needed to change money. The road from Vladivostok had exhausted my ruble supply. I only had one-hundred-dollar bills, the requisite currency for trade or travel in Russia. At least they were still in good shape, a little sweaty, but no tears, folds, or blemishes. Of course, they were late-model bills. Even the Japanese had heard the wisdom: No moneychanger in Russia, bank teller or street trader, would deign to accept a dirty or old-style C note. "Upstairs," the waiter instructed. Only upstairs could the bill be changed.

Sakhalin, it is claimed, has the highest level of syphilis in Russia. "Upstairs" I saw why. The top floor of the Eurasia yielded a single red door.

A black tassel hung from a brass nail in the middle of the door, just below a small sign that announced: NIGHT BAR.

Inside, a Russian pop tune blared, the lights were dim, and clouds of smoke twisted in the air. It was not, however, an establishment meant for drinking. No one danced, and no one laughed. The walls glowed with red satin. At banquettes arrayed across the darkness, Asian men in black suits and white shirts sat on red cushions. Young Russian women perched at their sides, two or three to a table. To the right a long bar, its metal top made rosy by recessed spotlights, stretched the length of the room. As I entered, the place fell silent, and all along the far wall, one by one a row of young girls rose. They stood long-legged in dispirited succession. They seemed like dolls come to life.

When I reached the bar, I felt the stare of a besuited gentleman seated across the floor. In a moment a woman in a diaphanous robe of purple silk, older and a foot shorter than the women behind her, emerged from the smoke. She puffed a thin cigarette through a tortoiseshell filter. She had black hair coiled high and painted eyebrows that nearly overran her temples. Her eyelids, shadowed lime green, hung low. The madam looked me over, less bemused than confused.

"What precisely are you doing here?" she asked.

Change, I said. I'd come to change money. When I showed her the hundred-dollar note, I suddenly understood the confusion. I'd walked in holding the bill, enough to buy a night, I later learned, with four of her charges. The madam wasted no time in dispensing with me. She waved an "at ease" to the girls standing along the dark satin, bade the bartender to count out my rubles, and retreated to the smoke. As I turned to leave, the girls sank back onto the couches, just as sullenly as they had risen.

CHEKHOV, AS HE made his way toward Sakhalin, did not turn his back on the bordellos. In Moscow, in the cold of the Lenin Library manuscript room, I had learned of his delight in the Japanese representatives of the Far East's sex trade. One winter morning in a drafty annex of the library, amid a half dozen elderly scholars poring over Old Church Slavonic tomes, I had read of Chekhov's proud lust. His letters home from stations along the road to Sakhalin, unexpurgated by blushing Soviet censors, would surprise devotees of the "dour," "sexless" playwright. In a June 27, 1890, letter to his friend, publisher, and patron Aleksei Suvorin, Chekhov shared his discovery in a Blagoveshchensk brothel. The lavender-colored paper was thin and small. Chekhov's handwriting was miniature, elegant:

The room the Japanese girl has is clean. Sentimental in an Asian way, it is decorated with all kinds of knickknacks, not with washbasins, rubber contrivances, or generals' portraits. . . . Modesty the Japanese understands in her own way. She does not turn out the light, and when asked how this or that is said in Japanese, she answers directly, and as she understands Russian poorly, she will point to things with her fingers, even take you in her hand, and she does not break up or blush like Russian girls. All the while she laughs and giggles this little "tse" sound. In the act she exhibits such sublime mastery that you feel as if you're not a customer, but a rider on an equestrian lesson of the finest school.[8]

Several of the letters were signed "Homo Sachaliensis." Even before he left Moscow in the spring of 1890, Sakhalin had taken hold of Chekhov. He spent months preparing for the trip. He filled his study with a Sakhalin library, hundreds of articles and sixty-five books on the island's exploration and history, its flora and fauna, geology and geography. He learned the origins of its coal mines and the schedule of its tides. But above all, he was interested in Sakhalin's *katorga*.

The *katorga*—derived from the Ionic Greek *kateirgo*, meaning "to shut in," and in the passive "to be kept down"—was the system of servitude, instituted by Peter the Great, whereby criminals and political undesirables were shackled into the service of the state. *Katorzhany*, the poor souls sentenced to *katorga*, wore iron chains on their hands and feet. On Sakhalin they were often shackled to the wheelbarrows they used in the mines. The *katorga*, no matter how the Bolsheviks cursed it, presaged the Gulag. In his *Gulag Handbook*, Jacques Rossi, the French survivor of Norilsk, offers a comparative "Table of Tsarist and Socialist Penal Servitude." Tsarist norms, Rossi notes, had exceeded the Soviets'.[9]

In 1881, after revolutionaries tossed a bomb under Alexander II's carriage, killing him, Alexander III, having heard reports of Sakhalin's riches and the impossibility of escaping it, established a penal colony on the island. By 1888 Sakhalin had become the empire's "most important penal establishment," in the words of the nineteenth-century American explorer George Kennan.[10] A great-uncle of the renowned diplomat of the cold war, Kennan the Elder, as he is known, crossed Siberia but never made it to Sakhalin. The tsarist censor banned his book on the exiles of Siberia, but a Russian edition did circulate, and Chekhov had studied it. He knew the American had promised that "as long as General Kononovich," the commandant of Sakhalin, whom Kennan had befriended in Petersburg, "remains in command of the Saghalin prisons and mines there is every reason to believe that they will be intelligently, honestly, and humanely managed."[11] Chekhov was not as convinced.

He spent three months and three days on Sakhalin. Each day, as summer stretched into fall, he rose early in an arduous attempt to interview every *katorzhan* and *poselenets*, or forced settler. Upon his arrival, Chekhov had a questionnaire printed for the purpose. On the thirteen lines of the "cards"–thin slips of paper, no more than four by six inches–Chekhov sketched the biographical contours of each exile and prisoner he met: address, name, age, sex, religion, work, education, marital status, and health. As I read through the cards, now badly foxed, in the little room that served as the manuscript repository of Russia's largest library, a strange realization hit. They bore a remarkable similarity to the gulag cards Volodya had written up each night in our cabin as we sailed north along the Yenesei.

In poor health and on foot, Chekhov succeeded in compiling more than seventy-five hundred cards.[12] He rose early and walked the island's settlements until late. Yet Devil's Island, for Chekhov, proved a tonic. Sakhalin, with its discontents and drunks, rapists and murderers, afforded the writer something that the editors and audiences of Moscow and Petersburg could not. Here, amid the forsaken at the empire's edge, Chekhov found his moral voice.

Sakhalin, he later said, was the breaking point. *Uncle Vanya, Three Sisters, The Cherry Orchard, The Seagull* came only later. Varvara Kharkeevich, a Yalta friend, remembered how Chekhov, asked why the island so rarely appeared in his work, was taken aback. Why everything, he replied, he'd written since had been *prosakhalineno*, saturated with Sakhalin.[13] Just as the young Tolstoy needed the Caucasus to escape Moscow's drawing rooms, so Chekhov found new purpose on the island. Wherever he went, he endeavored to see Sakhalin's worst–flogging, child prostitution, murder. For Chekhov, who traveled officially as a journalist with a letter of accreditation from his friend and publisher Suvorin, it was a reportorial baptism. The island, he later told Suvorin, was "the most depressing place in our land" he had ever seen.

In Moscow, Chekhov took years to write up his census. The misery of Sakhalin's prisoners and the arrogance of their guardians haunted him. He wrote in fitful spells. His heart at night began to beat irregularly. The book grew to become his longest work of prose, *The Island of Sakhalin*. It was not great literature, but it was a literary landmark—the first encyclopedia of Russian forced labor.

Today Chekhov's book is no longer read. Dry and impersonal, it appeared in English only in 1967. But his contemporaries devoured the tales from the islands. Sakhalin, after all, was a place where women wore chains, murderers were marked like Cain with their heads half shaved, and dark-skinned aborigines, Gilyaks and Ainus, survived on berries and seals. It was a hellish place, where Chekhov as doctor diagnosed an unknown fever that afflicted those laboring in its raw cold. "A genuine *febris sachalinensis*," he christened it.[14] Chekhov inspired muckrakers. In 1897 Vlas Doroshevich, a journalist from Odessa, came to file salacious dispatches from the wild land. But in Petersburg by then, Sakhalin had become more than parlor conversation. Officials vowed to reform the *katorga*, and a few hardy missionaries set out on pilgrimages. One daughter of aristocratic Petersburg even took the vow and as Sister Yevgeniya de Mayer journeyed to Sakhalin to minister to its wretched.

🐚 FOUR 🐚

WITHIN MONTHS OF the Soviet collapse the island again lured pilgrims. Sakhalin, at more than six hundred miles from tip to toe and one hundred miles across at its widest, is one of the world's largest islands. It abounds in timber and fur, salmon and crab, red caviar, and, above all, black gold. The new arrivals came for its riches. They soon formed a strange congregation, as provincial chieftains, gangland bosses from Vladivostok and Seoul, and a small battalion of executives from the world's largest oil and gas multinationals all vied for the post-Soviet windfall. Sakhalin now boasted the largest foreign investment project in Russian history.

In the late Yeltsin years, in Siberia and elsewhere on the mainland, the Russian oil sector, led by post-Soviet creations like Yukos and Lukoil, Sibneft and Surgutneftegas, had grown fat.[15] Oil and gas—Gazprom, the state natural gas monopoly dwarfed all other companies—were not simply part of the economy; they *were* the economy. As the world oil price remained high through the late 1990s, hydrocarbons kept the federal budget afloat. Yet few Russian oil companies, treasured fiefdoms of the oligarchs in Moscow, forged alliances with foreign partners. Russian oil barons, quipped the director of British Petroleum's mission in Moscow, preferred overnight riches to longevity. "They tend to live by one business plan," the Englishman explained, "pump as much oil out of the country as fast as you can." The Western oil giants, however, proved surprisingly eager to find Russian partners, to marry their technology, experience, and capital with the locals' old Soviet fields and turn a fine profit.

It was not to be. In Siberia and elsewhere, time and again Western bridegrooms were frustrated, jilted at the altar or betrayed thereafter. Yet all the while they kept a keen eye on Sakhalin. The island, they knew, held deep deposits of oil and gas. Japan, South Korea, and China, moreover, lay in profitable proximity.[16] Northeastern Asia, the oil companies reckoned, was the world's fastest-growing energy market, which could one day overtake the United States in consumption. After the Communist fall the foreigners wasted little time. The first major international oil alliance submitted a feasibility study to the Russian state in December 1992. The rush was on.

By the summer of 2000 a platoon of Western oilmen had descended on Sakhalin. Their home was called the American Village. A gated community, half hidden in the birch groves just south of the city, it sprouted almost overnight. The complex, in close proximity to the airport, impressed the Russians. Beyond its metal gates, guarded around the clock, the asphalt was graded and the grass thick. The new homes, forty-eight town houses and sixteen apartments, stood evenly appointed amid the gently sloping greens. A street sign, in English, read SAKHALIN ENERGY DRIVE. The oil executives in Yuzhno, ambitious men from Houston and London, Baton Rouge and Edinburgh, did not call it the American Village. But the name, devised by the locals, was apt. The tidy stage set seemed a mirage, a subdivision of sprawl from anywhere in America. Everything about the compound seemed to echo the words of the oil executive who planned it. "It's all you'd need on this island," he had told me. "Just like home."

Sakhalin had come of age. It was little known, on the edge of most maps in Houston, but it had become one of the top prizes in the new global oil game. The Russians had oil elsewhere, but nowhere was the promise of hydrocarbon riches as great as on Sakhalin's northeastern shelf.[17] With as many as thirteen billion barrels of oil in recoverable reserves, the Sakhalin shelf could rival, the Russians boasted, the fields of the North Sea and Alaska's Prudhoe Bay.[18] (America's oil reserves total some twenty-two billion barrels.)

Production sharing agreements, PSAs in the argot of the industry, were the key. Under Yeltsin, however, the Russians were not eager to sign the deals. First it was the Kremlin, fearful of giving up too much of the Motherland's riches. Then it was the Duma, *certain* the Kremlin was giving up too much of Russia's crown jewels. Then it was the *chinovniki*, the bureaucrats, who at every level thirsted for their own cut. So great were the red tape, xenophobia, and corruption few Westerners considered the barriers surmountable.

One consortium, however, did. Less than three years after the USSR had fallen, in April 1994, a small Texas oil company (Marathon) joined a giant (Royal Dutch Shell) and Japanese financiers (Mitsui and Mitsubishi) to form the Sakhalin Energy Investment Company, Ltd. Registered in Bermuda, the company was known by the Russians on Sakhalin for short, as SakhEnergiya, or SakhEnergy. The first foreign consortium to sign a PSA deal with the Russian state, it laid claim to two fields with recoverable reserves of one billion barrels of crude oil and fourteen trillion cubic feet of gas. Five years later, in July 1999, having sunk nearly a billion dollars into the venture, SakhEnergy struck first oil. The following year the Molikpaq, the refurbished drilling platform the company had towed thirty-six hundred nautical miles from the Beaufort Sea off Canada through the Bering Straits, was pumping out eighty thousand barrels a day. By the time I arrived on the island the bosses of SakhEnergy had grown giddy. They were preparing to celebrate their millionth ton of exported crude.

There was only one American Village on the island, but the fields were getting crowded. ExxonMobil headed a competing consortium, Chevron was also eyeing the Sakhalin shelf, and BP lagged not far behind. Even before September 11, 2001, Russia's petroleum fields–with forty-nine billion barrels of non-Arab proven reserves–seemed destined to supply a larger share of world demand. In the coming years, as the West seeks to wean itself of OPEC, and the environmental pressure in the United States inhibits oil drilling in Alaska's Arctic National Wildlife Refuge, Sakhalin is sure to seem attractive. Western oil companies, not surprisingly, have vowed to invest as much as fifty billion dollars in the coming decade to pull the hydrocarbons out of the Sakhalin shelf.

"WE ARE A RICH country of poor people," Vladimir Putin conceded not long after he settled into the Kremlin.[19] Nowhere in Russia was that paradox more evident than on Sakhalin. In the Yeltsin decade of license that beggared the provinces and stole Russia's dreams of reform, few regions fell farther faster. Sakhalin ranked near the bottom of every economic indicator. By the time I arrived in 2000, per capita income hovered at around thirty dollars a month. Nearly all its coal mines were closed. Fishing trawlers rusted in its quiet ports. And the pulp mills, as its clear-cut timber was sold off island as whole logs, were shuttered. Several of the mills, built by the Japanese in the 1920s and 1930s, were shells and turning fast to ruins. Worse still, with so many of its factories and military bases closed, the population had contracted sharply–from 714,000 residents in the last days of the Soviet Union to fewer than 600,000 in 2000.[20]

In Moscow government economists and Kremlin aides warned that Sakhalin was an aberration, an exceptional case exacerbated by the weight of the Soviet military collapse and the burden of its Japanese past. Yet in all the national plagues–crime, corruption, disease, and despair–the islanders scored high. For them, the onslaught of the oilmen and the accompanying talk of future reward offered little solace. The island's workers frequently had gone months without pay. For years they tried everything. They staged demonstrations, lay across railroad tracks, petitioned the bosses. Nothing worked. In their desperation they turned to drama. Viktor Lysenko, a mill-worker who had not seen a paycheck for two years, chained himself one winter day to the gates of the local mill. Then he drove a nail through his hand. His attempt at self-crucifixion failed. The police intervened. But Lysenko's coworkers were undeterred. They threatened to set themselves aflame. At last they did see a trickle of cash, not long before the bosses closed the mill altogether.[21]

You did not have to search far to see how the island that once haunted Chekhov continued to stagnate. Sakhalin was beset by an uncomfortable paradox. There was plenty of oil around, just none for local consumption. The paradox, in part, was the fault of the Soviet central planners. The old pipelines, first installed under Stalin, ran across the northern tip of the island, due west from the Soviet-era fields across the narrow Tatar Strait and over to the mainland. Sakhalin oil and gas had fed the defense plants of Komsomolsk and Khabarovsk, but not the apartment houses of Yuzhno. Little had changed since the Soviet collapse. Nearly all the gasoline on the island was still imported. And in the summer of 2000 Sakhalin boasted the highest gasoline prices in Russia.

THE OILERS' HUB in Yuzhno was the largest building in town. A seven-story business center on Kommunistichesky Prospekt, it was known as the Sakhintsentr, the Sakhalin Investment Center. The sign along its roof, in the place of honor where Soviet slogans once bade the populace to build a Bright Future or sang the praises of the Motherland's Aeronautics, left little to the imagination. Perched atop the all-caps Sakhintsentr sign was a giant S that boldly resembled—in red, white, and blue—a U.S. dollar sign.

One night in early September I walked through the soft warm air of Yuzhno, strolled into the Sakhintsentr, took a seat beneath the recessed lights of the Kona Bar on its ground floor, and met Ben. He was strumming his guitar before a forlorn gathering of five oilmen and nine local women. A Peace Corps worker from Southern California, Ben had taught English and environmental science in a Yuzhno high school for a year and a half. He understood the laws of economics. He realized that the oil companies knew no borders. All the same, he could not make sense of it. "How can it be," he asked, "that on one of the world's most beautiful islands, a place with whales and seals, where nearly anyone with a job is dependent on timber or fish, no one dares talk about the environment? Don't these guys ever learn anything?"

Ben had taken it upon himself to speak truth to power. He made an appointment with the head of one of the Western oil companies in Yuzhno. For several minutes he tried to tell the man, a nice enough guy who had adopted the local habit of avoiding neckwear and wearing flannel, about the need to preserve the island's ecology and the virtues of building a culture of environmental concern among the locals. It was more than the oilman could take. He interrupted Ben and explained, with sympathy, that he'd been on the island for years and had learned a thing or two about these locals.

"Let me tell you," he told Ben, "after you're here awhile, you'll see for yourself: On Sakhalin there is no culture, there is no history, and there is no environment."

✺ FIVE ✺

THE NEW RUSSIAN PRESIDENT could appreciate the value of the petrodollars. Days before I arrived, Putin had come visiting. He spent just six hours on the island, stopping en route to a G-8 conclave in Japan. He came to celebrate the island's new oil deals, and gave the keynote address at an international conference of oil executives that also lured the U.S. energy secretary. The conference fitted nicely into his calendar. Putin touched down on September 3, as the island was celebrating the anniversary of the day the Soviets seized the Kuriles in 1945.

Only once before had a Russian head of state visited. In 1990 Yeltsin had stumbled into Yuzhno for a long lost weekend. Valentin Fyodorov, Sakhalin's populist leader at the time, did not have fond memories of the visit. "It was a disaster," he said, "for me, for him, and for the revolution." Yeltsin was drunk the whole time. In Moscow, Fyodorov had given me a photo of Yeltsin on Sakhalin. He was slumped on a sofa. "And that was in the morning." He sighed.

Fyodorov was the first governor among the new generation of Russian political leaders. He had given himself the title even before the Soviet fall. Fyodorov had come to the island during perestroika as a progressive economist from an elite Moscow institute. Sakhalin, one of the first regions to protest the Communist Party's rule, attracted him. It seemed an oasis of prospects and promise. He came with a radical plan: "to achieve a revolution in one place." Once he'd become president, as he was sure he would, he'd apply the experiment to the entire country. In his office in Yuzhno, Fyodorov replaced the portrait of Lenin with one of Adam Smith. He chanted a reformist slogan, *Fermy, Firmy, Formy* (Farms, Firms, Forms), like an incantation. He made headlines in the West–*Le Monde* dubbed him the Napoleon of Sakhalin–and enemies on the island.

I went to see Fyodorov in Moscow, where he had retreated after losing his job on Sakhalin in 1993 and after stints as a deputy economics minister for Yeltsin and "prime minister" for the diamond satraps of the republic of Sakha in Siberia. He was in his sixties now, hectoring visitors in one of the myriad of half-furnished office buildings that the Academy of Sciences somehow, inexplicably and improbably, still maintained. He had traded politics for poetry–love ballads in the main. He gave me one of his latest tomes, *Gubernatorial Romances*. Inside, I found the "Hymn of Sakhalin":

> *In written speech words, no matter how you arrange them, are islands.*
> *Here floats one: Sakhalin.*
> *A place of damnation and suffering, tears and prison longing*
> *What other island could compare with its privations?*
> *Who at its birth condemned this place to such woe?*

Not the finest use of Pushkin's language, but the lines–penned, Fyodorov said, on the plane the day he touched down on Sakhalin–made their point:

> *We are breaking this fate, we are beginning the fight.*
> *So that the people of the East at last freedom shall find.*

Like the Yeltsin onslaught in the capital, Fyodorov's experiment had begun with grand ideals. Like his colleagues, the new mayors of Moscow and Leningrad, Gavriil Popov and Anatoly Sobchak, Fyodorov had stood in the vanguard of radical reform. But Popov and Sobchak, who rose in the euphoria of the new era, both left office amid allegations of corruption. Fyodorov suffered no such disgrace. But he had left Sakhalin in a hurry, run out by the voters who had soured on his gospel. Did he now, I wondered, look back and think it a failure?

"Why?" he nearly shrieked. "Everything that's now growing on the island–I planted those seeds. The oil companies, all of them–Shell, Exxon, BP–they came to see me first. And the market? Sakhalin had the first free market in Russia. We created the first exchange, first private farms, first private banya, and first enterprise fund. We were years ahead of Moscow and Leningrad. If Sakhalin's unfortunates ever have a future it'll be because of the earth I tilled then–as the first capitalist governor of the new Russia!"

❧ SIX ❧

ONE BY ONE, AS WE waited for the SakhEnergy charter to the hamlet of Nogliki in the north of the island, they appeared. Nearly all were rough-necks, veterans of years on rigs in the world's remote corners. They were guys with leathery faces and multiple marriages who had just flown from Seoul or Jakarta, Alberta or New Orleans and who still could not find their feet. To a man, they had made the most of the inflight bar, in a valiant attempt to stretch out their last day before camp.

"This is the grand hurrah," Buzz announced, as we sat side by side in the smoky waiting room. He was a tall man, slightly stooped. He had a long face scored by decades of sea air, salt, and winds. He explained that he'd soon be retiring. When Buzz spoke, verbs and definite articles seemed unnecessary accessories. He was from the Deep South–Natchez, Missis-sippi. He'd been in the oil business too long. Couldn't count all the coun-tries, let alone the oil platforms, on and offshore, he'd seen. He could only shake his head. "Never expected see inside of Russia." It wasn't the worst place, he allowed, just not for him. And so, he was pleased to announce, in recent days he had become living proof of the theory "Throw enough money at a man, he'll retire."

On the twin prop, an An-24 with the blue and gold emblem of SakhEn-ergy freshly painted on its side, Buzz entertained the crew. "Ever need a lady in Manila, he's the man." He pointed to an exhausted Filipino welder in the seat ahead of me. He did not look well. He tried to smile but managed only a grin. "He's the pimp of the Philippines!" Buzz shouted. The poor fellow sat in silence. As the solo flight attendant distributed rubber earplugs, the chatter died down, the small plane lifted up sharply, and the Filipino man turned gently to the wall and fell asleep.

Nearly everyone else passed out. We gained altitude and flew due north for more than an hour, between two verdant ridges carpeted with trees. To the east the green ran to the island's edge. To the west, where many of the old coal towns lined the coast, the forests grew sparse. As the sun slipped behind the horizon, we flew over an old Soviet timber collective farm, now a bald patch in the clear-cut heart of the island. In midflight the oil worker from the Philippines got sick. A paper bag was passed, hand to hand, to him. The mute camaraderie revealed a common fear—of the job the men had come back to do.

After an hour and a half we reached Nogliki. The landing was hard, so hard it roused the groggiest of the oilers and raised the specter of wheels exploding. The airport was a dirt field pitted with rocks. "Thank God," said Buzz, "they steamrolled it."

"HERE, ON RUSSIAN earth trampled by the Japanese, you will build a new, Soviet life," a brigade leader commands his new recruits in Aleksandr Chakovsky's *It's Morning Already, Here*, a 1950 Socialist Realist paean to the Soviet plans for Sakhalin. "If you know how to work and love to work, I promise you'll be up to your neck in it! You will pump out millions of tons of oil. You will load Sakhalin coal into tens of thousands of cargo containers. You will fill the shelves of Penza and Tambov with the splendid fish of the Far East. You will supply the USSR's printing presses with our paper. . . . You will turn our island into an island of happiness." The book earned Chakovsky, the pitiless and artless head of the Soviet Writers Union, the Stalin Prize.[22]

What a difference the end of empire had made. Half a century later the future of Sakhalin now rested on the shoulders of foreign oilmen. These men were not eager to get to Nogliki. Soon I learned why. "Camp" had all the comforts and freedoms of a modernized Stalag 19, a portable, secure barracks for the workers of the new century. Guards greeted us at the gate, the sole entry in a tall metal fence topped with concertina wire. In the middle of a barren acre, the corrugated metal containers were linked together in the shape of a U. For the men who worked the Molikpaq, this was their transit camp. Given the limited space on the offshore platform, the workers waited here to be ferried, by helicopter or boat, out to the platform. Sometimes they waited for days, sometimes for weeks. Two competing consortia, one led by Shell, the other by ExxonMobil, shared the camp's tight quarters. It seemed an odd arrangement; men who worked on rival rigs ate and slept under one roof.

It was a self-contained world, complete with generator, water treatment system, sewage works, and fresh-baked chocolate chip cookies. Inside, two long metal corridors led to the men's rooms. In the corridors, color photographs lined the walls of crenulated metal. *The Animal World of the Northeast Shelf of Sakhalin* was the title taped over a set of glossy images, tranquil scenes of seal rookeries and schools of gray whales, killer whales, and Pacific white-sided dolphins. The waters off Sakhalin, as everyone in camp knew well, were rich in marine life. Even its earliest explorers had told of the abundant whales. In 1805 the Baltic German circumnavigator Captain Adam John de Krusenstern wrote of his fears in exploring the island's bays, so abundant were the whales. "A larger quantity of whales is, perhaps, nowhere to be found than here . . . ," wrote Krusenstern.[23]

On the opposite wall of the camp corridor more photographs hung. Here were portraits of Al Gore and Viktor Chernomyrdin, Yeltsin's long-serving prime minister, rejoicing in Washington, D.C., at SakhEnergy's 1994 signing ceremony. Other images revealed the Moscow politicians who had come to Sakhalin on SakhEnergy pilgrimages. In one Boris Nemtsov, the former governor of Nizhni Novgorod and, for a time before Putin, an heir apparent to Yeltsin, sat on a plane. Nemtsov was smiling widely and wearing a white cowboy hat. Another photo showed Igor Ivanov, the foreign minister, visiting the American Village in Yuzhno. Next to Ivanov stood an American oil executive and the Sakhalin governor. Both men wore Russian fur hats.

The camp rooms held twin double bunks and one toilet/shower. You could sit in the middle of the room and almost touch its four walls. The bunks reminded me of a sketch Jacques Rossi had made of the zeks' barracks in Norilsk. Here, however, an invisible line separated the company men from the contract men. Company men were the managers and executives who came through only for a day or two, on quick field trips out to the platform. The rest of the time the company men kept to the American Village down in Yuzhno. The contract men were the grunts, the drillers, casers, and welders. They were foreign mostly–Asians and Americans, Australians, Scots, English, and Irish. Some, but a distinct minority, of the contract men were even Russian. They had come to the camp from Vladivostok, Khabarovsk, Moscow, and Yuzhno. The Russians expressed no joy at having won their coveted jobs. They were nonplussed about working with foreigners. They shrugged their shoulders and told me they had worked with foreigners before–in Vietnam.

The camp rules, posted on a wall near the entrance, were strict. They reminded me of the list of commandments I'd seen in a heroin detox center in Togliatti:

No smoking anywhere inside the facility.
No drugs or alcohol or guests.
No gambling is allowed in the camp.
No horseplay or loud behavior will be tolerated.
No visitors are allowed except for business purposes.

Number 8 was the most dreaded: "Guests permitted to the camp are not allowed to leave until it is time for their departure for offshore or other destination."

The rules were set by precedent, the most recent being the Incident. Two contract guys had gone "off camp." They hitched a ride into Nogliki, got blind drunk, picked up two girls, and brought them back to camp. Because the guards were asleep at the gate, they could not get back into the compound. The men were resigned to another night of celibacy, but the girls refused to give up. Hoping to wake the guards, they threw rocks at the windows. They broke the windows, but the guards slumbered on. The Incident led to the new regime: no unchaperoned excursions to town.

The oilers could, however, adjourn to the rec room. Here they could construct jigsaw puzzles, play pool, flip through magazines, and watch two large televisions that stood side by side. In a nod to the local contingent, one was tuned to a Russian station, the other to an English-language channel. The men naturally liked to keep both sets blaring simultaneously. This led to volume wars.

"Whatever they told you down in Yuzhno, don't believe it," said my dinner mate on the first night in camp. Hugh was English but lived in Vietnam. His company, though American-owned, had worked there for years. The trade embargo hadn't hindered it, he said. It just painted its trucks white and went to work. A shy man of ursine proportions, Hugh was a caser. Casers, he explained, ran pipe and poured cement around the drill hole. They made sure the hole did not collapse. It was not the best of jobs, Hugh said as he dipped a warm cookie into a glass of cold milk. The work was hard, and the days of waiting were long.

Joseph, Hugh's bunkmate, came from outside Aberdeen. Small, quick-eyed, and lithe, he looked like a wood sprite. He was also a caser. He had been waiting ten days in camp. If Joseph and Hugh ever got out to the rigs, they'd be working twelve-hour shifts. The schedule was rough. "Twenty-eight on and twenty-eight off"—a month on the platform followed by a month at home. Before camp, Joseph had sat for three weeks in Yuzhno. The wait was taking its toll. He'd begun to doubt that he would ever get offshore.

On the television in the English-speaking half of the room, a CNBC anchorman in Hong Kong told of the latest turns in the world petroleum market. "OIL RISE TO BOOST ASIAN MARKET," read the ticker across the bottom of the screen. "The price could rise to thirty-six or even forty dollars a barrel," the anchorman said, to which his colleague responded: "So there's still an awful lot of upside potential in this Asian market?"

Joseph watched the news and shook his head. He wore a black T-shirt that revealed twin tattoos on his biceps. He was not buying it. "Whether it's Russia or New Guinea," he said, "oil's oil, and the work's the same. First you wait forever, then you work like hell. The money, when you make it, is good. But when you're a foreigner trapped in a place like this, without a clue what's going on outside, it's like living in a well-paid hell."

Hugh sat on a chair that straddled the border between the two television audiences. He had fallen asleep. I asked Joseph if he wanted to join me on a walk outside. "No, thanks," he said. "I've walked the fence four times today."

That night in my bunk I returned to Chekhov's study of Sakhalin. I read of his encounter with a local householder. "Why are your pig and rooster tied up?" Chekhov asked. "In our Sakhalin everything is chained," the man replied. "That's the kind of land it is."24

❧ SEVEN ❧

I HAD BEGUN TO pick up the rumblings in camp. Like Ben, the Peace Corps teacher in Yuzhno, the oilers had pulled me aside and shared their fears. "Ask 'em about the spills," a welder whispered as we walked out back along the barren dirt beside the row of airboats shipped in from the Louisiana bayou. The boats, flat-bottomed metal shells powered by propellers, were built to move through the most shallow waters. Should there be a spill, the boats would constitute the first line of defense for Sakhalin's bays. "Gotta keep it outta the bays," the Canadian charged with devising the emergency cleanup plan told me. He had an open, cherubic face. He'd enjoyed Sakhalin. Here he'd found a Russian fiancée. "If it gets in the bays," he went on, "it'd be . . ." The Canadian could not bring himself to substitute "oil" for "it," nor could he fill in the prophecy. There was no need.

In Yuzhno I had learned that although the oilmen had brought the promise of transformation to Sakhalin, for many on the island the foreigners had also brought the threat of disaster. Even before I got to the camp, I had heard the worst fears: that a world-class oil spill not only would have a disastrous effect on the rich ecosystem of Sakhalin but could spread south to hit Hokkaido and Japan's fish industry. Concern for the future of Sakhalin's environment, oddly enough, pervaded conversations with the oilers. The company men went out of their way to detail how SakhEnergy had taken every possible precaution to avoid spills, while the contract men quietly told me otherwise. The confessions came from the most unlikely sources, at the most unexpected of times and places.

In a shack beside the steamrollered dirt airfield in Nogliki, as we waited to board the Mi-8 helicopter that was to ferry us out to the Molikpaq, SakhEnergy's primary offshore platform, an oil hand from Alaska unburdened himself. He wore blue jeans, a flannel shirt, and a baseball cap. As we pulled on full bodysuits of bright yellow rubber—protection against hypothermia in case of a water landing–the Alaskan began to conjure up the *Exxon Valdez*. Something about the island, he said, reminded him of that terrible Good Friday in March 1989, when forty thousand tons of Exxon oil spilled into Alaska's Prince William Sound. The environmentalists of course were still tallying the damage to the wildlife. But the Alaskan knew the cost of the spill. Prince William Sound had been his favorite refuge, "the most beautiful place in all Alaska." Ever since he'd arrived on Sakhalin, he said, shaking his head slightly, he'd been thinking about the *Valdez*. This island, he said as we zipped our safety suits tight, had brought the memories back. "Exactly where the *Valdez* spilled, there were always birds and animals, just real pristine nature," he said. "It was an awful lot, to be honest, like this place here."

TWO VETERANS OF THE Soviet war in Afghanistan piloted the helicopter. As we rose in the air, cows haplessly scattered. Nogliki grew small while the blades churned overhead and the helicopter gained altitude. Soon it was only a blurry patchwork of cinder block towers and tumbledown shacks. From three hundred feet the scars of Sakhalin's north became visible. To the left and right, abandoned logging roads and the red-brown empty patches of its green forests were revealed. The pilots seemed to trace the riverlets of the northern wetlands. We flew above looping lagoons, fishing boats with their great nets set in the shallow waters near the coast, and pristine sandy beaches. At one point, Okha, the island's northernmost city, appeared on the left. We passed over an abandoned Soviet antiaircraft station, its giant radar ears standing still. Then at the mouth of a sweeping lagoon a rookery of seals glistened in the midmorning sun. Tyulenii Island, just off the eastern coast, was famed as a home for fur seals, sea lions, and both common and thick-billed murres. In the 1840s and 1850s the small island had even lured seal hunters from America.[25]

"Forty clicks" up the coast from Nogliki, we turned due right and headed out over the dark blue Sea of Okhotsk. During the winter months the waters here froze. The men on the platform could drill year-round but pump out oil only six months of the year. "When the sea isn't frozen," said Alan Grant, the Scottish executive at SakhEnergy's helm, "we have to make the most of every minute." When the ice melted, there were no days off.

Eighteen miles east of the coast, the Molikpaq came into full view. The pilots circled its 1,234-square-foot deck, cutting a tilted circle around its towering derrick, before gently setting down on the platform's giant helipad. Darwin Storms, the stocky Canadian in charge of the Molikpaq's incident control center, was waiting for us. A ruddy-faced oiler from Alberta, Darwin had a hard time hiding how happy he was to see company. As he led me through the platform's safety precautions, I tried hard not to think of the *Kursk* submarine and the Mir space station. Darwin clearly had his work cut out. The Molikpaq sits on trillions of cubic feet of natural gas. "A cork stuck in one of the most pressurized man-made holes in the earth," a British caser had called it. For much of the year the surrounding waters are beset by storm winds and giant waves and blanketed by Arctic blizzards and extreme fog. On the platform it also gets cold—as low as forty below. In the late spring, when the iced-over sea begins to melt, the waves can climb to sixty feet. Darwin did not need to mention the earthquakes. The 7.6 quake that hit in 1995, wiping out Neftegorsk, the Soviet oil workers' settlement in the north of the island, had made headlines around the world. Of a population of some 3,000, 2,040 died. Neftegorsk is no more. The plowed-over land where the town once stood, however, lies almost due west of the Molikpaq.

As Darwin detailed the state-of-the-art computer-aided alarm system that alerted the command post to the slightest fluctuation in the levels and types of gases in the wells drilled far beneath the platform, I surveyed his office. On a blackboard on one wall someone had scrawled, in black erasable ink, a phonetic Russian cheat sheet to be employed in case of disaster:

> FIRE = paZHAR
> EMERGENCY = AVARijny
> HELP = paMOCH

Darwin had handed me a booklet that listed the dos and don'ts of life on the platform. The final page of the *Offshore Handbook* was an "epilogue" that ended with a plea: "We think our facilities are safe places to be. We would like to keep them that way. Please help us."

The Molikpaq had a history. Darwin, who had attended its christening in Canada in 1984, explained that in Canadian Indian the name meant "big wave." In its first life Gulf Canada had used the Molikpaq to good effect but in 1991 had mothballed it. The platform, ironically, had become another casualty of *Exxon Valdez*. Darwin explained: "Environmental was a big issue back then." The environmentalists, he said, forced a ban on supertankers, "like we've got here." The alternate was to build a pipeline, but the Beaufort Sea, he explained, has "multiyear ice." It made it too expensive to lay a pipeline on the seabed. In the end, Darwin said, after the government refused to subsidize a pipeline, Gulf Canada shut down operations altogether.

The Molikpaq sat off the Canadian coast, unused in the frozen sea for years, until the USSR collapsed and the need arose for a secondhand platform that could withstand the winds, waves, and ice hummocks off Sakhalin's coast. The Russians, however, had rechristened the Molikpaq. The Vityaz (Knight), they called it. The governor of Sakhalin, an aide explained, had given the name. "It conveys pride and patriotism," she said. Vityaz was also the name of a renowned Special Forces unit headquartered outside Moscow.

Darwin's boss, a tall Englishman with a gentle manner, appeared and offered a tour of the platform. Steve Frampton had not lived in his native England for years. Like many of the company men, he had come to Sakhalin from Houston. Frampton was the top man on the Molikpaq, the OIM, the offshore installation manager, "otherwise known," added Darwin, "as God."

Frampton wore a button-down shirt and square-framed eyeglasses. We toured the platform's four floors, home to 127 men. The Molikpaq, he explained with pride as we headed from the galley to the sleeping quarters, was "a one-off." It was an unprecedented feat of modern engineering. Unlike a typical offshore platform, it was not floating, nor was it anchored. It stood on sand. The fifty-eight-thousand-ton platform rested ninety-eight feet below the waterline on sand–three hundred thousand metric tons of sand. The sand had been "densified"–shot through with explosives for a month–to remove all air and water. The sand filled the submerged heart of the platform, a massive square hole 256 feet a side that the company men called the Core and the roughnecks called the Beach. Between the sand and the platform was a spacer, fifteen thousand tons of steel built in Komsomolsk-on-Amur by the men who in another era had made Soviet submarines. The spacer had been shipped to South Korea, home of the only dry dock in the world big enough to accommodate the Molikpaq. There four hundred welders had mated it to the Molikpaq. Finally, seventeen vessels from three continents had set the platform into its present position atop the Sakhalin shelf.

One of the contract men in camp had warned of the configuration. The platform, he cautioned, had "all the stability of a bar of soap." Yet as we climbed from the rig floor to the well heads, Frampton was all optimism. There'd been no troubles with the well, such as pockets of lethal gas that, if sparked, the roughnecks said, could blow the rig. Even if they did hit gas, Darwin's computers would trigger the "prepare to abandon platform" siren. The men would have only minutes to evacuate–a select few by helicopter, all others by lifeboat.

On the rig floor I at last found a few Russians. They were performing the most dangerous job on the platform. The three men worked fast. In silent unison they linked and unlinked giant pipes, extensions to the rig's drill, several times their size. The machinery they turned had come from Beaumont, Texas. Their faces and chests were dark with sludge. The air around them was filled with the bitter smell of chemicals. A notice, written in white chalk on a grimy sidewall, gave bilingual instructions: DON'T PISS HERE. *ETO NE TOILET* (THIS IS NOT A TOILET). Someone, it seemed, had been unable to wait.

The Russians, Darwin explained, were covered in mud. Mud, however, to oilmen is not mud. It is the chemical cocktail used to ease the drill bit's way into the rock below the sea. It is also, environmentalists warn, highly toxic. In camp, a mudlogger, the man charged with calibrating the precise and delicate state of the mud, explained to me its critical importance. Every rig had a mud-logging cabin, a high-tech corner where geologists manned computers. They measured the pressure of the mud pumped "down hole," the weight of the mud, and the weight on the drill while drilling. Mudloggers also kept a close eye on the return flow, the mud returning from the hole created by the drill. An increase in return flow could foretell a kick from the formation, a kick that could blow the rig. Given that the pressure on the drill bit was 50,000 pounds per square inch, the explosion was sure to be impressive.

We moved on, to the Molikpaq's rec room, where under fluorescent lights two dozen men, all Russian, sat on plastic chairs enjoying a smoke break. A heavy curtain of brown plastic was supposed to separate the two halves of the room. But the curtain was open. The smoke flowed freely, and the movie on the TV–*Titanic*–blared loudly. "We like this platform," one sallow-faced man, Volodya, said. "On some, we heard, the Americans don't even let you smoke."

In one of the offices on the main operational floor, I found Buzz, the tall engineer from Mississippi who had entertained the roughnecks on the plane up from Yuzhno. Unshaved and weary, he wore a black tie over a blue T-shirt. A cardboard pink flamingo stood behind his desk. Buzz was now rein-troduced as the man in charge of charting the eleven wells SakhEnergy had drilled thus far. Mapped out, the wells resembled a squid with elongated tentacles that reached for the pools of hydrocarbon beneath the seabed. Some of the wells, drilled at angles of sixty and seventy degrees, extended more than a mile. In all, Buzz explained, he had at his disposal enough pipe to drill through the porous rock as far as four miles from the rig.

Buzz would rather talk of his coming retirement than the work he had done his whole life. He had no desire, he said, to spend another Russian winter listening to the ice crush up against the Molikpaq's wall. He was excited about the B&B he and his wife would open back in Natchez. His wife was a tour guide–"does the antebellum thing"–and their boy was on his way to medical school. God, Buzz said, had heard his prayers and kept his son from following in his footsteps. There had to be a better way to make a living, he said, than the oil business. "The boy knows if I hear the word 'oil-field' out his mouth, I'll rip his tongue out."

Toward the end of the day Frampton led me up the metal staircase that wound around the uppermost level of the platform. Soon we stood beneath the flare tower, enveloped in its heat and noise. One hundred and eleven feet above us the flame was a deep orange banner whipping about in the wind. Black smoke wafted from its tip. The view from the flare tower was all pipes and metal, and at our backs were the aquamarine waters that sur-rounded the Molikpaq. The platform beneath us–bigger than a football field–looked like a maze, topped on the far corner by the helipad. Wherever you looked, amid the three cranes at work, steel squares and rectangles of all sizes wended in every direction.

"This could be the next North Sea," Frampton declared, sweeping an arm broadly across the sky. "We're just the first, but once the word gets out what we've done, the whole industry will come flocking in, trying to get a piece of this shelf."[26] To hear the company men tell it, theirs was the work of miracle workers, a spectacle of man and machine conquering nature in the pursuit of a utility good essential to the survival of the species. It was all, Frampton announced, so wonderful. Sure, there was the occasional hurricane and sixty-mile-an-hour wind that lifted the sea up onto the platform, but the Molikpaq was blessed. It sat, he said, "in such an environmental area." In winter, seals sunbathed on the ice nearby. In summer, whales, grays and killers, cavorted in the waters beside the platform.

"Such a gorgeous day," Frampton repeated, taking the measure of the late afternoon. "I'm not a whale person," he added, "but we do get a mix."

I had read about the whales that summered in these waters and the dangers the drilling posed to their future. Sakhalin Energy and ExxonMobil, sensitive to the potential for backlash, had reluctantly allowed a commission of Russian and American scientists to monitor the whales. Beginning in 1997 and led by Robert L. Brownell, Jr., a scientist from the U.S. National Oceans and Atmospheric Administration, the team made startling discoveries. It determined that the waters off the Piltun Lagoon were the only known feeding grounds for the western population of the species, the Pacific gray whale, *Eschrichtius robustus*. Moreover, it found that the whales constituted one of the most endangered marine mammal populations in the world. The Soviets had once estimated there were at least two hundred whales in the population. Brownell and his team determined the true number was fewer than one hundred.[27]

Now the oil companies were conducting seismic tests and drilling within miles of the waters where the whales dug troughs in the sea bottom to feed off its rich benthos.[28] Hunted to the edge of extinction, the whales faced the threat of the surveying, as well as the heightened ship and air traffic. The scientists began to find "skinny" whales. (Of the fifty-eight whales observed in 2000, twenty-seven were underweight.) Brownell could not hold the oil companies responsible for the weight loss—greater oceanographic changes, he posited, could be to blame—but the oilmen were certainly no help. The noise blasts of their seismic surveys were driving the whales from their feeding habitat. Worse still, in four years of monitoring the scientists had seen only twelve reproductive females.[29]

IT SEEMED A GOOD TIME to ask about the spills. Every precaution, Frampton assured me, was taken. He explained: "If we have a spill, if my radioman contacted me and said there was a spill on the main deck, some-body had knocked a tub of oil over, the first thing we'd do is stop what we were doing and we'd get as many people as we could there to contain it, keep it out of the drains. If I can keep it on deck, I can handle it. Once it gets into the drains, I can still handle it, but it's more difficult. We do everything, everything humanly possible, to stop it from going into the water."

But there had been a spill. It was small, yet big enough to gain the atten-tion of the local authorities and ecowarriors. It came one night late in the summer of first oil. Alan Grant, the head of SakhEnergy, was in Houston, briefing consortium members on the success on Sakhalin. The spill occurred on September 28, 1999, during the off-loading of the Molikpaq's second cargo of oil. Because the sea around the platform freezes for half the year, during the summer months the company stores its oil on a supertanker parked nearby. The supertanker in turn pumps the oil—via a subsea delivery hose—into shuttle tankers that ferry it to buyers in Asia.[30] It was nearly mid-night when the hawsers, the fat lines of steel that hold the supertanker in place, slipped free. The supertanker began to drift. The Molikpaq's comput-erized sensors went into action: They cut the oil flow and disengaged the hose from the supertanker. A major spill had been averted, but something had leaked into the sea.

Just how much oil spilled as the hose was retracted remained a matter of contention. SakhEnergy claimed it was two and half barrels, one of which was recovered. The State Ecological Committee said it was three and a half tons. In Yuzhno the spill made few headlines, but it was known. Among the environmentalists it gave rise to jokes that began with "Houston, we have a problem . . ." They knew, after all, that the supertanker could store 1,068,400 barrels—nearly four times the oil the *Exxon Valdez* could carry.[31]

In Yuzhno I had also heard tell of the Herring Affair. Earlier that same fateful summer local fishermen had found a mass of dead herring darkening the shallow waters of the Piltun Lagoon for nearly a mile. The fish washed up, just about the time they usually came in to spawn, at *Mys Golodnaya* (Cape Hunger). The inlet lay south of Okha and just north of the shelf where the oilmen were drilling.

At least a thousand tons of herring washed ashore. Government officials commissioned tests in Vladivostok and Moscow. The local environmental-ists ran their own tests. The oil company denied any blame. The governor and his men said it was the ice. The herring, they claimed, had got caught coming into the bay under a wave of ice and died from the lack of oxygen. The tests in Moscow, however, revealed high levels of metals–zinc, lead, cadmium–and DDT in the fish. The levels, some of the regional environmental officials said, fell within acceptable parameters, but the tests also turned up barium, a key ingredient in the drilling mud used on the Molikpaq. Still, even the environmentalists stopped short of blaming the oilmen. No one could say for certain, they conceded, why the fish had died.

As Frampton and I stood on the Molikpaq's uppermost deck, in the streams of heat that rushed from the flame tower overhead, I looked out over the railing and saw an ominous-looking effluent disgorging from the side of the platform. The discharge, an electric blue-green, swirled in the seawater, bleaching the surrounding blue a dove gray. I asked Frampton what the liquid was. "Oh, that," he said casually while we descended the stairs, "that's nothing serious." Everything discharged, he said, was guaranteed by a water use license. As we carried on down the stairs, he fought the roar of the flame overhead to reiterate his delight with the day. "If only," he cried out, "a killer whale would come by."

EIGHT

THE MORNING AFTER we returned from the rig, I was kicked out of the stalag. Company largess extended only so far. I decamped to the Nogliki Hotel, a fourth-class establishment hastily refurbished by an American entrepreneur eager to turn a profit on the oilmen. The hotel was a disaster, but I supported the endeavor. There in the cold, concrete-floored café of the hotel, I met Valery, Vitya, and Zhorzh. It was early in the morning, but they had already emptied a tableful of fat bottles of cloudy beer. They were in recovery, nursing bad hangovers. Yet somehow within minutes they had taken me in and I was in the back of their powder blue UAZik–the kind of Russian army jeep Yura had chauffeured across Chechnya–and we were heading to Okha, Sakhalin's northernmost city.

Something about the men–their short hair, alcoholic breakfast, or camouflage outfits—gave them away. They were, as I thought, military men. Valery was the deputy chief of police in Yuzhno. Vitya was a colonel in the border guards. They were great buddies. Valery had been on Sakhalin twenty-five years, ever since he left Kemerovo in Siberia. Vitya had been here eleven, ever since he left Vitebsk in Belarus. They almost looked like twins. Both were stocky, with sausage-size fingers, fresh buzz cuts, and jowly square faces. Zhorzh, a wiry man with heavy glasses and few upper teeth, was their faithful driver. The nature of his relationship to the two officers, as was soon revealed, was feudal.

Like Chekhov, I had learned that the only way to travel around Sakhalin was to appeal to the authorities. A century earlier Chekhov had supplicated to the wardens and the governor-general, while I begged rides from the police and oil executives. So far the road had been smooth. Yet within minutes of our leaving Nogliki, Valery ordered Zhorzh to stop at a roadside kiosk. The men plied me with three cans of rum and Coke, one after another.

Valery, Vitya, and Zhorzh had driven all the way from Yuzhno. They were headed for the tundra at the tip of the island. This was their annual fishing and hunting expedition. Behind me in the rear of the jeep five rifles lay atop the heap of bags. Vitya said the rifles were nothing. He spread his wide knees and revealed a rucksack full of bullets. "Two thousand." He laughed. "Just in case we come across the enemy."

The only road north was a strip of deeply rutted dirt. Dust filled my nose and burned my eyes, stirring memories of Chechnya. We closed the windows tight, but the heavy brown silt seeped through all the same, coating everyone in the groaning UAZik. As we drove on, we passed through abandoned logging settlements and collective farms long deceased. There were no road signs, let alone billboards, just an occasional portrait of Lenin fading into metal amid a row of dun-colored shacks that seemed to collapse in slow motion. Only the occasional field of rusting pump jacks betrayed any evidence that civilization had once spread this far north on the island.

Between rum and Cokes, Valery delivered an impromptu history lecture. He told how the Japanese before the war had controlled the south and how they had made it bloom with industry, skill, and discipline. Unlike the fear that pervaded the talk of their Asian neighbors in Vladivostok, Valery spoke of Sakhalin's former residents with admiration. And sympathy. After the war, he explained, the island's north was crowded with Japanese POWs.

They were put to work, like elsewhere in the Far East, building apartment houses and roads. But thousands of the prisoners were also killed–"just lined up," Valery said, "and shot."

As the UAZik bounced north, Zhorzh, the driver, did not dare say a word. Next to me, Vitya was asleep, snoring. His arms were sweating on my arms. On the turns his head flopped onto my left shoulder. I let it rest there. As we made our way north, the bald patches in the woods, acres clear-cut by enterprising outlaws, appeared with greater frequency. Before long the forests disappeared altogether. We crossed shallow rivers that swelled into swamps and yellowing fields of twisted scrub pine, dwarf cedar, and for long stretches, barren desert. I held a local map. Its legend pointed to the island's dark past and present woes. Among the items listed, "bay," "river," and "lake," I found "barrack," "mass grave," "abandoned village," and "ruins."

As the sun dipped, the landscape almost imperceptibly turned deep green, as a mossy carpet spread across the dirt on either side of the road. The Arctic tundra, with a fresh coat of foliage, took hold, and an odd sensation settled. I was sitting in the same type of military jeep that had carried me across Chechnya, while the landscape outside eerily resembled the stark plateau surrounding Norilsk. Even here on the country's far edge, one could not escape it–not its harsh clime, or its extreme geography, or its unfinished past.

"Ever hear the name Drekov?" Valery shouted as we passed through a one-street village known for the restorative powers of its mineral springs. I had. Sakhalin was famed for its sadistic wardens and executioners, but Vladimir Drekov was the most celebrated. In the 1930s, when Stalin ruled the mainland, Drekov ruled the north of Sakhalin. "This was his kingdom," Valery said. "His word was the law, and the law was merciless."

Drekov, from 1931 to 1938, ran the NKVD on Sakhalin. He lived in Aleksandrovsk, the town on the west coast that since the founding of the penal colony was the island's administrative center. Born in a Belarusian village, he had finished only six years in a provincial grammar school for future railroad engineers. But his hand, Valery said, was iron. A favored pastime was shooting the natives.[32] For centuries Sakhalin was home to three native peoples: the Gilyaks, whom Chekhov had seen and who were now called the Nivkh, the Oroki, and the Ainu, an ancient people related to the Japanese. Drekov, it was said, had taken special pleasure in ridding the island's rising Russian population of its first inhabitants.

As we drove, we passed now and then the spectral fishing hamlets where the native peoples had once lived. Nearly two thousand Nivkh still made their home on the island, surviving on miserly pensions, dried fish, and an annual hunting quota of one seal per family. The Ainu since 1945 had died out or moved to Japan. In Yuzhno, it was said, only one Ainu, an elderly woman, remained. In America, however, among archaeologists and forensic anthropologists, the Ainus had become well known of late. In the summer of 1996 two college students wading through the Columbia River in Kennewick, Washington, stumbled upon submerged remains. It was not a recent murder victim, but a ninety-three-hundred-year-old skeleton that scientists soon tagged Kennewick Man. One school of scholars posited that Sakhalin's Ainus were related to Kennewick Man. The ensuing debate engendered scientific and legal battles, as Native Americans claimed Kennewick Man as one of their own. Yet should his kinship to the Ainus be established, it would strengthen the long-held view that America's first inhabitants had come from northern Asia across a land bridge now submerged in the Bering Strait.[33]

Drekov did not end up well. In time, as it had to so many of the executioners of Stalinism, the terror turned back on him. Valery knew the story well. In 1938, Moscow summoned Drekov, said he'd been promoted. "The dictator of Sakhalin knew it was the end," Valery said, "but also he knew he had no choice." As soon as he stepped foot in Khabarovsk, Drekov was arrested, and in 1940 he faced his own firing squad.[34]

The UAZik filled with silence. No one said a word until, some five hours and six rum and Cokes after we set out, Valery barked at Zhorzh to slow down. We had at last reached Okha. A large metal sign crested the road, announcing the town's threshold. The billboard was painted with the Okha municipal emblem, an oil derrick towering over a giant fish energetically waving its tail, as if desperate to swim free of the inevitable slick. It seemed an apt, if accidental, symbol for the town's current predicament.

OKHA, ONCE UPON a time, was the oil capital of the Russian Far East. Even before you got to town, the roadsides filled with old Soviet derricks. On its outskirts the town resembled a miniature Baku, the capital of oil-rich Azerbaijan on the Caspian. The native peoples had long feared the "black lakes of death." But only in 1879 did Russians learn that Okha sat on oil. Filip Pavlov, a trader for a baron in Nikolaevsk on the mainland, carried home to his boss a bottle of Okha "kerosene water." The samples were sent on to Moscow, and by 1892, two years after Chekhov's visit, word had reached Europe. The Nobels, the famed Swedish clan who drilled the first wells in Baku and developed much of Russia's oil industry, never got this far. But prospectors from England and Germany were intrigued. The tsar, however, was loath to abandon Sakhalin's riches to a foreign concession.

The first derrick, built in 1910, the year of Tolstoy's death, was hard to reach. Even in a UAZik. Silent, but still standing, the landmark was hidden in the dead center of a swamp of mud, Sakhalin's first oil field, that blackened the southern edge of Okha. Hundreds of steel donkeys, most no longer nodding, dotted the hills everywhere. Some groaned heavily to pump out, by the miracle of Soviet technology, a gallon or two a day. Untended for decades and coated by years of petroleum runoff, the field swallowed trespassers up to the knee. As the mud sucked loudly at one's feet, the stench of crude oil came off the dark earth.

Downtown Okha was no less bleak. As far as Yuzhno is from Moscow, Okha seemed the same distance from the rest of Sakhalin. In Nogliki cows may have grazed on the weeds that filled the courtyards of its apartment blocks. But in Okha there were no cows in the yards, only weeds. The apartment houses were the same tired concrete stacks, five stories high, replicated in successive editions across the Soviet Union throughout the 1960s and 1970s. Everywhere heating pipes snaked above the ground, like veins connecting the apartment blocks. Covered with coarse wooden planks, the pipes filled the empty space of the treeless courtyards. Along the planks, barefoot children with muddy faces played. Others wore oversize old shoes and stretched-out sweaters. Like the *bezprizorniki* of Dostoyevsky's day, they would find their own way. The children were everywhere in Okha, but no one seemed to take notice of them.

A decade ago nearly sixty thousand people, almost all of them oil workers, fishermen, and their families, lived in Okha. No one now knew the population—it depended on how the fish swam—but more than a third of the town's residents had moved on. There were no cafés, no restaurants, no movie houses or theaters. The stores were few and mostly empty. The bazaar, a patch of dirt at a central street corner, was redolent of Grozny. The sellers greatly outnumbered the buyers, and the wares were scarce. Atop the back of an open Kamaz truck a man and a woman sold potatoes and cabbage. They found few takers. "Too expensive," a woman explained. "We all grow our own."

VALERY, VITYA, AND Zhorzh deposited me at the dormitory of the Okha Electric Company. It was not the worst hostelry I'd seen in Russia, but it ranked high. The lobby reeked of cat urine and mold. The corridors were dark and dank. The cots were thin, and the blankets threadbare, but at less than three dollars a night, no one could complain. Instead I set out in the driving rain in the direction of the only public institution that seemed to function in Okha.

I was eager to find Yuri Shvitsov. Yuri, I had heard, knew all about the Herring Affair. In camp and on the Molikpaq, no one had known anything of the dead fish. In Yuzhno the herring had been the talk of the fledgling anti-oil alliance, led by the city's few bona fide environmentalists, political activists, and journalists. They all had expressed grave concern over the "mass murder," as one ecowarrior, a young man who had recently painted a globe and the commandment "Save Our Sakhalin!" on the asphalt in front of the SakhEnergy headquarters, termed it. But none of them actually knew anyone, truth be told, who had seen the fish. If anyone did, I figured, it would be Yuri Shvitsov. Yuri was no Greenpeacenik. He was a hunter, the chairman for as long as anyone in town could remember of the Okha Regional Hunting Society.

The line of men outside Yuri's office was long. Inside, the air was thick with smoke and the smell of men who had worked hard all their lives and never cared for cologne or deodorant. Most wore worn jeans and faded flannel shirts. One stood stiffly in an old wool jacket that he could no longer button. Their hands were black, and their faces rough, darkened by stubble and the sun. Several had started to bald long before their time. All cursed as they waited. The men were Yuri's clients. They had stood for an hour to earn the right to shoot ducks.

"Just look at them!" Yuri barked, using his pipe to point down the line that stretched out the door. "Here's your goddamned suffering masses! Barely making it through the goddamned day!" He played it up for the audience, but he was not joking. Few of the men, once upstanding representatives of the Soviet work force, had held a job in years. Hunting for them was no longer an avocation. They all packed their own buckshot into used shotgun shells, scraped together the rubles for a license, and came to Yuri to vie for a chance to slog through the swampy shores at the tip of their island to shoot their dinner out of the sky.

Yuri was neither tall nor muscular, but as the referee among the daily supplicants, he tried his best to seem imposing. In his mid-sixties, he kept his gray hair trimmed short and favored a camouflage uniform: trousers, jacket, and cap. He wore heavy plastic-rimmed glasses and went nowhere without his pipe. He was forever sucking loudly on his pipe. If he resembled a cross between a physics professor and a marine commander, there was reason. Yuri had spent twenty-five years in the Okha Police Department, retiring six years previously as a major. But his first job, as he liked to remind visitors, had been as a surveyor. Yuri had charted each of the town's oil fields. He retained the stubborn certitude of a man of science and the aura, if not the authority, of a Soviet heavy in provincial law enforcement. At home Yuri might nurture a gentle streak, but in public he considered it a solemn duty to show his fellowmen his gruffest side.

Yuri had his own UAZik, a battle green antique that still ran strong at age twenty-seven. The metal dashboard was adorned with a row of seven naked girls, card-size stickers culled from kiosks. Yuri, however, was a traditionalist—a chauvinist, avowed and unabashed, and a Communist, proudly unreconstructed. In the last presidential election, the second since the Soviet fall, he had voted for the Communist Zyuganov over Putin. Yuri said he was tired of labels—what did "liberal" and "reformer" mean anymore?—but he affixed them to himself. He called himself a "patriot," a "dinosaur," and an "Old Believer in the old ways."

He was one of the diehards buried in the embers of the old party that held Stalin to blame for hijacking the Revolution. Lenin of course remained a hero. Yuri was particularly proud of his Lenin; a fine oil, it held a place of prominence in his office. The painting stood atop the double door safe where Yuri kept his hunting licenses. It was not a standard portrait. Lenin wore a felt hunter's cap and, resting beneath a birch tree, cradled a rifle in one arm while scanning the horizon. "A good hunter," Yuri called the founder of the Soviet state. "He just had too many enemies."

Yuri did not like the oilmen. It wasn't only the foreigners. He didn't care for any of the changes that had followed the Soviet fall. The rise of the *rynok*, the market, had brought only misery and woe. The *rynok*–he almost growled the word–had depleted Okha's stock of workers and increased, to his great dismay, its share of hunters. It wasn't just a matter of the fisheries, sawmills, and oil works shutting down. The gene pool, he was sure, would weaken over time. "Our little Okha will grow ever smaller," Yuri said, as we careered around its pitted streets in his UAZik, "and one day, if our oil never comes home, the whole town will disappear altogether."

He was only too pleased to be of help. He led me directly to a man who had been among the first to discover the swales of dead fish in the Piltun Lagoon. Like the anxious hunters, Volodya Baruzdin was a hard worker and slow talker. He had lived on the island for thirty years and never seen anything like it. "Dead fish everywhere," he said. "They were up to the tops of my boots." A fisherman friend who lived on the lagoon had phoned to tell him to come down and bring as many sacks as he could find. Volodya had only wanted to fertilize his vegetable garden. "We use it for fertilizer," he explained, "something we learned from the Japanese." He had gone home with fifteen bags of dead herring, which he shared with his neighbors. They all went out into their kitchen gardens, turned over the earth, and mixed in the dead herring. Sure, it had smelled terrible, but it'd been good, Volodya said, for the potatoes. The harvest that year was wonderful.

Volodya did not know what the lab tests had shown. He said he didn't need to know. He was a retired mechanic in desperate straits. The fingertips of his right hand were rusted burnt orange from *papirosi*. He had few teeth left, and one of them he moved with a thumb as he talked. His eyes, once blue, were now clouded by drink. As we talked, I could smell the vodka in his skin, and when we parted, his handshake left the acrid smell in my hand. Volodya had few people to talk to, but he had something to say. He said it again: He had never seen so many dead herring in his life, and he doubted that it was murderous ice, dumb luck, or blind coincidence that killed the fish. He had no savings and no paycheck, but Volodya wagered a bet that it was all the work of "the men out there," the men on the sea "drilling for gold."

THE OKHA MUSEUM was filled with relics from the first oil boom on the island. A plaque dating from the old order prominently claimed that "Russian and foreign merchants were only interested in the oil as a means of profit. . . . Until the establishment of Soviet power, the oil industry did not exist." The sign of course did not tell the whole story.

Unbeknownst to most of Okha and the oil executives down in Yuzhno, the Americans had been here before. In the early 1920s the Soviets had dangled the Okha fields before Harry Sinclair, a flamboyant Oklahoma oil baron who dreamed of overtaking John D. Rockefeller and the Nobels in Russia. Sinclair Oil had done well in Oklahoma, but was hardly a giant. The Soviets imagined that Sinclair's friendship with President Harding would ease his way around any Japanese obstacles. Sinclair in turn courted the Bolsheviks in style. In 1923 he arrived in Moscow with a Roosevelt–Teddy's son Archie–a U.S. senator, and an eighty-man entourage that filled two decks of an ocean liner and a two-hundred-thousand-dollar chartered train.[35] Sinclair met Lenin and made a pitch for the whole of the Soviet oil industry. The Bolsheviks offered a thirty-six-year lease on the oil fields of northern Sakhalin. However, since the spring of 1920, Japanese troops had occupied the north of the island, and Washington, fearful of riling the Japanese, lent no help. All the same, Sinclair bashed on, dispatching an exploratory team–two Sinclair officials and a translator–to the island.

J. P. McCulloch and D. T. McLaughlin left New York in September 1923. They traveled by ship, train, horse, and sleigh, before crossing the frozen Tatar Strait and stepping onto Sakhalin in February 1924. They did not get far. They spent their first night in a shack "less than twenty feet square, with cracks in the walls, broken panes in the windows, a single wood stove, and no facilities for personal cleanliness." McCulloch and McLaughlin scarcely slept. A coop full of chickens claimed one corner of the hut, while a dozen men–"Russian drivers, Chinese, Gilyaks and half-castes"–competed with the Americans for space on the floor. They awoke covered by snow. During the night a blizzard had hit.

Sinclair's dream died a quick and ignoble death. McCulloch and McLaughlin lasted two weeks on the island before the Japanese, refusing to recognize any agreement with Moscow, sent them packing.[36] By then President Harding had died and Teapot Dome, the scandal that centered on Sinclair's acquisition of the Wyoming oil fields of the same name, had erupted.

In a secret scheme not unlike the loans for shares devised by Potanin and his fellow oligarchs under Yeltsin, Harding's interior secretary, Albert B. Fall, had granted Sinclair rights to the Teapot Dome reserves in return for no-interest "loans." Congress investigated, and the Supreme Court ruled the deals illegal.

Sinclair retreated. He served six and a half months in jail and never again dreamed of entering the Soviet market. The Japanese, however, did well by Sakhalin. In 1925, in return for oil and coal concessions, they decamped from the north of the island. By 1928 they were pumping 150,000 tons of crude a year from the island's fields. Sakhalin by then was feeding Japan all the oil it needed.[37]

❧ NINE ❧

"A SAD, BUT NOT new picture," scribbled Alexander III, according to Kennan the Elder, in the margins of a secret report presented to him by the governor-general of eastern Siberia on the prisons of the region in 1882.[38] The same could be said today of life not only in Okha but all across northern Sakhalin. From the persepective of the island's north, Yuzhno, with its university, refurbished shops, frontier bars, and Internet access, seemed veritably cosmopolitan. In the north, life was not only more remote but darkened, as if the clouds had blocked the sun, by the pall of decay and uncertainty.

In Laguri, a one-street village just west of Okha, I discovered a strange phenomenon. The Soviet obsession with secrecy and the present vacuum of knowledge had unduly burdened the locals. They believed their village had been born as a Gulag camp. LAG-U-RI, they explained patiently, was short for *lager' usilennogo rezhima* (maximum security labor camp). The genealogy made sense, but it was not true. Sakhalin had Gulag camps, but not here. The origins of the name were far more prosaic. It derived from the Nivkhi *Lagi*, the name of the rocky creek that ran through the village.[39] It denoted not political prisoners but "autumnal salmon."

This apocryphal version of history, however, suited the residents of

Laguri just fine. Two women, strolling at sundown one Sunday evening, reflected on the limbo their lives had become. Natasha had just entered her forties. Her curls, dyed iced-lemon blond, bounced as she walked. Laguri, she said, once housed the men and women who built the pipelines in 1942 that carried Sakhalin oil and gas off the island. The pipes wound behind the little houses to Pogibi on the western coast, where the island jutted out just four and half miles from the mainland, and over to Komsomolsk on the Amur.

Natasha and her friend, Oksana, once worked in the oilmen's club. The club was shut down years ago, but they had stayed on in Laguri. Their roots ran deep. Their ancestors had first come as exiles, prisoners who worked the coal mines. Natasha's grandfather had fought the Japanese in 1905. Subsequent generations worked the oil fields, but today few of the old locals did so any longer. None of the young men worked at all. They hung around the village's lonely street, waiting for the vodka to come. Television antennas topped the little houses, and some of the kids, Oksana said, even had computers. But now so many families had left, the local school had only four classes. They had every reason to leave, the women said, but none of the wherewithal to do it. "Everyone who can," said Natasha, "moves away."

IN OKHA, BECAUSE the dorm had no café and the town no restaurants, I was left to forage for food in its kiosks. The kiosk must be a Russian invention. It surely sounds, and functions, like one. In the "transitional period," Russian merchants and traders did not build stores. They built kiosks. To retrofit an old Soviet store, almost always in the first floor of an apartment building, was costly. It demanded capital and clout. But erecting a metal kiosk on the sidewalk in front of an old empty Soviet store was an overnight venture. Kiosks sprouted everywhere in the early 1990s in Moscow. Soon they lined the streets across the country, in cities, villages, half-abandoned workers' settlements. By the mid-1990s the kiosk had become the primary point of purchase for Russian consumers. Food, beer, cigarettes, tampons, videos, Pampers and Bordeaux–they all were here.

Okha had the grandest temples of the street corner commerce I had seen in Russia. They ringed the town's mud-filled main square. In a city of charcoal streets and darkened apartment blocks, the lights of the kiosks glowed around the clock, every day. At night, however, the vendors worked behind metal bars.

In the Soviet era, kiosks everywhere sold the same goods: New Dawn perfume, Red October chocolates, Red Star sprats, Doktorskaya sausage, and heavy glass bottles of Zhiguli beer. Each night I scanned the shelves, like a menu, for dinner. Nearly everything now, except the water, vodka and black bread, was imported:

Can of corn from Nagykoros, Hungary (15 rubles)
Can of pitted black olives from Spain (28 rubles)
Half liter of apple juice from Chisinau, Moldova (14 rubles)
Jar of pickles from Bulgaria (9 rubles)
Poong Jeon Nice potato chips from Gwangju, South Korea (7 rubles)
Styrofoam cup of ramen with chicken bits. Two options: one from Ho Chi Minh City, Vietnam (10 rubles), the other from South Korea (12 rubles)

The ramen became a staple. The Vietnamese was far better than the Korean. You had only to boil water in the dorm room and pour it into in the square of styrofoam.

Every kiosk of course featured alcohol and cigarettes. The one across from the dorm, however, offered something I'd never seen in a kiosk: an entire shelf of *spirt*–the medicinal alcohol Issa had relied on in Chechnya. At roughly thirty cents a liter, it filled a shelf between the beer and the vodka. Behind the counter, a young girl with cotton candy pink hair said nothing when I asked if the *spirt* was always there. She only blushed. *Spirt*, she knew, was supposed to be sold by prescription. In Moscow some pharmacies even refrained from offering it. I had a friend, I explained to the girl, who would love her kiosk. He had to take the metro across Moscow to buy his *spirt* in an outdoor market. The next day, when I returned to the kiosk, the shelf had been emptied.

NINETEENTH-CENTURY travelers to Sakhalin often tallied similar lists of exotic sightings: wild savages and exiled revolutionaries, giant bears and mineral baths. Almost always they encountered murders. So did I.

The chief of the Okha police broke the news. On my first morning in town he paid a courtesy call on my companions at the electric company dorm, Valery, Vitya, and Zhorzh. In the nearby village of Tungor two men, both in their twenties, the chief explained, had gotten into a drinking bout. Valery, Vitya, and Zhorzh were themselves in the throes of a dedicated binge. The rum and Cokes had been the prelude for the opera to come. The trio sat and listened, but they could only give the Okha chief deadeye stares and leaden nods. Tall and dark with a wide grin half hidden by a bushy black mustache, the police chief reminded me of a Scotland Yard detective in a television show. He sketched out the murder, as much as anyone knew. There'd been vodka, an argument, then the eruption. One of the two friends had grabbed a kitchen knife and stabbed the other–seventeen times.

Two days later, in the chill rain Yuri and I came upon the funeral. Yuri pulled the UAZik off the road to wait for the crowd to pass. The whole village had come out. Through the windshield I could see men in black raincoats leading the procession. Umbrellas hid their faces. They lifted the pine coffin, its occupant open to the skies, onto the flatbed of a Kamaz truck. A dozen mourners clambered up to crouch in the rain beside the body. The boy's mother, who wore no coat and carried no umbrella, climbed on the truck last. She knelt beside the coffin and tried to cover her son with her wet arms.

The case, a homicide between friends ignited by vodka, was sadly a commonplace occurrence everywhere across Russia. But within days I learned from the two cops who worked the case that the murder story had a second act. They'd arrested the murderer with no trouble. But he'd been in jail only a few hours when his mother took the law into her hands. She went to the house of the victim's mother–and set her barn afire. The murder, the cops said, was a tragedy of course. One son was dead, another in jail. But torching a barn–that was another matter.

"Lose your barn," one cop said, "you lose your hay, you lose your livestock, you lose your stores for winter." A woman without a son or a barn, his partner added, had little else. The murderer's mother had exacted revenge because she believed the victim's mother had ratted out her son. After all, the boys were friends, she told the police. Who could blame them for drinking?

Now the cops feared "real trouble." They did not arrest the arsonist mother. Jail, they considered, would do her no good. They'd sit her down instead and give her a good talking to. If the women kept it up, the cops explained, the town would split into two camps. "And instead of a murder over vodka," one of the cops concluded, "we've got a war."

BY WEEK'S END Valery, Vitya, and Zhorzh had fallen to half-mast. Their room, never bright, was now dark. It reeked of vodka, cigarette smoke, urine, and potatoes fried in pork fat. Empty bottles, dirty clothes, open cans of meat, overflowing ashtrays, a sack of muddy onions, a bag of half-rotten tomatoes, and two skillets, one filled with freshly burned eggs and the other with the congealed grease of yesterday's sausage, littered the floor. By now it was clear the trio would not be going hunting. They had driven the length of the island to sit in the dormitory of the Okha Electric Company. But they were happy. In the room next door they had discovered a soul mate.

Seryozha came with his own vodka. He wore Chinese trousers and a shirt unbuttoned to his waist. He was scarcely in his twenties, with the soft smile and pale baby face of a college student who had lost his way in this dark wood. When we shook hands, however, I saw that deep scars lined his face. They ran north-south, east-west. One of his eyes was badly misshapen, its lid permanently half closed.

"Pay him no heed," Vitya, the border guard, instructed. Vitya was sitting on the floor, his back against the wall, in his underwear. No longer able to stand, he raised a forefinger to his temple and twirled it in tight circles. "He's lost it," Vitya yelled at me. "He's Chechen." It was not the first time I had heard Russians call their compatriots who had come home from the war in Chechnya "Chechens." It was intended as a slur of endearment.

As Valery, the deputy police chief of Yuzhno, poured a new round of drinks, Vitya hectored Seryozha. "You fucking Chechen!" he screamed. "You fucking Muslim!" Vitya ordered the boy to take his trousers off. In a moment, without a word, Seryozha let his trousers fall to the empty bottles at his feet. He stood swaying in his underwear in the middle of the room. Vitya grabbed him by the waist, dragged him onto the cot, and hoisted his naked legs aloft. Dark scars zigzagged down the boy's legs. Vitya smiled. "See these fucking ugly scars?" he yelled. "That's what makes him a fucking Chechen!"

The enthusiasm was not strictly for my benefit. Valery, who remarkably could still string two sentences together, explained: Vitya had done a spell in the border guards in Central Asia. The *dukhi*, the spirits, as the veterans of the Soviet war in Afghanistan called the mujahideen, lingered. When Vitya drank, his pal Valery explained, the *dukhi* returned. (The spirits had haunted the Russians in Chechnya as well; in Grozny the soldiers had also spoken solemnly of the enemy as the *dukhi*.) The unfolding scene, for all its drunkenness, offered an illuminating tableau: two generations of Russian men who had served the Motherland amid the infidels, naked with their wounds revealed. It was not long before the inevitable climax came. The aging border guard beat the young Chechen vet with his meaty hands until the boy's face bled.

Seryozha fled the room to smoke. I joined him in the dark corridor. As he took deep drags of the cigarette, he tilted his head back against the wall. Blood had filled his nostrils. He was from Chelyabinsk, the nuclear city that had inspired much of the black humor on the boat up the Yenisei. Yes, Seryozha laughed, "the warm heart of the nuclear world."

He had come to Okha to do a timber deal. A friend had put him in touch with a logging heavy in Vladivostok who knew a middleman in Okha who enjoyed the good favor of the head of the city administration. He'd won a license, no waiting, no paperwork, to clear fifty acres of pine from the woods. It was hard work, he said. But the money would be good. The fattest end of the margin, of course, went to the guy in Vladivostok, the guy who'd fronted him with the connection. But the work was within the law, more or less, and the only business he'd found since coming home to make money. In Chelyabinsk, Seryozha said, they didn't hire "Chechens." He'd been certified, after all, officially declared a victim of the "Chechen syndrome."

The plague was not restricted to the war zone but was a medical diagnosis all too common among conscripts returning from the war, the Russian version of the posttraumatic stress that preyed on America's Vietnam veterans. It was strange of course to meet one of its victims in this hovel so removed from urban Russia and the battlefields. But I was not surprised. The Chechen syndrome, I had learned, had spread far.

In Vladivostok, in a psychiatric ward that during the winter often went without heat, electricity, and hot water, a doctor had detailed the malady for me. Its symptoms ranged from rapid heart rates to hallucinations. But the most common sign, the soft-spoken doctor explained, was an inability to sustain personal relations, even with loved ones. The "Chechens," thin young men with long faces, filled the clinic's long corridors. Old rags, twisted around their wrists and ankles, bound them to the steel cots. The doctor explained. "The Chechens," he said, "tend to run."

❧ TEN ❧

TYMOVSKOYE MARKED the middle of the island. Here the road that linked Okha and Yuzhno met the byway that led to the west coast and Aleksandrovsk, once the headquarters of the penal colony in Chekhov's day. From Okha I had again hitched a ride with cops, this time two detectives sent down to Nogliki to report on the murder that had begat an arson that now threatened to ignite provincial unrest. From Nogliki I took a slow train south, a train so weary and tiny it would have been better suited for an African safari park. In Tymovskoye, I got out.

The village was once known as Derbinsk, after the master of its prison, Anton Derbin. The name lasted to Stalin's day, until in 1949 an enterprising Soviet citizen took it upon herself to inform the Kremlin of the oversight. Mariya Ivanovna Sherbak sent a letter to Stalin. "Dear Joseph Vissari-onovich!" she wrote, before explaining how she had pulled her *Small Soviet Encyclopedia* off the shelf and discovered a map in volume 9, 1941, still blighted by the village named Derbinsk. Mariya Ivanovna pleaded for jus-tice: "Is it possible to change the shameful name of this place, named to honor a tsarist executioner who was famous for his cruelty even in those dark times?" The Kremlin sent the letter on to the Party bosses on Sakhalin, who undertook an urgent investigation. Unfortunately, in the Yuzhno archives they unearthed little evidence to judge Derbin. In the end they too turned to Chekhov. They read his description of the merciless warden and made their decision. Within months the village of Derbinsk was renamed Tymovskoye.

As the sky darkened and filled with stars, I boarded an old bus, higher and shorter than any in Moscow, that carried me through the soft turns of the low mountains leading to the west coast. It was nearly midnight when the bus let me off in the deserted square that comprised downtown Aleksandrovsk. It was less a town square than a fat T formed by two streets, in the center of which stood a bust painted gold atop a pedestal painted blue: Chekhov.

I crossed the empty asphalt and checked into the Three Brothers Hotel, named after Aleksandrovsk's chief tourist attraction, three tall rocks that rose in a close row in the waters off its shore. The kind woman at the registration desk showed me to a room with a television and shower. The television did not work, nor did the shower. But in the morning, she promised, there'd be an hour of hot water. Perhaps, I wondered, they had another room? Oh, no, she said, it was her best. The governor himself, in town on a campaign swing, had slept there the night before.

I opened the pink curtains, pulled back the plastic drapes, and looked out the dirty window. Before me appeared the Chekhov monument, its back to the hotel. But now, in the darkness across the way, I saw the second statue. Both fixed in granite, they were staring at each other across the empty square: the writer who had begun his exploration of Sakhalin in this town a 110 years before and the founder of the Soviet state, the man who had seized power in Petrograd and promised to abolish the tsar's old prisons.

History everywhere on Sakhalin had a hard time hiding. Yet nowhere did the past manifest itself so keenly as in Aleksandrovsk. When the steamer *Baikal* docked here at dawn on July 11, 1890, and Chekhov first stepped on the island, the town was the Aleksandrovsky Post, a settlement of roughly three thousand inhabitants, two-thirds up the western coast. A sign that read 10,172 VERSTS [6,752 miles] TO PETERSBURG then stood in front of the post office. Now Aleksandrovsk was a forlorn hamlet, home to some thirteen thousand souls who liked to see their local history as a cautionary tale.

On the beach beneath the cliffs, still marbled with dark veins of coal, children dug in the sand. Every so often they unearthed rusted manacles, the chains once worn by the prisoners who worked the nearby mines. At the same time, pensioners scoured the same sands, culling bits of coal that had washed ashore after the storm.

Chekhov's arrival was ominous. From the boat he could scarcely see the settlement. Giant fires burned across the Sakhalin taiga. Black smoke covered the sea, masking the wharf and the prison beyond. "The horrifying scene," Chekhov wrote, "compounded of darkness, the silhouettes of mountains, smoke, flames and fiery sparks, was fantastic." To the uninitiated, it seemed "all of Sakhalin was on fire."[40]

On my first morning in town Aleksandrovsk again hid. The shower at the Three Brothers still ran dry, but outside, it was pouring. A gusty wind blew the rain in sheets. The uneven streets had turned into streams. From the crest of the hill that formed the town, whatever lay below was cloaked by the wet darkness. As I walked, slipping down a steep, gravelly road, I could only feel the hill falling away beneath my feet. I stumbled on, toward where I sensed the wharf lay, toward the flats.

This was the old Slobodka, the district, then a place of former convicts and teenage prostitutes, where Chekhov first stayed on the island. The Slobodka derived its wealth from bootlegging the vodka that nourished the prisoners and their guards. To Baron Korf, the governor-general of Amur, who visited the island during Chekhov's stay, the Aleksandrovsky Post was the Paris of Sakhalin. Chekhov concurred: "Everything that exists in this noisy and famished Paris—fornication, drunkenness, gambling, sickness, the buying of spirits and the sale of stolen goods, or selling one's soul to the devil—all this leads directly to the Slobodka."[41]

In the 1960s a museum was built to mark the spot where the great writer had slept. It was a modest wooden affair fashioned by Leningrad carpenters. Now rarely visited, it was kept well scrubbed and in 1990, for the centenary of Chekhov's stay, restored. It was a fine tribute. Only it was not the house where the writer had stayed. He had, however, visited the Trade Commission Warehouse that once stood here, the shop that sold "the little stars which go on epaulets, Turkish delight, crosscut saws, sickles and most up-to-date ladies' summer hats, very fashionable. . . ."[42] The shopkeeper, Karl Landsberg, a former guards officer in Petersburg, packed off to Sakhalin for murder, invited Chekhov to dine in his house.

The evening yielded one of the rare scenes in Chekhov's exhaustive study of Sakhalin that resembled one of his dramas. The trouble began when he asked when the snows had stopped. A debate ensued. In the end one of the guests, a doctor who bore a striking resemblance to Ibsen, closed the discussion with a dark legend: that the Gilyak shaman, offended by the Russians who occupied his native land, had cursed Sakhalin and vowed that "no good would ever come of it." The doctor related the tale as prophecy. "So it has come to pass," he concluded. The next day Chekhov moved in with the doctor.[43]

GRISHA SMEKALOV EXTENDED a beefy arm out the window of his Toyota minivan and pointed. "That's where we found the body," he said. We had passed the corner where the doctor's house once stood and forded a creek that had swollen across the Slobodka. The corpse, Grisha clarified, hadn't become a case. Just a murder among vagrants. "One less drunk, one less problem," he said as he leaned hard over the steering wheel, as if to lend his considerable bulk to the minivan's struggle up the gravelly hill.

Grisha–Grigori in his passport, Grisha to his friends, Grishenka to his wife, Lena–was a jovial fellow of forty-four. He had a broad chest and the girth that marked the onset of middle age. He had an unruly ginger beard and a bushy mustache and no reason, he said with pride, to own a razor. He wore an old T-shirt, stained jeans, and an orange baseball cap emblazoned with the black letters Y and G, the emblem of the Yomiuri Giants.

Grisha, I was hardly surprised to learn, was a cop. After weeks on the island I'd devised an equation: Any male resident with a car and a job was likely to be in the employ of the police, the border guards, the federal security service, or the armed forces. For fifteen years Grisha had worked as a detective tasked with serious crime, murder, and theft. He'd been promoted up the short ladder and now sat in the same office where Drekov, the dictator of the north, once reigned. The times, however, had changed too fast. Crime was no longer aberrant behavior but the norm. Grisha knew all about the troubles on the islands, from the poaching *mafiya* to the brothel that graced the top floor of the Eurasia Hotel down in Yuzhno. He was done with the job, but he was having trouble retiring. The old collective farms had once kept the town flush with timber and fish. Now, as nearly everywhere on the island, it was every man for himself. Aleksandrovsk, ever since it lost its prisons, had not known an industrial base. Yet in the decade of the changes, as Grisha called the era inaugurated by the Soviet fall, commerce had contracted to the limp line of kiosks beside the hotel. And so he stayed on the force. There was, he said, no other work.

Grisha was a third-generation islander, the son of a carpenter and grandson of a peasant who had come to Sakhalin of his own will. The male lineage, he was pleased to report, was martial. Like so many I'd met, his father fought the Japanese here in the Second World War. His grandfather had taken on the Whites in the Civil War and earlier, in the First World War, had slogged his way through the western front in Romania. When dekulakization came in the twenties, he had left his village near Irkutsk and headed for Sakhalin. It sounded strange, Grisha knew, but his grandfather had come in search of a better life. In America, he knew, folks went west for new beginnings. "But in Russia," he said, "we've always headed east."

He was devoted to tending the past. He had collected century-old photographic albums, letters, and diaries. He had also assembled an impressive array of artifacts: old locks and giant keys, iron cuffs and shackles. Some were heirlooms; others he had culled from neighbors, the beach, and the town's trash dumps. So great was his collection he had donated much of it to the fledgling one-room museum in town. Grisha had become Aleksandrovsk's unanointed historian.

The Smekalov home was a one-story rectangle of wooden planks, raised a foot off the marsh and shared with another family whose relations were muffled by a plywood wall. Grisha had painted the Seven Dwarfs in multicolor on the Smekalov side of the house. Inside, the living, he said in apology, was "simple." The small bathroom had no water. The toilet was flushed by a bucket filled with spring water and kept nearby. To bathe in winter, one heated a water tank by burning kindling beneath it. The yard was all vegetable garden: potatoes, tomatoes, cucumbers, squash (two varieties), onion, garlic, and beets. On a clothesline beside the house, fish and mushrooms were drying in the hot sun.

The home, however, was an idyll, a nest of tranquil warmth as any I had seen in Russia. Daughter Masha, a blue-eyed girl of fifteen, had long auburn braids, with twin strands woven tightly and beaded back in cornrows. She had postered Bruce Willis over her bed. She and her brother, Dima, a twelve-year-old with a quiet voice, shared a room. At night Masha played Russian ballads on the upright piano between their beds and sang, while Dima pumped an old accordion to accompany her. The children were studious and dutiful. They shared an assured air that filled the house. It was a confidence their parents lacked.

Lena, a stocky woman in her early forties, had lively blue-green eyes beneath heavy eyelids. She was embarrassed to shake hands, let alone trespass into political discourse. Like her husband, she had never met an American. But unlike her husband, she did not seem keen to have foreigners in her house.

Lena was a border guard. She had come from the south of the island to work the ships out in Aleksandrovsk Harbor. Whenever they came these days, and that wasn't often, she checked their manifests and vetted all onboard. This week she had Koreans. A few weeks earlier it had been Japanese. In the south her father had run a crane in a fishery and her mother had handled the paperwork in the same collective farm. Lena had done better, she conceded. Her salary was miserly, but it came. She had even splurged on six months of diet potions from Herbalife. But the border guards now owned her. Her years of service had made her *nevyezdnaya*, unable to leave the country. "Back then who would've known," she said, "that one day the door would open?"

ONE MORNING, WHEN the skies cleared and the rain let up, Grisha and I set out for Due. Founded in 1867, it had been the first Russian settlement on Sakhalin. It had never attracted many free men, but its rich veins of coal, first mined in the 1880s, gained fame even in Moscow. As the penal colony grew, Due became home to the island's worst prison and its most feared mines.

We had to wait for low tide, for Due lay hidden a mile or so down the beach, past bleak cliffs that jutted out into the sea. When the water was high, one could not walk through the tunnel. The passageway, a small hole cut in the rock above the shore, was once used for cargo wagons stacked with coal. The Toyota had no trouble on the hard sand of the beach. Grisha drove fast. The wet clumps flew in the air as we approached the opening in the cliff, the light barely visible through the rock.

Due impressed Chekhov as a well-ordered hell. "The street is straight and smooth," he wrote. "There are clean white cottages, a striped hut, striped posts." The settlement's single street reminded him of a parade ground. "All that is lacking to complete the impression," he noted, "is the roll of drums." The road remained, but little else did. The "coal breaks," the great fat layers of black, gray, and white exposed by the cliffs, still guided us, but Due was now nearly deserted. The stray dogs outnumbered the few spectral figures who stopped and stared beside their collapsing huts as we walked the lone road.

When Chekhov visited, he counted 291 inhabitants, excluding the guards. I counted 17 women, 4 men (three drunk), and 5 children (all barefoot and 4 without shirts). In the store at the road's end, where the narrow valley forked into two green gorges, 9 of the women stood in silence. The store was dimly lit. Its counters held dry crackers, dried fish, dry biscuits, Korean bubble gum, and Snickers. The women, inside and out, did not stand close to one another. They wore taut kerchiefs and plain skirts, and each carried a limp plastic bag. They were waiting, I sensed, but I didn't know what for. Bread was the answer. Twice a week, the women said, each staring off in a different direction, they brought the bread.

Due verged on extinction, but the women would live on. They had been here, after all, when Chekhov visited. It was easier, he reasoned, for the men. They were kept busy with hard labor. But how, he wondered, did the women survive? How did they not go mad in a place where "by reasons of poverty, the foul weather, the never-ending clank of chains, the unchanging view of barren mountains, and the roar of the sea, the moaning and wailing often heard from the prison when punishment is meted out with lashes and birch rods, time must seem far longer and more tormenting than in Russia"? The women, Chekhov concluded, suffered more than the miners: "There is nothing to do, they have nothing, they are tired of talking and arguing; it is boring to go out on the street because everything is equally cheerless and dirty. What an agony!"[44]

WE COULD HEAR the music from the graveyard. The tinny Russian pop boomed across the wharf, over the hulks of the rotting fishing boats. Grisha and I were sitting in the graveyard, as he called it, eating crab. An hour earlier the crab had been headed for a wedding, until Grisha's friend at the local fishery sold it to us on the side. Everywhere around us lay dead ships from the old days, when the hauls from the sea were set in Moscow. At the end of a long pier, a rickety affair that stretched as far as a football field, a single fishing boat had docked. The music, it seemed, was blasting from the boat. The fishermen in with the night's catch, surmised Grisha, who knew such things. Still, something was amiss. All along the pier people–women, men, children–were running back and forth.

Grisha negotiated past the security guards. "Fifteen years in the *militsiya* pays off at times," he said. As we walked down the pier, beside us ran an elevated metal trough that extended to its end. The fish should have been flowing down that trough, Grisha said. They were pumped out of the boat's hold all the way down into the factory on the shore. Something, he said, must be wrong. As we walked on, people hurried past us in both directions. Those rushing to the boat carried empty plastic sacks. Those rushing to the shore lugged the same bags, now full of fish.

When we reached the boat at the jetty's end, Grisha took in the state of affairs like a crime scene. "It's a blackout," he said. "If the plant had electricity," he explained, "they'd be pumping the fish down the pier. Instead, the catch is stuck on the boat and will have to be dumped back into the sea soon or it'll spoil." The fishermen had sent out the word. They had let their wives and neighbors know there was fish for the taking.

The deck of the boat was thick with men and flounder. The fishermen waded up to their knees in the shiny mass of silver. The men were tired. They had been out all night. The captain, however, was thankful. They hadn't had a good haul, he said. This was only eight, nine tons. Nothing like dumping a maximum load. A tall man with a broad grin, he seemed to speak from experience. As he spoke, all about him the fishermen raced to rescue the fish. Now and then, amid the flounder layered several feet deep, herring and squid surfaced. The men moved fast, as if pushed by the pulsating music, to stuff the fish into sacks.

Couldn't the fishery, I wondered, have radioed? Warned the men that the electricity was out, told them not to bother with fishing through the night?

Yeah, the captain said, they *could* have. But it wasn't so bad, he added. By now the men knew the drill. It wasn't the first time the electricity had gone down.

Overhead, the gulls already hovered. They circled in the warm currents, waiting their turn. People kept rushing down the pier. But the men had begun to dump the flounder, bailing it from the deck by the bucketful. Grisha was afraid to take the fish. He said he didn't need any. "Let the women take it," he said. "It's not right," he said, "for a cop to take charity." But as I talked with the captain, I saw Grisha ask one of the women for a sack. The men kept bailing. The waters around the old boat were fast dark-ening with the fish. The captain invited us into the bowels of his boat for a drink, but I begged off. I knew we'd be celebrating at the Smekalov house soon. I knew that night we would have flounder.

ELEVEN

I LEFT ALEKSANDROVSK as I had come, by bus. The old women and young couples—no one else ever seemed to travel on the island's buses and trains—were silent as we again climbed beneath darkening skies across the low mountains to Tymovskoye. In the warm dusk air, I bought a pack of cigarettes and a pound of sunflower seeds, dinner, from a woman who wore a black dress and could neither hear nor speak, and boarded a train that brought me south through the night, back to Yuzhno. I arrived at the station beside the Japanese-built hotel topped by the Korean-run bordello where I had spent my first night on the island. The circle was at its beginning. Yuzhno, however, now seemed like civilization.

In town I made the rounds. I saw the governor and heard tales of the munificence of the oil companies and the glory of their shared future. I vis-ited with his few brazen critics and filled a notebook with their fears. The oilmen had established an island development fund, which had handed over some sixty million dollars to date. Yet the fruits of the fund, the critics lamented, were hard to find. The roads were newly paved, it was true, but the steamrollers had come out only for Putin's visit. The new children's hos-pital, too, remained a source of strife. Begun in 1992, it was still unfinished five years later. The oilmen had given at least thirty million dollars to finish it off. But the local legislators had stalled—some said stole—and only last year, seven years late, had the hospital opened. No one, it seemed, knew where the time, and the money, had gone.

At a kiosk in front of the Chekhov Theater, I bought the papers. The most favored daily, *Sovietsky Sakhalin*—it hadn't bothered to change the name—held little news of Moscow, let alone the world beyond. It was filled with the latest murder—"another fish guy," the girl in the kiosk said with a yawn. She had been asleep, her head splayed across the papers, when I knocked. On a park bench I found *Sovershenno verno* (*Totally True*), a tabloid stuffed into every mail slot in town, and read unsubtle hints that the governor's chief rival, the mayor of Yuzhno, was campaigning on funds derived from a little-known nexus between the Chechen and South Korean mobs. This, I realized, was a smear campaign with a clever twist. It compounded the fear of "the blacks," as Russians termed almost anyone from the Caucasus, with the fear of "the yellow."

In the afternoon, I went to see Vera Boltunova, a local Duma deputy, a lapsed geophysicist, and the editor of the island's most independent paper. Vera had never meant to become a politician or a journalist. It was almost by instinct that in 1988 she'd helped lead the demonstations that removed the local Party boss. "We practically carried him out on our hands," she said with a smile. The joy had not lasted long. Under Yeltsin, Sakhalin sent another Communist, a former bulldozer driver, to the Duma in Moscow. Vera recited an impromptu eulogy to the romantic era: Yeltsin had been a lush; he'd not even watched as the oligarchs divvied up the land; he and his errant daughter Tatyana had sold the store and the country for a song. Vera did not trust the oilmen, but she feared "the three great Russian diseases"—greed, corruption, and bureaucracy—more. Russians, she said, didn't need any help to destroy their own opportunities. To put a single fishing boat on the water, Vera went on, one needed the signatures of forty-nine officials. To put up a kiosk, one needed twenty-two. I understood the calculus: the more signatures, the more bribes.

The next morning I drove out to an old government dacha that graced the hills above Yuzhno with Brezhnevian grandeur. With columns and a balcony that overlooked the city, it had once housed the Party boss Vera Boltunova had helped evict. Now it was the headquarters of the fisher king of Sakhalin, Anatoly Ivanovich Filipov. He was not a mobster or a politician, but all over the island Anatoly Ivanovich commanded respect. He was one of the few on Sakhalin who had crossed from the old era to the new on a bridge of his own making. Anatoly Ivanovich was as self-made as any man in Russia could be.

He had founded and now ran the Tunaicha fishery, one of Russia's biggest exporters of salmon and red caviar, which had just celebrated its tenth anniversary. However, he'd been trained to teach. For sixteen years, from Brezhnev to Yeltsin, he had taught the economics of dialectical materialism, and in the summers worked the boats to earn extra cash. Then in the first years of reform, even before the USSR fell, he made his move. Not many in his class had made it, but he was savvy, lucky, and, by his own admission, connected. He got loans, bought a boat, and took out insurance. First Governor Fyodorov, doling out small grants from his enterprise fund, backed him. Then a Moscow bank, flush in the early Yeltsin years, gave him a huge loan, one million dollars. Before long he had an American partner, an old Alaskan fishing family that hadn't seen salmon so plump and pink since the fifties. Now Tunaicha employed six hundred people—two thousand in season—and its eight boats hauled, on average per annum, fifteen thousand tons of fish. It was the only cannery in Russia to ship canned salmon to Europe—nearly four million tins in 2000. Still, staying afloat was far from easy. Anatoly Ivanovich, when he recounted his evolution, offered a litany that hit on each of Vera Boltunova's dreaded three great diseases. He had faced them all: the politicians, the mobsters, and, worst of all, the bureaucrats.

Anatoly Ivanovich wore a blue Lacoste cardigan buttoned over a silk tie, a stiff white shirt, plain slacks, and leather loafers. He had thick graying hair raked straight back, bushy eyebrows, and heavy Slavic lids. In his features, Asian brushstrokes balanced the European. He had been born in Tatarstan, the mostly Muslim republic in central Russia. His family came to Sakhalin after the war, when he was a toddler. As we drove out to his cannery, he embarked on an extended soliloquy on the problematic duality of the slogan Putin had made his grail, the Dictatorship of Law. "Either you're a dictator," he said, "or you're an elected official who governs by the law, right?" Anatoly Ivanovich was hardly the only one in Russia perplexed. But he was one of the few who had asked the president himself. So heralded was his success that Putin, during his Yuzhno stopover, had traveled thirty miles of rough gravel to see him at work.

Filipov had no illusions about the new man's capabilities, but Putin had impressed him—by how openly he admitted his ignorance and how strongly he sought to erase it. He explained. He'd given the president a tour, shown him how caviar was canned. At one point Putin was struck by how the cans fell along a conveyor belt into a water bath. "Why the water?" he inquired.

"So the cans will flow steadily," Anatoly Ivanovich replied, moving on to the next stage of the cycle.

Putin wanted a better answer. "No, really," he said, "what do you need the water for? Anatoly Ivanovich, kindly explain it to me."

So Anatoly Ivanovich kindly explained how the machine moved a big volume at once and that if there were no water, the cans could hit one another and dent. He told the president that if he had a dented can of caviar, he'd have to put it aside and sell it for less. It'd be second class.

Putin furrowed his brow and asked: "You mean, even if the caviar inside is fine, you'd still sell it for less?"

Anatoly Ivanovich nodded. "Appearance," he said, "also counts." If a can was even slightly dented, the price went down.

"OK," Putin said finally. "Now I understand."

It seemed comforting that the president of Russia had taken so acute an interest in the mechanics of canning. Putin could have learned a lot more from Anatoly Ivanovich, for he was something rare in Russia, a personification of the possible. He had survived the end of the Soviet Union, the hyper-inflation of the early Yeltsin years, the crash of August 1998, and, a month later, a bombing attempt on his life. As we toured the plant, a floppy-eared spaniel, copper and white, followed at his heels. The dog limped slightly and was blind in one eye. Anatoly Ivanovich owed his life to him. It had happened at the headquarters in town, right on the stairs to the office. He'd stepped out of his truck and started toward the steps when the dog came running, its tongue hanging out to greet him. Just as Anatoly Ivanovich stepped left to pet the dog, the stairs exploded.

The Putin years, he was certain, would prove a boon for business. Still, he had cautioned the president to be careful. Waging war against the oligarchs, he'd said, was not only stupid but futile. Putin couldn't change the way Russia had done business since the Soviet fall. He could change only how business would evolve in the future. Draw a line, he had told Putin, and the faster the better. There was no need for an amnesty, the kind Berezovsky had been pushing, that would allow the oligarchs to keep their "primitive accumulation of capital" and wipe the slate clean for all. It was useless, he'd told Putin, to go after select oligarchs, Gusinsky, Berezovsky, or Potanin. The fisher king had been blunt with the president: "Tell them all, 'It's over, boys, that's it. You've got your share. Now we're going to open things up for the rest of the country.'" Eighty-eight percent of the state's old enterprises now lay in private hands. Privatization hadn't been done right, of course. But only the country, not the oligarchs, would be hurt if the state launched a war to redistribute property. "That's one road," Anatoly Ivanovich said, "we've been down before."

ON AN AIRLESS MORNING a few days later, the papers blared the sordid details of a fresh murder–a timber guy this time–and I thought of the ever-bored girl in the kiosk. I walked along one of the anonymous cinder block walls of Yuzhno, entered a dark entranceway that reeked of beer and cats, and knocked on a clean white apartment door. Tatyana Shumilova greeted me with a wide smile. She had pale blue eyes, thick black doll's hair parted down the middle, and a doctoral degree from Moscow State. Tatyana taught sociology at the local university. She was so happy I'd come I feared she might kiss me. Her bow lips were painted thick with lipstick the color of burgundy.

The family album was waiting on the coffee table. "She was born Astafieva, but by marriage Sidorina," Tatyana said as she turned to the photograph of her grandmother. "Her father was exiled, just like her husband's father." Tatyana came from a long line of prisoners and exiles, on both branches of her family tree. "And that little one"–she pointed to a pudgy toddler at the photograph's edge–"that's me, right next to Grandma, always had to have my neck covered up tight." The image, from 1955, was yellowing.

We sat opposite each other, separated by a low table of dark wood. On it a tall crystal bowl held bananas, pears, and apples. The Turkish coffee, steaming in the stifling living room, cooled in tiny blue and white ceramic cups, treasures from a first trip abroad. Her husband filled an overstuffed chair in a far corner. Tatyana had introduced him, but he said nothing. This was, after all, her story. It was *her* grandfather who had met Chekhov.

After nearly a month on the island, dozens of interviews, and countless phone calls, I'd found at long last a descendant of the *katorzhany* Chekhov had met. Tatyana had grown up with the tale. It was one of the two most treasured memories from her childhood. The first was Pushkin, the lines from *Eugene Onegin* her father recited while he played the mandolin to her at night:

> *Tatyana, dear Tatyana! I shed my tears with you,*
> *for you have at so early a date,*
> *abandoned to a fashionable tyrant,*
> *for his sole keeping, your fate.*[45]

The Chekhov Story, as Tatyana called it, had always been a favorite. Her grandmother would sit her on her wool-covered knees and tell how Grandpa had not only met Chekhov, but been his guide, escorting the famous writer as he went visiting, from prisoner to exile to settler, in Grandpa's village.

Grandma certainly believed the tale. She had proof, she told Tatyana, evidence that wasn't pleasant to recall, but convincing. When her grandpa turned sixty, Tatyana said, he tried to make himself look younger. He wasn't indifferent, she explained, to a certain neighbor down the road. They'd had a dozen children, and he loved his wife dearly, but all the same he had these feelings for another lady. Grandpa had a long gray beard, but on his sixtieth birthday he shaved it to a modish goatee. When Grandma wondered why on earth he'd done that, Grandpa shot back: "I want to look like Antosha Chekhonte." Chekhov, in his earliest stories in *Strekoza* (*Dragonfly*), a Petersburg satirical weekly, had taken Antosha Chekhonte as a pen name. Because Grandpa scarcely read anything, Tatyana's grandmother took his knowledge of the writer's facial hair as proof that they'd met. For generations the tale had lived as a family legend, but Tatyana had always wondered if it was true.

Until the cards came. The guardians of the Soviet literary canon had celebrated Chekhov's study of Sakhalin as a landmark of his social conscience. Yet only recently had a small museum dedicated to the book opened in Yuzhno. From the first, Inga Tsupenkova, its prim director, was determined to acquire a complete set of Chekhov's census. She wrote Moscow and pleaded with the archivists at the Lenin Library. Years had passed, but at last, a few months earlier, the cards arrived. Inga scoured them for weeks, searching for familiar names. Tatyana looked as well. They did not need to hunt long. From the stacks that filled a tower of boxes in the one-room museum, Tatyana's ancestors—seven in all—soon emerged.

She poured the coffee slowly, lifting and setting my cup with a raised pinkie. Then, from a sheath of plastic, she produced with dramatic flourish the photocopied cards. "Sidorin, Andrei Nikonovich, 16 years old." The handwriting was Chekhov's. "That," Tatyana said triumphantly, "was Grandpa." He had arrived in 1881, the year the penal colony was founded. Chekhov had also written up Grandpa's brother and Tatyana's grandmother's sister and her great-grandparents. In all, Tatyana found four Sidorins and three Astafievs.

Tatyana wouldn't dream, and never had, of living anywhere else. She had fond memories of Moscow during her student days. She, too, was a child of glasnost; she had defended her dissertation in 1985, the year Gorbachev became general secretary. But she woke each day eager to get to her own classroom now. Her son, Sergei, at twenty-four, had just been made a correspondent at the Yuzhno television station. It was a new world now, she said, talking of his career. Yeltsin had gone, Putin had come, the ruble had crashed, and the oil price had soared. But to Tatyana none of it mattered. Yes, life had turned a bit more stable. The realm of the possible had perhaps expanded. But she had always had confidence in the future. It had come from her parents, she said. One always dreamed of escaping the island; the other wouldn't have been able to survive anywhere else. Tatyana imagined that she had found the golden mean.

Her father had lived on Sakhalin for forty years. He spent his life yearning to get out. In the end he did. He'd been born a Cossack, "a son of the Don," he liked to say. When he turned fifty-five, the pull of his native land was too great. He quit his job at the airport and went back to Russia's southern steppes. He had died not long after. He was buried there, Tatyana said, not quite on the Don, but close. She had seen to it. The grave was on a small hill bleached by the dry wind and hot sun. "All around," she said, "as far as you can see, there's nothing but the steppe."

Mama wouldn't leave. Not long ago she had turned eighty. The last of twelve brothers and sisters. Sakhalin, Tatyana said with sympathy, was all Mama had ever known. In her youth, it was true, she'd gone to Siberia, had even tried to live in Khabarovsk. But she just couldn't, Tatyana said with a soft laugh. She'd taken the boat right back to Sakhalin. Now in old age she wasn't about to leave. "Here," she liked to tell Tatyana, "are my roots, and here are my graves."

Tatyana had no idea where her grandfather, the man who met Chekhov, was buried. Some mass grave, she imagined. Caught up in Stalin's purges, he had been arrested as a Japanese spy. He had lived in a village in the north of the island and was in his seventies when he was taken away. He'd long quit the collective farm, but he had continued to farm his own small plot. There had been some kind of contact with the Japanese. Tatyana's mother remembered it warmly. A Japanese family had visited. She had played with the boy. "It was just trade," Tatyana said. "Bread for apples."

No one in the family had ever felt a need to search for Grandpa's grave. Tatyana certainly didn't. She had seen his file, the transcripts of his last days in the hands of the NKVD. In 1937, Drekov, the dictator of Sakhalin's north under Stalin, had sent her grandfather to the firing squad. As she remembered the documents, the color fell from her face. She had read the NKVD file closely. She had seen how her grandfather's strength and will had faded from his hand. The pages were filled with interrogations, each signed by the prisoner. The first was signed with a strong hand. Grandpa had written his surname boldly: "SIDORIN." The second time he could manage only three letters: "SID." The final interrogation had been brief. The transcript was just one page, the end of which was marked by a single, weary *S*.

For years few on Sakhalin talked of the *katorga*. Being a descendant of tsarist prisoners had not been a point of pride. But Tatyana, in Chekhov's census and the NKVD's archive, had unearthed a foundation, a heritage that she revered. As she spoke of the past now, there was pride in her voice. But there was inescapable sorrow as well. Tatyana had learned the perils of rummaging through her family history. She lapsed into silence and took her tiny cup into her hands. The coffee had long cooled. Her husband, as the talk moved beyond Chekhov, had left the room. He'd mumbled something about putting on the water. But he did not reappear, and in the kitchen next door no kettle sounded.

"After Grandma lost Grandpa"–Tatyana began again–"she developed the illness." Her mind, she said, went bad. As the sun went down each day, she would stand up straight and announce, "The black Maria is coming. Go open the door," she'd tell Tatyana. "Go out and look at the man. He's the devil," she'd say calmly. "You can tell it by his tail." In her last years, Tatyana told me, Grandma ate only when it got dark and never from a plate, only from a bowl. And every night she carried an ax with her to bed. "Strange, isn't it?" Tatyana asked, knowing she had not posed a question.

❧ TWELVE ❧

THE ENGLISHMAN Charles Henry Hawes, who followed Chekhov to Sakhalin at the turn of the nineteenth century, ended his work *In the Uttermost East* recalling the bounty of the Russian Far East and the obstacles to reaping it. "It is difficult for us to conceive," he said, "to mentally sympathize with the fatalistic element in the nature of the *muzhik*, living for centuries his life of isolation, fighting with the energy, not of hope but rather of despair. . . ." Hawes, too, had come at a time of opportunity. "Now this opening up of a new land," he wrote, "of fabulous resources, gold and silver, copper, coal and iron, of agriculture, cattle breeding and dairy produce, all this has come as the discovery of a new world, and you feel it in the air."[46]

Ivan Yuvachyov, one of the few political prisoners Chekhov met on Sakhalin, was another who left wishing the "sad island of miserables" well. A Petersburg native and a graduate of the esteemed Kronstadt Naval Academy, Yuvachyov was sentenced to hang as a member of the Narodnaya Volya, the underground People's Will movement that did away with Alexander II. His sentence was reduced, and in 1887, after years in the Schlüsselberg Prison, the jail that nearly a century earlier had been Sheikh Mansour's last home, he was sent to Sakhalin. On the island he took the pseudonym Mirolyubov (lover of peace) and turned to science and God. He ran the weather post in Tymovskoye, and later, back in Petersburg, his religious tracts gained fame. Before the Bolsheviks rose, his *Pilgrimage to Palestine* had been a best seller.[47]

In all, Yuvachyov spent eight years on Sakhalin, but he left it with a hopeful wish, dreaming of the day when its prisoners would reap its promise.

. . . I do not desire to see you as I left you! Perhaps you will remain, as always, a dumping ground for the refuse of our land, for all the unwanted limbs amputated from the body of Russia, or perhaps you shall become, on a par with other provinces, an independent region with a governor and a developed industrial life, and one day, eventually, with your own small fleet, your metal, coal, timber, fish and kerosene play no small role in the future of the Far East . . .[48]

Freedom and development have long competed in the world's most impoverished corners. But they need not always work in opposition. What law dictates that accommodation and cooperation cannot accompany economic development? After all, on Sakhalin I had discovered a paradox. More than a century after the birth of the tsarist *katorga*, the island of prisoners now harbored the freest men and women I had met in Russia. Freedom of course was a relative term. Anatoly Ivanovich Filipov personified the possible, but he was a rarity, and he knew he'd face hostility again. In my mind, as I walked Yuzhno those last days, lingered the image of the more prevalent predicament: the boatload of fishermen dumping their flounder. Wherever one looked, the old economy—fishing, farming, and forestry—lay in ruins. The prime consumers, moreover—the military men and their families—had left. Even the arrival of the oilmen had not stemmed the tide. The future lay in petroleum, with all its attendant perils. Yet try as I might, I could not block out Vera Boltunova's warning. "We've seen none of the oil money so far," she said. "Who's to say we ever will?"

For a month summer had extended its stay on Sakhalin. The cold fall rain came the morning I decided to visit the one corner of the island I had not seen. If Sakhalin, as its people said, was shaped like a salmon, I wanted to drive out as far as the dirt road would go, to its windswept tail.

Anatoly Ivanovich gave me a ride. As we headed out of town toward the southeastern coast, the wind rose and the rain pelted down. The car barreled on along the rutted road. Overhead, the clouds grew dark, closer. We came to Okhotskoye. Now a tired fishing hamlet, it had been born in the seventeenth century as Sakhalin's first Russian settlement, an outpost for fur trappers. A century later Vitus Bering, the Danish sea captain Peter the Great sent to chart the Far East, built his boats here before setting out to claim Alaska for the Russians. We drove on, fording the deep lagoon of Tunaicha. Here, on a cloudless afternoon only a month earlier, the salmon had spawned, flipping their plump bodies by the hundreds above the glistening blue, while the swans and ducks gathered, and the boys, naked and almond brown in their underwear, traded turns belly-flopping off a low bridge. Now the skies were heavy with rain, and waves slapped at the edge of the lagoon. On the sea the swans were flying in. A storm loomed. The boats were in, the canneries closed. The season was over.

Unlike at Aleksandrovsk or outside Okha, here the coast curved smoothly, one long beachy head stretching for miles. So plentiful was the salmon here once that nearly two centuries ago the explorer Krusenstern had marveled at how the natives caught them: ". . . they do not even employ a net for this purpose, but dip for them with a pail during the ebb."[49] We passed clusters of ramshackle buildings of rotting wood and aluminum roofs. They looked like abandoned warehouses, but they were fledgling fisheries." Sometimes, Anatoly Ivanovich explained, just a boat or two run by a few men. New people, he said, all along the coast, were coming in. First they bankrupted the old fisheries. Then they dismantled them—tore them apart, stripped them down to the earth. Slowly they'd begun to build something anew. Not far past the Tunaicha Lagoon a new aluminum shell gleamed in the wet. It was hardly a revival, but to Anatoly Ivanovich the row of shacks struggling to become canneries was heartening. He was impressed, buoyed even, by his new neighbors. "Initiative," he called their arrival.

The gravel road yielded to dirt, and then in the mud it ended. A stand of beeches, elegant and tall, stood three rows deep along the edge of the coast. The thin trees were bent forward. They grew that way, Anatoly Ivanovich said, so strong were the winds off the water. In the gusts the trees bowed ever lower, but they would outlast the storm. "You see," said the fisher king with the glee of a child, "even now, even in such a wind, they will not break."

V. WEST

THE *SKAZKA*

I gazed around me, and my soul was wounded by the suffering of mankind.

—Aleksandr Radishchev,
A Journey from Petersburg to Moscow, 1790

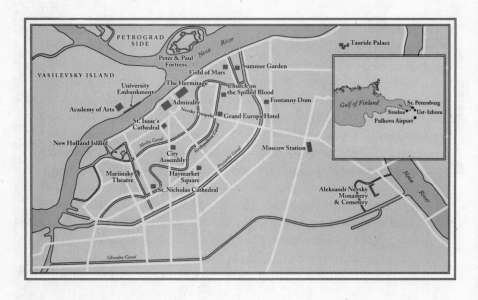

PETROGRAD SIDE

Neva River

Peter & Paul Fortress

VASILEVSKY ISLAND

Field of Mars

Summer Garden

Tauride Palace

University Embankment

The Hermitage

Church on the Spilled Blood

Academy of Arts

Admiralty

Fontanny Dom

Nevsky Prospekt

St. Isaac's Cathedral

Grand Europa Hotel

Moika Canal

New Holland Island

Griboyedova Canal

City Assembly

Fontanka Canal

Moscow Station

Mariinsky Theatre

Haymarket Square

St. Nicholas Cathedral

Obvodny Canal

Gulf of Finland

St. Petersburg

Strelna

Ust-Izhora

Pulkovo Airport

Neva River

Aleksandr Nevsky Monastery & Cemetery

✤ ONE ✤

AS WINTER SETTLED in, I boarded an overheated train that pulled out of Moscow at one minute before midnight and crawled through the night into the snowbound lands northwest of the capital where centuries ago few but the Varangians and wolves had trespassed. And in the winter of 2000, in a number of the settlements along the rail route to St. Petersburg, only the wolves remained.[1] In the village of Chernaya Gryaz' (Black Dirt), not far from the capital's limits, the packs had returned en masse. No one was quite sure why–a symptom of the years of excess, perhaps, a sign of provincial famine, or an omen on the cusp of the apocalypse–but the wolves now stalked not only farm animals but the streets. After years of nocturnal silence, the locals said, the wolves had returned to rule.

By now most Muscovites who could afford the train to Petersburg preferred the plane. Almost free when I first took it as a student before the days of Gorbachev, the train now cost nearly as much as the short plane ride to the "northern capital," as Petersburgers, with deliberate impertinence to Moscow, like to call their city. The price had gone up with the times, but the allure endured. Even the most jaded of Muscovites was not immune. Little in Russia delights like the night train to Petersburg in winter.

As in olden times, the passengers lined the red-carpeted corridor to bid long good-byes to those on the platform who had eased the burden of departure. As soon as the whistle wailed and the train jerked into motion, a new world, the world of onboard, came to life. Expectation swelled down the car as compartment doors slid open with excitement or closed hard for the night. Once the station had faded from sight, the *provodnitsa*, the uniformed attendant, surly and somnambulant as ever, sighed heavily and rolled up the long white trail of cotton that sheltered the corridor's carpet from the mud of her charges. The passengers meanwhile sat close on musty berths, sharing spirits, playing cards, or rereading old tabloids, before taking leave one at a time, to lend privacy to the ritual of changing for the night. The outskirts of Moscow endured for nearly an hour, their citadels of Soviet concrete glowing like Martian towers in the night, before the train at last reached the dark forests.

It was a routine secretly beloved by all. Swaddled in the communal conveyance, travelers tried on new roles. Strangers flirted; military men became gallant; illicit lovers played coy. Yet as the heavy sheets of snow fell softly outside, all aboard shared a rare moment of release, a balance, however temporal, between the worries at their back and the troubles ahead. At the end of the corridor, beside an electric samovar that steamed and hissed like the brass ones of old, the attendant retreated to her hovel to keep a reluctant vigil.

In the airless compartments the windows were forever locked, and the temperature fluctuated wildly and without cause. But by the time the train traveled far enough from Moscow that the stars and satellites arose in the black sky, the frost had stolen inside, spreading across the quarter inch between the double panes of the windows. Behind the icy gauze, the world outside turned to shadows and light. As the train barreled on, a wall of birch and fir streamed past the glass, interrupted on occasion by fields and villages frozen bone white, some forsaken centuries ago, others only since *privatizatsiya* became a Russian word.

Often I fell asleep in a sweat only to awake in the middle of the night numbed by the cold. Sleeplessness was compensated for by a rare sight. Somewhere in the stretch of ancient rail between the capital and the seat of the Revolution, a lone streetlamp gleamed, lighting a bright abyss in the dark. As the blue-gray flooded the car, I leaned hard against the glass to catch a sudden line of footprints. In the depth of the blur the tracks stood sharp, drawing a question mark in the woods. Inevitably there would be no one in sight.

🌼 TWO 🌼

IN THE HAZE of an early-morning arrival, Petersburg seemed a city reformed. The Nevsky Prospekt, its main drag, now glistened. The avenue was freshly repaved, its sidewalks rebricked–thanks, it was said, to an obscure alliance between the governor's wife and a local masonry firm—designer boutiques and neon-lit cafés lined its length, and a new hotel, at long last, had opened. Yet by noon the Petersburg paradox of old, the coincident reign of beauty and decay, would take hold. The street sweepers, burly women in orange vestments imported from Germany, relied, it seemed, on the brooms of their great-grandmothers—fat bundles of switches bound by twine. At their backs the palaces of crimson and ocher were as faded as ever and crumbling from Soviet neglect and the wet Baltic winds. Their dark archways still lent shelter to the drunks who had washed ashore after a thankful night of bingeing. Yet all the while, above the broad avenue, down near the Neva, the river that swells grandly between Russia's oldest prison and its greatest museum, the gilded spire of the Admiralty glistened. And the waterways that churned slowly around the city's forty-two islands still carried, to the relief of many among its five million residents, an unmistakable melancholy. History's return, though heavily billed, had brought little change to the old city of the tsars.

Anticipation had once run high. In the euphoric first years of the Yeltsin era, Russians everywhere turned to Petersburg and waited. They expected, as did many in the West, that if any corner of the country would be reborn, it would be the once-majestic city born of Peter the Great's grandiose dreams and unforgiving hand. With its birth name returned, the city would host an artistic renaissance, as poets and artists emerged from the underground to drink in the new freedom. There would be an architectural revival, as the cityscape regained its original glory. Most of all, there would be a political rebirth, as the bright young minds of the empire's westernmost city looked toward Europe and America and found hope and legislative paradigms to shape the new order. In short, Petersburg would, Russians imagined, lead the return of all that had been lost.[2]

To those who lived along the frigid shores of the Finnish Gulf, it had long been plain the revival would not live up to anyone's hopes. Yet few could have imagined the descent to come: that by 2002, as their city's third centenary neared, its first post-Soviet mayor, the once-beloved lawyer Anatoly Sobchak, would have been disgraced and dead of a heart attack at sixty-two; that the hopes for reform would have yielded to the ambition and muscle of the city's myriad criminal gangs; that the cemeteries holding the remains of Dostoyevsky and Tchaikovsky, Turgenev and nearly all of

Lenin's family would have been choked with the graves of those gunned down or blown up—bankers and brokers, port bosses and metals traders, district politicians and prominent academics; that the gangs would have grown so strong they would rule nearly every sector of the local economy, including the cemeteries; that even after the remains of the last Romanovs had finally been brought home, and after the stunning ascent of a native son (a middling officer of the secret police initiated in Dresden among the Stasi) to the Kremlin, their city, renowned the world over as the prerevolutionary heart of Russian culture, would among their saddened compatriots have acquired a new nickname: *Kriminal'naya Stolitsa* (the Criminal Capital).

THE DESCENT WAS long in coming, but one midwinter night, as the subzero cold sharpened to a glassy edge, the end came abruptly. At a quarter to eleven on the evening of November 20, 1998, Galina Vasilievna Starovoitova, a fifty-two-year-old woman of burly physique and cropped auburn curls, a Petersburg politician of national notoriety and international renown, an ethnographer expert in the peoples and troubles of the Caucasus, the defiant daughter of a prizewinning designer of Soviet tanks, the divorced mother of an adult son struggling in London to make it on his own, and the grandmother of a towheaded boy she doted on, stepped off the snowy sidewalk beside the Griboyedov Canal. She walked out of the dim light of the streetlamps through a long entranceway of arched brick and into the black courtyard of No. 91, a house sagging with soot and time near the bowed middle of a half-inhabited block along a curve in the waterway.

Starovoitova was heading home, escorted by Ruslan Linkov, a young aide who had met her flight from Moscow at around eight-thirty that evening. Tall and sweet-faced, Linkov had inherited his mother's dissidence. He had first met Starovoitova when he was seventeen. Rarely had a day gone by when he did not see or talk to her. He'd taken the usual Volga and the usual driver to the airport. They'd arrived just as the plane landed. After they'd given a lift home to a fellow Duma deputy, Starovoitova had asked to stop by her parents. They drove out along the Peterhof Schosse, the old road to Peter's Summer Palace on the Finnish Gulf. That afternoon her Duma aide, Lyudmila Yodkovskaya, had packed a bag of red caviar and smoked eel for Starovoitova to bring to her parents. "Keep the caviar for

New Year's," Starovoitova told her mother. They had tea and fried pancakes, talked of her little grandson in London, of Yeltsin and the snow. She teased her father that even at eighty he'd never lose his oxlike stubbornness. They laughed around a small table in the kitchen and left after half an hour. Then they drove back again to the center, to the Griboyedov Canal.

It was nearly a quarter to eleven when the driver let Starovoitova and Linkov off. The courtyard was dark. In fact, all the streets within two blocks were unlit. The Italians later recalled that even the lights at their consulate went out that night. As Linkov and Starovoitova stepped into the courtyard, they reviewed the weekend schedule. The Duma deputy was tired. A television interview awaited in the morning. The city elections were fast approaching. She was not running, but her party had a slate in the vote, now only weeks away. Starovoitova knew the campaign would not be easy, but she was in a buoyant mood, even laughing, when she unlocked the heavy steel door of her stairwell and went up the cement steps in the dark. They had nearly reached the landing of her two-room apartment on the second floor when out of the darkness emerged two figures, a man and a woman. Two shots, muffled by silencers, sounded. At first Linkov thought it was children playing with firecrackers at the top of stairs. Then he heard the voice. Someone cried out, "Kill off the snake!"

Starovoitova, who had faithfully served as the liberals' liberal in the Duma for nearly a decade, died instantly from three bullets to the head and neck. But the killers did not desire witnesses. They also shot Linkov–twice. Still, with one slug lodged below his left ear and another in the back of his skull, less than an inch from his brainstem, he lived. Bleeding profusely on the stairwell, he used his cellular phone to call a friend at the Petersburg office of Interfax, the city's most trusted wire service. Linkov had first dialed O2, to summon the police. But in a scene all too familiar, he encountered a belligerent dispatcher bent on interrogating him–"And who might *you* be? And who is this Galina *Starovoitova*?"–before he hung up.[3]

Within minutes the news spread across the country–and, quickly, the world. Just before midnight Sergei Stepashin, the interior minister, placed a call to the presidential dacha deep in the woods outside Moscow. He asked that Yeltsin, nearly bedridden for weeks, be awakened. It was one of the few moments, aides later recalled, that Yeltsin was genuinely stunned. He and Starovoitova had worked closely during perestroika. Yeltsin had even recruited her to serve as his adviser on minority issues when he first stormed the Kremlin. Yeltsin fumed. Vowing to take control of the case, he barked an order to Stepashin, Russia's top cop, that he fly at once to the crime scene.

Stepashin landed in Petersburg in the middle of the night. "I brought with me a team of experienced investigators," he assured the reporters gathered on the cold tarmac. "I think we'll clear this up soon." By morning the Kremlin had released a statement. The president, it said, was "outraged" by the murder "to the depths of his soul."

Starovoitova's body meanwhile lay prostrate on the cement landing throughout the cold night. The FSB inspectors and their German shepherds crowded the stairwell to dust and sniff. A local television producer, a muckraker who enjoyed cozy relations with the most rabid of Petersburg's nationalists, arrived to videotape the macabre still life. The next day the tape was broadcast on national television.

Even in a city steeped in the blood of tsars and Bolsheviks and in a country soaked in contract murders since the dawn of the new openness, Starovoitova's murder marked a new low. Since 1993 six Duma deputies had fallen to assassins. Starovoitova, however, was one of Russia's most prominent politicians. To the faithful, she was not just one of the country's first democrats. To them, she was its last.

Having been born in the first spring after World War II in Chelyabinsk, where her father had helped design Soviet armor, Starovoitova moved with her family as a young girl to Leningrad. Even as a child of privilege–both parents were devout Party members in the upper ranks of the nomen-klatura–she had gone against the Soviet grain. In 1964 Starovoitova entered Leningrad's Military Mechanical Institute but left after only two years. She had learned that Leningrad State had just opened a Psychology Department and was drawn to a new Soviet field, ethnopsychology, that married the old accepted disciplines of sociology and ethnography.

She had heard whisperings of dissonance before. As a teenager she had devoured a samizdat copy of *The Gulag Archipelago* in the dark of her bedroom. She had even briefly dated a dissident, a philosopher many years her elder and under KGB surveillance.[4] But the university meant change. The Khrushchev thaw was over, Brezhnev in power, and the writers Sinyavsky and Daniel had been jailed for publishing abroad, but for Starovoitova a new, political world had opened. She was to stay in the Soviet mainstream but quietly developed her contrarian voice. After graduating, Starovoitova was put to work as an "industrial sociologist" in several Leningrad factories. By the late 1970s, however, she had grown restless. As an ethnopsychologist she was selected for a series of expeditions to the Caucasus. She traveled to Abkhazia in Soviet Georgia and Nagorno-Karabagh, the largely Armenian enclave inside Azerbaijan, to study longevity among the mountain peoples.

Karabagh would decisively pull Starovoitova into politics just as a genuine political life was emerging in the USSR. The first turn, however, had come earlier. In 1986, not long after Gorbachev brought him home to Moscow, she met Andrei Sakharov, the physicist who'd been exiled to Gorky, as Nizhni Novgorod was then called, for nearly seven years. Sakharov became her spiritual godfather. "Galina had democratic ideals in her bones," her younger sister, Olga, said, but the soft-spoken elder dissident, the moral force of Soviet politics, brought them out. "Sakharov, by his example, encouraged her," Olga said, "to take on other people's causes, to fight in public for what she believed was right."

In 1987 the fighting first broke out in Karabagh. Soon it grew into war. Then, in December 1988, Armenia was hit by an earthquake of biblical proportions. Starovoitova not only had academic friends in Karabagh and Yerevan but understood the ethnic tensions at play. She spoke out in support of the Armenian minority. The Armenians at once adopted her. In 1989, running from Armenia, Starovoitova won a seat—with 75 percent of the vote—in the Soviets' experiment at a genuine legislative body, the short-lived Congress of People's Deputies. Before long, alongside Sakharov and Yeltsin, she helped found the Interregional Group of the People's Deputies, a collection of progressives who formed the vanguard of radical reform.

On the strength of her fight for Soviet minorities and human rights, Starovoitova gained fast prominence. In July 1991 Yeltsin named her his adviser on nationality issues. She soon fell out with him over the Ingush-Ossetian clashes outside Vladikavkaz in 1992. Yeltsin fired her, but she stayed loyal. Until December 1994. When Yeltsin ordered the first tanks into Grozny, Starovoitova withdrew her support.

By the time she won her Duma seat from Petersburg in 1995, Starovoitova had become the Bella Abzug of Russian politics. "A real tub thumper" Henry Kissinger called her after hearing her hold court at the Council on

Foreign Relations in New York. By then she had done battle with nearly every faction in the Duma and outside it. She battled nationalists and bureaucrats, unreconstructed Communists and would-be capitalists. "Galya," her sister, Olga, said, using the familiar nickname for Galina, "was always fighting. She fought with everyone." By the time that November night came, Starovoitova was not merely a household name in Russia but a conversation, one certain to provoke contention. Putin, in his official condolences, may have captured it best. Starovoitova, he wrote, "was either loved with devotion or hated with fury."

NOTHING BRINGS OUT Russians like a public funeral. At Stalin's farewell so many crowded the streets, thousands were crushed. During the Moscow Olympics in 1980, at the funeral of the actor and bard Vladimir Vysotsky, demigod of the Soviet underground, the police tried to keep the masses from taking over a central square. They could not. More recently mass funerals have marked the passing of eras: Sakharov's in 1989; the murdered television personality and executive Vladislav Listiev's in 1995.

Thousands—twenty thousand, the best estimates said—came to hear the leading lights of Russian reform bid farewell to Starovoitova. She was laid to rest in the Aleksandr Nevsky Monastery, the hallowed ground that anchors the eastern end of the Nevsky Prospekt. The governor of Petersburg, Vladimir Yakovlev, a man Starovoitova had long sparred with, stayed away—aides said his back was acting up—but Anatoly Chubais, Boris Nemtsov, Yegor Gaidar, Sergei Kiriyenko, Grigori Yavlinsky, all the so-called *Molodiye Reformatory*, the Young Reformers, turned out. The wishful politicians had given themselves the epithet. It had turned into a slur in vogue among those at the short end of their economic experiments. If the crew had ever been united, years of internecine warfare and unchecked hubris had long since rent them. Now they vowed to regroup, to carry the torch with renewed strength. Solemn talk of "our cause"—how it would march on, how no assassin could halt its momentum—rang out in the cool air.[5]

However, the prospects for reform—genuine and democratic turns that sought to better the citizenry's time on earth and not mere pledges of justice in the hereafter—had already darkened. The tragedy of Starovoitova's murder, as the men and women who lined the cemetery knew, was not that she was so powerful but that she was not. Once she had commanded influence and proposed radical change. Even before the Soviet fall, in 1990, she had helped found Democratic Russia, a movement that became the country's first party of progressives. In 1993 she had introduced a draft law on lustration, the screening process adopted elsewhere in Eastern Europe and the Baltics to bar former members of the secret police and, in some cases, the Communist Party from holding government office. In 1994 she became one of the first, and most vocal, critics of the military foray into Chechnya. In 1996 she even tried a long-shot run for president. In Yeltsin's second term, however, as popular disenchantment grew, the remaining liberals in the Duma formed a forlorn Greek chorus kept far offstage. In her last days, even as she fought for all that was good in Russia and railed against all that was wrong in the country—the evil of extremism was the theme of her final Duma speech—Starovoitova was ignored.

If the crash of August 1998 had marked the end of Russia's economic free-for-all, the murder of the country's leading liberal just three months later presaged the end of the idealism that had persisted against tall odds throughout the Yeltsin years. "How can we speak of reforming our country if bandits control it?" Nemtsov, once Yeltsin's favorite son, asked. The other Young Reformers could only nod. They knew they had lost more than a comrade-in-arms. They knew that the Great Romanticism, as many who outlived Starovoitova in the land's far-flung corners now called the first years after the Soviet fall, had been killed off as well.

Starovoitova herself seemed to see the end coming. Since the French Revolution, she said in a radio interview on Ekho Moskvy the summer before her death, it had been well known that revolutions devour their children. "And probably," she said, "that was only to be expected." The democrats of "the first wave," as she called herself and her comrades, should recognize that the law held for their revolution, however peaceful, as well. Yet she maintained a desire: that the fruits of their revolution—"free elections, a parliamentary system, freedom of speech and freedom of the press—that these institutions might not be swallowed up by the subsequent epoch as well."[6]

Starovoitova and the men and women who mourned her belonged to a generation raised in the strictures of Soviet norms. Since birth, their lives, and, even their food in the last Soviet years, had been measured out in state-sanctioned allotments. Once they could only torture themselves with dreams of freedom. Even then their imaginations could reach only so far. They could foresee the fruits of liberty but not the evils of license.

Their neighbors in Eastern Europe, those who had gone before them, could have warned them. They had already seen the confrontation, and few better knew its roots. Freedom, with the Soviet fall, had arrived. Starovoitova, wrote Adam Michnik, the Polish journalist and former dissident, "placed her faith in it with all the strength of the naïve romanticism of a Russian *intelligent*. But freedom," Michnik added in a eulogy to his fallen comrade, "is for everybody—also for rascals, cheaters and hooligans. When freedom is young, and not yet solid, it is always accompanied by an undeclared war between the idealist, who strives for truth and honesty in public life, and the gangster, who is satisfied with the freedom to rob. Galina Starovoitova fell victim in such a war."[7]

In the days after her death, as the airwaves filled with comparisons to JFK, Princess Diana, Gandhi, and Martin Luther King, Jr., in the streets of Petersburg, scruffy teens shuffled from car to car to hawk *Banditsky Peterburg*, a best-selling tome by a local tabloid journalist. Before long the book inspired a television series of the same title, while Starovoitova's endless campaign of causes became a receding memory.

THREE

PETERSBURG, LAMENT those who live there, seems burdened by a curse. Throughout its three centuries the city has endured calamities on an Old Testament scale: floods, disease, famine, and of course war. It suffered the enmity of Lenin, who hated its damp winds and imperial facades, and of Stalin, who distrusted its intelligentsia and despised its European aspirations. Most famously, it survived a nine-hundred-day siege at the hands of the Nazis. The troubles, however, as the locals like to say, were nothing new. They ran so deep they went all the way back to Peter the Great.

Russian biographies of Peter tend toward hagiography, but few cities anywhere more boldly bear the mark of one man. In 1703 Peter set forth a foolhardy idea. On the bogs of the Neva Delta—in Finnish, *neva* means "swamp"—he would raise a New Amsterdam. The city, an unprecedented union of Euclidean geometry, Karelian timber, and Russian slave labor, would stand on water. In a triumph long admired, Peter recruited Florentine architects and Parisian designers to build and decorate the grand houses lining his city's orderly avenues and squares. Sankt-Peterburg was to be the empire's "window on the West," Peter's opening to the world of art and trade, science and society, to the lands where wealth and reason fulfilled men's hopes and law governed their relations.[8]

The tsar-carpenter who founded the imperial navy and built its first boat, Peter was also the father of the country's Academy of Sciences, civil service, first museum, and greatest library.[9] He found time as well to take care of the Turks, Poles, and Swedes and to extend the empire to open on five seas. Yet Peter was a man of paradox: a six-foot-seven giant who relished the company of dwarfs, a son of Muscovy who learned Dutch and romped across Europe, an erudite ruler who delighted in debauchery.[10] Worst of all, he had a weakness for cruelty. In 1718, whether out of spite, parental exasperation, or despotic impulse, he murdered his own son.[11]

Yet it is not for his modernity or his brutality that Petersburgers revere Peter. They are grateful for his good taste. Like the tsars and tsarinas who followed him, they treasure the assembly of palaces, promenades, and gardens that adorn their city. Amid the Baltic marshlands, such luxuriant architecture, Italian rococo and French baroque, lends form to the native sense that the city, so populated with nineteenth-century literary heroes and antiheroes, is somehow unearthly.

Geography only enhances the illusion of the transcendental. In Norilsk's short summers the sun does not set, but no one in the Arctic speaks of the bright nights in tones of religious ecstasy. In Petersburg the locals do. White nights—the days from late spring to early summer when in the depth of night the lambent northern light glows pink across marble and cinder block; when, as Pushkin wrote, "one dawn hastens to relieve another, granting a mere half-hour to night," and when, as Joseph Brodsky, the city's last genius poet, noted, "It's hard to fall asleep, because it's too light and because any dream will be inferior to this reality"—are magic.[12]

Yet it is not the light alone that entrances. Helsinki after all has white nights, too. The splendor of Petersburg, its aged elegance, beguiles in any season: the stone revetments of the Neva; the canals that flow in concentric half circles through the heart of the city; the kaleidoscopic cupolas of the Church of Our Savior on the Spilled Blood (built on the spot where the People's Will terrorists blew up Alexander II); and the great gilded dome of St. Isaac's, the cathedral, named to honor Peter's saint day, that towers over the horizon. Everywhere the details only embellish the myth: the double-headed eagles braided into the bridge balustrades; the bare-chested cary-atids buttressing the crumbling balconies; the giant ebony horses on the Anichkov Bridge over the Fontanka Canal; the golden-winged griffins on the footbridge over the Griboyedov Canal; the giant sphinxes on the Neva's right bank. Given the scenery, it is hardly surprising the city has so famously fed the literary imagination, by turns offering its poets and writers solace or driving them mad. "There is no other place in Russia," concluded Brodsky, "where thoughts depart so willingly from reality."[13]

IN THE SUMMER of 1998, before Starovoitova was murdered and Putin promoted, Petersburg did try to move a bit closer to the present. Eighty years after their deaths before a Bolshevik firing squad the Romanovs came home. Following years of forensic sleuthing, fervent debate among ecclesiastical and secular powers, and an unseemly bidding war for their remains, Nicholas II, his wife, Alexandra, and three of their five children were interred in the small dank church inside the Peter and Paul Fortress. Just off the nave, where Peter and Catherine lie in white marble, the martyred last tsar and his family finally got their own little room.

The burial was marked with great pomp. Even Yeltsin, who as the Communist boss of Sverdlovsk had razed the house in which the Romanovs were killed, turned up at the last minute, bringing the Kremlin's seal of approval to the burial. The event was heavy with symbolism. Petersburg that day abounded in Romanovs—among them, Prince Michael of Kent, a relation through his maternal grandparents. On television the parade of aristocrats, no matter how thin their Russian blood, was long. Solemn speeches resounded, as Russia's leaders declared the past past.

On a Sunday morning a few months earlier I had entered a moldering entranceway and climbed a concrete stairway covered with graffiti to see the man who coaxed Yeltsin from hibernation. In Russia the wise say that one has to live long if one wishes to see any good come from all the upheaval. Dmitri Sergeyevich Likhachev, in his ninety-second year, savored his longevity. Russia's most prominent historian, he had outlived his tormentors to become the keeper of the golden age. Since 1954 Likhachev had headed the Department of Early Russian of the Pushkin House, as the leading literary institute of the Academy of Sciences was endearingly known. Under Gorbachev, he became a reluctant politician, serving for a time in the Congress of People's Deputies. After Sakharov's death, he had inherited the dissident physicist's mantle. Likhachev, on the cold morning I called on him, was known as the *Sovest' natsii* ("the conscience of the country").

He had earned the title. His life had mirrored nearly every turn of the Soviet century. Born in Petersburg in 1906, he once saw the tsarevich Aleksei, the ill-fated heir to the Romanov throne, and witnessed the Revolution. At the university he had done a stupid thing, read a paper on the Soviet desecration of the Cyrillic alphabet to a group of friends who called themselves the Cosmic Academy of Sciences. The "academy" was more a salon of satirists, he said, than the monarchist cell the secret police took it for. He was arrested and sent, long before the barracks rose in Norilsk, to the Solovetsky Islands in the White Sea, site of one of Russia's oldest monasteries and one of the Gulag's first labor camps.

Likhachev did not like to speak of the camps, above all, to tell how another man had died in his place. He clasped his hands together atop a silverhandled cane and recalled the night when the guards began to shoot the prisoners. Nearly three hundred were killed that night in November 1929. He had been warned of the executions–the guards' revenge for an escape– and had hidden behind a woodpile. The night still haunted him. He had lived with the terrible knowledge, as he put it, that a bullet destined for him had killed another.[14] In all, he served four years, including the frozen months when he helped dig the absurd White Sea Canal. He returned to Petersburg in 1932, only to suffer the scorn of his old classmates and the siege of the Nazis. Still, he did not lament the turns of the past. "No one," he said, "could have had a finer education."

The apartment house was tucked away in a far corner of town at the end of a long tram ride. The district was a Soviet eyesore, a product of Brezhnevian urban planning in the days when the Leningrad defense works were still on the rise. At the edge of the gray squat tower an old house of painted logs stood out in the copse of birches. Now a museum that seemed locked up forever, the house for Likhachev was an ironic landmark. Once it had hosted the Bolsheviks' first *soviet*, the inaugural council that in the fall of 1917 dreamed of overthrowing the old order.

Wearing a bolero tie, a billowy white shirt, and a hefty silver ring, Likhachev unlocked the door himself. Within the Soviet concrete, the apartment betrayed an amnesia of the present. Its small rooms were filled with musty leather, and its walls adorned with old oils, warm smells of the lost past. Here was a private re-creation of the old-world intelligentsia. Only the kitchen had seen renovation. "A disastrous gift," he explained, from Yakovlev the local governor.

He had once suffered a different kind of attention from the authorities. During his days as Party boss of Leningrad, Grigori Romanov, the old Politburo member I'd met in Moscow, had tormented the historian. It was Likhachev who had told me how Romanov once summoned him and he'd been amused to find the little man sitting at his desk on a raised stage. ("The Napoleonic complex again!" he cried.) The attention was not always benign. In 1975, on his way to give a talk on *The Lay of Igor's Campaign*, Likhachev was attacked on the stairwell outside his door—by a secret policeman wearing a fake mustache. It was a message, he was sure, from Romanov. The historian had had the last laugh, but he declined to ridicule his old nemesis. "Grigori Vasilievich must be a poor old man now," he said. Likhachev, by far his elder, spoke quietly. But his voice was strong, and his eyes, once a deep blue, sparkled beneath a glaze of milky white. Even in his nineties, he held office hours at the Pushkin House.

Few in Russia knew more of its past, and still fewer possessed greater levity in dispensing it. "Every city of world stature has a foundation myth," Dmitri Sergeyevich announced as Zinaida Aleksandrovna, his wife of more than half a century, sat by his side. He had embarked on a favorite riff, the historical illiteracy of his compatriots. "But few myths are as powerful, as lasting, as fateful as ours." The myth of Peter the Great and his creation, said Likhachev, was a *skazka*, a fairy tale. Stripped of its adornments, it was a story less about genius than about suffering. Everyone in Petersburg, he said, knew the myth. But few knew what it hid: that long before Peter, Russia had shown the yearnings and potential for individualism and a cultured civilization.

In Moscow a theory had come into vogue that the current order was neither democratic nor capitalist but feudal. I had often sat with a friend, Yuliya Latynina, one of the country's keenest business reporters, and weighed the evidence. Yuliya had become something of a literary celebrity. She had created a genre, the economic thriller. Taking her reporting as a starting point, she wove wild tales of murder, betrayal, and ornate offshore accounting. So true to life were her novels that her fans ranged from Kremlin aides to Siberian kingpins. "Don't expect any Renaissance," she liked to say. Russia had never even seen the Enlightenment. To understand the present morass, she argued, you needed to look only to the Middle Ages.

Latynina had a point. The new lords of the market, the oligarchs, did resemble the boyars, the wealthy elite of medieval times. And their bodyguards did seem to form a modern-day *druzhina*, the retinue that once protected princes. The new nobility, moreover, accumulated wealth only through grants of fiefs—once state-owned and still maintained by peasant serfs—that they had not earned by their own labor but won by pledging allegiance to the man on the throne. Even the primary growth industries of the new market—exploiting natural resources and reaping rent from protection—had advanced little from the economics of the Middle Ages. To Latynina the conclusion was clear. "In a land where commercial relations so heavily depend on personal relations," she said, "there is no law and no private property—only the word of the man in the Kremlin."

Likhachev did not suffer amateurs lightly. But he agreed the theory held promise. In truth, he said, things were actually worse. Russian society would be fortunate if relations lived up to medieval standards. The trouble was not in the order of commerce, he said. It was in the absence of a code of honor. Russia had always had men of great wealth, but honor had ruled the trade among them. In the nineteenth century, he said, the oligarchs had been the *kuptsy*, the wealthy merchants. "Timber, silver, gold, and vodka: They traded everything these men do now," Likhachev said. "But there was a difference. They lived by their word. Handshakes were done in public. Deals were blessed in church. And if one of their number dared break his word, no one would hire a hit man. They would simply never to do business with him again."

As his city descended into a den of thieves and compromised politicians, Likhachev did not disguise his nostalgia for tsarist days. He painted the pre-

Bolshevik past in warm hues, as a lost age when trust ruled human relations and the state breathed with the monarch's will and reason. The Russian people had suffered, he said, but suffering had become the national occupation. Suffering had bound the *narod* in a covenant with the Almighty. Now more than ever, he said, the people and the state lived in separate realms. Although he found it necessary to dispatch the occasional entreaty to the Kremlin, he tried his best not to pay any mind to the political charades of the day. Often, however, he could not restrain himself. He loathed, for instance, Luzhkov's resurrected cathedral in Moscow. "A prefabricated model" he called Christ the Savior. What was the logic, he wondered, of building a single church for three hundred million dollars when in great stretches of the country there were no churches at all? And yes, he would have preferred Yeltsin to have had the guts to ban the Communist Party. But things, he said, could have gone worse. Even given the best efforts of the governors and the president, the nation lived on.

Still, when Likhachev spoke of the future, there was fear in his eyes. Here at the end of the century the homeless children of his youth again filled Petersburg's streets. The gap between rich and poor, he said, was greater than even before the Revolution. Moreover, the terror of the Bolsheviks, bloody as it was, paled in comparison to the dangers now threatening the remnants of Russia's learned society. Today "the reserves" of the intelligentsia were running thin. Culture was on the wane, and commerce ever on the rise. Pushkin was right, he said. Ours was "the Age of Iron." The greatest threat, however, was not intellectual torpor but the moral vacuum. "We've always been a moral people," Likhachev said almost plaintively. "But how do we recover now? When education is neglected and thievery respected?" The options were limited. The country, he conceded, was not ready to revive the monarchy. Dictatorship of course was not the answer. Society needed order, but it would have to come from within.

The funeral of the Romanovs would mark the first step. "The act of the era," Likhachev called it. As the Soviet age had begun with murder, it was only fitting that eighty years hence the martyred be buried. Evil had been recognized, the historian said, and, in certain hearts, repented. A conscience, after all, he was sure, still dwelled in the country. It ruled the lives of people in towns across Russia whom nobody knew. They were not political leaders or generals or men of great wealth, but ordinary people working hard in everyday lives to keep the balance in the land. If not for them, the moral eclipse would be too great. Nothing less than the survival of the country, he warned, was at stake. "And if Russia edges over the abyss," he added, "she will not go alone." It was not a threat but a humble prediction.

🏵 FOUR 🏵

PETERSBURGERS, especially the police, liked to argue that their city's new nickname was unearned, that Moscow was the true mother of Russian crime. Body for body, they were right. Hit men, moreover, now worked everywhere in Russia. Yet in Petersburg, as Lev Lurie, local political columnist, teacher, and city historian, said, they worked "with style."

We sat in his local, a pizzeria disguised as a Mexican restaurant that was really a bar, on Vasilevsky Island. Lurie liked to have a beer here after class and kibitz about the dire state of his beloved city. The new lycée he'd helped found a few years back, Petersburg's first, where he now taught history, was around the corner. On the table were two squares of stale pizza, an ashtray overflowing with cigarette butts, and two pints of Baltika, the new brew of the modern Russian. Lurie never had much love for those who led his city—then or now. He had been a dissident, and his late father, Yakov, a medieval philologist who worked under Likhachev in the Pushkin House, had suffered the strictures of Soviet academia. The son, who had never fitted into Soviet society, had matured into a man of many vocations. When he wasn't teaching, or working to raise a Social Democrat party from the ruins of the city's intelligentsia, Lurie covered politics for the local edition of the daily *Kommersant*. Few better understood the canny ways that political power and underworld muscle had joined forces in Petersburg.

Lurie kept a running total of the city's most memorable contract murders, a list, as it were, of greatest hits. A favorite was the murder of Pasha Kapysh, a local oil baron who had succumbed in his forty-fourth year on the right bank of the Neva in the summer of 1999. Pasha had long lived in fear of assassination. He traveled in an armored Chevrolet Suburban–license plate 666–escorted by a corps of bodyguards. His murder had been arranged with military precision. As his convoy came to the intersection on the University Embankment in front of the Academy of Arts, his killers triggered the light to go red. Three gunmen opened fire. Two more stood on the embankment, between the giant sphinxes delivered from Thebes in 1832, and launched a pair of rocket-propelled grenades. The bullets preoccupied the bodyguards, while the grenades pierced the armored car. "All in all," Lurie said, "a spectacular job."

Nothing, however, had prepared the city for 2000. "A record year," Lurie called it, "even by our standards." Petersburg, it seemed, was awash in homicidal intemperance. CONTRACT GENOCIDE, a local paper called the flood in an inch-high headline. One after another, a stunning succession of *biznesmeny*, each among the city's most prosperous, met a violent death. The killing season began in early January, when the young financial director of Baltika, the Petersburg brewery and one of Russia's biggest, stepped into his kitchen to make a cup of tea and was shot by a marksman through the window. A month later the thirty-six-year-old CEO of Baltic Dawn, a timber company holding its own, went next–with two bullets in the back of the head. In March two of the city's top import-export barons went down, while April bade good-bye to the head of Russia's leading thread and yarn manufacturer as well as the chairman of an electronics plant, a former leader of Petersburg's RUBOP, the city's organized crime-fighting squad. As summer neared, down went the robust coowner of Hollywood Nights, a glittery nightclub on the Nevsky favored by Ukrainian prostitutes and Western businessmen. The club owner went to his death in swim shorts, shot on the stairs en route to the pool in the sports hall of the local Railways University.[15]

Lurie had witnessed, up close, the rise of Governor Yakovlev, the city's present ruler. Yakovlev had served as one of Mayor Sobchak's chief deputies–Putin had been the other–before running against his former boss in 1996. Yakovlev had won by twenty-seven thousand votes. "He's nothing but a *santekhnik* [plumber]," he said of the governor. Everywhere I went in Petersburg I heard the nickname. It was said that the governor, an alumnus of the Soviet school of construction, possessed an unparalleled knowledge of the city's steel bowels. To many, in a city notorious for water-borne bacteria, a plumber-governor was not a bad thing. If Luzhkov liked to talk building materials, Yakovlev could certainly talk pipe. Under his tenure, more than eight miles of new water pipes had been laid and six miles of sewage systems repaired, he liked to say. (The Danish and Finnish governments, eager to clean up the Baltic Sea, had covered a good share of the costs.) Lurie was fond of tracing the spiraling crime rate. Crime, to be sure, had begun to rise on Sobchak's watch, but under Yakovlev it became institutionalized.

If Russians elsewhere were perplexed by Petersburg's devolution, to Lurie it made perfect sense. Moscow was simple, he said. Moscow was owned by financial-industrial clans and the lesser *mafiya* groups that did the enforcement work. Petersburg, however, had languished for years as untitled land. Unlike Luzhkov, the governor here was weak. Petersburg lacked a *khozyain*, an all-powerful boss. There was only Yakovlev. Everyone in town talked openly of how his campaign had been funded by the *gruppirovki*, the city's organized crime gangs. Above all, unlike Moscow, Petersburg had the port. "A giant spigot," as Lurie put it, "for instant profits."

FOR YEARS, WHENEVER I came to Petersburg, I stayed with Dariya Petrovna. She was a gentle old woman long retired, who lived alone in a rambling and drafty flat on a dark side street a block from St. Isaac's and the city assembly on Senate Square. She had gained little and lost almost everything in the years since the old world ended. She did not cry, lament, or complain but may have been the loneliest person I knew in Russia. Brodsky had understood the paradox. "This is the city," he wrote, "where it's somehow easier to endure loneliness than anywhere else: because the city itself is lonely."[16]

Dariya Petrovna had read *Crime and Punishment* more than once, but she loved the company, and so did I. She didn't know what to charge for a room but shyly accepted ten or twenty dollars a night, depending on the guest's wishes, and every morning covered the kitchen table with bliny and pirozhki served hot on rose-edged china. Her flat took up much of the first floor of a nineteenth-century house where well-to-do merchants once lived. It was a narrow but elegant house, designed by a German architect of local renown and built, it was said, for a Polish princess. The floor tiles in the foyer testified to the pedigree. "*Jahre 1884*," announced the ceramic in faded black and white.

Like many in Petersburg, Dariya Petrovna had grown numb to the Noise, as she called the crime spiraling outside her door. She did not like it, of course, that legislators were killed in her neighborhood. But innocent people, she figured, did not die such violent deaths. She didn't care what was causing the corpses to pile up. Debts, betrayal, greed, they were all the same to her. A contract murder, she knew well, cost money, so these men surely deserved what they got. "The crime in the streets," she said, "is no different from the crime in the government." The city officials, she knew from her girlfriends who worked in the assembly, had grown fat on bribes. And the corruption in the state offices, when you got down to it, wasn't all that different from the evils that plagued nearly every home she knew. Dariya Petrovna had been spared, at great cost, but all her girlfriends faced the same plague: husbands who drank. For them, she'd say, the only thing worse than a husband's disappearance at night was his return by day. So whenever the conversation hit upon crime, corruption, or the future of the Russian family, Dariya Petrovna raised her tiny hand and, with a soft wave, dismissed it away.

She had other troubles. The decade of change had been a decade of loss. She'd lost her son, her only child, her husband, and her savings, and soon, she was sure, she would lose her apartment. She had only one dream now: to meet her granddaughter. In the last year of the USSR, in "those romantic days," her son had gone to America. He'd gone on a tourist visa for a month. Ten years had passed. He'd married a Mexican woman and they'd had a child, a little girl with huge black eyes and U.S. citizenship, whom Dariya Petrovna feared she would never see.

A photograph by the phone told the story. A young man, his blond hair wavy and long, sat on a bench on a shopping street lushly lined with bougainvillaea trees. He wore shorts, sandals, and sunglasses. And held a Starbucks cup. He was a long way from the foggy black-and-white picture that hung in the dark over the bed where I slept. That photograph was an army portrait from the old days—when the boy was eighteen perhaps—the kind that adorned the walls of quiet apartments in the distant corners of the old empire where too many men had left widows and grieving mothers. Dariya Petrovna's boy had served in East Germany. He had started, but never finished, the medical institute. By then perestroika had hit full swing, and somehow life for him had become impossible. He'd come home one day and said, "Mama I don't think I can live here again. Ever."

Her husband had died not long after their son left: a heart attack. "Fate, probably," she said. He was a native Leningrader, like his whole family. After the war he'd worked on the bases, while she worked in the factory. "We girls would make the parts he used to fix the MiGs and the submarines," she said. She allowed herself a soft laugh. "We met at a dance. In those days that's what you did. They were free, they were beautiful, and everyone went." Nowadays, she figured, no one went to dances anymore. Her husband had been blessed by the Americans. They'd given him a visa. But not her. She liked to show me the U.S. visa in his Soviet passport. "He died without ever seeing his son again," she said. "Wouldn't go without me. He was afraid."

Her son was now thirty-five. He lived in California, in Hollywood. Now and then he called. Sometimes he sent letters. But to Dariya Petrovna, he was invisible. She dreamed of seeing him, of meeting his wife and their girl, but knew a reunion was unlikely. "It's too late," she said. "Now he's illegal. He has to hide."

🎕 FIVE 🎕

"I'M CONVINCED THAT there are many people in St. Petersburg who talk to themselves as they go about," said Svidrigailov to Raskolnikov as they sat in the noisy saloon just off the Haymarket. "This is a town of semi-lunatics. If we had any seats of learning in this place, the medical men, the jurists and the philosophers would be able to conduct the most valuable investigations into St. Petersburg. . . . There aren't many places where there are so many gloomy, harsh and strange influences on the soul of man as there are in St. Petersburg."[17] Petersburg has long weighed on its inhabitants. The climate alone can warp a good mind. The natives forever complain of "the low sky" and the *davlenie*, the pressure. In the limbo that followed the Soviet collapse, and that for many seemed without end, the sense of doubt and despair may have grown more potent than ever.

One dark afternoon in late winter, on one of those days when the sun called it quits an hour or two after lunch and the trams and cars careered through black slush, while both driver and pedestrian recalled the days when they used to salt and scrape the walkways so clean even a toddler could run on them, I went to see Andrei Kurpatov, the twenty-eight-year-old psychiatrist who ran the city's main psychotherapeutic hospital. Founded in 1894, the clinic was once the working home of Pavlov, Pavlov of the dogs. When I opened the heavy iron doors at the entrance, old man Pavlov himself greeted me, staring out from an oversize oil painting that hung above the dark marble stairs.

Kurpatov was a young man of brooding intellect, a recent graduate of the Petersburg military medical academy, the alma mater of the Good Doctor of the Rostov morgue. He seemed at once to embody the possibilities of the new generation and an atavistic knowledge of its intellectual inheritance. He was slight and thin, and his face was long and pale, drawn tight beneath peaked dark brows and long sideburns. He wore black boots, black jeans, and a black turtleneck that exaggerated the length of his neck and the pallor of his skin. On a state salary of less than a hundred dollars a month, Kurpatov kept busy. He wrote academic textbooks (nine to date, the first when he was twenty-one), novels (the latest he summarized as "Zarathustra Meets a Psychiatrist"), and a weekly column for a local broadsheet (on intravenous drug use and its consequences). He also directed a quarterly devoted to the work of the educational theorist Lev Vygotsky and contributed articles on Dostoyevsky's psychology to the Petersburg chapter of the Russian Association of Dostoyevsky Scholars.

The clinic received a stream of patients. As we walked through long halls lit by large bulbs that swung slightly overhead, the place at first seemed empty. But it was full. Kurpatov's patients ranged from Russian veterans returned from Chechnya to rape victims to members of the city's burgeoning population of street youth. Wherever we walked, the stench of fermenting cabbage followed. So did a strange, distant groaning—muffled pleas, made unintelligible by iron doors. To supplement his income and enhance his research, Kurpatov had recently opened a small private practice, a response to the demand, he explained, for therapy among the newly moneyed entrepreneurs. A number of his clients, one of whom I knew, even came to him from Moscow. Business was good. He enjoyed his clinical rounds and the private hours. But most of his day was still taken up by "the suicides."

In Petersburg, Kurpatov said, the trouble was not murder but suicide. He cited the statistics. In the last five years of the twentieth century the suicide rate in Russia was four times higher than Europe's. In 2000 the number of suicides ran nearly double the number of murders. By way of example, he told of his new apartment. He had finally saved enough to buy a place. It was a great building, he had thought, because the local police station was on the first floor. But he had already learned of "the problem." The cops, he said, had taken to throwing themselves off the building's roof with regularity. Three had jumped in as many months.

The increase in suicidal ideation, Kurpatov claimed, didn't arise from an isolated neurosis. It stemmed from "the loss of self." He elaborated. Russians had never had the concept of, let alone the respect for, the individual. In the West there was a long-standing, time-honored cult of the individual. "Ever since Freud," he said, "desires, fears, depression have been of supreme concern in the West." Russians, on the other hand, never enjoyed such attention. "No one in our country ever treated fear," Kurpatov said. "No one ever *had* fears." Just as no one in Soviet Russia ever suffered depression: "They were simply '*lazy.*'" He took out a piece of white paper and placed it squarely in the center of his plain desk. He uncapped a black pen, seemed to consider making a line, but instead put the pen itself across the middle of the page. In the old days, Kurpatov said, for as long as anyone now alive could remember, the borders of the psyche were clearly drawn. "There were no individuals," he said. "Everyone belonged to the state."

Kurpatov came from a long line of doctors. His grandfather had headed the Northern Fleet's medical service. In 1997, when he completed his studies, he, too, was headed for a military career—on a nuclear submarine. It was a tradition. Many of his classmates served on the subs. One of his teachers had gone down with the *Kursk*. But Kurpatov had suffered an illness in the academy that briefly paralyzed his legs. He was spared the service. Yet even now he feared what would have happened to him in the military. He was, he conceded, not cut out for life underwater.

He almost seemed to relish the fear. After all, he said, fear was "the one thing that binds Russians everywhere now." In a land of troubles, fear was the most ubiquitous. Russians did not fear everything, Kurpatov said. No one really feared murder or burglary, airplanes or baldness, impotency or dictatorship. Russians now were burdened, he said, "by the most basic fears—of war, hunger, poverty." These were not fears of the future but of the past.

The trouble, Kurpatov went on, was that Russians had never been granted a rest. "In 1861, Alexander II ended serfdom. Then began a period of exploitation and poverty that lasted until 1914. Then the First World War with all its horrors and deprivations. After the Revolution, serfdom again. No one could move, everyone had to work and no one earned a kopeck. The suffering lasted of course until 1991, when we were rewarded with the revolutionary changes that now we see have led to a new feudalism and a complete loss of any unified sense of self."

Then there was Chechnya. The Chechen syndrome, which had crowded the halls of the Vladivostok clinic, here filled an entire wing. The illness exposed, he said, a fundamental fear that plagued all society. It was not the experience of battle, or a particular instance of brutality, that haunted the boys who came home from Chechnya. It was the loss of their guns. The war gave the Russian soldier a tool of survival. Once he was home, the state stripped him of it. The gun was not only power but the centerpiece of a new identity. "In Chechnya," Kurpatov said, "a Russian soldier learns to trust no one. Not his comrades, not his officers. He is alone, with one friend, his Kalashnikov. Naturally, when he comes home and steps out into the street, he feels naked, fearful, unable to cope. Unlike others, he knows what his life costs: nothing. If he cannot adapt, he goes into shock."

We sat in his small office that filled the dead end of a corner wing in the clinic. The patients' cries did not make it this far, but the rotting cabbage did. Kurpatov said he had made his choice. He worried most about the youth, the dispossessed who had nowhere now to turn but inward. "It is imperative to save these young people," he said with the solemnity of a field marshal. "They're trapped in a maze, with dangers in every direction and no one to help them out of it." Individuality was blooming. Young Russians faced choices their parents, who were not individuals but social objects, never had had. The old state was gone, and its ideology dead, and nothing but a limbo had replaced it. The returnees from Chechnya were not alone. Petersburg was plagued, Kurpatov said, by the identity crisis.

He lit a black cigarillo and told me of a recent case. He had a patient, Stepan, a thirteen-year-old boy with the intellect of a seven-year-old.

Thanks to the television that blared nonstop in his apartment day and night, Stepan had dreamed since the third grade of becoming a "*killer*," a hit man. Since birth the boy had been "slow." His mother, the school, no one knew what to do with him. Hence the television. One day his friend, Pyotr, a fourteen-year-old schizophrenic, told Stepan how much he hated his parents. He told him how they wouldn't let him play on their computer. So what did Stepan do? Maced his friend's father and stabbed him to death. And he tried, but failed, to kill the mother as well.

Both children of course were sick. But that, said Kurpatov, taking another long drag, was not the moral of the story. The point was they both were ignored—by their parents, their teachers, everyone but each other. They got no attention, let alone treatment. The case was extreme, Kurpatov admitted, but troubled children everywhere across Russia faced the same obstacles. They were being raised by fear and the television, not positive reinforcement—"like Pavlov's." For the youngest generation in Russia these days, there was "no reward for good behavior."

For a time we sat in silence. The longer we let it fill the room, the more comfortable the silence became. Then Kurpatov stubbed out the cigarillo, took off his white coat, and told another story. This was not one from his practice, but a *skazka,* a fairy tale every Russian knew, the tale of "Ivan Durak," Ivan the fool. Ivan, he argued, was the most influential antihero in Russian literature. And his tale revealed a shortcoming that lay at the heart of society. "Ivan encounters an evil dragon," he said, "that he must kill if he's to get a wonderful wife." He gets the girl in the end, but not of his own accord. "He has two brothers who are handsome and smart and work. But they don't get the girl. Ivan does and only because he does nothing. He gets a miracle."

Miracles, Kurpatov said, folding his thin hands under his sharp chin, had caused all the trouble. While fine for the church, the faith in miracles—not in individualism—lay at the heart of not only Russia's economic troubles but its psychoanalytic woes as well. He leaned in close to dramatize the point. Without his rounds coat, in his black clothes and boots he seemed a dark coil of intensity.

"You see, in Russia, everyone's always believed in miracles. Before 1917, it was the Miraculous Tsar. Under the Soviets, it was the Miraculous Collective."

And today? I wondered.

"Today," he said, "we have no more miracle workers."

THE IDENTITY CRISIS was not strictly personal. It was national. In recent years, among anthropologists of genocidal societies, "the search for a usable past" had become a cliché in demand. In the post-Soviet limbo, it became a Grail quest.

Only days after winning his second term in 1996, Yeltsin summoned campaign aides to the Kremlin. The time, he said, had come to find a new national idea. In the twentieth century alone, he told those assembled, Russia had gone from monarchy to totalitarianism to perestroika, before embarking on the democratic path. "Each epoch had its own ideology," he thundered. "Now we don't have one–and this is bad."[18] The country needed a new slogan, something pithy and unifying. Like "The Third Rome." Or the "Orthodoxy, Autocracy, and Nationhood" of Nicholas I.[19] Or the Soviets' "We Are Building Communism!" Yeltsin ordered up a commission. Historians, political scientists, and pollsters were enlisted. They were to rack their brains, search the "Civilized World" for historical models, and not return empty-handed.

Georgi Satarov, the avuncular political scientist who had been a chief strategist of Yeltsin's improbable reelection, served on the search committee. It was slow-going work, he recalled over tea at his apartment in Moscow. "The task wasn't impossible," Satarov said. "It's just that there weren't many historical analogies." They'd paid considerable attention to postwar Germany. West Germany, many of the commission members thought, might be the model. After all, as Satarov said, "After Hitler, they were even worse off than we were after 1991." For months they studied Bonn's policies in the postwar period. In the end they came to see the secret of the Germans' success. Yes, they'd had an economic miracle, but, said Satarov, "what united the West Germans, and gave them the strength to survive, was a moral force, the idea of national penitence." The notion, however, of making contrition the cornerstone of the new ideology for the new Russia did not grab many on the presidential panel.

THE SEARCH FOR a national idea–the Russian Idea, Dostoyevsky called it–has preoccupied, and divided, Russian thinkers since the early part of the nineteenth century. In 1836, when Pyotr Chaadayev published his scandalous "First Philosophical Letter," the intelligentsia split into opposing camps, Slavophiles and Westernizers. Chaadayev was not a major figure in the mercantile or political life of the day. He was a fallen officer of the Hussar Guards, a veteran of Borodino. Yet his letters—he never wrote anything else—ignited a debate that still burns. Herzen called him a martyr. Pushkin, a friend and early protégé, declared that all his own political ideas came from Chaadayev.[20] Wrote Pushkin:

> *By the lofty will of heaven*
> *Born in the fettered service of the Tsars,*
> *In Rome he would have been a Brutus, in Athens Pericles,*
> *But here he is an officer of the Hussars.*

Chaadayev took an extreme stand—one he later recanted in his *Apology of a Madman*—that Russia was a land apart, a "unique civilization" that had "not yet discovered truths that have elsewhere become truisms. It is the result of our never having walked side by side with other nations," he wrote. "We belong to none of the great families of mankind; we are neither of the West nor of the East. . . . Somehow divorced from time, we have not been touched by the universal education of mankind." Russia's early history, he theorized, was to blame: "At first brutal barbarism, then crude superstition, then cruel and humiliating foreign domination, the spirit of which was later inherited by our national rulers—such is the sad history of our youth."[21]

In the 1990s the Slavophile-Westernizer debate reignited. Petersburg gave rise to its post-Soviet chapter. Now the Westernizers were the technocrats, economists, and bankers—Petersburgers like Anatoly Chubais, German Gref, Aleksei Kudrin (Putin's finance minister); Russians who by their blood, manners, or surnames somehow did not seem wholly Russian to their compatriots. The Slavophiles were led, even posthumously, by Likhachev, who died at ninety-two in the fall of 1999. Solzhenitsyn, now resident in a dacha outside Moscow, weighed in with increasing regularity, while Nikita Mikhalkov, the film director and actor, appointed himself the Slavophiles' chief spokesman. The debate, as ever, concerned salvation. Russia's path, Slavophiles cried, lay in mystical asceticism and piety, while Westernizers preached the need to join the "Civilized World," to partake of enlightenment and humanism.

All too often, however, the fight, like almost everything in the country now, boiled down to money. The camps squared off along the economic front. Should Russians buy foreign goods? (The head of Nevskaya Kosmetika, a Petersburg shampoo and soap factory in business since 1839, lectured me for close to an hour on the sins of Procter & Gamble.) Should the country heed the advice of "experts" from the West? By Yeltsin's second term, Russians everywhere, even in the half-abandoned hamlets of the upper Yenisei, knew the translated names of the International Monetary Fund and the World Bank. They had become the favored objects of public derision. Should Russians, in short, follow Peter's path, continuing, as Stalin once put it, the "obsolete tradition of kowtowing before shitty foreigners"?[22]

Still a third camp emerged: the Eurasians, who saw Russians as neither European nor Asian, but as the ontologically unique "Eurasian." Eurasianism was not a new theory, but in the last Soviet years it had acquired a fast following thanks to the writings of Lev Gumilyov, the anthropologist son of the Petersburg poets Anna Akhmatova and Nikolai Gumilyov. His critics denounced Gumilyov's Eurasianism as little more than veiled nationalism, with anti-Western and anti-Semitic undercurrents. But the Petersburg historian Aleksandr Panchenko, a close friend of Gumilyov's who coauthored a number of works with him, defended the theory. "Don't listen to Chubais and Gaidar—or any of the new so-called Westernizers," he cried. "They all spout nonsense!" Eurasianism, he insisted, had no political colors. Yet in recent years it had united extremists of all stripes across Russia. It was especially strong among the upper ranks of the armed forces and secret services. Even Vympel, the elite *spetsnaz* antiterrorist squad, it was said, had adopted the theory as doctrinal.[23]

In the end, the Yeltsin commission in search of a national idea failed to find any suitable candidates. Academician Likhachev was not surprised. He simply smiled at the vain attempt. "In Russia one ideology cannot suffice to unify the country," he said. "Ours is a rich culture, but a culture of many peoples. Reality must dictate any political doctrine; a country so vast cannot be bound by a single idea. Each region—be it Vladivostok, St. Petersburg, the far north, or the Caucasus—has its own distinct culture. We must not try to disguise this truth, for the more diverse the culture, the richer it is."

In Petersburg, however, not all the historians and philosophers dismissed the Grail quest as merely another comic opera playing out in the Kremlin. For many, the search for a unifying idea revealed centuries-old fissures in the national psyche. Russians have long been possessed by the urge for a clean slate. "*Otrecheniye*," the historian Panchenko said, "may be our greatest vice." *Otrecheniye* means "renunciation." But Panchenko used it to mean denial or abandonment—in this case of one's past. He marked it as a fundamental Russian trait. "We've done it for generations, ever since that Viking"—the ninth-century Ruirik—"came down here," he said. "We've insisted on denying who we are for so long this denial just may make us what we are."

Nikolai Berdyaev, the religious philosopher and author of *The Russian Idea,* agreed. Berdyaev, from his Parisian exile, argued that the denial of the past had a twin: *samozvantso*, self-proclamation. He declared *samozvantso* "a purely Russian phenomenon."[24] By extension, someone who proclaims to be someone he is not is a *samozvanets*, a self-proclaimer, an impostor, a pretender. Russian history is crowded with self-proclaimers, but the most famous is the False Dmitri who came on the scene after Ivan the Terrible's death in the late sixteenth century, setting in motion a chain of events that led to the Time of Troubles.[25] Russians did not like self-proclaimers. As a rule, said Likhachev, the people feared them. But they fell for them all the same.

KURPATOV, THE PSYCHIATRIST at Pavlov's old institute, was on to something. I knew it because on most nights in Petersburg, I sat for hours in Dariya Petrovna's kitchen and listened to her talk of Dr. Konovalov and his breakthroughs. I would listen without questioning. Dariya Petrovna did not believe the politicians, she did not believe the police, and she certainly did not believe the priests. But she believed Dr. Konovalov. The doctor ran his own institute in town. He had devised a new treatment for cancer. He was now running, Dariya Petrovna related, a 60 percent cure rate—without surgery. The doctor, she explained, did not believe in operations. He believed in learning to live right, according to the needs and demands of one's organism. Years before, Dariya Petrovna had joined an experimental group under the doctor's close supervision. She attended the sessions religiously.

Dariya Petrovna had worked her whole life. She'd grown up in a village in Ukraine and, as a young girl, worked the fields. "It was the war," she said. "All the men were gone." She had come to Leningrad after World War II. She had studied construction engineering. For years, when she was still in school, she'd worked in the Big House, the Bolshoi Dom, as everyone in Petersburg called the old KGB headquarters on Liteiny Prospekt. (It still housed the secret policemen.) As an apprentice engineer she had run "from site to site all day." The sites were labor camps. "The prisoners were used to build all the factories. They built the cement factory, the furniture factory, the brick factory. That's how we rebuilt the whole city after the war." The job was hard, and she didn't much care for working with the poor prisoners, but she had earned the card that identified her as a veteran of the war effort. She was grateful for the card. It got her half off on the trains.

A few years earlier Dariya Petrovna had discovered an unexpected solace. One morning she started to paint. She created pastoral landscapes in primary colors, quiet scenes culled from remote memories: a girl and a boy atop a truck stacked with hay, an old lady sitting beside a thatched house, two women harvesting wheat. She painted on whatever she had: strips of canvas, cardboard, metal trays. She even painted her roasting pan. It hung in her kitchen. "It's the light I like best," she said. "It's the light of my childhood." She did not know why, but the light was what she had first painted, and now she could not stop.

Dariya Petrovna had made it to old age but won few of its compensations. Now she feared she would soon be forced from her home. It was a coveted address. In the seventies the city's KGB chief had taken over the top floor and added another floor with a view of St. Isaac's. In those days the director of the Museum of Atheism—as the Kazan Cathedral was called in Soviet times—had also lived in the building. Now it was only a matter of time before she would have to leave. A computer company, run by a crew of pony-tailed young programmers, had sprouted across the street. The company had spread fast down the street, taking over, one by one, the nineteenth-century houses left and right. "The siege," she said, "has begun."

She didn't travel far now, only across town to see Dr. Konovalov. The courses didn't cost much, and they gave her a sense of being alive. The group was working hard these days on physical rejuvenation. "The doctor's developing a new theory," she said, "a way to restore youth to mind and body." Expectancy had crept into her voice. Did it work? I wondered. Dariya Petrovna paused, as if to weigh the odds, and then said: "Just take a look around our blackened city, and tell me the truth, do you think it could hurt?"

❧ SIX ❧

NEARLY TWO YEARS had passed since Starovoitova's murder when I went to see Ruslan Linkov. His office was only a few blocks from Dariya Petrovna's house–past the city assembly, around the corner from the Astoria Hotel, and across the street from Peter Carl Fabergé's old jewelry store. The office was hidden, without signs, at the back of a pitch-dark courtyard. Linkov greeted me in a black suit. We entered a clean, newly renovated office, the headquarters of DemRossiya, the Democratic Russia party his late boss had helped found. Linkov had succeeded Starovoitova as head of the Petersburg chapter. The office was clean and spare, without any of the bric-a-bric that decorates bureaucratic warrens across Russia. No paintings, no calendars, no posters advertising the charms of a would-be "second Switzerland." On a desk veneered with birch, only a Finnish cellular phone rested. It was cold outside, early in January, but the windows of the office were wide open. The heat formed blurry rivulets in the air as it rushed out into the Petersburg street.

Linkov oddly had become an object of ridicule and suspicion in town. His appearance, his face, physique, and dress, did not serve him well. He was tall and thin, and he dressed smartly in clothes well pressed no matter the season. Although he was not yet thirty, gray hairs had appeared in his thicket of ink black hair. His chin was so prominent it jutted out below thin red lips that scarcely moved when he spoke. His eyes, framed by long black lashes and dark brows, were so green they startled. His fingers were thin and long, and his skin nearly translucent. So sharp were his features that some in Petersburg employed the word "Hollywood" in reference to him. Others called him doll-like. His critics ridiculed his voice as well; it was soft and high-pitched. Yet whenever he returned to that November night on the dark stairwell, his cadence took on gravity. When he spoke of Starovoitova, Linkov sounded like a man who had lived a lifetime.

He knew that by the laws of crime and the logic of power that governed his country, he should be in a grave. Only a miracle, he said, had spared him, keeping the bullet that grazed his spine from ripping through his cortex. He had lain in the White Nights Military Hospital for two months, under guard. FSB officers kept a vigil outside his door. They searched everyone visiting him. They welded iron bars over his windows–to keep grenades out. After he had come home, the guards stayed with him. They lived with him for months. Eventually he begged them to leave, and they did. Now his left side—from the shoulder to the hand—went numb on occasion, but only the faint scar that ran jaggedly down the left side of his long neck betrayed how close death had come.

Linkov had recovered. He could now revisit that night. He could walk calmly through its strange turns—"the signs" he called them. There was the car that pulled out of nowhere to cut in front of them as they drove along the Peterhof Schosse after they'd left Starovoitova's parents' apartment. It had sped ahead of their Volga. "Nearly caused an accident," he remembered. Then there was the strange company at the airport, the men who'd been on the flight from Moscow. Linkov had spotted the long-serving chief of the Petersburg FSB, Viktor Cherkesov. He was a figure of notoriety in town. In the days when the FSB was still the KGB, Cherkesov had overseen the apparatus of harassment and control in Leningrad, personally running a generation of cases against dissidents. More recently he had led the prosecution of Aleksandr Nikitin, the naval officer charged with treason for telling the world the truth about Russia's leaky nuclear submarines. After five years of torment and ten months in jail, Nikitin was acquitted in December 1999.[26] But Cherkesov, long a loyal Putin ally, was rewarded. The president in the spring of 2000 named the old KGB boss his envoy in the northwestern region. With Petersburg as his seat of power, Cherkesov took over the grand marriage palace in the center of the city as his headquarters.

Starovoitova had never met the FSB chief, but Linkov had. When he was eighteen, Linkov had been arrested for leafleting the Kazan Cathedral on behalf of DemRossiya. Cherkesov had ordered his apartment searched. Linkov was proud of the episode. It had been one of the last political cases in the USSR.

Next to Cherkesov at the airport had stood a Communist Duma deputy, Aleksei Aleksandrov. Linkov had overheard Starovoitova sparring with the men. Aleksandrov had so often changed his party, depending on the winds, Starovoitova could not help herself. She had made a characteristic jibe. "No, you never change your party," she told Aleksandrov, "you just stay with whoever's in power."

Lastly, Linkov remembered the "strange sense" that descended as the Volga turned onto the embankment of the Griboyedov Canal. The streets were dark, yes, but that was normal. Had they not been it would have been odd. It was the cathedral, St. Nicholas's, that stunned Starovoitova. The eighteenth-century church, its great blue and white dome rising above the elms on Glinka Street, was flooded with lights. The Italians–their consulate stood around the corner–had sponsored the spectacle. It was the first time Starovoitova had seen the church lit. "How glorious!" she said. "Such beauty!" The canal, Linkov said, always seemed to carry a sadness, its waters flowing darkly across town from the Church of Our Savior on the Spilled Blood, the site of Alexander II's demise. But that night as they neared her house, they both felt it, the combination of the radiance of the cathedral and the gloom of the canal. "It was a strange sensation," he said, "one of mournful beauty."

I met with Linkov often. The investigation passed from the old regime to the new. The FSB officers were still investigating. They had filled a room with binders containing interrogations written out in twelve copies. They had interviewed hundreds of "suspects" and thousands of "witnesses." But Linkov had little hope. "How long," he asked, "has the Men case been going?"

Father Aleksandr Men had been the first high-profile murder of the new era, killed, many suspected, for his dissidence. A liberal intellectual, a most unorthodox Russian Orthodox priest, Men was axed to death in the woods north of Moscow on September 9, 1990. It happened on a Sunday, early in the morning, as he was heading for the *elektrichka,* the suburban train that brought him each weekend to church. At the time I was living with Andrei and Lera in their communal apartment. Linkov was right. The Men investigation had stretched for more than a decade. No fewer than thirteen "suspects" had confessed to the murder. Many Muscovites, however, now had their answer. The KGB, they said, had killed Father Aleksandr.

In the Starovoitova case, however, clues abounded, had anyone cared to follow them. Before retreating into the darkness, the killers had left a Croatian-made submachine gun, an Agram 2000, with an internal silencer, and a Beretta pistol. Starovoitova's aides had also compiled a long list of her critics for the FSB to run down. It was a sizeable crowd. "Everyone from local political rivals to financial barons, Communists and nationalists in the Duma, anti-Semites and extremists at large," said Yodkovskaya, her Duma assistant. But the authorities from the start had proved inordinately inept.

Next door to Starovoitova's apartment house stood Petersburg's most fortified police station, the headquarters of the city OMON. Day and night OMON officers guarded its entrance and patrolled the embankment along the Griboyedov Canal. Even before I first visited Starovoitova's house, I had known about the OMON station. But I had not known about the bar. In the cellar of her house was a small bar, known only as the 777. Its electric shingle–three sevens lined up above a hand of playing cards as in a slot machine–glowed red. The 777, I learned upon entering, was a cop bar. It was crowded with OMON officers, smoking, drinking, trying their luck at a bank of electronic poker machines. To be sure, I asked the girl pouring beer behind the tall counter. Yes, she nodded. That Friday night when Starovoitova and Linkov were attacked in the stairwell above, the bar had been open for business.

A MONTH AFTER Starovoitova's death, an article appeared in *Komsomol'skaya pravda*, one of Russia's most popular tabloids, intimating, rather loudly, that she was carrying a million dollars the night she was killed.[27] The story was headlined STAROVOITOVA KILLED FOR $1,000,000? In the talk it stirred, however, the question mark was forgotten. The article was dressed up as an "interview" with Aleksandr Borisoglebsky, the television producer who had shown Starovoitova's videotaped corpse to the nation. Now he professed secret knowledge: The politician had been killed in a robbery. The million, he claimed, was to fund the upcoming city assembly elections. Soon the accusation gained a second voice. Aleksandrov, the Communist Duma deputy Starovoitova had sparred with at the airport, suddenly recalled in a television documentary seeing her carry "several big bags" on the plane.[28] Olga Starovoitova, infuriated by the *Komsomol'skaya pravda* article, sued to protect her sister's name. She won. Aleksandrov, by the time I contacted him, had already recanted his statement. By then he knew what the police had concluded. No money had been stolen from Starovoitova that night. In her purse, the police had found $1,820, a thousand German marks and a few Bulgarian levs left over from a recent conference in Sofia–on "Women in the 21st Century." Starovoitova, her sister and aides remembered, had savored the solidarity of the conference. Most of all, they said, she had enjoyed meeting the keynote speaker, Hillary Clinton.[29]

LINKOV KNEW WHY Starovoitva was murdered. As winter turned to spring, he held fast to what he called the Henry II theory. Since he was still under a gag order, Linkov could only say what was "generally known." But, he was quick to add, it was "generally known" that the good governor of Petersburg, Vladimir Yakovlev, and his good friend Gennadi Seleznev, the Communist speaker of the Duma, stood behind the murder. They had not conspired to murder Starovoitova, Linkov said, because there was no need. "Seleznev only had to say, 'This Starovoitova is making my life miserable.' Given his choices of colleagues, it would have been enough." The same held true for Yakovlev.[30] Linkov had shared his theory with Sergei Stepashin, the former prime minister, who three years earlier had opened the Starovoitova investigation and promised its swift completion. He had also shared it with another son of Petersburg, the president of Russia.

Linkov and Putin had enjoyed a long-running conversation. Linkov did not consider it protection, or providence, but the president had for years tendered a strange affection toward him. Whenever Linkov called, Putin agreed to meet. The two were not exactly friends, but they went a long way back. They had first met in 1990, when Putin was Sobchak's deputy. Anchored behind a desk outside the mayor's door, he had been the gate-keeper. "To get to Sobchak," recalled Linkov, "you had to get past Putin." When Putin moved on to Moscow, at first to work in the presidential administration in Yeltsin's Kremlin, he went home most weekends, and Linkov occasionally bumped into him on flights to Petersburg. Once, Putin told him to stop by his office the next time he was in Moscow. He did. In August 1998, when Yeltsin moved Putin to the Lubyanka, installing him as his new FSB director, Linkov was one of the first to come calling.[31]

It was Putin's turn next. After Starovoitova's murder, Putin, then still the FSB chief, visited Linkov in the hospital. Putin told him a story that Linkov was fond of. Putin recollected that back in the old days, as the walls around them were collapsing and new openings arising, he had once chauffeured Starovoitova and Linkov in his own Zhiguli when she campaigned for the Supreme Soviet in the region outside St. Petersburg. Putin, Linkov said, had sounded "almost nostalgic." Linkov had only the vaguest memory of the campaign trip. But to him, Putin's intention was clear. "I don't know why," he said, "but Putin likes to think he's one of us. He's always telling me how he supported Galina Vasilievna and our cause–from the very beginning."

Even once Putin ascended to the presidency, they had continued to meet. Most recently, one evening, when Putin was home in Petersburg on a short visit, he called Linkov. Would he go with him to visit Starovoitova's grave? the president asked. Putin had not come to the funeral. He stood now at her graveside for the first time. As they left the Nevsky Cemetery, Linkov told Putin of his suspicions: that Yakovlev and Seleznev were behind the murder, that the FSB investigation was a charade, that the case was headed for oblivion. "I'll look into it," Putin promised. "I'll ask them to dig harder."

❧ SEVEN ❧

"IF YOU REALLY WANT to understand Russia," the oligarch Boris Berezovsky once said, "all you have to do is watch the film *The Brother*." The 1997 film—*Brat* is its Russian title—not only was the runaway hit of the new era but proved to Russian filmmakers they could still work in their native land. (There was even a sequel, *Brat II*.) Lenin had understood the power of the big screen. In the old days Mosfilm and Lenfilm, the mainstays of the Soviet film industry, had churned out hundreds of films a year. But deprived of the state's sustenance, Russian directors foundered. They could not compete, they said, with the video pirates who had filled kiosks everywhere with cheap, black market Hollywood thrillers and Hong Kong action films. *Brat* and its sequel changed all that.

Both films starred Sergei Bodrov, Jr., a boyish-faced novice born to a Soviet film director of some renown. With his shaggy brown hair and blue eyes, Bodrov had become the first post-Soviet heartthrob. Berezovsky, however, was referring not to the actor's looks but to his character, Danila, a wide-eyed provincial who becomes, almost by accident, after coming home from Chechnya, a hit man in Petersburg. The film moves between the world of the knuckleheaded mobsters (whom Danila kills off one by one) and the drug-addled underground of young Petersburg (where he cannot hide the naiveté bred of the hinterland). The combination, for Russian audiences, proved irresistible. Before long politicians in Moscow and grunts in Grozny were quoting the film's nationalist, xenophobic lines as received wisdom.

Danila, the doe-eyed hit man with a heart, had become etched into post-Soviet culture.[32]

Vladimir Sergeyevich Kumarin was no fan of the Brother films. "Too simplistic," he said. They suffered "an insufficient depth in their knowledge of the context." For Vladimir Sergeyevich, I learned, many of life's misunderstandings arose from the same persistent problem. For him, the absence of context was disconcerting. We met on a sweltering Saturday afternoon in the middle of August in the atrium of the Grand Europa. The hotel was Petersburg's Plaza, and its air-conditioned atrium cafe, I had long noticed, the meeting place of choice for the city's *avtoritety*–its "authorities," as criminal chieftains in Russia are known. Vladimir Sergeyevich was punctual. I sensed his proximity before he appeared. Two bodyguards swept the room. Most often, bodyguards in Russia resembled the blue-chinned maulers of an undercard in the Bronx. These two were young, lean and dressed in European suits. One moved left, the other right. As soon as I noticed them, Vladimir Sergeyevich stood before me.

He was shorter than I'd expected. His face was small, undistinguished except for a pronounced grin and a thin, downward-sloping black mustache. His eyes were small and almond-shaped. His attire was far from flashy: plain gray slacks, a blue Polo shirt, black suede loafers. He bore a simple gold watch on his wrist. The word the late-summer outfit conjured was *sportif.* A pair of Ray•Ban sunglasses, tortoiseshell frames, rested atop his short dark hair, only enhancing the impression. The glasses hinted at a sensible side. They were attached to a black string. His fingernails were cropped, and his face was smooth. His skin revealed no trace of turmoil; only the base of his throat was marked by a knot of tissue, the vestige of a tracheotomy. As he entered the atrium café to clutch my right hand with his left, he did not swagger or saunter. He even carried a brown leather briefcase, quite like my own, on a strap across his shoulder. All in all, it was not the first impression I had expected. Reading my face, he smiled. Vladimir Sergeyevich knew he did not at all resemble the man many in a good position to know had assured me he was, no matter how firmly or frequently he denied it. He knew he looked nothing like the Godfather of Petersburg.

"Endru?" he asked.

I had recognized him, too. Vladimir Sergeyevich, as nearly everyone in town knew, had only one arm, his left. The right had been lost in an assassination attempt in 1994. We sank into plush couches, opposite each other, in the center of the atrium, his choice. After he'd ordered—pot of chamomile, please—he was still smiling. He spoke in an exceedingly polite, soft voice, taking time between phrases to look left, then right. Vladimir Sergeyevich, I learned, liked to smile. Every time he turned his head to yours and locked on to your eyes, an arresting movement that punctuated the end of his sentences, he smiled, and his eyes, shiny black like marbles, seemed to flicker.

Six stories above us loomed a vaulted ceiling of glass. The café was nearly empty. Tourists filled only a few tables. They were old-money Europeans, gray retirees in for the day from the cruise ships that lined the Neva in high season. We started with ease and talked for hours, throughout the afternoon, into the evening. In moments Vladimir Sergeyevich, as the waiters and bodyguards kept their distance, became Volodya, insisting I join him in employing the informal "you," *ty*, not the formal *vy*. It was odd. Only days earlier, I had thought he would never agree to meet. After all, the man known as Kumarin, not Volodya, did not give interviews. Certainly not to foreigners. Moreover, the timing did not seem propitious. Three days earlier Putin's interior minister, Boris Gryzlov, another Petersburg man freshly promoted, had thrown down the gauntlet at a press conference in town. On *Vremya*, the leading evening news program on Russian television, the declaration had seemed bold: "The Minister . . . highlighted the threat of the *Tambovskaya grupirovka* [the Tambov Gang] which runs up to one hundred industrial enterprises in St. Petersburg, making it the crime capital of the country."[33]

Kumarin, according to all I had heard and read, was the undisputed boss of the Tambov Gang. It was an appellation he steadfastly rejected. He denied any claim to the title and sued anyone who called him that in print. He did not, I had heard, enjoy the press. Only once had he met a foreign reporter. At the time he'd had little choice; he'd been in jail. Although the Kremlin's attention had left him nonplussed, he seemed grateful for the chance to burnish his image. And so, as we took turns taking sips from fine china in the middle of the most expensive hotel in Russia, we fell into a game of cat and mouse. Only I was not sure who was mouse and who was cat.

In *Banditsky Peterburg*, his preeminent study of the city's organized crime groups, the Petersburg investigative journalist Andrei Konstantinov maintained that the Tambov Gang, comprising some two thousand foot soldiers and controlling robust market niches in the city's gasoline, banking, and real estate sectors, was the dominant *gruppirovka* in town. The book was quite a read. It was amply illustrated with dozens of private Kodak moments between the bulls–men endeared with nicknames like the Baboon and the Elephant, the Broiler and the Iron, Kostya the Grave and Sasha the Shark–and their dolls. The book also offered a two-page flow-chart purporting to detail the ornate structure of the Tambov Gang. It was a maze of names and enterprises. But one name stood on the top line, Kumarin's, as "the undisputed leader who cannot tolerate collective leadership." To sum up the boss's stature, Konstaninov offered a literary allusion to Lermontov, the poet of the Caucasus. "Kumarin," he wrote, was "in a certain sense, A Hero of Our Time."[34] Kumarin did not dispute the book's claims. He had, in essence, dictated the chapter on his life and times. Still, it was not the best book, he said, as he dispatched a bodyguard to fetch it for me.

A few years earlier, a spate of articles in the Russian press had brought Kumarin greater fame than he desired. He had been embroiled in a pro-tracted struggle with "a competitor" that culminated with the attempt on his life. Was it a bomb? I asked, nodding in the direction of where his right arm would have been. "No," he said, ever grinning, "it was a Kalashnikov."

Kumarin had just left home on the first morning in June 1994, when a gunman wearing a wig opened fire on his Mercedes. One bodyguard was killed, and Kumarin woke up twenty days later in the hospital. While he lay in a coma, his arm, mangled by bullets, had been amputated. Bullets had also pierced his stomach, chest, and lungs. He had awoken in Hospital No. 26 on the edge of Petersburg, where, until the papers got wind of it, two dozen friends came to help out. They occupied the ICU, brought in their own doctor, medicine, and, of course, security. Once he came out of the coma, Kumarin was flown out of the country for further surgery. In Germany he had his lung reconstructed. He stayed among the Germans, with his wife and daughter, for two years. His daughter, now seventeen, had learned the language almost fluently. He'd gone back to Germany a second time. On the weekend the *Kursk* went under, he had suffered heart trouble. The doctors called it a heart attack. The sinking of the submarine had hit him hard, he said. He'd collapsed at home. When they revived him, they discovered a heart condition. In Germany he underwent another operation.

By now, Kumarin was grateful to the Germans. He liked their country, their doctors, and the way they did business.

INTERIOR MINISTER Gryzlov had not only singled out the Tambov Gang but announced plans to gut the RUBOP units, the regional police divisions formed to fight organized crime in the last years of the USSR, when extortion rackets began to take hold in Soviet cities. Kumarin was not concerned that Russia's top cop had all but named the Tambov Gang the prime force behind the city's criminal descent.[35] He had his own ideas on the restructuring. There was no need to get rid of all the RUBOP divisions, he said. "Just strip them of their corporate patrons." Every RUBOP in Russia was under the control, he said, of some industrial group. "That's how they work. They wait for an order from above. A company will say, 'So-and-so has to go down,' and they find a reason to bring so-and-so down. So when someone needs to go to jail, they find drugs, bullets, weapons, whatever on him." In his mind, the law enforcement system was as ruthless and arbitrary as under Stalin. I told him how the camp survivors in Norilsk liked to quote the Stalinist motto: "If there's a person, you can always find a charge." "Precisely," said Kumarin. "Only now it's all about the money."

IT WAS CALLED THE Tambov Gang for a reason. Volodya had grown up in a village—"no more than twenty houses"—outside Tambov, a city in central Russia, about eight hundred miles from Petersburg. Founded in 1636 as a fort on Muscovy's southern front, Tambov lay in the heart of the *Chernozemie,* the Black Earth region. Tambov officials were proud of their native sons, the composer Sergei Rachmaninov and the eighteenth-century poet Gavrila Derzhavin. The local music institute was named after Rachmaninov, the university after Derzhavin. Tambov even liked to lay claim to Andrei Platonov, the twentieth-century writer Brodsky ranked on a par with Joyce and Kafka. Born in nearby Voronezh, Platonov had lived there in his youth. But to the farmers of Tambov, no one was more famous than Kumarin.

He sipped a second cup of chamomile and told me of his parents. Papa drove a tractor on the collective farm. Mama milked the cows. She gave birth to him on a road. The horse cart didn't make it in time to the next village, where there was a doctor. "At thirteen," he declared with pride, "I earned my first ruble." He had worked with his father on the combine. Soon he had to leave home, to go to an *internat*, a boarding school crowded with orphans, "difficult" children, children whose parents couldn't provide for them, and children like Kumarin from villages without schools. He grew up "quietly." He had a brother a year older, a sister, few ambitions, and only one passion, music. He loved Soviet ballads and Western rock, especially Pink Floyd and, of course, the Beatles. He did his two years of military service in southern Siberia, down near Mongolia. In 1976, after the army, he came to Leningrad. He moved in with an aunt and uncle and enrolled at the Institute for Precision Mechanics and Optics. He liked talking about the institute, where he now sponsored the computer department. He had just graduated, two decades late, with honors.

We were interrupted often. First a man of about forty—barrel chest, short gray hair, double-breasted suit—stopped by. "Good to see you, Vladimir Sergeyevich," he said, shaking hands. As he waddled off, Kumarin followed him with his eyes. "Head of hotel security," he said, "colonel in the KGB." Enjoying his retirement, I commented. "Those guys never retire," he replied. "In once, in forever."

Every so often an unsmiling adjutant, his right-hand man, delivered a mobile phone. It was a fat Nokia, top of the line, with Internet connectivity, a screen, and a keyboard. Each time Kumarin courteously explained the calls. First it was "sugar stuck in the port," then "some guy trying to ship aluminum," then a Duma deputy, a leader in Vladimir Zhirinovsky's Liberal Democrats, who were neither, seeking advice. All squabbles, he said, minor and annoying, in need of sorting out.

Did the supplicants require his blessing? "Of course not," he said. "They just want to make sure no one rips them off." He told the story of a Russian émigré who got burned on a shipload of *nozhki Busha*, the Arkansas chicken drumsticks nicknamed Bush Legs, after George H. W. Bush, the U.S. president when they were first shipped east. In 1992 the United States sent 14,500 tons of frozen chicken to the Russians. By 2000 Bush Legs, at one million tons per annum, had become America's chief export to Russia. This poor guy, the émigré, Kumarin explained, hadn't known what he was doing. Trusted a local broker who'd tried to cut himself a fat margin. The deal had soured; the authorities stepped in; the chicken was confiscated. The émigré had sued, but the legal battle dragged on. And poultry parts, Kumarin added, did not last forever.

"So it's like soccer," I ventured. "You're just the referee."

Kumarin, pleased with the analogy, again smiled.

Behind us, two tourists, a sun-tanned couple from Manhattan, debated the virtues of the Hermitage's Matisses versus the new tomb of the Romanovs. The husband enjoyed the paintings more. The wife wished they had bought the video of the tsar's crypt.

Kumarin, I had heard, was not your average "authority." He did not care, it was said, about girls, money, or diamonds. He had been married to the same woman for twenty years. He did not smoke, did not drink, and rarely swore. He respected his partners and treated friends like brothers. Most of all, I was assured, he had a genuine vision of his work. He saw himself as helping rebuild his country. "He's far from typical," said an associate, trying to dissuade me from seeking him out. "Vladimir Sergeyevich is no thug."

Was the legend true, I asked, that he'd worked as a bartender when he first came to town? Not a bartender, he said. "The administrator." He'd been hired to keep order. The bar was only the beginning, he said. It was the late 1970s, Brezhnev was in his prime, and in Leningrad the Roza Vetrov, Rose of the Winds–was a hot spot.[36] The Roza was one of Leningrad's few "youth cafés," sanctioned refuges where students spent afternoons smoking *papirosi* and drinking the locally brewed syrupy Pepsi. The bar was long dead.

Was there a plaque on the wall outside? I wondered. Like the ones that everywhere proclaimed, "Lenin Slept Here"?

Kumarin laughed.

He didn't make money at the bar, but life was not bad. Then came Gorbachev's great try at prohibition, the antialcohol campaign in which he ordered the USSR's vineyards destroyed. Sensing the times were changing, Kumarin quit the institute. New horizons, he said, opened everywhere. "Russia woke up. Life began to develop in all directions. Wherever I looked, my old world turned into a new world." For every guy in town, life took a different path. For some, he said, it was their *zemliachestvo*, a brotherhood of guys from the same region. For others, it was the *gruppirovki*, the gangs. And for some, by the time the USSR collapsed, it was organized gangs. It was the era of cooperatives, the semiprivate small enterprises that marked the start of big money, real money.

"Everyone," Kumarin said, "went into cooperatives." He did, too. "We baked," he said. "Rolls, buns, cakes. And from there we moved on, first to flowers, then on to almost everything. You name it, we sold it."

"The big push," as Kumarin put it, had come much earlier, on the eve of the Moscow Olympics in 1980. Leningrad was flooded with foreign cigarettes and liquor. Before then such treasures were sold only in the *beryiozki*, the Soviet-era hard-currency shops that were the exclusive reserve of foreigners and diplomats. The Finns suddenly came to town on shopping sprees. They feasted on the cheap Western goods. It made sense. A pack of Marlboros at the time cost a ruble and a half, and the black market rate was six rubles to a dollar. Anyone who ran a kiosk or a shop made a small fortune. But Kumarin and his cohorts didn't sell cognac and cigarettes. "We made money a different way," he said, "by what in those days they called *mosheinichestvo*." It was a Soviet legal term, denoting fraud.

In time he was arrested. "The official charge," he said, "was extortion." By then a new business had emerged: protection. The rackets bloomed in every Soviet city. To open any business, one needed to pay for a *krysha* (a roof), a service provided by a force of local power, usually a gang or moonlighting law enforcement officers. (It was the obstacle that Grisha Smekalov still faced on Sakhalin.) In the early 1990s anyone with muscle, particularly the ethnic gangs and the sportsmen, got into the business. By now, however, the pioneers of "protection" had evolved. They were now in "security."[37]

Kumarin's version of events was more colorful. He'd been arrested because a friend had lost his temper. This guy, he said, had gone up to some other guy and told him, "Either you pay what you owe or we'll cut your head off and play soccer with it." The threat, he said, is what sent him to jail. In August 1991 he saw the coup attempt against Gorbachev unfold and collapse from the window of a KGB cell. He was due to be sentenced that day when a guard came and told him the news. "They've arrested Gorbachev," he said. His hearing was called off. He was still awaiting trial, sitting in the KGB jail, when his parents died. Finally, after nearly two years, in 1992 he was sentenced to four years in prison. He was packed off to the Kresty (Crosses) Prison, Petersburg's nineteenth-century red-brick fortress. "Where Brodsky was," he proudly noted. From there it was on to

Obukhovo, a local penal colony. In all, he had served two and one-half years.[38] Kumarin would not say if he was guilty. He only pulled a quote from American history, from one of the robber barons of the West. "What was it your man Morgan said?" (He meant J. P.) "'I'm prepared to defend my fortune, but not my first million'?"

THERE WAS A TIME, not long ago, when Kumarin handed out business cards. They announced that he had changed his name to his mother's maiden name and gotten a job. He had become "Vladimir Barsukov, Deputy Chairman of the PTK, the Petersburg Fuel Company." In the fall of 1994, not long after the attempt on his life, the city of Petersburg and several leading businessmen had formed the PTK. A Siberian oil giant, Surgutneftegaz, had once been the top supplier of fuel to Petersburg, but by 1998 its local subsidiaries had been subsumed by the new PTK.[39] Kumarin was only the number two man in the holding company. Yakovlev's vice governor was its chair. But when I asked for one of his cards, Kumarin said he no longer carried them. "Retired," he said. He could not control his grin.

In the first post-Soviet years Western reporters and scholars watched the rise of criminal groups in Russia with immense interest. Books were written on the gangs' rise, their prowess, and, above all, the threats they posed to the fragile shoots of Russia's free market. But the reverse influence—how business would recast the Russian criminal world—was largely ignored. The influence, however, was considerable. After the crash of August 1998, and the Bank of New York scandal the following year, any Russian trying to turn a profit—whether a Harvard-trained M.B.A. in a Moscow financial house or a young thug in a Rostov enforcement racket—faced a new world.

Crime of course persisted. But suddenly new terms—"transparency," "corporate governance," "shareholders' rights"—came to the fore. For most, the slogans were nothing more than the fashion of the day. Yet in time, as the Kremlin set a new course of selective prosecution of oligarchs and corrupt state officials (those who'd fallen out of favor), the criminal groups—perhaps more than anyone—reacted. The shift was pronounced. Some, like the Uralmash group in Yekaterinburg went into politics. The Uralmash boys, a muscular outfit led by former boxers and wrestlers, controlled a good slice of the local plant, Russia's largest machine-building complex.[40] Others took their economic portfolios aboveground and tried to burnish their images. "We're not criminals," they insisted, "but good corporate citizens."

When the Petersburg press acted up and started to accuse the Tambov Gang of taking over the local assembly, sponsoring Governor Yakovlev's reelection campaign, and using the city's gasoline holding company as a front, Kumarin, using the name Barsukov, took the unusual step of writing an article in the local newspaper, *Smena*. The headline made his point clear: TAMBOVIANS, LIKE PETERSBURGERS, ARE JUST RESIDENTS OF RUSSIAN CITIES. He declared the "Criminal Capital" sobriquet unfair. The Tambov Gang no longer existed, he wrote. He was now serving the city and its citizens well as a corporate officer of the PTK. The fuel company, he noted, fed 90 percent of Petersburg's public transportation and employed some 2,500 people, while the city itself owned 14.5 percent of it.[41]

Few were reassured, but the investigative articles soon receded. It had become obvious Governor Yakovlev would win reelection in the spring of 2000 with ease. The liberals failed to field a viable candidate, and Putin cut a deal with Yakovlev: Clean up your backyard, and we'll let you stay for now. With the reprieve, the governor handily won a new term. Kumarin had tried his best, but he soon stepped down all the same. Yet even in "retirement," he said he had learned lessons. He now knew the value of public relations, financial consulting, and accounting.

By 2002, Petersburg had 226 gasoline stations. The Petersburg Fuel Company, still the city's largest retail company, controlled 69 of them. The PTK now, for better or worse, behaved like almost any other Russian company. Its books were audited, and its shareholders made public. The shadowy reputation lingered, but in time, its officers were confident, it would fade. PTK officials now hoped, according to a business newsletter on opportunities in Russia prepared by the U.S. Commerce Department, of attracting "$100 million in investments to renovate two major oil terminals and its network of service stations."[42]

OUR FIRST TALK had stretched until darkness. We had moved far beyond Petersburg–to Kosovo (Why did NATO have to bomb?), Monica Lewinsky (Couldn't she have just kept quiet?), the WTO (Let us in, and Russian businessmen will have to play by the same rules as the rest of the world), the

Middle East (How could people blow themselves up and kill innocents in a pizzeria?), and Chechnya (Putin shouldn't call them bandits; they were terrorists, pure and simple). Yet when we met again, we spoke even longer.

We rendezvoused in the shadow of St. Isaac's, at the Angleterre. It was a hotel with character. Here, in 1925, the poet Sergei Yesenin, for thousands of Russian girls still their first crush, hanged himself. He had left a final poem in his own blood. I stood outside and watched Kumarin and his bodyguards pull up in a two-car convoy, a defiant show of modesty. The Mercedes was an armored 600, but used. (He'd picked it up second hand for a hundred thousand dollars from the former finance minister of Italy.) Kumarin saw me taking in the great gold-domed cathedral across the square. "What's higher," he quizzed, "St. Isaac's or Notre Dame?" I shrugged. "Ours is," he said, ever respectful of history, "by a hundred feet."

We sat again in the center of the restaurant, the bodyguards at their respectful distances. He ordered green tea and asked about the kitchen's range of ice cream. The waitress blushed when he asked her to describe the flavors. He chose vanilla, with chocolate sauce. It was a new Italian place, luxuriant in warm hues and recessed lighting. Once again Kumarin was dressed simply—Polo shirt and slacks. This time he wore a new watch, a fatter one. "One of the Moscow guys yesterday." He shrugged. "Wanted to give a present."

At the far side of the restaurant, a jazz singer sat at a grand piano. She was a beautiful African American, an exotic import recruited to entertain the local elite. Across the way I spied a familiar face, Brezhnev's. I had seen this poor soul before. His face so resembled the old, enfeebled general secretary that he dressed up in an old Soviet uniform, pinned on a chestful of medals, and worked as a Brezhnev double. Over the years I'd seen him—and "Lenin," "Stalin," and "Trotsky"—work the rounds in Moscow. Western companies hired them out to pose with happy partygoers at corporate events. (The Lenin double got the most work; he'd even appeared in Zhirinovsky's 1996 soft-porn feature film.)

I looked over at "Brezhnev" and decided the time had arrived. "So you're not really the Godfather of Petersburg?" I asked.

Across the table Kumarin feigned exasperation. "If I'm the Godfather, then who's the Godmother? And who are we going to baptize?"

If I called him "the leader of the Tambov Gang," what would he do?

"I'd sue you the same day," he shot back. We were back to cat and mouse.

"What's a Godfather anyway?" he asked. "If a Godfather is someone who heads an organization, he's got to have a big bureaucracy. And I have none."

I decided to lead him. If he had no organization, then of course he had no staff, no chief of staff, no cadres, and no directors, right?

He smiled. "None at all."

No board meetings, no congresses?

"No board meetings and no congresses. We don't meet once a week. We don't meet once a year. We don't meet for birthdays. We don't meet for weddings. Nothing–and everybody knows this perfectly well."

So there wasn't even a *gruppirovka* called the *Tambovskaya*?

"Well, of course there is," he said. "But when I hear some interior minister stand up and accuse us of controlling hundreds of businesses and ruling the city, I say to myself, 'What are they trying to tell me? That you can't spend time with your friends? That you can't do business with your friends? And that you certainly can't do business *well* with your friends, or it becomes a *gruppirovka*?'"

So it was that simple. He had gone into business with friends, done "well," as he put it, and gained a reputation for organized crime. He nodded, pleased that I had understood.

He lapsed into silence for a moment, before announcing that he had "nothing to apologize for." I thought of J. P. Morgan again, of his memorable words after the stock panic he caused in 1901 had left thousands in ruins: "I owe the public nothing."

"What should I be ashamed of?" Kumarin asked. "That we didn't let ourselves get taken advantage of? That we were the only guys who stood our ground and didn't let anyone insult us?" These days he paid his taxes and lived modestly. In 2000 he officially declared an income of four million dollars. He said he hid nothing, taking a jibe at the oligarchs. "No Swiss accounts, no villas in France."

He had been to France, however. Taken his wife to a resort in the south. Ritzy place, very exclusive. And guess whom they'd run into there? Hugh Grant and Liz Hurley. He'd swum out one day to a raft in the ocean. And there was Hugh. Kumarin had introduced himself: "Me Vladimir."

Hugh looked at the stump of his right arm and asked, "Afghanistan?" Kumarin went with it. But Hugh kept going: "Hero Russia, Afghanistan?" Kumarin nodded again.

"So the whole week we're there, here's Hugh and Liz introducing me to his friends, as 'My friend Vladimir, hero Russia, Afghanistan.'" Kumarin loved the story. It was a rare chance to enjoy the flip side of his old nemesis, the lack of context.

Life had indeed changed. He was now taking it slow, doing his part to help restore the city on the eve of its big birthday. He was rebuilding Ivanov's Tower. The Tower, the cupola-topped corner of the apartment house at No. 38 Tauride Street, was a literary landmark. From 1905 to 1912 Vyacheslav Ivanov, wild-eyed poet, critic, and high priest of symbolism, lived there. The building had flowed with culture. On the first floor was the Znamensky Dance Academy; on the second, a public reading room. But Ivanov, who lived in the top-floor flat, had put it on the map. Ivanov's salon, Wednesdays from midnight to dawn, was known as the birthplace of the silver age of Russian poetry. It became a nest for poets like Aleksandr Blok and Gumilyov and Akhmatova. In 1909, Akhmatova, just twenty, recited her first verses there.[43] Now Kumarin lived there. He had bought, communal flat by communal flat, the whole building. He was trying to figure out how to replace the wood roof beams, destroyed by a fire. He'd need a helicopter, he reckoned. He wanted to do it right, make sure the roof was exactly as it had been before the Revolution and would last.

It was a plan for a future. As I'd discussed the success of *Banditsky Peterburg* over black tea with Dariya Petrovna, it had occurred to me that Kumarin had no need to gild his past for my benefit. He needed to for his benefit. He had made a choice, as he put it, "to live a legal life." Each month, he said, brought more order to his life, to everyone's. "The noise," he said, echoing Dariya Petrovna's phrase, had lessened. He could not imagine a life without bodyguards, but things, he predicted, would only get more quiet. And quiet, he said, was good for anyone in business.

Night had descended, but outside, even in August, the sky still held sunlight. The tables to our left and right had cleared. Brezhnev lingered with a crowd of forlorn German businessmen. The jazz singer had long given up her serenade, and our waitress, whose thin hands trembled each time she replenished our mineral water, had disappeared. I could wait no longer. At a lone table nearby two couples, Brits, were finishing their cakes. A baby sat on one of the women's knees. The baby was crying. Its face was bright red.

I asked about Starovoitova. Who did he think killed her? "*Ne znayu,*" he said. "I don't know." For a moment he fell silent. He stared off, his gaze fixed on the baby at the far end of the neighboring table. The parents were fretting. The baby bawled ever redder. "*Ne znayu*," Kumarin repeated.

EIGHT

EVERYWHERE IN Russia the elderly carried history with them. But in Petersburg they carried a separate city that was no more. Nearly a third of the population, one and a half million people, were pensioners. More often than not they accepted the flood of crime without lament. It was a terrible thing, of course, that Starovoitova had fallen. But their city had always suffered, and its heroes had a long tradition of martyrdom. The city was ringed by vast burial grounds of the sacrificed. The Piskaryovskoye Cemetery on the outskirts of town was one enormous expanse of mass graves, the anonymous remains of nearly half a million Leningraders, only half the toll of the nine-hundred-day siege during World War II. For the survivors of the Nazi blockade, the *blokadniki*, the siege remained fixed in the present tense. To them, Petersburg was still Leningrad, and "the sunny side" of the Nevsky remained the side to avoid, the one more vulnerable to Nazi shells. The warning still hung at No. 14: "Citizens! During artillery bombardments, this side of the street is the most dangerous!"

Academician Likhachev and his wife, Zina, kept a notebook of memories from the blockade. They took turns setting to paper the macabre turns of those days. Romanov, the old Leningrad Party boss doomed to spend his final days tallying his losses in Moscow, had also survived the blockade. He'd volunteered at eighteen for the front and fought through the shelling, frostbite, and concussions. When Romanov spoke of those dark years, it was the one time he brightened. For him, the blockade was a usable past. Thanks to it, he had managed an executive takeover at last. He now chaired the Moscow Association of *Blokadniki*. He'd been welcomed. The survivors were getting on and scarcely getting by. They could use a lobbyist, and surviving the blockade was the one feat of Romanov's life that no one disputed.

Nearly everyone in Petersburg knew a *blokadnik*. Dariya Petrovna lived with her husband's memories, Lev Lurie with his parents'. To the survivors and those who loved them, the Nazi siege was not a historic event. It was a tragedy without end, a trail of suffering that lived on beneath the surface of their city, binding them to the victims it had taken, casualties no one else could now see.

IN JUNE 1941, when the Nazis attacked, Leningrad had nearly 3.5 million residents. In the first winter of the siege the city lived under a rain of bombs and shells that rarely paused. In the fall and winter of 1941, wrote the late historian W. Bruce Lincoln, more than a hundred thousand bombs and at least five thousand shells fell each month.[44] The siege, in its duration and devastation, was the worst suffered by any city since Roman times. No comparison suffices. "On a single day during January, February, March or April 1942," said Lincoln, "more people died in Leningrad than in the entire siege of Vicksburg" in the American Civil War.[45] When the siege ended in January 1944, fewer than six hundred thousand residents had survived. Tallies for the death toll vary—as in all mass murders, the true total will never be known—but the historians agree that the blockade took the lives of at least one million Leningraders.[46]

As the siege set in, the city was stripped one by one of the requisites of normal life. First the newspapers disappeared. Next the meat stores closed, and soon the lights went. Then the water and the plumbing and, as the snows came, the heating. A blockade routine took over. For water, Leningraders drilled holes in the frozen Neva. For heat, they built small makeshift iron stoves, *burzhuiki*, and fed them furniture, books, whatever burned. For food, they boiled wallpaper paste, glue, leather belts, whatever lent water a semblance of soup. The darkness came earlier than ever that first winter, as the city covered itself from the bombers' sights. Everyone nailed blankets over windows. Before long the cats and dogs disappeared. By spring even the mice were gone. Likhachev wrote of their death throes in his diary: ". . . in the silence of early morning, when most of us were in bed, we would hear a dying mouse scamper convulsively over by the window and then expire; it hadn't been able to find so much as a crumb in our room."[47] As hunger gave way to starvation, the corpses, sewn into sheets like mummies, piled up everywhere—in courtyards, on bridges, at the university. Many were dragged on children's sleds through the streets. Likhachev took his father's body to a makeshift morgue that way. He tied his daughters' sleds together and carted off the corpse.[48]

The deprivations were total. Cannibalism, the survivors said, was inevitable.[49] Yet among the *blokadniki*, one memory stood out: the hunger for bread. "Some were possessed by bread mania in its purest form. Just bread, our daily bread . . . ," wrote the literary critic Lydia Ginzburg in her moving diary of the siege. "Others elaborated their fantasies about bread. They had an urge . . . to sit in front of a dark loaf, cut thick slice after thick slice and dip it in sunflower oil."[50] The hunger for bread, "blockade bread," ruled all others.

Aleksandra Mikhailovna Morozova remembered the bread well. She could recite its recipe from memory and taste its bitter coarseness on her tongue, and whenever the need arose, she could also still bake it. I'd seen her handiwork in the Bread Museum near the rail station to Moscow. I'd gone to the museum on a hunch it would have a blockade room, a precise reconstruction of a typical Leningrad room during the siege. It did. The small window was covered by a black felt blanket. A *burzhuika* stood in the corner and beside the bed a radio, which had announced on any given day, as Ginzburg wrote, that "under enemy shelling, Leningrad carried on with its normal working and business life," just as "any one of us was killed by Hitlerite shrapnel."[51] And here, inside a Plexiglas cube, between a clipped ration card and a tiny handcrafted kerosene lamp, on a white dish with a pink lip, lay a hardened quarter slice–125 grams–of Aleksandra Mikhailovna's blockade bread. She'd baked the fortified loaf a year before, just as she had every day of the siege at Oven No. 6 in the Badaev bread factory.

Aleksandra Mikhailovna listed the ingredients–"barley husks, bran chaff, hydrolyzed cellulose . . ."–in a singsong voice that echoed the chanting of an Orthodox priest. Flour was so scarce, she explained, it had to be supplemented with "rye meal and millet dust"–and, while it lasted, wallpaper paste. A great-grandmother with chalky blue eyes and soft gray curls that fell about ample shoulders, she had a round face and an easy laugh. She wore a yellow floral dress, blue slippers, and tiny earrings painted bright orange. Little could shake her strength now. She had come to Leningrad on her own at sixteen, in 1937, the height of the purges. She had left her village near Yaroslavl to move in with her eldest brother, who welded tanks at a local factory. She'd had eight brothers in all. None had survived. The war had taken them all. Throughout the blockade she had stood by her oven. She had stayed there until she retired, after fifty-two years, a factory record. It was more than a good job, she said softly. It was a duty. The rewards had been more than ample. She'd earned a medal as a Defender of Leningrad and an albumful of certificates as a devoted worker.

Still, at times in her dreams, the years of hunger returned. Visions, she said, came back. How the factory bosses ordered the floorboards raised at the breweries and warehouses and she and her girlfriends scraped the "flour dust" from under the floors. "But by then," she said, "people had already grown inventive." They had started to boil the glue. Women, she now marveled, learned to melt lipstick into grease to fry their 125 grams of bread. She'd never been able to eat the glue. She always thought it was healthier to eat the berries, grass, and weeds.

During the siege Aleksandra Mikhailovna worked twelve-hour shifts in one of seven brigades that baked around the clock. After work, she helped wherever she could. She cut peat from the fields, "for heating and eating." She repaired roofs and dug trenches. She helped bury the dead. In the evenings, whenever she could, she went to the hospitals. She washed the bloodied floors and, whenever time allowed, played her balalaika for the wounded. It was a memory of rare joy. "Raised them all from the cots," she said with a laugh. "The boys called me the *Yaraslavskaya balalaika*." Her cheeks reddened, and her shoulders rose in a half laugh. In those days, she conceded, even with the horror she faced, she'd still been game for revelry.

Now she lived in one of the anonymous apartment blocks at the edge of the city. It had been built during the boom in the 1970s, when Leningrad expanded into the pines and birches. It was far from the center, she said, and the woods were mostly gone. But she liked her district all the same. It was where she used to come to gather grass and berries during the blockade. Like Dariya Petrovna, Aleksandra Mikhailovna longed for her son, her only child. He had died still a young man—food poisoning at a wedding—and she'd raised his kids, adopting them as teenagers. His wife, she said diplomatically, couldn't raise them alone. Now her grandchildren had grown up, and she had great-grandchildren, a pair of toddlers who kept her busy. All the same, when the ladies from the Bread Museum asked her to bake her blockade bread, she could not refuse. But she had encountered a problem. No one in the city baked anymore. The bread these days was all processed. So she had to take a train to an outlying village. Only out there, she said, waving off to a world far beyond the cinder block and concrete, do the babushkas still bake the old way, with ingredients like rye meal and barley chaff. "Out there," she said, "they have to, else they'd have died out long ago."

✦ NINE ✦

THE WEATHER IN Petersburg is prone to sudden shifts. A snowstorm can descend in the middle of a sunny spring afternoon and disappear just as abruptly. "The snow sometimes falls softly," wrote the historian Likhachev in his memoirs, "sometimes it whirls about or is driven into a blizzard. Sometimes it falls as wet flakes, sometimes as dry powder. At times it is cold enough to cut your face and at others it will caress it tenderly."[52] Early one Sunday morning, as a white tempest mysteriously cleared and the new asphalt of the Nevsky gleamed in the sunshine, a cop picked me up.

Valentin was squeezed in behind the wheel of the battered Volvo. He was well over six feet tall, and his forehead nearly touched the cracked glass of the windshield. The sides of his head were shaved, leaving only a thin strip of black hair, and his narrow blue eyes nearly closed when he smiled. A lone gold star adorned the shoulders of his jacket. A major in the police, he picked me up to earn a few rubles but refused any money once I told him I was American. Valentin didn't like that people called his city the Criminal Capital. Petersburg's worst problem, he said, wasn't crime. It was the loss of hope. The despair, he said, was "like a plague."

It was hard to miss the symptoms. One had only to walk down the Nevsky at night. The avenue was crowded, but the addicts—their faces drawn, their hands so deeply scratched they bled—were prominent. Many could not stand. Hunched over, they nodded out in the dark corners. Too many young people, as the psychiatrist Kurpatov said, now saw no way out. They had turned to the needle. Drugs—chiefly heroin—had flooded Petersburg.

The city, the medical experts estimated, was home to seventy thousand intravenous drug users. And thanks to a stubborn predilection to share dirty needles, a new siege had settled in.

In 1987 the first case of the human immunodeficiency virus, the virus known as HIV, was registered in the USSR.[53] For years Soviet authorities denounced the disease as a product of the West's debased culture and morality. Since sex among gay men was a Soviet crime, the disease entered Russia as a taboo. Yet even long after the fall of the USSR, health officials in Moscow insisted Russia faced no major HIV/AIDS threat. The country's isolation, they claimed, would quarantine it from the medical ills of the West. In Yeltsin's first years a false lull held. But by 2001 the myth of Russia's protected status had been shattered. The number of recorded HIV-positive cases remained comparatively low, but the truth was unavoidable: The virus was sweeping across Russia faster than anywhere else in the world.

In contrast with Africa and the United States, where the contraction of AIDS was primarily sexual, the major cause in Russia was through drugs. In Petersburg, as in the country as a whole, nearly 90 percent of the HIV cases originated through shared needles. One January night, at a corner on the city's desolate southern edge, I stood in line with a dozen teenagers. Their skin was so pale it shone in the night. They had come, as they did nearly every night, to queue up beside a retrofitted bus. Inside sat a volunteer doctor and two former addicts, now counselors. The kids had come to get clean needles, free condoms, and, for many, their first HIV tests. "I can't say this is how I hoped to die," said Kolya, who had just turned twenty. "But at least I'll have plenty of company where I'm going." The glow of the bus revealed his scrawny figure. He lived nearby, alone with his mother. His older brother was in the army. He didn't know where his father was. He had shot his first heroin at sixteen. He was tired of stealing from his mother to buy his fixes. A month before, he had tested positive for HIV.

Petersburg of course was not alone. Drug abuse was proliferating across the country. I'd seen its ravages everywhere, from Norilsk to Okha. Togliatti, a grim city of automobile workers on the Volga, may have been the worst. I'd crisscrossed the city one night with a paramedic crew. Togliatti was doubly cursed: It had a high youth population, and the car factory paid—by Russian standards—good wages. The doctor in the crew had grown tired of bringing junkies back from the near dead. "These are the kids who wanted to live free," he said sardonically. He answered seven calls that night. Four were heroin overdoses. The doctor had little hope for the addicts. "The ones the drugs spare now," he said, "the virus will take later."

The humor was black but held truth. The HIV epidemic was now progressing at an exponential rate. In 1999 Petersburg registered 400 new cases of HIV. In 2000 the total approached 4,000. By 2002 it had jumped to 17,000. Nationally, in each year since 1998, the number of reported HIV-positive cases nearly doubled. In 1998 the total number of cases reported was 10,993. By early 2003 it had grown to more than 200,000. That was the official count. Medical researchers estimated, conservatively, that the state's tally was only one-fifth to one-tenth of the true total.[54] By then the epidemic had entered a new phase, moving sharply into the heterosexual, non-drug-using population. HIV specialists had long seen the shift coming. Addicts not only shared needles but had sex, often selling their bodies for drugs. A confluence of factors now seemed certain to speed the virus's progression into the mainstream: Prostitution was ubiquitous, condom use rare, and needle exchanges were condemned even by medical specialists, let alone the Orthodox Church and the Duma.

Not all in Petersburg, however, were blind to the threat. "People like to dismiss the infected as social undesirables, but HIV will soon threaten every sexually active Russian," warned Yevgeny Voronin, the young doctor who ran the Republican Hospital for Infectious Diseases in Ust-Izhora, a village just beyond the city limits. Calling the two grim buildings, their windows covered by bars, a "hospital" was disingenuous. Russia's largest inpatient clinic for HIV-positive mothers and its only one for children with the virus, the center was hidden at the edge of the village behind a tall wall. "We're not exactly popular with the city officials," Voronin explained. Or the locals. In 1991, when it opened, the neighbors were outraged. They pelted the clinic with bottles and rocks, crying that they didn't want their water polluted with AIDS. The villagers had long ago relented—they had no choice—but the ignorance remained. The doctor still had trouble keeping his nurses. Fearing infection or public scorn, most did not stay with him long.

IN PETERSBURG AND across the country, grassroots support groups and prevention centers did appear. The government meanwhile succeeded in doing next to nothing to stave off the epidemic. For officialdom and most Russians, said Vadim Pokrovsky, the doctor charged with leading Russia's fight against HIV/AIDS since Gorbachev's days, the trouble remained on the horizon. Few Russians, he said, knew anyone who had died of AIDS. By June 2002 only 2,277 Russians had been known to have died of HIV-related causes.[55] "*Razborki* [criminal turf battles] claimed more lives in Moscow alone," Pokrovsky noted. But that will change, he was sure. By 2007, he projected, more than 5 million Russians will have HIV.

Pokrovsky's campaign was drastically underfunded. The state, he liked to remind reporters, spent $100 million to raise 120 bodies from the *Kursk* and set aside more than $1 billion for Petersburg's 300th birthday. However, the federal budget all but ignored the battle against HIV/AIDS. In 2001 the state spent less than $5 million on antiretroviral drugs–at a time when the United States devoted more than $5 billion annually to treatment. Prevention–at less than $2 million a year–was scarcely funded at all. In 2001 the World Bank, after years of hand wringing, at last offered Russia a $150 million loan to fight HIV, AIDS, and TB over ten years. The government, with renewed pride, refused the money, until finally accepting it in 2003.

In Petersburg the doctors knew they faced a Sisyphean battle. They saw the fight for what it was, an issue of national security. "We can do only so much," said Voronin, who each month took into his care additional babies abandoned by mothers with HIV. "It all comes down to economics and political will." Putin, he said, must make HIV a top priority. "Never mind Chechnya. This is our future, and we are losing it."

TEN

IF ANYONE WAS determined to ensure his city had a future, it was Valery Gergiev. If anyone could lead Petersburg's cultural revival, it was Gergiev, the artistic director of the Mariinsky Theater, known abroad by its old Soviet name, the Kirov. For decades the Mariinsky and the Bolshoi had been locked in a fierce rivalry, but by now the competition was over. The Mariinsky toured East and West, wherever Gergiev wished, while the Bolshoi fought off artistic and physical decay. As a result of Gergiev's musical and fund-raising genius, the Mariinsky had cut international recording deals, and its ballet troupe won raves in Europe and the States, evoking comparisons to Diaghilev's Ballets Russes. As his city prepped for its grand birthday, Gergiev had become one of the world's most sought-after conductors–since 1997 the first principal guest conductor at the Metropolitan Opera House in New York–and his house was one of the most dynamic in the world.

The theater, which stands not far from the Griboyedov Canal where Starovoitova lived, was built in 1860 as the tsar's palace of enlightened leisure. Its grand rotunda of pale chartreuse, flanked with stately wings laced with white moldings, was a monument to the lost era. Few theaters could claim greater history. Yet its rise from the Soviet ashes, as even his critics conceded, was all due to Gergiev. The maestro had become that rare species, a classical music celebrity.

His climb had not started easily. A son of the Caucasus, Gergiev came crashing on the gates of Leningrad's cultural elite in the 1980s. He was not welcomed warmly. A son of a Soviet colonel, he'd been raised among the hirsute footballers of Vladikavkaz. At twenty-three, after studying conducting under Ilya Musin, the Soviet master, at the Leningrad Conservatory, Gergiev won the Herbert von Karajan Competition in Berlin. Two years later he conducted his first opera, *War and Peace*. He was thirty-five when the Kirov voted him head conductor.

Gergiev now kept one of the busiest schedules in the music world. In addition to the Mariinsky and the Met, there were regular gigs in Washington, D.C., Vienna, London, and Salzburg. And "the Gergiev Festival" in Rotterdam. Critics accused him of overextension; friends worried about his stamina. But he was always eager to court the foreign press. We would meet often. We rarely talked opera, ballet, or symphonic orchestration. We talked politics. (After all, the new man in the Kremlin was an old friend from his days in the mayor's office. Moreover, one of Putin's best friends, the godfather of his elder daughter, played cello for Gergiev.) We talked soccer. (The game had been his first love. He'd dreamed of playing professionally and still liked to watch games on a small television backstage.) We talked finance. (He worried that the tech crash could soften sponsorship.) Yet no matter what the conversation, the final line was always the same, the future of the Mariinsky.

Zealous, stubborn, and savvy, Gergiev was, above all, ambitious. He religiously fought the slur that the Mariinsky was a provincial house that filled a niche market. He pushed his singers to new heights, forcing them to sing Verdi, Mozart, and Wagner, in addition to the standard Russian repertoire. Petersburg was no cultural backwater, he insisted. "Why can't Russians sing Wagner? And why not Verdi?" Verdi, he reminded one and all, had premiered *La forza del destino*, a Gergiev staple, in the Mariinsky. "We do more Verdi," he liked to boast, "than most Italian companies." If Russians could now sing Verdi at La Scala, Covent Garden, and the Met, he asked, "Why shouldn't they do it here?"

In 2000 Gergiev moved into megaoperas. He hired Andrei Konchalovsky to direct a revival of Prokofiev's *War and Peace*. Konchalovsky, brother of Nikita Mikhalkov, was once known as the director of *Tango & Cash*, a Sylvester Stallone vehicle that ran far off the tracks. The opera was an elaborate, lavishly funded production—with more than fifty soloists, a hundred choristers, and two hundred extras—all trying to keep their balance on a revolving stage. The audiences loved it, the critics raved, but rumors shadowed the production. On the eve of Putin's election, Gergiev and Konchalovsky had gone to the Kremlin. After an hour and a half audience, the two went out of their way in an interview on state television to bless Putin's rule. Russia had no troubles with free speech, freedom of the arts, anything of the sort, they insisted.[56] For many, it was an unseemly act of kissing the ring. Ever since, even in the corridors of the Mariinsky, the president's patronage was accepted as fact.

Gergiev did little to quell the envy of his compatriots. He had recently embarked on a new dream, annexing New Holland Island, an unused and decaying Soviet military complex, which lay across the canal behind the Mariinsky. He imagined a state-of-the-art music and arts center, replete with commercial subsidiaries, to rival Lincoln Center and Covent Garden. The undertaking, he conceded, would cost hundreds of millions of dollars. But Gergiev boasted an enviable record of reaping private and state support. The Cuban-born opera patron Alberto Vilar, a tech stock multibillionaire, had already dedicated millions to the Mariinsky, before he fell behind on his pledges to other major opera houses. "And the state," Gergiev said, would not "stay totally unmoved by the idea." The money to build it, he insisted, was out there. "How many billions left Russia illegally in recent years?" he asked. "Someone will take this chance. You can build a casino, an entertainment palace, or a factory. But it will be ugly. It is the nature of human beings to destroy. We would like to change that."

One summer night, well after midnight, we sat not far from the Neva in a stylish new restaurant, all white walls and wood tables, opened by a friend who'd recently moved home from New Jersey. It had been a long meal–of sturgeon and house vodka. Gergiev was enjoying a Cuban cigar. The tall windows were open, and the air was soft. He became philosophical.

"Think back a few years," he instructed me. "Russia was not enjoying its best days. Everything was in decline: stability, the state, the economy. The war in Chechnya took not only energy and money but lives. Almost nothing was possible. Every day then I told everyone here one thing: 'We are dancers, singers, musicians–performers. This is what counts. Perform, sing, dance. Dance, sing, perform. Sing, dance, perform. Then you will have people come to see you.'"

Gergiev understood the ironies of his position. He had become the country's most captivating cultural star, with political patrons at home and superrich devotees abroad, but he would always have to fight to earn respect in his own city. He would forever be a Caucasian at the helm of one of Russia's most fabled institutions. And as much as he railed against the city's reputation, even he could not ignore the criminal tide. He never traveled in Petersburg without a bodyguard. "Give us time," he said, almost pleading. "The business of culture here may still be unformed, but we have the tradition. We have a place to return to, to find the new foundation." It was not just the Mariinsky, he said. The whole city was changing. "Soon everywhere you look, the revival will come," he promised. "Everyone here is evolving at last. Things at last are moving in the right direction. Everyone's trying to rebuild his own world, to remake himself anew."

NO RESTORATION PROJECT would be more ambitious than the one just beginning out on the marshy lip of the Finnish Gulf. The Constantine Palace, an eighteenth-century gift from Paul I to his son Grand Duke Constantine, had stood for decades as an abandoned shell. When hints of the plan hit the papers, the locals who skied across its untended gardens and ice-fished in the frozen gulf nearby, dismissed the idea of reviving the thousand-room palace to its baroque grandeur as a farfetched dream. But the rumors persisted. The new president, it was said, the local boy who had made good, desired a country estate where he could unwind in style.

One morning in winter, after a regular visit to Linkov to check the status of the Starovoitova case (he no longer called it an investigation), I went to see the palace—Putin's Palace, as Yevgeny, the driver of the Volga, a round-faced engineer recently retired from the navy, called it. We drove out along the gulf's frozen edge on the Peterhof Schosse. The snow was wet. It fell in thick sheets, blanketing the tin roofs and barren streets in silence. We passed the old Soviet warships rusting in the wharves and the children skiing through the woods. Yevgeny had little patience for the Kremlin's latest reconstruction project. He had once made his living calibrating the missile guidance systems of the Northern Fleet. If NATO hadn't blocked Russia's deals to sell rockets to Cyprus and India, he said, he would still have a job. Putin should pay attention to the military, he grumbled, not to some dream of grandeur that was sure to cost more than all the officers of the fleet had earned in their lifetimes.

The palace had been lifeless when in August 2000, three days after the *Kursk* went down, the men from the Kremlin first came. They laced a ribbon of white plastic from oak to oak around the main house and erected a metal fence topped by concertina wire. Then they posted the laser-printed confirmation notices: "SITE IS GUARDED. By Order of the Property Department of the President of the Russian Federation." By then the Kremlin had made it offical. The president, who had taken to showing off his hometown to visiting dignitaries, required the seaside residence to host heads of state and royals. With helipad, drawbridges, and fountains, it would have to be done in a hurry; the city's birthday was fast approaching. The cost? The best estimates started at two hundred million dollars.

German shepherds now prowled the grounds, but it was plain to see the restoration would not be easy. Built in 1720 by Niccolo Michetti and Bartolomeo Rastrelli, it had once been a grand house with an arched grotto out back and sweeping gardens that sloped to the gulf. The estate even had its own arrangement of discreet canals that carried water from the grotto through the topiary to the shore beyond. Little remained of the original elegance. The gardens were iced-over hummocks. The Nazis had camped out in the palace and left it looted and scorched. Once the siege ended, the Soviets had revived it. For years the house had been a dormitory for the cadets from the next-door military academy. For a time it had housed juvenile delinquents. The hooligans had stripped everything, even the wallpaper. Now there was nothing inside, the guard informed me, but frozen empty rooms. No one could live in there. Except the vagrants. But they'd all been kicked out months ago.

In town many refused to believe the state could be so bold. Not Lev Lurie. When he spoke of Putin's Palace, he simply shook his head. It was the fateful allure of Petersburg's lost past. The *skazka,* the fairy tale Likhachev had warned of, was beguiling. We sat again in the Mexican restaurant. April was nearing, but winter had not abandoned its grip. Ice still coated the sidewalks. Lurie was enjoying a pint with a colleague, a gray-bearded poet. They'd been discussing the odds of raising a grassroots Social Democratic movement in Russia. The poet thought maybe the answer lay in the villages. Maybe there, he thought, the people were wiser. Maybe there, doubt, not loyalty, still ruled the day. Lurie wasn't hopeful. "The *skazka* of our great lost past has grown too fashionable," he said from under a cloud of smoke. Not only had politicians seized it as a usable past, but a lot of folks were making money off it. It was only natural, Lurie figured. A heritage industry was a sign of economic rebirth. Still, it could be dangerous, he mused, for "a whole city to remake itself in a false image."

🕸 ELEVEN 🕸

THE LENINGRAD SYMPHONY, as Shostakovich's Seventh is known, has no words. Yet according to his biographers, Shostakovich had once considering adding them. In an homage to Stravinsky and his *Symphony of Psalms,* he had entertained the idea of a soloist singing two lines from the Ninth Psalm:

> *When He maketh inquisition for blood, He remembereth them: He forgetteth not the cry of the humble.*

Have mercy upon them O Lord; consider my trouble which I suffer on account of them that hate me; thou hast lifted me up from the gate of death.

In a triumph of art over war, the symphony was performed in the city at the height of the Nazi seige. Shostakovich, however, chose not to include the lines. It is a shame. Although the religious themes remained in the music, the words would have resonated with poignancy during the blockade. They would also have lasted. Half a century later, in the composer's old town, even as memories of the siege and the purges faded with their survivors, the words had gained new relevancy. The longing for an "inquisition for blood" that might hear "the cry of the humble" remained as great as ever.[57]

Rimma Yakovlevna and Vasily Stepanovich Starovoitov wanted to believe otherwise, but they knew that those behind their daughter's murder would never face justice. Galina Starovoitova's parents lived in a Soviet apartment tower set off from the Peterhof Schosse, a sparse birch grove away from the Finnish Gulf. The apartment house stood on Ulitsa Chekistov (Street of the Chekists). Rimma was seventy-nine, and Vasily eighty-three. They saw nothing ironic, and nothing wrong, with their address.

"Not all the Chekists were necessarily bad, were they?" Rimma said. Starovoitova's mother was small, but a woman of big shoulders and few illusions. She squared up her tiny bright eyes and awaited a response.

We sat at a plain plastic-covered table in the middle of a bright living room. Vasily sat apart, in an armchair in a corner. He would have retreated to another room had Rimma let him. The murder had shattered his life. Vasily would rather Rimma do the talking, but on the subject of secret policemen he had to disagree.

"Most of them *were* bad," he said, "and the same is true now." He did not know who had killed their daughter, but he was sure *they* knew. "And they won't tell us a thing," he said. "Now is that justice?"

I had come on a Sunday visit with Olga, Galina's sister. When we first met, Olga had had faith in the FSB investigation. A few months later her faith had wavered. A year later she fumed that the case had been buried. By the winter of 2001, on the third anniversary of Galina's murder, she and her parents sued the FSB. They had wanted to see the hundreds of files the security service had compiled in the investigation. A Petersburg court rejected their case.

Vasily and Rimma had once believed in the old order. They had been Party members in high standing. Rimma had worked in the local apparat. She'd known Grigori Romanov well. Vasily had been one of the Soviet Union's most decorated tank engineers. He'd headed the country's premier tank design institute, had even won a Lenin Prize. The living room shelves were crowded with medals. Yet he was most proud of a small steel souvenir, a miniature model of the *lunokhod*, the Soviet moon buggy he had helped design.

They had met during the war in Chelyabinsk, the country's main tank production center, and married when peace arrived. Galina was born the next year. In 1948, they'd come to Leningrad. "My parents are a different generation," Olga had said. She had almost tried to apologize. "They genuinely believed in the system."

Yet even as the girls grew up, and Galina's stubborn independence emerged, Rimma and Vasily had supported her. "Papa wouldn't always agree with her," said Olga, "but he'd always demand that she carry on in her battles."

As Rimma recalled Galina's childhood in the placid, benign Leningrad that was no more, Vasily stared straight ahead. He kept his large hands together, the ends of his rough fingers touching. His health had long not been the best, Olga had said. But in recent months he'd gone deeper into himself. He sat unshaved in an old flannel shirt, beltless trousers, and slippers. It was always "opinions," he said. "Galya," he added, "never kept her opinions to herself." A smile flashed across the gray bristle. "She'd never take a no, never settle for a false yes. She'd only ever had her principles as weapons, but she had fought to the end." That was just the way, Vasily said, his daughter was.

Her parents knew that Starovoitova had long suffered tumult. There was the failed first marriage. Her ex-husband had moved to London, and her son, Platon, had joined him, taking her only grandchild. And although not long before her death she had remarried, the parents knew well that she had not been settled. Politics, not family, had always driven Starovoitova. And her parents had long witnessed the cost. They knew that her speaking out against the war in Chechnya and her railing against corruption, anti-Semitism, and nationalism would win her few friends. They had also known that even as her influence waned–in the Duma she could rally no more than two dozen votes–in her last days, perhaps more than ever, their daughter still stirred passions as few others did.

Her aides, however, had seen signs of renewal in her final days. Her 1996 presidential run was little more than a symbolic act of defiance, but Starovoitova, they said, had been pondering a race in 2000. The country had no interest in "a president in a skirt," she told Linkov. Yet she still dreamed of leading Russia's fractious liberals in a return to the idealism that had once united them and launched Yeltsin to the Kremlin. In the summer before her death there had even been signs of a warming from on high. On June 12, Independence Day, Starovoitova received an invitation, her first in years, to a reception in the Kremlin. It was a crowded affair in the gilded St. Catherine's Hall, but Yeltsin made a special effort to find her, no small feat given his medical status at the time. As Yeltsin approached, Starovoitova extended her hand to shake, but he kissed it. He took her elbow and led her aside. When they were alone, Yeltsin leaned forward and told her how much he missed her advice. Starovoitova by then had no great love for the president, but the gesture moved her. "They had gone through so much together," her Duma aide Yodkovskaya said. "The whole country had. That he would find her, in that crowd on that holiday, meant a great deal to her." In the days before her murder, she was preparing, her aides said, to meet again with the president. After kissing her hand, Yeltsin, with characteristic bravura, had barked to an aide that the lady from Petersburg should be granted a permanent Kremlin pass.

IN THE DAYS after Starovoitova's murder, bold proclamations on the ineluctable triumph of good over evil had filled the Petersburg air. As the years passed, however, the inevitability of that victory lost its certainty. Some still called the politician a martyr, but many now doubted the power of Providence and the promise of divine justice. Like most debates in Petersburg, it was not new. In the first years of the nineteenth century, a French Mason sent to Alexander's court as the envoy of the Sardinian monarchy, a jurist who until 1789 had faced a legal career of uncertain consequence and who had risen to prominence jousting in Petersburg salons, had asked the same question. Sadly, Joseph de Maistre's *Soirées de Saint-Pétersbourg*, a work that comprises nearly a dozen philosophical dialogues and stands as a landmark in the history of ideas, is little known in Russia.

In the first dialogue, on a gentle white nights evening, three confreres–a count, chevalier, and senator–float in a boat on the Neva. "Nothing is rarer," wrote Maistre, "nothing is more enchanting than a beautiful summer evening in St. Petersburg. . . . The sun, which in more temperate zones sinks quickly in the west leaving behind it only a brief twilight, here slowly brushes an earth it seems regretful to leave."[58] As the men savor the spectacle, the chevalier suddenly remarks, "I would like to have here in this boat with us one of those perverse men born for society's misfortune, one of those monsters that weary the earth. . . ."[59] The debate is engaged. The topic: "the happiness of the wicked and the misfortune of the just." Until midnight comes to the city's bright skies, the three men rock gently on the river, taking turns to assay the disbursement of good and evil on earth. Devotees of Maistre like to speak of his modernism.[60] Clairvoyance may be more apt, for nearly two hundred years later, few questions in the old city of the tsars carried greater urgency or ache.

EVEN KUMARIN, the man who assured me he was no more than the retired vice chairman of the Petersburg Fuel Company, had his own deeply held opinion on the debate. "Endru," he had said, leaning in, "I take it you've read *War and Peace*?" I had. "Do you remember Prince Andrei's dream?" I did.

Prince Andrei Bolkonsky, wounded at Borodino and suffering a terrible fever, dreams he is dying.

He was conscious of an aloofness from everything earthly and a strange and joyous lightness of existence. Without haste or agitation he awaited what was coming. That inexorable, eternal, distant, and unknown–the presence of which he had felt continually all his life–was now near to him and, by the strange lightness he experienced, almost comprehensible and palpable. . . .

He dreamed that he was lying in the room he really was in, but that he was quite well and unwounded. Many various, indifferent, and insignificant people appeared before him. . . . Gradually, unnoticed, all these persons began to disappear and a single question, that of the closed door, superseded all else. He rose and went to the door to bolt and lock it. Everything depended on whether he was, or was not, in time to lock it.

Terror comes over Prince Andrei in the dream. He knows that death stands behind the door, but he cannot lock it. Death enters and seizes him. But at that moment, just as he dies in the dream, Prince Andrei awakes in reality.

"Yes, it was death! I died—and woke up. Yes, death is awakening!" And all at once it grew light in his soul and the veil that had till then concealed the unknown was lifted from his spiritual vision. He felt as if powers till then confined within him had been liberated, and that strange lightness did not again leave him.[61]

Kumarin had had the same dream. Twice. First in the KGB jail. The cell, he said, was small—four by ten feet—with only a wooden bunk, bare mattress, pillow, and blanket. But the jail had a great library; its shelves were filled with "confiscated literature"—even Pushkin's uncensored works. Kumarin rose at six every morning and read. He had found *War and Peace* there. He'd read it before, back in the *internat*, but in jail he picked it up again and reread Prince Andrei's dream. That night he'd had the same dream. He dreamed that he woke up and was trapped alive in a grave. So when he truly woke up, he said, and saw he was only in a KGB cell, "life didn't look so bad." The second time was as he came out of the coma after the assassination attempt. He had fond memories of the coma. For twenty days he had lain there, enjoying, as he put it, "this sweet sensation, the sweetest of my life."

The dream had taught Kumarin something. "You know how they say only the good get to heaven and the rest go to hell? It's not true. There's another realm, this world after death, and it's a wonderful feeling. Bliss." He knew, he said, because that was where he had been those twenty days. "It's only here on earth that they try to scare you, tell you only the good make it up there. It's not true. We all go to heaven. God forgives everybody. He sees all, and He accepts all. That's what I saw in my dream."

The wisdom struck an odd echo. Above the entrance to an eighteenth-century palace now fading in its former elegance along the Fontanka Canal, its facades sprouting cracks and its courtyards weeds, one could still find the motto of the Sheremetev family, once one of the richest in the land: "DEUS CONSERVAT OMNIA." Akhmatova, who for nearly thirty years lived in a drafty wing in the rear of the palace, called it the Fontanny Dom, the Fountain House.[62] The poet had made famous the motto of the house of

Sheremetev, the hope of a merchant dynasty. She took it for the epigraph to her "Poem without a Hero." Few who visited her old rooms, now a museum that breathed with life, failed to hear the words translated from the dead language. The Latin, they learned, means "God saves all."

PETERSBURG HAD DONE its best to spruce up. It put on new lipstick and here and there a bit of gloss. But when you walked a block or two off the Nevsky, you found the same lean landscape Brodsky had left three decades before. The city, he wrote, had "almost a starved look, with, as a result, more definite and, if you wish, nobler features. A lean, hard face with the abstract glitter of its river reflected in the eyes of its hollow windows."[63] Petersburg, however remains the city of perseverance. It may suffer a crisis of identity, a rising flood of crime, and unchecked epidemics of HIV and drug abuse, but the city somehow thrives. As Aleksandra Mikhailovna Morozova, the great-grandmother who every year still baked blockade bread, put it, "the city seems to live to suffer."

One blustery blue sky afternoon in April, I walked out to the unguarded flame in the middle of the Field of Mars. The field, the largest open space in the center of the city, is a grassy rectangle, sparsely adorned by a few wane lilacs, that stretches, a short walk from the Nevsky, between the Moika Canal and the Neva Embankment. A marsh before Peter ordered it filled with earth in 1710, the field was originally called the Tsaritsyn Meadow. By the century's end Paul I had built the magnificent guards barracks, complete with Doric porticoes along the field's western edge, and renamed it in honor of the Roman god of war. It long served as the imperial parade grounds, the dusty site of annual spring reviews. Hussars, Cossacks, cuirassiers, and dragoons, by the tens of thousands, had charged here on horseback in front of Romanovs kept at a safe distance in loges.

I joined the half circle of young people in the center of the field. Some stood; others sat on a bench pulled close. The flame danced high and wild. Some kept their feet near its base; others stretched their hands to its tip. Some sipped warm beer in fat brown bottles; others smoked. But all stared at the undulating thread of heat. They were as silent and motionless as if in prayer. It was a tradition dating from the 1960s–back when Leningrad youth were hip–hipsters with no place to go. Day and night, throughout the long months of the Petersburg winter, the young still converged here. Strangers, they sought company and warmth.

The field had always been a place of sacrifice–to the imperial order, to revolution, to war. During its days as a parade ground, so great were the numbers that took part in the cavalry exercises that many–spectators and participants–had died here. The Soviets had refashioned it a memorial to those who gave their lives to their cause. The flame was squared at a distance by four walls, low and open, great blocks of red granite. Chiseled into the stones were purplish lines from Anatoly Lunacharsky, the People's Commissar for Enlightenment:

> *The immortal fallen shall have eternal life with the people*
> *for their noble deed.*
> *He who laid down his life for the people has toiled, struggled,*
> *and died for the greater good.*

The field was the Bolsheviks' first burial ground. Here in the spring of 1917, the martyrs of the February Revolution were buried in a mass grave. Soon they were joined by the fallen of Great October and later of the Civil War. Locals now called it the Red Cemetery. During the blockade, as some still remembered, they grew vegetables here.

IN MY MIND IT had become "The Song from the Yenisei":

> *This is all that will remain after me,*
> *This is all that I will take with me,*
> *Two dreams and a glass of sorrow*
> *That we, arisen from the dead, drank to the end.*

It was the mournful ballad the crew had sung on my last night on the river. Olga from the Krasnoyarsk museum had called it depressing. The boys had paid her no notice and kept singing. Ever since Norilsk I heard the song everywhere. In Moscow it blared from tape decks in underground passageways. On a night train to Samara, it came through the compartment's thin wall, sung by new recruits drinking their way to daylight. It was played across Russia, but it was a Petersburg song by a Petersburg band, DDT. This was the city of poetry, but to many, its greatest poetry was song.

> *I don't know why I am given to you.*
> *The way of war rules me.*
> *Don't cry now, but if you can, forgive.*
> *Life is not sugar, and death is not tea.*
> *I will bear my way. So good-bye my friend, and farewell.*

The congregation at the flame remained silent. But as the spring sun fought the dusk for the last of the day, the cold air broke. The blue sky dissolved at its edges into orange and red, and snow filled the air. Giant white flakes flew like feathers breaking free of a pillow. The sun's rays gained sudden strength, streaming through the sheets of white. As the snow gently settled, it whitened black leather, laced eyelashes, disappeared on tongues. And as the sun slipped behind the glistening roof of the Pavlovsky Barracks, I again heard "The Song from the Yenisei."

> *Memory sits with us at the table, the candle's flame is in its hands*
> *You were so good, look at me, don't be silent*
> *On the white wall the black moon rings the seagulls' cries*
> *Draw something on the window and, by the river, whisper good-bye.*

Akhmatova had provided a beguilingly simple answer: memory. But everywhere in Petersburg others talked of forgetting. Amnesia, they said, relieves pain like little else. The wish to forget, in fact, to repress memory, in a city that had suffered so much, made sense. It was a balm the whole country would choose, if allowed to. Shalamov, in his *Kolyma Tales*, had recognized the strength of forgetting: "A human being survives by his ability to forget. Memory is always ready to blot out the bad and retain only the good."[64] So had Lidiya Ginzburg in her *Blockade Diary*. The law of forgetfulness, she wrote, is "one of the cornerstones of civilization." Yet like Akhmatova, and the survivors of the massacre in Aldy, Ginzburg had favored the law of remembrance. She had quoted Herzen: "He who could live through it must have the strength to remember."[65]

Peter's city, for all the bloodshed and corruption of its reformation tragedy, still strove for a new age. For some, the transformation would come with the rise in small business and Internet connectivity; for others, with the decrease in suicide and drug abuse; and for a delusional few, with the restoration of the imperial order. But for many, the city already breathed anew, resigned to its singular fate, to live less as a modern metropolis than a fictional creation. Spectral souls had long inhabited its streets, haunted the imperial palaces and Soviet communal apartments. The myths–from the benevolent tsarist past to the present *mafiya* rule–would surely live on.

"Petersburg lives on myths," warned Lurie. "It may need them to survive."

"Something about the place," said Kumarin, "it breeds legends."

"Ours is a city of spirits," Likhachev had long ago concluded.

They were of course right. Petersburg celebrated both the dead and the imagined.

VI. MOSCOW

"EVERYTHING IS NORMAL"

We wanted the best, but it turned out as always.

–Viktor Chernomyrdin,
Russian prime minister, 1992–1998

☙ ONE ❧

IT WAS ONLY NATURAL, said Oleg Orlov. "You want to find a rational explanation for the inexplicable. So you search. But it doesn't mean there is one." Orlov should know. We first met more than a decade earlier, back in the buoyant days of perestroika, when Memorial was just getting started and I was a grad student in Moscow. Perhaps more than anyone, he had investigated the human rights abuses wrought by the combatants in the "hot spots," as the war zones that ignited across the old USSR were called. In the months after the massacre in Aldy, Orlov and his colleague Aleksandr Cherkesov had written a seventy-one-page report documenting the terror. I had come to Orlov to compare notes. I had also told him the sad tale of Andrei Sazykin, the young conscript killed in Grozny on August 6, 1994, the boy whose parents had looked at me and wondered why their son had died. We had sat together in the Moscow headquarters of Memorial, in an airless office lined with dissidents' memoirs and files of alleged injustice, and wondered when Russian jurisprudence would shed its Soviet past.

I had tried to understand it in Chechnya as well. In Aldy, I had sat in the courtyard of Aset Chadayeva's house, under the trellis heavy with overripe grapes, and searched. As the tea her mother poured grew cold, I sat in the still heat with the survivors and tried to separate horror from reason, grief from fact. Together we had tried to find a cause for the Fifth of February. But we could not.

I confessed to Orlov that after a year of searching, I still knew little. I had looked for answers: They were drunk; they were high; they were avenging dead comrades; they were settling old scores; they'd been told that behind every old man and young woman lurked a well-armed rebel. Yet a year later no answer seemed more credible than any other. It wasn't enough, I came to realize, to go to the site of the massacre, to interview witnesses and survivors. I wanted to follow the road from Aldy, to see where it led.

"Why bother?" the American diplomat, that sober-minded veteran of years in Russia, had asked. He'd seemed bemused by my pursuit. "So you write up the story, 'Another massacre of innocent Chechens'? What does it add? By now the whole world knows the Russians hate the Chechens."

Even Sergei Kovalyov, that rare voice of reason in the Duma, knitted his brow. "Why Aldy?" he wondered. Kovalyov had been one of the first to warn of the generals' madness in Chechnya. He had done more than carp. He had borne witness. In the first weeks of the first war, Kovalyov had spent nearly three weeks in Grozny, from December 16, 1994, to January 5, 1995. He had been there when the Russians first stormed the capital. Yet as he spoke, I heard the common sense of the American diplomat. "After all," Kovalyov said, "Aldy was just one of many massacres."

They were right: the human rights advocate, the Duma deputy, the diplomat. Even before September 11, 2001, in the inconvenient "small" wars of the post–cold war era, mass murder had made a remarkable comeback. Massacres now arise so often they have become a staple of modern journalism. The news that the blood of innocents has again been shed is nearly certain to make the front page. Such prominence, however, may reveal a predilection for sensation over substance. For as often as such massacres appear in the headlines and flicker across the television screens of the West, they are not given the limelight for long.

By now we have a postmassacre routine. Be it in Africa, the Balkans, the Middle East, or Asia, the bloodletting is depicted in full color and its players are tidily divided into teams: killers and the killed. The body count is tallied, weighed against precedent, and then tucked away in the ever-expansive catalog of atrocity. As we struggle to explain such crimes, we reach for the convenient clichés of the failed new world order, while the victims and their murderers fade from view. We blame "global geopolitics," an "ancient ethnic hatred" or a "religious divide." Rarely do we pause long enough to seek the cause of the horror. With the exception of the Israeli-Palestinian conflict, which often takes center stage, rarely does our interest in massacres sustain us. It may turn from revulsion to curiosity, but rarely do we reach examination before acceptance, and resignation, settle in.

Aldy was no different. From Washington think tanks to Chechen kitchens, even the best informed reached for the catchphrases of the post–Soviet era to explain Aldy. To many, it was true that what had happened in the village on February 5, 2000, was "just another massacre." But this time even Russian officials recognized it was a war crime. Common Article 3 to the Geneva Conventions, the protocol governing internal armed conflicts, is eminently clear.[1] Summary executions, even of armed combatants, even in war, are not acceptable practice. It was true, of course, civilians had been slaughtered in Chechnya before, and more would be afterward. Yet this time, at least in the first weeks that followed the massacre, the official response took a hopeful turn. Families of thirteen victims received death certificates stating that their relatives had been killed in a "mass murder." The yellow-white slips of paper read:

On February 5, 2000, the mass murder of civilians took place during a passport inspection by sub-units of the Ministry of Defense and the Ministry of the Interior of the Russian Federation in the village of Novye Aldy, Zavodskoi District, Grozny.

 T. A. Murdalov
 Investigator for Especially Important Matters,
 Office of the North Caucasus Prosecutor General of the Russian Federation

A second unprecedented move followed. The military prosecutor of the North Caucasus dared blame Russian forces for the killing–specifically, OMON units from Petersburg and Ryazan. Yet because OMON units belong to the regional police forces, they do not come under the purview of the military prosecutor. So, even as he blamed the Russian police units, the military prosecutor washed his hands of Aldy. The case was transferred to the civilian prosecutor, who in turn shuffled it from Gudermes to Moscow to a backwater district in southern Russia and back again to Grozny, where, in 2002, it quietly came to rest.[2]

Despite the death certificates issued, and the finger pointed at the Petersburg and Ryazan OMON, few in Aldy had expected a genuine investigation. The villagers had told of the daily trail of investigators, imperious men from the FSB, MVD, and Defense Ministry and too many prosecutors to keep straight, who paid regular visits in the weeks after the massacre. They exhumed bodies. They took notes. Above all, they interrogated the survivors. "They seemed more interested in learning if we could identify the murderers than in finding them," Bislan Ismailov said. But the survivors had been too afraid to talk. "If you told them you remember the Russians' faces," added Timur Chadayev, "you could be sure they'd come after you."

The FSB had kept a close eye on Aldy after the Fifth. The day after I'd left, Russian forces staged a raid and detained the mullah Shamkhan and Timur. Both were taken away for interrogation. What had they told the American? the Russians wanted to know. Timur was held for a week, then released with his upper body bruised. Shamkhan fared worse. He was let go within a day, unharmed. The villagers now feared the mullah was an informant. How could he not have been beaten? they wondered.

Not long after the dead in Aldy were reburied for the final time, Yuri Dyomin, Russia's chief military prosecutor, told an audience of Western human rights advocates in Moscow that he regretted "the time I have wasted" investigating reports of abuses "based on disinformation." He went on to accuse Chechen refugees of spreading *skazki*, fairy tales.[3]

A YEAR HAD PASSED since the massacre when I went to see the man who ran one of the OMON units officially named, but never formally accused, of being in Aldy on February 5, 2000. The headquarters of the St. Petersburg OMON stood on the Griboyedov Canal, one house away from the stairwell where Starovoitova was assassinated. After weeks of frustration—every time I called I was told to "call back a little later"—I finally got through. The commander did not hesitate. "Step outside in three minutes," he said. "There'll be a car there for you. An Audi, a black Audi." It was.

At the guard booth I was greeted by four OMON officers, each cradling an AK-47. Another officer appeared to vet my press card and usher me through the gates. We entered a broad blacktopped quadrangle. The facing wall featured a mural of OMON officers in full dress, on guard. The figures were topped by their motto, painted in red block letters: "THE HONOR OF THE DIVISION STANDS ABOVE ALL ELSE." The first OMON units were formed in the late 1980s, when the Soviet authorities faced new threats of urban turmoil, twin outbreaks of political demonstrations and violent crime. OMON stands for *Otryad Militsii Osobogo Naznacheniya* (police unit of special designation). It was hailed as an urban rapid reaction force, the Soviet version of riot police or, as many OMON officers would have you believe, SWAT teams in the United States. It was not long before OMON troops, under the Interior Ministry's command, were dispatched to the hot spots. The Petersburg OMON was one of the first formed. By 2000, with more than a thousand members, it had become the second largest in Russia.

Lieutenant Colonel Viktor Kabatsky, commander of the Petersburg unit, had sandy blond hair and sharp blue eyes. For a commander, he seemed surprisingly slight and unusually sunny. But as we shook hands, I felt the coiled strength of a flyweight. He was eager for me to learn about the history and prowess of his unit. He detailed its extensive training. He traced the rise of crime in Petersburg, how it had grown to an epidemic. He told me how the OMON fought it. The bandits in the Caucasus, he said, were no different from the bandits in the backyard. They responded to only one thing, force. He showed me the present his men had given him on the occasion of the unit's tenth anniversary. It was a sword, inscribed in cursive: "HE WHO COMES TO US WITH A SWORD IN HIS HANDS SHALL DIE BY THE SWORD."

When a call interrupted, I scanned the commander's desk. A hunting license. A stack of journals, topped by *Psychology and Social-Rehabilitation Work*. Nearby, a CD: *Songs from the Front*, Soviet Army classics. To the side, an MVD calendar. This month's photograph depicted an OMON officer karate chopping eight cement bricks with his bare hands. The commander hung up the phone and said he was sorry, he'd have to go. "Grozny," he said of the call. One of his men had just been killed.

WE MET AGAIN LATER, for lunch. The commander treated me to a meal in a new Russian fast-food restaurant. "Our own McDonald's," he said. "Only cheaper and fresher." He was sure I'd love the homemade *pelmeni*, meat dumplings. His wife joined us. She was a polite blonde who said little but kept her eyes fixed on mine. Commander Kabatsky was not in uniform. He was taking his wife, he said, by way of apology, to a Jet Ski competition on the Neva. The Petersburg OMON, he wished me to know, was the only OMON unit in Russia that had to guard waterways. He wore a white short-sleeve shirt, pressed beige trousers and Polish-made gray loafers. A pair of gold metal-rimmed sunglasses hung from the top button of his shirt.

In his office he had seemed taciturn, talking quickly through clenched teeth. But in the closeness of the café, huddled with strangers around the grease-spattered tables, he spoke openly. He told of his laments. He could have retired by now, could have gone into private security, like all the others. Could have made a much better living for his wife and their two kids. He expounded on the state of the nation. He favored Putin's "Dictatorship of the Law." "If the state can't enforce its laws," he said, "we're left with the law of jungle." He also backed Putin's campaign against the oligarchs. The time had come, he said, to show people that stealing from the state was not the only way to make their fortune.

He retraced his career. Born near Vladikavkaz, he'd grown up in the Caucasus. Then came the famed paratrooper academy in Ryazan, where General Lebed had been his company leader. In the Interior Ministry troops, he had risen fast. He'd been "lucky," Kabatsky joked, to come up just as the wars broke out everywhere. Shrapnel scars laced his body. He'd been to nearly all the hot spots–Afghanistan, Karabagh, North Ossetia, and, of course, Chechnya.

Kabatsky had made twenty-three "business trips" to Chechnya. Like Shvedov, he called it the Zone. In the first war he'd been among the first troops who entered Grozny in the winter of 1994. That campaign had been a miserable failure, he admitted. But he had done well. He rose to deputy head of the Interior Ministry's intelligence forces in Chechnya. General Anatoly Kulikov, then running the war, took notice. He promoted Kabatsky, sending him to Petersburg.

For more than an hour the commander talked expansively. But when I asked about his men's conduct in Chechnya, he fell mute. Questions about the war, he said, had to be cleared with Yastrzhembsky. "No exceptions." Sergei Yastrzhembsky, as any reporter in Russia knew, was the Kremlin's chief spokesman on Chechnya, the well-groomed spin doctor who prided himself in keeping journalists as far as possible from military sources. "I'm sorry," Kabatsky added, "I wish I could help you." Instead, he asked me to pass the sour cream. Our dumplings had arrived.

IT WAS NOT THE FIRST I'd heard of the Kremlin ban. On an earlier visit to the OMON headquarters in Petersburg, I had met with one of the commander's adjutants. He read me the riot act, refusing even to tell of the unit's whereabouts on February 5, 2000, unless I had the Kremlin's blessing–certified with an official seal. All the same, over the months I managed to pry a few details of the service of the Petersburg OMON in Chechnya.

They had in fact been in Chechnya that week. Nearly three hundred of Kabatsky's men had left Petersburg weeks earlier, embarking on a three-month tour. One morning in the middle of January 2000, they had boarded a snow-covered train and traveled for three and half days before reaching Khankala, the sprawling Russian base on Grozny's eastern edge. On January 27, a week before the massacre in Aldy, the Petersburg OMON suffered their first casualty of the second war. During a *zachistka* of the village of Michurinsky on Grozny's eastern edge, the men found no Chechen fighters. At least none they could see. They split up into small units, three or four men each, to search the village. One unit did not come back.

All the men heard the explosion. Three of their comrades had entered the courtyard of a house and shot their way inside the house—empty. On their way out, they checked the pit dug deep into the frozen ground where the former residents, like so many Chechens during the war, had distilled kerosene into a poor man's petrol. They tripped a booby trap and triggered a bomb. One OMON officer was killed instantly, and two were wounded. The officer killed, Aleksei Stepanov, was twenty-seven. The blast had been so strong, a colleague explained, it left little of him to retrieve. Stepanov had a young wife and six-year-old son. After his death the OMON hired his widow. Her brother, too, had been killed in Chechnya. Now Svetlana Stepanova also worked as an OMON officer.

The Petersburg OMON, with others from around the country, moved into Grozny as the rebels retreated at the end of January. They were among the first federal forces to reach Minutka Square. Other units, Interior Troops and Defense Ministry forces, moved with them. For the Russians, the retaking of Minutka was a momentous occasion, reported that night on state television with pride. The rebels had left, crossed the minefield and were now surrounded in Alkhan-Kala to the southwest of the city.

In the days that followed, from Khankala the officers from the Petersburg OMON moved out, said one who was there, "from suburb to suburb around the city." They followed the perimeter of Grozny, beginning on its eastern edge and moving clockwise. As the OMON officer told of the travails he and his comrades faced from the last days of January into early February, he spoke of hard work, exhaustion, and little sleep. He retraced their movements on a map. It was the same map that had made Ilyas, the young would-be Wahhabi fighter, grow wide-eyed when he told me where the Chechen commanders were based. Its creases had worn into holes, but Ilyas's pen marks remained. The OMON officer's right forefinger circumscribed a crescent moon around the city. The unit's "zone of responsibility" he called it. Aldy fell squarely within it.

AFTER WE HAD FINISHED our *pelmeni*, the commander dismissed his wife. His driver drove her off in a black Volga. Kabatsky suggested we go for a stroll. We walked alone through the leafy square beside the zoo. It was a warm day in August. Thin young boys, pants covered with dirt, kicked a rubber ball amid the drunks sprawled on the patches of grass. We passed a small bulletin board that stood between two benches. On it were stapled advertisements for films and concerts. The Night Snipers, two female rockers who nodded wryly to their city's criminal reputation, were performing soon. The afternoon had grown hot. The square reeked of stale beer, cigarettes, boredom. We walked its length in silence. But as we neared its edge and the black Volga reappeared as if by magic before us, the commander spoke again.

He squatted on his haunches, and I joined him. Muscovites, with the insistent air of urbane sophisticates, like to note that the pose is not native to Russia. Balancing yourself on your heels, often for hours, to wait or talk is a custom of the Caucasus and Central Asia, but one that Russians at some point ages ago seem to have taken as their own.

"Listen to me," Commander Kabatsky said. "I can't tell you where we were and what we did in Chechnya."

I looked hard into his drawn face. His blue eyes shone like agate.

Duty was duty, he said. He could not talk about the "work" of his men in Chechnya. He could tell me only one thing: Chechnya was like no other place he'd fought. He had spent twenty-four months and five days in Afghanistan. With the Afghans, he said, "things were clear." They hated the Soviets, and the soldier's job was to eliminate the enemy. In Chechnya, "everything was so much more complex." It was hard, he said, to know where the enemy lurked. War was not simple anymore. Everything had changed. Even at home nothing was simple now. His was not an easy job, he said. His men didn't even have enough weapons, ammunition, and armor to do what was asked of them in Petersburg. Who could compete with the crime bosses for budgets? Who could match their arsenals? He had only his men, no budget, no new hardware, nothing. And these were the same men who had had to fight in Chechnya since the first war. He could no longer count how many times he'd sent units to the south. Often, several units, each more than two hundred men, went at once. Of course they got paid "almost nothing." He knew what SWAT officers earned in the United States. The information vacuum was over. There'd been exchanges; the American cops had come for a tour. He knew, he said, "what law enforcement officers make in the civilized world."

It was a breathless rant, an inventory of complaint not easily aired by a reticent man of duty. The commander fell quiet. Eager to take his leave, he looked over to the waiting Volga. We were still doubled low to ground, squared up over our feet. The kids, the drunks, the old ladies, no one seemed to notice us. The world on a bright summer Petersburg day seemed to shine, and the mass murder of innocents seemed a remote nightmare of another realm. Crouching low, we could smell the grass, the earth even, lifted by the heat.

"What do we do in Chechnya?" he said. "I'll tell you what. We do *zachistka* operations. That is our job."

TWO

A FEW WEEKS AFTER Boris Yeltsin stunned his compatriots and the world with his New Year's Eve resignation, Mia and I hosted a wake for him. It was a night in deep winter when fresh snow had just mantled the city. Everyone came all the same. The apartment was packed, and the mood buoyant. In Moscow, as John Steinbeck noted on his 1947 visit, "parties are very desirable things." This one, however, was different. Everyone wanted to celebrate, but also to mark the passing of the man who had ushered in the end of the old empire and presided over the worst years of hardship Russia had seen since the Great Patriotic War.

It must have been nearly three in the morning when I called upon my friend Pavel Lobkov for a toast. One of the longest-serving correspondents for Gusinsky's NTV network, and a Petersburg botanist before perestroika, Pavel was, by his own estimation, Russia's first openly gay journalist. He was also among its best. I found him in the kitchen, entertaining the crowd en route to finishing off a bottle of single malt. "Can't you just smell the bogs?" he asked a bemused Serbian refugee as he sniffed another glassful. But when I ushered him into the living room, and he saw the faces turned to him, Pavel found his form.

"Let us raise our glasses," he said in his best on-air tenor, "not only to Boris Nikolayevich Yeltsin but to the years of his reign. They were sweet, and they were bitter, but tonight I'm reminded of the words of one of Russia's greatest historians, Vladimir Ilych Lenin."

Laughter filled the room.

"You may think of Vladimir Ilych as a brilliant revolutionary or a ruthless coup plotter. But he wasn't a bad historian. It was sometime in 1917, between the February and October revolutions, when Lenin wrote—it's in one of the forty-five volumes of his *Collected Works*—that Russia had become the freest country in Europe."

Pavel paused, and the room fell silent.

"Tonight I hear these words again," he said. "Because under Yeltsin Russia again became the freest country in Europe, a place where everything was allowed and anything could happen. With his departure, I fear we've missed our chance yet again. Under Yeltsin, Russia was ugly. It grew fat, greedy, and corrupt. But these last few years may well prove to be the freest of our lives. So let us drink to their passing." The room broke into cheers, as the celebrants drained their champagne and the eyes of at least one or two hardened journalists brimmed with tears.

THREE

"THEY'RE NEARLY GONE now," Semyon Vilensky said. "All the Kolyma girls."

I had known Semyon for years and never seen him cry. He was the former zek who had dedicated his life to publishing the literature of the camps.

On a Saturday morning in midwinter I stood with him before an open coffin and wondered when he had cried last. In the plain pine casket, her cheek-bones blushed, her thin gray hair neatly parted and her eyes closed for good, lay one of his closest friends, Zoya Marchenko. "Our Zoya" Semyon called her. Always. "Now that our Zoya's gone," he said, "who's left?" For a time we stood there, heads slightly bowed, hands clasped behind our backs, in contemplation. But he knew the answer.

In the Moscow winter, little, save the cars crawling along the thinly peopled streets, divides day from night. At every hour a dusky pall hangs close overhead. I stood beside Semyon in an old church on the grounds of the Botkinskaya Hospital, a sprawling pre-Bolshevik relic, where Zoya Marchenko had died.

We stood beside the coffin in the middle of a sparse crowd. Not many had turned out, but they all were veterans of the struggle for human rights in the USSR. Some were famous to their comrades, others unknown. But all their faces, set aglow by the reedy church candles in their hands, looked weary, depleted. The cold air of the church, its red brick blackened by soot, was laced with sweet incense. A young priest—so young his beard but a wispy goatee—chanted the Orthodox rites. He clanked a golden censer on a chain as he circled first Zoya's coffin and then a second coffin. The two coffins lay head to toe. In the second, a bald man no more than sixty was stretched out in a black suit. A sudden death and a beloved father and grandfather, to judge from the swell of keening relatives. They doubled them up now, Semyon explained. It was cheaper for the family. Zoya had almost no family, someone said, only a niece. On the steps outside, I had seen the line forming, pallbearers patiently bearing still more coffins, their black covers whitening in the snow.

ZOYA MARCHENKO died in her ninety-fourth year. Outside of Moscow's dissident circles and historians of the Gulag, she was not well known. Thanks to the reign of the secret police, Solzhenitsyn could not have given Zoya her due, but she was an important source for his *Gulag Archipelago*. Arrested three times, she had spent more than twenty years in the camps and exile. In the far north she had worked on the Railroad of Death near Igarka. She had been a devoted fighter of the Big Lie, as Solzhenitsyn called the ideology that varnished Soviet power. But above all, as Semyon liked to say, she was a Kolyma girl. It was not a nickname he had invented. It was what the women, even in their nineties, had called themselves.

Returning to Moscow after the camps, the "girls" had sought one another's comfort to forge a life on the outside. They formed a sisterhood of strength, once more than a dozen women, who convened in a tiny flat near the old Stalinskaya metro. Their host was Bertha Babina-Nevskaya, at one time a young Petersburg Socialist Revolutionary who'd been hauled off early on. Arrested in 1922, Babina-Nevskaya spent seventeen years in Kolyma. The best known of the group, however, was Yevgeniya Ginzburg, author of *Journey into the Whirlwind* and mother of the émigré writer Vasily Aksyonov. Ginzburg's memoir of the camps was one of the works that first ignited my interest in Russia. I'd read it on the lawn at Wesleyan in a single afternoon. I was unable to put it down. When I came to its last page, the trees, the grass, the sky seemed different. With Zoya gone, the last survivor of the Kolyma sisterhood was Paulina Myasnikova. In her mid-nineties, she still appeared—as herself—in the stage version of Ginzburg's *Journey* that had played for years in a theater downtown. "The Kolyma girls were like sisters," said Semyon, who'd been a brother to them. "But they were more: They were a collective living memory. Each one testified to her own survival and to the women who never made it back, to those they left behind."

Now they were nearly all gone. Semyon, however, would not cry. He would make good on his promise. He would publish their works. Zoya Marchenko was honored, of course, that her Kolyma had gone into Solzhenitsyn's *Gulag,* but she had written her own book, a memoir that remained unpublished.[4] As the mourners dispersed, threading out of the church left and right onto the snow-muffled street, Semyon said he would now publish it. He'd long wanted to do it, he explained, but never had the money. "Of course I still don't," he said as the snow fell, its flakes floating big and soft like the little motes inside a plastic-domed model. "But Our Zoya needs her book."

❦ FOUR ❦

ONE SPRING MORNING, as the frozen sidewalks began to melt and the streets turned into swales of icy black soup, I called again on General Numerov. Nearly a year had passed since our trip up the Yenisei. I dreaded suffering his arrogance again, but I had to. I had to give him a chance to respond. Nikolai Numerov had survived the camps of Stalin and the jails of Hitler. But he would have to face one more interrogation. In my hands I held a card that told the story, at least the state's story, of his years in Norilsk.

In the capacious, near-empty headquarters of his Association of the Victims of Political Repression, we sat at the same long table where I first met him. The photographs of Marshal Zhukov and the Patriarch still hung on the walls. The portrait of Putin, however, was new. It seemed even larger than the old one.

The general, now eighty-one, was in an expansive mood, nostalgic already for our days on the *Matrosov*. He had drawn up a list of a couple more points—Putin's athletic prowess, the impossibility of rapprochement between the Orthodox and Catholic churches, and Mayor Luzhkov's poorly disguised Zionism—that he wanted to be sure I hadn't missed in our conversations. He was freshly tanned, having just returned from a holiday at an old Soviet resort on the Black Sea. He sat across from me, peeling a persimmon with a rusty hunting knife. He was eager that I try the fruit—"the only good thing the Turks ever gave us." No need to be shy, he said. He'd brought back a whole box.

In Norilsk none of the women who heckled the general at his book party had trusted him. They considered him a big shot who, to be sure, had suffered a terrible fall but who'd climbed back nicely, and extraordinarily quickly, to the top of the Soviet heap. His Norilsk, the survivors said, had not been theirs. Some disliked the general for his pressed suit, others for the sheen of his pomaded hair. More than one confided they wouldn't rule out the possibility that he'd served in the camps as an informant, monitoring the politicals. Even my cabin mate Volodya Birger did not hide his doubts. "Our general," he said, "is not a clear case." Numerov, Volodya said, did not fall into any of the usual categories of camp survivors. There were, he said rather ominously, "too many exceptions in his story."

All through the trip to Norilsk and later in Moscow, I tried to fit together General Numerov's story. It was easy to conclude he had received preferential treatment. After all, almost immediately upon arriving in Norilsk, he'd been made head of the drilling team at its biggest mine. He had also spent at least several years in Norilsk living not in the camps but in town. Moreover, after his release Numerov returned to Lithuania and was given a job running a large construction materials plant. Later he won a fine Soviet sinecure, moving to Kaluga, a city just south of Moscow, to head a secret institute. The institute's mandate was to develop a protective wrapping for food that could survive a nuclear war. For decades, Numerov ran the Kaluga institute, until he retired. All in all, it was not the typical zek résumé.

Then Volodya sent me the general's camp card. He had compiled it from the archives in the Krasnoyarsk police files. The card only raised more questions. The dates of his arrest, arrival, and departure from Norilsk, even of his time in transit jails en route, all jibed with the general's telling. Two points, however, did not. The first was the destination to which he was granted permission to travel after his release from the camps in the summer of 1954: Lyubertsy, Moscow Oblast. I consulted the historians. It was rare, very rare, they said that a former zek was allowed to live in the Moscow region. They referred me to the strict rule on resettlement: A returnee could live only a hundred kilometers from a city center. In the town of Pereslavl, just across the Moscow perimeter, there was even a new 101-Kilometer Museum dedicated to the returnees who had settled there. But Numerov, it seemed, was granted an exception. The second point was even more discomforting. It was the official charge for which he'd been arrested: "Service in the execution squads of the occupying forces."

Volodya expected my call. I reached him in Krasnoyarsk at his day job in the computer store. (He still had no home phone.) "I figured you'd find the card of interest," he said in a flat voice. He had not known what to make of it himself. He could say only that it meant the NKVD had accused Numerov of killing Soviet soldiers on behalf of the Nazis. Many of the officers who'd fallen into Nazi hands had of course returned only to be arrested and sent to the camps. But, Volodya added, they were usually accused of treason, not of working in German death squads. The accusation did not seem to clarify anything. It only further obscured the general's story, darkening its mystery.

When I handed the card to him, the general's hands still dripped with persimmon juice. He read it once, then a second time. When he got to the line accusing him of lending the Nazis a hand in killing his own kind, he bent close to the paper and said softly, "Oh my Lord . . ." He went over each word slowly, aloud. After a moment he said, "Anders, I must thank you."

I had expected anger, outrage, shock, not gratitude. But he had never seen the charge made against him more than fifty years ago. He was relieved. Now at last he knew why he'd been hounded his whole life, twice kicked out of the Party, once even after he'd been rehabilitated and headed one of the most important scientific institutes in the Soviet Union! "This," he said shaking the card, "is why they never gave up." Of course, he said, the charge wasn't true. It was just the worst they could think up to throw him away. He dropped his voice to a whisper. "Even now they're still after me."

The general may have had a sinister air, but he did not resemble a collaborator. After all, he was no dissident. He was a true believer. Like many of those sent to the camps, he had helped build the system that imprisoned him. The general never made a secret of it; having to surrender his Party card had been his greatest regret. "I remain faithful to Lenin," he thundered. "It was the Jews who hijacked the Party and brought us Stalin. . . ."

He was already back in the present, peeling a second persimmon, ordering his aged secretary to brew a pot of tea, and once again recalling how as a young partisan in the Lithuanian woods he dressed as a German officer, slipped behind Nazi lines, and led a crew that blew up an armored train carrying German ammunitions to the western front. The tale was a favorite. Soon, too, he was again arguing the need to translate his memoirs into English. It was imperative! "After all, Solzhenitsyn only had the Gulag. I have the Gulag and the Gestapo! I fought on the southern front, suffered a concussion, was captured, became a POW, was thrown in the worst of Hitler's jails, joined the Berlin antifascist underground! What's Solzhenitsyn got? One long tale of Stalinism! I've got my escape from the Nazis, joining the partisans in Lithuania, leading the guerrilla attacks behind enemy lines!"

We had come full circle. I tried to return him to the question of the execution squads. He only shook his head, disappointed in his dear American friend. The masters of the Gulag, he said, were evil, not stupid. They had known his résumé: He was a mining engineer, had graduated from the top mining school in the USSR, knew "a thing or two about explosives." It was only natural, he said, that they'd send him to Norilsk and not waste him

there. As it happened, early on he'd run into an old friend at the mines, who
had helped him get the job at the Medvezhka. As for after the camps, being
allowed to come to Moscow, he'd never lived in the city, had only returned
straightway to the Baltics, where he'd had to fight to become head of that
plant. He'd always had good relations with the Party bosses in Lithuania.
They were *muzhiki*–real men–and recognized another who'd been done a
terrible wrong. Had he been graced with luck? Some might say that. He preferred to call it destiny.

General Nikolai Numerov leaned across the desk. He had some advice:
Don't listen to those longhairs at Memorial and the old biddies up in
Norilsk. "I suffered because I was strong," he said, anger buckling in his
voice. "I was sent to the camps because they needed *muzhiki* to run those
mines." He cocked his jaw, looked into my eyes, and said, "My record's
clear, and my conscience even more so."

Tea was served, in chipped china into which the general dunked dry biscuits, one after another. We drank in silence, the first I had ever experienced
in his company. Then, ever the gentleman, the general rose to escort me out.
At the door he reiterated his desire to see the *Golden Star of the Gulag* in English. It was high time, he said, Solzhenitsyn lost his monopoly. He realized, of
course, the competition was unfair. Solzhenitsyn had friends in the West. The
CIA still published him. Even his wife, he'd heard somewhere, was Jewish.

🕸 FIVE 🕸

AS THE NEW CENTURY opened, after the years of upheaval and excess,
an unexpected quiet settled in Moscow. Putin and Luzhkov, once bitter foes,
now spoke in one voice about the new patriotism and the need for Russia's
economic independence. NO ONE WILL HELP US EXCEPT OURSELVES,
announced the slogan on billboards everywhere. Western Union outlets and
dentist offices sprouted everywhere in town. The ruble seemed to obey the
Central Bank's desires, and the stock market rose, slowly, from the ashes.
Stability, however, threatened to ruin Moscow's Night Town. The party
would continue but be refined.

It was no surprise that when the time came to celebrate the Bolshoi Theater's 225th anniversary with a gala, there was only one maestro in Russia up to the task, Gergiev. Only the ruler of the Mariinsky could lure nearly every star in the political firmament–save the old man convalescing at his dacha–out to the opera in the dead of winter.

The small square in front of the theater glowed white, the snow blanketing its trash. An icy wind had glazed the naked branches of its few trees. Mia and I made our way through the cordon of security agents and metal detectors arrayed in the Bolshoi's lobby and found our seats. Mia had been photographing backstage at the theater for months. Her girlfriend in the press office had been good to us. The scalping along the barricades outside had started at five hundred dollars. We were seated dead center, in the parterre. Two rows in front of us sat the girlfriend.

The Bolshoi never ceases to stir a sense of awe, if only in its grandeur. Its gold and red curtain is massive, the hammer and sickle still prominent and the letters *CCCP* embroidered in gold. On either side, the theater rises six tiers, closely stacked, each a balcony brocaded in gold leaf and shimmering beneath miniature chandeliers. I knew the gala would bring out the cream of Moscow finance and culture, but I had not expected a pageant of Kremlin heavyweights. Gergiev, it seemed, had attracted the entire Putin government and most of the old regime as well.

In the cloakroom I ran into the beet-faced General Manilov, the Defense Ministry spokesman for Chechnya, the man who had steadfastly assured the world that Russian troops would never harm civilians. They were only after the bandits, Manilov had insisted. They would never take the Radio Liberty reporter Andrei Babitsky hostage, let alone hand him over to Chechens working for the FSB. One could never believe Manilov, a nonplussed Babitsky told me when I asked if he'd ever discussed his ordeal with the general. He was hopeless, Babitsky said. "Manilov cannot even get the party line right."5 As the general checked his wool overcoat, I saw him for the first time in civilian clothes, a crisp gray suit. Yes, he smiled, he was stepping out, taking in a night of culture with Mrs. Manilov.

As the parterre filled, the Manilovs settled into seats three rows in front of us. Throughout the first aria I could hear Mrs. Manilov, her purplish white bouffant freshly coiffed, furiously unwrapping sweets. A few rows ahead of them, the men from Petersburg assembled. Anatoly Chubais, as always, stood at the center of the cluster. Once they had been called the Petersburg Team. By now, however, given their preponderance and power, the men from the northern capital were known in Moscow's political and business circles as the Petersburg *Mafiya*. Near Chubais milled two former protégés who had risen fast in Putin's backdraft: Aleksei Kudrin, minister of finance, and German Gref, minister of economics and trade. To the far right sat Nikolai Aksyonenko, minister of railways, a onetime Yeltsin favorite who carried a heavily compromised reputation—even by the local standards. (A year later Aksyonenko was to depart under a cloud of accusations involving missing state funds.)[6] Nearby stood the deputy prime minister, the man who had run the *Kursk* investigation and gone gray in months, and next to him, the venerable head of TASS, who had served every Kremlin chief since Brezhnev.

The Yeltsin crowd was relegated to the first tier. Andrei Kozyrev, the first foreign minister after the Soviet fall, now in the employ of a Western pharmaceuticals giant, sat beside Andrei Makarov, the corpulent superlawyer Yeltsin had tapped to prosecute the Party after the 1991 coup. Nearby sat Dmitri Yakushkin, Yeltsin's former press secretary, and a few seats down, Vladimir Shevchenko, the Kremlin subaltern who handed Yeltsin his every paper and cup of tea—and would doubtless continue to do so until his boss breathed his last.

Putin was not to turn up until the second half, but the tsar's box, high above the gallery of luminaries, was full. Up front sat the prime minister, Mikhail Kasyanov, his wife, and their pudgy-cheeked teenage daughter. Beside him glowered Sergei Ivanov, the president's closest confidant ever since their days in KGB finishing school. Yet all eyes, even in this crowd of jaded elites, were fixed on the bald-headed man sitting in the shadows, stroking his little beard, Aleksandr Voloshin. An erstwhile associate of Boris Berezovsky's, Voloshin had come to the Kremlin in Yeltsin's final years. With the Kremlin in disarray and the government paralyzed every time Yeltsin disappeared for an extended stay at his dacha, Voloshin, the forty-four-year-old chief of the presidential staff, had virtually run the government. A former aide called him a master of "creating compromises and accommodations by sabotage and strong-arming." A number of the former ministers seated in the parterre had sparred with him and lost. By now he was known as the Gray Cardinal. Not only was he one of the prime movers in orchestrating Putin's rise and Yeltsin's early exit into a safe retirement, but Voloshin was one of the last men of the ancient regime still in power.[7]

For the occasion, Gergiev had culled the Mariinsky's greatest hits. He opened with the Overture from Verdi's *La forza del destino* and offered something for everyone: A scene from *Don Carlos*, one of Violetta's arias from *La traviata*, Tomsky's ballad from Tchaikovsky's *Queen of Spades*, a scene from Mussorgsky's *Boris Godunov*, the Overture to *Tannhäuser*. "Moscow after all is not Milan," the maestro later told me. "The more fireworks the better."

While the clock tower scene from *Boris Godunov* played out on the stage, the history of Russia resounded in the Bolshoi. As the Kremlin bells tolled, Tsar Boris flopped from wall to wall, burdened by guilt over the murder of the tsarevich Dmitri, the true heir to the throne. Prince Vasily Shuisky made his entrance. Shuisky, leader of the boyars, the gentlemen-schemers who surrounded the court, yearned for the tsar to entrust Russia to his guidance. The scene reenacted the early-seventeenth-century coup known as the *semi-boyarshchina*, the Rule of the Seven Boyars, that grew from the power vacuum of the Time of Troubles. Shuisky failed to become tsar but succeeded in ruling Russia almost single-handedly. It all sounded so modern, so post-Soviet. Moscow pundits had long ago caught the historical echo. They had dubbed the reign of the oligarchs during the Yeltsin era the *semibankir-shchina*, (the rule of the seven bankers). Voloshin, with his narrow eyes, peaked bald head, and trimmed beard, bore an uncanny resemblance to the tenor singing Shuisky's entreaties to the tsar.

At the bar during the entr'acte the city's worlds of finance and politics mixed. There was no deal making, lobbying, debate, or dissent. Rather, the politically powerful simply commingled with the financially powerful in a mutually reassuring display that the improbable world of Moscow's neocapitalist elite lived on. Men smiled, clasped hands, and threw looks of feigned astonishment at finding one another at so cultural a celebration. In overly polite tones they traded jibes–"So you're not in Paris after all?" "That tan from the salon or Cyprus?" "The Alps too crowded this year?"–before they clapped backs, shared airless laughs, and moved on.

In the center of the chandeliered room, the head of a Gazprom bank stood draining champagne flutes with the chairman of the state bank, Sberbank. Behind them, looking lost and lonely as ever, stood the Central Bank chairman. A stolid Communist holdover and a last-ditch compromise candidate, the Central Banker always seemed to stand alone. In a corner sat the Ossetians. Oversize men with necks as big as bulls', they had filled the row in the parterre in front of us. Their women, young beauties with black eyes that smoldered, had sat across the aisle. Even before the curtain rose, the men were sweating. For Gergiev's gala, they had stuffed themselves into Italian suits. They had waited patiently for the curtain to rise, folding their programs into fans and talking of the recent arrival of the maestro's firstborn. "Thank God it was a boy," they said, as all agreed fatherhood had done wonders for him. By the second aria the Ossetians had shed their ties and decamped to the buffet.

In line at the bar a Putin foreign policy aide chatted up a film actor. The actor, who wore black leather trousers and a white leather jacket buttoned with rhinestones, seemed eager to reach the truffles. Crossing the room, I ran into another top banker, fabulously wealthy, but by his own description, "a tier below the oligarchs." He had come out to me the year before. "Those years I served as an economics attaché at the embassy in London," he'd said, veiling his face with a copy of *Time* so that only his eyes peered out above Katie Couric on the cover. "Well, I was actually in foreign intelligence." He had dropped his voice to a whisper and said he'd never told a journalist the truth. But things were different now: The president had returned honor to the services, and the banker was peddling his memoirs. In the buffet he stood dapper as ever, steering a skeletal redhead by the elbow. The woman was tall and draped in little but sable and emeralds. We exchanged salutations. How wonderful the music was! the former spy-cum-banker cried. And the singing! It almost made you wonder why one traveled anymore. Even the market was heating up again, he said, scanning the bar while keeping a hand on his companion, as if he feared she might float away. Espying the foreign policy aide, now piling large slabs of smoked salmon on small plates, the banker made for the bar. But he was too late. Just as he reached him, the bell sounded.

The rest of the gala passed without fanfare. Only our view was greatly enhanced. The Ossetians never reappeared. Even the balconies, by the time Gergiev's head fell on the last note of Strauss's Overture to *Die Fledermaus*, had half emptied. When the lights went up, the ushers, elderly women faithful to the old ways, shooed their charges from the seats. Mia and I made for a side corridor, where to our great surprise, we ran into a dowdy couple tacking their way through the throng arm in arm. Viktor Chernomyrdin, the former prime minister, and his wife brushed past us. Once king of the Soviet Gas Ministry and never far from the Gazprom nest, Chernomyrdin had done well by Yeltsin. And the gas giant had done well by him. Despite years of pleas from its Western investors, advisers, and creditors for reform, the Soviet behemoth had lived on, grown ever fatter. In retirement, Chernomyrdin reaped what he had sown. He had returned to the Gazprom board.

Now he and his wife were eager to get backstage. Gergiev would be hosting the aftergala party. The door, however, was closed and guarded by a sallow-faced man with stooped shoulders. "Invitations, please," he said. The former prime minister was taken aback.

He gasped. "Don't you know who I am?"

The guard hazily scanned the face. "Oh, so sorry," he said calmly. "I did not see you."

As he opened the door for the Viktor Chernomyrdins, the murmur of the crowd inside, the elite of the Moscow elite, filled the corridor. As the couple marched on, the former spy-cum-banker turned the corner, now leading his female companion by a thin wrist. How marvelous it'd all been! he exclaimed. Gergiev was marvelous, the Bolshoi was marvelous, and, yes, the crowd was so marvelous. The enlivened pomp of the evening had left him beaming. A sign of the new times, he called it. "Don't worry," he smiled icily, "Russia is back."

✸ SIX ✸

BY THE TIME MIA and I left Russia, Putin was no longer a phenomenon. Against all expectations, the former lieutenant colonel in the KGB, who had never held elective office and boasted a popularity rating of less than two percent when Yeltsin named him his chosen heir, had fashioned a new era. "Under Putin" now began people's sentences.

Roy Medvedev, the Marxist historian whose 1971 *Let History Judge* stands as a seminal work on Stalinism, spoke of "the Putin miracle." I went to visit him at the once-elegant sanatorium of the Soviet Writers Union in the village of Peredelkino outside Moscow. Formerly the reserve of writers and poets, Peredelkino now reflected the changing times. The writers were graying, and the New Russians had moved in. The telltale red brick mansions now towered amid the ramshackle old dachas of rotting wood.

Medvedev had nothing but praise for the new man at the helm. After all, upon his taking over the FSB in the summer of 1998, one of Putin's first acts was to invite the historian to the Lubyanka to lecture on Andropov, the last KGB master to rise to the Kremlin. At the time, Medvedev had just published a biography of Andropov, who had ruled the Soviet Union for fifteen months before succumbing to kidney failure.

We sat beneath the pines and talked of Putin. Andropov, Medvedev said, was "clearly a hero." During his tenure at the KGB, from 1967 to 1982, the secret police kept a grip on dissent, yet his fans liked to argue that when Andropov succeeded Brezhnev in 1982, he ushered in a generation of younger, more modern thinkers, one of whom was Mikhail Gorbachev. The myth, which gained new currency in the last years of Yeltsin, held that Andropov had an iron hand but a humanist soul. He was even, devotees insisted, a closet Westernizer. The fable derived from the days when the Western press corps, fed KGB tales, helped ennoble Andropov's image abroad. The new Soviet boss, Western readers were told, was a "scholar" (he wore Coke bottle glasses) who flourished fluent English and conversational German and nurtured secret loves for tennis, the tango, fine scotch, abstract art, Glenn Miller, and American fiction. His was an extensive library, it was said, that even included *The Valley of the Dolls*.

Recalling the Western profiles of Andropov, Medvedev chuckled. But one had to be careful, he warned. The "Good Andropov" was not the Andropov Putin admired. Putin's Andropov was the man who had foreseen the need to restore law and order. "Putin," he said, "like Andropov, understands the need to keep order above all. He realizes the state collapsed with the end of the USSR, and for years, we lived in essence in a failed state." The Yeltsin years managed only a semblance of law, of political order, of democratic institutions. "Putin came in, surveyed the chaos and said, 'We need to go back and learn from Andropov.' We have learned, alas, that the state cannot hold itself together on its own." Putin understood, the historian said, that to survive, the state needed a centralized, strong authority—or else the centrifugal forces would tear the federation apart.

Medvedev was in his seventies now, frail and gray. He had never won the trust or the admiration of the dissidents and historians of Memorial. The author of *Let History Judge* still imagined, as he conceded in a nostalgic moment, that Marxism in Russia was possible. Before I took my leave, we walked back to his room in the sanatorium. He wanted to give me a present. He had just published his thirty-second book, this one a slim political biography of the new president. It was called *The Putin Riddle*.

WHEN YELTSIN CALLED upon Putin to become his prime minister in August 1999, Putin turned white. At the time he had headed the FSB for only a year. The televised scene in the Kremlin was remarkable. Putin's first words were: "*My lyudi voennie* [We are military men]." The message was clear: "We will carry out our orders." Yeltsin had seen the dedication to duty. "The First President," as he would now be known, needed a guarantee of immunity from future prosecution, and Yeltsin got it as soon as Putin took over on New Year's Day 2000.

Putin, however, is more than loyal. The first Russian leader born after World War II, he is above all a *gosudarstvennik*, a believer in the state and in its precedence over the individual. After the crash of 1998, as Yeltsin faded from view, many in Moscow openly feared that the Russian Federation—eighty-nine regions, including Chechnya—could go the way of the USSR. Those who had suffered devaluation and default now feared atomization. Early on Putin spoke of the danger. The talk was not political hyperbole, the new president's aides assured me, but a genuine concern. Yeltsin had dismantled the state, the Putin men said, but built nothing in the void. The new men who moved into the Kremlin and the White House, the seat of the government, spoke with singular confidence of what ailed Russia. They spoke not only with the benefit of hindsight but out of a need to justify what was to come.

Putin moved swiftly, in unprecedented fashion, to strengthen the state. He made it his mission to rebuild the *Vertikal*, as the new men in power longingly called the hierarchy of state control that once tied the far-flung regions to the center and the center to one man. He took on the most unruly of the regional governors. Yeltsin had told them to take "as much sovereignty as you can swallow." In short order Putin reined in those who had: Shaimiyev in Tatarstan, Nazdratenko in Primorye, Aushev in Ingushetia, and Yakovlev in Petersburg.

Before long, he turned his attention to the Duma, reducing it to a supine body dominated by one faction, his. Yedinstvo, the Unity party created as an electoral vehicle for Putin, wielded such parliamentary power that even a high-ranking member of the presidential legal staff winced. "We may be only the country in the world that has a parliament but no pluralism," he conceded. Next, the president reconstituted the upper house, the Federation Council, turning an unpredictable assembly of 178 governors and regional leaders into a hall of rubber-stamping political appointees from the regions.

Putin soon extended his reach far from Moscow. To tighten control in the restive regions, he carved the country into seven federal super districts and dispatched seven plenipotentiaries to run them. Five of the seven Putin envoys were generals—from the army, Interior Ministry, and FSB. To Moscow historians, the plan struck an echo. The borders of the new federal regions closely resembled the military districts Peter the Great had devised in 1708. The press even took to calling Putin's envoys by the tsarist appellation "governor-generals."[8]

At the same time, Putin went after the oligarchs—at least those who no longer nodded at his every word. The two who fell the hardest, and fastest, happened to run the only national media empires that the state did not control. Neither Vladimir Gusinsky nor Boris Berezovsky was well suited for martyrdom. When the need arose, law enforcement officials had little trouble finding fault with their financial evolution over the past decade. On June 13, 2000, Gusinsky found himself locked inside Moscow's notorious Butyrka Prison.

For the titans of the once-heady Moscow market, Gusinsky's arrest signaled the end of an era. Even Potanin, the banker who controlled Norilsk Nickel, never one to roil a cozy relationship with state power, spoke of "a new chill." Potanin rallied seventeen of Russia's most prominent businessmen to draft an appeal to the prosecutor. "Until yesterday," they wrote, "we believed we lived in a democratic country; today we have serious doubts."[9] Detained on suspicion of embezzling "at least ten million dollars" in state funds, Gusinsky stayed in jail four days. Putin, conveniently out of the country, feigned surprise at the arrest. At first he pleaded ignorance. "If there's a political aspect to this case, I am unaware of it," Putin said in Madrid, the first stop on a European tour, ironically intended to lure investors to Russia. The next day he revealed a surprising familiarity with the details of Gusinsky's finances. The mogul, Putin claimed, had failed to repay loans, and his debts totaled $1.3 billion. Only when he had reached Berlin did Putin allow that Gusinsky's arrest had been "excessive." He said he had tried to reach his prosecutor general by phone but failed to find him.

Gusinsky came out of Butyrka fighting, but the experience had left him shaken. (He vowed to start a foundation to improve prison conditions.) He talked of regrouping, but he knew the winds had changed. Aleksei Venediktov, news director at Ekho Moskvy, Media-MOST's radio station, was convinced Gusinsky's arrest came in retaliation for President Bill Clinton's participation on a call-in show during a recent Moscow visit. At the time White House aides did not hide the aim of Clinton's appearance: to lend support to Gusinsky's embattled media in the aftermath of an earlier raid on his headquarters and to underscore the importance of a free press. Just days before Gusinsky's arrest, Venediktov had met with Voloshin in the Kremlin. "He said we were playing dangerously by taking an antistate position and hosting Clinton," Venediktov told me. "He went so far as to warn that the Kremlin 'would be returning fire.'" Commenting on the arrest, Strobe Talbott, then the U.S. deputy secretary of state, found rare public candor. "There is a pattern here, and we have seen it for some time," he said. "It has a look and feel to it that does not resonate rule of law. It resonates . . . intimidation."

Oddly enough, perhaps Sergei Dorenko, then the rabid mouthpiece for Berezovsky on ORT, the national channel that ostensibly belonged to the state but was controlled, in a sleight of hand few understood but all acknowledged, by Berezovsky, described the cold shift best. On the night of Gusinsky's arrest, NTV had rushed to air a special edition of its political talk show *Glas naroda* (Vox Populi). Dorenko had been in his car when he heard of the arrest. He raced to the NTV studio. As he entered the soundstage, surrounded by bleachers filled with politicians and journalists, nearly all of them anxious Gusinsky supporters, Dorenko wore jeans and a sweater and was perspiring heavily. I sat a few seats from him. Once a sworn enemy of Gusinsky and NTV, Dorenko won applause just by showing up. Yet when he spoke, on air without a script for the first time, he rose to the occasion with undiscovered eloquence.

"We thought something had happened these past ten years," Dorenko said. "We thought the old system was broken, that we'd thrown all the robots on the scrap heap. But they've been lying there, and now they've stirred and begun to move again. They're starting to stand up and act. They hear a new music . . . that's how the *siloviki*"–the officers of the "power ministries," the armed forces, police, and security services–"across the country understand Putin's rise to power. Independent of whatever Putin says, they hear a music that we do not hear, and it rules them. They're standing up again, walking like zombies, and surrounding us." Only the new president, the newscaster concluded, could stop them. "If Putin remains silent, they'll just carry on and on–because they've been given the signal."[10]

Gusinsky's arrest shocked even his worst enemy. I spoke with Berezovsky while Gusinsky sat in jail. The days when the two had been allies, partners, even, in a common enterprise, were long gone. They were now bitter rivals. Berezovsky, himself long under prosecutorial scrutiny, knew the crackdown had begun and the prosecution would be selective. "That the state should fight its opponents is normal," he said, but "the methods in this case were inappropriate." Anyone who had done business in Russia since the Soviet fall, he argued, "had broken some law somewhere at some point." Berezovsky liked the line; he used it often. Russia after the Soviet fall was wild, and what passed for business within its borders obeyed its own rules, not the laws of the country. Few could argue. Yet even Berezovsky knew the ruse would hold only so long.

Did he fear for his future? I wondered.

"I'd be a fool if I told you I felt safe in Russia today."

Within months, Gusinsky and Berezovsky were living abroad. Theirs was not the exile of Soviet writers or dissidents. Both still enjoyed lavish residences. Berezovsky maintained, among other properties, a château in the south of France, while Gusinsky retreated to a lavish Spanish villa on the Mediterranean. They tried to cloak themselves in the mantle of free speech. They tried to decry Putin's Russia as a revanchist police state. They tried to salvage their empires. Both had been stripped of nearly all their media properties in Russia.[11] Berezovsky, however, did not lose all his Russia assets, maintaining, Moscow financiers attested, interests in oil, aluminum, and even media.[12] Yet both Gusinsky and Berezovsky knew was what plain to every-one else: Their days as two of the country's prime movers were over.

PELEVIN, THE YOUNG WRITER, the "voice of the new generation," also felt the winds shift. In the winter of 2002 his influence on Russia's young minds won official recognition. *Idushchie Vmeste*, the pro-Putin youth group Moving Together, added his name to their list of "garbage" writers. (Marx was another.) Moving Together launched a campaign to encourage young readers to trade in "trash literature" in exchange for patriotic novels. Earlier, on the first anniversary of Putin's inauguration, the group had rallied on Red Square. They'd sported T-shirts emblazoned with the official presidential portrait and carried placards that read, CLEAN OUT THE GARBAGE IN YOUR HEAD. Pelevin was more than pleased his works were among those chosen for such high-profile criticism. He had seen the reckoning coming.

One night he woke me, as always, from the depths of sleep. He could barely control his excitement. "I have a new joke," he said. "You know the two fateful questions of Russian history?" Every student of Russian history did: "'What is to be done?' and 'Who is to blame?'" He had come up with a new one, he announced, the question that defined the age of Putin: "What is to be done . . . with those who are to blame?"

PUTIN, ECHOING A TRADITION prevalent in Russian history, had done more than revive the spirits of the security forces. His success went deeper than taming cabinet ministers, Duma members, the governors, Berezovsky and Gusinsky. Even as the war in Chechnya churned on, Putin had renewed Russians' sense of themselves. For a great many of his compatriots, he cured their identity crisis.

Medvedev, the historian of Stalinism, spoke of "Putin's nation building." He was not alone. Sergei Kiriyenko, the young technocrat who had served briefly, and disastrously, as a Yeltsin prime minister, said Putin had united the country. The president had dispatched Kiriyenko to the Volga region, enlisting him as one of the new seven presidential plenipotentiaries. When he took the job, Kiriyenko later said, "we weren't living in a unified country—not in any sense, economic or legal."[13] It was not, however, merely a matter of bringing the local and federal laws into conformity. The change went far deeper, said Oleg Khlevnyuk, the young historian whose works on Stalin's Politburo had won him a following at Oxford and Yale.

We met one night for a beer in a fluorescent-lit café across from Solzhen-itsyn's old apartment off Tverskaya Street. By then the balance had been struck. Political life had become more stable, but few dared call it more democratic. There would be no return to Soviet totalitarianism, yet the fear of a backslide remained. In Moscow, Putinian democracy was termed, by his own men, as "controlled." Pluralism, they knew, was a virtue of the "civilized world," something to strive for. Russia was just not ready yet. Khlevnyuk understood the criticism well enough—"It's a police state, and we'll have to sacrifice personal liberties, the rights of minorities, and so on"—but for Rus-sia, right now, he said, the alternative "was just too dangerous." The nation at long last was coming together. For the first time in his memory. Putin, moreover, even with the carnage in Chechnya, had averted the greater threat. "Chechnya would look like a minor squabble," Khlevnyuk said, "if the country had fallen apart." Democracy, he said, took time.

MORE THAN HALF A century ago an American diplomat looked to Soviet Russia and warned Washington against foolhardy attempts to pro-duce in short order a replica of the Western democratic dream. "It behooves us Americans," he wrote, ". . . to repress, and if possible to extinguish once and for all, our inveterate tendency to judge others by the extent to which they contrive to be like ourselves."

George Kennan had foresight. "When Soviet power has run its course," he wrote in 1951, ". . . let us not hover nervously over the people who come after, applying litmus papers daily to their political complexions to find out whether they answer to our concept of 'democratic.' . . . Give them time," he counseled, "let them be Russians; let them work out their internal problems in their own manner. The ways by which peoples advance toward dignity and enlightenment in government are things that constitute the deepest and most intimate processes of national life. There is nothing less understandable to foreigners, nothing in which foreign interference can do less good."[14]

Kennan could imagine the end of Soviet power but not the slaughter in Chechnya. Read today, his argument might be regarded as an apologium for the Western leaders who shunted Chechnya aside as "an internal Russian matter." Yet when read in the wake of the West's ardent attempt to export democracy and the free market, of the failed dream that the good men and women from the "Civilized World" could transplant Western practices and have them take root overnight in Russian soil, Kennan's words ring true.

After the debauchery of the Yeltsin era, the West's romanticism with reform cooled. By 2002 the powerful in Washington, London, and Paris no longer worried about, "Who is Mr. Putin?" After the attacks on the World Trade Center and the Pentagon, they fretted about "losing Mr. Putin." Putin, after all, had made a historic choice. He had sided, however tactically and temporarily, with the West. He had given his blessing to the United States to use former Soviet bases in Central Asia to wage war in Afghanistan against the Taliban and Al Qaeda. Washington's criticism of Russian excesses in Chechnya, never very vocal, became muted. Chechnya was suddenly not just a Russian problem but another front in the global fight against Islamic terrorism.

There was, yes, the sticky problem of George W. Bush's "axis of evil." Iran, Iraq, and North Korea held central positions in Russia's axis of trade and cooperation. Kim Jong Il even took his armored train to see Putin twice inside a year—first in the summer of 2001, then again the following August.[15] Iran meanwhile remained a primary consumer of Russian nuclear technology and expertise. Early in 2002 Moscow reiterated a desire to finish the Iranians' eight-hundred-million-dollar nuclear plant in Bushehr, long a source of contention with Washington. (The Americans feared the plant would be capable of producing weapons-grade fissile material.) But soon the Kremlin went further, announcing in July 2002 a ten-year plan to build five additional reactors in Iran.[16] Within weeks, just as talk of a U.S.-led move to effect "regime change" in Baghdad hit fever pitch in Washington, the Russians made another sudden announcement, disclosing a forty-billion-dollar trade agreement with Iraq.[17] With the Iraqis, the Russians had more than old friendships. They had multibillion-dollar deals to develop their oil fields. Within days of the disclosure of the Iraqi trade pact, Kim Jong Il was back in Russia, on his second pilgrimage, now triple-kissing Putin in the Russian Far East.

For many in the Bush White House, it was all too much to take. Yet others, especially those who had watched Putin closely since his days in Petersburg, recognized the dance. The man from the State Department, a high-ranking official who knew the Russian president as well as any in

Washington, was blunt. "Big *D* or little," he said, "we know Putin's no democrat." Yeltsin, he said, had always proclaimed himself a democrat, always promised the world and produced little. "The thing about Putin is," the diplomat added, stopping just short of apology, "he never promises more than he can deliver—and this guy delivers."

Kremlin advisers had awaited the Republican administration with anticipation. The Clinton team, they liked to say, suffered from the vacillation of the fainthearted. Texans, as one Putin foreign policy aide put it, are "known for their decisiveness."[18] George Bush had proved the Russians right. In June 2001, in their first meeting in a sixteenth-century Slovenian castle, he looked into Putin's eyes and pronounced himself pleased with what he found. "I was able to get a sense of his soul," Bush enthused. "He's an honest, straightforward man who loves his country. He loves his family." Asked if the Russian could be trusted, President Bush replied, "I wouldn't have invited him to my ranch if I didn't trust him."

The Bush administration, even before the exigencies of the war on terrorism, brought a new expediency to relations with Russia. The symmetry was striking. In Moscow the sobriety had begun with Yeltsin's exit. Both Putin and Bush were sports fanatics and teetotalers and not great men of rhetoric. Clinton and Yeltsin had met eighteen times—by Strobe Talbott's count—as many times as the nine previous U.S. presidents had met their Kremlin counterparts, since Truman's first face-to-face with Stalin. Bill and Boris had been great friends, unlikely counterparts who found much in common. Both shared gargantuan appetites and a flair, to put it mildly, for the dramatic. But Clinton and Yeltsin had left the stage of Russian-American relations in disarray. By 2000 charisma was out. The era of romantic intentions and ambitious aims had ended. In both capitals a new pragmatism, lean and cold, ruled.[19]

🕸 SEVEN 🕸

EARLY ONE JULY morning I flagged down a battered Volkswagen and drove out of town with a Serbian carpenter. He'd been dry-walling a dacha colony for the Ministry of Defense and hadn't been paid in weeks. He had fled Milosevic's Republika Serbska a few years before and come to Moscow. Now his ancient VW, its Belgrade plates rusted over, had to cover the rent. Before the crash he'd done well. (He showed me a photo album of his handiwork, snapshots of marble Jacuzzis set into teak.) But now he wondered why he'd ever come. As we negotiated the thicket of Ladas and Mercedes on Prospekta Mira, he cursed the Russians–"They hate each other," "They produce nothing of their own," "They'll never rise from this swamp"–before telling me he had married a Russian, his kids spoke only Russian, and he feared he would never go home.

After an hour we arrived in Star City, the cosmonauts' training center deep in the fir forests northeast of Moscow. Vasily Tsibliyev was happy to see me. Star City was quiet, nearly deserted. He seemed alone. Once upon a time his name had resounded in every Russian home. He'd been as famous as Gagarin or Armstrong or Laika, the space dog. Tsibliyev would rather the world forgot him, but he was the poor fellow at the controls of the Mir space station that terrible day in June 1997 when a supply craft crashed into the station and nearly blew it to bits.

The Russians had recently had brought Mir back to Earth, ending its fifteen years in orbit. To much of the world, the station was an accident-prone dinosaur, an apt metaphor for a onetime superpower in the terminal stages of decay. Yet to Tsibliyev, Mir was simply a mirror of his nation's sad predicament. Ever since we first spoke, only days after he had returned to Earth, the commander had articulated his theory. Mir, he said, was the perfect symbol for Russia's capacity to endure more suffering than Job. Strapped for cash and long overworked, the station, like the country, somehow stayed in orbit against tall odds. Mir he argued, deserved its place in Russian history–alongside the Leningrad blockade, the Battle of Stalingrad, and the Tatar yoke.

Even before the crash, Tsibliyev's final trip to the station had been eventful. Throughout the troubles–the fire, the defiant oxygen generator, the broken toilet, the nonfunctioning coolant system (for a month it was eighty-six-degrees onboard)–I kept in touch with Tsibliyev's family. The world hungered for news from Mir, and mission control was mute. Almost daily, I called in for updates from his wife. Once he returned to Earth, I reached Tsibliyev at home. It was late, but he was gracious. He kept his fury at the world–and the American press in particular–in check. He did not enjoy his new notoriety. He did not like being made a scapegoat. But he expected it. He knew that his country, ever since Lenin, had made a sad habit of finding people to blame. "There are those," he said, "who would've been happy to see me come back in a coffin." Time, he promised, would tell who had done what up there.

WHILE THE SERB washed his VW outside, I sat in a spacious office, its decor unchanged since Brezhnev, and heard an unlikely Russian sequel. Tsibliyev seemed as big as ever, with the broad chest and hard stare of an aging boxer. But now the shock of black hair combed back was graying, the widow's peak more pronounced, the cleft chin fuller. Tsibliyev said he bore no grudges. He just could not stand to hear the phrase "human factor." (It was what Yeltsin had said had caused the accident.) He considered himself fortunate. His partner, Sasha Lazutkin, had gone on a home shopping channel to help retail a cosmonaut spacesuit, but Tsibliyev had been promoted. Gold stars sat on his square shoulders. A month earlier he'd made major general. Now he sat behind a broad desk in a big office, a new computer to his right, six phones to the left. Tsibliyev was first deputy head of Star City.

He lit a Marlboro. After the crash he had developed an irregular heartbeat. Mission control proscribed sedatives and rest. Back on earth he had started to smoke. "For forty-three years," as he put it, he did not smoke. American astronauts, he knew, never did. It was a bad habit, one he had to get rid of, but Moscow was not Houston, and his life was "not the easiest." I remembered hearing Michael Foale, the British-born NASA astronaut, say that the Russians think Americans soft. "They believe," Foale had said, "that Russians have a natural ability to suffer, to take hardship and surmount it."[20]

"It was a mistake to try the manual docking," Tsibliyev said. "No one now disputes that."

We had been down this road before, in the days after he landed. But there was something else I wanted to know, something he'd only hinted at then. He retraced the moments after the crash. At first the siren had gone off. The crew had known then they were losing pressure. The errant cargo ship had punctured the Spektr module at the far end of the station. If Lazutkin and Foale failed to seal it off, Mir would depressurize and they'd all die.

"The station started to spin, slowly," Tsibliyev said. "The solar panels had been knocked out of alignment with the sun. The batteries ran out." Mir was traveling around Earth at sixteen thousand miles per hour. The ventilation system was off; the lights were off; even the radio was off. That was when the silence had settled over the station.

It was hard to imagine, he said, so absolute was the silence, so strange. He had never heard such a silence before. "We sat in the dark, listening to nothing but our breathing. The silence was so loud it pounded against our ears. Then, all of a sudden, through the portholes we saw the northern lights," a curtain of color against the black dome of space. In the impossible silence, with death so close, suddenly, he said, here was such beauty. He took the auroral vision as a sign. Tsibliyev, like many Russians, was superstitious. On the eve of his last launch, he had consulted a short chestnut-haired woman known as Globa, one of the country's most famous psychics. Before the crash he contacted her from Mir as well. She took the call on her kitchen phone. "You're about to enter a strange new period," she warned.

In time of course they managed to right the station. Foale, the NASA guest, came up with the idea of using the thrusters on the Soyuz module, the escape craft, to stop Mir's spin. Mission Control helped, as did his partner, Lazutkin, but it was Tsibliyev who powered the Soyuz thrusters to slow the spin and regain the station's orientation. Now he sat in his new office and said that was the easy part.

Cosmonauts, he explained, knew their stars. They memorized all eighty-eight constellations, and in each they learned the stars one could navigate by. It was part of basic training. Always. "You've got to know your stars," he said, allowing himself a wide grin. Foale's idea to use the Soyuz thrusters was critical, he said. But navigating by the stars was nothing new for Mir pilots. No one ever talked about it, but almost every crew had had to do it. You just looked out the windows and followed the stars. There was, he said, "nothing miraculous or superhuman about it; it's just our life."

THE SPACE PROGRAM had long mirrored the arc of the nation's history. On April 12, 1961, the day Yuri Gagarin entered space, Tsibliyev was six years old, a boy living in a village in the Crimea. For Soviet officialdom, Gagarin's flight broadcast the achievements of Soviet science. For his compatriots, it stretched the realm of the possible. Tsibliyev remembered the day well. It was imprinted in his mind. "If Gagarin had come from a village," he had thought, "I could do it, too." In time he won entry to the military academy in Kharkov. He'd risen fast, become a jet pilot, flown MiGs in the air force, before joining—the only one of his class—the elite ranks of the cosmonauts. There followed six years of training at Star City, before his first space flight in 1993. In all, Tsibliyev had spent 382 days among the stars. Six times he had climbed out of Mir and performed space walks. He was one of the few cosmonauts who had served from Gorbachev to Putin. Now he knew he would never return to space. Life had not ended after Mir, but regret hung in the air.

Did he ever miss it? I wondered.

He took a deep drag of the cigarette.

"Of course," he said as the smoke billowed between us. Now and then, however, he still took a training jet out for a spin. (In the States his American colleagues had even let him take the wheel, to and from Houston, of one of NASA's T-38s.) But the time had come, he said, to think about the future of the country's program, not his own. There was no need to hide it anymore: With Mir gone, Russia's space program faced subordination to America's. The new International Space Station (ISS) was fine, but why should the Americans rule space? Lately Tsibliyev had given a lot of thought to the problem.

Space tourists, he said, were the answer. The American billionaire Dennis Tito had already made history as the first paying space traveler. Tsibliyev, however, was thinking more boldly. Why just ferry wealthy civilians up to the ISS when you could build your own small space station—"say, two or three modules"—to host tourists? He imagined the day when the Russian Space Agency sponsored a cosmic resort, offering round-trip rides for anyone willing to pay his or her way. It was the only way he could see the Russian program's earning its keep. It would not have to be the exclusive domain of foreigners. There were rich Russians now, too, he noted. Why not give them an alternative to the south of France?

It seemed a farfetched idea. But Tsibliyev was serious. Russians should invest in the country's future. Putin, he said, understood this. The president had come to Star City not long ago for the fortieth anniversary of Gagarin's flight. Tsibliyev had met Yeltsin—he'd awarded the cosmonaut a medal for service to the Motherland–but Putin he admired. He was a military man, Tsibliyev said, who had put the country at last back on the right track. But space travel, he understood, was expensive. The state, of course, was not as poor as it once had been. The oil price was feeding the budget, tax receipts were up, and the Central Bank's reserves were higher than ever. It was Chechnya, he said, that sapped so much of the state budget.

If they could only end the war, the space program's financing woes would have been solved long ago. But Chechnya, of course, was "a matter of *politika* [politics]." And politics, the military man had learned ever since he had landed in the barren Kazakh steppe and heard Yeltsin invoke the dreaded "human factor," was far more treacherous than space travel. Politics was merciless. It had nothing in common with the beauty of the silence that had deafened him on that fateful day in space. He had survived a collision in space but feared the political exigencies that compromised the men around him more. "*Politika,*" said Tsibliyev, uttering the word with caution as if it were toxic, was something he had "already suffered once."

🎕 EIGHT 🎕

The people have already freed themselves from the fear that they harbored just a few years ago. I call on all my fellow citizens, in the name of unity, to get to work for the renewal and resurrection of Russia, to work for the victory of Democracy over reactionary forces, so that things can be as they were in the times of [ancient] Rus'! Hurray!
  –Boris Yeltsin rallying a triumphant crowd on August 23, 1991,
    after the collapse of the coup against Gorbachev[21]

Ten years had passed since the putsch that sought to bring down Gorbachev but ended up launching Yeltsin. Moscow, for many, had become a city at last revived–if not quite European, then certainly livable. Its pockets of wealth and glamour remained the domain of the few, but as Luzhkov kept up his drive to build and rebuild, the city at times could even look modern.

One warm luminescent night toward summer's end in 2001, Mia and I were out on a walk when we noticed a cluster of people gathering on a narrow side street in the center of town. Soon the crowd formed a column, two dozen across, and began to march. We walked close, first along the procession's edge, then in among the crowd. An honor guard, six soldiers in full dress, led the way. Tall and lean, their legs in black leather to the knee, the soldiers marched in somber, formal step. Among those at the head of the crowd was a man familiar to millions of Russians. He had not been seen much in Moscow of late. He had once charmed Western correspondents, sporting a Harvard sweatshirt and a perpetual smile. On this night he wore a black shirt and no expression. His hair was thinner now. No longer was he a Young Reformer, the bearer of hopes. Fearful of retribution at home, he had spent years abroad. Accused of a ten-thousand-dollar bribe—embarrassingly small by Moscow standards—he had fled to Poland. Now the saga had ended—some said thanks only to Putin's intervention—and he had come home.

The silent parade moved slowly past the American Embassy. As we turned onto the Garden Ring Road, the ranks swelled. The Garden Ring, the vast artery that encircles Moscow's center, has little greenery. Nearly always it is packed with traffic. On this evening two lanes had been cleared for the occasion. As the endless line of cars passed beside us, we marched on.

On August 21, 1991, the lives of three young men had ended here. A gray granite cross and a Russian tricolor now stood above the dark underpass where the three were killed, at the point where the Novy Arbat intersects the Garden Ring. Few in the flood of cars that passed it each day ever noticed the memorial. The cross was the gray of the sidewalk, and the flag was coated with exhaust. On this night, however, the flag had been cleaned and lowered to half-mast. As we approached the cross, the column of marchers unfurled, opening into a congregation of mourners. The evening air was strangely sweet and warm. As twilight settled, the crowd grew. I looked up and saw an illuminated billboard advertising ELITE HOMES WITH PRIVATE YACHT CLUB. Across the street a sea of small lights, candy blue and white, streamed from the Arbat casino. Parked in buses in front of the fun house, cops played cards. Across the street, a truckload of soldiers, their shaved heads stubbled with a day's growth, watched in silence.

I walked among the crowd and eavesdropped on three black-clad monks, members of the patriarchate's male choir. Their eyes were bright, and their beards long and unruly. Young and animated, they were talking of Putin.

"No, no, it can't be true," said one.

"But it is!" another insisted. "Vladimir Vladimirovich has opened a chapel in the Kremlin. For his use only. He goes there alone."

"How can you know such a thing?"

"I have sung there."

"Then he's truly a believer?"

"Belief or no belief, at least he prays."

On the stone cross, a single sentence was inscribed: "Here died in August 1991 the defenders of democracy in Russia. Komar, Krichevsky and Usov." Ilya Krichevsky was twenty-eight, a hopeful poet and, like his father, an architect, when he was hit by a bullet in the forehead. He fell on the second day of the coup, after midnight. Tens of thousands had formed a human chain to protect the White House, the parliament building nearby. Inside, Yeltsin's supporters clutched Kalashnikovs, while he ranted, issued commands, and waited out the tense night. Among those in the White House was a young Radio Liberty reporter, later awarded a medal as a Defender of Free Russia, Andrei Babitsky. When the tanks and armored personnel carriers of the Tamanskaya Division churned the asphalt of the Garden Ring, they had come to a halt in the underpass here. Dima Komar, a twenty-three-year-old Afghan vet, got on top of one. He tried to get inside but was forced off and crushed by its steel treads. Volodya Usov, a thirty-seven-year-old accountant, the son of a retired rear admiral, was the next to fall. He had tried to save Komar. The last to die was Krichevsky, hit by a bullet fired from inside the armored vehicle.

In the crowd I found Krichevsky's parents. I did not know what they looked like. I had only to read their faces. Inessa, his mother, was short, a soft wave curling her gray hair. Marat, his father, was no taller, a gentle man with large hands and a neatly trimmed white goatee. They were not crying. Standing together, to the side, they were taking in, acutely and resolutely, the spectacle that surrounded them.

Wreaths shingled the low wall behind the cross. Stapled across the green were fat black ribbons that announced who had paid for them: the government of the Russian Federation, the president of the Russian Federation, the mayor of Moscow . . . The honor guards had arranged themselves on either side of the cross. They stood rigid in their knee-high boots. (I realized why the guards were familiar. They usually stood beside the Tomb of the Unknown Soldier at the Kremlin wall.) A single icon rested against the stone cross, while the sidewalk before it had become a floor of candles. As the monks prepared to sing, people came up to place more small candles in front of the stone.

It was a Monday night in mid-August. Moscow was empty, and the dachas were full. Some in the crowd wore T-shirts and baseball caps made for the occasion that declared "Ten Years without Communism." But this was more than a reunion of the veterans of the White House stand. Street cleaners hung up their brooms on their plastic carts and joined the assembly. So did the shopkeepers from across the road. So did the teenagers, kids on Rollerblades and skateboards, kids with arms tattooed and eyebrows pierced. The crowd gathered tight, as the monks started to sing and a tall priest in silver finery began to chant an Orthodox prayer. It was a rare moment in Moscow, one of public solemnity, of remembrance.

A FEW DAYS LATER I went to see the Krichevskys. The apartment was on a far edge of Moscow, and the living room dark, lit only by the mottled sunlight that fought through the heavy curtains. Inessa and Marat had lived here since 1965. They had moved in when Ilya was a year and a half. It had been a long week of commemoration. Even the coup plotters, the feeble Gang of Eight, as the members of the self-proclaimed State Committee for a State of Emergency had come to be known, had returned to the limelight. They had staged a press conference. This one went better than their first, the one a decade earlier when the hands of Gorbachev's vice president, Gennadi Yanayev, trembled so that the world imagined him either drunk or terrified. (He was both.) I opted to forgo the reprise. Later, when I called to get a transcript–the *Patriot*, a nationalist anti-Semitic newspaper, had hosted the press conference–I was told it would cost me a thousand dollars. Even the Communists most nostalgic for the old days had caught up with the times.

The Krichevskys were tired. They had attended too many public perorations, weathered an all-day rock concert–the liberals' attempt at celebration—and stood at their son's grave with Gorbachev. Inessa and Marat did not enjoy the attention. They were restrained, reticent people. I had offered to visit later, but they were eager for me to come. They wanted me to see Ilya's room.

Everything was just as he left it. The Beatles poster still hung on the wall, next to a vintage shot of Ozzy Osbourne. Ilya loved music, his father said. An old tape recorder—a reel to reel—sat on a shelf. His father spun the plastic reels with two fingers one after the other. Ilya, he said again, loved music. Albums were stacked against a wall. He loved heavy metal, but also the bards, the poets of the underground who sang with humor of the sad absurdities of Soviet life. "Even more than the music," his mother said of the album collection, "he loved to listen to the words." Inessa and Marat did not claim their son was another Brodsky. They did not use the words "talent" or "gift." They said only that Ilya loved to write poems. It was fitting, of course, that in its last gasp Soviet power had taken the life of a young poet. Once he had tried to get a book of his poetry published. He'd titled it "A Conversation with the Wall." The title, his father said, came from "some English rock band." Marat had never heard of Pink Floyd. Ilya had gone to all the publishers in town—without success. He was working then as an apprentice architect after he'd come home from the army. Oddly enough—Marat smiled at the irony—he served in a tank division. "In the south," Inessa added. "In Chechnya."

He had served in Shali, the town where Issa's mother had lived, where his sisters still swept the broad concrete courtyard of the family house three times each day. Ilya had served in another age, when a modern war between Chechens and Russians was unimaginable. Yet his poems and drawings were filled with the Russian envy of the mountaineers. Like the nineteenth-century masters, he had written of Elbrus, of love and longing. A few years ago his parents had delved into their savings and published a thin volume of his poems and drawings. Ilya's charcoal sketches were of robust nudes, ancient churches, deserted Moscow street corners. His poems were filled with fire, light, and blood. The words and images seemed discordant, the distance between heaven and hell the only governing theme. "He must have seen something," his mother said, her small fingers lingering over the drawings. "He must have foreseen the worst."

We sat in their living room and talked through the long summer afternoon. It may have been the first time I had visited a Russian home and not had tea. At the memorial march the Krichevskys had seemed out of place. Even in their own home they seemed displaced. Their son's death had left a dark vacuum they had struggled to fill. The living room walls were covered with Marat's paintings—quiet scenes of a far-off serenity, of white stone monasteries and tumbledown huts. Marat had worked as an industrial architect on grand Soviet projects. Most of the 1970s he'd devoted to drawing a new Kamaz truck plant on the Volga. But he'd had a separate passion: Every summer for twenty-five years he had traveled the northern reaches of the USSR. He'd filled a backpack and ventured across some of its most remote provinces, wandering by train, steamer, and often foot. He had loved painting the north, the rural villages from another age and the unknown rivers that suddenly arose to divide a boundless plateau in two. Above all, he had loved the open space and the light. The north had stirred, he said, "a sense of freedom." Now he could no longer paint. Not a thing since the death. It was easier, Marat said, for his wife. "She believes."

The morning after the three young men were killed, the Soviet minister of defense, one of the putsch leaders, ordered the troops withdrawn from Moscow. The three were the sole fatalities of the coup. Gorbachev made them all Heroes of the USSR. The state issued stamps illustrated with their portraits. The papers were filled with eulogies, and thousands marched in their honor. But in private, some did not consider Ilya Krichevsky a Russian hero. Ilya, they said, was a Jew.

Inessa said it was because of her. Her family, not Marat's, was Jewish. Marat was even a Tatar name, she said. She had been born Jewish but no longer knew what to believe. Now, she said, she put her faith "in anything that brings solace." She had been reading the works of Aleksandr Men, the humanist priest murdered so long ago in the woods north of Moscow. "Father Aleksandr helps," she said. A friend had sent a Bible, but Inessa preferred the works of the slain theologian. "Father Aleksandr," she said, "gives me peace."

THE TENTH ANNIVERSARY of the coup proved problematic for Russia's politicians. They knew that only a minority of Russians still saw the failed putsch as the first landmark on Russia's path to democracy. A recent survey had revealed that 43 percent of those polled agreed with the proposition that those three days in August 1991 had been "just an episode in the history of the struggle for power in the government." The same number thought Yeltsin had merely "used the disorder in the country to seize power."[22]

During the week of celebration and commemoration, the undisputed hero of those dramatic days, Boris Yeltsin, remained in hiding at his dacha. Putin meanwhile left town altogether. First he went trout fishing in Karelia. Then he joined the Patriarch on a boat trip that the Kremlin billed as "historic." Putin and the Patriarch traveled to the fifteenth-century monastery in the Solovetsky Islands, the site of the labor camps where Academician Likhachev and Vasily Romashkin, the engineer who had set so much of Norilsk's cement, among countless others, had once been interned. Putin was not avoiding the coup anniversary, his press team insisted. The pilgrimage, they said, was the president's way of honoring the victory over the coup.

Putin would seem to have nothing to hide in his role during August 1991. Linkov and others in Petersburg recalled Putin, then Mayor Sobchak's deputy, coming to Sobchak's aid during the putsch. When Sobchak flew back to lead Petersburg's defense, Putin brought bodyguards to meet his plane. But on the tenth anniversary he kept silent. Putin, more than any Russian politician since the Soviet fall, had been careful to appeal to everyone—both those who loathed the Soviet days and those who longed for their return. He liked to recycle an appealing nostrum: "Anyone who does not regret the collapse of the Soviet Union has no heart, but anyone who wants it restored has no head." The line never failed to raise thunderous applause.

To Marat and Inessa Krichevsky the wisdom was one of the simple verities of Putin's rule. Their son had been a victim of the old regime, the system that had schooled and trained the KGB lieutenant colonel who for years had given directives to the Stasi in East Germany and now, against all odds, had risen to the Kremlin. Yes, they saw the irony. But to Marat and Inessa it did not matter. They liked Putin.

Inessa was seated at a small table, her thin arms folded close. Marat sat in a wooden chair nearby. Inessa said that at the memorial that night a woman had come up to her with a question, "What did your son die for?" For ten years, she said, countless people had asked the same question. Inessa understood. She did not begrudge the questioners. The woman, she explained, had just been to the store to buy sausage, and the price had risen again. Perhaps, she said, her answer was not the best, but she had turned to the stranger and said, "What do you mean, 'What for?' "

A silence filled the room. I recognized it. It had filled another living room equally sparse and heavy with loss, another private void within the Soviet cinder block at the city's opposite edge. Viktor and Valentina had also lost a son to the state, their Andrei, who had been sacrificed that fateful August morning in Grozny in 1996. They, too, had called it a crime and never seen justice.

Marat stared at his wife. The room remained dark, but his eyes now shone with the light of the afternoon outside. Viktor and Valentina had also struggled to smile but ended up crying. On a side table beside Inessa sat a heavy volume of poetry, the *Complete Works of Akhmatova*, a new edition. Of course Ilya had fought for the right thing, his parents said. He'd wanted democracy, free speech, a free press, the right of people to have a say in their own government—all the good things rational Soviets had long yearned for but never imagined they would see. It wasn't their son's fault, Marat and Inessa said. He never could have imagined what would come later. After all, the miracle did befall them. The Soviet Union had collapsed. But the morass that followed—the industrial descent, the flood of crime, corruption, and poverty, Chechnya, the rising toll of drug abuse, TB and AIDS, the sex on TV, the sex in the streets, the casinos—"How could our Ilya have foreseen all that?" his mother asked.

They realized that for many of their compatriots life had become worse, not better, in the decade since the coup. They knew that the vast majority of Russians now equated the liberal forces that won the day in August 1991 with the decay that followed. Gorbachev, they knew, was hated, but they would defend him, and their son, forever. The last Soviet leader had brought a wreath to Ilya's grave that week. They were especially grateful for its inscription: "From the Soviet President to the Victims of August 1991." Gorbachev, they said, was the only one still brave enough to call the boys who'd died "victims."

"These victims saved many more," Marat said. "The small blood saved the big blood. If the coup had lasted a day longer, rivers of blood would have flowed."

Inessa nodded. She had no doubt heard the conclusion a thousand times, but she listened to her husband with all her attention.

"Once the boys were killed," he said, "the coup leaders got scared."

In the age of Putin it had become fashionable for Russians to say, "What putsch?" Many had taken to proclaiming those three days in August 1991 "an operetta," "a harmless farce" that never had a prayer of success. The coup plotters, according to the revisionists and the forgetful, had never intended to shed Russian blood. The talk infuriated the Krichevskys. The coup plotters, they knew, had in fact planned to storm the White House, the parliament where Yeltsin and his supporters had holed up. In court the prosecutors had elicited the details from the conspirators' own mouths. As evidence of their crime the state's lawyers had introduced the murders of Krichevsky, Usov, and Komar. Now in their return to the spotlight, the coup plotters had blamed everything on Gorbachev and the West. At their press conference the Gang of Eight had offered a simple equation: Whatever plagued Russia now it was all because Gorbachev had opened the country to the West. The conspirators even had the nerve, Inessa said, to claim they'd only wanted the state that Putin wanted now.

"'Did your son die in vain?'" Marat said, his voice rising. "Are they blind? We now live in a completely different country! Not just the bankers and mobsters and oil barons. We do as well. We can travel. We can say what we want. We can meet foreigners–a reporter even!–in our apartment. We can shop in stores that are full of goods and open twenty-four hours every day. And to think people still think it was all in vain!"

Inessa and Marat had voted for Putin. Theirs was a straightforward logic, in line with the new pragmatism. Under Yeltsin, they said, the state ceased to function. In the chaos, said Marat, the criminal *gruppirovki* sprouted like mushrooms, and the oligarchs grew fat. But with Putin, he was sure, a new temperance had come at last. All those generals and admirals who rose with Putin were men of honor, of conscience. They would not stand for the stealing that had eaten away at the heart of Russia ever since their son had died.

"Russia's a rich country," Marat said, his voice rising ever higher, "but we've lived like the lowest dogs for more than eighty years." In the old days, everyone worked, but everything went to the Party bosses. Then after the coup the country had plunged straight into *privatizatsiya*, the mass privatization scheme that soon became known among the *narod*, Marat reminded me, as *prikhvatizatsiya*–a pun on the verb "to grab." The devolution to him was clear. "One group got the oil, another the timber, a third the fish, and so on. Now that they've divvied everything up, they only have to live off the interest."

Inessa was less pleased with the prevalence of the men from the KGB in positions of power everywhere. She still had a fondness for the Yabloko party, now one of the last liberal refuges in Russian political life. Once the party held promise, but it had long since been pushed to the margins, become a reserve of interminable naysayers. Inessa, like many in Moscow and Petersburg, still nurtured hope for Yabloko. But something about its leader, Grigori Yavlinsky, the clever economist whom perestroika had spawned–his arrogance? his sense of entitlement?–rubbed the wrong way. She, too, in the end had voted for Putin. "What choice did we have?" she said, drawing her arms tighter. It was the sad conviction I had heard everywhere since Putin first rose. The restless young governor of Novgorod, Mikhail Prusak, an unabashed Westernizer, had aired the doubts others hid. "Our president," he said, "was nominated by a handful of people. The rest of us only voted for him."

Marat, however, held hope. Putin offered the sole path to revival, he said. He was insistent now, nearly yelling. For too long, he said, Russians had lived not *po zakonam,* but *po ponyatiyam.* It was a rhythmic phrase that had come into fashion, a diagnosis that resounded in the Duma, the papers, and kitchens and buses across the country. Russians, it held, did not live "by the law" but "by an understanding," an unwritten code of behavior. *Pony-atiya* most often meant "a notion" or an "idea," but in this usage, it conjured up the underworld. *Ponyatiya* was the law of thieves. In Petersburg, Kumarin had explained the trouble: Society had taken the rule of *ponyatiya* out of its context and tried to transplant it to politics, to business, to everyday life. Of course it failed. A code of understanding among like-minded comrades, *ponyatiya* demanded one thing above all, honesty.

Putin understood that Russians were not renowned for honesty, Marat said. That was why loyalty and obedience were the new coins of the realm. Putin would see to it the law was obeyed. Of course a raft of problems remained. It was only to be expected. The country had gone through a new Time of Troubles, a period of wild capitalism, of wealth accumulation that had been primitive, even barbaric. Much of what Putin had already done, it was true, did not encourage optimism. But the path was correct. Putin would right the country. Marat was certain of it. The whole world, he said, had gone through the same evolution.

"The whole *civilized* world," Inessa cut in.

A small woman with a face lined by regret, she had sat across from her husband, scarcely moving for hours. Evening had come. She pulled at the ends of her white sweater. She did not share her husband's confidence in the future. She told of a man she'd heard the other day on the radio. He had said that when the demonstrators tore down the statue of Dzerzhinsky, the founder of Lenin's secret police, from in front of the Lubyanka, the square had become freer but in people's heads everything had stayed the same. "It was a lot harder," the man had said, "to tear down the statues in someone's head."[23]

Their son was a victim. Inessa knew that. But was he a hero? She did not know. She said she could never forget what came after the coup. Moscow, she said, was not Russia. She knew that "out there," in the provinces, most Russians did not live as she and Marat did. The hyperinflation of 1992, it was true, had sapped the couple's savings. Whatever they had left then disappeared in the devaluation of 1998. Yet they continued to receive compensation for Ilya's death, twelve hundred rubles each month. It was less than forty dollars, but they couldn't complain. They managed to cover their bills. Still, Inessa worried about the millions out there, the ones who failed to make ends meet. She understood how the chaos had happened. If you lived in a town that lived off a single factory and one day it suddenly went under, the whole town fell with it. It wasn't the fault, of course, of the democrats. Still, she wondered: "There had to have been some other way, some other way to build a normal life."

NINE

IT HAD BEEN NOT only an epochal but a cataclysmic shift. When the empire fell, 25 million Russians had found themselves stranded in the former Soviet republics. Since 1991 millions–3.7 million–had flooded into Russia from those lands. The country's borders had contracted dramatically, nearly to where they stood in the days of the Romanovs, while NATO had expanded ever eastward. Inside a decade a new economy had emerged, crashed, and risen from the ashes. Germany, Russia's chief trading partner, had replaced the United States as the economic model to emulate. Russia had become the world's number two oil exporter. Many of the men who once called themselves oligarchs had survived, but the most unseemly phase of the country's neocapitalism, the period of the "primitive accumulation of capital," had come to a close. Russian scientists had been among the first to exchange digitized information by computer. Now 4 million of their compatriots, nearly half of them women, logged on to the Internet. If not a middle class, then a business class–a new generation of bankers and lawyers, dentists and dry cleaners, Web designers and travel agents–had emerged.

The state, too, sought to keep pace. Putin forced through a host of new legislation: a flat tax (at 13 percent, the envy of Western conservatives), a law on land sales (nearly all the country's one billion acres of farmland remained state-owned, but it was a start), and a new criminal procedure code. By 2002 Putin could claim, though few believed him, that for the first time in history Russia would spend more on education than on defense. After all, war with the West was now unthinkable. Russia had shrunk its nuclear arsenal to one-third of what the Soviets wielded in 1991. The country even had a seat, if not membership, in the NATO Council. The horizon, the Kremlin announced, had brightened.

The U.S. Department of Commerce agreed. On June 6, 2002, it officially declared Russia a free market economy. The optimism was shared by few Russians. The poverty line after all still cut through a third of Russia's households. Per capita GDP, at twenty-one hundred dollars in 2001, was nearly a thousand dollars shy of Panama's. (Portugal's was more than six times higher at sixteen thousand dollars.) True, stocks were up again, but who owned stock? The capitalization of Russia's entire stock market, moreover, equaled less than a sixth of General Electric's. True, the fall of the Soviet bloc had opened new markets for the men who now controlled Russia's oil and gas, but the rest of the populace discovered only the downside of globalization: the onslaught of foreign brands and the competitive advantage of exporters East and West.

Russia, moreover, still looked longingly at the World Trade Organization, while Mongolia was already a member. Foreign investment, all the while, remained dismally low. China during the years 1992 to 1999 received some $350 billion in direct foreign investment. Russia over the same period earned $11.7 billion. Poland, the Russians were loath to admit, won nearly four times the foreign investment Russia did in 2001. Investors did not fear the crime and corruption–they could live with those hazards–but the legal vacuum. Russians understood. After all, the richest among them had been sending their cash abroad for years. From 1995 to 2000 capital flight, the best estimates held, averaged $20 billion a year. The state budget meanwhile survived on oil and gas receipts. When the price for a barrel of oil on the world market fell by a dollar, the Russian budget lost $1 billion.

All the while the country veered toward the demographic abyss. Russia's mortality rates had gained fame, topping any in Europe. TB and HIV grew ever more prevalent, while the birthrate fell to among the lowest in the world. The body politic was not only diseased but dying. In the first decade of the "transition," the population had contracted at a staggering rate, falling from a peak of 148.7 million in 1992 to 144 million in 2002.[24] In 2001 alone it fell by 846,600 citizens. By 2050, sober-minded scholars projected, Russia's population could fall by a third: to 100 million. Ever since the first years after the Soviet collapse, the birth and death rates had begun to head in opposite directions. Demographers looked at the intersection of the rising mortality rate and the falling birthrate and discovered a name for the national health crisis. "The Russian Cross" they called it.

Likhachev had looked out at his native Petersburg and recognized the danger. "Once we had too many people," he said, recalling the days when thousands waited years for apartments in Leningrad. He had doubted the dire predictions, but in the last year of his long life he saw the threat. The state might grow strong again, he said, but should the population continue to fall, no amount of political power, centralized or not, could reverse the trend. A sustained boom of course could slow the decline. But demography, as the French nineteenth-century philosopher Auguste Comte noted, is destiny.

Putin, all the same, remained blithely optimistic. The oil price stayed high, the ruling elite clung to their offshore accounts, and the common folks relied, as in the days of Pushkin, on ingenuity, resilience, and sheer will to survive. Some had found the elusive usable past; others had at last discovered a leader they could believe in. Yet in the four corners of the country where I had traveled, little changed for the better.

In the Far East, even after Putin had pried Nazdratenko from his fiefdom, the economic woes continued. For millions, the winters were still cold and dark, with electricity and gas scarce as ever. Poaching remained the chief source of local income. On Sakhalin the illegal trade even came to the attention of the Kremlin. Putin dispatched his own man, Border Guard Commander Vitaly Gamov, to Yuzhno to clean up the mess or at least to lend it a semblance of order. In December 2001, at thirty-nine, Gamov became one of Russia's youngest generals. By May 2002, however, he was dead, killed by burns suffered when three Molotov cocktails landed in his kitchen.

After September 11, 2001, Grisha Smekalov, the gentle cop with a passion for history whom I'd befriended in Aleksandrovsk, sent an e-mail message. He expressed sympathy and solidarity and had good news to report. At last he'd found a life after the *militsia*, a means of providing for his wife and children. Did I remember those tired fishermen, he wondered, who had dumped all their flounder? The next time they had to throw their night's haul back into the sea it would be his problem. He'd been made deputy director of the town's biggest fishery. The boat and its crew were Grisha's dominion now. He had no illusions–the fish business was all blood and money–but he'd been lucky, the first to quit the force and get a new job. The family was fine. Dima and Masha were growing tall, studying hard, attending Sunday school. Two young priests had come from the mainland. Father Roman and Father Piter had recruited a work force of men rescued from the streets, and they were now resurrecting the white church that once graced Aleksandrovsk's bald hill. By spring, the priests promised, the bells of the first mass would sound across the harbor below, out along the desultory shore where Chekhov had landed more than a century ago.

IN PETERSBURG THE years since the murder of Galina Starovoitova had yielded no justice. Then on November 6, 2002, as the fourth anniversary of Starovoitova's death neared, the FSB suddenly announced that it had arrested six men and charged them with the murder. The news, however, only further clouded the case. The authorities refused to identify the suspects. The FSB, moreover, had made similar claims before, claims that later had proved unfounded. Olga Starovoitova, the politician's sister, complained that the investigators continued to share scant information. She said that she knew only one thing: that the men detained, if in fact they were culpable in her sister's murder, were merely the ones who had carried it out, not those who had ordered it. Ruslan Linkov meanwhile held fast to his suspicions. In February 2002 he had even taken them public. To find Starovoitova's killers, Linkov declared on the radio station Ekho Moskvy, "You don't have to go to Riga or Prague [where Russian investigators had said two suspects were living]. You only have to look in the entourages of the Duma chairman Gennadi Seleznev or the Governor of St. Petersburg Vladimir Yakovlev."[25]

Vladimir Sergeyevich Kumarin, in early retirement from the Petersburg Fuel Company, sent notes by electronic mail every so often. After the attacks on the World Trade Center and the Pentagon, he wrote: "September 11th changed everything. America and I are on the same side now." Kumarin survived the interior minister's verbal assault and the reports, leaked by the FSB, that the men arrested in the Starovoitova case were connected, in some fashion, to the Tambov Gang. He remained a "simple pensioner," but one always assaying the options for a future turn in a remarkable career.

RAIBEK TOVZAYEV, the Good Chechen, as imagined by the generals orchestrating Putin's War, did not fare as well. Any man in Raibek's position had to know he would not live long. He survived two more ambushes, one that came only days after I visited.[26] In the end, however, Raibek had only eight lives. In August 2001, the rebels got him at last. Fittingly, it was not an ambush. This time Basayev and Khattab's men launched a full-scale operation. In one day they hit a Russian convoy making its way up the Vedeno Gorge, raided the occupiers' military headquarters in town, and stormed the office of the regional administration. Their timing was opportune. Just as he was quitting for the day, getting ready to collect his bodyguards, and drive his steel-plated Patrol back up to his mountain redoubt, they shot Raibek dead.

Chechnya burned on. Yet in the wake of September 11, as the world learned of the global campaign of terror sponsored by Osama bin Laden and Al Qaeda, whatever vestigial sympathy the Chechens enjoyed in the

West disappeared overnight. Few wished to consider the plight of a Muslim minority in Russia, no matter how embattled, as long as Putin sided with the West and the U.S. secretary of defense spoke with certainty of "Chechens" fighting alongside the Taliban in Afghanistan. It did not matter that no bodies, documents, or witnesses had emerged testifying to the presence of Chechen fighters in Afghanistan. The Chechens had never hidden their affinity for the Taliban's cause, and Al Qaeda, conversely, certainly saw the Chechens' plight as another front to man and arm. Yet if Chechens had fought in Afghanistan, theirs had never been a sizable contingent.

All the same, in the mountains around Vedeno, Basayev and company were keen to sever even the appearance of a tie to bin Laden. So it did not surprise many, certainly not Issa or Ilyas, when the FSB in April 2002 aired a videotape of Khattab, the Saudi-born commander who had once boasted of meeting bin Laden, in his final repose. The fearsome commander who had tormented the Russians since the first war, the reports from Chechnya held, was fatally poisoned—by one of his own.[27]

For Moscow, the cost of the war only grew. Putin and his generals had long declared "the military phase" of their endeavor in Chechnya over. But in the fall of 2002 the war hit Moscow itself. On October 23 a group of more than forty Chechen terrorists seized a theater in a southeastern corner of the capital. The popular *Nord-Ost* musical, a love story on a World War II theme, was five minutes into the second act when the Chechens took more than eight hundred men, women, and children hostage. The terrorists, heavily armed and equipped with more than two hundred pounds of TNT and two hundred-pound bombs, demanded that Russia withdraw its forces from Chechnya. One of the terrorists was an Arab, and the group made several calls to Saudi Arabia. However, the gang leader, twenty-five-year-old Movsar Barayev, declared pointedly that "our war is not against foreigners, our war is against the Russians." On the fourth day of the seige, just before dawn, the Russian security forces pumped a military gas through the theater's ventilation system, and one hundred special forces troops stormed the building. The Russians killed all the terrorists. One hundred and twenty-nine hostages died as well. They never recovered from the gas.

Aset Chadayeva, the nurse who had survived the *zachistka* in Aldy, was by then living as a refugee—thanks to the munificence of private sponsors, Russian human rights workers, and the U.S. government—in a one-room artist's studio in lower Manhattan. At night on the street below her window transgender sex workers paraded their wares. Aset lived alone, making ends meet as a nanny and cook. That night in October she came home late, turned on the television, and saw the footage shot by an NTV crew inside the theater. She was stunned. There among the Chechen men wearing camouflage and balaclavas were women—eighteen in all. One, a woman in her twenties, stood tall and thin, a four-pound bomb tied to her waist and a pistol in her hand. A black headband emblazoned with Arabic script declared her a mujahideen. She told the NTV reporter she was prepared to die. "We won't be stopped by anyone or anything," she said calmly. "We are on the path to Allah. If we die here, that won't be the end. There are many of us. It will continue."

VLADIMIR POTANIN, the man who controlled Norilsk's future, fared incomparably better than his fellow oligarchs Gusinsky and Berezovsky. Potanin not only survived his legal skirmish with the prosecutor general in 2000 but soon came back into political favor. Moreover, after the death of Governor Lebed in a helicopter crash in April 2002, Potanin even saw his own man—Aleksandr Khloponin, the technocrat he had installed at the helm of Norilsk Nickel—win election as the new governor in Krasnoyarsk. In time, with Norilsk Nickel's revenues more robust than ever, Potanin searched for a more cost-effective means of bringing the riches of the Kombinat to market. He was looking into employing a few of the Northern Fleet's nuclear submarines to cut through the frozen north. By 2002 Potanin once again graced the *Forbes* list of billionaires, as the fourth-richest Russian in the world, with a net worth of $1.8 billion. Then, in February 2002, in a move that stunned many in Moscow's business circles and the Petersburg art world, Potanin was named to the board of the Guggenheim Museum in New York, the first Russian on any major museum board in America. Potanin was not simply one of the few surviving oligarchs. He had acquired a commodity a New York financier had once told him he could never buy, respect in the West.

Of all those I met on the trip up the Yenisei, I kept in closest touch with Volodya Birger. We exchanged e-mail and talked often on the phone; after a decade of waiting for a home telephone, he'd finally gotten one. During the day Volodya continued to work in the software store, and at night, in the

Krasnoyarsk branch of Memorial. Then, one winter day in 2002, I got the news. I called Krasnoyarsk and spoke with his wife, Tanya. It had been sudden, she said, at five in the morning. Volodya had died in his sleep–"like the righteous," they say in Russian. A heart attack. At fifty years old. As she related her husband's passing, Tanya's voice was calm and strong. "He lived like a righteous man," she said, "and he died like a righteous man."

In Moscow, Andrei and Lera, the young couple who had hosted me in their communal apartment the year before the Soviet fall, had divorced. They both were overjoyed to be free of their marital bonds. It once had been love, of course, but there was also the need for the residency permit, then the baby. Now life had changed so. Lera went to work in a sculptor's studio on the Arbat and raised their two girls on her own. Andrei in short order got a law degree, remarried–a German–and joined a top Western firm in town. The Tito devotee with peroxided hair had become a corporate lawyer in a European suit. But Andrei had not changed. He had never "found a place," as he put it, in either the Soviet world or the new one.

One humid night in the second summer under Putin, we met for dinner in the center of town. Andrei announced that he was leaving Russia for good. Emigration in the age of Putin was no longer a topic. Real estate, vacations, boarding schools: These were the talk of the Moscow business class. Only Chechens now talked desperately of leaving. For Andrei, however, it was all he could think of. Things had gotten better, of course, he said, pouring another glass of wine. Life was fine, "in the details." You could go to a restaurant, drink Bordeaux, and eat *foie gras*. You could work hard, or steal well, and buy your own apartment and travel the world. It was just in general that life remained as impossible as ever. "No matter how far you get here," Andrei said, "you still face a deadend."

🐾 TEN 🐾

IT WAS ONE OF those summer evenings in Moscow when the air can suddenly turn soft and, if you round the right corner, you can catch the rare scent of trees, genuine grass, earth even. I decided to walk home, along the boulevard. The promenade arched through the city in a half circle around the Kremlin. A fortified line of defense in the seventeenth century, the boulevard had been laid out after Napoleon, after the fire of 1812. Its arrival had marked a respite from turmoil. Even now it remained a preserve of release.

The sky had gone a brilliant crimson. Above the crooked line of rooftops and smokestacks, a new moon had joined the last of the sun. On the pale gravel of the boulevard an old couple shuffled with care. Nearby stood a tall man smoking a cigar, three Borzois leashed to one hand. They huddled close, master and dogs, ghostlike in the rosy dusk. Farther on, at the edges of the path, teenagers gathered in private assemblies. They perched atop low benches long and white that they'd dragged close to face each other. They drank beer and smoked and flirted. As I passed, giggles rippled in the growing darkness.

At Pushkin Square, halos filled the sky. Bronze Pushkin, roses on his pedestal, stood in the center of the square. It was the city's meeting place. At the poet's feet, assignations began, politicians rallied, and drunks came to rest. Glasnost had first surged onto the streets here. Pushkin had served as the centerpiece to the first public debates in the USSR, as his square became a Soviet Speaker's Corner. The career of Mikhail Leontiev, one of Russia's most popular television commentators, had begun here. A provocateur who wore a black jacket of buttery leather and a well-groomed stubble, Leontiev was now the Kremlin's chief pit bull on state television. In those days he'd been a graduate student in economics when an essay of his, foretelling the nationalist storm that was to come in August 1991, turned up glued to the lampposts beside Pushkin. Leontiev had told me it'd all started by accident. He had never intended the article to be published. But the brave souls at *Atmoda*, the broadsheet of the Popular Front of Latvia, had got hold of it. "The Balts were always ahead of us," he said, "even then."

Leontiev's career mirrored the rise and fall of the free press in post-Soviet Russia. In 1989 he joined the first independent paper, *Kommersant*. Soon he moved on to *Nezavisimaya gazeta* (*Independent Newspaper*) to head its economics desk. He and the society editor shared a typewriter. ("We put it in the middle of a desk, sat across from each other, and spun it around when we had to use it.") He went on to help found the leading paper of the Yeltsin years, *Segodnya*. Leontiev had worked, at various times, for Gusinsky, Berezovsky, and Luzhkov. For a time he even moonlighted for Radio Liberty (in five minutes on the air he made more than half his monthly salary). Eventually of course he ended up working for Putin.

He now anchored the one political commentary program in Russia that reached every television in the land. While Putin rose, few advertised the new bloodlust with more gusto than Leontiev. He had hosted many infamous evenings. However, the programs that aired shortly after Putin had launched his war in Chechnya stood apart. He had applauded Putin's threat to "rub out" Chechen bandits even "in the outhouse." The support did not go unnoticed; when Putin became acting president, Leontiev won the first interview with him. By now, he said, he'd learned that "there's no such thing as 'free speech.' " It didn't matter if you were in New York, Ulan Bator, or Moscow. "Every word you write or broadcast," Leontiev said, "is paid for by someone."

It was a new age. That was certain. Yet now, as ever, the "black-voiced silence," the peril Mandelstam had seen gathering in his years of exile amid the black earth of Voronezh, reigned on. Rarely did they rally anymore at Pushkin Square. Once, at the height of perestroika, I had stood here beside Oleg Rumyantsev, a bearded graduate student passionate about legal reform. He had asked me to smuggle his scholarly articles out to the West. Rumyantsev's evolution was not unlike Leontiev's. In the final Soviet years he'd risen fast. He had stood close to Yeltsin, served in the Congress of People's Deputies, and even led a team that helped draft the new constitution. But by the time Yeltsin shelled the White House in October 1993, he had moved to the far side of the barricades. Only recently, after years out of view in Moscow, had he resurfaced. The beard was gone, and he had a new job, but Rumyantsev was as ardent as ever. Now, however, he spoke fervently about chocolate bars. He had become the chief lobbyist for Mars, helping fill kiosks across the land with Snickers.

On the eastern edge of the square the kiosks still lined the front of the *Moscow News* offices. In the days of Gorbachev, they all had held newspapers and magazines—and sold out a fresh title in an instant. Two of the old kiosks remained. One was filled with more than eighty different magazines—Russian glossies on hunting, e-business, car racing, expectant mothers, teen music, real estate, beauty aids, homeopathic remedies, island travel, macramé, Hollywood divas, and Russian stars of the NHL—but only three on politics. The second kiosk had long been a trove of dissident literature and the latest offerings from Memorial. In the glass window it showcased four new volumes: *Who Ruled the NKVD, 1934–1941*; *Godfather of the Kremlin*, the Russian edition of a new Berezovsky biography; *Two Hundred Years Together*, volume one of Solzhenitsyn's latest, a history of the Jews in Russia; and the cheapest of the four, at less than two dollars, *The Jewish Question through the Eyes of an American*, the Russian edition of David Duke's *My Awakening*.

What was the problem with the assortment? the girl in the kiosk asked. It was *normal'no*, she said. Perfectly normal. Everything in Russia after all was always normal. It was the understatement the cosmonaut ascribed to his crash in space—and the recovery that followed. It was the charity the miners and survivors of Norilsk lent to their impossible lives. It was the illusion shared by the Russian soldiers who sorted the corpses from the Zone and the Chechens who bathed and buried the dead in Aldy. It was the resignation of the great-grandmother who still baked blockade bread even as she watched the criminal tide rise in the city she would always call Leningrad. *Normal'no*. It was the one-word reply that resounded across the land, the hollow comfort of the first resort for those who had little left to believe in other than Providence or fate.

Across the square lived a longtime veteran of Norilsk I had visited a few weeks earlier. An ethnic Greek, he was the grandson of immigrants who'd crossed the Sea of Azov and settled in Taganrog. He'd been born in the warmth of the Aegean and spent most of his life in the Arctic. He wasn't a survivor of the camps. He was a survivor of the system. He'd been a top boss, at one point the head of the port in Dudinka. Then "the trouble" had interrupted his career, something about his ethnic background, something "not worth going into after all these years." Now he lived in two rooms above McDonald's. He had told me of his years in Norilsk, how the white of the tundra had imprinted itself on his eyes, how the prisoners had become his friends, how it had all turned out so strange. Now a banker, a man less than half his age, owned the whole town. The Greek's apartment was nearly barren, filled only with the mementos from his days at the Kombinat and the stench of the Big Macs below.

It was a historic McDonald's. Back in the winter of 1990 the Golden Arches had risen here first. As a student I had joined friends to stand in the long line that curled around the block. Often our entire class came, and

443

lunch swallowed the day. McDonald's of course had done well. It had just opened its thirty-fourth restaurant in Moscow. Forty more had opened in eighteen cities across Russia. But the Pushkin Square restaurant remained the flagship and, with some fifteen thousand customers a day, the busiest McDonald's in the world.

The sky had grown dusky blue. The neon billboards that ringed the square, atop the old *Izvestia* building and the Stalinist stone apartment blocks across the way, had come alive. Pushkin's bronze was now streaked with the blue, white, and pink of the neon. Big Macs had long ceased to be souvenirs. Luzhkov had nurtured an indigenous fast-food chain, Russkoe Bistro, that offered hot piroshki and cold *kvas* in dozens of little cafés everywhere across the city. But the New Russians had moved on; they had fallen for sushi. It was a problem, a friend had said. He was a well-tattooed chef from Brooklyn who ran one of the restaurants on Moscow's high end. His supplier in Tokyo could no longer keep pace with his orders. Moscow, he lamented, now sold more sushi than Paris.

I crossed under Tverskaya, angling through the commuters and venders, cops and Rollerbladers in the underground passageway. The labyrinth led to three metro stations. It smelled of beer and tobacco and the long-stemmed roses that filled the kiosks even in the depths of winter. A year earlier a bomb had ripped through the crowds here, killing thirteen and wounding more than a hundred. A small plaque marked the spot. Strangers, pausing for a moment in the rush, left flowers beneath it.[28] At the far end of the passageway the concrete wall above a bank of pay phones was stickered with ads: "Become a dancer in Turkey"; "Buy an engineer's diploma"; "Get your children off heroin"; "Lose 5 kilos in 7 days"; "Avoid the draft."

On the far side of the square the boulevard began again. The evening was darkening, the traffic thickening. Two boys and three girls competed in selling their wares to the cars frozen in place. In the summers the kids sold tight bunches of wildflowers, blue, yellow, and pink, that the babushkas culled from their dachas. For a time they hawked detective novels, Internet guides, and Dale Carnegie in Russian. Now they were showcasing new goods, compact discs of classified state databases. "State Customs Committee!" shouted a short girl with a dark face. "All national imports, '98 to 2000!"

The promenade stretched on, past more teens crowded on benches usurped from the old chess players who had battled until the last light of the day. The boulevard led on, past the TASS headquarters to the statue of Gogol. Here, on a granite step, I had tasted my first sip of Soviet champagne. Two decades had passed. It had been on my first trip to Moscow. The pair of would-be punk rockers had been gracious. The *gastronom* where they'd bought the champagne now sold Finnish sofas and German track lighting. A block on, however, the metro station still carried the name of a nineteenth-century anarchist no longer honored, let alone read. Every so often a crowd, newly released from the dank realm below, streamed from the exits. The dead weight of the glass doors slowed the flow, throwing the weary off-balance one last time before they reached home.

The end of empire had ended a world. Yet so much of course remained the same. ". . . people are weary of endless promises of economic flowering in the very near future, and have ceased altogether to believe in fine words," wrote Sakharov nearly thirty years earlier on New Year's Eve 1973. His diagnosis still carried currency: "The standard of living (food, clothing, housing, possibilities for leisure), social conditions (children's facilities, medical and educational institutions, pensions, labor production, etc.)–all this lags far behind the level in advanced countries. An indifference to social problems–an attitude of consumerism and selfishness–is developing among the broad strata of the population. And among the majority, protest against the deadening official ideology has an unconscious, latent character."[29] Sakharov's words, had the leaders of the shambolic liberal opposition recalled them, could have added force to their muted critique of the new day.

Beyond the metro, as the boulevard bent to the left and sloped toward the unseen river below, the giant gold dome rose. Christ the Savior, Luzhkov's gift to his city, loomed above all else. In the darkness, the cathedral's glow cascaded on the listless figures beneath it. Moscow was once a city of churches. "There are seven hills," wrote Marina Tsvetaeva of Moscow in 1916, "like seven bells."

> *Seven bells, seven bell-towers. Every*
> *One of the forty times forty churches, and the*
> *Seven hills of bells have been numbered.*[30]

Before Lenin and company, churches, more than five hundred in all, stood on nearly every corner.

Weeks earlier I had stopped at a kiosk across from the metro and watched a priest in the middle of the road. When the light went red, he paced among the cars. He wore a black robe belted by a white string. Around his neck hung a tin box. A man at the wheel of a polished German sedan—chauffeur, bodyguard, or banker, the distinction had become hard to make—slipped a handful of ruble notes into the tin. The priest crossed himself and offered a prayer. The car window shut tight before the benediction ended.

It was now getting late. The evening breeze remained warm but had gained strength, becoming a wind as night settled. On the boulevard the dust swirled. The wind possessed a sound now, and a force. It slapped at my face and climbed into my sleeves. I bent forward and walked on, not to fight the wind but to feel it. In the sudden warmth the city, like the land surrounding it, seemed as dark and wondrous as ever.

✦ ACKNOWLEDGMENTS ✦

I am in the debt of all those across Russia who opened their doors and shared their the tales of memory, loss, and hope. I am also grateful to those who provided support along the way–whether historical levity, navigational tips, archival documents, hot meals, or long talks–as well as to those writers, some legendary, some unknown, who traveled these regions before me.

Although it is impossible to thank all deserving–many prefer anonymity–even a partial list is in order. Among those not listed in the text who gave generously of their time, ideas, or information were:

For the Moscow chapters: Pyotr Aven, Denis Babichenko, Charles Bausman, Andrei Bogolyubov, Al Breach, Umar Djabrailov, James Fenkner, Yegor Gaidar, Danila Galperovich, Pyotr Glanz, Craig Kennedy, Yuri Kotler, Lyona Krutakov, Veronika Kutsyllo, Otto Latsis, Owen Matthews, Igor Moukhin, Boris Nemtsov, Aleksandr Oslon, Olga Oslon, George Pachikov, Raisa Pestova, Nathan Pettengill, Nikita Petrov, Lena Popova, Joe Ritchey, Inna Shchekotova, Yermolai Solzhenitsyn, Bernie Sucher, Vladimir Syomin, Oleg Sysuev, Lev Tabenkin, Yuri Tavrovsky, Zurab Tsereteli, Glenn Waller, Aleksei Venediktov, Dmitri Yakushkin, Sergei Zverev.

Chechnya: Usam Baisayev, Hassan Baiyev, Shamil Beno, Yelena Bonner, Maksharip Chadayev, Georgi Derluguian, John Dunlop, Kristel Eerdekens, Jason Eskenazi, David Filipov, Maria Fedulova, Dmitri Furman, Moshe Gammer, Stanley Greene, Malcolm Hawkes, Abdulla Khamzayev, Robert King, Sonya Kishkovsky, Vera Krolikova, Diederik Lohman, Timur Muzayev, Johanna Nichols, Emil Pain, Sasha Petrov, Petra Procházková, Dmitri Trenin, Lyoma Usmanov, Bagrat Tekhov, Tom de Waal, Ruslan Yanderov, Layla Yanderova, Marcus Warren, Anna Zelkina, Yelena Zubrovskaya.

Norilsk: Igor Aristov, Oleg Bukharin, Darya Chapkovskaya, Alan Cullison, Irina Danilenko, Yulia Dorinskaya, Georgi Dorinsky, Svetlana Ebizhants, Chrystia Freeland, Joshua Handler, Tim Heleniak, Diane Nemec Ignashev, Michele Kelemen, Oleg and Tanya Krashevsky, Tatyana Lengyel,

Alan Lolaev, Alla Makarova, Masha Makhanova, Jadwiga Malewicz, Natasha Mirimanova, Ludmila Novikova, Vera Pristupa, Tony Suau, Sergei Skaterschikov, Olga Yaremchuk, Larissa Zelkova.

The Far East and Sakhalin: Robert Brownell, Nonna Chernyakova, Aleksandr Chudakov, Pavel Fomenko, David Gordon, Aleksandr Kostanov, Marat Khabibullov, Dmitri Lisitsyn, Vladislav Latyshev, Dave Loran, Timur Miromanov, Yelena Uspenskaya, Lawrence Uzzell, Slava Titov, Mikhail Vysokov, Russell Working.

St. Petersburg: Afrika (Sergei Bugaev), Arlen Blum, Kathy Charla, Mila Gladkova, Dmitri Golynko-Volfson, Boris Grebenshikov, David E. Hoffman, Pilvikki Kause, Aleksandr Kitaev, Nikolai Kovarsky, Irena Kuksenaite, Toby Latta, Katya Novikova, Yevgeny Pshenichny, Gennadi Suspitsyn, Irina Titova, Marina Yakovlova, Vadim Znamenov.

At *Time*, I am indebted to my Moscow bureau chief, Paul Quinn-Judge. Few men, native or otherwise, know more about the land. Among *Time* editors, Chris Redman was unduly generous. Jim Kelly, Howard Chua-Eoan, Rick Hornik, and Joshua Ramo were ever encouraging. To the late Brigid O'Hara-Forster, as great a Russophile as any I have known, I owe special thanks. My colleagues in the Moscow bureau all deserve thanks for enduring me under close quarters for so many years: Andrew Keith, Marina Malyugina, Andrei Polikanov, Boris Tyunin, and Yuri Zarakhovich.

Having begun my career as a Moscow stringer fresh from Oxford, I owe great thanks to David Remnick, who as a *Washington Post* correspondent did me the outrageous favor of extending visa support, thereby granting me a start in journalism. Since we met ringside at a Moscow boxing match in 1988, his encouragement has been unstinting. Thanks too to editors for advice and commissions along the way: Sandy Close, Katrina vanden Heuvel, Clara Jeffery, Lewis Lapham, Andrew Sullivan, and Paul Wilner.

I cannot imagine a better place to have written this book than the Woodrow Wilson International Center for Scholars in Washington, D.C. A rare meeting ground for thinkers and policymakers in the capital, the Center was even gracious to a journalist, affording me more resources and quiet than I had ever enjoyed. The Center's Kennan Institute, named in honor of George Kennan's nineteenth-century relative, the explorer of Siberia, remains one of the preeminent homes in the West for the study of Russia and the former Soviet lands. My thanks to the Wilson Center's enormously generous staff, in particular, Director Lee Hamilton, Blair Ruble, Mike van Dusen, Ben Amini, Arlyn Charles, Steve Lagerfeld, John Tyler, and the superb library team of Michele Kutler, Dagne Gizaw, and Janet Spikes. Thanks also to my fellow Fellows for their comradeship and counsel.

Thanks as well to the Alicia Patterson Foundation, the most munificent source of independent funding for journalists in the United States. As a Patterson Fellow in 1996, I was able to return to Russia and travel the war zones of the former Soviet Union and Afghanistan. Thanks also to the Open Society Institute, in particular Anthony Richter. At Oxford, thanks are due to Mike Nicholson and Paul Foote.

A number of people have aided in the writing and research of this book. Above all, I am grateful for the privilege of working with Bob Weil of W. W. Norton. His faith and exuberance were only exceeded by his patience and guidance. Thanks too to the entire Norton staff and associates, especially Jason Baskin, Brendan Curry, Julia Druskin, Nancy Palmquist, Don Rifkin, and Renee Schwartz.

In Moscow, Anna Masterova devoted care and a long winter to the task of transcribing miles of taped interviews. Yekaterina Lebedeva, among the youngest but toughest veterans of the Moscow press corps, was unparalleled in checking the most obscure of facts. In Washington, Alexei Porfirenko, Nora Khan, and Iren Sargsyan were able research assistants.

Thanks as well to the Georges Borchardt Agency. Georges, Ann, and their daughter Valerie not only work in the best tradition of the American book world, they are vital forces in keeping it alive. Many thanks as well to Lourdes Lopez, for her unflagging faith and friendship.

For their sharp eyes, thanks are due Kostantin Akinsha, Neela Banerjee, Catherine Barnett, Peter Carwell, Yuri Koshkin, Andrew Reynolds, and Eugene Rumer. For their unending encouragement and ever-open doors, great thanks to Ed and Jill Kline, Doug Hamilton, Tom Hulce, Sherry Jones, Betsy Klein, Joe Oliveira, Julia Rask, Michael Smith, Jonathan and Katya Sparrow, and Bill Wrubel.

Among those to whom I am most indebted, Mark Franchetti, Moscow correspondent of the *Sunday Times* of London, stands alone. As colleague and friend, he brought his great sense of the country to bear on the manuscript. Not only were his comments invaluable, his humor was a source of sustenance. His friendship has been a great boon to my life.

My toughest readers, however, remain my brothers David, Daniel, and Jeremy and my parents, Gerald and Gretl Meier. I am blessed to have their support and love; without it I never would have made it to Moscow in the first place. I am grateful as well to Shelagh Meier, Hazelle Fortich, and Jacqueline Jensen. Their love enriches our family, strengthening the promise of our shared future.

I reserve utmost thanks for my first reader and closest traveling partner, my wife, Mia. Her strength not only sustained me throughout our Russian journey, it carried me to the last page of this book. Her love is the greatest gift I have known. This book, as she alone knows, would not exist without her.

❧ NOTES ❧

PART I. MOSCOW: ZERO GRAVITY

1. In October 1996, Yeltsin fired Tarpishchev as Russia's minister of sport amid reports of alleged corruption concerning Tarpishchev and Yeltsin's onetime bodyguard and confidant Aleksandr Korzhakov (NTV, October 6, 1996; ORT, October 7, 1996). In 2002, Tarpishchev initially had trouble in securing a U.S. visa to attend the Salt Lake City Olympic Games even though he was a member of the International Olympic Committee and the coach of the Russian national tennis team. Reuters, on February 1, 2002, reported that Tarpishchev blamed "political problems" for the delay. In the end, after an embarrassing controversy over the visa, he did travel to the games.

2. For an excellent review of Luzhkov as *khozyain*, see Donald N. Jensen, "The Boss: How Yury Luzhkov Runs Moscow," *Demokratizatsiya, Journal of Post-Soviet Democratization*, v. 8, no. 1 (Winter 2000).

3. Richard Pipes, *Russia under the Old Regime* (New York: Collier Books, 1992), p. 73.

4. My thanks to Steven Zwirn, curator at the Dumbarton Oaks collection in Washington, D.C., for researching the role of the double-headed eagle in Byzantine heraldry.

5. Vasily Nikolaevich Malinin, *Starets Eleazarova Monastyria Filofei i ego poslaniia* (Kiev: Tipografia Kievo-Pecherskoy Uspenskoi Lavry, 1901), appendix: p. 55.

6. The oligarchs were not the only ones to give alms. The state arms trading company, Rosvooruzheniye, donated $235,000.

7. Transcript of Putin's meeting with the Kursk families, *Kommersant-Vlast*, August 29, 2000.

8. In the years that followed, the four financiers never again met around one table. Derby soon abandoned his dream of making a fortune in Moscow. His bank was swallowed by a Luzhkov-backed bank, and he disappeared from the local scene. At the dinner he had spoken longingly of relocating to his native Long Island and taking his chances in the wilds of its local politics. Ryan, Browder, and Jordan became three of the market's last survivors. Ryan suffered a protracted dispute with Gazprom, Russia's natural gas monopoly, over how best to use the minority stake his financial group, UFG, owned in the company. In time, however, UFG rose from the ashes. Browder, too, saw his Hermitage Fund come back. In 2001 the Russian stock market, although still small, at less than one-sixth of the market capitalization of General Electric, again topped the world's emerging markets for best returns. Jordan perhaps rose highest. In 2001, when the Kremlin moved against Vladimir Gusinsky, stripping him of his beloved independent television network NTV, officialdom turned to Jordan to run it. Putin of course kept Jordan at arm's length as the struggle raged over NTV's fate. But his minions adopted the banker as a long-lost son of the Motherland, touting him as a American executive with fluent Russian. At the

reins of Gusinsky's old network, Jordan quickly regained his old form. He assured officials in Washington that the independent network would survive and that the Kremlin would not control its news policy. The takeover of NTV, he told all who would listen, was purely a matter of economics. Before long, however, he too would earn the Kremlin's wrath. In January 2003, Jordan was fired from his post at the helm of NTV.

9. In February 1966, Sinyavsky and Daniel were arrested for the crime of having smuggled out their writing to the West, where it appeared in a French journal. The trial was a Soviet milestone, the first time officialdom blatantly jailed writers for publishing abroad. Sinyavsky, perhaps best known for his brilliant essay *On Socialist Realism*, served six years in the camps. He left the USSR in 1973 and lived in Paris, teaching at the Sorbonne, until his death in 1997. Daniel, an author and translator best known for his short stories, among them "This Is Moscow Speaking," died in 1988 in Moscow.

10. Radio Free Europe/Radio Liberty, November 8, 2001. VTsIOM poll, November 2–6, 2001.

11. The German philosopher Karl Jaspers examined the notion of a national *Vergangenheitsbewältingung* in his seminal 1947 work, *Die Schuldfrage* [*The Question of Guilt*]. Jaspers delineated four species of guilt: criminal, political, moral, and metaphysical. Nanci Adler, in *The Gulag Survivor* (New Brunswick, N.J.: Transaction Publishers, 2002), gives a good précis of Jaspers's description of the process and its aims. See Adler, pp. 15–16.

12. Kobzon has twice won immunity by winning a Duma seat, the second time with 92 percent of the vote. The singer claims to have visited the United States some thirty times, before being denied a tourist visa in 1995. In May 2000 he did get a visa, as part of a Duma delegation that attended a Harvard conference. He left early. (For a recent profile of this Soviet survivor, see Alison Smale, "The Smoothest Soviet Crooner, Still in Good Voice," *New York Times*, April 25, 2002.)

PART II. SOUTH: TO THE ZONE

1. The Soviet armed forces were renowned for an abundance of generals. Dudayev, however, was the sole Chechen general, a major general since 1987. Born in the Chechen village of Permomaiskoye in 1944, as an infant he was sent into Central Asian exile with his family. He rose through the ranks of the air force to command, for a time in the last Soviet years, a squadron of Soviet nuclear bombers stationed in the town of Tartu in the Soviet republic of Estonia.

2. Ichkeria became the politically correct name for Chechnya, employed to mark a speaker's pro-independence stance.

3. Dumas traveled across the Caucasus just months before Imam Shamil, the famed leader of the mountioneers' nineteenth-century resistance, surrendered in 1859.

4. Detained by Russian soldiers on January 16, 2000, as he left the ruins of the Chechen capital, Grozny, Babitsky was held incommunicado for twelve days. He was jailed in a filtration prison in the village of Chernokozovo, where the Russians claimed to sort terrorists from civilians. Human rights groups reported widespread torture in the prison. On February 3, the day he was to be released, the Russians suddenly swapped Babitsky for two Russian POWs. The exchange, videotaped by the FSB, was later shown on Russian

television. His colleagues, who saw Babitsky handed over to masked men in camouflage, purportedly the same Chechen fighters Moscow terms terrorists, were outraged. "What kind of state arrests a journalist and then uses him in a POW swap?" Radio Liberty's Moscow editor, Mikhail Sokolov, asked me. Later, few doubted that the FSB had faked the handover.

5. The ban on press travel was total. It extended even to Russian reporters. Any reporter who wished to travel to Chechnya was required to get a special Kremlin military accreditation and travel in the company of official Russian military escorts. The result: Much of the reporting, both foreign and Russian, came from reporters stationed in Khankala, the Russian military command headquarters outside Grozny. In Khankala the Russians conveniently maintained their own press center and the only television satellite relay dish in Chechnya. All those who violated the Kremlin's strict rules on access to the war zone—and many Western and Russian reporters did—did so at their own risk. Some, like Babitsky, suffered extreme consequences. Others, like my colleague Petra Procházková, were denied entry visas to Russia. In 2000, Procházková, a Czech journalist who during the first war had worked in Chechnya as much as any foreigner, decided to abandon journalism and move to Grozny to set up a food distribution center for the elderly and most vulnerable returnees. In 2001 the Russians denied her an entry visa to Russia for five years, although her husband was a Russian citizen, residing in Ingushetia. In the spring of 2002 the *Novaya gazeta* reporter Anna Politkovskaya, after investigating reports that Russian officers in the Shatoi region had killed a number of civilians, received death threats and had to flee the region.

6. Like Elbrus, Mount Kazbek, after a century of isolation, was now enjoying the attention of the world's most enterprising climbers and skiers.

7. See Daniel Yergin, *The Prize: The Epic Quest for Oil, Money, and Power* (New York: Simon and Schuster, 1991), pp. 334-39.

8. Historians note the participation of the so-called Viking Division, a Nazi division that comprised a "volunteer" battalion of Finns and other Nordic and European volunteers. The question of how many Chechens, Ingush, and others from the North Caucasus aided the Nazis, at the center of Russian contentions about the Chechens' loyalty, has been explored at length in recent years. Western, Chechen, and even Russian historians, however, do not believe that substantial numbers of Chechens sided with the Nazis. See Dunlop, *Russia Confronts Chechnya: Roots of a Separatist Conflict* (Cambridge, U.K.: Cambridge University Press, 1998), pp. 58-61, who cites among others the Chechen historian Abdurahman Avtorkhanov.

Avtorkhanov writes: ". . . during the Second World War not one single German soldier ever appeared on Chechen-Ingush territory, with the exception of a brief occupation of the frontier locality of Malgobek, where the population was Russian" (Avtorkhanov, "The Chechens and the Ingush during the Soviet Period and Its Antecedents," in *The North Caucasus Barrier: The Russian Advance Towards the Muslim World*, ed. Marie Bennigsen Broxup [London: Hurst and Company, 1992], p. 147).

9. Dunlop, *Russia Confronts Chechnya*, pp. 61-67.

10. Robert Conquest, *The Nation Killers: The Soviet Deportation of Nationalities* (London: Macmillan & Co., 1970), p. 67.

11. In November 1989, the South Ossetian parliament voted to elevate the region's status

to an "autonomous republic" within Georgia. The leader of Georgia at the time, the ultranationalist former philologist Zviad Gamsakhurdia, could not tolerate such insubordination among an ethnic minority. In days, Georgian troops marched on the South Ossetian capital, Tskhinvali. The ensuing conflict lasted, on and off, for three years, leaving thousands dead and forcing thousands more—both Ossetian and Georgian—from their homes. A cease-fire was struck in 1992, with Russian, Ossetian, and Georgian peacekeepers installed along the disputed region's borders. No peace deal, however, was signed, and as became the rule in the ensuing conflicts across the Caucasus, the crucial question of the region's status was left undetermined. South Ossetia meanwhile, cut off from Georgia, survived on little save a robust trade in bootleg vodka. The new Georgian president Eduard Shevardnadze, still beloved in Western capitals as Gorbachev's foreign minister, managed an uneasy peace with the first South Ossetian leader, Ludvig Chibirov. However, when Eduard Kokoyev, a thirty-eight-year-old Moscow businessman and Russian citizen, was voted his successor in December 2001, tensions again heightened. Kokoyev, a former Komsomol leader who headed the largest contingent of South Ossetian fighters in the war, wasted little time in striking a new strident tone. In an interview published on March 6, 2002, in the Moscow newspaper *Vremya novostei*, he denounced Shevardnadze, saying he bore responsibility for genocide. "He ought to recognize the genocide of the Ossetians and personally apologize," Kokoyev said. The region, moreover, had gained new prominence. In 2002, as part of America's war on terror, a handful of U.S. Special Forces arrived only some sixty miles away, in Georgia's Pankisi Gorge. Long a sanctuary for Chechen refugees, the Pankisi was now reputed to be—most vocally by Moscow—a haven for Chechen fighters and Al Qaeda operatives. Chechen fighters, specifically the band under the occasional control of the warlord Ruslan Gelayev, were seen in the gorge in late 2001, but just how many Chechen fighters were hiding out among them remained a matter of dispute. See Jean-Christophe Peuch "2001 in Review: Shevardnadze Loses Room to Maneuver," RFE, January 18, 2001; Alan Parastayev, Institute for War and Peace Reporting, Caucasus Reporting Service, "US Deployment in Georgia Angers South Ossetia," March 22, 2002.

12. In his excellent book on the Caucasus, Sebastian Smith writes of the importance, and irony, of Wasterzhi in North Ossetia. See *Allah's Mountains: Politics and War in the Russian Caucasus* (London: I. B. Tauris and Co., 1998), pp. 80–83.

13. For a wonderful explication of the founding and inner workings of Ingushetia's *ofshornaya zona*, see Chrystia Freeland, *Sale of the Century: The Inside Story of the Second Russian Revolution* (London: Little, Brown & Co., 2000), pp. 94–104.

14. In my travels elsewhere in the former Soviet states, particularly Uzbekistan and Tajikistan, I had encountered the Wahhabi movement before. Begun by Abdul Wahhab (1703–1792), Wahhabism intended to cleanse the Arab Bedouin from the influence of Sufism, wrote Ahmed Rashid in his *Taliban*. "The spread of Wahhabism became a major plank in Saudi foreign policy after the oil boom in the 1970s" (Ahmed Rashid, *Taliban: Militant Islam, Oil and Fundamentalism in Central Asia* [New Haven: Yale Note Bene, 2002], p. 85).

15. Susan Layton, *Russian Literature and Empire: Conquest of the Caucasus from Pushkin to Tolstoy* (New York: Cambridge University Press, 1994), p. 142.

16. Troshev's remarks made headlines in Russia. They were also broadcast on the Voice of America, December 2, 1999.

17. Michael Whittock, "Ermolov–Proconsul of the Caucasus." *Russian Review: An American Quarterly Devoted to Russia Past and Present*, v. 18, no. 1 (January 1959), p. 59; John F. Baddeley, *The Russian Conquest of the Caucasus* (London: Longmans, Green and Co., 1908), p. 93.

18. Whittock, "Ermolov," p. 59; Moshe Gammer, "Russian Strategies in the Conquest of Chechnia and Daghestan, 1825–1859," North Caucasus Barrier, ed. Bennigsen Broxup, pp. 45–61.

19. Baddeley, *Russian Conquest*, p. 97.

20. Gammer, *North Caucasus Barrier*, p. 47; Whittock, "Ermolov," p. 58.

21. Baddeley, *Russian Conquest*, pp. 106–7.

22. Layton, *Russian Literature and Empire*, p. 108.

23. The Chechen among the three men in the statue was Aslanbek Sheripov. Next to him was an Ingush, Ghapur Akhriyev. The third man, naturally, was Russian, Nikolai Gikalo. All three were ardent Bolsheviks. The trio was intended to symbolize the unity of the three major ethnic groups of the Soviet province of Checheno-Ingushetia.

24. Maskhadov, like Dudayev, the political leader of the Chechens' rebellion, was a former Soviet officer–in his case, a former artillery officer.

25. "We are absolutely independent," a Basayev envoy told me in mock seriousness after the first war ended, "because absolutely no one depends on us." General Lebed was well aware that his deal was faulty. But he claimed that the Kremlin had hindered his negotiating leverage. "We could only wait and let the smoke clear," Lebed later told me. "Yeltsin would not allow me to do anything more."

26. The ties between Khattab and bin Laden have yet to be clearly established. Khattab, however, in an interview with the Chechen rebels' main Web site, Kavkaz.org, less than a month after September 11, 2001, was quoted as saying that bin Laden was "a good mujahid and scholar" and a "very decent" man, whom he had known when both fought the Soviets in Afghanistan, but that Khattab had not seen nor spoken with bin Laden for eight years (Kavkaz.org, October 10, 2001; see also *Jamestown Monitor*, v. 7, issue 187, October 11, 2001).

27. The fighters reportedly moved into the Dagestani regions of Botlikh and Buinak, taking over the villages of Karamakhi, Chabanmakhi, and Kadar. When serving as Yeltsin's interior minister, Sergei Stepashin had met with the Wahhabi leaders of Karamakhi and Chabanmakhi on August 20, 1998. For prescient reporting, see Mikhail Roshchin, "Wahhabism in Dagestan and Chechnya," Keston News Service, March 2, 1999.

28. The portfolio of the Kremlin Property Department ranged from the sprawling dacha complexes outside Moscow to luxury hotels to the presidential airlines. By his own hyperbolic estimation, Borodin oversaw property worth a total of $600 billion dollars. The so-called Mabetex scandal was an immensely complex affair but centered on allegations of money laundering and corruption at the highest level of the Yeltsin Kremlin. Borodin was detained in January 2001 at New York's JFK Airport on a Swiss warrant. The Swiss had accused him of involvement in a multimillion-dollar kickback and money-laundering scheme arising from Russian state construction jobs. Swiss authorities had alleged in court documents that Borodin had used "his position to obtain approximately

$30 million in kickbacks from Swiss companies to which he awarded contracts." Prosecutors also claimed that Borodin had "attempted to conceal these kickbacks through a series of transfers along bank accounts belonging to offshore companies controlled by him and certain members of his family" (AP, April 2, 2001).

After three months, in April 2001, Borodin abandoned his extradition fight. In Geneva, he was released on bail. In March 2002, Geneva Cantonal Prosecutor Bernard Bartossa found Borodin guilty of laundering $22.4 million through Swiss banks while he ran the Kremlin property empire under Yeltsin. Bartossa fined Borodin 300,000 Swiss franks ($175,000) and closed the case (AP, March 15, 2002; RFE Newsline, March 7, 2002).

29. The Bank of New York affair, another of the great scandals of the late Yeltsin years, exploded on the front page of the *New York Times* on August 19, 1999 (see Raymond Bonner and Timothy L. O'Brien, "Activity at Bank Raises Suspicion of Russian Mob Tie"). The *Times* ran a series of extensive investigative articles, as the rest of the Western media joined the chase. The BoNY scandal dragged on for months, yielding voluminous articles in the press, but few indictments, let alone convictions. A former bank executive, Lucy Edwards, and her husband, Peter Berlin, both Russian émigrés, did plead guilty to money laundering, saying they were paid $1.8 million in commissions (Reuters, February 16, 2000). In the end, however, the scandal proved an unduly inflated story.

30. In a rare occurrence, the bombing in Buinaksk resulted in a trial. In March 2000, a court in Makhachkala sentenced two men to life in prison for their roles in the blast. On November 14, 2001, the trial of five Karachaevo-Cherkessia residents accused of preparing terrorist acts ended. Three were sentenced to fifteen years, one to thirteen and one-half years, and another to nine years in prison. The court held that the men had graduated from a Wahhabi terrorist training camp run by Khattab in Avtury, Chechnya. The trial, however, failed to link the men to the apartment house bombings in Moscow and Volgodonsk. By 2004, although the federal prosecutor's office had completed its investigation of the 1999 bombings, and claimed to have apprehended at least two suspects, the crimes' initiators remained unknown.

31. After Patrushev's remarkable statement on September 24, 1999, a number of Duma deputies moved to open an inquiry into the Ryazan case. But in March 2000 the move failed, blocked by the pro-Putin Unity party. In the spring of 2002, Boris Berezovsky, by then a fallen oligarch out of favor with the Kremlin and in opposition to Putin, the man he had helped make president, financed an elaborate public relations campaign that sought to blame the FSB for the bombings in Moscow, Volgodonsk, and Buinaksk. On March 5, 2002, Berezovsky told a London press conference that the FSB had masterminded the bombings to justify the second war in Chechnya. Other than generate publicity for himself, Berezovsky's campaign added little depth to the hunt for the culprits behind the bombings.

32. In 2002, after the arrival of American military advisers there, the Pankisi Gorge gained some notice in the U.S. media. The gorge lies inside the former Soviet republic of Georgia, in the valley formed by the Alazani River in Georgia's northeastern province of Kakheti. Long before the Russian offensive in Chechnya, ethnic Chechens–known as Kisty in Georgian–had made the gorge their home. The Kisty first began to settle the small mountain villages, often no more than a handful of stone houses and a few flocks of sheep, more than a hundred years ago. During the second Chechen war, military officials in Moscow talked of hundreds, even thousands of Chechen and Taliban fighters who had taken refuge in the gorge to heal their wounds, train recruits, and smuggle arms, sup-

plies, and money into Chechnya. Rumors continue to emanate from the gorge, but one fact is undisputed: During the second war, the Pankisi became a critical lifeline for the Chechens to the outside world. The Chechens came by the myriad of trails through the mountains, but also by car. They traveled along the newly paved road, one of Shamil Basayev's construction projects, that linked the Chechen mountain village of Itum-Kale with Shatili on the Georgian side. When I visited the village of Duisi at the mouth of the Pankisi in October 1999, the war had forced a first wave of as many as two thousand refugees. UN relief workers in the Georgian capital, Tbilisi, provided them with supplies and plastic sheeting. The Georgian government preferred to ignore their presence. In October 1999, the main road from Tbilisi to the Pankisi Gorge was nearly unmanned by Georgian police.

33. Moscow's previous puppet regime was headed by Doku Zavgayev, the republic's Communist Party chief from 1989 to 1991. Zavgayev's attempt at administration lasted from October 1995 to August 1996, when the rebels retook Grozny. For more on Zavgayev's abortive regime and Koshman's role in the "nonrestoration of Grozny," see Carlotta Gall and Thomas de Waal, *Chechnya: A Small Victorious War* (London: Frank Cass, 1997), pp. 314–15.

34. Present-day Chernorechiye and Novy Aldy, both districts of Grozny, encompass the territory of the original Aldy. Residents on both sides of the dam are descendants of those who lived in the eighteenth-century village of Aldy. Novy Aldy was founded only in the 1950s, when the Chechens were allowed to return from their Central Asian exile.

35. Anna Zelkina, *In Quest for God and Freedom: Sufi Responses to the Russian Advance in the North Caucasus* (London: C. Hurst & Co., 2000), pp. 59–60.

36. Ibid., p. 64; See also: Dunlop, *Russia Confronts Chechnya*, pp. 11–12.

37. Zelkina, *In Quest for God and Freedom*, p. 66.

38. In April 1996, Khattab organized and led the ambush that trapped and destroyed a large Russian armored convoy near the village of Yaryshmardy. Nearly one hundred Russian soldiers were killed. Khattab, in a self-congratulatory video, marched with a beaming smile beside a long line of Russian corpses. The video, quite likely made for fund-raising purposes in the Middle East, was broadcast often on Russian television. After September 11, 2001, the charges that bin Laden and the Chechen rebels were in league grew by the day. The reports, vigorously promulgated by Moscow but amply seconded by Washington, ran from the probable–that Al Qaeda financed and recruited men for Khattab–to the fantastic: that bin Laden had offered unknown Chechen agents "$30 million and two tons of opium" for twenty Russian nuclear warheads (*Christian Science Monitor*, October 30, 2001). A series of reports, beginning with a UPI article in August 2000, held that a man known as Abu Daud, reportedly a bin Laden associate, had claimed to have trained four hundred fighters at an Al Qaeda camp in Afghanistan and sent them to Chechnya. While Abu Daud's claims went unproved, a number of Islamic militant groups had long been interested in Chechnya both as a cause and a potential center of operations. English-language Web sites, such as Qoqaz.net, openly conducted fund raising for the Chechen insurgency. It is also known, moreover, thanks to an Al Qaeda computer acquired in Kabul after the fall of the Taliban by my colleague in the Moscow press corps Alan Cullison, of the *Wall Street Journal*, that in December 1996 bin Laden's chief deputy, Dr. Ayman al-Zawahiri, tried to enter Dagestan. A letter Zawahiri sent to his colleagues in Egyptian Islamic Jihad, the militant group he helped found in Cairo years

before allying with bin Laden, reveals that he had tried to resettle the group in Chechnya. In Dagestan, however, Zawahiri and two assistants were arrested for entering the Russian Federation without visas. He spent six months in jail in Makhachkala, the Dagestani capital, before being released. At the trial in April 1997, Zawahiri stated his aim in coming to Dagestan was "to find out the price for leather, medicine, and other goods." Only after his failed Dagestani escapade did Zawahiri turn to Afghanistan as a base of operations, and eventually establish a formal alliance with bin Laden, in early 1998. Egyptian Islamic Jihad and Al Qaeda officially merged into Qaeda al-Jihad in June 2001. The *Wall Street Journal*, on July 2, 2002, published the first detailed account of Zawahiri's failed mission, "How a Secret, Failed Trip to Chechnya Turned Key Plotter's Focus to America and bin Laden," written by Alan Cullison and Andrew Higgins. See also Lawrence Wright's piece on Zawahiri, "The Man behind Bin Laden," *New Yorker* (September 16, 2002.)

39. The administrator was Ruslan Khamidov, killed in Alkhan-Yurt on July 16, 2000. Such reprisals for siding with the Russians became widespread. In February 2000 in Grozny the Russians established an OMON unit made up of three hundred Chechens aligned with Moscow. By the end of 2002, however, sixty of the Chechen OMON officers had been killed by rebels in ambushes and assassinations. The youngest victim was Katya Batayeva, the eighteen-year-old secretary of the Chechen OMON commander. Batayeva died from sixteen bullet wounds in January 2001.

40. The filtration camps have been amply documented. Babitsky was the most vocal witness of the Chernokozovo prison, but Memorial, Human Rights Watch, and Amnesty International all have published numerous reports on the human rights abuses visited on the Chechens in these jails. See, for example, Amnesty's March 23, 2000, report, "Chechnya: Rape and Torture of Children in Chernokozovo 'Filtration Camp.' "

41. The film, *War in Chechnya: A Strange War*, was produced by the pro-Russian Information Center of the Chechen Republic in 1997.

42. Chechen *teips* are clans, but the word denotes more than familial history. A *teip* signifies one's ancestral land. Gall and de Waal, *Chechnya*, p. 26. The Russian scholar Jan Chesnov has written extensively on the history and significance of the *teips*.

43. *Sheikh Kunta Khadzhi: zhizn' i uchenie*. Against great odds, it was published in Grozny in 1994.

44. Ibid., pp. 28–31; Zelkina, *In Quest of God and Freedom*, pp. 229–30.

45. Anna Zelkina, "Some Aspects of the Teaching of Kunta Hâjjî: On the Basics of the Manuscript by Abdal-Salâm Written in 1862 AD," *Journal of the History of Sufism* (2000), p. 491.

46. Akayev, *Kunta*, p. 61.

47. Leo Tolstoy, *Master and Man and Other Stories*, tr. Paul Foote (London: Penguin Group, 1977), p. 226.

48. Lev Tolstoi, *Dnevniki (1847–1894), Sobranie sochinenii v dvadtsati dvukh tomakh* (Moskva: Khudozhestvennaia literatura, 1985), v. 21, p. 37.

49. Layton, *Russian Literature and Empire*, pp. 284–85.

50. Edmund Spencer, *Travels in Circassia, Krim-Tartary, & C.* (London: Henry Colburn, 1839), v. 2, p. 20.

51. Alexander Chudakov, "Dr. Chekhov: A Biographical Essay (29 January 1980–15 July 1904)," in *The Cambridge Companion to Chekhov* (Cambridge, U.K.: Cambridge University Press, 2000), p. 3.

PART III. NORTH: TO THE SIXTY-NINTH PARALLEL

1. *Krasnoyarsky krai,* as the region is known in Russian, is a complex creature. Officially both the neighboring *okrugs,* a Soviet-era administrative term for a smaller province, the Taimyrsky and Evensky *okrugs,* are subordinate to the *krai. Krasnoyarsky krai* covers some 903,000 square miles. Only Yakutia, the region to the east, is bigger in landmass.

2. In 1992 the Russian government fined the complex $135 million for contaminating the local environment with radiation. Environmentalists estimated that the fine would cover the costs of cleaning the Yenisei and spreading seventy million cubic meters of clean topsoil around the Krasnoyarsk facility. There is no evidence the cleanup was ever done. In the Yeltsin years, the Ministry of Atomic Energy finished a storage plant, but a reprocessing complex, first authorized in 1977, remained unbuilt in 2002.

3. Despite polls that showed nearly eighty percent of the population opposed the new law, the Duma passed it in June 2001.

4. The Moscow historian was Boris Ilizarov; the girl was Lydia Pereligina. The long-buried document, signed by Igor Serov, then head of the KGB, was written to Khrushchev in June 1956. The KGB had stumbled on the story of the illegitimate son in the course of digging in Kureika after an article in *Life* magazine claimed that Stalin had been an informant for the Okhrana during his exile there. The only surviving grandson in Novokuznetsk was Yuri Davidov.

5. *The Protocols of the Elders of Zion,* a work cited by Hitler and Henry Ford, and still widely disseminated by anti-Semitic groups the world over, was a fake promulgated by the Okhrana. First printed in 1897, it was sold in book form in 1905. Its plot–a Jewish cabal seeks world dominion–was cribbed from various sources, including an 1868 German novel, *Biarritz,* by Hermann Goedzsche. See Walter Laqueur, *Black Hundred: The Rise of the Extreme Right in Russia* (New York: Harper Collins, 1993), ch. 3; Norman Cohn, *Warrant for Genocide: The Myth of the Jewish World Conspiracy and the Protocols of the Elders of Zion* (Encino, Calif.: Scholars Press, 1981; published in Russian in 1991 in Moscow); and Philip Graves, "The Truth about the Protocols: A Literary Forgery," *Times* (London), August 16–18, 1921.

6. Adriadna Efron, *Miroedikha* (Moskva: Vozvrashchenie, 1996), p. 150.

7. Fridtjof Nansen, *Through Siberia–The Land of the Future,* tr. Arthur G. Chater (New York: Frederick A. Stokes Co., 1914), p. 193.

8. Las Cases, Emmanuel, comte de, *Lesage's Historical, Genealogical, Chronological and Geographical Atlas,* 2d ed. (London: 1818).

9. József Lengyel, *Acta Sanctorum and Other Tales,* tr. Ilona Duezynska (London: Peter Owen Ltd., 1970), p. 133.

10. For centuries nomads roamed the ice fields around Norilsk. Then came Soviet power. The Bolsheviks classified them as "Peoples of the North"–rich material for museums and

dissertations, but not of much use to the Soviet experiment. I spent two days on a "reserve" north of Norilsk among the Nganasani, one of the region's native peoples, who rank among the most endangered in Russia. The northernmost of the Samoyeds, the Nganasani are first mentioned by the monk Nestor in his twelfth-century chronicle *A Tale of Bygone Years*. Theories vary on their origins, but they are considered the oldest nomads of the north, dating from the fourth century B.C. The Arctic was not exactly fertile, but fish and deer provided enough nutrition, and the isolation kept the Russians at bay. Only in the seventeenth century did Russian traders, hungry for their furs, come upon the Nganasani. At their peak, some kept vast herds of reindeer. The Soviet century, however, devastated them. First came an outbreak of influenza, then collectivization and Russification, and finally, the smelters of Norilsk. Today no Nganasan owns a single deer, and few are fluent in their native tongue. Once numbering more than four thousand, today there are only some seven hundred Nganasani alive.

11. Schmidt also helped map out Sakhalin. Nansen, *Siberia*, p. 156.

12. Urvantsev wrote two memoirs, one published in 1969, the other in 1981. Neither mentioned a word about prison labor. Urvantsev's first trip was in 1919, but it was not considered a full-scale expedition; successive crews came throughout the early 1920s.

13. Palladium, one of the PGMs, platinum group metals, rose in value almost tenfold from 1999 to 2001, from about $120 an ounce to almost $1,050 an ounce on the main international market, the London Metals Exchange.

14. On Norilsk's pollutants and their volume, see Andrew Bond, "The Russian Copper Industry and the Noril'sk Joint-Stock Company in the Mid-1990s," *Post-Soviet Geography and Economics*, v. 37, no. 5 (May 1996), pp. 305–8. See also D. J. Peterson, *Troubled Lands: The Legacy of Soviet Environmental Destruction*, in particular, ch. 2: "The Air" (Boulder, Colo.: Westview Press, 1993). For a historical perspective on the region's pollution, see an earlier article by Bond: "Air Pollution in Noril'sk: A Worst Case?," *Soviet Geography*, v. 25, no. 9 (November 1984).

15. Boris Kolesnikov, director of the Kombinat from 1973 to 1987, provided extensive data on the geometric growth of the 1970s.

16. Rossi, *Gulag Handbook*, p. 176. Rossi spent 1937 to 1961 in Soviet prisons and exile, ten years in Norilsk. When he got out, he decided to compile the notes he had kept in two decades of interviewing his fellow zeks. The result was his *Gulag Handbook*. Stretching more than six hundred pages, it is, as Solzhenitsyn has remarked, not a glossary but an encyclopedia of camp life. Jacques was still alive, in his nineties, when I went to see him in his flat on the edge of Paris. Among French anti-Communists he had become a living affidavit on the evils of Bolshevism. I asked about Norilsk. "It is useless to try to describe the life," he said, "because it was not life." He did not like to talk about the camps. He only said that he had accepted his sentence as "an opportunity, a chance to learn how wrong he had been." He preferred to talk of the present. He had returned to Norilsk, long before General Numerov, in the early 1990s. He had even written a new book of tales, *Qu'elle était belle cette Utopie!* (Paris: Le Cherche Midi Éditeur, 2000), which was followed by an autobiography, *Jacques, le Français: Pour mémoire du Goulag*, written with Michéle Sarde (Paris: Le Cherche Midi Éditeur, 2002).

17. Evfrosiniia Kersnovskaia, *Skol'ko stoit chelovek: povest' o perezhitom v 12 tetradiakh i 6 tomakh* (6 vols.; v 1–2: Moskva: Fond Kersnovskoi: Novosti, 2000; v. 3–6: Moskva: Fond

Kersnovskoi: Mozhaisk-Terra, 2001), v. 4, p. 25. In the 1960s, in an attempt to tell her mother what had happened to her, she drew seven hundred drawings–cartoonlike illustrations–of the camp's horrors. Kersnovskaia, whose drawings were first published during glasnost in *Ogonyok*, died in 1994. Her complete memoir, nearly fifteen hundred pages in twelve notebooks, only recently appeared in Russian. It was published–with a print run of a mere two thousand copies–in six volumes in 2000–2001. In 1991 selections of her drawings were published in a Russian-language album, *Naskal'naia zhivopis'*, (*Cave Drawings*) (Moscow: Kvadrat, 1991).

18. I was able to get copies of the statistical documents pertaining to the Norilsk camps from the Russian state archives. Some state documents pertaining to the Norilsk camps have been printed in works published by Memorial, both in Moscow and in Norilsk. Unfortunately, not all these documents have been declassified.

19. The *ukaz*, or decree, of the Presidium of the Supreme Soviet, passed on February 21, 1948, was signed by Stalin.

20. *MVD Prikaz*, (Interior Ministry Order) top secret, dated February 28, 1948.

21. David E. Hoffman, *The Oligarchs: Wealth and Power in the New Russia* (New York: PublicAffairs, 2002), p. 315. Hoffman gives an in-depth account of the loans-for-shares scheme. As does Freeland; see *Sale of the Century*, ch. 8, "The Faustian Bargain."

22. Hoffman, *Oligarchs*, p. 362.

23. Ibid., pp. 306 and 522; Thomson Bankwatch, report, September 27, 1996.

24. According to analysts at the Hermitage Fund and TroikaDialog, the company's net income for 2000 was $2.16 billion (using Russian accounting standards) and $1.42 billion (using the international standard, GAAP method), while dividends totaled $10,460,000. Figures, however, varied wildly. The *Moscow Times*, for example, in a May 22, 2001, article, "Norilsk Pans Minority Investors," reported its 2000 profits as $3.06 billion.

25. Urvantsev survived. He lived into his nineties, with his wife in Leningrad. After the camps, he was able to return to the Institute for Arctic Geology. He even had a mineral named after him: Urvantsevite; Pd (Bi, Pb)2. In 1985 an urn with the ashes of the Urvantsevs was flown to Norilsk and interred at the site of the First House. The First House was later moved, and there is no sign of the plaque where their ashes once lay. Urvantsev, however, fared better than some. In 1926 Pavel Alliluev, older brother of Stalin's second wife, was Dzerzhinsky's secretary when he was dispatched on a Norilsk expedition, no doubt to keep an eye on Urvantsev. Alliluev did not have a kind fate. He died early in Paris in 1938–of an "apparent" heart attack; Robert Conquest, *The Great Terror: A Reassessment* (New York: Oxford University Press, 1990), p. 58. Dzerzhinsky had also considered another Stalin brother-in-law, Stanislav Redens, then head of the Moscow secret police, for the trip. Anatoly Lvov, *Noril'skiye sud'by 1815–1995* (Moskva: Presto, 1995), p. 34.

26. The Stasi files, taken together, stretched 125 miles. The commission, known as the Gauck Authority for its head, the former East German pastor Joachim Gauck, was established in June 1990. By late 1993 it had received more than two million requests by citizens seeking to see their files. See Tina Rosenberg, *The Haunted Land: Facing Europe's Ghosts after Communism* (New York: Random House, 1995), pp. 290–97.

27. The issue of moral complicity and how German society, particularly reunited Germany, has faced it is of course enormously complex. German *Vergangungsheitbewältigung* is by no means a uniform, tidy process. Nor, of course, have all those devoted to national socialism recanted. Extremist groups continue to find followers, especially among the young. Yet the scale of the attempt to come to terms with the past in German society far dwarfs any such attempt in Russia. For more on Germany's "official exorcism," as she terms it, and its achievements and failings, see Rosenberg, *Haunted Land*, pp. 306–55.

28. Aleksandr I. Kokurin and Nikita V. Petrov, eds., *GULAG, 1918–1960* (Moskva; Materik, 2000), p. 10.

29. On July 14, 1953, in the Vorkuta camps more than ten thousand prisoners went on strike. Then, in May 1954, the largest insurrection hit in the Steplag camps in Kengir, Kazakhstan. The Steplag strike lasted forty days and was halted only by military force. Interior Ministry troops and tanks quelled the uprising. Solzhenitsyn devoted a chapter in *The Gulag Archipelago* to the Steplag strike, "The Forty Days of Kengir." See also Aleksandr Kokurin, *Otechestvennye arkhivy*, no. 4 (1994), pp. 33–86.

30. The tension had begun to increase in the fall of 1952, when a new *etap* of a mixed contingent–hard-core criminals and politicals–arrived from Karaganda, Kazakhstan. The new arrivals, survivors told me, were motivated and soon organized into "opposition cells" of five men each. They even devised their own arms, small hammers and axes. Ukrainians, Lithuanians, and Russians led the planning, but among them were ethnic Germans, Poles, and Belarusians. There exist a number of memoirs by zeks who participated in the strike. Yevhen Hrycyak and Rygor Klimovich, two of the revolt's leaders, wrote book-length memoirs.

In addition to the survivors in Norilsk, I was also able to interview former prisoners who now lived elsewhere. Among those who shared their memories of the strikes were Josef Halski, who had lived in Norilsk from 1946 to 1959 and now lived in Kraków, and Bronius Zlatkus, a Lithuanian who had arrived in Norilsk in 1948 and now lived in Vilnius, the Lithuanian capital. Igor Sobolyov, who now lived in the Russian city of Yaroslavl, told of the last and largest camp revolt. Sobolyov had been a leader of the Kengir strike, which lasted from May 16 to June 24, 1954, and in which nearly six hundred prisoners were killed. Interviews with Aleksei Loginov, the long-term Kombinat official, and Vasili Ksintaris, a former deputy head of the Norilsk complex and head of the Dudinka port, were also helpful in understanding the conditions before and after the strikes. Alla Makarova, a Norilsk journalist, has compiled a useful summary of the available material on the strikes, from memoirs, letters, and state archives. See Makarova, *Noril'skoe vosstanie: Mai-Avgust 1953 goda. In Soprotivlenie v Gulage. Volia*, v. 1, pp. 68–108. Moskva: Izdatel'stvo Vozvrashchenie, 1993.

31. Makarova, p. 78.

32. The camp and prison record of Leysia Zelinskaya, also known as Aleksandra Matveevna Zelinskaya, or Zelens'ka in Ukrainian, was reprinted by Memorial in Krasnoyarsk. See its Web site: www.memorial.krsk.ru.

33. Zlatkus interview, January 19, 2001.

34. Nanci Adler, *Gulag Survivor* (New Brunswick, N.J.: Transaction Publishers, 2002), p. 79.

35. In their demands, the strikers asked only for a relaxation of the camp's strictures. Among them: to shorten the workday to nine hours, to remove the stitched-on numbers

from their trousers and jackets that marked them as politicals, and to receive letters from relatives.

36. Zverev begged his bosses to rid him of his greatest problem, guards who drank. "The collective of the camp sector includes around 12,000 members in all, including the Party and Komsomol workers . . . but the cadres working in the maximum security camp divisions were poorly selected. This mistake must be corrected quickly. We must quit nannying certain guards who drink excessively." Zverev's 1953 report reveals that officials were aware the Norilsk camps needed reform—not to ease the lot of the prisoners but to survive as an economic concern. Additionally, I found a number of documents in the archives of the Soviet prosecutor's office, an unlikely source of human rights activism, detailing infractions by camp bosses and guards, ranging from drunkenness to embezzlement to endangering the life of a female prisoner. (Zverev's 1953 report was published in a collection of documents by the Norilsk chapter of Memorial in August 1991.)

37. Figures come from Kolesnikov and materials he provided from his tenure as director of the Kombinat, 1973–1987.

38. József Lengyel, *From Beginning to End* (Englewood Cliffs, N.J.: Prentice-Hall, 1968), p. 99.

39. M. S. Gorbachev, *Memoirs*, (New York: Doubleday, 1996), p. 264.

40. To my surprise, many of female prisoners I met had married their guards. Jadwiga Malewicz told me how her future husband had proposed to her. "He was one of the guards who took us to the factory every day," she said. "One day he yelled out to me, 'Hey Anya! My service time is finished in a week. I know you've got a year and half left of your sentence. So I'll stay here in town and wait for you. Then we'll get married.'" They did. Jadwiga said he had called her Anya because he could not pronounce her name. (It was Polish.) Her whole life that was who she was to him, Anya.

41. Romashkin's lament was common to many of the former prisoners. Often, they were deprived upon release of their rights to travel, to move, to work in city centers (where the work was), and to vote.

42. IEvhen Hrytsiak, *The Norilsk Uprising: Short Memoirs*, (München: Ukrainisches Institut für Bildungspolitik, 1984), p. 28.

PART IV. EAST: TO THE BREAKING POINT

1. Anton Chekhov, *Polnoe Sobranie Sochinenii i Pisem* (Moskva: Nauka, 1924–1968), v. 14–15, p. 28.

2. VladAvia suffered a crash the following year, in July 2001, when a Tupelov 154 fell from the sky near Irkutsk, halfway through a flight from Yekaterinburg in the Urals to Vladivostok. All 145 on board were killed.

3. See John Stephan, *The Russian Far East: A History* (Stanford: Stanford University Press, 1994), pp. 87–88.

4. A fascinating, rare account, written by one Junius B. Wood, of life within the short-lived Far Eastern Republic, appeared in *National Geographic* in June 1922.

5. The writer Varlam Shalamov was perhaps the most famous of the countless thousands of prisoners who went through the Second River transit camps en route to Kolyma. Another was Semyon Vilensky, the Moscow poet-publisher, head of the Vozvrashchenie publishing house.

6. Owen Lattimore, "New Road to Asia," *National Geographic* (December 1944), p. 657. Lattimore, whom McCarthy called the Soviets' top agent in the United States, is credited with coining the term "McCarthyism." Wallace later, in his 1946 book *Soviet Asia Mission* (New York: Reynol and Hitchcock Publishers, 1946), written with Andrew J. Steyer, recalled the trip in positive hues that virtually parroted Lattimore's words. Dalstroi, Wallace wrote, was "a combination TVA and Hudson's Bay Company" (p. 33), and the Kolyma gold miners were "big, husky young men" who, much to his surprise, wore American-made rubber boots (p. 35).

7. Stephan, *Russian Far East*, p. 71.

8. Chekhov began the June 27, 1890, letter to Suvorin: "When out of curiosity you hire a Japanese girl, you begin to understand Skalkovsky, who, they say, has a photograph of himself with some Japanese whore." Konstantin Skalkovsky, a contemporary of Chekhov's was a Petersburg critic. Further on in the letter, Chekhov provides his publisher and friend Suvorin with intimate details of his encounter in the brothel: "When you come, the Japanese girl will tug out a little piece of cotton with her teeth from her sleeve and catch you by the 'boy' (remember Mariya Krestovskaya?) and surprise you by performing a wipe-down, during which the cotton even tickles your stomach. All this she does coquettishly, laughing and singing with these little "tse" sounds. . . ." (Krestovskaya was an actress and an early love of Chekhov's.) The letter, absent from Soviet editions of the writer's collected works, was published by the Russian scholar Aleksandr Chudakov in " 'Ne prilichnie slova,' i oblik klassika," in *Literaturnoe Obozrenie*, v. 11 (1991), p. 54. Donald Rayfield, in his biography of Chekhov includes a somewhat different translation (Rayfield, *Anton Chekhov: A Life* [New York: Henry Holt & Co., 1998], p. 220).

9. Rossi, *Gulag Handbook*, pp. 524–25. For tsarist prison rations, Rossi cites Vlas Doroshevich's book on Sakhalin, published in 1901.

10. George Kennan, *Siberia and the Exile System* (New York: Century Company), 1891), v. 2, p. 221.

11. Ibid., p. 222.

12. The Sakhalin state archives are compiling a book of Chekhov's cards. The archivists in Yuzhno-Sakhalinsk and in Moscow believe the total is not ten thousand, as Chekhov claimed. The children's cards were at some point separated, and some may have been lost. Yet it was clear, as I read through the cards in the Lenin Library, that Chekhov had had help in filling out the thousands of cards. Not every card was written in his distinctive hand.

13. G. I. Miromanov, "Sakhalin v tvorchestve Chekhova," in *Sibir i Sakhalin v biografii i tvorchestve A. P. Chekhova* (IUzhno-Sakhalinsk: Dal'nevostochnoe knizhnoe otdelenie, 1993), p. 77.

14. Chekhov, *Polnoe sobranie, Sochinenii i pisem*, v. 14–15, p. 361.

15. All the Russian oil companies were associated with oligarchs. Yukos was founded by

the former Komsomol leader Mikhail Khodorkovsky, Sidanco acquired by Potanin, Lukoil run by Vagit Alekperov, and Sibneft controlled first by Boris Berezovsky and then by his erstwhile protégé Roman Abramovich. In time, a few, like Lukoil, Surgutneftegas, and Sidanco, did attract–with varying degrees of transparency and corporate governance–sizable foreign investment.

16. Hokkaido, at its closest point, is just twenty-five miles to the south of Sakhalin.

17. In early 2003, Russia was producing more than 7 million barrels of oil per day, second in the world only to Saudi Arabia. At the same time, the country's total exports, after a low in 1994 of 3.16 million barrels a day, topped 5 million. Oil executives in Moscow may talk of the day when the Russians will overtake the Saudis in exports, but few in the industry foresee it happening. Most Russian oil still does not go for export–beyond the borders of the former Soviet Union. The Saudis' reserves, moreover, dwarf the Russians': The Saudis have 264.2 billion barrels of proven oil reserves (more than a quarter of the world total), while the Russians have oil reserves of some 49 billion barrels.

18. The governor of Sakhalin, Igor Farkhudinov, told me that the island's total recoverable reserves of oil, gas, and condensate, including both on- and offshore fields, totaled nearly nine hundred million tons. If true, this would be approximately equal to one-half of the reserves of Prudhoe Bay in Alaska. See Judith Thornton, "Sakhalin Energy: Problems and Prospects," in *Russia's Far East: A Regional Risk*, ed. Judith Thornton and Charles E. Ziegler (Seattle: University of Washington Press, 2002), p. 8.

19. "An Open Letter from Vladimir Putin to the Russian Voters," Feb. 25, 2000. Published in numerous Russian newspapers and Web sites on the eve of the 2000 presidential election.

20. Only Magadan, Komi, Chukotka, and Yakutia lost more residents in absolute numbers.

21. The mill worker's attempt at self-crucifixion, alas, did not get much press. It was noted, however, in small stories in *Novye izvestiya*, November 27, 1997; *Vladivostok*, November 28, 1997, and *Pravda 5*, December 1, 1997.

22. Years later, in February 1973, Chakovsky, ever the court scribe, then editor in chief of *Literaturnaya gazeta*, in a "review" of a new Harrison Salisbury book, attacked Andrei Sakharov, claiming the dissident physicist "coquettishly waved an olive branch," "played the holy fool," and "willingly accepted the compliments of the Pentagon" (Andrei Sakharov, "How I Came to Dissent," first published in English in the *New York Review of Books*, March 21, 1974).

23. Adam John de Krusenstern, *Voyage Around the World in the Years 1803, 1804, 1805 & 1806* (London: John Murray, 1813; facsimile edition, Tokyo: Tenri Central Library, 1973), v. 2, p. 66.

24. Anton Chekhov, *The Island: A Journey to Sakhalin*, tr. Luba and Michael Terpak (New York: Washington Square Press, 1967), p. 37.

25. John J. Stephan, *Sakhalin: A History* (Oxford: Clarendon Press, 1971), p. 179.

26. ExxonMobil in the summer of 2001, with Putin's vocal blessing, announced plans to develop its own fields. British Petroleum also soon set its sights on the shelf.

27. Brownell, who studied the "eastern" population of the species that migrates from Alaska to Baja California, had known of the Sakhalin whales for years, but could see them only after the USSR collapsed. He and his colleagues first traveled to Sakhalin in 1995. They worked under a U.S.-Russian environmental agreement, initiated by Nixon in 1972 and renewed under the Gore-Chernomyrdin Commission. They were the first to use small boats to monitor the whales during their feeding months; the Soviets had always used helicopters to survey, an inexact science. Camping out each summer at the Piltun Lighthouse at the mouth of the lagoon, the Russian and American scientists managed to photograph the whales in such detail that they could tell each animal by its spots. The team of scientists reached an accommodation with the oil companies. ExxonMobil and Sakhalin Energy even funded the whale research in part. Brownell worked with Dr. Aleksandr Burdin of the Kamchatka Institute for Ecology and Nature Management and Dr. David Weller of Texas A&M University. See D. W. Weller, S. H. Reeve, A. M. Burdin, B. Wuersig and R. L. Brownell. "Western Gray Whales (Eschrichtius robustus) off Sakhalin Island, Russia: Spatial Distribution as Determined by Aerial Surveys," *Journal of Cetacean Research and Management.* Special Issue on Gray Whales, no. 3, forthcoming.

28. The whales' feeding ground is north of the Molikpaq, the primary offshore platform run by the Sakhalin Energy consortium. But the Odoptu field, where the consortium that is led by ExxonMobil is searching for oil, overlaps the area where the whales feed each year from June to November (Robert Brownell interview, July 11, 2002; David Gordon, "Suckered at Sakhalin," *Ecologist* [February 2002]).

29. In 1999 the scientists started to see "extremely skinny whales," about ten in all, in the population. In 2000 the number rose to twenty-seven. In 2001 it fell to seventeen. Russian and American environmentalists wanted to blame the oil companies for the weight loss. But Brownell found the same decreased weight among the eastern population—some twenty thousand whales—that migrated along the West Coast from Alaska to California to Baja. He and other scientists posited that greater oceanographic conditions—more ice cover, etc.—may be affecting the food base and reducing the chances to feed. Still, the appearance of skinny whales raised concern. In summer 2001, ExxonMobil conducted a series of seismic surveys, sending loud blasts of noise through the ocean waters. Within days the whales swam south to an area they had not previously used for feeding. To Brownell, the move was alarming. "For whales that are skinny, and some who are calves, having to move from their feeding ground to a place of poor quality food is detrimental," he said. Swimming away from the feeding ground during the seismic testing, he explained, "meant a big metabolic drain on the calves; they need the maximum number of days on the feeding grounds." Also that summer the team's research resulted in a resolution from the intergovernmental International Whaling Commission to protect western Pacific gray whales. In a letter to the Russian Ministry of Natural Resources, the scientists wrote: "We believe that seismic operations have displaced whales from their preferred habitat. It is quite likely that they have been forced to use less preferred areas that may be characterised by food resources that are more limited or of poorer quality. That is, although the whales observed continue to feed, their food intake may be decreased as a result of the noted shift in distribution to the south." Finally, late in the summer, ExxonMobil stopped the testing. Almost immediately the whales moved north again.

30. As the ice closes in, the supertanker itself then leaves for Asia with the last oil shipment of the season.

31. The Pacific Environment and Resources Center (PERC), a California group involved in efforts to protect Russia's environment, commissioned a team of independent experts to write a report on the dangers posed by oil production on Sakhalin and described the September 1999 spill. One Yuzhno-Sakhalinsk environmentalist, Nikolai Shugaipov, argued that the amount spilled in 1999 far exceeded two tons. Dmitri Lisitsyn, director of the Sakhalin Environment Watch in Yuzhno, claimed that the environmental inspector on board the Molikpaq during the off-loading did not at first know about the spill. Instead, Sakhalin Energy informed its Houston office, which relayed the news to Natalia Onischenko, the head of Sakhalin's Committee of Ecology at the time, who happened to be in Houston visiting Sakhalin Energy. The local environmental inspector found out about the spill only when Onischenko, calling from Houston, woke him in the middle of the night. Judith Thornton also describes the spill in "Sakhalin Energy: Problems and Prospects."

32. Stephan, *Russian Far East*, p. 235. A book, paid for in part by the local KGB, was published on Sakhalin devoted to Drekov's crimes: Mikhail Voinilovich, *Delo No. SU-3246 (zhizn' i smert' kombriga Drekova)* IUzhno-Sakhalinsk: Transport, 1991.

33. See "Expert Panel Recasts Origin of Fossil Man in Northwest," *New York Times*, October 16, 1999. A long legal battle ensued, as Native American groups fought to claim the remains found in the Columbia River as their own.

34. *Kto rukovodil NKVD*, p. 180.

35. The Sinclair fiasco is described by several sources: Robert Tolf, *The Russian Rockefellers: The Saga of the Nobel Family and the Russian Oil Industry*, (Stanford: Hoover Institution Press, 1976), p. 223; Floyd J. Fithian, "Dollars Without the Flag: The Case of Sinclair and Sakhalin Oil," *Pacific Historical Review*, v. 39, no. 2 (May 1970), pp. 205–22; Stephan, *Sakhalin*, pp. 101–03.

36. In the National Archives in Washington, D.C., I found copies of the affidavits given by McCulloch and McLaughlin at the U.S. Legation in Peking on May 8, 1924.

37. Fithian, "Dollars Without the Flag," p. 221.

38. Kennan, *Siberia and the Exile System*, v. 2, Appendix G, p. 555.

39. Vladislav Latyshev, director of the history museum in Yuzhno, related the history of Laguri.

40. Chekhov, *The Island*, p. 16.

41. Ibid., p. 45.

42. Ibid., p. 20.

43. Ibid., pp. 21–22.

44. Ibid., p. 100.

45. Vladimir Nabokov, in his *Onegin* translation, offers: "Tatiana, dear Tatiana!/I now shed tears with you./Into fashionable tyrant's hands/ your fate already you've relinquished." Aleksandr Pushkin, *Eugene Onegin*, tr. with commentary by Vladimir Nabokov (Princeton: Princeton University Press), ch. 3, stanza XV.

46. Charles H. Hawes, *Uttermost East: Being on Account of Investigations among the Natives*

and Russian Convicts of the Island of Sakhalin, with Notes of Travel in Korea, Siberia, and Manchuria (New York: Harper and Brothers, 1903), p. 464.

47. Yuvachyov was a "soft radical," according to Aleksandr Kostanov, Sakhalin's chief archivist. He did not appear to have had a direct role in Alexander II's assassination. On Sakhalin, Chekhov was much taken with him, and in 1901, Chekhov's publisher, Suvorin, printed Yuvachyov's memoir, *Eight Years on Sakhalin*. It was never reprinted. Not until 2000 did the village elders of Tymovskoye produce an offprint. In Yuzhno I bought the last of the two hundred copies they printed. In 1903, back in Petersburg, Yuvachyov sired one of the great absurdists of the Soviet century. His son was also best known by a pseudonym, Daniil Kharms. An irreverent author of experimental prose and poetry, in 1920s Petersburg Kharms was a leading voice in the OBERIU group, writers and poets who paraded their disdain for the canon. Although never outwardly political, Kharms, too, incurred the wrath of the state. He died–of starvation, it is said–in a Leningrad cell in 1942.

48. Ivan Miroliubov (Yuvachyov), *Vosem' let na Sakhaline* (St. Petersburg: Tipografiia A. S. Suvorina, 1901; offprint, IUzhno-Sakhalinsk: Sakhalinskaia oblastnaia tipografiia, 2000), p. 287.

49. Krusenstern, *Voyage Around the World*, v. 2, p. 67.

PART V. WEST: THE *SKAZKA*

1. The rails followed, more or less, the old road made famous by the writer Aleksandr Radishchev in 1790, when he published an account of a journey from Petersburg to Moscow. Radishshev's *A Journey from St. Petersburg to Moscow* was a radical work, an abolitionist treatise.

2. In 1991 the people of Leningrad began to debate returning to their city its first name. The name had of course changed several times since the city's birth. As a Soviet riddle asked, "Who was born in a swamp and baptized three times?" In 1914, at the outset of the World War I, when Nicholas I considered the German suffix "burg" no longer acceptable, St. Petersburg became Petrograd. In 1924, after Lenin died, Petrograd was renamed Leningrad. Lenin, however, hated the city. He feared its damp air and blustery winds, considered its ornate facades and gilt interiors obscene reminders of the imperial past. When Lenin moved the capital to Moscow in 1918, he earned the gratitude of Peter's heirs. He had saved their grand buildings and parks from the Bolshevik urban planners. The vote to return the city's original name came in the summer of 1991, just weeks before the putsch against Gorbachev. Solzhenitsyn, playing midwife to history's rebirth, put forth his own choice: Svyato-Petrograd, or St. Petrograd. The name, the writer argued, would be both linguistically correct (i.e., purebred Slavic) and true to its founder's desires. To many in the city, however, their hometown had always been just *Piter,* the nickname its residents had used for generations.

3. The tape of Linkov's emergency call was later aired on television in the NTV film *Chista rossiiskoe ubiistvo [A Purely Russian Murder]*, made in time for Starovoitova's forty-day memorial, the Russian Orthodox tradition of mourning the dead forty days after their death. The call to Interfax was taken by Linkov's colleague and friend Irina Krupenie.

4. The dissident philosopher had served a decade in prison for anti-Soviet agitation. Once, after they had met in a café, Starovoitova was called into the Big House, as Petersburg residents still call the city's secret police headquarters. The agents showed her photographs of herself with the dissident. They told her she'd better be careful whom she chose as her friends. Starovoitova had taken pride in the encounter. The KGB men had driven her home in a black Volga. "See how they escorted me!" she boasted to her younger sister, Olga. Their father, however, for the first time drew the line. "Papa had no illusions, but we did," Olga told me. "He sat us down and said, 'Girls, you can do want you want, but we live in a police state. Don't ever forget that.' "

5. Starovoitova's was not the first grave the Young Reformers had convened at. A year and a half earlier they had buried thirty-six-year-old Mikhail Manevich, a close protégé of Chubais's and a Petersburg deputy governor who had run the city's privatization program. If Starovoitova's murder shocked for its target, Manevich's, in August 1997, stunned the city for its audacity. Manevich was killed in his Volvo by a sniper as he was driven to work in morning traffic on the Nevsky Prospekt. So precise was the shooter that he hit Manevich five times while the back window of the sedan did not shatter. Governor Yakovlev's comment on Manevich's murder struck a typically hollow note: "I believe this is an attempt at a threat of sorts, and it will not lead to anything good" (*St. Petersburg Times*, August 25, 1997). At Manevich's funeral, Chubais found rare passion. "I want to tell those who pulled the trigger," he declared, "and those who paid for this with their dirty stinking stolen money, we will get you, all of you." Ruslan Linkov, I was not surprised to hear, had a theory about why Manevich was killed. Manevich was murdered on August 18, 1997. The next day he was to meet with Starovoitova about a racket run by a local parliamentarian concerning prospective privatization projects. Manevich, Linkov told me, had documents on the scam and wanted Starovoitova to publish them. On the day Manevich was killed, Linkov was to call him to arrange the meeting. August 19 was the anniversary of the 1991 coup. Starovoitova had asked Linkov to set up the meeting in a café. "Manevich was going to give Galina Vasilievna the documents on the racket," Linkov claimed, "and they were going to celebrate the victory over the coup plotters."

6. Radio interview with Galina Starovoitova, Ekho Moskvy, June 23, 1998.

7. Adam Michnik. "A Death in St. Petersburg," *New York Review of Books* (January 14, 1999), pp. 4–6.

8. Peter christened it not, as is popularly thought, after himself, but in the Orthodox tradition, after the saint he was named for.

9. Peter initiated modern Russia's attempt at a meritocracy, the Table of Ranks. While the move intended to give men rank according to their abilities, not to their blood, Peter also believed in the need to strengthen both the aristocracy and the institution of serfdom. Dreaming that he could foster a European nobility in Russia, he ordered Russian men to lose their Muscovite caftans and shave their beards.

10. Peter and his mates founded the Drunken Synod, whose orgiastic feasts mocked the rituals of the Orthodox Church. During his stay in England in 1697 as a young man, he and his party trashed Sayes Court, John Evelyn's estate. Evelyn passed the bill on to the crown "for a destroyed lawn, smashed furniture, torn curtains, and family portraits that had been used for target practice." Priscilla Roosevelt, *Life on the Russian Country Estate: A Social and Cultural History* (New Haven: Yale University Press, 1995), p. 12.

11. Peter so despised the feeble tsarevich Aleksei, he leaped at the chance to accuse him of treachery. The record is unclear, but it seems that the closest poor Aleksei ever came to treason was to impregnate a Finnish lover.

12. Alexander Pushkin, *The Bronze Horseman and Other Poems*, tr. D. M. Thomas (NewYork: Penguin Books, 1982), p. 248. Joseph Brodsky, *Less than One: Selected Essays* (New York: Penguin Books, 1986, p. 94.

13. Brodsky, *Less than One*, p. 76.

14. Likhachev wrote of the execution night, the formative event of his life, in his memoir, *Reflections on the Russian Soul: A Memoir* (New York: Central European University Press, 2000).

15. The toll of the first months of 2000 was extraordinary:
January 10: Ilya Vaisman, thirty-six, financial director of the Baltika brewery in Petersburg. Shot–in the head and heart–in his kitchen by a marksman who had stood on the ledge of his fifth-floor apartment. It was not the first time the brewery had lost an executive; the summer before, its marketing director, who had once been a political activist in Vladikavkaz, Aslanbek Chochiyev, was shot dead as he alighted from his Mercedes.
February 2: Valery Potapov, thirty-six, head of the Baltic Dawn timber company. Shot twice in the back of the head near his house.
March 11: Dmitri Varvarin, forty, head of a Russian-American venture, into everything from shipbuilding to tea. Shot point-blank in the back of the head.
March 22: Sergei Krizhan, forty-four, head of an import-export outfit. Shot to death while driving his jeep with his twenty-year-old son, a university finance student.
April 4: Gennadi Ivanov, forty-five, head of Kvarton, Russia's biggest thread and yarn company. Killed by automatic-weapons fire on his way to the office.
April 10: Igor Bamburin, forty-seven, head of Viton, a Petersburg television factory. Shot in the head four times as he arrived at his daughter's home. Bamburin had previously served in Petersburg's RUBOP, the regional organized crime-fighting squad. At least five passersby witnessed his murder.
April 26: Georgi Pozdnyakov, forty-four, part owner of the Hollywood Nights nightclub. Shot three times in the head and chest at the Petersburg Railways University sport complex.

16. Brodsky, *Less than One*, pp. 89–90.

17. Fyodor Dostoyevsky, *Crime and Punishment*, tr. David McDuff (London: Penguin Books, 1991), p. 540.

18. Mikhail Lantsman, "Prezident poruchil doverennym litsam naiti natsional'nuiu ideiu," *Segodnia*, July, 13, 1996; interview with Georgi Satarov.

19. "Nationhood" is *Narodnost'*, often translated as "nationalism"; first used in 1832 by Sergei Uvarov, Nicholas I's minister of education.

20. Pipes, p. 266; Peter Yakovlovich Chaadayev, *Philosophical Letters & Apology of a Madman*, tr. Mary-Barbara Zeldin (Knoxville: University of Tennessee Press, 1969), p. 6.

21. Chaadayev (Zeldin), *Philosophical Letters*, p. 34.

22. S. Volkov, *St. Petersburg: A Cultural History*, tr. Antonina W. Bouis (New York: Free Press, 1995), p. 452, cites K. Simonov, *Glazami cheloveka moego pokoleniya* (Moscow: "Kniga," 1990), p. 111.

23. For more on Lev Gumilyov's Eurasianism and its nationalist undercurrents, see Viktor Shnirelman and Sergei Panarin, "Lev Gumilev: His Pretensions as a Founder of Ethnology and His Eurasian Theories," *Inner Asia*, v. 3 (2001), pp. 1–18.

24. N. A. Berdyaev, *Russkaya ideya sud'ba Rossii* (Moskva: Svarogik, 1997), p. 14.

25. The House of Romanov ruled for three centuries, but the legacy of the False Dmitri outlived their reign. Pushkin took it as material for his play *Boris Godunov*, which Mussorgsky later turned into the opera of the same name.

26. The Nikitin case came to a final resting point only the following summer. On September 13, 2000, Russia's Supreme Court dismissed the state prosecutor's move to overturn the St. Petersburg City Court's acquittal of December 29, 1999, which the Supreme Court had upheld on April 17, 2000.

27. Tatiana Maksimova, "Starovoitovu ubili iz-za $1,000,000?" *Komsomol'skaya pravda*, December 22, 1998.

28. *Chista Rossiiskoe Ubiistvo*, NTV.

29. The Sofia conference was held on October 10–12, 1998.

30. It was not the first time I had heard the accusation. Many in Petersburg had aired it. The evidence, however, was circumstantial. Seleznev, a Petersburg native, was a veteran of the old school who had taken fast to the new orders. In the months before the murder, he had announced his intention to dislodge Gennadi Zyuganov as leader of the Communists. Seleznev had already publicly entertained the next move, a run for the presidency. But his career had suffered a setback. A disconcerting number of his adjutants had fallen prey to contract hits. At the same time, a shadowy entity calling itself the Academy for National Security emerged in Petersburg. The academy had held one seminar—on "Insurance & National Security"—and was soon to convene a fund-raising meeting for another seminar, this time on "Telecommunications & National Security." On October 17, 1998, the academy held the fund-raiser in the Tauride Palace. A gift from Catherine to her most treasured lover, Prince-Field-Marshal Grigori Potemkin, in 1789, the neoclassical palace was Potemkin's home for just a year, the last of his outsize life. Now the Tauride, its facade and colonnade restored, belonged to the city government. Starovoitova and Linkov were headed for a meeting in the palace when thanks to an errant guard, they learned of the fund-raiser. They ducked inside and could not believe what they heard. The scheme, Linkov claimed, was to extract private funds in exchange for political patronage. "Seleznev just threw it out there," Linkov said. " 'Become a sponsor of our academy.' " Linkov and Starovoitova surveyed the crowd. An array of local business luminaries filled the rows. Among them sat the regional bosses of the FSB, police, tax police, and customs. The contributions, Linkov said, ranged from "General Sponsor" (thirty thousand dollars) to "Official Sponsor" (ten thousand dollars) to "Regular Sponsor" (one thousand dollars). Before long, the interlopers were discovered. By then, however, Starovoitova and Linkov had done a tally. They had seen pledges totaling half a million dollars. Outraged, Starovoitova set out to expose the scheme in *Severnaya stolitsa* [*Northern Capital*], the weekly broadsheet of her own political party. The article,

"New Russian Communists: The Union of the Sickle and Dollar," appeared the day before her murder. The byline read "Anna Prokhorova and Pyotr Glebov," but behind the pseudonyms stood Starovoitova and Linkov. Seleznev expressed shock at the article, sued for libel, and in May 1999 lost his case.

When it came to Governor Yakovlev, Linkov's list of motives ran long. There were the World Bank credits. UNESCO had put Petersburg's city center on its list of heritage sites. In 1997 the city received the first tranche of three hundred million dollars for rebuilding projects. Starovoitova did not doubt the need for the funds. The roof of the National Archive, after all, was caving in. She wrote Governor Yakovlev to suggest establishing a commission of historians and architects to study which buildings deserved restoration. Academician Likhachev, she wrote, should head it. To her surprise, Starovoitova got a quick reply. Not to worry, the governor wrote, the commission was in place, and he was its director. In February 1998, another front opened. Starovoitova engaged Yakovlev in a shouting match in Smolny, the former convent that had served as Lenin's war room and was now the governor's office. The fight, said her longtime Petersbug aide Galina Markelova, had become personal. By spring Starovoitova had engaged Yakovlev in a legislative crisis that paralyzed the local assembly for months. Hoping to weaken Yakovlev's power to rule by decree, the assembly's liberal members had moved to revise the city charter. The governor and his allies saw no need for any changes. Starovoitova revived the Russian tradition of the open letter to challenge the assembly members. "Whether we will live in a city with a European-style rule of law or just another nameless provincial town depends on each of your positions in this conflict," she wrote (Brian Whitmore, "St. Petersburg's Reformers Battle a Russian Tammany Hall," *Prism*, v. 4, Issue 22 [November 13, 1998]).

Another source of contention with the governor was the two-hundred-millon-dollar line of credit from a British bank earmarked for his pet construction project, a new train station with a deluxe hotel, the terminus of an envisioned high-speed link with Moscow. The company founded to build the complex had asked the city to guarantee the loan. (The railroads had long been a source of scandal. RAO VSM, a fast-train company founded by a Yeltsin decree in November 1991, lasted five years before going bankrupt. It had cost the state five hundred million dollars.) The summer before her death, Starovoitova had learned of the project and spoken out against it. She knew, her Duma aide Yodkovskaya said, how the deal would go: Once the city backed the loan, the company would get the cash, the cash would be diverted into private pockets, and the company would go bankrupt. In the end, all the players would disappear, and no station, deluxe or otherwise, would be built. Starovoitova, as everyone in Petersburg knew, had succeeded in scuttling the deal.

31. Their meeting took place a week after Yeltsin named Putin to replace Nikolai Kovalev as the director of the FSB. Yeltsin had tasked Putin with a crackdown, or at least a perceived crackdown, on extremist groups. Putin, Linkov recalled, spent most of the meeting complaining of the "cold shoulder" he had first felt at the helm of the FSB.

32. I spent an afternoon in February 2001 with Bodrov at Lenfilm. He was finishing work on his directorial debut, *Sisters*. By then he had appeared in more than two dozen films. The best known in the West were Regis Wargnier's *East-West*, in which Bodrov acted alongside Catherine Deneuve, and the 1996 Oscar-nominated *Prisoner of the Caucasus*, which was directed by his father. Yet it was Bodrov's role as the insouciant hit man in the *Brother* films that had earned him a singular place in the Russian popular imagination.

For my sake, he tried to explain the public's immense affinity for his hit man. The popularity weighed on Bodrov. He recalled a conversation with a priest who had complained that the films did not comport with Russian Orthodoxy. "He said that in the Russian tradition a hero had to repent, to have a conscience–you know, like Raskolnikov." He had pleaded with Bodrov to make another film in the series, to have his character repent. Bodrov had begged off.

The *Brother* films, he told me, tried to make a different point: "Imagine a time in the primeval world when people were still living in caves. They're sitting around the fire when suddenly someone gets up and says, 'Enough. This is the way it'll be. . . . We need to defend our own, to defend our brothers and our women. We've got to stand together, simply to survive.' It's like a proto-law. . . . Later, of course, other codes will follow. They'll find Christ and repent and so on. But at this point there still was no law–like it was, and in essence still is, in Russia today." His hit man, yes, did not always act equitably–some of his victims were innocent; some were murderers–but it was only a first attempt, he said, "to introduce some kind of justice into this world." The following year Bodrov joined the seemingly endless line of Russian cultural stars who died too young. In September 2002 he was killed in an avalanche in North Ossetia. He and a film crew had been filming in the area at the time. His death was mourned as a national tragedy.

33. *Vremya*, August 8, 2001.

34. Andrei Konstantinov, *Banditsky Peterburg* (Moskva: Olma Press, 1999), p. 347.

35. The interior minister was rather specific in his public accusations: "In St. Petersburg the Tambov organized crime group controls as many as one hundred industrial enterprises–including the fuel and energy sector." The press conference was widely covered. See Viktor Matveev, "Tambovsky Peterburg," *Vremya novostei*, August 9, 2001, p. 1.

36. On eighteenth-century maps, the *rosa ventorum* was a legend marker, divided in thirty-two points, of cardinal directions. Once a symbol of boundless exploration, of the romance of the seas, in the mind of an enterprising Soviet planner it evoked the far-flung reach of the Soviet Navy.

37. A number of works have appeared on the rise of Russian organized crime. A great many suffer from inaccuracies and hyperbole. But the most detailed academic study is a recent book by Vadim Volkov, associate professor at the European University in Petersburg, *Violent Entrepreneurs: The Use of Force in the Making of Russian Capitalism* (Ithaca: Cornell University Press, 2002). Volkov in an earlier article in a leading Russian business magazine, "Ne slovo o proshlom [Not a Word about the Past]," *Ekspert* (April 15, 2002), summarized the complex evolution of the Tambov Gang.

38. The 1990 arrests–seventy-two members of the Tambov Gang in all–resulted from a police special operation. See V. Volkov, *Violent Entrepreneurs*, ch. 5, "Bandits & Capitalists," pp. 97–125.

39. V. Volkov, "Ne slovo o proshlom."

40. In May 1999 the Uralmash group registered as a political organization with the Justice Ministry, now calling itself the Social-Political Union–Uralmash or OPS in its Russian acronym. It was a wry joke. Law enforcement had long called the gang by the same initials, standing for "organized criminal society" in Russian.

41. Vladimir Barsukov, "Tambovtsy, kak i peterburzhtsy–eto vsego lishch' zhiteli rossi-iskikh gorodov," *Smena* (April 20, 2000). By 2003 the city had sold nearly all its shares in the fuel company. It now held, according to Kumarin, "a little more than one percent" of the PTK.

42. "St. Petersburg, Russia Retail Gasoline Market," U.S. Foreign Commercial Service, St. Petersburg, Russia, April 16, 2002. Report by Business Information Service for the Newly Independent States (BISNIS), U.S. Department of Commerce.

43. Anna Benn and Rosamund Bartlett, *Literary Russia: A Guide* (London: Papermac, 1997) pp. 296–98; S. Volkov, *St. Petersburg*, p. 177.

44. W. Bruce Lincoln, *Sunlight at Midnight: St. Petersburg and the Rise of Modern Russia* (New York: Basic Books, 2000), p. 276.

45. Ibid., p. 290.

46. On the deaths, see ibid. but also Harrison Salisbury's book on the siege, *The 900 Days: The Siege of Leningrad* (New York: Harper & Row, 1969), and most recently, a new military account: David M. Glantz, *The Battle for Leningrad, 1941–1944* (Lawrence: University of Kansas Press, 2002).

47. Likhachev, *Reflections*, p. 220.

48. Ibid., pp. 248–51.

49. Ibid., pp. 234–35. Likhachev described how a woman on the Academy of Sciences staff was "eaten." She was lured to a market by a promise of meat and never returned. "She'd looked comparatively healthy," he noted. "We were afraid to take the children out into the street even in daytime."

50. Lidiya Ginzburg, *Blockade Diary*, tr. Alan Myers (London: Harvill Press, 1995), p. 65. Among literary accounts of the siege, Ginzburg's may be the best known. Another is Natalya Baranskaya's *A Week Like Any Other*. A recent compilation of women's memoirs and diaries from the blockade is *Writing the Siege of Leningrad*, edited by Cynthia Simmons and Nina Perlina and published by the University of Pittsburgh Press, 2002.

51. Ginzburg, *Blockade Diary*, p. xx.

52. Likhachev, *Reflections*, pp. 26–27.

53. HIV/AIDS researchers believe the virus first entered the USSR in 1986, but 1987 was the first year that cases were officially recorded.

54. Russian Health Ministry statistics as of January 2003. The number of registered cases, however, rose so fast the federal figures often failed to incorporate the latest totals from the regions. See also UNAIDS, "Report on the Global HIV/AIDS Epidemic 2002" (The Barcelona Report, July 2002). In late 2002 the World Bank office in Moscow said that according to its best estimates, the true number of HIV cases was between 800,000 and 1.2 million.

55. Health Ministry press release, June 2, 2002.

56. After the Kremlin meeting, Gergiev announced, "For Vladimir Putin, as a politician and as a person, the most important thing is the fate of his country–its people, its culture and its morale." "Nepravitel'stvenniy doklad," *Novaya gazeta*, March 6, 2000. Days later,

on March 10, 2000, Putin hosted British Prime Minster Tony Blair at the Mariinsky, to take in the premiere of the Gergiev-Konchalovsky *War and Peace*, a coproduction with the Metropolitan Opera. The presidential election was held on March 26, 2000.

57. S. Volkov, *St. Petersburg*, pp. 427–28. In Volkov's telling, the lines from the Ninth Psalm were to be sung by a soloist. However, Sofia Khentova, Shostakovich's Russian biographer, maintains that the composer, before arriving at the Seventh, had "started to compose a work for soloist, choir and orchestra with a text based on David's Psalms" (Khentova, *Shostakovich, zhizn' i tvorchestvo*, 2 vols. [Leningrad: Sovetskii kompozitor, 1985–1986] v. 2, p. 18).

58. Joseph de Maistre, *The St. Petersburg Dialogues, or Conversations on the Temporal Government of Providence*, ed. and tr. Richard A. Lebrun (Montreal and Kingston: McGill-Queen's University Press, 1993), p. 3.

59. Ibid., p. 5.

60. Composed between 1809 and 1813, the *Dialogues* were published only posthumously in 1821. Ever since, Maistre has been hailed as a genius and condemned as an archconservative "lion of illiberalism." Yet his influence has been considerable. Isaiah Berlin tried to trace the roots of modern fascism to Maistre (see Berlin's "Joseph de Maistre and the Origins of Fascism," *New York Review of Books* [September 27, 1990]). George Steiner has called his *Dialogues*, alongside Galileo's *Dialogo*, "the most powerful philosophic-dramatic dialogues written in the West after Plato." Tolstoy's thinking on war was shaped in part by his reading of Maistre. Steiner also noted Maistre's "night-vision": "The age of the Gulag, and of Auschwitz, of famine and ubiquitous torture . . . is exactly that which de Maistre announced" (Steiner, *Darkness Visible, London Review of Books*, v. 10, no. 21 [November 24, 1988], p. 3). See also a review of a 1989 biography of the thinker: "The Lion of Illiberalism," *New Republic* (October 30, 1989), pp. 32–37, by Stephen Holmes.

61. Leo Tolstoy, *War and Peace*, tr. Louise and Aylmer Maude (New York: W. W. Norton, 1996), Book 12, ch. 4, pp. 868, 871.

62. Akhmatova spent her childhood in Tsarskoye Selo, the imperial summer residence outside the city, and many of her poems resound with the rhapsody of her years there. But to Petersburgers, Akhmatova and the Fountain House are inseparable. She first lived in the house for a time with her second husband, Vladimir Shileiko, in 1918, and later returned to live there from 1926 to 1941 and 1944 to 1952.

63. Brodsky, *Less than One*, p. 4.

64. Varlam Shalamov, *Kolyma Tales*, tr. John Glad (London: Penguin Group, 1994), p. 43.

65. Ginzburg, *Blockade Diary*, p. 21.

PART VI. MOSCOW: "EVERYTHING IS NORMAL"

1. Common Article 3 of the four Geneva conventions (noninternational armed conflict) reads, in part: "To this end, the following acts are and shall remain prohibited at any time and in any place whatsoever with respect to the above-mentioned persons: a. Violence to life and person, in particular murder of all kinds, mutilation, cruel treatment and torture; b. Taking of hostages; c. Outrages upon personal dignity, in particular humiliating and

degrading treatment; d. The passing of sentences and the carrying out of executions without previous judgment pronounced by a regularly constituted court, affording all the judicial guarantees which are recognized as indispensable by civilized peoples."

2. As of April 2003, no Russian officer had been sent to jail for the murder of any civilians in Chechnya. In 2001 Colonel Yuri Budanov was brought to trial in a military court in Rostov for the March 27, 2000, murder of Kheda Kungaeva, an eighteen-year-old high school senior who had been taken from her home in the Chechen village of Tangi-Chu and beaten, raped, and killed. (The events occurred on the day that Putin won election to the Kremlin; that night Budanov, a tank commander, held a party to celebrate the birth of a daughter.) Budanov did not stand trial for rape, only for the kidnapping and murder. He admitted strangling Kungaeva but said it was not a premeditated act; he had become carried away during a difficult and emotional interrogation. Fifteen of his men had been killed by a sniper in the preceding days, and he claimed that he suspected Kungaeva of being the sniper.

Budanov found widespread support among the military and political elite. General Vladimir Shamanov, by then governor of Ulyanovsk, traveled to Budanov's trial to shake his hand. Shamanov called the case an "ideological intervention of the West against Russia." In a May 17, 2001, interview with *Izvestiya*, Defense Minister Sergei Ivanov also expressed sympathy for Budanov. Ivanov called him a victim of circumstances and imperfect law. Two postmortem certificates emerged after Kungaeva's autopsy. One held that she was first raped, then killed. The second certificate, antedated according to some sources, claimed that the rape occurred after her death–by the soldiers whom Budanov had ordered to bury the Chechen.

The case stretched more then three years. In late 2002 Budanov was evaluated, for the second time, at Moscow's Serbsky Institute for Social and Forensic Psychiatry, where doctors concluded he had been temporarily insane when he killed Kungaeva. (Military doctors had previously twice found Budanov competent to stand trial.) In the Soviet era, the Serbsky Institute had gained renown for its leading role in the state's abuse of psychiatry to silence dissenters. In the Budanov case, human rights advocates and the lawyer for the victim's family, Abdulla Khamzaev, suggested that the Serbsky had once again subverted medical science to the service of the state. On December 31, 2002, as Russia prepared to celebrate the biggest holiday of the year, the court in Rostov absolved Budanov of criminal responsibility on the ground of temporary insanity and committed him to a psychiatric hospital, but added that he could be released as soon as doctors found him sane. In April 2003, however, Budanov was yet again brought to trial. By then, however, the case had become so politicized few believed–whether the officer was eventually found innocent or guilty–that justice would be served.

3. Human Rights Watch meeting with Yuri Dyomin, March 10, 2000.

4. An excerpt of Zoya Marchenko's memoirs appeared in the anthology of women's writing that Semyon Vilensky published at the height of glasnost, *Dodnes' tiagoteet: zapiski vashei sovremennitsy,* 1989, published in English, as *Till My Tale Is Told: Women's Memoirs of the Gulag,* tr. John Crowfoot (Bloomington: Indiana University Press, 1999), pp. 201–10.

5. Putin seemed to have agreed with Babitsky. Before long, in August 2001, General Manilov was retired. With the Kremlin's heavy lobbying, he won a sinecure in the Federation Council, representing the chastened post-Nazdratenko Primorsky krai. The local Duma in Vladivostok tepidly endorsed Manilov as its representative in the upper house

of the national parliament. Manilov, who had first visited the region only that July, won the local vote with three votes more than the minimum. See Roman Dyablov, "Duma Votes General into Parliament," *Vladivostok News*, September 7, 2001.

6. Aksyonenko had long been seen as a protégé of Yeltsin's and at one time a proxy of Boris Berezovsky's in the Kremlin. After Putin came to power in 2000, Aksyonenko lost his job as deputy prime minister but retained the railways ministry. Reports of corruption, however, had long dogged him in the Russian press. In October 2001, Putin's prosecutor general, Vladimir Ustinov, announced that he had opened a criminal case concerning Aksyonenko's abuse of power. The investigation centered on the alleged misappropriation of $2.3 million in state funds and an unpaid tax debt of $370 million. Aksyonenko denied any wrongdoing and called the case against him politically inspired. In January 2002, Putin fired Aksyonenko, who accepted "moral responsibility" for the troubles at the railways ministry and soon faded–along with the reports of embezzlement–from view.

7. In November 2003, after the dramatic arrest of Russia's richest man, the oligarch Mikhail Khodorkovsky, Voloshin would depart the Kremlin. He resigned as head of the presidential administration in protest over the arrest, and the accompanying state campaign against Khodorkovsky's oil giant, Yukos.

8. The five regional presidential envoys who were generals were Viktor Kazantsev, Konstantin Pulikovsky, Pyotr Latyshev, Viktor Cherkesov, and Georgi Poltavchenko. Peter the Great in 1708 carved Russia up into eight military districts. If you drop the modern-day Baltic nations, you very nearly have the borders of Putin's seven federal districts. Mikhail Prusak, governor of Novgorod, told me the redistricting idea was originally Andropov's. Andropov, he said, had had a secret plan to carve the USSR into thirteen administrative regions but died before he could implement it.

9. The group included Anatoly Chubais, now head of Russia's electricity monopoly, UES; Rem Vyakhirev, chairman of Gazprom, the natural gas giant; banker Pyotr Aven, of the Alfa Group; and even oilman Mikhail Khodorkovsky, head of the Yukos oil giant.

10. *Glas naroda*, NTV, June 13, 2000. Official transcript. The shift that began with Gusinsky's demise, and marked the rise of the secret policemen to power, only grew. In December 2002 the Russian government terminated its participation in the U.S. Peace Corps program. Since 1992 more than seven hundred volunteers had worked in Russia; most had taught English and business education in the regions. Earlier in 2002, Russia had denied visa renewals to half the country's Peace Corps contingent. By way of explanation, the FSB director Nikolai Patrushev declared that among the volunteers were "persons who were engaged in gathering information about the sociopolitical and economic situation in Russian regions, about employees of organs of power and administration and about elections." In a speech in Washington, D.C., in January 2002, the U.S. ambassador to Russia, Alexander Vershbow, said Russia had the sovereign right to end the program, but that "unfortunately the decision was accompanied by groundless allegations by the head of the FSB." The ambassador termed Patrushev's comments "not only outrageous but an ominous departure" from the commitments previously affirmed by Presidents Bush and Putin to expand nongovernmental links.

11. Gusinsky lost NTV, Ekho Moskvy, and the newsweekly *Itogi*.

12. Berezovsky was never one who understood the virtues of transparency. He lost control of ORT, the state television channel, but by the end of 2002 many in Moscow's financial circles believed that he maintained at least $1.5 billion in Russian assets, includ-

ing stakes in oil and aluminum companies, as well as the *Kommersant* publishing group, and the newspapers *Nezavisimaya gazeta* and *Obshchaya gazeta*. In an interview in February 2003, Berezovsky hinself put his net worth at $3 billion ("Exiled Russian Oligarch Plots His Comeback," *New York Times*, February 17, 2003). On March 25, 2003, Berezovsky's exile took a turn for the worse–the British police arrested him on fraud charges that had originated in Moscow. Also arrested was Yuli Dubov, the man who had once run Berezovsky's LogoVAZ network of car dealerships. Both men were released on bail and faced extradition to Russia, a process that in the U.K. could last years.

13. Kiriyenko, Speech at the Woodrow Wilson Center, Washington, D.C., January 30, 2002. The former prime minister noted that his new federal administrative region, the swath in the center of the country along the Volga, had "at least two thousand local laws that contradicted federal laws." A region like Yakutia, for example, had even passed a law establishing two official languages, Yakut and English. It was repealed only in 2001.

14. George Kennan, "America and the Russian Future," *Foreign Affairs*, v. 29, no. 2 (April 1951).

15. In the summer of 2001, Kim Jong Il traveled the length of Russia by train. In August 2002 Kim came only to the Far East.

16. The MinAtom announcement, made on July 26, 2002, caught the Bush administration off guard. The plan called for Russia to build an additional five reactors–two at the Bushehr complex and three in Ahvaz near the Iraqi border.

17. While the Russians did not disclose the dollar amount of the ten-year deal with Iraq, the Iraqis did. Iraqi Ambassador Abbas Khalaf said the agreement was worth forty billion dollars. "Russia Defends Deal with Iraq," *Washington Post*, August 20, 2002.

18. Kremlin aides made little attempt to disguise their support for George W. Bush over Al Gore–despite the great interest and efforts in Russia Gore had extended over two terms in the White House. "We tend to prefer conservatives to liberals," said Mikhail Margelov, a young Putin campaign aide and onetime Arabic-language professor at the KGB Academy, who rose to chairman of the foreign affairs committee in the Federation Council. "Maybe the Republicans give us a harder time, but at least we know where we stand." Russian policy makers like to note that Nixon went to China and Reagan to Moscow.

19. Many in Moscow, however, doubted the post-September 11 partnership would last long. Even before a year had passed, some influential voices in the West called for foreign involvement in resolving the Chechen conflict. "Moscow," the *Financial Times* intoned in an editorial on August 20, 2002, "cannot reap the full benefits of closer ties with the West without giving up on barbarity." No one, however, could imagine Putin accepting foreign mediators in Chechnya, let alone peacekeepers. At the same time, the accusations of rampant human rights abuse in Chechnya–of both Chechen civilians and Russia's own soldiers–continued. In 2003, the U.S.-led war in Iraq brought new strain to U.S.-Russian relations. The Russians, siding with the French and Germans, became vocal opponents of the military action. Putin called the war a "political mistake" that had provoked the worst crisis of the post–cold war period.

20. *Mir Mortals*, BBC Horizon program, April 23, 1998.

21. RFE, December 10, 2001.

22. VTsIOM poll, August 2001.

23. In September 2002, Luzhkov even called for returning the statue of Dzerzhinsky to Lubyanka Square. Interfax, on September 13, 2002, reported that at a planning meeting concerning construction projects in Moscow, Luzhkov declared: "This excellent monument was the highlight of Lubyanka Square. . . . It is a shame that this outstanding sculptor was so unreasonably insulted." Regarding the founder of the Soviet secret police, Luzhkov said: "Some associate this man with the KGB, others with the crackdown on child neglect and railroad restoration," references to Dzerzhinsky's initiatives to remove homeless children from Soviet cities and employ prison labor to rebuild Russia's railways.

24. A new census, the first since 1989, was conducted in the fall of 2002; the provisional 2002 figure was only an estimate.

25. Ekho Moskvy, February 15, 2002. Fourteen months later, one of the Starovoitova's strongest former allies fell. On April 17, 2003, a contract hit took the life of Sergei Yushenkov, one of the most prominent liberals remaining in the Duma. At fifty-two, Yushenkov, a former lieutenant colonel with a Soviet Ph.D., who for years had chaired the parliament's Defense Committee, was shot four times as he entered his apartment building in northwest Moscow. Hours earlier he had announced that the Justice Ministry had registered his Liberal Russia movement, which he co-chaired, as a party in advance of the Duma elections scheduled for the fall of 2003. In May 2001, Yushenkov had joined Liberal Russia, a movement funded by Boris Berezovsky in a vain attempt to build an opposition to Putin. In 2002, he allied with the self-exiled Berezovsky in a public relations campaign aganst Putin and the FSB, alleging that the security services has orchestrated the apartment bombings of 1999 in Moscow and elsewhere. Yushenkov, the ninth Duma deputy killed in as many years, was the second leader of Liberal Russia murdered. In August 2002, Vladimir Golovyov was killed in similar fashion. As of June 2003, none of the cases had been solved.

26. On July 20, 2000, as Raibek Tovzayev and his men drove home along the road we had taken to his checkpoint in the hills above Vedeno, his Nissan Patrol came under fire. Thirty bullets pierced the car before his men dragged Raibek from it. He'd taken two bullets, one in the hip, another just above his heart. Still, he lived. On General Troshev's orders, Raibek was flown by helicopter to Gudermes, where the Russians pretended to keep him in a field hospital. They put someone else in his bed, while Raibek was secretly flown to Moscow for surgery in the Interior Ministry's hospital. He recovered, only to suffer yet another ambush nearly a year later. In June 2001 he and his men were driving into the town of Vedeno when a line of antitank mines exploded beneath their car and gunfire burst from the woods along the road. Two of his bodyguards were killed, but once again Raibek managed to survive.

27. In late April 2002, Russian state television broadcast images of Khattab's body and claimed that he had been killed in an FSB "special operation" on the night of March 19–20. Reports surfaced that Khattab was killed by a poisoned letter in the FSB plot. Chechen sources presented a different take: that after September 11 the Chechens had little desire for an Arab mercenary, with admitted ties to bin Laden, in their midst. As for his origins, Khattab's biography remains shadowy. After reports of his death, a man claiming to be his brother came forward. Mansour al-Suwailem told the London-based *Asharq al-Awsat* Arabic newspaper that Khattab's real name was Samir bin Saleh al-Suwailem and that he had been born in 1969 and had left Saudi Arabia at seventeen to fight in Afghanistan. See Isa Mubarak, "Woman Inspired Chechen Warlord's Fight–Brother," Reuters, May 2, 2002.

28. In time, as Russia yearned for full partnership in America's war against terrorism, the plaque would change. On August 8, 2002, the second anniversary of the bombing, Luzkhov unveiled a new memorial. The simple plaque had been replaced with a white marble tablet dedicated to the victims of "the terrorist act." Before September 11, however, numerous officials, including the FSB and the Moscow prosecutor's office, had told a different story: that the bombing may well have resulted from another *razborka*, a settling of scores among criminal gangs.

29. Andrei Sakharov, "How I Came to Dissent," originally published in English in the *New York Review of Books* (March 21, 1974). Translated by Guy Daniels.

30. Marina Tsvetaeva, "Moscow Verses," in *Selected Poems,* tr. Elaine Feinstein (Oxford: Carcanet, 1999), p. 18.

❦ BIBLIOGRAPHY ❦

NB: Where possible, I have listed English translations of works originally published in Russian, German, or French.

ARCHIVES

GARF: State Archive of the Russian Federation, Moscow

Memorial Society Archive, Moscow and Krasnoyarsk

National Archives, Washington, D.C., and College Park, Maryland

RGALI: Russian State Archive of Literature and Art, Moscow

RGASPI: Russian State Archives of Social and Political History, Moscow

MOSCOW

Aron, Leon. *Boris Yeltsin: A Revolutionary Life*. London: HarperCollins, 2000.

Aslund, Anders. *How Russia Became a Market Economy*. Washington, D.C.: Brookings Institution, 1995.

Berlin, Isaiah. *Russian Thinkers*. London: Hogarth, 1978.

Billington, James. *The Icon and the Axe: An Interpretive History of Russian Culture*. New York: Vintage, 1970.

Blasi, Joseph R., Maya Kroumova, and Douglas Kruse. *Kremlin Capitalism: The Privatization of the Russian Economy*. Ithaca, N.Y.: Cornell University Press, 1997.

Bobkov, Filip. *KGB i vlast'*. Moscow: Veteran MP Publishers, 1995.

Boyko, Maksim, Andrei Shleifer, and Robert Vishny. *Privatizing Russia*. Cambridge, Mass.: MIT Press, 1995.

Burrough, Bryan. *Dragonfly: NASA and the Crisis aboard Mir*. New York: HarperCollins Publishers, 1998.

Dunlop, John B. *The Faces of Contemporary Russian Nationalism*. Princeton: Princeton University Press, 1983.

——. *The Rise of Russia and the Fall of the Soviet Empire*. Princeton: Princeton University Press, 1993.

Freeland, Chrystia. *Sale of the Century: The Inside Story of the Second Russian Revolution*. London: Little, Brown and Company, 2000.

Gaidar, Yegor. *Days of Defeat and Victory.* Seattle: Jackson School Publications in International Studies and University of Washington Press, 1999.

——. *Gosudarstvo i evolutsiia.* Moscow: Eurasia Foundation, 1995.

Gorbachev, Mikhail. *Memoirs.* New York: Doubleday, 1996.

Herzen, Aleksandr. *From the Other Shore and The Russian People and Socialism: An Open Letter to Jules Michelet.* Introduction by Isaiah Berlin, 1st American ed. New York: George Braziller, 1956.

——. *Socheneniia v deviati tomakh.* Moscow: Gosudarsvtennoe izdatel'stvo khudozhestvennoi literatury, 1956.

Hoffman, David E. *The Oligarchs: Wealth and Power in the New Russia.* New York: Public Affairs, 2002.

Josephson, Matthew. *The Robber Barons: The Great American Capitalists: 1861–1901.* New York: Harcourt, Brace and Company, 1934.

Kapuscinski, Ryszard. *Imperium,* tr. Klara Glowczewska. London: Granta Books, 1998.

Khlevnyuk, O., A. V. Kvashonkin, et al. *Bol'shevistskoe rukovodstvo. Perepiska. 1912–1927.* Institut Gosudarstvennogo Upravleniia i Sotsial'nikh Issledovaniy Moskovskogo Gosudarstvennogo Universiteta Im. M. V. Lomonosova. Moskva: ROSSPEN, 1996.

Korzhakov, Aleksandr. *Boris Yel'tsin: Ot rassveta do zakata.* Moskva: Interbuk, 1997.

Kotkin, Stephen. *Armageddon Averted: The Soviet Collapse 1970–2000.* Oxford: Oxford University Press, 2001.

Kovalev, Sergei. "A Letter of Resignation," tr. Catherine Fitzpatrick. *New York Review of Books* (February 29, 1996). Originally published in *Izvestia,* January 24, 1996.

Krichevskii, Ilia. *Krasnye besy.* Kiev: Oberig, 1992.

——. *Spasibo, drug, chto govorish' so mnoi.* Moskva: Moscow Worker, 1998.

Kutsillo, Veronika. *Zapiski iz belogo doma.* Moskva: Kommersant Publishing House, 1993.

Layard, Richard, and John Parker. *The Coming Russian Boom: A Guide to New Markets and Politics.* New York: Free Press, 1996.

Lloyd, John. *Rebirth of a Nation: An Anatomy of Russia.* London: Michael Joseph Ltd., 1998.

Malia, Martin. *Russia under Western Eyes: From the Bronze Horseman to the Lenin Mausoleum.* Cambridge, Mass.: Belknap Press, 1999.

——. *The Soviet Tragedy: A History of Socialism in Russia, 1917–1991.* New York: Free Press, 1994.

Malinin, V. N. *Starets Eleazarova Monastyria Filofei i ego poslaniia.* Kiev: Tipografia Kievo-Pecherskoi Uspenskoi Lavry, 1901.

Matlock, Jack. *Autopsy of an Empire: The American Ambassador's Account of the Collapse of the Soviet Union.* New York: Random House, 1995.

Medvedev, Roy. *Let History Judge: The Origins and Consequences of Stalinism,* ed. George Shriver. New York: Columbia University Press, 1989.

——. *Neizvestnyi Andropov*. Moskva: Prava cheloveka, 1999.

——. *Zagadka Putina*. Moscow: Prava cheloveka, 2000.

Obolensky, Dimitri, ed. *The Heritage of Russian Verse*. Bloomington: Indiana University Press, 1962.

Pelevin, Viktor. *Buddha's Little Finger*, tr. Andrew Bromfield. New York: Viking Press, 2000.

——. *Homo Zapiens*, tr. Andrew Bromfield. New York: Viking Press, 2002.

——. *Omon Ra*, tr. Andrew Bromfield. New York: New Directions Publishing, 1994.

——. *The Yellow Arrow*, tr. Andrew Bromfield. New York: New Directions Publishing, 1993.

Pipes, Richard. *Russia under the Old Regime*. New York: Collier Books, 1992.

——, ed. *The Unknown Lenin*. New Haven: Yale University Press, 1996.

Platonov, Andrey. *Happy Moscow*, tr. Robert and Elizabeth Chandler with Angela Livingstone, Nadya Bourova, and Eric Naiman. London: Harvill Press, 2001.

Putin, Vladimir. *First Person: An Astonishingly Frank Self-Portrait by Russia's President*, tr. Catherine A. Fitzpatrick. New York: PublicAffairs, 2000.

Remnick, David. *Lenin's Tomb: The Last Days of the Soviet Empire*. New York: Random House, 1993.

——. *Resurrection: The Struggle for a New Russia*. New York: Random House, 1997.

Schmemann, Serge. *Echoes of a Native Land: Two Centuries of a Russian Village*. New York: Alfred A. Knopf, 1997.

Shevtsova, Lilia. *Yeltsin's Russia: Myths and Reality*. Washington, D.C.: Carnegie Endowment for International Peace, 1999.

Simonov, K. *Glazami cheloveka moego pokoleniia: razmyshleniia o I. V. Staline*. Moskva: Kniga, 1990.

Skidelsky, Robert, ed. *Russia's Stormy Path to Reform*. London: Social Market Foundation, 1995.

Solnick, Steven. *Stealing the State: Control and Collapse in Soviet Institutions*. Cambridge: Harvard University Press, 1998.

Solzhenitsyn, Aleksandr. *Invisible Allies*. London: Harvill Press, 1997.

——. *Rossiia v obvale*. Moskva: Russkii put', 1998.

——. *The Russian Question at the End of the 20th Century*. London: Harvill Press, 1995.

——. *Slovo probivaet sebe dorogu*. Moskva: Russkii put', 1998.

Steinbeck, John. *A Russian Journal*. New York: Viking Press, 1948.

Wilson, Edmund. *Travels in Two Democracies*. New York: Harcourt, Brace and Company, 1936.

Yeltsin, Boris. *Against the Grain: An Autobiography*, tr. Michael Glenny. New York: Summit Books, 1990.

——. *Midnight Diaries*, tr. Catherine A. Fitzpatrick. New York: PublicAffairs, 2000.

——. *The Struggle for Russia*. New York: Times Books, Belka Publications Corp., 1994.

CHECHNYA

Abubakarov, Taimaz. *Rezhim Dzokhara Dudaeva: pravda i vymesel*, Moscow: INSAN, 1998.

Akaev, V. *Sheikh Kunta-Khadzhi: zhizn' i uchenie*. Groznyi: Ichkeriia, 1994.

——. *Sufizm i vakhkhabizm na Severnom Kavkaze*. Moskva: Institut etnologii i antropologii im. Miklukho-Maklaia RAN, 1999.

Anderson, Scott. *The Man Who Tried to Save the World: The Dangerous Life and Mysterious Disappearance of Fred Cuny*. New York: Anchor Books, 1999.

Ascherson, Neal. *Black Sea*. New York: Hill and Wang, 1995.

Avtorkhanov, Abdurahman. "The Chechens and the Ingush during the Soviet Period and Its Antecedents." In *The North Caucasus Barrier: The Russian Advance towards the Muslim World*, ed. Marie Bennigsen Broxup. London: Hurst and Company, 1992.

Baddeley, John F. *The Rugged Flanks of the Caucasus*. London: Oxford University Press, 1940.

——. *The Russian Conquest of the Caucasus*. London: Longmans, Green and Company, 1908.

Bagalova, Zuleikhan, et al. *Chechnia: prava na kul'ture*. Moscow: Polinform-Talburi Publishers, 1999.

Barrett, Thomas M. "Lines of Uncertainty: The Frontiers of the North Caucasus." *Slavic Review*, v. 54, no. 3 (Fall 1995).

Bennett, Vanora. *Crying Wolf: The Return of War to Chechnya*. London: Picador, 1998.

Bennigsen, Alexandre. *Narodnoe dvizhenie na Kavkaze v XVIII v. : "Sviashchennaia voina" Sheikha Mansura*. Makhachkala: Fond "Tarikh," 1994.

——, and S. Enders Wimbush. *Mystics and Commissars: Sufism in the Soviet Union*. London: C. Hurst & Company, 1985.

Bey, Essad-. *Twelve Secrets of the Caucasus*, tr. G. Chychele Waterson. New York: Viking Press, 1931.

Blanch, Lesley. *The Sabres of Paradise*. New York: Carroll and Graf Publishers, 1960.

Blinushov, A., A. Guryanov, O. Orlov, Ya. Rachonsky, and A. Sokolov. *By All Available Means: The Russian Federation Ministry of Internal Affairs Operation in the Village of Samashki: April 7-8, 1995*, tr. R. Denber. Moscow: Memorial Human Rights Center, 1996.

Burrell, George A. *An American Engineer Looks at Russia*. Boston: Stratford Company Publishers, 1932.

Cherkasov, Aleksandr, et al. *"Zachistka": Poselok Novye Aldi*. Moscow: Memorial Society, February 5, 2000.

Chudakov, Alexander. "Dr. Chekhov: A Biographical Essay (29 January 1860–15 July 1904). In *The Cambridge Companion to Chekhov.* Cambridge, U.K.: Cambridge University Press, 2000.

Conquest, Robert. *The Nation Killers: The Soviet Deportation of Nationalities.* London: Macmillan and Co., 1970.

Derluguian, Georgi. "Che Guevaras in Turbans: Chechens versus Globalization." *New Left Review*, no. 237 (September–October 1999).

Ditson, George Leighton. *Circassia: or, a Tour to the Caucasus.* London: T. C. Newby. New York: Stringer & Townsend, 1850.

Dudaev, Dzhokhar. *Ternisty put' k svobode.* Vilnius: Vaga, 1993.

Dumas (*père*), Alexandre. *Adventures in the Caucasus*, ed. and tr. A. E. Murch. London: Peter Owen Limited, 1962.

Dunlop, John B. *Russia Confronts Chechnya: Roots of a Separatist Conflict.* Cambridge, U.K.: Cambridge University Press 1998.

Furman, Dmitrii, et al., *Chechnia i Rossiia: obshchestva i gosudarstva.* Moskva: Polinform-Talburi, 1999.

Gall, Carlotta, and Thomas de Waal. *Chechnya: A Small Victorious War.* London: Pan Books, 1997.

Gammer, Moshe. "The Introduction of the Khalidiyya and of the Qâdiriyya into Daghestan in the Nineteenth Century." In *Daghestan and the World of Islam*, eds. Moshe Gammer and David J. Wasserstein. Helsinki: Finnish Academy of Sciences and Humanities (forthcoming).

——. *Muslim Resistance to the Tsar: Shamil and the Conquest of Chechnia and Daghestan.* London: Frank Cass, 1994.

——. "The Qâdiriyya in the Northern Caucasus." *Journal of the History of Sufism*, no. 1 (2000).

Graham, Stephen. *A Vagabond in the Caucasus, with Some Notes of His Experiences among the Russians.* London: John Lane, Bodley Head, 1911.

Hartmann, R., R. Virchow, and A. Voss, eds. *Zeitschrift für Ethnologie: Organ der Berliner Gesellschaft für Anthropologie, Ethnologie und Urgeschichte.* Berlin: Verlag von Paul Parey, 1882.

Hawkes, Malcolm. *Russia/Chechnya: February 5: A Day of Slaughter in Novye Aldi.* Moscow: Human Rights Watch, June 2000.

Henze, Paul. *Chechnia: A Report of an International Alert Fact-Finding Mission.* September 24–October 3, 1992. London: International Alert, 1996.

——. "Marx on Russians and Muslims." *Central Asian Survey*, v. 6, no. 4 (1987).

Herbert, Agnes. *Casuals in the Caucasus: The Diary of a Sporting Holiday.* London: John Lane, Bodley Head, 1912.

The Ingush-Ossetian Conflict in the Prigorodnyi Region. New York: Human Rights Watch/Helsinki, May 1996.

Karny, Yo'av. *Highlanders: A Journey to the Caucasus in Quest of Memory.* New York: Farrar, Straus, and Giroux, 2000.

Layton, Susan. *Russian Literature and Empire: Conquest of the Caucasus from Pushkin to Tolstoy.* New York: Cambridge University Press, 1994.

Lermontov, Mikhail. *A Hero of Our Time,* tr. Paul Foote. London: Penguin Group, 1966.

Lieven, Anatol. *Chechnya: Tombstone of Russian Power.* New Haven: Yale University Press, 1998.

Longworth, John A. *A Year Among the Circassians.* London: Henry Colburn, 1840. 2 vols.

Maclean, Fitzroy. *To Caucasus, the End of All the Earth: An Illustrated Companion to the Caucasus and Transcaucasia.* London: Jonathan Cape, 1930.

Marsden, Philip. *The Spirit Wrestlers: A Russian Journey,* London: HarperCollins, 1998.

Mazaeva, Tamara. *100 Dnei Prezidenta.* Groznyi and Sankt-Peterburg: SEDA, 1997.

Musaev, Timur, and Zurab Todua. *Novaia Checheno-Ingushetia.* Moskva: Panorama, 1992.

Nichols, Johanna. *The Indigenous Languages of the Caucasus,* ed. Rieks Smeets. In *Northeast Caucasian Languages,* v. 4. Delmar, N.Y.: Caravan Books, 1994.

——. *Who Are the Chechen?* U.C. Berkeley Slavic Studies Bulletin, January 13, 1995.

Nivat, Anne. *Chienne de Guerre: A Woman Reporter behind the Lines of the War in Chechnya.* New York: PublicAffairs, 2001.

Orlov, Oleg, and Aleksandr Cherkasov. *Behind Their Backs: Russian Forces' Use of Civilians as Hostages and Human Shields during the Chechnya War,* ed. T. I. Kasatkina, tr. Paul LeGendre. Moscow: Memorial Human Rights Center, 1997.

Politkovskaya, Anna. *A Dirty War: A Russian Reporter in Chechnya,* ed. and tr. John Crowfoot. London: Harvill Press, 2001.

Potto, V. A. *Kavkazskaia voina v otdel'nykh ocherkakh, epizodakh, legendakh i biografiiakh.* St. Petersburg: Tipografiia R. Golike, 1885–1891. 5 vols.

——. *Utverzhdenie russkogo vladychestva na Kavkaze.* Tiflis: Tipografiia Ia.K. Libermana, 1901–1904. 3 vols.

Rashid, Ahmed. *Taliban: Militant Islam, Oil and Fundamentalism in Central Asia.* New Haven: Yale Note Bene, 2002.

Slezkine, Yuri. "The USSR as a Communal Apartment, or How a Socialist State Promoted Ethnic Particularism," *Slavic Review,* v. 53, no. 2 (Summer 1994).

Smith, Sebastian. *Allah's Mountains: Politics and War in the Russian Caucasus.* London: I. B. Tauris and Co., Publishers, 1998.

Spencer, Edmund. *Travels in Circassia, Krim-Tartary, & C. Including a Steam Voyage down the Danube, from Vienna to Constantinople, and round the Black Sea.* London: Henry Colburn, 1839.

Stalin, J. V. *On the Road to Nationalism. (A Letter From the Caucasus.)* In *Works* [*Sochineniia*], v. 2. Moscow: Foreign Languages Publishing House, 1953.

Lev Tolstoi. *Dnevniki (1847–1894), Sobranie sochinenii v dvadtsati dvukh tomakh,* v. 21. Moskva: Khudozhestvennaia literatura, 1985.

Tolstoy, Leo. *Hadji Murad.* In *Master and Man and Other Stories,* tr. Paul Foote. London: Penguin Group, 1977.

——. "A Prisoner of the Caucasus." In *How Much Land Does a Man Need? And Other Stories,* tr. Ronald Wilks. London: Penguin Group, 1993.

Whittock, Michael. "Ermolov–Proconsul of the Caucasus." *Russian Review,* v. 18, no. 1 (January 1959).

Wilson, A. N. *Tolstoy.* New York: W. W. Norton, 1988.

Yergin, Daniel. *The Prize: The Epic Quest for Oil, Money, and Power.* New York: Simon and Schuster, 1991.

Zelkina, Anna. *In Quest for God and Freedom: Sufi Responses to the Russian Advance in the North Caucasus.* London: C. Hurst & Co., 2000.

——. "Some Aspects of the Teaching of Kunta Hâjjî: On the Basis of the Manuscript by 'Abd al-Salâm Written in 1862 AD." *Journal of the History of Sufism,* no. 1–2 (2000).

NORILSK

Adler, Nanci. *The Gulag Survivor.* New Brunswick, N.J.: Transaction Publishers, 2002.

——. *Victims of Soviet Terror: The Story of the Memorial Movement.* Westport, Conn.: Praeger Publishers, 1993.

Agranovskii, Valerii. *Poslednii dolg.* Moskva: Academia, 1994.

Alekhin, Petr. "Golubaia os'." *Severnye prostory,* v. 1 (January–February 1994).

Bond, Andrew. R. "Air Pollution in Noril'sk: A Soviet Worst Case?" *Soviet Geography,* v. 25 (November 1984).

——. "Northern Settlement Family-Style: Labor Planning and Population Policy in Noril'sk." *Soviet Geography,* v. 26, no. 1 (January 1985).

——. "The Russian Copper Industry and the Noril'sk Joint-Stock Company in the Mid-1990s." *Post-Soviet Geography and Economics,* vol. 37, no. 5 (May 1996).

Bridges, Olga, et al. *Losing Hope: The Environment and Health in Russia.* Brookfield, U.K.: Ashgate Publishing Co., 1996.

Cohn, Norman. *Warrant for Genocide: The Myth of the Jewish World-Conspiracy and the Protocols of the Elders of Zion.* Chico, Calif.: Scholars Press, 1981.

Conquest, Robert. *The Great Terror: A Reassessment.* New York: Oxford University Press, 1990.

——. *The Harvest of Sorrow: Soviet Collectivization and the Terror-Famine.* New York: Oxford University Press, 1986.

——. *Kolyma: The Arctic Death Camps.* London: Macmillan, 1978.

Courtois, Stéphane, Nicolas Werth, et al. *The Black Book of Communism: Crimes, Terror,*

Repression, tr. Jonathan Murphy and Mark Kramer. Cambridge, Mass.: Harvard University Press, 1999.

Craveri, Marta. "The Strikes in Norilsk and Vorkuta Camps, and Their Role in the Breakdown of the Stalinist Forced Labour System." In *Free and Unfair Labour: The Debate Continues*, ed. Tom Brass and Marcel van der Linden. New York: Peter Lang, 1998.

Dallin, David, and Boris I. Nicolaevsky. *Forced Labour in Soviet Russia*. London: Hollis & Carter, 1948.

Ebedzhans, Svetlana. *Norilskiy Memorial 4. Oktiabr' 98*. Izdaniie Muzeya Istorii Osvoeniia i Razvitiia NPR i Noril'skogo Obschestva: Memorial, 1998.

Efron, Ariadna, *Miroedikha* and Ada Federol'f, *Riadom s Aley*. Moskva: Vozvrashchenie, 1996. (Found in same volume.)

Feshbach, Murray. *Russia in Transition: Ecological Disaster: Cleaning Up the Hidden Legacy of the Soviet Regime*. New York: Twentieth Century Fund Press, 1995.

Forsyth, James. *A History of the Peoples of Siberia: Russia's North Asian Colony 1581–1990*. Cambridge, U.K.: Cambridge University Press, 1992.

Gabris, Roberts. *Norilsk-Baltic Katyn*. Riga: Liesma, 1990.

Heleniak, Timothy. "Migration from the Russian North during the Transition Period." Social Protection Discussion Paper No. 9925, World Bank, September 1999.

——. "Out-Migration and Depopulation of the Russian North during the 1990s." *Post-Soviet Geography and Economics*, v. 40, no. 3 (April–May 1999).

Hochschild, Adam. *The Unquiet Ghost: Russians Remember Stalin*. New York: Viking, 1994.

Hrytsiak, IEvhen. *Istoria Noril'skogo vostaniya*. [*A Short Account of Recollections: A History of the Norilsk Uprising*.] Baltimore and Toronto: V. Symonenko Smoloskyp Publishers, 1980.

——. *The Norilsk Uprising: Short Memoirs*. München: Ukrainisches Institut für Bildungspolitik, 1984.

Jackson, Frederick George. *The Great Frozen Land: Narrative of a Winter Journey across the Tundras and a Sojourn among the Samoyads*. London and New York: Macmillan and Company, 1895.

Kersnovskaia, Evfrosiniia. *Skol'ko stoit chelovek: povest' o perezhitom v 12 tetradiakh i 6 tomakh*. 6 vols. v. 1–2: Moskva: Fond Kersnovskoi: Tipografiia Novosti, 2000; v. 3–6: Moskva: Fond Kersnovskoi: Mozhaisk-Terra, 2001.

Khlevniuk, Oleg V. *Politbiuro: mekhanizmy politicheskoi vlasti v 1930-e gody*. Moskva: ROSSPEN, 1996.

Klimovich, Rygor. *Konets Gorlaga*. Minsk: Foundation Nasha Niva, 1999.

Kokurin, A. I. "Osoboe tekhnicheskoe biuro NKVD SSSR." *Istorichesski arkhiv*, no. 1 (1999).

——. "Vosstanie v Steplage Mai–Iul 1954." *Otechestvennye arkhivy*, no. 4 (1994).

Kokurin, Aleksandr I., and Nikita V. Petrov, eds. *GULAG (Glavnoe Upravlenie Lagerey) 1918–1960.* Moskva: Materik, 2000.

Kozlov, Aleksandr. *Massovyie besporiadki v SSSR.* Moskva: GARF, 1998.

Kuchaev, Andrei. *Teploe mesto.* In *Shest'desat deviataia parallel'* Moscow: Molodaia Gvardiia, 1972.

Laqueur, Walter. *Black Hundred: The Rise of the Extreme Right in Russia.* New York: HarperCollins, 1993.

Las Cases, Emmanuel, comte de. *Lesage's Historical, Genealogical, Chronological and Geographical Atlas,* 2d ed. London: 1818.

Lengyel, József. *Acta Sanctorum and Other Tales,* tr. Ilona Duczynska. London: Peter Owen Ltd., 1970.

——. *Confrontation,* tr. Anna Novotny. London: Peter Owen Ltd. 1973.

——. *From Beginning to End,* tr. Ilona Duczynska. Englewood Cliffs, N.J.: Prentice-Hall, 1968.

Loginov, Aleksei Borisovich. *Noril'sk: moi zvezdnyi chas.* Moskva: Polimedia, 2000.

L'vov, Anatolii, *Noril'sk.* Krasnoiarsk: Krasnoiarskoe knizhnoe izdatel'stvo, 1985.

——. *Noril'skie sud'by, 1815–1995.* Moskva: Presto, 1995.

Makarova, Alla. *Noril'skoe vosstanie: Mai–Avgust 1953 goda.* In *Soprotivlenie v Gulage.* Volia, v. 1, pp. 68–108. Moskva: Izdatel'stvo Vozvrashchenie, 1993.

Mishechkina, M. V., A. I. Toshchev, et al. *Stroika N. 503 (1947–1953).* Igarskiy Kraevedcheskiy Kompleks. Grotesk: 2000.

Nansen, Fridtjof. *Through Siberia–The Land of the Future,* tr. Arthur G. Chater. New York: Frederick A. Stokes Co., 1914.

Numerov, Nikolai Vladimirovich. *Zolotaia zvezda GULAGa.* Moskva: Moskva, 1999.

Pavlovskii, Evgenii. "Vinovata trevozhnaia pamiat'." *Noril'sky Memorial,* no. 2 (August 1991).

Peterson, D. J. *Troubled Lands: The Legacy of Soviet Environmental Destruction.* Boulder, Colo.: Westview Press, 1993.

Pryde, Philip R., ed. "Environmental Problem Areas." In *Environmental Resources and Constraints in the Former Soviet Republics.* Boulder, Colo.: Westview Press, 1995.

Roginskii, Arsenii, et al. *Kto rukovodil NKVD, 1934–1941.* Obschestvo Memorial, Rossiyskiy Gosudarstvenniy Arkhiv Social'no-Polit'icheskoy Istorii, Gosudarstvenniy Arkhiv Rossiyskoy Federatsii. Moskva: Zvenia, 1999.

——. *Sistema ispravitel'no-trudovykh lagerei v SSSR 1923–1960: Spravochnik.* Obschestvo Memorial, Gosudarstvenniy Arkhiv Rossiyskoy Federatsii. Moskva: Zvenya, 1998.

Rosenberg, Tina. *The Haunted Land: Facing Europe's Ghosts after Communism.* New York: Random House, 1995.

Rossi, Jacques. *The Gulag Handbook: An Encyclopedia Dictionary of Soviet Penitentiary Insti-*

tutions and Terms Related to the Forced Labor Camps, tr. by William A. Burhans. New York: Paragon House, 1989.

Shalamov, Varlam. *Kolyma Tales*, tr. John Glad. London: Penguin Group, 1994.

Shentalinsky, Vitaly. *The KGB's Literary Archive*. London: Harvill, 1997.

Shumuk, Danylo. *Life Sentence: Memoirs of a Ukrainian Political Prisoner*. Edmonton: Canadian Institute of Ukrainian Studies Press, 1984.

Smolka, H. P. *40,000 Against the Arctic: Russia's Polar Empire*. New York: William Morrow and Company.

Solzhenitsyn, Aleksandr. *The Gulag Archipelago 1918–1956: An Experiment in Literary Investigation*, tr. Thomas P. Whitney (parts I–IV) and Harry Willetts (parts V–VII). London: Collins Harvill, 1986.

Thubron, Colin. *In Siberia*. New York: HarperCollins, 1999.

Toshchev, Aleksandr, ed. *My iz Igarki*. Moskva: Vozvrashchenie, 2000.

Urvantsev, N. N. *Noril'sk*. Moskva: Nedra, 1969.

——. *Otkrytie Noril'ska*. Moskva: Nauka, 1981.

Vilenskii, S. S., ed. *Soprotivlenie v Gulage–vospominaniia, pis'ma, documenty*. Moskva: Fond Vozvrashchenie, May 1992.

——. *Till My Tale Is Told: Women's Memoirs of the Gulag*, tr. John Crowfoot. Bloomington: Indiana University Press, 1999.

——. *Volia*. Zhurnal uznikov totalitarnykh syst'em. v. 4–5 (1995) and v. 6–7 (1997). Moskovskoe Istoriko-Literaturnoe Obschestvo Vozvrashchenie, 1995 and 1997.

Vitman, Boris. *Shpion, kotoromu izmenila rodina*. Kazan': Elko-S, 1993.

SAKHALIN

Arseniev, V. K. *Dersu the Trapper*, tr. Malcolm Burr. New York: E. P. Dutton and Company, 1941. First American edition.

——. *Po Ussuriyskomy krayu dersu'uslala*. Moscow: Pravda Publishers, 1983.

Bogdanov, D. *Putevoditel' po Vladivostoku i promysly Primorskoi oblasti*. Vladivostok: Kamchatki i Sakhalina, Ekspress, 1909.

Chakovsky, Aleksandr. *U nas uzhe utro*. Moskva: Sovetskii Pisatel', 1950.

Chekhov, Anton. *The Island: A Journey to Sakhalin*, tr. Luba and Michael Terpak. New York: Washington Square Press, 1967.

——. *Notebook of Anton Chekhov*, tr. S. S. Koteliansky and Leonard Woolf. New York: Ecco Press, 1921.

——. *Polnoe sobranie sochinenii i pisem*. Moskva: Nauka, 1974–1988. 30 vols.

——. *Zapisnye knizhki*. Moscow: Vagrius, 2000.

Chesalin, Vasilii. *Zdes' nachinalas' istoriia.* IUzhno-Sakhalinsk: Dal'nevostochnoe knizhnoe izdatel'stvo, 1987.

Chudakov, A. "Neprilichnye slova i oblik klassika." In "Erotika v russkoi literature ot Barkova do nashikh dnei," *Literaturnoe obozrenie.* (Special Edition.) Moskva: Literaturnoe obozrenie, 1992.

Doroshevich, V. M. *Kak ia popal ia Sakhalin.* Moscow: Tipografiia tovarishchestva I. D. Sytina, 1903.

——. *Sakhalin (Katorga), Izbrannye Ocherki.* Sakhalin: Vserossiiskii fond kul'tury, 1991.

Fithian, Floyd J. "Dollars without the Flag: The Case of Sinclair and Sakhalin Oil." *Pacific Historical Review,* v. 39, no. 2 (May 1970).

Fedorov, Valentin. *Gubernatorskie romansy.* Moskva: Moskovskii pisatel', 1994.

——. *El'tsin, politicheskii portret.* Moskva: INFRA-M, 1995.

Gitovich, N. I. "Khronika prebyvaniia A. P. Chekhova na Sakhaline." *Literaturno-khudozhestvennii sbornik Sakhalin.* IUzhno-Sakhalinsk: Dalnevostochnoe knizhnoe izdatel-stvo, Sakhalinskoe otdelenie, 1990.

Hawes, Charles H. *In the Uttermost East: Being an Account of Investigations among the Natives and Russian Convicts of the Island of Sakhalin, with Notes of Travel in Korea, Siberia, and Manchuria.* London: Harper and Brothers, 1903.

Hingley, Ronald. *A New Life of Anton Chekhov.* London: Oxford University Press, 1976.

Kennan, George. *Siberia and the Exile System.* New York: Century Company, 1891. 2 vols.

Kostanov, A. I., ed. *Gubernatory Sakhalina.* IUzhno-Sakhalinsk: Arkhivnyi otdel adminis-tratsii Sakhalinskoi oblasti, 2000.

Kostanov, Aleksandr. "Iz istorii Sakhalinskikh arkhivov," in *Chitaia 'Ostrov Sakhalin,'* no. 2, IUzhno-Sakhalinsk: Sakhalinskii oblastnoi kraevedcheskii muzei, 1990.

——. Samaia vostochnaia doroga Rossii. Moskva: Transport, 1997.

Kropotkin, Peter. *In Russian and French Prisons.* London: Ward and Downey, 1887.

Krusenstern, Adam John de. [Kruzenshtern, Ivan Fedorvich] *Memoir of the Celebrated Admiral Adam John de Krusenstern: The First Russian Circumnavigator. Translated from the German by his Daughter Madame Charlotte Bernhardi,* ed. Sir John Ross, C.B. & C. London: Longmans, Green, Brown, and Longmans, Paternoster Row, 1856.

——. *Voyage Around the World in the Years 1803, 1804, 1805 & 1806.* London: John Mur-ray, 1813. Facsimile edition from Tenri Central Library, Tokyo, 1973.

Kuzin, A. T. *Sakhalinskii Revkom.* IUzhno-Sakhalinsk: Sakhalin Book Publishers, 2000.

Lahusen, Thomas. *How Life Writes the Book: Real Socialism and Socialist Realism in Stalin's Russia.* Ithaca: Cornell University Press, 1997.

Lawn, D., R. Steiner, and J. Wills. "Sakhalin's Oil: Doing It Right." *Pacific Environment and Resources Center.* Valdez, Alaska: Lawn, Steiner & Wills, 1999.

McConkey, James. *To a Distant Island.* New York: E. P. Dutton, 1984.

Miromanov, G. I. "Sakhalin v tvorchestve Chekhova." In *Sibir i Sakhalin v biographii i tvorchestve A. P. Chekhova (Sbornik nauchnikh statey)*. Institut Mirovoi Literaturi Rossiyskoi Akademii Nauk. Yuzhno-Sakhalinsk: Dal'nevostochnoye Knizhnoye Otdelenie, 1993.

Miroliubov, I. P. (Yuvachyov). *Vosem' let na Sakhaline*. Sankt-Peterburg: Tipografiia A. S. Suvorina, 1901; offprint, IUzhno-Sakhalinsk: Sakalinskaia oblastnaia tipografiia, 2000.

Pilsudskii, B. O. *Dogoroi Lev Iakovlevich*. Yuzhno-Sakhalinsk: Sakhalinskii Oblastnoy Kraevedcheskii Muzei, 1996.

Ponomarev, Sergei. "Sakhalinsky tonnel'." *Problemy Dal'nego Vostoka*, no. 9 (1990).

Rayfield, Donald. *Anton Chekhov: A Life*. New York: Henry Holt and Co., 1998.

Rosenthal, Erika, and Vera L. Mischenko. "Conflicts over International Oil and Gas Development off Sakhalin Island in the Russian Far East: A David & Goliath Tale." In *From Concept to Design: Creating an International Environmental Ombudsperson*. Berkeley: Nautilus Institute for Security and Sustainable Development, 1998.

Saktaganov, Sergei. "Vosem' dnei, kotorie potriasli Sakhalin." *Sakhalin: Literaturno-khudozhestvennyi sbornik*. Yuzhno-Sakhalinsk: Sakhalinskoe otdelenie, Far East Book Publishers, 1989.

Stephan, John J. *The Russian Far East: A History*. Stanford: Stanford University Press, 1994.

——. *Sakhalin: A History*. Oxford: Clarendon Press, 1971.

Thornton, Judith. "Sakhalin Energy: Problems and Prospects." In *Russia's Far East: A Region at Risk*, ed. Judith Thornton and Charles E. Ziegler. Seattle: University of Washington Press, 2002.

Tolf, Robert. The Russian Rockefellers: *The Saga of the Nobel Family and the Russian Oil Industry*. Stanford: Hoover Institution Press, 1976.

Voinilovich, Mikhail. *Delo No SU-3246, Zhizn' i smert' kombriga Drekova*. Yuzhno-Sakhalinsk: Transport, 1991.

Vysokov, Mikhail. *The Sakhalin Region*. Yuzhno-Sakhalinsk: Sakhalin Book Publishing House, 1998.

Wallace, Henry A. "The Era of the Pacific." *Vital Speeches of the Day*, v. 10, no. 19 (July 15, 1944).

——, with Andrew J. Steiger. *Soviet-Asia Mission*. New York: Reynal and Hitchcock Publishers, 1946.

PETERSBURG

Akhmatova, Anna. ed., tr., and intro. Stanley Kunitz with Max Hayward. London: Harvill Press, 1970.

——. *Selected Poems*, tr. D. M. Thomas. London: Penguin Books, 1988.

——. *The Complete Poems of Anna Akhmatova*, ed. Roberta Reeder, tr. Judith Hemschemeyer. Boston: Zephyr Press, 1992.

Anschel, Eugene, ed. *The American Image of Russia: 1775-1917.* New York: Frederick Ungar Publishing Co., 1974.

Babey, Anna M. *Americans in Russia, 1776-1917: A Study of the American Travelers in Russia from the American Revolution to the Russian Revolution.* New York: Comet Press, 1938.

Bely, Andrei. *Petersburg: A Novel in Eight Chapters with a Prologue and an Epilogue,* tr. David McDuff. London: Penguin Group, 1995.

Benn, Anna, and Rosamund Bartlett. *Literary Russia: A Guide.* London: Papermac, 1997.

Berdayev, Nikolai. *The Russian Idea.* London: Lindisfarne Press, 1992.

Berlin, Isaiah. "Conversations with Akhmatova and Pasternak," *New York Review of Books* (November 20, 1980), pp. 23–35.

Brodsky, Joseph. *Less than One: Selected Essays.* New York: Penguin Books, 1986.

Capote, Truman. *The Muses Are Heard.* New York: Random House, 1956.

Chaadayev, Peter Yakovlevich. *Philosophical Letters & Apology of a Madman,* tr. Mary-Barbara Zeldin. Knoxville: University of Tennessee Press, 1969.

Clay, Cassius M. *The Life of Cassius Marcellus Clay: Memoirs, Writings, and Speeches Showing His Conduct in the Overthrow of American Slavery, the Salvation of the Union, and the Restoration of the Autonomy of the States,* v. 1. New York: Negro Universities Press, 1969.

Chukovskaia, Lydia. *Zapiski ob Anne Akhmatovoi.* 1938–1941. Moscow: Soglasie, 1997. 3 vols.

Dostoyevsky, Fyodor. *Crime and Punishment,* tr. David McDuff. London: Penguin Books, 1991.

Figes, Orlando. *A People's Tragedy: The Russian Revolution, 1891-1924.* New York : Viking, 1997.

Gelman, Marat, et al. *Neofitzialnaia stolitsa.* Sankt-Peterburg: Tipografiia Pravda, 2000.

Ginzburg, Lidiya. *Blockade Diary,* tr. Alan Myers. London: Harvill Press, 1995.

Glantz, David M. *The Battle for Leningrad, 1941-1944.* Lawrence: University of Kansas Press, 2002.

Gogol, Nikolai. *The Overcoat,* tr. David Magarshack. London: Journeyman Press, 1979.

Khentova, Sof'ia, *Shostakovich, zhizn' i tvorchestvo.* Leningrad: Sovetskii kompozitor, 1985–1986. 2 vols.

Konstantinov, Andrey. *Banditskii Peterburg.* Moskva: Olma Press, 1999.

Lemkhin, Mikhail. *Joseph Brodsky, Leningrad: Fragments.* New York: Farrar, Straus, and Giroux, 1998.

Likhachev, D. S. *Novgorodskii albom.* Sankt-Peterburg: Russko-Baltiyskiy Infomatsionny Tsentr, BLITs, 1999.

——. *Reflections on the Russian Soul: A Memoir,* tr. Bernard Adams. Hungary and New York: Central European University, 2000. First published in Russian as *Vospominania.* Sankt-Peterburg: Logos, 1995.

——. *Stat'i rannikh let.* Tver': Tverskoe oblastnoe otdelenie Rossiiskogo fonda kul'tury, 1993.

Lincoln, W. Bruce. *Sunlight at Midnight: Sank-Peterburg and the Rise of Modern Russia.* New York: Basic Books, 2000.

Lurie, Lev, et al. *Real'niy Peterburg.* Sankt-Peterburg: Limbus Press, 1999.

Maistre, Joseph de. *The St. Petersburg Dialogues, or Conversations on the Temporal Government of Providence,* ed. and tr. Richard A. Lebrun. Montreal and Kingston: McGill-Queen's University Press, 1993.

Mandelstam, Nadezhda. *Hope against Hope: A Memoir,* tr. Max Hayward. London: Harvill Press, 1999.

Mandel'shtam, Osip. *The Collected Critical Prose and Letters,* ed. Jane Gary Harris, tr. Jane Gary Harris and Constance Link. London: Collins Harvill, 1991.

——. *Selected Poems,* ed. and tr. James Greene. London: Penguin Group, 1991.

Merridale, Catherine. *Night of Stone: Death and Memory in 20th Century Russia.* New York: Penguin Group, 2000.

Montefiore, Simon Sebag. *Prince of Princes: The Life of Potemkin.* New York: St. Martin's Press, 2000.

Muchak, Ivan. "Tri kitelia Podpolkovnika Kabatskogo." *Bratishka,* no. 4 (1999).

——. "Mech Piterskogo OMONa." *Bratishka,* no. 5 (1999).

Popova, N. I., and O. E. Rubinchik. *Anna Akhmatova i Fontanny Dom.* Sankt-Peterburg: Nevsky Dialekt, 2000.

Prince, Nancy. "A Narrative of the Life and Travels of Mrs. Nancy Prince: A Machine-Readable Transcription." *Schomburg African American Women Writers of the 19th Century.* New York: Schomburg Collection, Digital, 1997.

Pushkin, Alexander. *The Bronze Horseman and Other Poems,* tr. D. M. Thomas. New York: Penguin Books, 1982.

Radishchev, Aleksandr N. *Puteshestvie iz Peterburga v Moskvu.* Sank-Peterburg: Nauka, 1992.

Roosevelt, Priscilla. *Life on the Russian Country Estate: A Social and Cultural History.* New Haven: Yale University Press, 1995.

Ruble, Blair A. *Leningrad: Shaping a Soviet City.* Berkeley: University of California Press, 1990.

Salisbury, Harrison. *The 900 Days: The Siege of Leningrad.* New York: Harper & Row, 1969.

Simmons, Cynthia, and Nina Perlina, eds. *Writing the Siege of Leningrad: Women's Diaries, Memoirs, and Documentary Prose.* Pittsburgh: University of Pittsburgh Press, 2002.

Starovoitova, Galina. *Natsional'noe samoopredelenie: podkhodi i izuchenie sluchaev.* Sankt-Peterburg, 1999.

Tolstoy, Leo. *War and Peace*, tr. Louise and Aylmer Maude. New York: W. W. Norton, 1996.

Tsvetaeva, Marina. *Selected Poems*, tr. and intro. Elaine Feinstein. Manchester, U.K.: Carcanet Press Ltd., 1999.

Volkov, Solomon. *St. Petersburg: A Cultural History*, tr. Antonina W. Bouis. New York: Free Press, 1995.

Volkov, Vadim. *Violent Entrepreneurs: The Use of Force in the Making of Russian Capitalism.* Ithaca: Cornell University Press, 2002.

PHOTO CREDITS

Frontispiece:	Ural Mountains, Russia (1998). Josef Koudelka/Magnum Photos.
Part One:	St. Basil's. Moscow, Russia (2000). Jacqueline Mia Foster.
	Tram Stop. Moscow, Russia (1993). Anthony Suau.
Part Two:	*Zachistka*. Grozny, Chechnya (February 2000). Vladimir Velengurin.
	Civilian. Grozny, Chechnya (January 1995). Luc Delahaye/Magnum Photos.
Part Three:	Nickel Worker in the Crematorium. Norilsk, Russia (2000). Jacqueline Mia Foster.
	Acid Rain Forest. Norilsk, Russia (1997). Anthony Suau.
Part Four:	Duck Hunting on Piltun Bay. Sakhalin, Russia (2000). Jacqueline Mia Foster.
	Factory. Okha, Sakhalin, Russia (2000). Jacqueline Mia Foster.
Part Five:	Peter and Paul Fortress. St. Petersburg, Russia (2000). Jacqueline Mia Foster.
	The Russian Museum. St. Petersburg, Russia (2001). Jacqueline Mia Foster.
Part Six:	Advertising Exhibit. Moscow, Russia. (2001). Jacqueline Mia Foster.
	Kremlin Honor Guard, Tenth Anniversary of the Coup against Gorbachev. Moscow, Russia (2001). Jacqueline Mia Foster.

※ INDEX ※

INDEX

Chechnya, 57–157
  author's visit to, 57–65, 87–157, 275
  checkpoints in, 57–60, 84–85, 89, 100,
    115, 130–31, 139, 142–44, 149–50
  deportations from, 58, 78, 80–81, 126,
    155, 226
  independence movement in, 58–59, 64,
    66, 80–81, 87–89, 95, 119, 123–24
  Islamic fundamentalism in, 59, 62, 84,
    89, 91, 92, 94, 119–24, 127–33, 134,
    139, 140, 146, 155, 396, 437–38,
    439
  journalists in, 59, 85, 118, 127, 132–34,
    142–44, 151
  maps of, 56, 129–30, 395–96
  minefields in, 98, 124, 141, 156–57
  population of, 115
  relief organizations in, 82, 83, 85, 86
  reputation of, 61, 62–63, 87–88
  Russian administration of, 58, 63, 66, 78,
    99, 115, 131–32, 135–37
  tsarist military control of, 87–89,
    121–23, 144–46, 155
  warlords of, 123–24, 140
  as the "Zone," 74, 81, 127, 134, 140, 394
  see also Grozny
Cheka, 185, 374
Chekhov, Anton, 70, 156, 157, 160
  Sakhalin visited by, 168–69, 237–38,
    248, 249, 251–52, 258, 265–66, 275,
    276, 278, 289, 290–92, 294, 301–4,
    305, 436
Cherkesov, Aleksandr, 389
Cherkesov, Viktor, 344
Chernenko, Konstantin, 30–31, 32
Chernomyrdin, Viktor, 263, 386, 408–9
chernozem (black earth), 67–68, 352
Cherry Orchard, The (Chekhov), 253
Chikatilo, Andrei, 66
Childhood (Tolstoy), 147
Christ the Savior cathedral, 23, 328, 445
Chubais, Anatoly, 320, 339, 340, 405–6
Church of Our Savior on the Spilled
    Blood, 324, 345
Clay, Cassius Marcellus, 37
Clinton, Bill, 37, 413, 418
Clinton, Hillary, 346
cold war, 175, 177, 241
collectivization, 197–98, 227, 303
Communist International (Comintern),
  205

Communist Party:
  ban on, 31, 42–43, 321, 328
  elite of, 26, 29–33
  in post-Soviet Russia, 24, 30–33, 166,
    172, 426
Comte, Auguste, 435
Conboy, Jim, 175, 176, 181
Congress of People's Deputies, 319, 325,
  442
Conquest, Robert, 78
Constantine Palace, 371–73
Constantine XI, Emperor of Byzantium,
  19
Conversation with the Wall, A (Krichevsky),
  427
"Cossack Lullaby" (Lermontov), 87
Cossacks, 87, 121, 139–40, 147, 148, 155,
  169, 170, 303
Cossacks, The (Tolstoy), 148
Crime and Punishment (Dostoyevsky), 331
Cuny, Fred, 127

Dagestan, 76, 89, 92–93, 94, 95, 98, 117,
  140, 144
Daniel, Yuli, 43, 318
de Mayer, Yevgeniya, 254
DemRossiya (Democratic Russia), 321,
  343, 344
Derbin, Anton, 289
Derby, Peter, 34–36
Derzhavin, Gavrila, 352
Dokuchaev, Vasily, 67
Dorenko, Sergei, 413–14
Doroshevich, Vlas, 254
Dostoyevsky, Fyodor, 315, 331, 334
Dragonfly (Chekhov), 302
Drekov, Vladimir, 276, 277, 304
Dudayev, Djokhar, 58, 59, 74, 85, 99,
  119–20, 123–24, 146
Dudayev, Lecha, 98, 182
Dudinka, 163, 191, 194, 195, 197, 203, 214,
  443
Duke, David, 443
Duma, Russian, 39, 42–43, 94, 178, 256,
  298, 317, 318, 319–21, 344, 347,
  375–76, 412, 415, 432
Dumas, Alexander (père), 61
Durin, Viktor, 3–5, 430
Durina (née Sazykina), Valentina, 3–5, 430
Dyachenko, Tatyana, 298
Dyomin, Yuri, 392

501

❧ ABOUT THE AUTHOR ❧

Andrew Meier was a Moscow correspondent for *Time* magazine from 1996 to 2001. A recipient of an Alicia Patterson Fellowship to report from the war zones of the Caucasus and Central Asia in 1996, he was most recently a Fellow at the Woodrow Wilson Center for International Scholars in Washington, D.C. His writing on foreign affairs has appeared in *Harper's*, *The New Republic*, and the *New York Times*, among other publications. A graduate of Wesleyan and Oxford, he is married to the photographer Jacqueline Mia Foster.